The Specter
of the
Absurd

Sources and Criticisms
of Modern Nihilism

Donald A. Crosby

State University of New York Press

Published by
State University of New York Press, Albany

For information, address State University of New York Press, State University
Plaza, Albany, N.Y., 12246

Library of Congress Cataloging-in-Publication Data

Crosby, Donald A.
    The specter of the absurd: sources and criticisms of modern nihilism/ by
Donald A. Crosby.
        p. cm.— (SUNY series in Philosophy)
        Bibliography: p.
        Includes indexes.
        ISBN 0-88706-719-0. ISBN 0-88706-720-4 (pbk.)
        1. Nihilism. I. Title. II. Series.
B828.3.C76   1988
149′.8—dc19   87-20917
                                                                              CIP

10 9 8 7 6 5 4 3 2 1

To Charlotte

In gratitude for the meaning she gives to my life.

Contents

Anyone who is to think creatively today has to be able to confront the nothingness of positivism and existentialism and appropriate them; and this means, not destroy them without a trace, but lift them up into a new ownness in which the very strength of their bitter opposition feeds the growth of a new affirmation.

Albert Hofstadter
(1974:146)

Acknowledgments

I am indebted to my colleagues in the Department of Philosophy at Colorado State University for their interest in this work and for their insightful advice and criticism during its preparation. James W. Boyd, Willard O. Eddy, and Holmes Rolston, III, labored tirelessly on successive chapters of an earlier draft of the entire manuscript. Robert W. Jordan and Ron G. Williams each criticized some of the pages of that draft. An expression of thanks is also due to Judy Schindler, who rendered invaluable assistance in editing the manuscript and preparing the index, as well as in suggesting ways to improve the book's content. My wife, Charlotte, not only gave me the benefit of her own careful readings of the emerging book but also provided a constant encouragement and support for which I am deeply grateful.

I wish to express my appreciation to the Endowment Fund of the Department of Philosophy and the Professional Development Program of the College of Arts, Humanities, and Social Sciences at Colorado State University for grants to defray expenses of putting the manuscript in its final form. My thanks go as well to William Eastman, Director of the State University of New York Press, for his early support and his unfailing patience and courtesy in working with me on this project. In addition, I want to acknowledge the contributions of many friends in the Rocky-Mountain—Great Plains Region of the American Academy of Religion and Society of Biblical Literature, friends who faithfully attended my readings of papers based on sections of the book and raised provocative questions about some of my interpretations and claims. Finally, I thank the students who through the years have been enrolled in versions of a class on "Nihilism in the Modern Age." Whatever may be of value in this volume is due in no small measure to these students' thoughtful reactions to my often groping attempts to shed light on a dark subject.

PART ONE

Introduction

Chapter 1

Experiencing the Absurd

In posing a question, a certain negative element is introduced into the world.
—*Jean-Paul Sartre (1966:28)*

1. A STUDENT'S DREAD

A few years ago, a freshman came to my office to talk about a paper he had failed to hand in on time. I was prepared for the usual excuses, but this student surprised me. He explained that he had not been able to bring himself to write the paper—on an aspect of Plato's philosophy—because he was a Christian. I asked with some puzzlement what that had to do with it, and he replied that he considered writing such a paper a waste of time. As a Christian, he saw no point in studying the thought of someone such as Plato, who was not a Christian and had no way of knowing about the Bible or its teachings. Because he was firmly convinced that the Bible already contained all the truth needed for understanding oneself and the central issues of life, he did not think that anything could be gained by trying to comprehend Plato. He could put the time to better use by studying the Bible or some of the great Christian thinkers.

I responded by pointing out that Christian thinkers over the centuries had found much of value in Plato's philosophy, drawing on it in many ways to enhance and give expression to their faith. I then went on to stress the importance of what a colleague had called "letting one's understanding outreach one's convictions,"[1] of trying to grasp from within and in their own terms outlooks different from one's own, as a way of widening one's intellectual horizons, sharpening one's critical skills, and learning to test one's beliefs so as to allow them to develop and mature over time. I stated that I regarded this process of critical reflection and sympathetic consideration of many different points of view as the lifeblood of higher education.

My student friend remained unconvinced. As we continued to talk, I realized that his persistence in clinging to his original position expressed more than simple unreflective stubbornness. He had given this matter a lot of thought. He explained that it was not exactly Plato's philosophy that bothered him so much, but the habit that his hero, Socrates, had of asking questions about everything. This habit had been taken over by professors in universities; and philosophy professors, in particular, practiced it with a vengeance. They seemed to have no firm convictions of their own and to take delight in questioning and criticizing everything in sight. Students who took seriously their example of endless questioning and criticizing would soon lose whatever convictions they had and be left with nothing in their place. They would slide helplessly into relativism and skepticism, wallowing in a sea of "options," no one of which could withstand critical doubt.

For all the acclaimed values of intellectual openness, was it really worth it? Was the gain of sophistication worth the loss of what had formerly given structure and meaning to one's life? After all, *anything* could be questioned. Once set in motion, the process of questioning could come to but one end, the erosion of conviction and certitude and collapse into despair. This process could also prove fatal, this student continued with all earnestness, to moral conviction and social consensus, thereby contributing to civilization's general decline. He thought that he could see such a deterioration already taking place on an increasingly wide scale, as people graduating from the colleges and universities carried into society the spirit of unrestrained questioning and criticism they had absorbed from their professors.

Writing off his view as provincialism, fanaticism, or adolescent simple-mindedness, or condemning him as lacking the courage to accept even the most elemental risks of intellectual inquiry would have been easy. But I tried to practice what I had just preached and to understand from within and in its own terms the outlook he had sketched.

For one thing, I clearly could not longer hope to satisfy him with a few familiar slogans about the aims of education, because these slogans were based on assumptions he did not share. What for me was a positive vision of growth and enrichment was for him a bleak prospect of erosion and negation. He was responding to this prospect in the only way he knew, by embracing "faith,"[2] which he interpreted to mean belief in an exclusive, absolute body of truth, divinely inspired and accepted unquestioningly on the basis of authority. The sole alternative, as he saw it, was a welter of contending views that could only cancel each other and result in a complete annihilation of objective truth and value. Reason, with its merciless questioning of assumptions and beliefs, could only undermine the foundations of "faith." With that undermining would vanish without a trace all that could give sense and orientation to one's life. Behind my confident scenario of rationality, active self-criticism, and openness to many viewpoints there lurked for him the specter of the absurd.

Our discussion came to an end soon thereafter, for we both realized that our differences ran deep and that we were not going to be able to resolve them that day. The memory of the conversation, however, has stayed with me. This particular student, with his painfully desperate attempt to avoid asking questions and to shield himself against the uncertainties of intellectual inquiry, stands out in my mind as a vivid image of the mood of nihilism, or at least of acute susceptibility to nihilism, which is a mark of our times.

One might object that he was far from being a nihilist, given his belief in God and unquestioning reliance on the authority of the Christian tradition. I do not claim that he was a professed or conscious nihilist, only that he was a victim of the nihilist mood, and that he can therefore be viewed as a telling symbol of the presence and power of that mood in today's world. The fact that he was a freshman makes the symbolism all the more compelling, for it suggests the pervasiveness of this mood, showing how it seeps into the consciousness even of the unsophisticated young and strongly colors their outlook on the world, although they know nothing of its specific character as a movement in contemporary culture or of the multiple intellectual and social forces lying behind it.

My using this student as a symbol of the nihilistic mood can be more readily understood if we pause to consider two distinctively nihilistic themes implicit in his viewpoint.

2. TWO NIHILISTIC THEMES

The first nihilistic theme is that human reason is bankrupt and incapable of resolving any of its own significant questions. As we will see in the following chapter, this conviction is one of the main meanings of the term *nihilism*. The student thought that he could avoid the skeptical despair his radical mistrust of reason implied by turning to "faith." But a moment's reflection shows that what he took to be a decisive alternative to the absurd outcomes of rational inquiry is not really an alternative at all, but an especially poignant expression and confirmation of the very absurdity he sought to avoid. For why should one "faith" be chosen rather than another? Why this particular authority instead of some other? By his own claim, reason can give no help whatever in answering such a question, and the raising of it is just one more trap that reason lays in our path. All that is left, then, is the essentially arbitrary act of the will the student called "faith."

He was advocating, although unwittingly, a version of the "therapy of arbitrariness" (Hauck 1971: 222) that John Barth parodies so mercilessly in his novel, *The End of the Road*. A character in the novel, Jake Horner, goes to a doctor of rather dubious credentials who runs a clinic for mental patients called "Remobilization Farm." The doctor tells him that because choices are necessary for life, unless one is to become completely "immobilized," and because no rational basis exists for choosing one alternative over another, he should follow the principles of "Sinistrality, Antecedence, and Alphabetical Priority." This means that if "the alternatives are side by side, choose the one on the left; if they're consecutive in time, choose the earlier. If neither of these applies, choose the alternative whose name begins with the earlier letter of the alphabet" (Barth 1969: 85). My student friend seemed to be commending something embarrassingly similar to the doctor's approach as a protection against absurdity. Seen in this light, his safeguard of faith turns out to be heavy with unintended irony, a sand castle molded from the very stuff of the absurd. Any new act of the will can wash it away without a trace, even in the next moment. And any two opposing acts of the will can cancel each other out at least as thoroughly as can the opposing conclusions of reason that he was so anxious to point out and deplore.

The student's statements also echoed a second nihilistic theme. This is the idea that atheism and nihilism come down to the same thing—that the only alternative to belief in God and adherence to traditional Western religious teachings is nihilistic despair—coupled with the notion that an alleged rapid decline of Western civilization in recent years can be attributed directly to loss of faith in God and the fading of the Christian vision. Fyodor Dostoevsky, the nineteenth-century Russian novelist, hammered at the two aspects of this theme throughout his life. Ivan Karamazov's allegation in *The Brothers Karamazov* that if belief in God and immortality be relinquished, then all things will be "lawful" or "permitted" has been widely cited (1933: I, 92, 111, 311). No longer could there be any basis for distinguishing morality from immorality, or any norms to guide the decisions of individuals or groups. Hence, atheism is viewed as a recipe for personal and social lawlessness and chaos. For those who do not believe in God, nihilism is seen as the only remaining option.

A necessary connection between belief in God and the meaning of life is assumed by Kirillov, a character in Dostoevsky's *The Possessed:* "I can't understand how an atheist could know that there is no God and not kill himself on the spot" (1931: 582). It is also implied by Stepan Trofimovitch, another character in the same novel, when he says:

> The one essential condition of human existence is that man should always be able to bow down before something infinitely great. If men are deprived of the infinitely great they will not go on living and will die of despair. The Infinite and the Eternal are as essential for man as the little planet on which he dwells (1931: 624).

As for the tie between the ebbing of traditional religious faith and the demise of Western civilization, this characteristic entry appears in Dostoevsky's 1871 *Notebooks*: "The West has lost Christ, and that is why it is dying; that is the only reason" (quoted Lubac 1963: 184). I will return to the question of the legitimacy of such claims later; I note them now as constituting an important nihilistic theme implicit in the student's statements.

3. REASONS FOR THIS BOOK

These, then, are two forms a nihilistic view can take, and they can serve to give a first glimpse of the topic of this book. But why have I decided to write a book on nihilism at all? What is the justification for this work? Many reasons could be given, but the following I deem most important. First, nihilism is among the most prominent trends of thought in recent times. Although its roots lie in the beginning of the modern era, it has come to fruition in the last one hundred years and particularly in the period since World War I. Far from being the preoccupation of only a few disenchanted intellectuals, the nihilistic mood is part of the air we breathe today. One of my purposes is to show that this is so; another is to explain why it is so. Still another is to ask whether it *must* be so.

A second reason for this book is the response of students to a course called "Nihilism in the Modern Age," which I have taught in many versions over the past decade. Their responses have been, for the most part, intense interest and concern, even immediate recognition and sympathy, which is surprising for a topic often thought of as esoteric. It becomes even more surprising when we reflect that most of these students are from prosperous middle-class families in the American heartland. Good jobs and a reasonable share in the good things of life await them. Advances in medicine promise to reduce their susceptibility to disease and pain. Communications media provide unprecedented access to the riches of culture, present and past, national and global, and their educations and opportunities for leisure time equip them to take advantage of these riches. They live in a democratic society affording them wide latitude for thought and action. It seems that they have much for which to live and hope.

And yet, the mood of many is one of dark disquiet and extreme discouragement. They despair of the future and have an acute sense of being at the end of an age. They are cynical about the motives and competence of the decisionmakers of society and have scant confidence in their ability as ordinary citizens to make any impression on important public planning or policy. They feel themselves to be swept along by forces entirely beyond their influence or control. Many have concluded that a canker of absurd incompetence and indifference to fundamental moral and human concerns is eating away at our political and economic institutions, at our relations to the natural environment, and at the whole fabric of social existence. These students view as inevitable, or nearly inevitable, what they see as an impending total bureaucratization and dehumanization of life, wholesale political corruption and incompetence, universal terrorism and crime, economic collapse and environmental disaster, world population glut and famine, and nuclear holocaust.

Many of these students also lack religious faith or any other sustaining vision of a meaningful life. When they do have a religious outlook, they often cling to beliefs that must be held in defiance of modern culture instead of helping to give integration and purpose to it. So baffled and overwhelmed are they by the pluralism and complexity of the modern world and the fragmentation of fields of knowledge that they tend toward radical skepticism about the mind's capacity to know, especially in the realm of values. The result is profound feelings of disorientation and rootlessness, leading to a consuming perplexity about the focus and direction of their own lives and of human life in general.

Not all the students of my course have been of this state of mind, but a significant number have. They have welcomed a course that focuses directly on these kinds of problems and tries to give some aid in dealing with them. Even those who did not share in that state of mind found the course challenging and relevant, illuminating a way of thinking whose influence is widely felt in contemporary society. I have concluded that a book of this kind, which draws upon my experiences in teaching the course, will be of value for a wider audience.

A searching question posed by Paul Roubiczek suggests the last and most important justification for this book:

> What can the philosopher do to prevent the irrational from invading our lives in a meaningless and destructive way, what can he do to ensure that it is approached in a manner which contributes to the enrichment of our lives in such a way as to give meaning to them? (1964: 179).

Writing this book not only provides an opportunity to highlight and put in perspective some of the lessons learned from the philosophy of nihilism, but also to develop as strong a case as I can against its claim to be the final word on the human condition or the tendencies of the present age.

Despite its name, not everything in the nihilistic philosophy need be considered purely destructive or negative, because it contains important truths that can be put to positive use. For example, its relentless tracing to their bitter conclusions of certain long-held theories and assumptions about humans and their relations to the world can help to make us more critically aware of those theories and assumptions and where they lead. Moreover, while its preoccupation with deeply perplexing and threatening aspects of experience may strike us as being overwrought, it can give insight into our situation as human beings, serving as a counterweight to the elements of superficiality, sham, and false optimism that infect our culture. Finally, against those who recommend unquestioning acceptance of one or another *absolute* as the antidote to the limitations of the human condition, the nihilistic philosophy reminds us that the very act of affirming or adhering to such a putative absolute, or of trying to apply its meaning to our lives, is the act of a finite being and can find expression only within the limited perspectives of human conceptuality and awareness. The uncertainties of our finitude cannot be escaped, and we must be on guard against those who would delude us into thinking otherwise. I will return to these and other lessons of nihilism in the final chapter.

However, just as we should not dismiss nihilism out of hand, so we should not succumb to it without thinking it through to its assumptions and asking whether it has told us all we need to know if we are appropriately to ponder the problems and prospects of our lives. I will argue that the philosophy of nihilism is rooted in historically-conditioned assumptions and beliefs open to fundamental criticism and that, far from being an adequate comprehensive analysis of the human situation, it suffers from gross overstatement and onesidedness. I will present some major criticisms of nihilism and propose in its place the outlines of a more balanced and cogent philosophical perspective.

Of course, this perspective and its own assumptional foundations can also be questioned. Does not that fact itself give fuel to nihilism, by indicating that no positive position can be trusted, because none is immune to radical doubt? I dispute this conclusion because the act of questioning can be viewed in another way. One of the assumptions I make is that creative inquiry and progress in reasoning can take place only where there is the willingness to question deeply. Thus, I welcome questions about the book's conclusions because the very act of questioning is in keeping with one of its assumptions.

But this response does not quite get to the heart of the matter. I make another assumption that I willingly put to the test in this book. Raising questions need not run in a meaningless circle or undermine and level all belief. It can add refinement and strength, as well as clarity of recognition, to those beliefs that are fundamentally sound. All that I aspire to in this work is premised on the conviction that while the regimen of questioning has its risks and may well expose us to the specter of the absurd, it can also contribute, in Roubiczek's words, "to the enrichment of our lives in such a way as to give meaning to them."

Chapter 2

Types of Nihilism

What does nihilism mean? That the highest values devaluate themselves. The aim is lacking. "Why?" finds no answer.

—*Friedrich Nietzsche (1968:9)*

Like so many words designating some kind of *ism*, the term *nihilism* is ambiguous and vague. This is not surprising, because it has been in use for some time by persons of different persuasions in a wide variety of contexts. Some have not bothered to define it, assuming perhaps that its meaning was already apparent or that it would become clear in context—not always safe assumptions. Others have defined the term quite narrowly; still others, very broadly. In addition, the word fairly crackles with evaluative significance and has often been used in prescriptive rather than purely descriptive ways.

In this chapter I take the term's ambiguity into account by sorting out its different meanings into five types of nihilism—political, moral, epistemological, cosmic, and existential—and commenting on their interrelations. All but the first (presented mainly for historical reasons) will figure prominently in the rest of the book, but I give greatest attention to existential nihilism.

Three reasons for this emphasis on existential nihilism are as follows. First, because this is probably the most commonly assumed meaning of the term, giving it my principal attention seems appropriate. Second, moral, epistemological, and cosmic nihilisms, especially when considered together, tend to coalesce into and culminate in the last type of nihilism. Third, existential nihilism, by definition, encompasses the whole of human life, while each of the other forms relates to but one of its aspects. The second and third reasons suggest that existential nihilism is the most basic and inclusive, and therefore the most important, form of nihilism.

1. POLITICAL NIHILISM

On Sunday, March 1, 1881, Czar Alexander II was returning to his Winter Palace in St. Petersburg, having ridden out to review the troops at a cavalry parade ground and to visit with his cousin, the Grand Duchess Catherine. He rode in a carriage surrounded by mounted cossacks and accompanied by the chief of police and others on two sleighs. Suddenly, a young man leaped out and threw a bomb. It narrowly missed destroying the Czar's carriage. When the coachman had regained control of the horses, the Czar commanded him to stop and stepped out of the carriage to return to the scene of the explosion. The perpetrator had already been apprehended, and a small crowd had begun to gather. Assuring his guards of his safety, the Czar turned toward his carriage again, only to be blasted by a bomb thrown at his feet by another assassin who had lurked unnoticed at the side of the road. Mortally wounded, the Czar was rushed back to the palace, where he died about an hour later. This assassination was the culmination of six earlier attempts on the Czar's life plotted by a group who called themselves "People's Will." Five members of the group were brought swiftly to trial and publicly hanged on April 3, 1881. In the parlance of the day in Russia, this group and other political revolutionaries and terrorists like them had come to be called nihilists.

A fair number of such secret revolutionary societies had emerged in Russia after the accession of Alexander II in 1855. Two groups established in the early 1860s were "Land and Freedom" and "The Organization." A subgroup of the latter, called "Hell," took as its main task plotting the death of the Czar. One of its members, a student named Dmitry Karakozov, tried to shoot the Czar with a pistol in 1866. The 1870s saw the establishment of groups such as the "Troglodytes," the "Revolutionary Populist Group of the North," a second society named "Land and Freedom," and the "People's Will" itself. None of these groups was very large; most lasted only for a short period of time; new groups were often recyclings of more or less the same members from earlier ones.

The groups also disagreed among themselves on strategy. Some were satisfied with publishing radical journals and distributing revolutionary propaganda in the cities. Members of other groups donned peasant garb, hoping to teach peasants about revolutionary attitudes and tactics. Still other groups resorted to terrorism. Terrorist activities came to a peak between 1878 and 1881, when a number of public officials were attacked and several were killed. Shortly before the many attempts of People's Will to kill the Czar, terrorist Alexander Solovyov managed five pistol shots at him on the grounds of the Winter Palace. Solovyov missed with his first shot, and the Czar was able to dodge the others while running away.[1] Why were these groups and individuals regarded as nihilists?

The term *nihilism* first came into prominent use in Russia with the 1862 publication of Ivan Turgenev's novel *Fathers and Sons*. Early in the novel, Arkady, the young disciple of Bazarov (the novel's chief character), refers to his hero as a nihilist. Arkady's father inquires into the meaning of this term, and the son explains that a "nihilist is a man who does not bow down before any authority, who does not take any principle on faith, whatever reverence that principle may be enshrined in." Later, Bazarov himself declares to Arkady's father and uncle, "We act by virtue of what we recognize as beneficial. . . . At the present time, negation is the most beneficial of all—and we deny. . .everything." Arkady's father then states, "You deny everything. . . .But one must construct too, you know." Bazarov responds with a scornful air, "That's not our business now. . . .The ground wants clearing first" (Turgenev: 24, 56). It is not hard to understand how this statement of the nihilist outlook, which became widely known because of the influence of Turgenev's novel, came to be associated with programs of political revolution and terrorism in which negation or destruction for its own sake seemed to be the dominant aim. This is precisely the first sense of the term *nihilism*.

The association of nihilism with revolutionary action and sentiment was reinforced in the public mind by conservative journalists (e.g., M. N. Katkov) and antinihilist novelists (e.g., A. E. Pisemskii, N. S. Leskov, V. P. Kliushnikov, and Dostoevsky). But it was also endorsed by influential radicals such as Dmitry Pisarev, who regarded the fictional nihilist Bazarov as a splendid model of the revolutionary "realist" or "new man" (Hingley 1969: 48-49; Moser 1964:29). 1860s' revolutionaries often styled themselves nihilists, meaning that they stood for the negation of traditional beliefs and practices obstructing radical reform and for destruction of the institutions in which these beliefs and practices were embedded.

The fact that they hoped for reform and for the dawning of a new social order indicates that these revolutionaries were not committed to destruction merely for its own sake. However, they were often extremely vague and inarticulate about the way wholesale negation and destruction could bring in the new day and about what form the new society would take.[2] Their preoccupation with destruction and the naive assumption many of them seemed to have that once everything had been cleared away something better would automatically take its place left the revolutionaries open to the charge that they had no positive program at all and simply delighted in lawlessness and destruction as ends in themselves. Their conservative detractors, including the "Third Section" or Secret Police, showed no hesitation in levelling this charge against them and dramatizing it in any way they could. An 1869 Third Section report stated that the typical nihilist deserved to be condemned as a "confirmed enemy of political and social order" (Brower 1975: 31-32). By the early 1870s, *nihilism* had a mainly pejorative meaning; as a result, most revolutionaries were no longer willing to apply it to themselves. The pejorative sense of the term was greatly strengthened by the outbreak of terrorist acts toward the end of that decade that climaxed with the Czar's assassination.

2. MORAL NIHILISM

I have begun my discussion of the various meanings of *nihilism* with political nihilism, because this sense of the term was the main one it had when it first came into common usage in the West. I turn next to moral nihilism, which can take at least three forms. The first is the rejection of all moral principles and the determination to live without morality altogether. The second is the theory that moral judgements are purely individual and arbitrary and admit of no rational justification or criticism. The third is the view that the sole obligation of any individual is to himself. Therefore, he need have no moral concern for the effects of his actions on others, except to the extent that he perceives these effects to bear on his private interests. These three forms of moral nihilism can be termed *amoralism, moral subjectivism,* and *egoism*, respectively.

Amoralism can be said to be nihilistic in that it negates all the standards and constraints of a moral life. An example of one who takes, defends, and seeks to live out this outlook is the character Wolf Larson in Jack London's novel *The Sea Wolf*.[3] Larson is not entirely consistent, for he seems sometimes to be arguing for egoism and condemning those who do not live up to the code of an egoist. But it is his amoralism with which I am concerned here.

Its premise is Larson's conviction that "life is a mess."

> It is like yeast, a ferment, a thing that moves and may move for a minute, an hour, a year, or a hundred years, but that in the end will cease to move. The big eat the little that they may continue to move, the strong eat the weak that they may retain their strength. The lucky eat the most and move the longest, that is all (1981: 35).

Later he contends that life, objectively considered, is totally devoid of value. "Of cheap things it is the cheapest. Everywhere it goes begging. Nature spills it out with a lavish hand. Where there is room for one life, she sows a thousand lives, and it's life eats life till the strongest and most piggish life is left" (48). Larson rejects the idea that one is obligated to respect the lives of others, but even the view that one has some moral obligation to oneself he regards as a delusion, for one's own life has no value either. And yet, one is in the absurd position of not being able to *help* valuing one's life and of continuing to crawl and squirm for "piggish" advantage in its yeasty ferment. Morality, for Larson, evaporates into the instinctive claim of might against weakness: "it is pleasurable to be strong, because of its profits; painful to be weak, because of the penalties" (55). He is an extremely strong and self-confident individual and shows no hesitation in trying to gratify his whims and desires at whatever pain to those around him. He is capable of acts of great cruelty, which he carries out with a delight unhampered by moral qualms.

Humphrey Van Weyden, who was taken aboard Larson's ship *Ghost* after an accident at sea and forced to sail on her toward the sealing grounds off the coast of Japan, asks Larson at one point, "You are a man utterly without what the world calls morals?" The captain responds, "That's it" (57). On other occasions, Van Weyden muses that Larson is "not immoral, but merely unmoral," or that he is not so much black-hearted as possessed of no heart at all (68, 40). Larson is thus portrayed as a moral nihilist in our first sense of that term: a man devoid of moral conscience or concern, seeing no reason to submit his actions to any moral principle. He seeks to live entirely for himself but can claim no obligation to do so, because dispassionately conceived, his life, like all forms of life, is absurd and worthless in its blind striving to conquer and endure. By his reckoning, he simply does what he cannot help doing. But he prides himself on his honesty at being able to accept his situation and that of all living beings just as it is, stripped of the gauze of irrelevant moral sentiment.

Moral subjectivisim, the second kind of moral nihilism, can be said to be nihilistic in its denial of any rational way of deciding among conflicting moral claims. According to this view, moral utterances are not really claims at all but expressions of choice, preference, attitude, emotion, or desire (or the attempt to evoke such in others), which thinking of as being either true or false, or as subject to any kind of rational test, makes no sense. "If by nihilism one means a disbelief in the possibility of justifying moral judgments in some rational way," observes Robert G. Olson, "and if philosophers reflect the intellectual climate of the times in which they live, then our age is truly nihilistic. At no period in Western history, with the possible exception of the Hellenistic age, have so many philosophers regarded moral statements as somehow arbitrary" (1967: 515).

An example of moral subjectivism is the position laid out in 1935 by Bertrand Russell in a chapter from his *Religion and Science* entitled "Science and Ethics." Here he defends a form of the "emotivist" theory of ethics. He rejects the idea that some sort of empirical or rational evidence can be adduced to resolve disagreements about basic moral claims. Such claims are inescapably "subjective," in the sense that each disputant in the ethical arena "can only appeal to his own emotions, and employ such rhetorical devices as shall rouse similar emotions in others" (1961: 229). Because ethical utterances make no assertions but only express emotions or desires, they are not open to confirmation or refutation. This does not mean that they are irrational; it only means that they are nonrational, i.e., neither rational nor irrational.

What demarcates ethical desires from other forms of desire, in Russell's view, is that when a person speaks ethically, as when he says, "This is good in itself," he means, "I wish everybody to desire this" or "Would that everybody desired this." Thus, ethics "is an attempt to give universal, and not merely personal, importance to certain of our desires" (235, 232). Despite the universal scope of ethical desires, however, the desires themselves are incurably subjective, as Russell strongly emphasizes:

> This doctrine consists in maintaining that, if two men differ about values, there is not a disagreement as to any kind of truth, but a difference of taste. If one man says, 'oysters are good' and another says '*I* think they are bad,' we recognize that there is nothing to argue about. The theory in question holds that all differences as to values are of this sort . . . . The chief ground for adopting this view is the complete impossibility of finding any arguments to prove that this or that has intrinsic value (238).

He illustrates the thoroughly subjectivist character of his theory from another direction by calling attention to the ethical views of Jeremy Bentham and Friedrich Nietzsche. Bentham advocated democracy, says Russell, on the ground that one person's pleasure has the same ethical importance as another's, while Nietzsche held that only the great man can be regarded as important on his own account and that others should be subservient to him. This is an important kind of moral disagreement, to say the least, but Russell declares that "we have absolutely no means, of a scientific or intellectual kind, by which to persuade either party that the other is in the right" (230). We are left to decide such crucial matters solely on the basis of our emotional preferences.

Russell asserts that these preferences are conditioned in us by our early childhood training. Nursemaids, parents, schools, and other social influences cause us to associate pleasure with certain courses of action and discomfort with others. In these feelings of pleasure and discomfort, and only in them, the sense of moral "ought" resides (226-227; also Copleston and Russell, in Edwards and Pap 1965: 487). Faced with such deeply rooted, socially inherited feelings about right and wrong, appeals to reason can have no relevance. Russell ends his chapter in *Religion and Science* with a forthright statement of the positivistic presupposition that colors it throughout. He argues that because knowledge can only be attained by the methods of science, "what science cannot discover, mankind cannot know" (1961:243). Among the things that mankind cannot know are rational answers to basic moral questions, for these questions lie wholly outside the domain of science and hence outside the domain of knowledge and rationality altogether. It is this radical unknowability in the sphere of morals, and the radical undecidability of basic moral questions, that constitutes Russell's moral nihilism.

Radical subjectivist about moral judgments though he was (at least by the 1930s[4]), Russell lived an intensely moral life and wrote prodigiously on practical moral problems relating to areas such as war, nuclear proliferation, social and economic organization, sex and marriage, euthanasia, and freedom of expression. He was thus at the farthest possible remove from the ruthless amoralism of a Wolf Larson. Yet, by his own theory, any inclination we might have to commend Russell's high committment to moral principles, to say nothing of our attitude toward those principles themselves or toward ways in which he sought to apply them, rests ultimately on the contingent grounds of our socially induced moral feelings.

Had we been conditioned like Larson, then it would be Larson's stance we would be predisposed to praise, not Russell's. And we could not help ourselves. To look at the matter in another light, were we to find Russell deploring (as surely he would) Larson's delight in cruelly taking advantage of others and his utter lack of regard for moral principles, we would be witness to no more than a sparking and sputtering of one set of ardent emotions against another set in which the currents of passion run equally strong. If Russell's theory of moral judgments is correct, the distance between his fervent moral outlook and life and the perspective of the amoralist is not so great as we might initially have supposed. Such differences have now lost all conceptual content and are shrunken to a mere impasse of contending feelings that reason has no power even to address, much less resolve.

The third form of moral nihilism, *egoism*, differs from amoralism mainly in that it purports to be a moral position in its own right, not a denial of all moral positions. One is morally obligated to realize or to fulfil *oneself* at whatever price to others. Egoism differs from moral subjectivism primarily in that this obligation is taken to be objective and universally binding. One would simply be mistaken if one thought of having a moral obligation to anything or anyone other than oneself. But, as with the other two positions, egoism can be regarded as nihilistic. The reason is that it rejects what is commonly regarded as the moral point of view.

What is this point of view? According to Kurt Baier, it is that we should follow "rules designed to overrule reasons of self-interest whenever it is in the interest of everyone alike that such rules should be generally followed" (1965:155). At the root of morality is a view of things in which no person is entitled to preference or special treatment—even if that person is oneself—because each is seen to be equal to the other in dignity and importance just by virtue of being human. To be moral is thus to look at the world from the perspective of *anyone*, not just of oneself. It follows that we should try to put ourselves in the place of others who will be affected by our actions and to seek for them exactly what we would seek for ourselves (107, 150).

Something like this understanding of the nature of morality is reflected in Russell's notion that moral desires differ from other desires in that they are universal or impersonal. A moral wish is for everyone and not just for oneself.[5] C. S. Lewis captures the logic of the moral viewpoint with a vivid analogy: to prefer my own happiness to that of my neighbors would be like thinking that the nearest telephone pole is really the largest (1955: 226). One might *seem* to oneself to be more important than anyone else, but morally speaking this is only an illusion, a distortion of proximity.

It is precisely the moral point of view, so interpreted, that egoism flatly dismisses, as can be seen from the writing of a resolute egoist of the nineteenth century, Max Stirner (born Johann Caspar Schmidt). Stirner's one major work, *The Ego and His Own* (first published in 1845 as *Der Einzige und sein Eigentum*), is devoted to a vigorous defense of the idea that the entire obligation of each individual is to himself and not to any external principle, person, institution, or authority.

> To the egoist nothing is high enough for him to humble himself before it, nothing so independent that he would live for love of it, nothing so sacred that he would sacrifice himself to it. The egoist's love rises in selfishness, flows in the bed of selfishness, and empties into selfishness again (1971: 203).

The egoist's sole aim in the world, Stirner declares in another place, is to use it for his private enjoyment. He strives to make the world his "property" and to "win" it for himself. He goes on to say, "I do not want the liberty of men, nor their equality; I only want *my* power over them, I want to make them my property, *material for enjoyment*" (222). Other people have no value *in* themselves; their only value is *to* themselves. Thus, Stirner insists, "We owe *each other* nothing, for what I seem to owe to you I owe at most to myself" (205).

Stirner's negation of the moral viewpoint is made more explicit by his repudiation of the whole notion of the equality of persons before the moral law. Only the newborn are equal to one another, he contends. Adults differ from one another with respect to their "earned rights"; i.e., rights of superior might and power that entitle some to dominate and exploit others for their own ends (129-130). These earned rights permit hypocrisy, cheating, lying, or the breach of any conventional moral principle when that is required for the strong individual to have his way. These egoistic rights extend even to power over the life and death of others (120, 122).

This outright dismissal of the moral viewpoint can also be seen in another light. Central to Stirner's thesis is his conviction that each person is altogether "unique." No such thing exists as a common *humanity* or *human nature* in which we all share. *Humankind* is a fiction, and to make it the ideal of one's life would be to live for an illusion. Consequently, while the moral viewpoint takes an impartial stance in its attitude toward persons, assuming that each is to be regarded alike, Stirner proclaims:

> I am not an ego along with other egos, but the sole ego: I am unique. Hence my wants too are unique, and my deeds; in short, everything about me is unique. And it is only as this unique I that I take everything for my own, as I set myself to work, and develop myself, only as this. I do not develop men, nor as man, but, as I, I develop—myself.
> This is the meaning of the—*unique one*. (256).

He grounds his position in a thoroughgoing nominalism, denying reality to universals, essences, or relations and claiming that only particular individuals exist. Even the relation of resemblance among persons he rejects out of hand. No person resembles another. Each is entirely unique.

Thus, a view of morality premised on the idea of equality before the moral law can be claimed by Stirner to have no ontological standing. Nominalism, in his view, requires egoism as the only possible kind of morality. Because each individual is totally unique, no general predicates can be applied to any given individual. All persons are "nothing" and found their lives on "nothing" (257, 259, 261). They must each create their individual characters and courses of life through unique acts of will, and only an ignorance of their irreducible uniqueness could cause them to think that they could be obligated to something external to themselves, such as other human beings. Only people with something in common can be obligated to anything in common.

Stirner even compares his egoistic ideal with the concept of God. Just as it has been said of God, "Names name thee not," so it is true of human individuals that no universal predicates can be used to describe them (40). And just as God was thought to serve "no higher person" and to satisfy "only himself," so should individuals attend only to their private desires (40). Stirner does not believe in God, but this kind of reasoning enables him to make a strong nominalistic critique of Ludwig Feuerbach's plea for bringing the idea of God down to that of humanity. Feuerbach was right to reject belief in God, but he did not go far enough in analyzing the consequences of atheism. In Stirner's judgment, his replacement of God with humanity is half-

baked, and as fanatical and ill-founded as the traditional belief in God he
sought to overthrow. For, as already seen, Stirner thinks that "humanity,"
like all universals or essences, is a figment of the imagination. To accept it as
the moral or religious ideal for one's life is to fall prey to one more way of
eclipsing the inalienable prerogatives of one's uniqueness. He puts the point
with characteristic forcefulness: "My concern is neither the divine nor the
human, not the true, good, just, free, etc., but solely what is *mine*, and it is not
a general one, but is—unique, as I am unique. Nothing is more to me than
myself!" (41).

This statement suggests similarities between egoism, on the one hand,
and amoralism and moral subjectivism, on the other, that need to be kept in
mind along with the differences mentioned earlier between it and the other
two views. Egoism is similar to amoralism in that it repudiates what
commonly count as fundamental moral concerns (e.g., goodness, justice, and
freedom), to say nothing of concern for the well being of others. We also saw
that Wolf Larson's brand of amoralism has a similarity to egoism in that
Larson is an egoist in practice, even though he denies having any moral
obligation to be such. Egoism is similar to moral subjectivism in that the
specific content of egoistic morality is relative to individuals. It must be
worked out by them entirely on their own and in ways peculiar to themselves.

Before leaving moral nihilism, I must note an important difference
between it and political nihilism. The difference is that political nihilism
makes claims about current political or historical facts and tendencies, while
moral nihilism is a more strictly philosophical position, focusing on what is
taken to be the human condition as such. Thus, it is one thing to reject as
bankrupt the moral practices or traditions of a given place and era, as did
mid-nineteenth century Russian nihilists, and quite another to write off
morality altogether, in the manner of a Wolf Larson. The former is a view of the
contingent facts of politics and society; the latter is a philosophical view. This
difference also applies to the three types of nihilism yet to be considered, for
they too are philosophical, making general claims about knowledge, the
cosmos, or the human situation, and not particular claims about existing
political institutions or social circumstances.

Because this book is concerned with the philosophical forms of nihilism,
I will not devote further attention to political nihilism. However, the
difference I am emphasizing does not preclude the possibility of mutual
influence between the philosophical types of nihilism and political nihilism.
For example, Stirner's moral nihilism may have influenced some of the
political nihilists in Russia, forming "an important component of the egoist-
nihilist-anarchist complex of doctrines" that influenced their thinking (see
John Carroll's "Introduction" to Stirner 1971:28).

3. EPISTEMOLOGICAL NIHILISM

Epistemological nihilism can be divided into two main forms. The first makes claims to truth entirely relative to particular individuals or groups, while the second holds semantic intelligibility to be entirely relative to self-contained, incommensurable conceptual schemes. Because this relativism to individuals, groups, or conceptual schemes is seen as bedrock and inevitable, it follows that the scope and power of reason is sharply restricted. Reason can operate only within systems of belief or meaning, each of which gives it a particular character; it has no power to address fundamental disagreements arising from the conflict of systems. This implies that no basis can be found for arguing the truth of one system as over any other system or for comparing the patterns of meaning of one system with those of another. It also implies that all such systems are themselves ultimately arbitrary in the sense of being beyond rational criticism or support. We are thus reminded of the first nihilistic theme implicit in the student's comments in the previous chapter. The student had no confidence in the power of reason to settle basic questions of truth and felt that his only recourse was to an essentially arbitrary act of "faith."

An example of one who asserts a radical relativism of truth is Nietzsche. But before looking at his theory of truth, let me note two important similarities between his outlook and that of Stirner. Nietzsche's views on morality are in many respects quite similar to Stirner's. Each holds conventional moral standards in contempt, seeing life as a perpetual struggle for power, self-expression, or self-aggrandizement, where all the rights belong to the creative and strong.[6]

Second, Nietzsche's epistemological views closely resemble Stirner's. Stirner contends that there are no objective truths to which thought must be held accountable, and that truth is completely relative to each human subject. Properly understood, truth is nothing other than a *de novo* construction whereby each subject seeks to "consume" the world and to subjugate the data of experience to itself (see Patterson 1971:152). This concept of truth is the direct outgrowth of Stirner's nominalistic egoism, as can be seen in the following passage from *The Ego and His Own*:

> As long as you believe in the truth, you do not believe in yourself, and you are a—*servant*, a—*religious man*. You alone are the truth, or rather, you are more than the truth, which is nothing at all before you. You too do assuredly ask about the truth, you too do assuredly 'criticize,' but you do not ask about a 'higher truth'—to whit, one that should be higher than you—nor criticize according to the criterion of such a truth. You address yourself to thoughts and notions, as you do to the appearances of things, only for the purpose of making them palatable to you, enjoyable to you, and your own... (1971:251).

Nietzsche's concept of the nature and status of truth is much like this, as we will see. Important differences characterize the two thinkers,[7] but the similarities are striking enough to have encouraged some scholars to argue for a direct influence of the earlier philosopher on the later one, despite the lack of any clear evidence of Nietzsche's having read Stirner at firsthand (see Patterson 1971:148-149).

At the heart of Nietzsche's theory of truth are two concepts: the "will to power" and "perspectives" as focal manifestations of the will to power. Like Friedrich Schelling and Arthur Schopenhauer before him, Nietzsche believes that "will" pervades everything or, in the final analysis, *is* everything.[8] This is as true on the inorganic level as it is on the level of conscious life. The world is a chaos of contending forces or wills, each struggling for dominance over others challenging and threatening it on every hand. As a restless, featureless flux of "egoistic" centers of energy, the world is a radically Heraclitean realm of dynamic process and surging change where each center "construes all the rest of the world from its own viewpoint" and makes its bid for being the privileged or definitive perspective on reality (Nietzsche 1968:339-340). But no reality exists as such, no world of enduring facts or intelligible structures or essences to which perspectives can be related as more or less adequate representations. *Only perspectives* exist, and each human interpretation or claim to truth, no matter how familiar, obvious, or convincing it seems, is just one more perspective or expression of will, "a means of becoming master of something" (342).

Because all interpretations of the world are merely expressions of the will to power, and because there is no intelligible world as such, but only a welter of perspectives vying with one another for dominance, asking if a given perspective is true, or whether this perspective is truer than some other one, makes no sense. Truth is purely relative, a creature of this or that perspective and wholly immanent in it. Each perspective expresses what is true for that center of will or energy; thus, there are as many truths as perspectives.

The search for transperspectival criteria of truth or for "objective knowledge" is doomed to failure, for it wrongly assumes that truth can be gained independently of particular perspectives or that there is a "world out there" to which perspectives are approximations. Take away perspectives and nothing is left. The "world" for any individual or group is nothing other than the set of values and beliefs constituting its perspective.

One perspective may come to prevail over others for a time and to gain widespread acceptance as true, but only because it succeeds in dominating other perspectives as a more potent expression of the will to power. Nietzsche regards the dominance of Newtonian science in his day in this way, differing sharply with those who, like Turgenev's character Bazarov and many of the nineteenth-century Russian nihilists, considered science unquestionably true and based on it a positivistic, materialistic conception of reality (Nietzsche 1968:301-302, 332-341; Moser 1964:29-35). Nietzsche also insists that so-called common sense is but one perspective among others, one whose long dominance has given it a familiarity shading off into obviousness. It must be said without qualification, then, that "*every* belief, every considering-something-true, is necessarily false because there simply is no *true world*" (1968:14). Nietzsche's theory of truth thus leads to the conclusion that "there is no truth," by which he means there can be no transperspectival truth, no inherent nature of things or reality-itself to which our claims must be held responsible, and no means of rationally adjudicating among conflicting perspectives (14, 330). These denials constitute the central thrust of his epistemological nihilism.[9]

We are bound to ask whether all of this does not apply with as much force to Nietzsche's own philosophy as to any other perspective or point of view and, if so, why we should hold his philosophy in any special regard. He nowhere directly addresses this question. Perhaps part of his answer is that because he denies that there is such a thing as a true world, his claims do not suffer from the necessary falsity of those perspectives purporting to portray the world, or some aspect of the world, as it really is. However, given his theory of truth, what is the epistemic status of his denial of a true world? How or in what sense could it be shown to be, or even be said to be, more entitled to the claim of truth than those perspectives that assume a knowable structure for the world?

But this may be the wrong way of posing the question. Instead of posing it in terms of truth, perhaps we ought to pose it in terms of value. Nietzsche's statement, "Our values are interpreted into things" (323) offers a way of better understanding his somewhat elusive claim that perspectives are manifestations of the will to power, as well as pointing to the valuational basis of perspectives. He insists that our perspectives are rooted in our value commitments and orientations and that these, in turn, are based in fundamental drives and needs, and ultimately in the life-force itself. He frequently equates the life-force with the will to power, or argues that life should be viewed as an instrument of the will to power (331, 375).

The close connection of perspectives, on the one hand, with valuations, fundamental drives and needs, life, and the will to power, on the other, stands out clearly in the following three passages from *The Will to Power:*[10]

It is our needs that interpret the world; our drives and their For and Against. Every drive is a kind of lust to rule; each one has its perspective that it would like to compel all the other drives to accept as a norm (267).

...the value of the world lies in our interpretation;... previous interpretations have been perspective valuations by virtue of which we can

> survive in life, i.e., in the will to power, for the growth of power...(330).

> All valuations are only consequences and narrow perspectives in the service of this one will; valuation itself is only this will to power (356).

In light of statements like these, one ought to ask, not whether this or that perspective is true, but in what way or to what extent it is valuable. And of two different perspectives, while asking which is more true makes no sense, Nietzsche seems to think asking which contains the most value does make considerable sense.

The latter question must be answered in terms of which perspective best subserves life and the will to power. In this way, and only in this way, is a comparative appraisal of different perspectives possible. Nietzsche firmly believes that his own philosophy best meets this test of value. It most fully supports and enhances the life-force, or the overbounding energy of the will to power, in two principal respects: (1) it requires us to come to terms with life as it is, in all its terrifying strife and change, danger and uncertainty, rather than allowing us to dissipate our energies in the futile quest for a more secure world lying behind or beyond immediate experiences; and (2) by its rejection of a world-in-itself to which our beliefs and values must be held accountable, it removes all barriers to individual freedom and creative self-expression. Nietzsche thinks that the old picture of truth, with its stolid commitment to permanent essences and fixed standards, pales into insignificance beside his bold vision of humans become like God, introducing into an unstructured chaos their own freely invented patterns of meaning, positing goals and molding facts according to them (317, 319, 327).

This is a nihilism, to be sure, but it is an *active nihilism* that stands in sharp contrast with the resigned, despairing mood of *passive nihilism* into which Western culture has been led, partly because of its debilitating pursuit of the phantom of objective truth. It is a nihilism in which the will to power can be given completely free rein, one where those possessed of the strongest and most persistent life-force can be expected to prevail. Thus does Nietzsche's theory of truth coalesce with his prophecy of the coming of the Superman, whose sun lies just over the horizon of a culture now settling into its twilight gloom.

The notion that some justification can be found for choice among alternative perspectives, depending on which of them best gives free rein to the will of power, might be taken to mean that while no objective truth exists for Nietzsche, at least one objective value (namely, that of the will to power itself), does exist. This interpretation has a certain validity, although it drives too much of a wedge between truth and value and needs to be qualified in other ways as well.

Objective value connotes for Nietzsche a value or set of values imposed on the individual from without, by an external authority such as God or nature, and it also suggests the idea that the values thus imposed possess universal form or content. He rejects both of these senses of objective value. The will to power is not imposed from without, but wells up from within each individual and is, in fact, the very root and meaning of individuality. Moreover, the values the will to power posits have no universal form or content but vary among individuals, depending on the ways each expresses itself through constantly changing circumstances. Thus, no moral values reside in the nature of things and await discovery by human beings, subjecting them to specific duties or standards of behavior—only the restless volatility of the will to power. Values, as well as truths, must be freely invented, not discovered, as wills confront wills in ceaseless struggles for dominance.

Nietzsche teaches that not just individuals but groups and whole cultures become vehicles for the will to power. This is not surprising, for the weak far outnumber the strong, and is only to be expected that large numbers of weak individuals will band together for the mutual enhancement of their slight powers of will. Nietzsche believes that the concept of objective value (along with that of objective truth) is one of the most characteristic ways in which impotent individuals seek to nullify the threat of the few strong individuals in their midst. Seen in this light, the concept of objective value is the sworn enemy of the full and free expression of the will to power.

An unresolved tension in Nietzsche's thought remains, however. He seems to want to say that the will to power represents the ultimate truth of things as well as the final value of the universe. And he seems to want to say this while at one and the same time denying that any such thing as ultimate truth or final value exists. The second half of this paradox is one expression of his epistemological and moral nihilism. But even that part of the first half of the paradox asserting the will to power as the final value does not detract from the earlier suggestion that Nietzsche's view of morality has close affinities with Stirner's egoistic brand of moral nihilism. Stirner thinks that we are all obligated to serve our private interests, just as Nietzsche believes that we *are* our perspectives (see Danto 1965:227) and that these, in turn, are nothing more than manifestations of each person's will to power.

I turn next to the second main kind of epistemological nihilism. The focus of this kind of nihilism is on semantics or conceptual meaning. It asserts an incommensurability of fundamental meanings among different conceptual schemes and contends that cultures, historical periods, groups, or individuals are locked into such schemes. Because no commonality of meaning is discoverable for the basic concepts of different schemes, their claims cannot even be comparatively understood, much less assessed for their comparative truth value. Nietzsche's theory of perspectives can be taken to imply this kind of epistemological nihilism as well as the first kind, as Danto suggests when he states that for Nietzsche it would make no sense to say that the world is the sum of perspectives, because these "are altogether incongruent" (1965:78). But Nietzsche's emphasis throughout seems to be on the relativity of *truth*, not *meaning*.

A contemporary of Nietzsche, Fritz Mauthner, gives considerable stress to the relativity of meaning, so we can use his philosophy to illustrate the kind of epistemological nihilism that denies general standards of meaning valid for everyone. His principal work is *Beiträge zu einer Kritik der Sprache (Contributions to a Critique of Language)*, first published in three volumes in 1901-1902 and going through three editions, the third appearing in 1923. Like Stirner, Mauthner is a resolute nominalist. He bases on this nominalism a theory about the thoroughgoing relativity of conceptual meanings, both at the level of individuals and at the level of different linguistic communities.

I look first at the level of individuals, then at the level of communities. Finally, I note Mauthner's reasons for thinking that language, and hence reason or thought, is incapable of describing reality—the point at which his radical meaning-relativism blends into the first kind of epistemological nihilism, with its denial of the possibility of objective truth, conceived as true descriptions of the world. Because at this point, Mauthner and Nietzsche clearly join hands, I also want to reflect on the connections between the two kinds of epistemological nihilism.

Nominalism denies independent reality to essences, universals, or general concepts, viewing them merely as collective designations for particulars. Therefore, asking what those particulars are for Mauthner is important. He insists that they are not substantial entities like physical objects or selves, but only the fleeting, momentary data of sensate experience. Even though no two such data are ever entirely alike (in fact, each is in some significant sense unique), we come to associate general terms in language with certain groupings of data, and this association is what it means to have a concept. Because no two individuals have the same experiences or memories, these associations vary among persons, with the result that each gives different meanings to the same linguistic terms (1901-1902:I, 54).

Mauthner makes the same point in a later work by stating that all of the terms of the language function as "metaphors," in the sense of being necessarily vague or ambiguous in the meanings they connote among persons (1910:xi). This indeterminacy of meaning constitutes Mauthner's conceptual relativism or nihilism at the level of the individual. We each live in our own world, with our own conceptual scheme or distinctive set of meanings and associations built out of our unique experiences and uses of language. No two individuals share the same fund of meanings, even with respect to the simplest concepts. If some way existed whereby individuals could know reality as such, they could never succeed in clearly communicating their knowledge of it to one another.

If we protest that Mauthner's view is belied by the fact that we do communicate with one another quite successfully through the use of language, his response is that we are confusing language as a vehicle of meaning with its function of providing stimuli for action. Mauthner considers language a part of our biological equipment and a principal means of securing our survival. For that function, it is not necessary that shared meanings, i.e., common associations of terms with sensate images, be available, as long as common responses of action can occur. Thus, while language is a barrier to mutual knowledge and understanding among individuals, it can still work effectively to facilitate cooperative activity (see Janik and Toulmin 1973:127-128).

Just as each individual lives with a private conceptual scheme, which is to a large degree incommensurable with the schemes possessed by other individuals, so do basic language groups constitute, for Mauthner, self-contained, incommensurable worldviews. Each language community is closed off from the others by inherent canons of truth and meaning unique to itself. Logic and science are but conventions of discourse accepted at present among members of a particular linguistic tradition, so no scientific study of language as such can be carried out, and searching for logical structures or principles common to all languages is futile.

Mauthner's position of extreme linguistic relativism and conventionalism rests not so much on the careful empirical study of languages as on a theoretical basis. He reasons that any association of terms with groupings of the data of sensate experience is completely arbitrary and that each linguistic community will thus reflect an arbitrary selecting of patterns of meaning. There is no reason why language groups should be similar or have common structures, and there is every reason for them not to, in view of the countless possibilities of association and meaning presented by the chaotic welter of sense data. Once set off in a certain direction by its initial assignments of meaning, each language community is destined to develop in its own idiosyncratic fashion, forever set apart from the communities of other places or times. Furthermore, because we cannot avoid assuming the perspectives and beliefs of our own language group, whatever it may happen to be, there is no way in which we can make comparisons between our groups and others without begging all the questions. For Mauthner, any claim to objective meaning or truth is based on a delusion, for all such questions will inevitably be decided in terms of the established patterns of thought of a particular linguistic tradition.

A certain incoherence can be detected in Mauthner's account of the incommensurability of individual schemes, on the one hand, and of the schemes inherent in linguistic groups, on the other. His discussion of the second seems to presuppose more commonality of understanding among the members of the same linguistic group than his analysis of the first allows. The problem can be partly resolved by saying that it is all a matter of degree. There will be a much closer approximation to shared meanings among the members of the same linguistic group than among members of different groups, although in neither case can the indeterminancy of meaning relations be completely surmounted. However, this resolution seems to accord to a given language group more of the role of being a vehicle of shared meanings (as opposed to a mere facilitator of common actions) than Mauthner seems at other times to want to grant it. So his conceptual relativism on the individual level remains inconsistent with his argument for the relativity of different linguistic groups.

The last aspect of Mauthner's position I want to examine is his claim that language (and hence reason and thought, for these come down to the same thing as language or the uses of language, given his nominalistic view of concepts) is incapable of expressing any knowledge of the world. First, we cannot know the world as such, but only its effects on our senses. Second, these effects vary greatly among individuals. Third, our possession of five senses is purely "accidental." Were we possessed of different senses, the world would appear very different—perhaps completely different—to us (1901-1902:III, 535-536). Fourth, languages themselves, which make concepts and beliefs possible, are mere conventions or games, based on rules as arbitrary as those of any other game (1901-1902:I, 24-25). And fifth, Mauthner shares in Nietzsche's emphasis on turbulence and change, stating that words are forever being born and developing in new ways (1906:109). As Janik and Toulmin note, this means for him that not "only language, but the whole of culture as well, is continually in a state of transformation. Nothing stands still" (1973:128). With these changes in language and culture, our perspectives on the world also undergo constant change, implying the futility of claiming for any one stage of this process some special access to the world.

Thus according to Mauthner, all we have is the turmoil of our "accidental" senses, ordered by the arbitrary concepts and structures of our particular ever-changing linguistic heritage. We have no means of knowing the world or even of knowing whether there is such a thing as world existing in and of itself. This being the case, speculating about the nature of reality and purporting to give it even partial linguistic expression are pointless. Here Mauthner sounds much like Nietzsche, who drew from different premises the same nihilistic conclusion.[11]

The fact that Mauthner and Nietzsche come to the same conclusion about the relativity of truth to different perspectives and the impossibility of giving true accounts of the world suggest that the two kinds of epistemological nihilism we have been discussing are closely connected. I end this section by briefly noting two important respects in which this is so. Clearly, if conceptual relativism of the sort espoused by Mauthner is assumed, the question of the possibility of objective truth has already been decided in the negative. For if claims from two different schemes can have no significant overlap of meaning, then they can never be said to be in conflict, and the issue of comparing their truth can never arise. Thus, problems of truth-assessment can have meaning only within perspectives, not between or among perspectives. This signifies that no such thing as objective truth can exist—only truth completely dependent upon and relative to a given perspective. Conversely, if we assume with Nietzsche that claims to truth are merely expressions of perspectives and that no way is available to assess comparatively the truth-content of claims which seem to be in conflict, then we have already relegated people of different perspectives to different worlds, leaving them with little or nothing of significance to say to one another. Considerations like these show that the two kinds of epistemological nihilism have a natural drift toward one another.

Finally, we should note the fact that a species of epistemological nihilism, one bearing on questions of moral value, enters crucially into the thinking of the representatives of the three types of moral nihilism whose views were discussed above. Larson, Russell, and Stirner all deny that we can have knowledge of basic moral principles expressive of the moral viewpoint. For Larson, there is only the piggish ferment of the life-struggle, utterly devoid of moral significance. Hence, no moral values can be known. Russell defends moral subjectivism on the ground that moral disagreements cannot be rationally resolved, meaning that moral principles cannot be said to be matters of knowledge, only matters of feeling. Stirner's claim that no two individuals are ever alike means that there can be no knowledge of moral principles applying equally to all human beings. On this basis, he rejects the moral viewpoint. More generally, epistemological nihilism seems to entail moral nihilism. If interperspectival adjudications of fundamental differences about truth or meaning are impossible, it follows that shared knowledge of moral principles is impossible as well.

4. COSMIC NIHILISM

Cosmic nihilism asserts the meaninglessness of the cosmos, either in the absolute sense of denying it any intelligiblilty or knowable structure at all, or in the relative sense of denying that it gives any place or support to the kinds of valuative and existential meanings to which human beings aspire. Nietzsche's dictum, "There are no facts, everything is in flux, incomprehensible, elusive; what is relatively most enduring is—our opinions" (1968:327), gives expression to the first kind of cosmic nihilism. Mauthner's position also comes down to something like cosmic nihilism in this first sense, because even if the world had an intelligible structure, it would be forever inaccessible to us, for reasons already given. Illustrated here is a connection between epistemological and cosmic nihilism. A world that cannot in principle be known is for us a meaningless surd.

Stirner's radical nominalism, which lies behind his ethical egoism, also leads to the conclusion that the world cannot be regarded "as a comprehensive structure of objective meanings" but must rather be seen "as a metaphysical chaos" (Patterson 1971:217). The world is chaotic because no general concepts or principles of interpretation can legitimately be applied to it. It is a mere aggregation of unique particulars or individuals, each sufficient to itself, exhibiting no intelligible patterns of interdependence or interconnection.

But there is also the more qualified nihilistic view that the cosmos, while amenable to scientific and mathematical understanding, is utterly devoid of value and provides no sanction for the ideals and goals so important to human beings. Russell takes this view in his essay "A Free Man's Worship," first published in 1903. He claims that the cosmos is alien and inhuman and that the values we cherish have no realization in it. We must learn to accept the fact that the natural world is oblivious to all distinctions between good and evil and that it is nothing but an arena of blind forces or powers (here he reminds us of Nietzsche) that combined by sheer chance in the remote past to effect conditions conducive to the emergence of human life. These same forces are now leading inexorably to humanity's extinction. Each human being is a "helpless atom" (1957:47) and insignificant pawn in the cosmic processes described by science, writes Russell, and he does not seem to doubt for a moment science's competence to give us the final and complete word on the character of the natural universe.

How are human beings to live in the face of this cold and uncaring cosmos? Russell's answer is that we must reject the brutal play of natural forces as a pattern for our own lives[12] and cultivate instead those ideals which make human community possible and ensure some measure of shared happiness, however precarious and fleeting. We must erect walls of civilization to protect us for a time against the ravages of nature, knowing all the while that the savage foe assailing us from without will eventually break through and crush us, both as individuals and as a species.

His bleak view of the antagonism between the cosmos and human life is summarized in these poignant words:

> Brief and powerless is Man's life; on him and all his race the slow, sure doom
> falls pitiless and dark. Blind to good and evil, reckless of destruction,

omnipotent matter rolls on its relentless way; for Man, condemned to-day to lose his dearest, to-morrow himself to pass through the gate of darkness, it remains only to cherish, ere yet the blow falls, the lofty thoughts that enoble his little day; disdaining the coward terrors of the slave of Fate, to worship at the shrine that his own hands have built; undismayed by the empire of chance, to preserve a mind free from the wanton tyranny that rules his outward life; proudly defiant of the irresistible forces that tolerate, for a moment, his knowledge and his condemnation, to sustain alone, a weary but unyielding Atlas, the world that his own ideals have fashioned despite the trampling march of unconscious power (1957:54).

We can discern in this dichotomous view of nature and humanity the same sharp separation of scientific fact from moral value encountered earlier in Russell's ethical subjectivism. This suggests a line of connection between Russell's moral nihilism and his cosmic nihilism, namely, that if facts have nothing to do with values, it follows that the world of fact described by science will be lacking in any valuative significance. It is but a step from this conclusion to the further one that human culture, with the central place it must accord to aims and ideals, stands in sharp contrast to a scientifically depicted natural world which, in the words of the eighteenth-century philosopher David Hume, "has no more regard to good above ill than to heat above cold, or to drought above moisture, or to light above heavy" (Hume 1957:79).

Another version of the relative (or valuative) form of cosmic nihilism is defended by the nineteenth-century German philosopher, Schopenhauer. Like Russell (and Nietzsche), Schopenhauer believes that the world is steered by blind impulse or energy. But he goes further than Russell when he declares that the world exhibits such a tragic overbalance of pain and suffering as to require us to brand it, not merely oblivious to matters of good and evil, but malignant throughout. The impulse of "will," which constitutes the inner nature of every individual thing and is manifested in human life as a restless craving or desire, produces universal suffering among human beings in a number of ways.

All striving is rooted in deficiency and need, and thus in pain. Each organized form of nature, including human beings, everywhere encounters resistance to its strivings and must struggle to wrest from its surroundings whatever satisfaction it can achieve. Thus "a constant internecine war is waged" throughout the world, and the price of every satisfaction is the pain or deprivation of someone or something at whose expense the satisfaction is attained (Schopenhauer 1957:I, 399). Moreover, the experience of pain is so much more pronounced and intense than that of pleasure that pleasures must be viewed negatively, as the temporary absence of pain. This absence can only be fleeting, because the respite from pain quickly becomes the starting point for the pain of a new striving. In our own case, for example, satisfied desire soon produces boredom, and "life swings like a pendulum backwards and forwards between pain and ennui" (402). If there is no end of striving in the world, then "there is no measure and end of suffering" (399).

The overbalance of suffering plaguing all life is made most evident by the fact that even if an organism manages to survive the threats and dangers that imperil the course of its life on every side, it cannot escape the finality of its death. Human beings suffer most of all, because they are acutely aware of their own impending extinction, and thus of the aimlessness and futility of the life struggle as a whole. This point is brought out powerfully in the following two passages:

> Life... is a sea, full of rocks and whirlpools, which man avoids with the greatest care and solicitude, although he knows that even if he succeeds in getting through with all his efforts and skill, he yet by doing so comes nearer at every step to the greatest, the total, inevitable, and irremediable shipwreck, death; nay, even steers right upon it; this is the final goal of the laborious voyage, and worse for him than all the rocks from which he has escaped (1957:I,403).

> That this most perfect manifestation of the will to live, the human organism, with the cunning and complex working of its machinery, must fall to dust and yield up itself and all its strivings to extinction—this is the naive way in which Nature, who is always so true and sincere in what she says, proclaims the whole struggle of this will as in its very essence barren and unprofitable. Were it of any value in itself, anything unconditional and absolute, it could not thus end in mere nothing (1942:V, 24).

Schopenhauer's view of the universe is thus nihilistic or "anticosmic" (1957:III, 435) in the extreme. He speaks of the world as a kind of penal colony or place of punishment and expiation for the crime of being born. Once we come to see the world in this way, we will give up the futile hope of happiness. We will no longer regard life's "disagreeable incidents, great and small, its sufferings, its worries, its misery, as anything unusual or irregular"; instead we "will find that everything is as it should be, in a world where each of us pays the penalty of existence in his own peculiar way" (1942:V, 17).

If the crime is individual existence, how are we to find release from its harsh sentence? Should we commit suicide? Schopenhauer rejects this option, arguing that it does not get at the heart of the problem. "The suicide wills life, and is only dissatisfied with the conditions under which it has presented itself to him. He therefore by no means surrenders the will to live, but only life, in that he destroys the individual manifestation" (1957:I, 515). His solution is rather that we should take up lives of asceticism and self-negation, lives in which we expose ourselves unflinchingly to the pain of abject humility and unsatisfied desire. Only in this way can we escape the power of the restless craving that holds us in thrall and causes us so much wretchedness and misery.

Schopenhauer's answer to the question of how we are to live in the face of a meaningless, valueless, or malignant cosmos is thus quite different from the course of life recommended by Stirner, Nietzsche, and Russell, each a cosmic nihilist after his own fashion. Where Stirner advocates egoism, Schopenhauer sees it as the source of all suffering. Where Nietzsche celebrates the will to power as the highest value, Schopenhauer rejects it as the essence of evil. And where Russell recommends civilized existence as a fortress against an uncaring world, Schopenhauer would have us cast aside the characteristic concerns of civilization and seek instead reclusive lives of severe personal hardship and self-denial.

His ideal mode of human existence is the discipline of the Trappist monk, who practises "denial of the will, aided by the severest renunciation and an incredibly hard and painful manner of life..." (1957:III, 455). He also stresses the importance of sympathy with the sufferings of others, for we all alike share in the same misery. Identification with and compassion toward others, when coupled with rejection of all self-seeking, can provide a way out of the pangs of individual existence. For those in whom the will to live turns upon and renounces itself, "this our world, which is so real, with all its suns and milky ways—is nothing" (1957:I, 532). And if nothing, it can threaten us no more with anxiety and hurt. Rid of passion and striving, the flame of life is reduced to a vague flicker, and we can await with equanimity our final extinction at death.

5. EXISTENTIAL NIHILISM

The existential nihilist judges human existence to be pointless and absurd. It leads nowhere and adds up to nothing. It is entirely gratuitous, in the sense that there is no justification for life, but also no reason not to live. Those who claim to find meaning in their lives are either dishonest or deluded. In either case, they fail to face up to the harsh reality of the human situation.

Schopenhauer's cosmic nihilism (in contrast to Russell's) quickly shades off, as we have seen, into existential nihilism. For him, life is riddled with disappointment, frustration, and pain. Whatever small significance it might have been thought to have is nullified by the inevitability of death. Our dreams of happiness and fulfillment are soon turned into nightmares by the mocking malignancy of the universe. The only feasible goal for anyone who understands the human condition is the abandonment of all goals and the cultivation of a spirit of detached resignation while awaiting life's last and greatest absurdity, an annihilating death that wipes us so cleanly from the slate of existence as to make it appear that we had never lived.

The mood of existential nihilism has nowhere been more vividly conveyed than in the lament William Shakespeare puts on the lips of Macbeth, as he anticipates the siege of Malcolm's avenging forces against his castle at Dunsinane:

> To-morrow, and to-morrow, and to-morrow,
>
> Creeps in this petty pace from day to day,
>
> To the last syllable of recorded time;
>
> And all our yesterdays have lighted fools
>
> The way to dusty death. Out, out, brief candle!
>
> Life's but a walking shadow; a poor player,
>
> That struts and frets his hour upon the stage,
>
> And then is heard no more; it is a tale
>
> Told by an idiot, full of sound and fury,
>
> Signifying nothing (*Macbeth*, Act V, Scene V).

This mood also finds striking expression in a passage from Leo Tolstoy's *Confession* in which he talks of the "arrest of life," which convinced him that human life is nothing more than a "stupid and spiteful joke."

> I could give no reasonable meaning to any single action or to my whole life. I was only surprised that I could have avoided understanding this from the very beginning—it has been so long known to all. Today or to-morrow sickness and death will come (they had come already) to those I love or to me; nothing will remain but stench and worms. Sooner or later my affairs, whatever they may be, will be forgotten, and I shall not exist. Then why go on making any effort? And how go on living? That is what is surprising! One can only live while one is intoxicated with life; as soon as one is sober it is impossible not to see that it is all a mere fraud and a stupid fraud (Tolstoy 1940:19-20; see also 15).

This passage shows that Tolstoy, like Schopenhauer and Macbeth, is intensely preoccupied with the relentless passage of time and the finality of death. It also strikes another theme of existential nihilism in its claim that meaning can be affirmed in human life only to the extent that one allows oneself to be intoxicated by unreflective naïveté and illusion.

The spirit of existential nihilism also controls the reasoning of the young Emperor Caligula, in Albert Camus's play, when he observes that nothing is more important than anything else, whether we are speaking of Rome's grandeur or someone's arthritis. Therefore, everything is on an equal footing.

And if everything is equally important, he points out, it follows quite logically that nothing is important (Camus 1947:18-19).

Of course, we can attribute Macbeth's despairing mood to his wretched, guilt-racked state of mind, as he contemplates the doom his perfidy and folly of ambition is bringing down upon his head. Were he not in that state of extreme agitation, perhaps he would be less likely to brand life in its totality as aimless and futile. Further on in his *Confession*, Tolstoy recounts how he came to the realization that it was not human life as such that was meaningless; rather, it was his own self-centered and parasitical life that lacked meaning (1940:58). As for Caligula, his mind was deranged, so perhaps we should not take too seriously his rantings about the absence of anything of importance or value in life. The possibility remains, however, that Camus wishes for us to understand that the demented sometimes see things more logically and clearly than the rest of us.

In any event, existential nihilism, as I define it here, is beyond all such ambiguity or qualification. It purports to describe, not some passing mood or phase of life, not the contingent situation or outlook of some human beings, but the human situation as such. Therefore, of all the examples of this position cited above (Schopenhauer, Macbeth, Tolstoy, and Caligula), Schopenhauer stands as its most forthright and categorical exponent. For him, as for existential nihilists in general, human existence in all its manifestations exhibits an inescapable and unalterable absurdity. Strut, fret, and delude ourselves as we may, our lives are of no significance, and it is futile to seek or to affirm meaning where none can be found.

When Camus speaks clearly for himself, and not ambiguously through one of his characters, such as Caligula or Meursault (the chief character in his novel *The Stranger*), he is an interesting example of an existential nihilist. This interest for us stems from two main directions. First, he argues for an intimate connection between existential nihilism, on the one hand, and epistemological and cosmic nihilism, on the other. Second, while he does not doubt for a moment that human life is doomed to absurdity, Camus still insists that life is worth living. That is, he tries to convince us that it makes more sense to live than to commit suicide. These two aspects of his existential nihilism are developed in *The Myth of Sisyphus* (first published in French in 1942). Let us consider each of these aspects in turn.

Camus gives expression to cosmic nihilism when he speaks of the world as "dense" and "strange," or when he refers to it as "a vast irrational," exhibiting "primitive hostility" and remaining stubbornly unresponsive to our yearning to feel at home within it and to reduce it to unity and clarity of understanding (1955:24, 27-28, 50-51). He sees human beings as hopelessly alienated from their world, claiming that it can never be made their own or rendered familiar to them. Implicit in these statements of cosmic nihilism is

Camus's epistemological nihilism. The reason the world is totally alien to us is that we lack the capacity to know it, except in superficial ways that make it only too clear that we cannot find in it that fullness of meaning for which we yearn (36, 40).

We want desperately to have everything explained, insisting that we must have that or nothing (27). But our insatiable appetite for clarity and unity runs up against fragmentation, contradiction, and absurdity. The history of human thought's attempts to pierce through appearances and to attain objective knowledge (which for Camus means complete certainty and comprehensiveness of understanding) is a sad story of "successive regrets and ... impotences" (18; see also 53). This long history of bold and ingenious but utterly futile efforts to understand the world shows clearly that "reason is useless and there is nothing beyond reason" (35). It leads to the unavoidable conclusion that "the end of the mind is failure" (25).

The unrelievable tension between our craving to understand and feel at home in the world, on the one hand, and the world's density and strangeness, on the other, entails for Camus a situation of existential absurdity. It is not so much the world itself that is absurd, he tells us, but our peculiar relation as humans to the world. A tree or cat, for example, experiences no absurdity, for plants and animals make no attempt to comprehend the world or their place in it. They simply exist. They exist as part of that very world to which we humans are unalterably opposed, just by virtue of our unrelenting attempts to find clarity and meaning where none can be found. The "ridiculous reason" which sets us "in opposition to all creation" causes a predicament of existential absurdity from which there can be no escape so long as we continue to live and strive as human beings (51).

Camus supplements this argument for the absurdity of life with references to the wearisome routine of everyday existence (one thinks of Macbeth's lament), the ludicrous spectacle of a man's mechanical gestures in pantomime while talking in a telephone booth where he cannot be heard,[13] the sudden revelation of the ineluctable strangeness of some aspect of nature before it retreats again behind the "stage scenery" of habitual attitudes and expectations, and the fact that we must live always with an eye to a future that will one day bring the unthinkable moment of our death (12-16).

He also bemoans the passing of a time when belief in God was possible, for this passing has deprived life of a principal source of meaning. Ivan Karamazov's cry, "Everything is permitted," should not be construed as "an outburst of relief or of joy, but rather a bitter acknowledgment of fact." Could there be the "certainty of a God giving meaning to life," this would far surpass "in attractiveness the ability to behave badly with impunity. The choice would not be hard to make. But there is no choice, and that is where the bitterness comes in" (67). Camus often speaks of the human desire to make sense out of life and the world as a kind of "nostalgia," and these statements about God convey that sense of nostalgia with exceptional sadness.

What are the consequences for Camus of his conviction of the meaninglessness of life? In contrast with Schopenhauer, he denies the consequence of resignation, saying that he "cannot conceive that a skeptical metaphysics" like his own "can be joined to an ethics of renunciation" (55). He asserts that the "absurd man is the contrary of the reconciled man" (59, note 2). Instead of passive renunciation, the first consequence of the meaninglessness of life, in Camus's view, is revolt or defiance. This spirit of revolt also militates against suicide, meaning that for Camus life is worth living despite its absurdity. To commit suicide implies meek acquiescence to the absurdity of life, and that is the last thing he wants to recommend. Both passive resignation and suicide are cowardly, undignified, and unmanly. The life of revolt gives life value by creating

> a constant confrontation between man and his own obscurity. It is an insistence on an impossible transparency. It challenges the world anew every second. Just as danger provided man the unique opportunity of seizing awareness, so metaphysical revolt extends awareness to the whole of experience (54).

In other words, one must live unreconciled to the absurdity of life. And one must die in the same spirit of defiance, not by one's own hand but at the hand of fate. The other part of the spirit of defiance is that one must live without illusions. There is an air of contradiction in this mode of life Camus advocates, but it is precisely his intent to sustain the tension between our stubborn demand for meaning and the cold unresponsiveness of the world. This tension gives a peculiar zest to life. Yet it can take fully into account all the evidence of life's absurdity.

A second consequence of the meaningless of life for Camus is that it allows for "the only responsible freedom" (60). Rid of the delusion of eternal life and realizing that no prior plan, purpose, or meaning to life exists, we are released from all barriers or inhibitions to freedom. Now, no scale of values constrains us (as Caligula says, nothing is more important than anything else), so we are free to create our own values and to concentrate with "unbelievable disinterestedness" on "the pure flame of life," maintaining it entirely as we see fit (158-160). Because we are well aware that no external authority can give value to our lives, we are freed to determine the path of our own responsibility. This claim of completely unrestricted liberty arbitrarily to define the principles of one's conduct shows Camus to be committed to a kind of moral nihilism akin to Russell's subjectivist view of ethics. We could term Camus's position "voluntaristic subjectivism," because values are posited by our wills rather than by our emotions. Camus points out, however, that "if all experiences are indifferent" (i.e., not subject to a prior scale of values), the experience "of duty is as legitimate as any other. One can be virtuous through a whim" (67). This statement chimes in with the student's conception of "faith" in Chapter One.

The third and final consequence Camus draws from the meaninglessness of life is that we should seek to attain the most intense consciousness and feeling of the "present and the succession of presents" (63). Because we are all doomed to die and because death can come at any moment, living for the future is pointless. We can only live for the present and try to experience as much of life as we can in the present. Awareness of our impending death, which Camus calls "the most obvious absurdity" (59), can enable us to focus our attention fully on the present, so as to extract from it all the richness of feeling and awareness it can afford. This is to live without hope, but it is also to live with a proud defiance and freedom. So it is to live without despair. Camus thus concludes that life is worth living after all, and that it can be lived wholly "without appeal" (60).

There is more than a suggestion of Nietzsche's conception of active nihilism in Camus's version of existential nihilism. Both take vigorous exception to an "ethics of renunciation" (as Camus terms it) of someone like Schopenhauer, calling for bold and aggressive living in the face of the absurd (see Nietzsche 1968:17, 319, 536). Similarly, as we noted earlier, Bertrand Russell lived an earnest moral life despite his defense of a brand of moral nihilism, and he did not allow his cosmic nihilism to reduce him to despair. Life, or substantial parts of life, may be deemed absurd, but thinkers such as Russell, Nietzsche, and Camus (as well as others discussed above) contest Schopenhauer's judgment that this absurdity requires that life can only be lived in a dispirited and docilely resigned fashion. Hence, Camus can claim that an existential nihilism, which negates the meaning of life, need not negate life itself.

Common to the types of nihilism discussed in this chapter is an attitude of negation or denial, as is implied by the term *nihilism* itself. Each type denies some important aspect of human life. *Political nihilism* negates the political structures within which life is currently lived, as well as the social and cultural outlooks that inform these structures. It has little or no vision of constructive alternatives or of how to achieve them. *Moral nihilism* denies the sense of moral obligation, the objectivity of moral principles, or the moral viewpoint. *Epistemological nihilism* denies that there can be anything like truths or meanings not strictly confined within, or wholly relative to, a single individual, group, or conceptual scheme. *Cosmic nihilism* disavows intelligiblilty or value in nature, seeing it as indifferent or hostile to fundamental human concerns. *Existential nihilism* negates the meaning of life.

I have identified all but the first type of nihilism as philosophical in character and noted that these four philosophical forms of nihilism will be my concern in what follows, with greatest emphasis accorded to existential nihilism. I stipulate that nihilism be conceived primarily as existential nihilism, i.e., as the denial of meaning in human life (or stated positively, as the conviction that human life is pointless and absurd). While I will continue to discuss the other philosophical types of nihilism, I do so largely in order to determine the extent to which each bears on existential nihilism. Let us keep this strategy in mind, then, as we turn in the next two chapters to some important arguments for the nihilistic viewpoint. Certain of these arguments have already been sketched or alluded to in our discussions to this point, but we now want to examine them in greater detail.

PART TWO

Arguments For Nihilism

Chapter 3

Arguments About God, Nature, Suffering, and Time

The moments follow each other; nothing lends them the illusion of a content or the appearance of a meaning; they pass; their course is not ours; we contemplate that passage, prisoners of a stupid perception. The heart's void confronting time's: two mirrors, reflecting each other's absence, one and the same image of nullity . . . .

—E. M. Cioran (1975:13)

The case for the meaninglessness of human life has been made in numerous ways by a host of writers in this and the preceding century. I make no attempt to do justice here to all of the arguments that have been given, or that could be given, in support of the nihilistic position. But I will examine some of the most prominent of these arguments, in order to portray as fully and sympathetically as I can the nihilistic frame of mind and its accompanying rationale. In doing so, I not only seek to understand the typical sorts of reasons that nihilists give for their outlook (or that others claim must lead to a nihilistic conclusion) but also to gain insight into the key assumptions implicit in the presentation of those reasons. The assumptions tell us much about the cultural and historical background of the mood of nihilism that has come to exert such pervasive force and influence in the modern world.

The arguments for nihilism to be considered in this chapter and the next fall into several main classes: those relating to God, to the place of human beings in nature, to suffering, to temporal existence, to reason, to will, and to life with other persons. Each class of argument is developed in a separate section.

1. ARGUMENTS RELATING TO GOD

Probably the most important difference between the medieval and modern periods in the West is that the unperturbed confidence in the reality of God characterizing the Middle Ages and playing such a pivotal role in its life has given way in the modern period to a growing mood of uncertainty and doubt that has led an increasing number of people to abandon belief in God altogether. In a later chapter I will critically analyze some assumptions behind various statements about connections between belief in God and the meaning of human life. But I am interested now in arguments that purport to show that loss of belief in God leads necessarily to nihilism.

The thrust of the first argument is that without belief in God as its creator and sustainer, the world can no longer be regarded as a *uni*verse but must be seen rather as a jumble of discordant events that exhibit no underlying unity, pattern, or significance. A world without God must lack the intelligible structures and purposive goals of a creative mind. It has no personality at its center and no "human face." It has become an opaque cipher, a chaotic and inhospitable realm that derides the desire to comprehend it as an ordered whole or to find in it a meaningful context for human aims and aspirations. Nietzsche's vision of the world as a blind and featureless flux of contending centers of energy on which we can only impose arbitrary "perspectives" is one version of what, according to this argument, a world without God must be like. Nietzsche contrasts his picture of the world with "the Christian moral hypothesis" that "granted man an absolute value, as opposed to his smallness and accidental occurrence in the flux of becoming and passing away" (1968:9). Russell's, Schopenhauer's, and Camus's visions are similar to Nietzsche's in their portrayal of a Godless cosmos indifferent or inimical to human concerns.

In this kind of universe, the persistent search for coherent understanding and preoccupation with seemingly urgent questions of purpose and value becomes comic and absurd. For like everything else in a bleak and uncaring world, human life is suspended in a meaningless void. Humans are born into and must live and die in a world where all that happens occurs capriciously and without reason. Jean-Paul Sartre's character Antoine Roquentin, in the novel *Nausea*, gives us his perception of the status of human beings in such a world when he states, "I hadn't the right to exist. I had appeared by chance. I existed like a stone, a plant or a microbe." He also expresses his sense of bewilderment and frustration "before this life which is given to me—given for nothing" (1964:116, 203). The radical contingency of a world without God, a world which cannot be viewed as an expression of purpose or design but in whose context human life must be lived, implies for Roquentin, as for many others, an existence doomed to emptiness and futility.

The contemporary theologian Hans Küng presents a form of this first argument. He reasons that by "denying God, man decides against a primary ground, deepest support, and ultimate goal of reality." This means that "assent to" or "fundamental trust in" reality is left "ultimately unjustified," with the further consequence that atheism runs the grave risk of being exposed to the "possible disunion, meaninglessness, worthlessness, hollowness of reality as a whole." The final result is that the atheist is made vulnerable "quite personally to the danger of an ultimate abandonment, menace and decay, resulting in doubt, fear, even despair" (1980:571). Küng's strategy is to defend theism on the ground that its opposite, atheism, leads through what we have called cosmic nihilism to the *reductio ad absurdum* of denying all significance to human life and reducing human beings to despair. He argues on the other hand that by "boldly trusting in God's reality, despite all temptations to doubt, man experiences the reasonableness of his trust" in reality and reason and is able confidently to affirm the meaningfulness of his life (1980:574, 567-568).

A second argument tying atheism to nihilism yields two interconnected conclusions. The first is that no objective ground for values can exist apart from belief in God as the source and standard of all value. The second conclusion is that if humans are required to exercise their freedom with no objective values to guide their choices and define their responsibilities, then their lives are absurd. Nietzsche speaks to both conclusions when he observes that one of the features of the Christian worldview was that it "posited that man had a *knowledge* of absolute values and thus *adequate knowledge* precisely regarding what is most important" (1968:10). With the demise of Christianity and collapse of belief in God, however, people in the West now must come to the realization that "There is nothing to life that has value, except the degree of power..." (1968:37). Nietzsche's position closely resembles that of Stirner, who concluded from his own stance of radical atheism that there are no general patterns or norms to guide human life or to be used in appraisals of the meaning of life, leaving only the willful acts of each unique and completely isolated ego.

Küng spells out from his own perspective the consequences of atheism for moral values when he insists that "fundamental trust in the identity [unity], meaningfulness and value of reality" is the presupposition of "autonomous ethics," and that this trust can be justified or supported only by belief in God (1980:476). He grants that atheists can live moral lives, but denies that they can give convincing justification for the absoluteness of moral obligation or for the unconditional observance of moral norms. Without such justification, the way is opened to relativism, rationalization, and the arrogance of power: "what is to stop a power holder, a criminal, a group, a nation, a power bloc from acting against humanity if this serves their interest?" Küng is convinced that the unconditionality of moral obligation "can be justified only in the light of an unconditioned: of an absolute that can convey an overall meaning and that cannot be man as individual, as human nature or as human community, but only God himself" (578-579). His purpose in pointing this out is similar to Dostoevsky's, when the latter warns us through the lips of Ivan Karamazov that if belief in God and immortality is lost, then all things will be permitted, because there will be no absolute measure for demarcating right from wrong actions and no conviction of the everlasting consequence and import of the distinction between good and evil deeds.

Sartre tells us in his essay "Existentialism is a Humanism" (first published in 1946) that Ivan's statement is the "starting point" of his own view of human life and values (Kaufmann 1956:294-295). One of the "conclusions from a consistently atheistic position" is that no *a priori* values exist to determine human choices. We are "condemned to be free" to invent our own values and thus at every moment, "without any support or help whatever, . . . to invent man." Neither within us nor outside us do we "find anything to depend upon" (294-295, 310). Sartre reasons that if humans can no longer be thought of as creatures of God, then they cannot be assumed to have a created nature or essence which prescribes the proper course of their lives. Their existence precedes their essence; their essence must be seen not as something antecedently given but as the outcome of their choices. "Man is nothing else but that which he makes of himself." He also states that the only sense we can give to something being a "value" is that it is chosen (290-292, 297).

Sartre does insist, presumably as against egoists like Stirner, that when an individual chooses a course of action, he chooses not merely for himself but for all humankind. The basis for his insistence is that he views each free act (which is also an act of evaluation) as having an implicit universality about it, regardless of whether this is recognized or taken into account by the chooser. Despite this qualification, it remains true for Sartre that in the absence of God, there is no context of prior value to define the path of moral obligation. Values are created (and old values may be as readily uncreated) moment by moment with each individual's choices. The conclusion Sartre draws in this essay from a "consistently atheistic position" is thus very much like Camus's view of the character of human values. It is another instance of what we have termed "voluntaristic subjectivism."

A radically subjectivist view of values like that taken by Sartre and Camus can be related to the nihilistic outlook on life in the following way. If no objective standards are available to distinguish responsible from irresponsible uses of freedom, then it seems to follow that no way exists to distinguish a meaningful life from a meaningless life. And if not, then it does not make sense to speak of any human life as having meaning, because to speak in this manner implies the availibility of standards on whose basis such an assessment can be made.

Of course, we can *invent* values and use them to appraise the quality of various lives, including our own. In terms of his own theory of values, Sartre must be doing this when he assumes values like honesty, "good faith," and a strong sense of personal freedom and responsibility for the image of humankind in his writings, and mocks or condemns those who lack such virtues. However, because he holds all such values to be purely subjective and groundless, any case that might be made through the use of them for the greater meaningfulness of some lives as over against others would suffer from a fatal arbitrariness. Someone else could make an exactly opposite appraisal, deriving from different chosen values, and there would be no basis for showing that appraisal to be wrong. Sartre does say that "in certain cases choice is founded upon an error, and in others upon the truth. One can judge a man by saying that he deceives himself" (e.g., into thinking that he is not radically responsible or free). But he quickly adds that this is only a "logical" judgment, and he would not presume to judge such a person morally (Kaufmann 1956:307). In other words, no basis exists for the value judgment that this or that life either has or lacks meaning. One might deliberately choose dishonesty, for example, because he views the truth (or what Sartre calls the truth) as too threatening or inconvenient. If a person thinks that this kind of life is meaningful, then it is for that person, and that must be the end of the matter. Making a mistake in such evaluations is impossible, precisely because they are without basis or ground.

A somewhat different way of linking radically subjectivist theories about the status of values (moral or otherwise) with the absurdity of life has been developed by Karl Britton, in his book *Philosophy and the Meaning of Life*. Britton contends that an important criterion of meaning in life is that we must be free to make and to be guided by our own decisions in living our lives. But, he adds, we must be able to make these decisions in the context of common standards of value and responsibility, standards not merely posited on the spot by each individual's solitary choices, but discovered to be worthwhile on their own account. This means that we must be capable of giving *reasons* for our choices and evaluative claims, "and if this giving reasons ends up by appeal to a principle for which no reason can be given, then we must at least claim that this basic principle is generally or at the very least widely accepted" (1969:13). If our decisions are of necessity arbitrary and capricious and if no way to identify a mistaken action can be discovered, then our choices and the patterns of life that result from these choices can have no meaning.

In arguing for this position, Britton uses the analogy of language:

> Speech is meaningless if there is no way of showing when it is correctly used and when not. So that to reject the whole enterprise of having rules in common with others, and applying them to the best of our ability—to reject all this would be to deprive life of all meaning. It is to isolate oneself: to pose as the only person or the only non-person. To this plight a man may be driven

by extreme fear or pain or confusion: and in this state life for him is without meaning (182).

Britton himself does not think believing in God is necessary to justify the conviction that there are such standards, but others do think it necessary, as we have just seen. If we couple their reasoning with his criterion, we have made explicit another line of argument which leads from atheism, through valuative subjectivism (which includes what we called *moral nihilism*), to denial of the meaning of life.

A third argument is that without belief in God, the deep religious needs of human beings cannot be met, and if these needs are not met, then life ceases to have meaning. Nietzsche alludes to some of these needs when he reminds himself in *The Gay Science* of the staggering price of his own philosophy:

> You will never pray again, never adore again, never again rest in endless trust; you do not permit yourself to stop before any ultimate wisdom, ultimate goodness, ultimate power, while unharnessing your thoughts; ... there is no avenger for you any more nor any final improver; there is no longer any reason in what happens, no love in what will happen to you; no resting place is open any longer to your heart, where it only needs to find and no longer to seek; you resist any ultimate peace ... (1974:229-230).

Using as our point of departure these words of Nietzsche, so full of the "nostalgia" of which Camus speaks, we can elucidate this third argument as follows. In the absence of God, there is no one to whom one can pray for guidance or forgiveness, no supernatural strength for the transformation of life. There is no one to guarantee the victory of goodness over evil or to give purpose and direction to human history. There is no assurance of an afterlife to take away the sting of death or to counterbalance the sufferings and tragedies of earthly existence. There is no response to the restless yearnings of the human spirit for answers to the riddles of existence and for a lucid understanding of life's purpose and destiny. There is no final and pervasive wisdom, goodness, and power of the universe to be worshipped and obeyed as the focus of one's life, as that summit of meaning that gives other meanings their meaning. Human beings without God are abandoned and forlorn, left with their own pitifully meager resources to deal as best they can with the terrible shocks and uncertainties of their lives. It is a grim picture, with little in the way of solace or hope, so grim in fact as to render human existence essentially pointless and absurd.

Tolstoy is one who came to feel this way. He recounts in his *Confession* how he had failed utterly to find sustenance in the secular attitudes and preoccupations of his life as urbane author and nobleman and had come to the inescapable conclusion that "for man to be able to live he must ... have such an explanation of the meaning of life as will connect the finite with the infinite" (1940:51). This statement is similar to that of Stepan Trofimovitch in Dostoevsky's *The Possessed*, quoted in Chapter One. Tolstoy's reason for claiming that the finite must be brought into relation with the infinite is that finite human existence by itself is radically unsatisfying and incomplete. It requires connection with "an infinite meaning, a meaning not destroyed by sufferings, deprivations, or death" (50). He insists that this infinite meaning can be found only through belief in God:

> I do not live when I lose belief in the existence of God. I should long ago have killed myself had I not had a dim hope of finding Him. I live, really live, only when I feel Him and seek Him ... He is that without which one cannot live. To know God and to live is one and the same thing. God is life (65).

For those who think as Tolstoy does, atheism and nihilism come down to the same thing. Life is without point or purpose unless it finds its fulfilment in God. As Charles Hartshorne puts it, persons with an acute sense of their religious needs require but one certainty for the living of their lives, and that is assurance of "the world-embracing love of God." "Everything else we can take a chance on; everything else, including man's relative significance in the world, is mere probability" (1937:44; quoted Ogden 1966:x). Without this assurance, life becomes an abyss of uncertainties and insecurities.

The last argument connecting nihilism with loss of belief in God takes as its central premise the idea that the essence of any culture is its dominant religious tradition, meaning that when the religious tradition is eroded away, the culture it sustains must also collapse. Nietzsche, for example, contends that "the advent of nihilism" in the West is rooted in the demise of the "Christian-moral" interpretation of reality (1968:3, 7). Oswald Spengler, in *The Decline of the West* (first published in German in 1918), argues to the same effect. He holds that a culture and its religion are synonymous, because religion is the essence of a culture. Thus when one dies, so must the other (1932:I, 358).

Spengler compares cultures to biological organisms, with their predetermined courses of birth, growth, decay, and death. For each, its "mode of spiritual extinction ... follows of necessity from its life as a whole" (1932:I, 356). Thus, the vibrant culture of ancient Greece was destined to become senile with the onset of the Hellenistic period. A similar fate befell Brahmanic culture with the coming of Buddhism. The symptoms of a culture's breakup are everywhere the same. At its height, a culture's "whole vast form-world of art, religion, custom, state, knowledge, social life, [is] . . . easy." The people of the culture can "carry it and actualize it without 'knowing' it." For them, culture "is the self-evident." But when decay sets in, the cultural forms come to be felt as strange and as "a burden from which creative freedom requires to be relieved." What before had been spontaneous and natural now becomes labored; what before was instinctive must now be questioned, intellectualized, and haltingly defended. Spengler sums up the point trenchantly: "Only the sick man feels his limbs" (I, 353). What Nietzsche saw as the arrival of nihilism in the history of the West is for Spengler just this feeling of self-doubt, alienation, and desperate groping, a sure symptom of the West's decline.

As noted in the first chapter, Dostoevsky is another thinker who attributes what he sees as the dying of the West to the waning of traditional religious faith. If loss of belief in God and in the fundamental tenets of traditional religion portends the perishing of Western culture and if this fading of belief is already becoming widespread (as Nietzsche, Spengler, and Dostoevsky believed), then Western culture must be close to collapse.

If it is, then by further development of the argument we are now considering, individuals in the West are in imminent danger of falling victim to the corrosions of the nihilistic mood, because few of them will be able to withstand the debilitation and extinction of their culture. Most are going to experience the death of meaning in their lives as their culture begins to fall into ruin around them. This fourth argument thus ties together atheism, a position about the future of the West (the position can also easily be extended to other cultures experiencing a radical weakening of their own traditional forms of religious belief), and nihilism as the denial of meaning in life. Berger *et al.* sum up the main thrust of the argument when they describe the religious traditions that today are so sorely threatened by modernity as playing "a vital role in providing the overarching canopy of symbols for the meaningful integration of society," and when they speak of "the essential ordeal of modernization," whether in the West or elsewhere in the world, as "the collective and individual loss of integrative meanings" (1973:79, 158). Because belief in God occupies such a central place in the religious vision of the West, its loss is seen by this fourth argument as the dissolution of the principal source of "integrative meanings" for the people of the West. This argument does not have the complete generality or thoroughly philosophical character of the preceding three arguments, but it does claim a necessary connection between belief in God and the meaning of life in the West.

The four arguments considered in this section regard belief in God as the linchpin of life, without which it goes nowhere and simply falls apart, its deepest problems and concerns left either unaddressed or unresolved. This implies that those in the contemporary world (or at least those in the Western world) who find themselves no longer able to believe in God are doomed to lives of absurdity. Accordingly, theists like Dostoevsky, Tolstoy, and Küng, who insist upon a necessary connection between belief in God and the meaning of life, do not have to go far to explain the nihilistic malaise infecting an increasingly secular Western culture. And the nihilistic (or nihilist-tending) philosophies of thinkers such as Stirner, Schopenhauer, Nietzsche, and Sartre give strong confirmation from their side to this alleged connection, at least to the extent that each purports to be simply spelling out the inevitable consequences of a "consistently atheistic position."

2. ARGUMENTS RELATING TO THE PLACE OF HUMAN BEINGS IN NATURE

The arguments of this section take as their focus the concept of nature that emerges from the methods and findings of natural science. The general conclusion of these arguments is that scientific accounts of nature give such slight status or support to distinctively human experiences, values, and endeavors as to radically undermine confidence in the meaning of life. This remains true whether we accept a dualistic or a reductionistic interpretation of the relation of human beings to nature.

The central assumption of this mode of argument is that science provides us for the first time in human history with a comprehensive and accurate description of the cosmos in which we live. But the sad truth is that nature viewed through the lens of modern science is not at all what we would wish for it to be. *Sub specie naturae*, human civilization and all its accomplishments, to say nothing of mere individual attainments, must be seen as peripheral and insignificant, regardless of how important they may appear from a purely human perspective. If nothing else, the incredibly vast spatial and temporal sweep of the universe disclosed to us by science makes the history of the earth and of human beings upon the earth seem trivial and ephemeral by comparison. As Thomas Nagel says, "Nothing we do in this out-of-the-way corner of an unremarkable galaxy would be likely to have cosmic significance, if there were such a thing" (1972:770).

To think otherwise is to fall prey to the illusions of a naive anthropomorphism and an outmoded medieval way of envisioning ourselves and our place in the world. In the words of Max Otto, the scientific account of nature demands that "we assume the universe to be indifferent toward the human venture that means everything to us" and "acknowledge ourselves to be adrift in infinite space on our little earth, the sole custodians of our ideals" (1924:289, quoted Titus 1964:218). The price of accepting the scientific way of thinking is thus to abandon any delusions about the instrinsic value of human life and to realize that human beings have no more importance in the cosmic scale than do the lowliest of nature's living creatures or inorganic productions. Specks of dust, bacteria, the human species—all alike result from a reckless profligacy of indifferent forces and mechanical operations that grind aimlessly on as long as the universe endures.

To view nature scientifically, according to this way of reasoning, is to view it in a purely "objective" manner. The methods of science are by their very nature detached, dispassionate, and impersonal. They are designed to filter out distortions of human bias, preconception, and wishful thinking and to present us with an unvarnished description of the facts, those facts that would remain were human beings to vanish from the universe. The scientific facts are the elements of nature that can be quantitatively analyzed, subsumed under formal laws, comprehended as the outcome of efficient causes or statistical probabilities, and subjected to rigorous empirical tests. These elements, taken collectively and in the network of their relationships, constitute the whole of nature as scientifically conceived. Existential meanings, values, and the qualitative dimensions of human experience have no place in this picture of nature, because they are not among the objective facts of the "world out there" but only projections of human subjectivity. Just as scientific methods of investigation and confirmation are meant to filter out distortions of subjective preference and value, so the scientific descriptions that result from these methods are descriptions of a nature completely objective and value-free.

If we add to this reasoning the assumption already alluded to, namely, that the techniques of science are the *only* ones suited to give us reliable information about nature, it then follows that nature as properly understood is devoid of value and oblivious to human purposes and non-scientific meanings. A.N. Whitehead underscores the nihilistic implications of this view of the universe when he notes that from the standpoint of the scientific philosophy of the late seventeenth century (a philosophy still widely taken for granted in many of its respects today), nature in and of itself, considered only with reference to what are thought to be its objective or "primary" mathematical properties, "is a dull affair, soundless, scentless, colourless; merely the hurrying of material, endlessly, *meaninglessly*" (1948:55; emphasis added).

The French biochemist Jacques Monod, in a widely read book called *Chance and Necessity* (first published in 1970 as *Le Hasard et la Nécessité*) sums up for us his sense of the "essential message of science" when he says that its objective portrayal of nature "outrages values" by making them "seem to melt into the world's uncaring emptiness." This portrayal requires that man abandon his anthropocentric and "animistic" biases. He must

at last wake out of his millenary dream; and in doing so, wake to his total solitude, his fundamental isolation. Now does he at last realize that, like a gypsy, he lives on the boundary of an alien world, a world that is deaf to his music, just as indifferent to his hopes as it is to his suffering or his crimes (1972:172-173).

Monod makes explicit the connection between science's objective mode of knowing, which he takes to be "the *conditio sine qua non* of true knowledge," and the view of nature as empty of values, when he tells us that "knowledge itself is exclusion of all value judgment. . . , whereas ethics, in essence *nonobjective*, is forever barred from the sphere of knowledge" (174). This means that the sharpest of dichotomies must now be drawn between the values on the basis of which human beings make their decisions, direct their lives, and determine their cultural aims, on the one hand, and the cold austerity of the universe brought into view by the objective methods of scientific research, on the other. That humans tend to see the scientific account of nature as opening up an "abyss of darkness" or that they react to it with a "profound ache" of misgivings and regret is no wonder (169-170). Although Monod is sympathetic to these feelings, he nevertheless insists that we must follow scientific objectivity wherever it leads, for only in this way can we hope to have firm knowledge of the world and our situation in the world, and to avoid the vain delusions of the past.

Monod's view of nature, and of the role of humans in nature, is to a significant extent the same as that of Russell. We saw earlier that it was Russell's assumption of a radical separation of scientific fact from moral value, as well as his unquestioning acceptance of the scientific description of nature as a domain of brute facts blind to values, that led to his characterization of human life and civilization as an ultimately futile endeavor to maintain an oasis of purpose and meaning in the face of the vast encroaching desert of the natural world.

Acceptance of this bleak vision of nature, arrived at on the basis of strict demands of scientific objectivity, has given rise to two ways of conceiving the relation of human beings to the natural order. One way is to emphasize the differences between human consciousness and nature to such a great extent as to relegate each to a separate domain of reality. The other way is to place so much stress on the continuities of the two as to argue for the complete subsumption of human life and experience under the scientific description of nature. The first alternative is the way of dualism, and the second is the way of reductionism. Both alternatives have strong nihilistic overtones, as we will see.

The first alternative establishes two dichotomous realms. First, there is the objective world of nature, scientifically conceived. It is a barren world of sheer facts resolved into mathematical quantities and relations. Then there is the subjective realm of human consciousness, saturated with immediate qualitative experiences of fragrance, taste, color, beauty, joy, sorrow, and the like and guided by an instinctive sense of purpose and value. Because the world as it objectively is can allow no place to such central human experiences and concerns, they must be regarded as free-floating products of the human mind, set over against the properties of nature and having no purchase or support in nature itself (even though they are believed somehow to be produced and sustained by natural processes).

An image this dualistic view brings to mind is that fascinating childhood toy, the kaleidoscope. When you look through the toy from its "correct" end and begin turning the barrel at the other, you are treated to a dazzling display of ever-changing patterns of color and design. This "world" overflows, as it were, with significance and value. But turn the kaleidoscope to its other end and you see only a few scattered, nondescript pebbles, analogous to the blank and valueless world of objective scientific description. Which is the real world? According to the hypothesis of dualism, *both* are real. Yet the contrast between them could not be more complete. The discussion of Russell's cosmic nihilism in the preceding chapter gave indication of how sharp the distinction between the two realms of science and value, cosmos and culture, is assumed by the dualistic thinker to be.

This separation of the two realms can lead readily to a nihilistic conclusion. However real in its own right the realm of human consciousness may be assumed to be, the dualistic hypothesis implies a deep estrangement of human beings from nature. How can we feel at home in a natural order that is foreign to our deepest impulses and needs and contrasts utterly in its stark objectivity with the purposiveness and panoplied vividness of our subjective experiences? How can we have any confidence in the value or significance of our lives if they are suspended in a void and radically cut off from the rest of reality? It is not as though we can retreat blithely into the separate realm of mind and ignore the aloofness of nature. Our minds are embedded in our bodies, and our bodies are part and parcel of the natural world. Thus, we are at one and the same time intimately conjoined with nature and yet radically alienated from it. We must depend upon it in every moment of our lives, despite its indifference to all we cherish. This stark incongruity seems to give the lie to assurance of someone like Russell that the scientific view of nature need pose no hindrance to the strivings and achievements of human culture, the latter having their legitimacy and importance in a separate order of reality. For many moderns, this kind of assurance carries no conviction. They sense a direct link between the scientific description of nature and a crushing sense of the absurdity of human life.

Not only does the dualistic hypothesis contain the seeds of alienation of human beings from nature, and thus of profound feelings of rootlessness and homelessness, but it also suffers from a seemingly ineradicable incoherence that compounds the sense of strangeness and absurdity. Dualism is open to the charge of incoherence on the ground that it seems unable to give convincing answers to questions like the following. If the two realms of consciousness and nature are as radically dissimilar and distinct as the dualistic theory claims, what commonality, overlap, or basis of interaction can there be between them? What explanation can dualism offer for the intimate dependence of mind on body, or for mind's capacity to affect and to be affected by events of nature through the mediation of bodily processes? How can it account for the human capacity to arrive at an objective knowledge of nature, a knowledge paradoxically assumed in its sharp separation of mind from nature; or for the scientific prediction and control of natural phenomena, undeniable achievements of human culture? Or how can human awareness and culture, if viewed as belonging to a completely different type of reality, ever have arisen from nature or be sustained by nature, even in a purely objective or scientific sense?

This seeming incoherence of the dualistic position has given strong impetus to reductionism as a second kind of response to the scientific description of nature. But the reductionistic hypothesis only brings us to a nihilistic conclusion by another route. In this response, everything human is brought under a scientific description and completely absorbed into the objective facts of nature. The significance of human subjectivity is greatly diminished, if not eliminated altogether. It is no longer seen as a separate order of reality capable of independent action and creation, but is viewed as a mere epiphenomenon or spin-off of natural processes, rather like the mist of sublimating snow rising from the earth on a warm winter day. What looks like purpose, value, and meaning, or the capacity of free decision, is nothing more than a subjective registration of bodily processes, a passive display of neural firings, muscular tensions, visceral churnings, and the like. The mind is a pawn of the powers of the body and can be reduced without residue to scientific, physicalistic descriptions. Thus subjectivity is swallowed up into objectivity, and a monistic theory replaces the theory of dualism. Now the scientific descriptions of nature are believed to encompass the thinker and perceiver as well as what is thought about and perceived. Purpose becomes a veil of illusion cast over purely mechanical operations; cultural meanings become nothing more than genetically inherited survival strategies of one more species of organism, naturally selected for their success in adapting the organism to the environment; values, to the extent that they have any significance at all, become mere facts to be causally explained.

To the reductionist, scientific descriptions and explanations of the facts of nature do not allow for acts of purposive freedom, because these facts are thought to be entirely lawlike in their functions and relations, a pattern of effects flowing with complete predictability from their antecedent causes. Even when elements of indeterminacy are conceded to be operative in nature, as in current quantum theory or evolutionary theory, these are believed to be the workings of blind chance, rather than instancing anything like purpose or design, and to have probabilistic effects at the macroscopic level of ordinary human experience that are still entirely lawlike and predictable in character. So no foothold in seems to exist in nature as scientifically conceived for purposive freedom, in the sense of ability to act for the sake of future goals or to make genuine choices among alternative possibilities in a given context of efficient causes.

The contemporary psychologist B. F. Skinner, speaking for his own conception of "the scientific view," rejects the idea that a person "is free to deliberate, decide, and act, possibly in original ways" and that "he is to be given credit for his successes and blamed for his failures." He holds it to be in the nature of scientific inquiry that we assume that "a person's behavior is determined by a genetic endowment traceable to the evolutionary history of the species and by the environmental circumstances to which as an individual he has been exposed." The more we learn "about the effects of the environment," the less reason we have "to attribute any part of human behavior to an autonomous controlling agent" (1971:96).

H. J. Paton calls our attention to the nihilistic undertone of such reductionistic treatments of consciousness and freedom, carried out in the name of scientific objectivity, when he remarks that man

> displays his intelligence in discovering laws of nature and then awakes, perhaps with horror, to the fact that these laws apply to himself: for science he is only one object among many others and has to be understood in the same way as the rest. Thus man is finally entangled in the meshes of the net that he himself has woven; and when we say this, we must add that it is true, not merely of his body, but of his soul. Science is, as it were, a machine constructed by man in order to master the universe; but the machine has turned against its maker and seeks to master him as well (1955:109-110).

Skinner apparently has little sensitivity to the "horror" of being swallowed by the objective processes of nature, for he dreams of bringing scientific techniques of prediction and control to bear upon human beings in order to program them to want to do only those things that are in their own and society's best interest. This prospect inspires him with optimism, for he thinks it contains the long-sought secret of enduring human happiness. To persist in the belief in human freedom is to be hopelessly unscientific and to place a foolish impediment in the way of those programs of behavioral conditioning that must be put into effect if we are to resolve the chronic problems of human existence. After all, says Skinner (through his spokesman Frazier, in *Walden Two*), "you can't have a science about a subject matter which hops capriciously about" (Skinner 1948:257; see also 1953:6).

But others can find no cause for celebration in a scientific reductionism that views human beings not as free agents but as automata, and sees all their individual and cultural achievements, to say nothing of their failures and crimes, as following inevitably from their genetic make-ups and the conditioning influences of their natural and social environments. This remains true even if they are assured that they can be programmed to become unconcerned about their lack of freedom and to accept without question the conditioning factors in a scientifically planned social environment like Skinner's Walden Two. In their judgment no amount of programmed "happiness" can substitute for genuine freedom of action. Such people are painfully attuned to the nihilistic horror of which Paton speaks, because to them a life without freedom is also a life without purpose or value of any kind.

The philosopher William James tells of a critical period in his life, in the year 1869, when he felt himself "swamped in an empirical philosophy," i.e., a reductionistic determinism asserting that "we are Nature through and through, that we are wholly conditioned, that not a wiggle of our will happens save as a result of natural laws" (1920:I, 152-153). This philosophy, far from instilling in him any feelings of optimism, shook him to the core and brought him perilously close to a mental breakdown. He was able to find confidence and hope only by rejecting scientific reductionism and developing a philosophy of reality that gives a central place to human freedom. Dostoevsky was another who felt the nihilistic shudder and and debilitation of the reductionistic view. He observes in his *Notes From Underground* that anyone resigned to the idea that all his actions without exception can be explained in terms of natural laws and mathematical formulas has become "a man without desires, without freewill and without choice. . . ." He is no longer a human being but "something of the nature of a piano-key or the stop or an organ"(Kaufman 1956:72, 70). For thinkers like these, to go "beyond freedom and dignity" in the name of science, as the title of one of Skinner's books boldly proposes that we must, is to extract the core of meaning from life.

Another proponent of the reductionistic response to the scientific description of nature is Monod, even though he seems to lapse rather frequently into the language of dualism (see Lewis 1974:27-50). For him, as we have already seen, what things really (objectively) are is what they scientifically are. This includes human beings and all their activities. It encompasses the whole sweep of human evolution, history, and cultural development. In a British Broadcasting Company lecture, Monod announces his reductionistic perspective in no uncertain terms: ". . . anything can be reduced to simple, obvious, mechanical interactions. The cell is a machine; the animal is a machine; man is a machine" (quoted Lewis 1974:ix). In *Chance and Necessity* he argues that cultural achievements like language, religion, and philosophy can be fully explained in evolutionary terms, i.e., in terms of the survival advantages they have conferred on the human species (1971:129-133, 167-169). Like everything else in the universe, the evolution of human beings and the emergence of their distinctive form of life has resulted from the interworkings of pure chance, on the one hand, and existing physical laws, genetic structures, and environmental factors, on the other. Nothing remains, therefore, which cannot be accounted for in a strictly scientific fashion. The human brain, Monod tells us, is not different in kind from a cybernetic machine, and its higher functions, involving conscious awareness and intricate uses of language, can all be brought down to mechanistic explanations, at least in principle, if not in the present state of scientific understanding (148). He speaks in one place of "the dualistic illusion" that distiguishes mind from brain and insists that "objective analysis" requires us to rid ourselves of this illusion, even though we have great difficulty resisting its spell (159).

Monod concludes his book with a vision of a "scientific socialist humanism" that will give authenticity at last to human existence by refusing any claim to knowledge not grounded squarely on scientific evidence or on what he proudly terms "the postulate of objectivity." This postulate is the foundation of the new social life and outlook he recommends. It prohibits any mixture of facts and values, and removes values *qua* values altogether from the category of truth. While we can give scientific *explanations* for the presence of human values in general, as well as for given sets of values, no *justifications* are possible for these values. All values, including even the value implicit in the positing of the postulate of objectivity itself, are arbitrary and indefensible, for they can never be objectively (i.e., scientifically) grounded or criticized (173-176, 180). In contending that values cannot be scientifically supported, Monod differs from Skinner and agrees with Russell (Skinner 1971:ch. 6). But he shares in Skinner's reductionism and in his dream of salutary social reform based on a thoroughgoing application of scientific principles.

The nihilism inherent in Monod's reductionistic outlook is close to the surface. It is obvious, for example, that science as he interprets it can give us no help deciding how we shall live. The postulate of objectivity consigns individuals and societies to an abyss of existential meaninglessness, a vacuum of value in which we must nevertheless continue to choose. Moreover, Monod fails to address the critical question of whether there can even be anything like choice, given his claim that human beings are, at bottom, nothing but machines. He seems to assume a capacity for choice while at the same time denying it by implication with his overall theory. It is notable that nowhere in the five functions of the central nervous system he lists and discusses is any suggestion of a capacity for purposive choice. So whether human beings are free arbitrarily to invent their values, as Sartre holds, is not even clear. Consciousness itself tends to be portrayed by Monod as a mere epiphenomenon, a capacity for subjectively "representing" and "simulating" external events while not having any effect of its own upon them (149-152). In short, Monod's reductionistic approach and conclusions do little to alleviate, and much to support, a consuming sense of the absurdity of the human situation. This suggests from yet another direction how readily the scientific view of nature can gravitate toward nihilism.

In an article entitled "Science in Modern Culture, or the Meaning of Meaninglessness," Eric Weil defines *scientism* as the fundamental attitude that

> only what can be established scientifically is true, objective, and valid everywhere and for everybody (madmen excepted), whereas the remainder of human discourse has nothing to do with truth, although this remainder is in fact the greater part and the more important one for human beings as such (scientists not excepted) (1965:185).

Scientism as thus defined and Monod's postulate of objectivity come down to the same thing. Weil goes on to note that scientism either dismisses all questions of value to the sphere of subjectivity, where nothing can be truly or objectively known, or sees values as mere contingent facts of history to be causally explained, the view that he calls *historicism*. By splitting facts from values, scientism also creates split personalities, especially among the well educated in society, and it divides culture into two tightly sealed compartments—the one having to do with scientific explanations, and thus with knowledge proper, and the other involving arbitrary expressions of valuational opinion (e.g., ethics, the arts, religion) that are ultimately meaningless because they lie beyond the bounds of knowledge. Science, regarded as the sole repository of truth, can do "an admirable job of pointing out both the conditions for success and the consequences of possible decisions," but a culture under the grip of scientism is left with no source of understanding when it comes to weighing the valuative dimensions of its options and decisions (186). As a result, says Weil, "Science as interpreted by scientism... has become a disruptive factor in our culture on a profound, probably the profoundest level" (185).

This last statement can be taken as a fitting summation of the arguments of this section, since the import of each of them is that the scientific view of nature, as undergirded by the attitude Weil calls *scientism*, must introduce profound disturbance into contemporary society by casting a nihilistic pall over all that is of greatest importance in human life. As we have seen, the scientifically inspired outlook and program of complete, all-encompassing objectivity undercuts our values, renders insignificant and irrelevant most of our conscious experience, and impugns our sense of purpose and freedom. We seem to be led to but one conclusion by the cosmic and moral nihilism implicit in the scientific description of nature and approach to value, as well as by science's overall view of the place of human beings in the universe: human life in all its essentials is hopelessly and pathetically absurd.

3. ARGUMENTS RELATED TO SUFFERING

"It destroys your whole world—not just your child, but everything you believed in." These words, spoken by the distraught parent of a son shot and killed by his junior high school classmate (see Stene 1984), epitomize the arguments of this section. They express the feelings of bewilderment and absurdity that can sweep over us when we are forced to acknowledge the pitiful fragility of human life, its susceptibility at any moment to wrenching pain, catastrophic loss, or death. The theological problem of evil is that of having to explain how the presence of evil in the world can be reconciled with belief in its creation by a just and all-powerful God. The problem posed in this section might be termed the "existential problem of evil." It is the problem of whether we can find any reason for living in the face of so much actual and potential suffering in the world. Those who reason from this problem to a nihilistic conclusion contend that it is impossible that lives like our own, so vulnerable to devastating shocks, sorrows, disappointments, and pains, can have any meaning.

Schopenhauer was brought to just this conclusion. His denial that life is worth living is based largely on his sensitivity to the great amount of seemingly senseless suffering and sorrow which is the lot of human beings. We saw earlier that he contends that suffering so exceeds pleasure as to be the positive principle of our existence, and that pleasure is nothing more than momentary respite from pain. Even these brief respites are frequently wrested from others at the price of their own pain. When we are not experiencing pain, we tend to be plagued with boredom, which is but another form of suffering, in some ways more torturing than pain itself. And Schopenhauer is distressed beyond consolation at the thought that we survive the multifarious dangers and evils of life only to be brought to the absurd end of death. Life for him, then, is a "disappointment" and a "cheat," and he believes that we become ever more acutely aware of this fact the longer we live. He muses that it would be an act of mercy to spare unborn children the burden of existence, an existence whose miseries will inevitably swamp whatever momentary satisfactions they might be able to attain (see Schopenhauer 1942:V, 3-5).

There are those who find Schopenhauer's case to be entirely convincing. They see him as cutting through a fog of romantic delusion and forcing us to take our actual situation as human beings plainly into account. How can we have any sense of safety in the present or confidence in the future when we know that our deepest loves and most cherished undertakings can be destroyed or brought to naught in an instant by some wholly unexpected event? Even if we are so fortunate as not to experience exceptional suffering in the present, we know that there can be no guarantee that we will not be subject to it in the future. In fact, there is a good statistical likelihood that we will, especially if we live long enough to confront the ravages of old age. We also know that at this very moment the lives of countless others are filled with agonies of body or spirit, whether as a consequence of the malice or indifference of other human beings, or because of the workings of natural processes that bring in their train congenital mental or physical defects, debilitating diseases, and various horrible accidents and disasters—all happening with no discernible reason, arbitrarily selecting some while leaving others, at least for the moment, unscathed. In the face of their own actual or potential sufferings and the widespread suffering in the world, how can sensitive persons hope to attain lives of happiness or contentment, or how can they think for a moment that human existence is meaningful or worthwhile?

We have only to scan the daily newspaper or read the routine records of any hospital to be reminded of how pervasive the problem of human suffering is. Babies are born blind, deaf, disfigured, or mentally retarded. A young child wanders into the path of an oncoming truck and is crippled for life. A teenager is paralyzed from the neck down in a skiing accident. An adult in the prime of life is diagnosed as having incurable cancer that will mean either slow and agonizing dying or a stupor of pain-killing drugs. Another person's steadily increasing bouts of severe depression, for which doctors seemed unable to find a cause or cure, have led finally to suicide. We can easily recall similar cases from our own experience, sad cases of affliction of body or mind which defy analysis or justification. Such cases are not confined to isolated individuals here or there, but sometimes involve large groups. For instance, as I write these lines, hundreds of thousands of people are starving to death in central Africa due to a prolonged drought.

So much routine suffering and deprivation makes the conclusion seem unavoidable that, when all things are said and done, our lives are fundamentally absurd. E. M. Cioran marshalls the evidence for this conclusion in a bleakly compelling way. Here is his judgment about the world of our existence, a world he, like Schopenhauer, regards as blighted irremediably by gratuitous agony and pain:

> Of all that was attempted this side of nothingness, is anything more pathetic than this world, except for the idea which conceived it? Wherever something breathes there is one more infirmity: no palpitation which fails to confirm the disadvantage of being; the flesh horrifies me: these men, these women, offal

that moans by the grace of certain spasms; . . . each moment is merely a vote in the urn of my despair (1975:142).

He argues that language conceals from us the hard truth that life is a mere "euphemism for Evil." Alone with ourselves, beyond the comfort of words, "grand expressions" such as "fate, misfortune, disgrace" lose their abstract luster and their power to distance us from their inescapable references to the misery of our own concrete existence. We are then forced to confront "the unqualified universe, the pure object, the naked event; where find the boldness to face them?" (121).

We usually take for granted the predictable course of our projects and concerns, ignoring how suddenly and easily they can be thrown off track. We are generally oblivious to the precarious equilibrium of highly complex functionings, both psychic and physical, which maintains our mental competence and sanity. We forget how quickly these delicate bodies, with their paper-thin flesh, can be damaged and torn; how open they are at every pore to invasions of senseless deprivation and pain. We fail somehow to notice or to take seriously the fact that they are all that stand between us and absurd, irrevocable mutilations, the nothingness of our own death, or the maimings or extinctions of those we love. Yet the evidence of widespread suffering and loss is all around us. Even if these bodies remain intact for awhile, their relentless ongoing decay spells our coming dissolution and doom. Thus, to live is to teeter for a few brief moments over an abyss, and then to be hurled indifferently into its depths; some sooner than others, but all inevitably in the end. Only pretense or dull stupidity can lull us into thinking that such an existence gives basis for any enduring confidence or hope.

We must add to our catalogue of the ills afflicting human life all the calamities that result from the deliberate actions (or sometimes, callous inactions) of human beings toward one another. Our extreme vulnerability to the destructive deeds of our fellow human beings calls into serious question from a somewhat different direction the meaningfulness of human life.

In his book *Murder U.S.A.*, John Godwin describes the murderous rampage of two drifters of the Southwest during three weeks of 1973. They first killed two people in a trailer house in Arizona, blasting their heads beyond recognition with shotguns held at close range. Having earlier overpowered and bound two of their partners in a drug distribution scheme and put them in the back of a van, they now transported these two to a fishing spot in California, stripped them naked, strangled one with a piece of rope, and slit the other's throat ear to ear. The blood lust fully upon them, they turned again toward the east, picked up two hitchhikers in Arizona, and promptly killed them. Then they broke into the apartment of two students and shot them dead.

Returning once more to California, they went to a small town in the San Joaquin Valley. Here they forced their way into the home of a couple and held their children and those of a neighboring couple hostage until the two sets of parents returned from bowling. After forcing one of the fathers, who owned a grocery store, to go to the store and give them money from the safe, the drifters systematically killed every one of the people in the house, shooting each one twice—once in the head and once in the chest. There were nine of them in all. Godwin notes that slayings such as these often seem to lack clear motive, or that at least the motive is not a simple desire for cash. It seems rather to be a weird gratification or feeling of release in the act of killing itself (1978:299, 303, 305-307). Speaking of the moments just before the drifters shot their nine victims in the home in California, he reflects,

> Perhaps they savored those moments: that glorious surge of power when the last frantic seconds of your victim's life are measured by the slowly increasing pressure of your trigger finger—when the helpless being before you has heard the shots and knows what's coming but can do nothing, absolutely *nothing*, to stop you. It was something to look back on, to relish retrospectively in those years to come (307).

What if we or someone we loved fell victim to men like these? Could we still make sense out of life? Some might be able eventually to come to terms with the experience, perhaps seeing it as a mere aberration. But those who are persuaded by the arguments of this section would insist that the shock of such experiences peels away the veneer of distraction and delusion that normally hides from us the absurdity of life. They would observe that it does not help to blame the men, their parents, or their society. The real point is that we must live day by day in a universe in which such atrocities happen, and in which the demonic distortions of mind and spirit that produce them develop. We note here an intimate connection between cosmic nihilism and the conviction of life's meaninglessness. Even the contingent circumstance of these two men meeting and staying together, each reinforcing the most malevolent tendencies of the other, can only heighten the sense of absurdity.

But crimes like these, crimes of individual against individual, pale into insignificance when compared with the amount of suffering which modern nation states can inflict on humankind. It is surely one of the major anomalies of the modern age that, while natural science has solved many natural evils, such as the Plague, smallpox, whooping cough, and appendicitis, and is now even capable of replacing defective major organs, it has at the same time spawned a whole new capability of moral evil with its weapons of mass destruction.

Someone has estimated that the combined firepower of World War II, including the two atomic bombs dropped on Japan, was about three megatons (three-million tons of TNT). At the time of this writing, in the nuclear arsenals of the United States and the Soviet Union, there exists a total firepower of approximately twelve-thousand megatons (Broad 1984). This means that the U. S. and the U. S. S. R. have the total destructive capability at this moment for four thousand World War II's. Or to put the point in a slightly more comprehensible way, one Poseidon submarine has a destructive capacity of three World War II's. Moreover, nations other than the United States and the Soviet Union either now have, or will soon attain, the capability for nuclear war. Most of us are citizens of nation states that would become embroiled in a global nuclear conflict, were it to take place. And even if some are not, we must all live on the same earth. So there is no way we can be immune to the threat of unimaginable suffering and devastation posed by these weapons. How can we live secure, meaningful lives in the face of a threat of this magnitude, a threat which can not only wipe out whole cities and millions of lives in a few minutes, but also places in dire jeopardy the structures and resources of human civilization itself?

Knowing what we already know about human nature and human history, and especially given our knowledge of the recent tragic history of nation states, the likelihood of a truly catastrophic (if not apocalyptic) World War III seems so undeniably high as to be fatal to the peace of mind and optimism of any thoughtful person living in the world today. How, then, can our lives be thought to be meaningful or worthwhile? We seem doomed either actually to suffer the unimaginable carnage of another world war, this time fought with nuclear weapons, or to be consumed by the constant anxiety of our realization that such a war can begin at any moment. In either case, our susceptibility to a global insanity already well underway, and to its threatened stupendous suffering, makes our condition as human beings appear grotesque and absurd. Even if we do not go so far as to conclude that our fate is sealed, the high probability of such universal devastation is enough to bring us to the brink of despair.

But suppose that all this modern technology were to disappear. Suppose further that the amount of physical suffering resulting from the laws of nature and the cruelty or callousness of human beings was drastically reduced. Would we then have reason for living? In the judgment of thinkers such as Franz Kafka, it is highly doubtful that we would. For he seems to believe that our greatest suffering stems, not from our susceptibility to out-of-the-ordinary deprivations and pains, but from an excruciating mental conflict and anguish built into our make-up as human beings. We find that we cannot live without our ideals, but we also find that the unattainability of these ideals forever condemns us to lives of radical dissatisfaction and unease. Stephen D. Ross finds this to be a major, if not *the* major, motif of Kafka's enigmatic novel, *The Trial* (first published in 1925). Our ideals (symbolized by Kafka's "the Law") are what give promise of meaning to our lives, but, "[i]t is a failure in any and all ideals—that they necessarily either make impossible demands on men, or lose their capacity to function as ideals" (Ross 1969:135).

The impossibility of the Law's demands on K., the main character of *The Trial*, is symbolized by his continuing inability to ascertain what crime he is charged with, to confront his accusers, to examine their evidence against him, or to defend himself in court. He is always kept off-balance, never able to understand how he should behave or what is expected of him. His protestations of innocence are never quite believed by those with whom he comes in contact, and his own self-doubt and lurking sense of guilt increase steadily as the elusive "trial" proceeds. He is told that the outcome of these trials is usually a foregone conclusion, and at the end he seems almost resigned to the inevitability of his condemnation.

Ross explains, "To exist as human is to strive toward something—be it divine or simply some natural ideal of self-realization. But the very existence of such goals is and must be a torment to consciousness—thus contradicting their very purpose of existence." From suffering like this, no avenue of release can be found. We seem condemned either to the misery of guilt, remorse, and an ever-present sense of frustration and failure, or to the emptiness of lives "incapable of self-confrontation and challenge." Consciousness of being trapped in a situation like this, a situation from which there is no escape as long as we remain human beings, is, according to Ross, "utterly the most frightening thing possible to contemplate" (135). Lives doomed to such a consciousness, and to the pervasive, ineluctable suffering it implies—and what sensitive person's life is not?—can scarcely be deemed satisfying or fulfilling.

Finally, we need also to consider the sufferings of animals, some of these sufferings brought on by the actions of humans but others woven into the tapestry of animal existence itself. In a moving passage from *The Varieties of Religious Experience*, William James takes note of the ordeals of animal experience, by way of exhibiting the melancholic side of life:

> To believe in the carnivorous reptiles of geologic times is hard for our imagination—they seem too much like mere museum specimens. Yet there is no tooth in any one of those museum-skulls that did not daily through long years of the foretime hold fast to the body struggling in despair of some fated living victim. Forms of horror just as dreadful to the victims, if on a small spatial scale, fill the world about us today. Here on our very hearths and in our gardens the infernal cat plays with the panting mouse, or holds the hot bird fluttering in her jaws. Crocodiles and rattlesnakes and pythons are at this moment vessels of life as real as we are; their loathsome existence fills every minute of every day that drags its length along; and whenever they or

other wild beasts clutch their living prey, the deadly horror which an agitated
melancholiac feels is the literally right reaction on the situation (1958:138).

A similar point could be made about some people's mistreatment of their
domestic animals or pets, the harsh regimens imposed on animals being raised
for food in many modern high production food "factories," and the flagrant
abuse of animals in various types of research (see Rollin 1981:84, 89-148).

Schopenhauer notes that none of our attempted explanations or
justifications for at least some human suffering (e.g., misuses of freedom, the
Fall of Man, criminals viewed as the products of bad social environments)
have application to animals. That is, there is no way in which they or any of
their species can be held responsible for even a part of their own sufferings.
And yet, as he points out, animals must endure great torment and agony, both
at the hands of humans, and because of the natural "gradation of
phenomena" whereby the stronger prey by instinct on the weaker, and the life
of the one is given to it by the death-throes of the other (1942:V, 11). If we
possess even a modicum of compassion, how can we affirm a world in which
the sufferings of innocent living beings are so rampant and routine?

The great religions have always been acutely attuned to the inexplicable
sufferings of the world that we have been concentrating on in this section. For
example, Buddha saw the human experience of the turning of the Wheel of
life as "a mass of suffering" and spoke often of the "old age and death, grief,
lamentation, suffering, dejection and despair" that beset human existence
(*Vinaya Texts*, quoted Noss 1969:137). And Walter Kaufmann reminds us
that "Jewish piety has been a ceaseless cry in the night, rarely unaware of 'all
the oppressions that are practiced under the sun'" [Ecclesiastes 4:1]. This
piety is "born of suffering so intense" that Jews "cannot contain it and must
shriek, speak, accuse, and argue with God—not about him—for there is no
other human being who would understand..." (Kaufmann 1963:168).

Of course, each religion has also claimed a means of redemption and
release from the sufferings it recognizes as a central problem of existence. But
what if there is none, or none seems adequate, or we cannot be convinced that
a means of salvation is available to us? Then our situation is stark and
desperate indeed, and nihilism seems to be the final, inescapable truth of our
lives. This at least is the burden of the arguments I have sketched here,
arguments that only scratched the surface of a problem that probes to the
deepest roots of the question of the meaning of life.

4. ARGUMENTS RELATING TO TEMPORAL EXISTENCE

I just mentioned the fact that the religions of the world are intensely
concerned with the problem of suffering; each has claimed to provide some

definitive way of dealing with it, if not conceptually, then at least existentially. Religions have also given a great deal of attention to the problem of existence in time, which I discuss in this section. In another work, I note that "a large part of what salvation means in the religious traditions is being able effectively to cope with such threats of time as the accumulation of evil deeds, the bondage of birth and rebirth, the terrors of death, the disintegration of things of value, and the anxieties of an uncertain future" (1981:263). This preoccupation with the problem of time is understandable because it, like the problem of suffering to which it is closely allied, can pose profound dangers to the integrity and stability of human existence. Thus many who despair of finding solutions to various aspects of this problem also come to despair of the worth of their lives.

The first aspect of this problem I discuss is the ephemerality of events in time, or as Schopenhauer expresses it, the perception that "the ever-passing present moment" is "the only mode of actual existence" (1942:V, 19). If this is true, then there seems to be no warrant for placing any value on the events and experiences of our lives, because each is too fleeting and evanescent to have value. As soon as an event or experience takes place it is immediately absorbed into the past. Then it "exists no more; it exists as little as that which has never been." We may have attached great importance to it, but as past, it is inferior to anything that is now present. The latter is at least "a *reality*" and is therefore "related to the former as something to nothing. . . ." Schopenhauer concludes this line of reasoning by saying, "that which in the next moment exists no more and vanishes utterly, like a dream, can never be worth a serious effort." Because every moment of our lives is like this, and because life is nothing more than an aggregation of such moments, it follows that our lives are completely devoid of value (19-20).

Antoine Roquentin, in Sartre's *Nausea*, is also afflicted with this despairing feeling of being "cast out, forsaken in the present" (1964:49). At work on his biography of the Marquis de Rollebon, he notices that the letters he had "just inscribed . . . were not even dry yet and already they belonged to the past." He looks anxiously around and can find only "the present, nothing but the present." In his diary he writes of this experience, observing that it had revealed to him the "true nature of the present." The present "was what exists, and all that was not present did not exist. The past did not exist. Not at all. Not in things, not even in my thoughts" (130).

Early in the novel Roquentin recounts a scene that brings the ephemerality of the present vividly to mind. He describes the scene in minute detail, almost in the manner of an impressionist painter intent upon capturing the sensations of the passing moment before they vanish forever into the past:

. . . Saturday, about four in the afternoon, on the end of the timbered sidewalk of the new station yard, a little woman in sky blue was running backwards, laughing, waving a handkerchief. At the same time, a negro in a cream-coloured raincoat, yellow shoes and a green hat, turned the corner of the street and whistled. Still going backwards, the woman bumped into him, underneath a lantern which hangs on a paling and which is lit at night. All at once there was the paling smelling strongly of wet wood, this lantern and this little blonde woman in the negro's arms under a sky the colour of fire....

Then everything came asunder, there was nothing left but the lantern, the palisade and the sky; it was still rather beautiful. An hour later the lantern was lit, the wind blew, the sky was black; nothing at all was left (15-16).

The citizens of Bouville, the town in which the events in *Nausea* take place, are said to suffer acutely from this sense of the fleetingness of the present moment. Roquentin describes how many of them seek respite from the strains of their workaday week by strolling along the seashore on a Sunday afternoon. But they find that their holiday brings them no enjoyment. They can feel "the minutes flowing beneath their fingers," as they try in vain "to store up enough youth to start anew on Monday." At last they return to their homes distracted and discontent, to read the evening paper or listen to the radio. Their "Sunday has left them with a taste of ashes and their thoughts are already running towards Monday" (74, 76).

So it is with all our longed-for pleasures, attainments, and moments of fulfilment. They disappear as soon as they have come, and we must learn to live with the fatal realization that nothing can last. Time erodes everything that happens, not just in the distant future but even as it is taking place. In a world where, as Schopenhauer states, "unrest is the mark of existence," and where each instant is continually being swallowed up in a "hurrying whirlpool of change," the attainment of anything approaching happiness seems inconceivable. Doomed to life in time, our situation as human beings is both barren and ridiculous. "We are like a man running downhill, who cannot keep on his legs unless he runs on, and will inevitably fall if he stops...." At the end of our days we will have nothing to show for our lives, seeing that they were "never anything more than a present moment always vanishing" (1942:V, 20-24).

Because the present is all that is real, and it is forever being churned under in the millrace of time, nothing can persist even for a short period. Among other things, this means that there can be no enduring self or coherent pattern of life, but only the constantly shifting perceptions and moods of a series of present moments. Edouard, a character in André Gide's *The Counterfeiters*, witnesses to a feeling of self-disintegration resulting from his awareness of being caught up in a temporal existence in which only the frail and fickle present is real:

> I am never anything but what I think myself—and this varies so incessantly, that often, if I were not there to make them acquainted, my morning's self would not recognize my evening's. Nothing could be more different from me than myself (Gide 1973:70-71).

Edouard has come to regard belief in the identity of one's self through time asa an illusion; there are as many "selves" as there are moments of one's life. But not even the expression "one's life" makes sense anymore. For there is no enduring "one" to have a life, and the "life" itself can have no genuine unity, being only a medley of detached episodes, each of which must cease to exist as soon as it has become, in order to make way for the equally volatile moments of experience that are to follow. The fleeting transience of events in time adds strong support to the nihilistic conclusion because time, like some universal solvent, dissolves the sense of self and destroys any basis for belief in a coherent pattern or encompassing meaning in one's life.

Even though the past is no longer real, perhaps we can at least relive it in our memories and preserve it in our retellings of it, and in that way give some measure of substance and continuity to our lives. Roquentin takes this possibility seriously for a time but finds at last that he must reject it. Our attempts to restore the past in memory or to embody it in words are bound to fail, partly because little of the vivid detail of past experiences remains with us, and more of it continues to evaporate with the passage of time. Also, we cannot help distorting the past even as we try to preserve it, because we unconsciously impose upon it the perspectives and expectations of each new present. We add to it or subtract from it without being fully aware that we are doing so, and our "reminiscences" of the past become more and more the whole-cloth fabrications of the present. The problem is only exacerbated by frequent attempts to remind ourselves of the specifics of past experiences, for with each attempt there is more embellishment and distortion, more substitution of the general and abstract for the particular and concrete. Finally, we become completely unable to distinguish fiction from fact. So what looks like continuity with our past is only a story of our own invention we tell ourselves in the present, a story that is in process of constant, though largely unconscious, revision.

Roquentin reluctantly comes to this conclusion with regard both to what he calls his "adventures" and the "experience" that people believe themselves to have accumulated with age, and which they think they can draw upon and share with others as a source of understanding and wisdom. As far as his so-called adventures are concerned, Roquentin travelled widely in the world and thought for a long while that he had experienced "great moments" in exotic places, moments that, by being stored up in his memory, could give continuity and significance to his life. But he finally realized that the "rare and precious quality" he sought in these adventures was an illusion. Our life in time does not come neatly packed in adventures, with a beginning, middle, and end, but is actually helter-skelter and confused. Only the embellishments and abstractions of "memory" give apparent order to that confusion. Even more basically, belief in the meaning of adventures is based on belief in the irreversibility of time. But there is no such thing. The past is not at all fixed but is continually being altered by the reconstructions of the present. Hence, it has no enduring meaning, and thinking of it as giving continuity to our existence is a mistake. Finally, an adventure is not such until it is past; so we cannot even live our adventures the first time around, much less "relive" them, as though they were something intrinsically real and fixed in time. The futility of trying to find meaning in one's adventures is for Roquentin a crucial reminder that the past is dead and beyond recall. It is an "enormous vacuum" that we try in vain to retain. "I wanted the moments of my life to follow and order themselves like those of a life remembered," he laments. "You might as well try to catch time by the tail" (Sartre 1964:54, 80, 89, 58).

A similar realization applies to the idea of "experience." Starting about age forty, people "would like to make us believe that their past is not lost, that their memories are condensed, gently transformed into Wisdom." But this belief in experience, commonly regarded as "the right of old men," is, like the belief in adventures, nothing but an illusion. Forsaken in the present, we try in vain to rejoin the past. But there is no escape from our imprisonment in the here and now (94, 118, 49). The past sheds no light on the present, nor can it bestow order and connectedness on our lives. "My memories," says Roquentin, "are like coins in the devil's purse: when you open it you find only dead leaves" (47).

If we cannot hope to make sense out of our lives on the basis of the present or the past, what of the future? Perhaps it can be a source of reassurance and hope. For while it is true that something is continually being lost in the passage of time, it is equally true that something is being gained: a new moment of experience and the moments which are to follow. Can we not find refreshment and challenge in a feeling of freedom before an open future, and in the promise of novel experiences yet to come? Anticipation of the future seems to be the other side of the tarnished coin of time, a welcome corrective to the ephemerality of the present and the nonrecoverability of the past.

According to the outlook we are now considering, however, a strategy of looking to the future is no less abortive than that of trying to freeze the present or preserve the past. This strategy not only overlooks the fact that future moments have no reality until they enter the present and then, like all present experiences, vanish irrevocably into the past. It also assumes a comfortable predictability about the future, foolishly oblivious to the fact that it is fraught with perils. The future is a dark unknown that can at any moment bring the annihilation of those loves, tasks, and commitments that give at least some semblance of sustenance and order to our lives. In the preceding section, which focused on the problem of suffering, I wrote about the threats the future can hold and the impossibility of feeling confident or secure in the face of these threats. If that reasoning remains sound, how can anticipations of the future be of any use in giving meaning to life? It is akin to basing one's life on successive throws of dice. As Roquentin never tires or reminding us about the future, "*anything* can happen" (106-107). If he and others are right who speak of the unlimited malleability of the past and the detached autonomy of the present, it could hardly be otherwise.

The upshot of these considerations about the present, the past, and the future is that there can be no such thing as what John Wisdom has called an "order in the drama of Time" (1970:40-41). Instead of being a steadily unfolding drama or "an extension directed toward a goal," life in time can only be seen as "a sum of discontinuous moments which must be endured here and now" (Thielicke 1969:31). There is no enduring meaning of the past, no reliability of the future, and no repose in the present. The events of our lives do not flow smoothly from the past and serenely into the future; instead, each event is radically disconnected from those preceding and following it, and only in the fleeting present is any actuality of experience to be found. To attempt to live in the past is to succumb to the illusion of its reality, or what amounts to the same thing, of its fixity. To live for the future is to assume against all experience that future events will be different, i.e., that when they occur they will somehow exhibit more permanence or have more lasting significance than the events of an ever-perishing present. And it is to underestimate the fickleness of fate. To live for the present is to live for something that by its very nature can provide no fulfilment or repose, because it is forever restless and incomplete, endlessly annulling and transcending itself in the direction of that which is yet to come (see Sartre 1966:152, 658).

Therefore, whether we approach our lives in retrospect, in prospect, or from the standpoint of the present moment, it seems impossible to find in them any coherent pattern or sustaining purpose. Earlier in this chapter, we made use of the first of Karl Britton's four criteria for a meaningful life. The fourth one is relevant here. In Britton's judgment, if a person is to live a meaningful life, he must be able "to direct and accept a particular pattern in his own life" and be guided by that pattern (1969:189). But if the foregoing analysis is correct, any conviction we may have of such a persisting pattern or organizing purpose in our lives must rest on a misconception of the nature of time. It accords to our temporal existence far too much in the way of continuity, predictability, and enduring value. It follows that the criterion cannot be fulfilled, and that our lives cannot be meaningful.

Two other aspects of temporal existence remain to be discussed: boredom and the threat of death. These give further reason to doubt the meaning of life. In the preceding discussion, emphasis is placed on our inability to find satisfaction or repose in our life in time, given the lack of connectedness in temporal events and the fleeting instability of the present moment. But what if we were able to attain the satisfaction and repose for which we long? By Schopenhauer's reckoning, it would only mean being rescued from one scourge of temporal life in order to be made victim to another: monotony. Our first task in life, he observes, "is to win something," i.e., the satisfaction of some yearning or need. The second task is that "of doing something with that which has been won—of warding off boredom, which, like a bird of prey, hovers over us, ready to fall wherever it sees a life secure from need." It is a law of life that "to gain anything we have longed for is only to discover how vain and empty it is." The experience of boredom makes it evident that "existence has no real value in itself," and boredom can best be defined as "the feeling of the emptiness of life." What better proof do we need of the absurdity of existence than our constant susceptibility to craving, on the one hand, and boredom, on the other? "If life were possessed of any intrinsic value, there would be no such thing as boredom at all: mere existence would satisfy us in itself, and we should want for nothing" (1942:V, 22-23).

Both Schopenhauer and Cioran insist that misery is better than monotony, and that it is better to be beleaguered than to be bored. Schopenhauer asks what human beings would do with their time if all their wishes were fulfilled and if the world were a paradise of luxury and ease. He answers that they "would either die of boredom or hang themselves; or there would be wars, massacres, and murders . . . ." He concludes that enduring pain at the hands of an indifferent nature is more acceptable than being condemned to a static life of monotonous surfeit, a life with no torment of anxiety, dissatisfaction, or desire (1942:V, 3). Cioran speaks of ennui as "the revelation of the void" lying at the heart of life, and he too considers any amount of want or suffering to be preferable to it.

> The man suffering from a characterized sickness is not entitled to complain: he has an occupation. The great sufferers are never bored: disease fills them, the way remorse feeds the great criminals. For any intense suffering produces a simulacrum of plentitude and proposes a terrible reality to consciousness, which it cannot elude; while suffering without *substance* in that temporal mourning of ennui affords consciousness nothing that forces it to fruitful action (1975:14).

Cioran goes on to say that in comparison with boredom, which he describes as "this displacement in time, this empty and prostrate languor in which nothing stops us but the spectacle of the universe decaying before our eyes," the agonies of hell could only be welcomed as a "haven" (15).

Sartre's *Nausea* is filled with statements about the feelings of torpidity and languor which plague our life in time. In one scene Roquentin exclaims: "Nothing happens while you live. The scenery changes, people come in and go out, that's all. There are no beginnings. Days are tacked on to days without rhyme or reason, an interminable, monotonous addition" (1964:57). Whereas from one standpoint, the problem of temporal existence is that of trying to "catch time by the tail" and to prolong the fleeting moments, from another the problem is that time "is too large, it can't be filled up. Everything you plunge into it is stretched and disintegrates" (32). Our desperate need for "adventures" can be interpreted, not only as an attempt to package and relive the past, but also as an effort to stave off this unbearable sense of monotony and ennui.

In fact, any program or project, no matter how ridiculous it may be in itself, is preferable to being bored, with time hanging heavy on our hands and no prospect of anything to do. Roquentin tells us of a particularly pathetic example. The so-called Self-Taught Man spends his days in the library with the project of reading every single book on the shelves, from "A" to "Z," in a frantic attempt to fend off boredom and to find a sustaining challenge and purpose for his life. The library also provides a flimsy shelter for Roquentin from the aimless monotony of his own existence. On one occasion when he is sitting in the library trying to absorb himself in reading a novel by Stendhal, he becomes suddenly aware that it is nearly seven o'clock, the library's closing time. Face to face with the yawning emptiness of time, he is seized with panic. "Once again I was going to be cast out into the town. Where would I go? What would I do?" (110).

It can be argued that many of the things with which all of us try to fill our lives can be explained in this way, from games, hobbies, television, conversations, shopping trips, books, flirtations and passing love affairs, on down to our most protracted and "serious" pursuits. A prime motive, and perhaps the dominant motive, for all these activities is that of willingness to do almost anything to escape the horror of boredom, with its stark unmasking of the barrenness of our existence. Cioran even goes so far as to claim that the flight from boredom is the key to human history. He views it as the major incentive of the thrust toward pillage, conquest, and the glory of battle; and the principal cause for the otherwise inexplicable eagerness of the many to idolize or follow the few mad despoilers of the earth such as Napoleon. Was it not Napoleon who complained that the vapid life of Paris weighed on him "like a leaden garment?" (1975:101-103).

But if our lives in time were rid of these afflictions of ephemerality, discontinuity, hazard of the future, and the vacuum of ennui, they would still not have eluded the threat of death, that ultimate absurdity to which every temporal existence inexorably leads. "Wherever there is life," says Keiji Nishitani, "there must be death." And in the face of it, "all life and existence lose their certainty and their importance as reality, and come to look unreal instead". (1982:7). In *Être et Avoir*, Gabriel Marcel tells us just what this dizzying loss of certainty and importance means on the concrete level of one's own existence. He records a "sad Sunday" in March 1931, when he became intensely conscious of "time as open toward death—toward my death—toward my doom. Time-abyss; vertigo in the presence of this time at the bottom of which is my death which sucks me in" (Marcel 1935:120; quoted Choron 1963:255). We have seen already how the transitoriness and disconnectedness of temporal events threaten the sense of self. But there at least we have the thread of an ongoing consciousness and memory, however tenuous that thread may be. With respect to our impending death, there can be no such qualification. The maelstrom of time will hurl us at last to a shipwreck so absolute that not only must we jettison much of the cargo and content of life, such as is lost to memory all along; but our biological organisms themselves, the vessels and bearers of our conscious lives, must be dashed into ruin.

The prospect that one's own familiar body, so long warm with pulse, breath, and feeling, and so immediately responsive to one's every impulse and intention, will someday become nothing more than a blankly staring lump of matter, is a prospect awful to behold. It brings home to us as perhaps nothing else can the chilling indifference of nature of which the cosmic nihilist speaks. In *The Idiot*, Dostoevsky describes Prince Muishkin's reaction to a painting of Christ just taken down from the cross. It was to him a "dreadful picture," because it exposed the stark ugliness of death, in this case a death following upon great suffering. The spectacle of that mangled body, says Muishkin, makes nature appear "as some huge, implacable, dumb monster; or still better ... some enormous mechanical engine of modern days which has seized and crushed and swallowed up a great and invaluable Being, a Being worth nature and all her laws, worth the whole earth ... " (1967:391-392).

Similar feelings of horror about the dead body are evoked by Milan Kundera, in his novel *The Book of Laughter and Forgetting*. One of his characters dies in the night and is removed from the hospital room by being unceremoniously dragged along the floor, his head bumping over the threshold on the way out. His wife, hearing later about how the body of her husband has been treated, reacts with both terror and disgust.

> Being a corpse struck her as an unbearable disgrace. One minute you are a human being protected by modesty—the sanctity of nudity and privacy—and the next you die, and your body is suddenly up for grabs. Anyone can

tear your clothes off, rip you open, inspect your insides, and—holding his nose to keep the stink away—stick you into the deepfreeze or the flames (1980:170-171).

Kundera sums up: "Death has two faces. One is nonbeing; the other is the terrifying material being that is the corpse" (1980:171).

To contemplate one's death, therefore, is to contemplate one's total undoing. Because this wholesale calamity awaits each of us at the end of our days, how can those days add up to anything meaningful or worthwhile? If we acknowledge, as we must, the unalterable fact of death, how can we persuade ourselves of the reality or importance of any of life's concerns?

In an article on "Meanings of Life," published in 1936, William Ernest Hocking helps us to comprehend the enormity of death's threat to our perception of the value of life. His thesis is that if death is final and there is no hope of immortality, then there can be no overall meaning to life. Such value as remains to it will be reduced to a series of momentary "spotwise enjoyments" (1936:256), with no unifying context of long-range purpose and plan. For Hocking, the questions of the meaning of my life is not a question which someone else can answer: "What is more melancholy than to feel bound to take the public view of one's self?" (280). I alone can answer this question, and only in the context of my own firsthand memories and ongoing aspirations.

As for its memories, "the self makes its own memory by its unconscious selection of what it deems significant, as data for its ultimate answers" (274). These memories, thus selected and evaluated, provide the basis on which the self projects its hopes and plans for the future. An essential part of life's meaning, according to Hocking, is what it means in prospect to this self. It is the conscious self, then, facing both to the past and to the future, which continues to assess and discover the overall meaning of life, as the context in which the failures and achievements of particular times gain their enduring significance.

For the conscious self to cease to exist "at the point of *any* attainment is to lose the full meaning of that attainment," because the attainment can no longer be placed in the comprehensive framework of the self's remembered past and envisioned future. Thus Hocking contends that "from the mere logic of meaning, . . . there is *no moment* at which conscious existence could appropriately cease" (273). He states this same conclusion in a slightly different way when he says, "there is no meaning at all except in the being of the self. (And if this self vanishes, and all like it, meaning vanishes out of the world. No achievement can keep the person alive. . . . It is the person who perpetuates the achievement, not the achievement the person)" (280). The meaning of a particular life is therefore something inescapably personal, and for the person who is the subject of that life to cease to be is for the meaning of his life to be extinguished, as though it had never been.

If follows from Hocking's reasoning that death as the extinction of self and the meaning of life are completely and unalterably opposed. He presents his argument in the interest of showing the necessity of immortality. But it can easily be turned around to show that if the hope of immortality be groundless and the finality of death the fate of us all, then we have no basis for believing in the meaning of our lives. And there would seem to be little in the way of convincing evidence to support belief in an afterlife. Its probability is so slight as to leave us no alternative but to conclude from Hocking's own premises that our lives are petty and insignificant, of no more lasting value than the mayfly, which today is and tomorrow is not.

In *Being and Nothingness* (first published in 1943, as *L'Être et le Néant*), Sartre makes some statements that, at first, sound strikingly similar to Hocking's analysis of the relation between death and the meaning of life. Sartre asserts that there can be meaning to one's existence only so long as one is conscious and alive, because only then is one free to decide what the meaning of one's life is or will continue to be: "life decides its own meaning because it is always in suspense; it possesses essentially a power of self-criticism and self-metamorphosis which causes it to define itself as a 'not-yet'..." (1966:664). He connects this point with death by saying that because "a meaning can come only from subjectivity, death must *remove all meaning from life*" (659). These observations seem close to Hocking's contention that "there is no meaning at all except in the being of the self," consciously drawing from its past and projecting itself toward its future, and that death must therefore pose an absolute threat to the meaning of life. But there is a difference between Hocking's reasoning and that of Sartre, the significance of which we need to weigh.

Hocking, it will be recalled, argues that if I am going to die at any time in the future, my life must cease to have any meaning right now. The reason is that the context giving meaning to the particular events of my life, and without which they cannot have comprehensive meaning, is a context which must by its very nature be dynamic and unending. Were that context (the context of my ever-developing conscious existence) to cease, my life as a whole would be deprived of meaning. Sartre, on the other hand, argues that my life has meaning as long as I am here to give it meaning, as long as possibilities for choice await me in the future which I can act upon in the present. Death is not one of my possibilities because, logically speaking, I can *do* nothing with my own death when it has occured. As the "nihilation" of all my possibilities, death is "always beyond my subjectivity." Thus, "I can neither discover my death nor wait for it nor adopt an attitude toward it...." On this ground, Sartre rejects Martin Heidegger's notion that my death is my peculiar possibility, something which can happen to me alone, and that "being-unto-death" is the authentic mode of being for a finite individual. Pushing the point further, he contends that the projects with which I define the meaning of my life are independent of death. It is true that death is their final *limit*, because with death my projects will cease. But in no way is death to be viewed as an *obstacle* to these projects while I am alive to plan them and carry them out (1966:667-668, 670). Implicit in these statements is the idea that thinking of death as a threat to the meaning of my life so long as I live makes no sense. Death lies wholly beyond life and subjectivity, so it cannot threaten them.

These are reassuring words, but there is a less easily disposed of similarity between Hocking and Sartre which makes one wonder whether the latter has entirely resolved the problem of the putative threat of death to life's meaning, even in his own mind. It is well known that the major emphasis of Sartre's philosophy is on the reality of freedom and the responsibility this reality gives to the individual. But death must entirely eclipse my freedom and with it, any possibility of continuing to be responsible for the meaning of my life. As Sartre puts it, death imposes upon my life "an arbitrary and definitive totalization," as over against the dynamic, ever-evolving context of which Hocking speaks. When I die, nothing more can happen to my life from within; "it is entirely closed; nothing more can be made to enter there . . . . " Will my life then be wholly beyond change? No, says Sartre, for "its meaning does not cease to be modified from the outside." Its meaning is now open to modification by others, and there is nothing I can do to prevent their modifications and interpretations of my life. My life is out of my hands; it is no longer my responsibility. Thus "the very existence of *death* alienates us wholly in our own life to the advantage of the Other. To be dead is to be a prey for the living." Sartre concludes that "the one who tries to grasp the meaning of his future death must discover himself as the future prey of others" (665).

Is this frightening prospect—one we would think to be especially disturbing to someone like Sartre, given his insistence that freedom lies at the heart of human existence—something which he or we can regard with equanimity? To believe that all that we have made of our lives in the course of living them is now at the point of our deaths to be subject to the freedom of others, and not at all to our own; and that those others can size up our lives at will, with no possibility of correction or protest from our side—does not this prospect threaten the meaning of our lives here and now, and in the most far-reaching and fundamental manner? In a way, this prospect is more dreadful than that of simply being forgotten. We feel here the shudder of Hocking's statement that nothing is "more melancholy than to feel bound to take the public view of one's self." Furthermore, it is obvious that Sartre or anyone else is perfectly capable of entertaining this prospect; he has, after all, written as some length about it. Public figures, in particular, can understand fully from the perspective of their present experience the melancholia of which Hocking speaks. Oscar Wilde, for example, said of biography that it "lends to death a new terror" (quoted Oates 1984). So Sartre's claim that death, which entails having our lives someday fall prey to others (if they do not vanish completely, as forgotten), is something entirely outside our subjectivity and irrelevant to our present existence, seems facile and unpersuasive. This is at least true if he means to include the prospect of death, and not just the ontological fact of death. To the extent that his analysis of death fails to convince and reassure us, the prospect of our dying must continue to fill us with dread and to be seen as a preeminent threat to the meaning of our lives. Or so it can be argued by those who reason from the fact of death to a nihilistic conclusion.

There is no way in which we can do justice to the various dimensions of the threat of death in this brief section. We can only touch lightly on a few of them. But one other dimension does need some discussion, because it seems to differ significantly from the fate of eventual death which is common to us all, as troublesome as that fate is. I refer to so-called premature or untimely death. It should be noted that in order to address the problem of premature death we will have to bracket some of the other problems of temporal existence already discussed, because posing this problem requires us to make some assumptions those other problems would call into question (e.g., the assumption that there can be such thing as an enduring self, or that a connected pattern of life is possible).

It is one thing to contemplate the course of one's life from the vantage point of old age and to feel that it has been a good life overall, with much of what one had hoped to experience, contribute, and attain now fulfilled. But it is quite another to be cut off in one's childhood, youth, or prime, with a large part of one's potential unrealized and much that one could have accomplished left undone. In the case of living to a ripe old age, one can have the satisfaction of having had sufficient time to learn how to respond to life's possibilities in one's own way, creating a unique self-identity and pattern of personal accomplishment by the cumulative effects of one's choices and activities stretching over a long period of time. Not all lives in old age achieve this kind of satisfaction. But some do and others may. They may, however, only if death stays its hand. And there is no assurance that it will. People are every day made victims of fatal car crashes, hit by lightning, swept away by flash floods, caught in tornadoes, attacked by virulent organisms, seized with heart attacks, suddenly choked to death on their food, killed by accidental falls, or subjected to the slings and arrows of a thousand other outrageous fortunes. Because such things can happen to any of us at any time and are happening to someone else all of the time, and because it is impossible to predict when or whether they will occur, it is clear that our lives hang from a thread.

Writing this book, for example, is an activity of some importance to me at this moment. But I have no way of knowing right now whether I will live to complete it. There may be some disease lurking in my cells or some accident on the horizon of my near future that will mean my death. I must live and work, not only with the constant awareness that my existence in time will end, but with no knowledge of *when* it will end. It may end suddenly and with no warning, leaving no opportunity to make the contributions I hope yet to make, to complete those projects important to me and that may have some value to others as well, or to bring the pattern of my life to the kind of resolution I would like for it to have. I may not be around to give company to my wife in her old age, or to see my grandchildren or watch them grow. We must live, in other words, in the face of a terrible uncertainty that threatens to annihilate us before the fulness of time and bring to ruin much on which we now stake our hopes and focus our energies.

The magnitude of this calamity is greatest in childhood and decreases as we move toward old age. Were my life to end right now, the event would not be as calamitous as it would have been earlier on, or as it would be for someone far younger. I have lived for more than one-half a century and have been given the opportunity to do many things that I wanted to do. The menace of time is unremitting for us all, but the young and unfulfilled are especially at the mercy of its pitiless caprice. The fact and prospect of premature death makes our existence indisputably tragic. For some its presence does more; it pronounces a sentence of meaninglessness on life as well. Not only must we feel grief beyond solace for those to whom untimely death does occur and for those who had loved them. We must despair of a temporal existence in which this calamity never ceases to find new victims, and in which it continues to loom as an omnipresent danger to people of nearly all ages, sparing only the very old.

When all this is said and done, however, we can still raise the question of how significant the distinction finally is between premature death and death in old age. The fact that the severity of the threat of untimely death is on a sliding scale for given individuals does not appreciably diminish its insult to life in general, or the aura of absurd contingency it imparts to human existence as a whole. Even to the very old their impending deaths may seem untimely. For example, some of them must face death frustrated and unfulfilled. Others may resent having to die in their old age when they continue to be in possession of their faculties, feel that they still have much to live for and much to contribute, or perhaps strongly believe that they have finally arrived at a mastery of their powers which it has taken them the whole span of their long lifetimes to achieve. Pablo Picasso in his eighties and nineties is one good example of the second kind of case (see Richardson 1984).

Those among the very old less gifted than Picasso take with them to their graves irreplaceable perspectives and backgrounds of experience on which they could have continued to build, and from which others might have derived inestimable benefit. And we should not forget that deaths of the elderly, as well as of the young, can produce feelings of deep sorrow and loss on the part of their families and friends. Even the debilitation of body and mind in old age does not make death then more fitting, because it is part of the problem of death and signalizes one more absurd aspect of our lives in time. So we are brought back to death itself, and not just so-called premature death, as the final atrocity and ultimate surd of our temporal existence.

Chapter 4

Arguments About Reason, Will, and Other Persons

... I was engaged to come here as a Land-Surveyor, yet that was only a pretext, they were playing with me, I was driven out of everybody's house, they're playing with me still today . . . .
—Franz Kafka (1969:258)

1. ARGUMENTS RELATING TO REASON

Aristotle begins the most brilliant and probably the most influential of his many works with the observation, "All men by nature desire to know" (*Metaphysics* 980a). His definition of human beings as "rational animals" is well known. But, as we have already seen, epistemological nihilists believe that thinkers such as Aristotle drastically overestimate our powers of reason, and that we can either know or understand precious little. I will soon consider ways in which their conclusion relates to despair of the meaning of life, but first let me present a case for what one writer has called "despair of the intellect" (Heller 1966:279). In doing so, I will recall arguments presented earlier on behalf of epistemological nihilism, elaborating on these when appropriate, and also take note of some additional arguments. My intent is not so much to probe the arguments in depth as to suggest the variety and range of such arguments.

The first argument was mentioned in the discussion of Camus's existential nihilism in Chapter Two. The French writer contends that it is the sad but clear lesson of human history that the mind's ravenous appetite for clarity and comprehensiveness of understanding has found no nourishment. The contradictions, absurdities, and fragmented character of thought and experience are just as intractable today as they have ever been; hence, there is no basis for hoping that we will ever make any progress in trying to resolve them.

Cioran adds his voice to Camus's, arguing as the latter does that history's exposure of the poverty of reason is plain for all to see. It shows that we can as well argue against, as for, any position whatever; and that no firm conclusions ever have been or ever will be established by the human mind's dogged quest for knowledge.

> The history of ideas, like that of deeds, unfolds in a meaningless climate . . . . This earth, a place where we can confirm anything with an equal likelihood: here axioms and frenzies are interchangeable; impulses and collapses are identified; exaltations and depravities participate in the same movement. Show me a single *case* in support of which nothing can be found. The advocates of hell have no fewer claims on truth than those of heaven— and I should plead the cause of madman and sage with the same fervor (1975:118-119).

He states in another place, in reference to the Greek sage with whose words we opened this section, "The merest illiterate and Aristotle are equally irrefutable—and fragile" (146).

Yet we do not give up this search that history shows to be completely hopeless. We allow hope to triumph over logic. Having all the evidence we need to realize that truth is inaccessible, we continue to believe that "it must be searched for, aspired to, fought over." No one could be more simple-minded, asserts Cioran, than one who takes account of the history of human attempts to know and still "speaks of Truth with *conviction*" (167).

According to this first argument, then, an honest appraisal of the history of thought reveals a bizarre parade of ingenious systems of thought, each with its insistent claims to truth and elaborate arguments, but each taking basic issue with the systems that preceded it and differing just as essentially with those that have followed it in the course of time. No consensus has ever been achieved on the great recurring questions, despite our most deeply probing investigations. The mystifications of the mind have not been reduced, but only made worse, by the steady multiplication of striking but incommensurable schemes. What reason have we to think that the situation will change now or in the future?

The second argument for epistemological nihilism concludes that there are no transperspectival truths or meanings, i.e., that all claims to truth and structures of meaning are relative to the idiosyncratic assumptions and standpoints of particular persons, groups, epochs, or systems. We saw how Nietzsche argues for this view with respect to persons and groups, each regarded as a center of its own will to power, and how Mauthner develops it in relation to language as the instrument of thought and expression. We also saw how Stirner's nominalistic egoism leads him to the view that truth is completely relative to each human subject, and thence to contempt for the concept of truth itself.

Spengler, an author strongly influenced by Nietzsche, defends the position that claims to truth are relative to different periods of human history. He takes Western intellectuals to task for lacking "insight into the historically relative character" of their beliefs and for being unaware "of the necessary limits of their validity." He argues that the so-called unshakable and eternal truths assumed by people in the West are in fact only true for them and eternal for their particular worldview. Other cultures have evolved similar convictions about the absolute, unchanging truth of their own quite different basic beliefs. A proper understanding of history shows that "there is nothing constant, nothing universal." Spengler concludes that "we must cease to speak of the forms of 'Thought', the principles of 'Tragedy', the mission of 'The State'," and all such unqualified, universal topics. "Universal validity involves always the fallacy of arguing from particular to particular" (1932:I, 23).

More recent thinkers such as the anthropologists Emile Durkheim, Robin Horton, and Clifford Geertz have contended for an ineradicable relativity of the conceptual systems of different cultures, each system laying down in its own particular fashion the path of what is thinkable and believable (see Godlove's sketch of their reasoning and his bibliographical references in 1984:290-294). The general conclusion of positions and arguments of this sort is that an ultimate arbitrariness attaches to all assertions of truth and/or patterns and assumptions of meaning. Reason is the pawn, not the master, of the particular contexts and circumstances in which it happens to find itself.

A third line of argument follows closely upon this second one. The idea that truth and meaning are purely in us—mere constructs of the mind, arbitrary creations of human language, culture, and history—leads to the conclusion that the world itself is radically unknowable. If unknowable, it can only be regarded as alien to all that is human. We are divorced from the world as something nonsensical, something devoid of those intelligible principles and patterns of meaning we unconsciously project upon it in our anxious craving to discover in it that which is homelike and familiar. We saw earlier that Camus's despair of reason's ability to find in the world an answering response to its search for meaning leads him to brand the world as hopelessly "dense" and "strange," a "vast irrational" inaccessible to understanding. We also noted how Nietzsche's perspectival theory of truth is accompanied by the conviction that there are no facts in reality itself, only a chaotic, featureless flux; and that the only thing that endures, even for a short period of time, is our opinions. (Camus and Cioran, as noted above, seek to show how changeable and conflicting these opinions can be, when viewed against the backdrop of the history of thought.)

Similarly, the fundamental discovery Roquentin makes in *Nausea* is that "the world of explanations and reasons is not the world of existence." There is an unbridgeable gap between names, concepts, descriptions, and explanations, on the one hand, and the brute, unintelligible giveness of things, on the other. Even distinctions among things, or the idea that this is one thing and that another, are baseless impositions of the mind, as are notions of spatial, temporal, and causal relations, and all discriminations of quality and character. The world of existence, as it presents itself in the experience of "nausea," is symbolized by Roquentin as a kind of oozing heavy paste or sluggish larva, which can be brought under any scheme of interpretation whatever. We can know that it is, but it makes no sense to ask what it is, or what it means. As such, it contrasts utterly with the lightness and transparency of understanding for which reason yearns.

Roquentin announces that this realization of the bare giveness or absurd contingency of the world of existence (i.e., its amenability to any and all interpretations) is "the key to Existence, the key to my Nauseas, to my own life. In fact, all that I could grasp beyond that returns to this fundamental absurdity" (Sartre 1964:173-174). His view of the separation of knowledge from reality, and of the consequent divorce of human beings from the world, is thus closely akin to the views of Nietzsche and Camus. For all three, so-called knowledge is not a window opening out upon a world of intelligible qualities and relations (as it was for Aristotle, for example), but an opaque screen reflecting conceptions and schemes of our own invention.

In the preceding chapter, I described the dualistic view of human consciousness and world, which is one kind of inference from the scientific vision of nature. Sartre's dualism, as expressed both in his novel *Nausea* and in his lengthy treatise *Being and Nothingness*, is much more radical, because it drains the world even of the "objective" properties and relations science ascribes to it, and thus of the remotest resemblance to the contents of human awareness. The hiatus between the world as it is in and of itself (or what Sartre calls being-in-itself) and human consciousness (being-for-itself) could not be more thoroughgoing or complete. While the former is characterized as dense, compact, full, undifferentiated, and radically contingent—or in a word, completely unknowable—the latter is seen as the sole repository of possibilities, distinctions, logical and causal connections, and meanings.

It is true that Sartre does not interpret his position as being dualistic, for at least three reasons. First, he claims that thought and object are always experienced together, because thought is inescapably intentional, or fastened upon objects. Second, he argues that the for-itself has no substantial or independent being of its own but is completely dependent on the in-itself which it "nihilates," meaning that the for-itself attributes characteristics to the in-itself, whereby the latter can be distinguished from things it is not, or from things it might have been or could be, but now is not. Also implicit in the for-itself's nihilating activity is consciousness of its not being the in-itself. Reality in itself just *is*, but thought imparts to it a context of contrasts and alternative possibilities, a context upon which all conceptualiztion and awareness crucially depend. Were there no reality to be nihilated, there could be no thought, showing that the for-itself has being only in a derivative sense and cannot be dualistically conceived. Third, he asserts that both kinds of being are somehow part of a more inclusive context.

But Sartre gives us no clear analysis of this context, and so sharp and complete are the distinctions he draws between the two types of being that there is serious question as to how they can possibly be brought into the kind of synthesis or interaction he claims them to have (see Blocker 1979:69-72). Moreover, it does not seem that the attribution of properties and relations to a blank and characterless reality can be anything but arbitrary. Sartre seems to admit as much when he lays stress on the radical contingency and massive, nauseating facticity of the in-itself, the way in which it eludes all of our conceptions, discriminations, and patterns of interpretation, not just in the sense of being more than we are capable of comprehending, but in the sense of having no inherent comprehensibility whatever.

A fourth argument for epistemological nihilism is that there is no ground of certainty or complete justification of belief on which we can base our claims to knowledge, and that without such a ground our arguments and appeals must be sucked into an infinite regress. This argument depends on the asumption that we can be said to know something only when we are certain of it or only when our belief in it is completely justified. The rationale for this assumption is that if we are less than certain of what we claim to be true, or if it is something less than completely justified, then it is to that extent doubtful to us. But if something is doubtful to us, we can hardly be said to know it. The next step in the argument is to show that we can never be certain about anything. The reason is that certainty is an absolute state, admitting of no degrees, and we always have some reason to doubt, however slightly, what we claim to know. The same thing can be said about beliefs that purport to be completely justified.

No empirical proposition can be entertained with complete certainty, for instance, because some future experience might call it into question. Even in the case of the so-called truths of reason, such as fundamental logical propositions or the basic propositions of mathematics, we can say either that they are true only in a trivial, purely formal sense of "true" (i.e., true merely by definition or by derivation from arbitrarily posited axioms, rules of operation, and primitive definitions), or that our certainty about them may not be warranted. As soon as the latter possibility is seriously entertained, then we cease to have the attitude of absolute certainty about the propositions in question.

For example, in the seventeenth century, René Descartes introduced the possibility that we may be deceived by an evil demon into being certain about propositions that are not true. Keith Lehrer, a contemporary philosopher, gives us a modern rendering of this skeptical hypothesis by suggesting the possible existence of creatures of another galaxy (he calls them "Googols"), with an intelligence many orders higher than that of humans, who send out a peculiar kind of wave that causes us to believe what we believe (which would include those things about which we are certain). These beliefs are close enough to being correct to enable us to survive in our environment, but they are also infected with some degree of error. "However," says Lehrer, "whether any belief of any man is correct or even nearly correct depends entirely on the whimsy of some Googol rather than on the capacities and faculties of the man" (1971:292). Thus, a fatal tinge of arbitrariness marks the beliefs, meaning that there is no way in which we can ever be sure about the truth (or falsity) of any of them.

The Googols, in their turn, derive their beliefs from galactic beings with an even higher order of intelligence who similarly amuse themselves by partially deceiving the Googols. And so it goes, *ad infinitum*. Lehrer's thesis is, to the extent that this or a similar hypothesis is even slightly conceivable, to that extent we must call our certainties into question. Hence, we cannot be truly certain of anything. From this it follows that we cannot have any knowledge at all, in the sense of having at least some completely justified (and thus unquestionable) beliefs.

Peter Unger, in a book fittingly titled *Ignorance*, gives us a slightly different perspective on this same path of argument when he contends that for a person really to know anything requires that the person be absolutely certain about what he claims to know. His reason is that he considers it to be a contradiction for us to say of someone, "He really *knows* it, but he *isn't* absolutely *certain* of it" (1975:87; see 82-87). Unger goes on to insist that for anyone to be absolutely certain that something is so, is for that person to embrace dogmatism. To be absolutely certain, one must have "the attitude that *no* new information, evidence, or experience will now be seriously considered ... to be *at all* relevant to any possible change in how certain one should be in the matter ...." But to have such a "severe" view, foreclosing in advance the possibility of changing one's mind on the basis of new information in the future, is arrogant close-mindedness that can never be justified. Hence, there can be no such thing as a warranted absolute certainty (1975:105-106). And because knowledge requires absolute certainty, there can be no such thing as knowledge.

The same kind of conclusion follows from the perspective-relative view of truth and meaning considered earlier. Beliefs that are thought by us to be absolutely certain and unassailable could turn out to be nothing more than the contingent products of our linguistic, historical, or cultural conditioning. Or they might be beliefs which were posited arbitrarily by an individual or group at some time in the past and seem "certain" simply through long familiarity and lack of critical reflection. Because we can never be entirely sure that these beliefs are not so conditioned or arbitrarily posited, we cannot be said to possess any genuine knowledge; beneath our claims to truth is no sure foundation, but only a morass of sinking sand.

In summary, however hard we may try to justify a given belief, we can only do so in terms of other beliefs. Because we can—or should—always call these latter beliefs into question, as per the above, we are trapped in an infinite regress of doubt. Cioran gives us an apt statement of this endless regress, and of the void of reason and understanding it opens up, when he observes that "[e]very problem, if we get to the bottom of it, leads to bankruptcy and leaves the intellect exposed: no more questions and no more answers in a space without horizon. The interrogations turn against the mind which has conceived them: it becomes their own victim" (1975:78). The student whose comments were discussed in Chapter One was led to a similar conclusion by his reflections on the process of rational criticism and questioning.

Other arguments for epistemological nihilism could be considered, but these four should be sufficient for our purposes. I turn now to the question of how this position can be related to the conclusion that life has no meaning. One obvious relation is that if nothing can be known, it follows that nothing can be known about values. And if nothing can be known about values, then there are no knowable standards for making our choices or giving direction to our lives. That is, all values are completely arbitrary, and so must be all value commitments. This consequence of epistemological nihilism for values has already been mentioned in connection with moral values, at the end of the third section of Chapter Two. Clearly, it applies to values of any sort whatever, including those values involved in knowing how we ought to live our lives so as to find purpose and meaning in them.

The intimacy of this first connection between intellectual despair and despair of the meaning of life is illumined further by Peter Heller:

> It is a commonplace to say of a person in despair that he does not know where to turn or that he will turn his hope everywhere and anywhere and yet find no answer. And while 'despair' (désespoir, desperare) emphasizes the general failure of hope, the German term Verzweiflung would seem to accentuate the intellectual aspect by conceiving of all manners of despair in the image of despairing doubt (Zweifel) (1966:279).

Richard Hauck also speaks to this relation between the two types of despair when he says, "A man's awareness of total absurdity depends upon the failure of his intellect to discover that rightness and meaning which his inner sense suspects" (1971:4). And there is at least a suggestion of a connection between a complete relativism of values and the perspectival view of meaning and truth in another of his statements: "The absurd view is relativistic: it depends partly if not wholly on the assumption that any value can be judged arbitrary when seen from a point outside the framework which produced the value in the first place" (6). If values are arbitrary, then so must be any and all courses of life, to the extent that the outlooks, choices, and actions of those courses of life are rooted in, and expressive of, fundamental value commitments. To say of a course of life that it is purely arbitrary is, as Hauck remarks, no different from saying that it is absurd.

The two kinds of despair are related in a second way, alluded to in our discussion of the attitudes toward nature taken by Nietzsche, Camus, and Sartre. The epistemology of these three makes nature completely inscrutable and tends to set it in sharp opposition to human beings. This divorce of humans and nature stems from a position in which nature is dense and absurd and thus utterly unresponsive to those concerns about truth and meaning which lie at the core of human existence. Nature seems to vanish altogether with Nietzsche's claim that there is no world in itself but only a meaningless flux of innumerable contending perspectives, each giving transient focus from its own standpoint to the restless energy of the will to power. All three views have the effect of casting humans adrift in a meaningless world, a world oblivious to everything they hope for and value.

We saw in the previous chapter how a similar vision of the world can result from another epistemological viewpoint, namely, the assumption that scientific knowing is the only objective and reliable form of knowing. But regardless of its epistemological pedigree, the view of the world in question is one that removes from it any human aspect and fails to find in it the slightest shelter or support for the human spirit. Such a view cannot help but endanger feelings of rootlessness and abandonment, and an accompanying conviction of the pointlessness of human life.

I conclude by noting a third important connection between epistemological nihilism and denial of life's meaning. It is suggested both by the quotation from Aristotle with which I began this section and by the philosopher-emperor Marcus Aurelius's confident assertion (in the second century A.D.) that it is our capacity for "reason which gives us our status as human beings" (*Meditations* iv.4, quoted Cochran 1944:166). The implication of these statements is that if we cannot rely on our reason to give us knowledge of the world and our place within it, and to achieve at least some significant degree of resolution for our urgent questions of truth, meaning, and value, then our existence as human beings ceases to have any importance. If it is in our very nature to know, or at least to aspire to know, as all human history and culture so plainly show that it is—and knowledge is impossible—then the human project is a dismal failure, a built-in contradiction, a tragicomical "tale told by an idiot."

2. ARGUMENTS RELATING TO THE WILL

In this section, I turn from the reason to the will. The two topics are not entirely unrelated, however, as we shall see. Considered here are two major types of argument for a nihilistic outlook. The first moves from determinism or fatalism (or at least from a claim of fundamental weakness or inadequacy of the human will) to nihilism, while the second arrives at a nihilistic conclusion on the basis of a doctrine of radical, unrestricted freedom. Some of the elements of these two types of argument were examined earlier, but I want to bring them into sharper focus, making the comparisons and contrasts between them more explicit.

We encountered two versions of the deterministic position in Chapter Three. It is implicit in Monod's reduction of mind to brain and in his treatment of organisms in general, and human beings in particular, as intricately structured cybernetic machines. It is also a prominent feature of Skinner's scientific reductionism and dream of a new society founded on the principles of behavioristic psychology.

Schopenhauer is another advocate of determinism, holding that all the incidents of each human life, from the least significant to those of the greatest moment, "occur, strictly speaking, with the same necessity as the movement of a clock" (1942:VI, 67; see also 57). The character of every person is predetermined, and each action proceeds unalterably and predictably from that character and its associated motives, in response to the circumstances of the environment. Given the same environmental circumstances, an individual will act again and again in the same way. This is in keeping with Schopenhauer's doctrine that individual entities of whatever sort are but objectifications or manifestations of the workings of a universal cosmic Will (1942:VI, 64-67, 70-71). Schopenhauer's views acord with more recent Freudian psychoanalytic theory, which teaches that our characters are shaped in their entirety in the very early years of childhood before we have any awareness of what is going on, and which claims ample clinical evidence for the domination of our conscious "choices" by the hidden forces of unconscious motivation. As John Hospers remarks, the Freudian image of human existence is that "of the puppet whose motions are manipulated from behind by invisible wires, or better still, by springs inside..." (Hospers, in Edwards and Pap 1965:80).

When presented with the deterministic thesis and its robot-like depiction of human behavior, we might well ask the question Schopenhauer himself poses: "What is the meaning of life at all? To what purpose is it played, this farce in which everything that is essential is irrevocably fixed and determined?" His reply is not reassuring. He says the best we can do is to observe the unfolding of our lives, and in that way come to an understanding of who and what we have been destined to become. Thus, the determinist must be resigned to being a spectator of his own life (1942:VI, 75, 67).

The only exception to this bleak picture of total determination of character and behavior, according to Schopenhauer, is the prospect of freeing ourselves from the hold of the universal cosmic Will by arduous lives of unstinting asceticism. That can afford only a negative freedom of resignation and denial, a freedom from, rather than a freedom for, the challenges of life. We mentioned this possibility earlier, in our discussion of Schopenhauer's cosmic nihilism. The idea that we can somehow be free to escape the constraints of an all-encompassing determinism is, as Schopenhauer himself admits, something of a contradiction (see 1957:I, 371; and Copleston 1965:VII, Pt. II, 49-51).

At any rate, whether we are well-adjusted and productive persons, or deeply disturbed criminals of the sort described in our earlier discussion of the problem of suffering, is, according to determinism, a matter of the luck of the draw (see Hospers's article in Berofsky 1966, esp. 37, 39, 45). We are stuck with the characters and behaviors we possess and manifest, unless something in the external environment, wholly beyond our control, happens to come along and cause us to change. There is no independent power of will within us, no ability freely to choose our own course of life. We are cogs in the machinery of a closed world system, devoid of any capacity for alternative courses of action when the causal conditions within us (e.g., our character and motives) and the circumstances of the external environment remain the same.

I do not have space to delve in detail into the arguments for determinism but will briefly indicate two arguments that seem particularly important. The first is that the deterministic hypothesis enables us to avoid the notorious incoherencies of a dualistic juxtaposition of causality and freedom— determinists can claim the virtue of parsimony over against an indeterminism they see as inherently dualistic and needlessly complex in the problems it poses. The previous chapter noted that avoidance of the problems of dualism is one of the principal advantages claimed for the reductionistic response to the scientific view of nature and that determinism is usually seen as a necessary concomitant of this response. Schopenhauer reasons similarly when he contrasts his position with those who set the moral will in opposition to the causal necessities of nature, thereby establishing a seemingly unresolvable antinomy of final and efficient causes, or of mysteriously free human subjects, on the one hand, and the lawlike processes of the physical world, on the other. He proposes to overcome this dichotomy with his doctrine that all that occurs, whether in the inorganic or organic realms, and including every detail of the behavior of human beings, is the manifestation of the inexorable workings of one and the same cosmic Will (1942:VI, 70-71).

A second, closely related line of argument is to the effect that only determinism can allow, at least in principle, for thoroughgoing knowledge of the world, because everything without exception can now be regarded as amenable to causal, and thus scientific, explanations. No enigma of causeless freedom is left over to defy understanding. (Hospers, for example, professes himself entirely unable to comprehend what encountering an uncaused event would be like; see Berofsky 1966:41.) The argument thus sets in opposition concern for the capacities of reason and concern for the powers of the will. If we are to put complete confidence in our reason and get on with the task of probing the laws of the physical universe and the principles of human behavior, so the argument goes, then we must give up our concern for freedom. Skinner seems to have this trade-off in mind when he complains, as against defenders of freedom, that it is impossible to have a science of "a subject matter which hops capriciously about" (see Section 2 of the previous chapter). Monod's insistence that human organisms be construed as machines, and in that way be treated as susceptible to objective understanding, is in the same spirit, as is his claim that teleological approaches to explanation and understanding are outmoded and take us nowhere.

Of course, many other arguments for determinism have been made. We mentioned in passing, for example, the clinical evidence cited by psychoanalysts in support of their brand of determinism. The successes of efforts in the behavioral sciences to find predictable correlations of stimulus and response in human and animal behavior could be brought in as another kind of proof for the deterministic thesis. Also worth mentioning are the spectacular achievements of modern technology in gaining control over the processes of nature, evidencing the predictability and lawlike character of these processes. Are not human beings a part of nature, and thus subject to the same lawlike processes? But we will have to leave such arguments behind and go on to consider the bearing of determinism on the question of the meaning of life. Some of what we will have to say about this topic has also been anticipated by our earlier discussions.

Bernard James spells out clearly one nihilistic consequence of the deterministic rejection of autonomous powers of the human will when he asserts, "where there is no place for will there is no place for good and evil, and where good and evil are not realities it is meaningless to speak of human dignity or indignity" (1973:93). This point is closely connected with Weil's observation, cited in another connection, that causal (e.g., historical, cultural, biological, psychological) explanations of the values implicit in our actions have nothing to do with the issue of justification or criticism of those values (except, we might add, in cases where normative biases are implicit in the explanations). But in the deterministic view the significance of our actions is reducible without residue to the causes that produce and explain them. Therefore, the whole enterprise of seeking valuative reasons for or against any course of action, as though it were possible for us to act freely in accordance with our evaluations or even to arrive at those evaluations as an outcome of free inquiry, becomes nothing more than an illusory overlay, one more instance of completely determined behavior.

This means that human life is left without justification. A life is what it is, and once we have exhausted our causal explanations of its course, bringing in considerations of genetitic disposition, character, motive, and influences of the environment, that must be the end of the matter. On the issue of intrinsic appraisals of the values implicit in a given life, or of the valuative dimensions of life in general, we can only remain silent. Thus determinism deprives human life of dignity, as Bernard James insists it must, by stripping it of all but the most superficial meaning.

A further consequence of the deterministic view also underscores this loss of human dignity. That consequence is that we must cease regarding ourselves as autonomous subjects or centers of autonomous thinking, valuing, and acting. We must learn to view ourselves and others from a purely external standpoint as functioning automata, and to accept the demotion of our subjective experiences (including experiences of apparent freedom of choice and weighing of alternative values) to the status of irrelevant epiphenomena, or what Monod calls "representations" and "simulations" of wholly objective causal laws and functions (see Chapter Three, Section 2). In other words, determinism implies the unreality of one's own self. In it there is no place for the sense of personal responsibility for the direction of one's own life. A character in Salman Rushdie's novel *Midnight's Children* sums up the main thrust of this argument from determinism to nihilism when he says that if determinism is true, we might as well "give up right here and now, understanding the futility of thought decision action, since nothing we think makes any difference anyway; things will be as they will" (1981:79).

But we need not go so far as to assume with determinism a total eclipse of the freedom of the will, to arrive at the nihilistic conclusion. We need only recognize a fundamental weakness or impairment of the powers of the will to be brought to this outcome. This recognition is a central motif in Kafka's *The Trial*, as we noted in the preceding chapter. K's experiences can be seen as emblematic of a basic inadequacy in us all: the weakness of will that dooms us to the perpetual frustration and guilt of not being able to live up to our highest ideals, and thus to the agony of always expecting far more from ourselves than we seem able to attain.

The theme of gross impairment of the human will is also recurrent in Dostoevsky's novels. We cannot help but feel pity for even the most despicable of his characters because, in the words of Ross, he shows us "that evil and malice, destructiveness and cruelty, are always the result of an inner desperation that men cannot cope with" (1969:142). Even if we are to some extent free, and thus capable of feeling responsibility for the direction of our lives, of what use is our freedom if it is insufficient for us to attain the good and overcome the evil, or to triumph over the despondency, guilt, and sense of failure that seem to lie at the center of our being?

Here again, a religion such as Christianity can offer some sort of an answer with its doctrine of the availability of divine grace. But what if there is no such answer? What if we do in fact have to go it alone, without the help of God or gods, or with no way to find the strength of will we need? What sense can we then make of our lives? "Precious little," is the nihilist answer, for it denies all paths of redemption and supernatural sources of aid which could serve to make life meaningful and worthwhile. So we are brought by one more route of argument to the nihilistic dead end.

If determinism puts all of its emphasis on the object side of the subject-object dichotomy, virtually eliminating subjectivity from consideration in its drive to explain every aspect of human behavior from a purely external standpoint, by means of objective processes and laws, the doctrine of radical, unrestricted freedom of the will does just the opposite. It comes down so squarely on the side of the subject as to diminish almost to the vanishing point the significance of causal constraints or objective restrictions of any kind on our freedom of choice and autonomous responsibility for the course of our lives. It is clear from our previous discussions, for example, that Stirner, Camus, and Sartre not only take for granted, as against the determinists, that we are genuinely free, but also reject the idea that there is anything like a prior human nature or antecedent scale of values to place constraint upon the exercise of our freedom by defining our duties and obligations in advance of our choices. In the thinking of all three, it can safely be said, the role and power of will is paramount; so much so, in fact, as to put the claims of knowledge or reason in a decidedly inferior place. With them we see the other side of the trade-off mentioned above, where, as in the cases of Skinner and Monod, concern for the capabilities of will seems to become completely overshadowed by a passion to maximize the powers of reason, and in particular, scientific reason.

"Indeterminism" is not a strong enough word to characterize the position I am now bringing under discussion; therefore, I term it "radical voluntarism." I will first examine the position in more detail, noting some of the arguments that can be presented in its support. Then I will consider its negative implications for the meaning of life.

Sartre is a foremost exponent of radical voluntarism, so we will look at a series of arguments in support of this view based on some of his reasoning in *Being and Nothingness*. The first argument begins by observing that determinists arrive at their position on the basis of an act of questioning the reality of freedom. But the fact that freedom, and its opposite, determinism, can both be doubted or questioned is itself a tacit admission of the reality of freedom. To assume otherwise, and to say that the questioning itself is determined by causes, would be to make the questions raised "unintelligible and even inconceivable" (Sartre 1966:28). This is so because the act of questioning implies freedom, in the sense of openness to alternative possibilities.

Posing a question, says Sartre, manifests the freedom of the for-itself in its nihilating role. It requires "a kind of nihilistic withdrawal" of the questioner from the questioned whereby the questioner shows that "he is not subject to the causal order of the world; he detaches himself from being" (28). Thus the freedom to question, to assess, and to arrive at conclusions is ironically inescapable even in the act of denying the reality of freedom; it is present by implication in the claims and arguments of the most convinced determinists. Attempts on their part to persuade themselves or others of the truth of their theory, and to respond to objections to it, is either a free activity or it ceases to have the meaning of intelligent activity. If wholly determined by causes, it becomes nothing more than a series of movements. Sartre sums up the point by saying that determinism destroys the very notion of conduct or action, because the "existence of the act implies its autonomy" (583). It thereby undermines itself as an outcome of the activity of questioning and reasoning.

The argument so far has only contended for the reality of freedom and the falsity (or meaninglessness) of the deterministic theory. We have not yet arrived at the above-mentioned *radical* voluntarism. The next phase of the argument introduces the radical note. Sartre thinks that we become aware of how all-embracing and unrestricted our freedom really is in the experience of "anguish." He states his thesis in this way: "In anguish I apprehend myself at once as *totally free* and as not being able to derive the meaning of the world except as coming from myself" (48; emphasis added). When he says, "from myself," he could just as well have said, "from my freedom," for that is what he intends. Let us try to understand, then, what Sartre means by the experience of anguish and how he reasons from it to this doctrine of total freedom.

Anguish is awareness that, regardless of what activity I am currently involved in, and regardless of what course of life I am now pursuing, I could be acting or living differently. Thus, what I do, I do completely by my own choice, and the responsibility is entirely mine. Sartre illustrates the point with a vivid example (1966:35-39). Suppose I am on a narrow path running along a precipice, without a guard rail. A motive of fear may (but only if I allow it to) strongly influence me to pay close attention to the stones in the road, to keep as far away from the precipice as I can, and to tread with great care. But I am aware that this motive, strong as it may be, does not *determine* my actions. Anguish presents itself in the form of vertigo, which for Sartre is more than the fear of falling. It is my awareness that I can, in my freedom, hurl myself over the precipice if I decide to do so. I am fully capable of making this choice despite all of the elements of character, motive, common sense, custom, and so on that ordinarily incline me away from it. To be *afraid* is to be aware of threats from outside myself, but to be in *anguish* is to be aware of the full extent of my freedom. The possibilities of choice the sense of anguish lays before me, "because they are *my* possibilities, do not appear to me as determined by foreign causes" (35, 37). If we stop to think about it, he says, this heady sense of freedom pertains to everything in our lives.

It pertains, for example, to character and motive. Far from it being the case that they determine our actions, their significance for action in every new moment is problematic and uncertain, awaiting the assessments and decisions of the nihilating for-itself, which insinuates itself between them and the act. In other words, we are always free to question the role that character and motive shall be allowed to play in our lives. They are, as it were, mere raw material for the ongoing and unavoidable enterprise of having continually to remake the self and its forms of life by fresh acts of freedom. Thus Sartre can speak of the "spontaneous invention of *motives* and *causes*" through acts of freedom, by way of objecting against the view that motives or causes have an inherent weight or force of their own which must be given due consideration in accounting for our actions (575, 550-551).

We saw earlier that Sartre denies that there is any such thing as an essence of the self, or a human nature, existing antecedently to free acts. As the outcome of past free choices, "[e]ssence is all that human reality apprehends in itself as *having been*" (42). That essence we fashioned for ourselves in the past can be unmade by new decisions of the present and future. Thus, we are entirely capable of transcending our characters (or the "essences" which we gave to ourselves in the past) and their associated motives. We are in no sense constrained by them to behave in predictable ways.

Others may regard us in terms of our characters and expect typical modes of behavior from us, but from the standpoint of our anguish and freedom, character presents itself more in the form of a vow, something we sustain in being by successive free reaffirmations. "In this sense," Sartre remarks, "there is no character; there is only a project of myself" (675). Or as he says elsewhere, in flat repudiation of the whole deterministic thesis, "the meaning of the past is strictly dependent on my present project. . . . I alone in fact can decide at each moment the *bearing* of the past. . . .[B]y projecting myself toward my ends, I preserve the past with me, and by action I *decide* its meaning" (610). As for the psychoanalyst's claim that our conscious choices are only the manifestations of hidden forces of the unconscious, and thus of the characters we inherited from our early childhood experiences, Sartre dismisses it out of hand. He claims that attributions of our behavior to influences of the unconscious are acts of bad faith whereby we try to cancel out the sense of anguish, with its message that we are completely responsible for our lives. Such "explanatory" schemes as that of Freud, with its ego, id, and superego, and its insistence on the determining role of the unconscious, "can succeed only if I distrust every kind of intuition, only if I apply to my case *from the outside*, abstract schemes and rules already learned" (61).

Sartre pushes the role of freedom even further, making it the ground of all value and meaning, and even the basis of what count for humans as the intelligible structures of the surrounding world. The values by which we live have no "objectivity" or independent being. They are not contained in an antecedent human nature, nor do they await discovery as givens of a world in which we find ourselves existing. Instead, they are the fruits of free choice, the reflections of "an original projection of myself which stands as my choice of myself in the world." Realizing this,

> I emerge alone and in anguish confronting the unique and original project which constitutes my being; all the barriers, all the guard rails collapse, nihilated by the consciousness of my freedom. I do not have nor can I have recourse to any value against the fact that it is I who sustain values in being (1966:47).

Consequently, the values by which we live our lives, and the whole course of those lives, are left "without justification and without excuse" (47). Sartre elaborates this idea in the following way:

> As a being by whom values exist, I am unjustifiable. My freedom is anguished at being the foundation of values while itself without foundation. It is anguished in addition because values, due to the fact that they are essentially revealed to a freedom, can not disclose themselves without being at the same time 'put into question' [,] for the possibility of overturning the scale of values appears complementarily as *my* possibility. It is anguish before values which is the recognition of the ideality of values (1966:46).

Thus, no values of any kind exist that can lay objective claim upon my life or constrain my freedom in any way. I am obligated to the values implicit in my "original project" only so long as I choose to be, and the meaning of my life is whatever I decide it will be, in the solitary sovereignty of my unrestricted freedom.

To think otherwise, e.g., in terms of a prior human nature we are obligated to act in accordance with, or in terms of values with some basis other than the free acts that create them and sustain them in being, is, for Sartre, to contemplate "a total slavery" (659; see also 51-52). One measure of the radicality of his conception of freedom is this adamant either-or. Values are either sheerly invented or freedom is completely unreal. There can be no middle ground. As Sam Keen explains, in reference to Sartre's view of freedom, "If there are any 'oughts,' any given standards of good or evil, or any invasions of human life by powers beyond its control, there is no freedom" (1969:112).

While I am on the subject of this either-or, I should note that what holds for the objectivity of values also holds for causal constraints of any kind (as is implied by the last part of Keen's statement). Sartre expresses the dichotomy of causality and freedom in this way: "either man is wholly determined (which is inadmissible, especially because a determined consciousness—i.e., a consciousness externally motivated—becomes itself pure exteriority and ceases to be consciousness) or else man is wholly free" (1966:541). His insistence on the total freedom of the for-itself is tied closely to his idea that the for-itself is "nothingness." Were it to be influenced by given standards of value or by its past in any way that lies outside its complete control, then it would cease to be consciousness in his technical sense of the term and would become an in-itself, a something, rather than a sheer nothingness. It is fundamental to his whole system of thought in *Being and Nothingness*, therefore, that only freedom can limit freedom. Values gain their obligatoriness, and the past derives its force, urgency, or meaning, purely from the for-itself's free choices of the future (658, 617).

Radical voluntarism joins hands with determinism in depriving values of any objective status or obligatory role. Determinism does so by its reduction of the language of justification to the language of causes, as well as by its denial of any ability on the part of human beings to adjudicate rationally or choose freely among valuative possibilities. Radical voluntarism does so in the interest of maintaining its doctrine of absolute freedom. Also worth noting in this connection is that one determinist, Skinner, insists that no such thing as human nature exists, holding that we are simply what our social environments condition us to be (1971:202-206). Their common rejection of the concept of human nature—although from quite different premises—shows another striking agreement between radical voluntarism and at least this one version of the determinist view.

What is true of values is also true of the world in which I live, according to Sartre. That world is constituted in its patterns of meaning by acts of freedom. We saw earlier that reality in itself has no inherent structure or character. It is purely contingent and absurd, in the sense of admitting of any number of possible interpretations. It is the for-itself's nihilations that produce those interpretations and give meaning to the world, or indeed, that introduce the very notion of *world*. These nihilations are, at bottom, acts of freedom; the structures they create have ongoing significance on account of their rootage in the "original projects" of human beings (1966:47). Thus, like the nihilations which create values, they are without justification.

It is true that we are surrounded by antecedently given "presences," notes Sartre, but these presences are incomprehensible in themselves, i.e., they have status and knowability as independent existences only in the context of acts projected by us:

> We are separated from things by nothing *except by our freedom*; it is our freedom which is responsible for the fact that *there are* things with all their indifference, their unpredictability, and their adversity, and for the fact that we are inevitably separated from them; for it is on the ground of nihilation that they appear and that they are revealed as bound one to another. Thus the project of my freedom adds *nothing* to things: it causes *there to be* things; that is, precisely, realities provided with a coefficient of adversity and utilizable instrumentality (623).

The last part of this statement means that aspects of the lived-world impose limitations on our freedom or prove useful to our freedom only to the extent that we allow them to do so. The "facticity" "of my birth, of my place, of my past, of my environment," and of the actions and productions of my fellow humans, including those embedded in language, culture, and institutions, acquire their significance and role for me solely on the basis of "my freedom without limits." Sartre insists that "there is no situation in which the for-itself would be *more free* than in others." For example, if I have been made a slave, I am always free to risk the worst in order to rid myself of slavery (672-673).

Not even the red-hot pincers of a torturer can exempt us from being free. The impossibility of our resisting the torture (by continuing to withhold information, for example) is a "freely constituted" impossibility. "This impossibility comes to things by means of our free renunciation; our renunciation is not induced by the impossibility of maintaining the behavior." This is once again to deny to situations or causes any fixed character or inherent power. The only role or significance they can have is that accorded to them "by the motivating-consciousness which is itself a free choice of an end" (619).

Whatever "brute givens" there might be in our environments, or whatever changes might take place within it, are therefore not to be construed as obstacles to freedom but rather, as Joseph Catalano states, as "the very context and ground from which freedom arises as a nihilation" (1980:210; see also Sartre 1966:619-620). Were there no givens, there would be nothing to be nihilated, and freedom in Sartre's sense of the term would be impossible. World, space, time, qualities, potentialities, all structures and patterns of meaning whatever, are thus instated "by our very upsurge" of uninhibited freedom, working with the opaque density of the in-itself (1966:623). And as Catalano comments again, "The in-itself can be projected differently according to the lived purposes of the for-itself" (1980:141). For Sartre, therefore, the very nature of the world is constituted for the individual by the hierarchy of relations, importances, obstacles, and instrumentalities he imposes upon it through the projects and ends implicit in his free choices (see 1966:596). He puts the point quite succinctly when he says, "The end illuminates what is," and then goes on to add, "What is . . . takes on its meaning only when it is *surpassed* toward the future" (608).

We can sense here the extent to which the claims of knowledge are subordinated to the claims of freedom in Sartre's philosophy, and in radical voluntarism in general. In this connection Barrett calls our attention to Sartre's "secret kinship with Nietzsche." Nietzsche "declares that knowledge of the object-in-itself is unnecessary" (Immanuel Kant having told us earlier that it is impossible), concluding that "all we need is to be able to master it, and hence the Will to Power." Sartre's radical voluntarism, Barrett suggests, is the direct analogue of the will to power in Nietzsche's thought (1958:220-222). We can add that Sartre's pivotal concept of the "original projects" of human beings, regarded as acts of absolute freedom, is not far from Nietzsche's concept of "perspectives," viewed as expressions of the will to power. Sartre does say in one place that "[w]e must not confuse our necessity of choosing with the will to power" (1966:577). But as the context of this statement shows, he means only that we may choose to be sad, resigned, humiliated, or indecisive; we may not happen to choose to be joyful, resolute, noble, or powerful. The point of Barrett's comparison still pertains.

Thus, while with determinism we gain unrestricted knowledge of the world and lose the self, in radical voluntarism we abandon all possibility of an objectively knowable nature of things, opting instead for the self and its freedom. We must now learn to accept, not only what Sartre calls "the ideality of values" (see above), but the ideality or ultimate subjectivism and arbitrariness of everything. He repeatedly denies that his philosophy is a species of idealism or subjectivism, arguing that the for-itself and the in-itself "form a dyad" in which self and world come into being together, and wanting to speak of a synthesis or unity of "*the things themselves* and myself among things" (111, 671). But the subjectivist conclusion seems unavoidable. Its unavoidability turns to a significant degree on his failure to overcome the dichotomies of his own basic categories of the for-itself and the in-itself, a matter which we commented on in the preceding section. But its taproot is the primordial and unrestrained role he assigns to human freedom, or to the nihilating power of the for-itself.

One more aspect of the general argument for radical voluntarism ought to be noted before weighing its nihilistic implications. This relates to the social context within which we must exercise our freedom. This aspect will not modify the ultimate subjectivism and arbitrariness of freedom, and of the fruits of freedom, implied by Sartre's overall system of thought in *Being and Nothingness*. But it does remind us of the fact that the freedom of the individual is not exercised in a vaccum, but must find expression in the context of those values, meanings, symbolic expressions, and noetic structures that are the projections of other free subjects, one's fellow human beings. But once again, these social and cultural constructions in the midst of which individuals find themselves, including the roles to which they are relegated and by which they are objectified by others (e.g., Black, Caucasian, Aryan, Jew, crippled, ugly, beautiful, criminal, saint, shopkeeper, civil servant; see Sartre 1966:645) are givens to be transcended, as all givens are necessarily transcended, by the nihilations of the for-itself.

It is not that I can freely alter or control the view that others have of me; that is the result of their own free activity, not mine. But I must freely choose how to respond to their conceptions of me, just as I must freely choose how to think and act in relation to those social and cultural constructions which are the products of the free choices of human beings who came before me or are my contemporaries. The freedom of others imposes limits on my situation in the sense that I cannot change at will the way my person or behavior will be regarded from the outside, or the canons of value and meaning assumed by those who do the regarding. But Sartre insists that "I can *experience* these limits only if I recover this being-for-others which I am and if I give to it a meaning in the light of the ends which I have chosen" (645). He persists, therefore, in his contention that the freedom of each human being is "total and infinite," in the sense that the "only limits which freedom bumps up against at each moment are those which it imposes on itself..." (650).

Now that we have analyzed the position of radical voluntarism and have some of the arguments for it in view, we can consider its connections with the nihilistic outlook on the meaning of life. One connection is implicit in the recognition that a doctrine of absolute freedom such as Sartre's is also a doctrine of *absurd* freedom. Because any and all of the modes of human life must have their origin in acts of absolute freedom and must continuously be reconstituted by such acts, the conclusion seems unavoidable that human life is totally and inescapably absurd. The connection between an absurd freedom and the absurdity of life has been spoken of earlier, especially in Chapter Three, Section 1. But we are now in a position to examine it more closely and from a different angle.

Sartre himself readily proclaims that the choices which lie at the base of our existence not only appear absurd, but are in fact completely absurd. Consequently, he judges our very being as absurd. Other choices are available to us at any moment, and because the choices we make, and those others which we could have made, are equally normless and groundless (freedom being "that by which all foundations and reasons come into being"), we must reconcile ourselves to living with "the feeling of unjustifiability." Furthermore, we cannot escape the absurdity of having arbitrarily to choose, and continuing to choose, the form of our life: "human-reality can choose itself as it intends but is not able not to choose itself." Even an attempt to avoid having to make a choice is "to choose not to choose." Hence "human reality participates in the universal contingency of being and thereby in what we may call absurdity" (586-589). So Sartre is unequivocal in his recognition that the nihilistic outlook as we have defined it follows necessarily from his position of radical voluntarism.

This connection is also implicit in Hocking's contention that sheerly invented meanings and values, arbitrarily imposed on an "incommunicative environing world," cannot require commitment; and thus that any appeal to them by way of trying to find some justification for one's life is circular (1936:264-265). Sartre contends in one place, for example, that the fact of radical freedom does not entail that life is nothing more than "a series of capricious jerks," because our choices are made within the context of our so-called original projects, which give fundamental focus and orientation to our lives. But each individual's original project is entirely groundless and arbitrary, and Sartre even insists that it cannot be arrived at on the basis of conscious deliberation. His reason is that the original project *gives rise* to consciousness and *defines* the world of ends, discriminations, and meanings within which reflective choices must operate (see 1966:564-565). Thus, Sartre's radical voluntarism can save the passing moment from caprice only by rooting it in a more ultimate caprice. The pronounced circularity here bears resemblance to the attempt on the part of some determinists to persuade us that we are free because we are usually capable of doing what we want, while reminding us in the same breath that all our wants are completely determined.

Barrett makes a point similar to Hocking's when he notes that a will naked of conviction is hardly capable of willing at all; it is suspended among its alternatives like Buridan's ass between its stacks of hay, with no reason to choose any one alternative over the others. He also remarks that acts of significant freedom can take place only in the context of a "consciousness that can irradiate them and give them meaning" (1979:309, 286-287, 86). Without such conviction and context, freedom becomes empty and pointless, and the life resulting from it must be characterized in the same way. By placing the freedom of the original project before knowledge, meaning, or value, and making it their sole ground, Sartre robs freedom of its purposive significance, thereby obliterating the basic distinction between freedom and chance. It is hardly surprising that he is then driven to the conclusion that life is absurd.

Furthermore, persistence in a course of life, which Sartre regards as not only possible but usual, seems difficult to account for if on the one hand (as Hocking suggests), there can be no such thing as *commitment* to a course of life which is arbitrarily chosen, and on the other hand (as in Sartre's reasoning), the causal influences of motive and habit are denied any significant power to channel or constrain our freedom. In Sartre's analysis, every new moment of choice is seen in the experience of anguish to pose a crisis of freedom every bit as fundamental as that implicit in the constitution of our original projects, for anguish makes us fully aware that those projects have no basis or support. In our pristine, virtually causeless freedom, we can as readily undo our whole previous course of life by our next act as we can continue it. And absolutely no reason can be found not to do so. Why then, in the absence of any basis for commitment to that course of life and the values it contains, do we continue in it over long periods of time?

Sartre's only answer to this important question is that we tend not to want to pay the price of changing the course of our lives or reorienting the goals of our existence in the radical way which would be required, and this despite the fact that we are completely capable of doing so at any time (1966:555, 567-568). But if past acts of freedom have no inherent consequences or connections, but only those *chosen* as such by the present act of freedom in its drive toward the future, and if that act is not the act of a self with intrinsic continuity over time, but rather the act of a sheer "nothingness" which creates temporal connections anew moment by moment, the notion of a "price" of radical change in the course of our life from one moment to the next remains opaque. Indeed, the very notion of an original project somehow structuring or surrounding our present acts of freedom seems impossible to account for. The fact that Sartre can give no persuasive explanation for our persistence in a course of life only serves to put into bold relief the connection between radical voluntarism and an absurdist view of human life. We persist in our courses of life because we inexplicably choose to do so; beyond this, absolutely nothing can be said. It could not be otherwise if every new act is, as Sartre so repeatedly insists it is, one of total freedom.

No writer brings home to us more vividly the connection between radical, contextless freedom and the absurdity of life than Dostoevsky. He does this with many of his characters, but most particularly with Kirillov, Shatov, and Stavrogin, in the novel *The Possessed*. Kirillov has become convinced that in the absence of God, human beings must act like God. This means to him that they must take on God's attribute of unbridled self-will. His way of expressing and proving this new-found independence and "terrible freedom" is to commit suicide, first leaving behind a note confessing to a crime he did not commit (see Dostoevsky 1931:582-583). Our reaction as readers is to say to ourselves, "But that's absurd." And this is precisely Dostoevsky's point. An absolute wilfulness, without the guidance or constraint of any objective context of conviction or value, is a "terrible" freedom that leaves us no reason to prefer life over suicide.

The experience of the second character, Shatov, makes evident our inability to create conviction by acts of choice, and thus to give to our lives a significance that they would otherwise lack. He desperately yearns to abandon his old way of life and to "believe in Russia" and her orthodoxy, to "believe in the body of Christ" and in God (235). But try as he may, he cannot will himself into belief; he cannot create the conviction that would reorient his life. He dies a sad death in the end, murdered by his former comrades in a nihilistic revolutionary society. Perhaps he was on the verge of genuine faith. Who knows? But the point is that he could not create that faith, nor can we create conviction of any kind by sheer acts of will. If freedom is all we have, and if knowledge, meaning, and value must flow directly from our freedom, then our lives are as unquestionably absurd as Sartre claims them to be.

The third character, Stavrogin, is beset with a vacuous freedom closely allied with feelings of insufferable ennui. Yet he has a strange hold over the other nihilists of the novel. He finds himself unable to believe in anything in particular, or to commit himself to any course of life. He is aloof from the world and from the society of other human beings, including those of his nihilistic comrades who admire him to the point of worship and will do anything he asks, or even hints at. He finds all attachments and causes boring and floats through his life with nothing to compel his attention or to challenge his considerable powers. He is attracted neither to great debauchery nor to great accomplishment. He is hopelessly lukewarm.

Just before his own suicide at the end of the novel, Stavrogin confesses in a letter to a woman who loves him with all-abandoning passion that there is no way in which her love can make him different. His love will always be detached and as petty as himself; he will in the end only make her unhappy. Thus, although he asks her to go away with him, he also counsels her not to bury her life with him. Still, he states that he expects her to come, saying that indicates how little respect he has for her (634-635). In light of his account of his own life and outlook, and of what is said of him elsewhere in the novel, we would perhaps not be far off the mark in concluding that Stavrogin is an embodiment of the Sartrean ideal of absolute freedom, and even of perfect "good faith." He is, after all, not the victim of passion or of dogmatic, uncritical belief. He does not kowtow to anybody, and he is unaffected by the way others objectify him. He is remarkably neutral and thus, we would think, capable of exercising his freedom without bias or restraint. Yet his life is miserable, and there seems to be nothing he can do about it, despite his freedom.

Again, Dostoevsky's point is that freedom is not enough. It alone cannot confer meaning on life. A life based only on freedom is "vertiginous," to borrow an apt word from Phillip Fandozzi's illuminating discussion of Stavrogin (1982:39), a word reminiscent of Sartre's reference to the experience of vertigo in his analysis of the anguish of freedom. Such a life exists in an impasse of unlimited possibilities, no one of which has anything to commend itself over the others. A freedom like this, says Roquentin in *Nausea*, "is rather like death" (1964:209). It is no wonder that the lives of two of these three representatives of groundless freedom in Dostoevsky's work end by self-inflicted death, and that the life of the other is extinguished by an act of pointless murder. In this way the author impresses upon us one of his fundamental themes: the uselessness and absurdity of lives without the sense of obligation or conviction, lives in which there is nothing but an insipid freedom to which all things are permitted.

A second connection between radical voluntarism and the nihilistic view of life grows out of the idea, constantly emphasized by Sartre, that because we are radically free, we are totally responsible. It is one thing to say that we are, to a significant degree, responsible for our own actions; it is quite another to hold that we are *totally* responsible for them, and that our motives, beliefs, values, commitments, and the whole course of our lives are at every moment fully within our control and completely of our own making. If I am absolutely free, I can make no appeal to any kind of mitigating circumstances or explanations for my actions, such as peculiarities of my biological make-up, aspects of my upbringing or environment, factors in my unconscious of which I am unaware, the weight of the past or force of habit, my singular susceptibility to certain kinds of temptation, or the influence of others over me. To the extent that I fail to act according to the goals and ideals implicit in my life project, or to abandon a morbid, self-destructive project (see Sartre's discussion of the so-called inferiority complex, 1966:577-582), I alone am to blame. I have chosen to fail where I could just as well have succeeded.

A profound sense of loneliness and isolation, to say nothing of a potential for consuming guilt and self-condemnation, is latent in this view. Not only does it make any compassion of others toward my failings of will inappropriate and imply that there is nothing that they can do to help me, thereby effectively severing one of the most common and significant bonds of human fellowship. It also renders any compassion I might feel toward myself wholly out of place. I must continue to tell myself that whatever weakness of will I seem to be experiencing is an illusion fostered by bad faith, and I must resolutely resist any inclination I may have to forgive myself, even in the slightest degree, for my past mistakes. I must just as resolutely fight off attempts on the part of others to share the burden of my guilt, and can only dismiss as irrelevant and misguided any attempts they might make to assist me in finding resources for the strengthening of my will. The reason is that the responsibility and guilt is completely mine, and so cannot be shared; and that my will stands in no need of strengthening because I am already radically free. I have no alternative, therefore, but to accept all failures as mine and mine alone, and to continue to do battle against them completely on my own, through solitary exertions of will. Others may help me to understand my situation better and to perceive the range of options open to me, perhaps by helping me to bring into focus just what my original project is, but the choice among those options is entirely up to me, and it is entirely within my control (see Sartre 1966:699-704).

This second connection between radical voluntarism and nihilism is made quite explicit by Sartre when he states that by my freedom I am "condemned to be wholly responsible for myself" and to "carry the weight of the world by myself alone without anything or any person being able to lighten it." To discover the full meaning of radical freedom is to experience "abandonment," in the sense of finding "myself suddenly alone and without help" (680-681). Or, as he states in another place, "for human reality, to be is to *choose oneself*; nothing comes to it either from the outside or from within which it can *receive or accept*. Without any help whatsoever, it is entirely abandoned to the intolerable necessity of making itself be—down to the slightest detail" (538-539). I spoke earlier of the guilt, frustration, and despair that can flow from a sense of the weakness of one's will. But the problem here cannot be attributed to any inherent weakness of the will; it stems rather from a will so sovereign and free that it can brook no suggestion of weakness of any kind. Hence, it is immune to help of any kind and is left without any possibility of excuse.

The full extent of the loneliness and guilt implicit in the doctrine of radical freedom can be understood in light of an example. Let us imagine that a woman has been going to meetings of Alcoholics Anonymous and finally seems to be making progress in conquering her alcoholism. In the past, she frequently "slept around," largely to get drinks from men. It is a past about which she is deeply ashamed. Some of the men who slept with her before, and who are fully aware of her attempts to break with her past, continue to offer her drinks, hoping to seduce her when drunk, as before. Suppose she finally succumbs to one of them by beginning to drink with him, and then ends up in bed with him. Is he not partly responsible for her failure, because he has played on her weaknesses? Not according to the concept of radical freedom. The responsibility is completely hers, and she can lay no blame whatever at the feet of the man. Nor can she plead, because of her alcoholism, any weakness of will. In fact, she must even deny that her impairment of will has been helped by Alcoholics Anonymous, for no impairment of will existed in the first place. She was at any moment completely free to abandon her drinking and to change the course of her life.

But to convince her that this is true is to load her down with a burden of guilt and despair even more devastating to the meaning of her life than the feeling of powerlessness and shame associated with the alcoholism itself. For her to seek help for her problems anywhere but in the soverign strength of her will is for her to be in a state of illusion and bad faith. To the extent that she fails to solve her problems on her own, she is completely without excuse. If she protests that she has long been trying with all her being to stop drinking, but with no success, and if she is then told that she has not tried *hard enough*, is this likely to be anything but a message of despair? All she has to do is exert her will, and yet she has up to now stubbornly and inexplicably refused to do so; if this is the true account of her situation, how can she avoid holding herself in total contempt? How can she help feeling completely isolated from those who, according to the doctrine of radical freedom, can give her no aid, even if she desperately wants their aid; and especially from those who appear able to choose with such ease to refrain from the practices which seem to hold her so much in thrall?

Because this example applies in some sense to us all (none of us succeeds in living up completely to his ideals or accomplishing all that he intends), the doctrine of radical voluntarism would seem, by a similar process of reasoning, to assign all of our lives, in one degree or another, to absurdity. It is an absurdity of inexcusable failure and of a consequent burden of guilt that must be shouldered by each of us in complete isolation, because there is no way in which we can be of comfort or help to one another. It is also an absurdity of infinite debt and responsibility, not only because we are totally responsible for all that we are and do, but also because we can and do recreate ourselves *in toto* in each new moment. Hence, everything we are at any given moment is entirely of our own doing at that moment.

We can give ourselves no credit, and deserve from ourselves only blame, to the extent that we make only gradual progress in bringing our lives more into line with our ideals. For according to the doctrine of radical freedom, we could just as readily have completely remade our lives by any new act of freedom. Therefore, the doctrine affords us no middle ground. It is all or nothing. Because we invariably find ourselves somewhere in between, with nowhere to turn but to ourselves, and no one to blame but ourselves, the doctrine contains the seeds of bitter self-condemnation, agonizing loneliness, and utter despair. Our only relief seems that of deliberately choosing to lower our ideals so drastically that they no longer condemn us or threaten us with failure. But this means that we can escape from the devestating consequences of our freedom only by deciding to sharply restrict its range of options, thus severely reducing our freedom's scope; which is but another way of grasping the absurd situation to which the concept of radical voluntarism consigns us.

Sartre attempts to deal with the seeming insufficiency of our wills when we are in the grip of a problem like that of alcoholism or some severe obsessional neurosis. But his explanation for this experienced insufficiency poses a dilemma of its own. His explanation is that the conscious will can only operate within the parameters of the original project and hence cannot alter that project itself. The project can be altered only through an experience of conversion, an experience in which "the prior project collapses into the past in the light of a new project which rises on its ruins . . . ." Sartre speaks of such experiences as being quite "extraordinary and marvelous," and he claims that they "furnish the clearest and most moving image of our freedom" (1966:582). But how can they, if they lie beyond our conscious control? Either they are subject to our conscious control, in which case there should be no basis for the seeming insufficiency of our wills, or they are not, in which case we are not as totally free as Sartre elsewhere argues that we are.

If we must await a mysterious conversion to change the course of our lives, no matter how intent and desperate we are to effect that change (the situation of Shatov, cited earlier, is a case in point), then we cannot be said to be radically free. The root difficulty here is the ambiguous way in which Sartre uses the word *freedom*. On the one hand, it involves conscious deliberation and reflective choice; on the other, it involves a kind of purely spontaneous happenstance or contingency (as in the case of the emergence of an original project, or the replacement of one project by another) quite beyond intentional control. This latter sense, as already suggested, seems indistinguishable from mere chance. If our liberation depends upon some chance event like a conversion and not on our radical purposive freedom, then we have simply substituted one absurdity for another in our attempt to account for our failure to make the choices that would be (or that we believe to be) in our own best interest.

A third connection between radical voluntarism and nihilism is that this view of human freedom seems to require denial of the reality of the self, and with that, of the pattern and connectedness—hence, the meaning—of one's life. We have already seen (in Chapter Three, Section 4) how this consequence can flow from a conception of time that holds only the present moment to be real, and, as a result, deprives even the expression "one's life" of any clear significance. There is a loss of selfhood implicit in determinism too, as we have also noted, on account of its rejection of autonomous powers of the will and its putting human beings in the position of puppets drawn hither and yon by inner strings of conditioned character and motive, and by outer factors of environmental context and influence.

But where determinism denies the existence of self by rejecting any personal capacity for directing courses of action or endowing them with elements of novelty (by which I mean some degree of independence of causes flowing from the past), the concept of radical voluntarism denies selfhood from the opposite direction, namely, by placing such great stress on the novelty of each new choice as effectively to deny any inherent causal connectedness to those choices over time. In this second view, the self is in a position of such radical dominance over its past as to reduce that past to a kind of figment whose only semblance of continuity and influence consists in its *de novo* (and, as we have seen, wholly inexplicable) replications by untrammeled acts of an absolute freedom. But a self this free of its past is no single self existing over time but a mere loose collection of detached and momentary episodes of awareness and freedom; in other words, it is hardly anything like a self at all. Sartre speaks advisedly in calling it a *nothingness*, although how a nothingness can do all those things he attributes to it is unclear (on this see Desan 1960:144-159, esp. 156).[1] Nor can we speak of it as having anything like the connectedness and continuity of its own unique "life."

This glaring lack of connectedness is as fatal to a concept of an enduring self capable of being a genuine subject of its ongoing pattern of life as is the absence of any degree of autonomy in relation to the causal past. Thus, even though radical voluntarism, as was said earlier, comes down squarely on the subject side of the subject-object dichotomy, when this view is followed through to its logical conclusion it ends up ironically destroying the subject that is its central focus and preoccupation. What is left is not the freedom of a self but a bare freedom, mysteriously upsurging and inexplicably replicating itself over the course of time. Against this background, the connectedness of time itself becomes elusive and enigmatic, taking us back to the subject of the last section of the previous chapter. What could be more destructive of the meaning of one's life than the denial of one's very selfhood, a denial we now see to stem as much from the doctrine of radical voluntarism as from that of causal determinism? So we are brought by two directly opposed interpretations of the nature and capacities of the human will to the same nihilistic result.

The nihilistic arguments relating to the will discussed in this section bring to mind yet another (the second in his list) of Britton's four criteria for a meaningful life, namely that life can have no meaning unless it is possible that oneself and one's own life matter *to* oneself: "Rocks and stones and trees matter if they matter to somebody. A person inevitably matters just because he matters or might matter to himself. If this were not so, life would have no meaning" (1969:183). In the determinist or radical voluntarist views of the human will, there seems to be no way in which this criterion can be fulfilled. We just saw that neither view allows for a meaningful concept of a self, in the sense of an autonomous persisting subject and agent, to whom life can matter; or conversely, for a "oneself" to be cherished or accorded significance over time. The concept of a free self requires both an inherent causal continuity linking its present to its past, and a capacity for genuine choice among alternatives in the context of that continuity. Contrary to the determinist belief, a free self must be capable of choices and actions which cannot in principle be exhaustively explained by analysis of causal factors in the individual or his environment. But in contrast to the view of radical voluntarism, this self must also have a continuity of existence over time that is more than a cinematographic illusion of resembling presents, each arising from a totally unconstrained and enigmatic act of freedom. Furthermore, I spoke a short while ago of the supreme self-contempt in the face of one's failures that seems to be entailed by the doctrine of radical freedom. And I discussed the seeds of despair contained in the conviction of a fundamental weakness or impairment of the powers of the will. If we take Britton's highly pertinent second criterion into account, therefore, either view of the will that we have discussed makes it impossible that life have meaning.[2]

3. ARGUMENTS ABOUT OUR RELATIONS TO OTHER PERSONS

"There is no love among human beings; only power and fear." In the BBC's *Masterpiece Theater* version of Paul Scott's *The Raj Quartet*, a British Superintendent of Police makes this statement to an Indian man he has arrested and is soon to flog brutally, partly for information but mainly for revenge. It is an apt summation of the theme of this section. In its immediate context the statement is intended as a justification for the subjugation of India by Great Britain and as a reminder of the necessity for maintaining the sharpest line of separation between the rulers and the ruled, so that the latter will be forced always to know and to keep their place. But in its broader significance, it expresses a rejection of the possibility of genuine human community, perceiving each person as sealed within himself and forced to defend as best he can the citadel of his solitary being against the threats and incursions of others: a situation of all against each and each against all. If we are not to succumb to manipulation and fear, then our only recourse is to try to subdue and dominate those around us, to convert them into instruments for the attainment of our private ends. But in no case can we ever hope to surmount to any significant degree the terrible isolation and vulnerability that is our fate as human beings.

I will first survey some of the main arguments for this view, then make explicit its nihilistic consequences. The first argument calls attention to the inescapable solitariness of our lives by reminding us that we must each experience, suffer, and die completely alone. No one else can share in my immediate experiences or pains, nor can anyone else know what it means to me to contemplate my own death.

A physician tells me that I will have "some brief discomfort" when he sticks me with a needle in the sensitive tissues of my face, but I remind him that his "brief discomfort" is my stab of real pain, which I must endure in private. He may assure me that he knows what I am going through, but even if he has experienced similar trauma in the past, all he can do now is to try to recall it in faded memory. The experience is not immediate for him as it is for me. More to the point, he has no way of knowing what my pain feels like to me; he can only know what his pain feels like to him.

From a trivial case of this sort, it is but a step to more severe instances, for in all cases the situation is the same. You can no more share my excruciating than my simple pains, and this is true whether the pains be those of body or spirit. If I have just received news of my betrayal by someone to whom I had always given unquestioning trust and love, it is in vain for you to try to comfort me. I must accept the agony of my loss alone; only I can live through what this shocking breach of trust means to me. The same holds true for all my experiences—those of anxiety, embarrassment, and failure, as well as those of joy, pride, and accomplishment. You must remain forever an onlooker and outsider to the experiences which only I can suffer or undergo at firsthand, against the background of my particular memories and hopes. I am as shut off from your experiences as you are from mine.

Now that the novocaine has taken effect, the doctor can cut away at my skin with his scapel and I can be relatively unperturbed. We talk about a mutual acquaintance; he tells me that the man has been diagnosed to have incurable intestinal cancer. We each give indications of concern and sympathy. But are not our statements just so much cant? How can he and I come anywhere near imagining the shattering impact on our acquaintance of his physician's announcement that his condition, which lately has been causing him so much distress, is much worse than he had allowed himself to believe; and that by every indication it will be only a very short while before he must lose his life? Or in more commonplace terms, how can anyone else know what it means to me to have always in the back of my mind awareness of my irrevocable sentence to death, whether through inoperable disease or by some other means? You can know of your coming extinction and its impact on you; but only I can contemplate what my death means to me. And whether the actual process of my dying, through disease, accident, or old age, be mercifully brief or long and painful, I must again suffer through it alone. Each much face his sentence of death in the solitary confinement of his own being.

This sad fact is exemplified by the experience of Colonel Aureliano Buendia, in Gabriel García Márquez's *One Hundred Years of Solitude*. The Colonel has devoted the prime of his life to leading a revolution against the conservatives of his country in the Caribbean. He has survived extraordinary dangers, including one occasion on which he faced a firing squad, only to be rescued at the last minute by his brother; and another on which, in a fit of despair at the disappointing outcome of his battles, he tried to take his own life by shooting himself in the chest with his revolver. Now his days of fighting are over. He is old and tired, disillusioned with war and the dreams which had once filled him with shining hope and fervor. His sole preoccupation in his advanced age is the death, eluded for so long, that still lies in wait to claim him. "Taciturn, silent," he isolates himself as much as he can from the activities of his household, understanding "that the secret of a good old age is simply an honorable pact with solitude." Sitting moodily in the doorway at dusk, someone dares to disturb his solitary reveries with the question, "How are you, Colonel?" "Right here," he answers, "waiting for my funeral procession to pass" (Márquez 1971:190-191).

The second argument rests upon the position I earlier termed *epistemological nihilism*: the denial that there are or can be common truths or shared cognitive meanings among human beings. It is especially clear from Mauthner's version of this position that human community is an impossibility, except in the most superficial sense of the term, because community presupposes communication. In his view, what passes for communication among humans is counterfeit coin, despite all seeming indications to the contrary. His basic reason for saying this is that no person can avoid giving to language or any other putative means of public expression an interpretive significance that is shaped through and through by her own distinctive background of experiences and memories. Thus, each of us is necessarily consigned to her private world. Stirner's uncompromising nominalism leads to the same conclusion, not only because there are only unique particulars and no universal meanings to be shared, but also because there can be no such thing as a truth higher than the individual. Each individual constructs his own "truth" as he strives to subject the world, including all other human beings, to himself and his own interests.

Nietzsche's rejection of the concept of a "true world" to which our claims must be held responsible, and his teaching that the world for each individual is constituted out of those values and beliefs that express that individual's idiosyncratic perspective and will to power, also have the effect of shutting each person within himself. Instead of community, we have individuals vying with one another for dominance and control; and in place of common truths or meanings that could provide a basis for social cohesion, we have a welter of egoistic centers of energy. Sartre's approach to knowledge and truth bears a close resemblance to Nietzsche's, as we have already noted. This is but one of the many ways in which Sartre's philosophy poses profound problems for the possibility of human community, as will be seen elsewhere in this section. The effect of each of these versions of epistemological nihilism is to block human beings from one another by denying to them any fund of knowledge or understanding transcending the particularities of their individual thought, experience, or expression.

The third argument for the necessary alienation of individuals from one another and the impossibility of human community stems from what I called *moral nihilism*, expecially in two of its forms, *amoralism* and *egoism*. We saw earlier that London's character Wolf Larson assumes that all forms of life, including the human form, are absurd and worthless, and yet that they are all by nature caught up in a blind striving to conquer and endure. Holding this to be the case, Larson rejects the idea that one individual has moral obligations to another and holds it to be inevitable that the strong will seek to dominate and control the weak. That they will sometimes do so with exceptional callousness and cruelty is a matter of no consequence to him, because if one takes a realistic view of the world this is only to be expected. It is obvious that Larson's position allows no foundation for genuine community among human beings. Each person is left to go it alone; his only hope for avoiding the debilitating effects of cruelty and intimidation at the hands of others is to struggle for whatever mastery over them he is capable of achieving.

Stirner's egoism also destroys any basis for common values to which all human beings can be held accountable, values which could help to create a climate of mutual concern and obligation and thus provide essential bonds of social unity. Each individual is obligated only to himself, and he is entitled to use any means at his disposal, however much it might offend conventional standards of morality, to achieve his personal aims and to frustrate attempts on the part of others to gain power over him. In an "anything goes" situation of this sort, there can be no trust, only universal suspicion accompanied by cautious and calculating maneuvering for private advantage. Whatever semblance of community there might be in the world, the underlying reality is that of isolated individuals who must concentrate anxiously on their self-aggrandizement and survival. Anyone who thinks otherwise suffers from fatal delusion and makes himself easy prey for exploitation. No matter how many solemn agreements individuals may make with one another, each can only expect that the other will ignore these agreements when he thinks it suits his purpose to do so. It is bound to be extremely difficult, if not impossible, to foresee in advance when or under what circumstances this breach of agreements will occur, though it is predictable in general. Each individual is therefore precariously exposed and alone and can hope to rely on no one but himself.

Sartre's stance of *atomic individualism* (to use Copleston's phrase) with respect to moral values also contains the seeds of the dissolution of human community. It follows from his view that "in the long run no one set of values is intrinsically superior to any other set of values," a proposition that must also encompass the values upon which Sartre himself places such great emphasis, e.g., responsibility to society and concern for the ideal for all humankind implicit in my choices, or the value of freedom itself (see Copleston 1966:194-195; and our discussion of this same point in Chapter Three, Section 1). Consensus on these and all values is contingent on the arbitrary decisions of human beings; it has no basis in human nature or in the nature of the world. Moral values are sheerly invented, not discovered. We have also seen that Sartre's doctrine of pure freedom does not admit of antecedent restraints. Thus, it seems that for him obligation as such cannot exist. I am in no sense bound to respect your humanity, nor are you bound to have any respect for mine. We are each free to do to one another as we choose. Common acceptance of this concept of morality would make the bonds of community tenuous indeed; it has a negative consequence for human society similar to that we have already recognized in the outlooks of Larson and Stirner.

Cioran makes this consequence crystal clear when he addresses the following question to an imaginary figure (perhaps himself) who takes a position on moral values akin to that of a Larson, Stirner, or Sartre: "Since for you there is no ultimate criterion nor irrevocable principle, and no god, what keeps you from committing any and every crime?" He answers the question by concluding that the only constraint is apathy, an unwillingness to take the trouble to act consistently with the view that one has assumed concerning the status of moral claims (1975:156). Larson or Stirner could add that it might not suit their personal goals or needs at a given time to engage in criminal acts, and Sartre could only say that he chooses arbitrarily not to do so. (Or as Camus states, "One can be virtuous through a whim;" see Chapter Two, Section 5.) The concept of social groups and institutions entailed by the general view of morality now under discussion is that they can at best represent only loose and fragile associations of essentially withdrawn and competing individuals, each entitled to be a law to herself and each with philosophical license to dismiss the idea that moral standards have intrinsic importance or obligatory character. The moral basis for community is thereby obliterated, and the individual is left to assert and defend herself in the presence of others as best she can.

Sartre's doctrine of radical freedom calls the possibility of genuine human community into question, not only with respect to its negative implications for shared truths, meanings, and moral values, but in other important respects as well. One of these other respects was indicated toward the end of the previous section: the acute sense of separation and loneliness implicit in Sartre's insistence that each of us is condemned to be wholly responsible for herself. We have already discussed this claim and its implications in some detail; it can stand here as a fourth argument for the ineluctable isolation of human beings from one another.

A fifth argument for this conclusion also grows out of Sartre's doctrine of radical freedom. According to him, the freedom of others is a constant threat, enigma, and embarrassment to me, just as my freedom is to them. I cannot avoid converting them into objects for the utilization of my freedom, and they cannot avoid doing the same in relation to me. Conflict between or among individuals is thus insurmountable; each atomic center of freedom works relentlessly to absorb all other centers of freedom into the orbit of its projects and concerns. Sartre speaks in one place (1966:311-313) of the overwhelming feeling of danger and vulnerability I experience when I become aware that every center of freedom and subjectivity external to myself is a kind of drain hole that sucks the world into itself, thus robbing me of my world and my freedom. I am robbed of my world because it now becomes the world of the other, viewed from his unique perspective, in terms of relations and distances that flow from him; and it is brought within the controlling compass of his priorities, purposes, and meanings. I am robbed of my sense of freedom because the other's stare transfixes and freezes me, transforming me into an object, one more in-itself to serve as fodder for the grinding mill of his own object-transcending nihilations.

On such occasions I become aware of being a "self," constituted and given settled character by its past acts construed from the standpoint of the other, and no longer a volatile focus of unceasing flight toward the future. This awareness creates either shame or resentment. By the one I am tempted toward absorption into the world of the other (though it is still by my own act of freedom that I acquiesce in his view of me); by the other I reassert myself as center, endeavoring to swallow him into the objectifying vortex of my own freedom. So once again, the sole alternatives are fear or power, submission or domination, neither of which is conducive to community. "My original fall is the existence of the Other," says Sartre, because by the other's agency I come to "have an outside" or a "nature," and to envision the "solidification and alienation of my own possibilities" (322). It is a prospect I must fight against in the only way possible: by doing to the other precisely what he strives to do to me.

The melding of such stubborn centers of freedom into genuine community is an impossibility; the closest approximation to it is when I and another have the sense of being threatened by the objectifications and dominations of a third person (or group of persons). This is not a "we-subject" kind of mutual empathy, cooperation, and sharing; rather, it is an "us-object" sense of mutual petrification by the Medusa-like stare of another. Any "we-subject" awareness is at best shallow and unstable. Sartre concludes, therefore, that "[i]t is . . . useless for human-reality to seek to get out of this dilemma: one must either transcend the Other or allow oneself to be transcended by him. The essence of the relations between consciousnesses is not the *Mitsein* [of Heidegger]; it is conflict" (525). Or, as he states the point in another place, "While I attempt to free myself from the hold of the Other, the Other is trying to free himself from mine; while I seek to enslave the Other, the Other seeks to enslave me . . . . Conflict is the original meaning of being-for-others" (444-445). His despair of the possibility of community, at least in *Being and Nothingness*, is made quite explicit in these statements.

An assertion of Sartre that we referred to in another context, "To be looked at is to apprehend oneself as the unknown object of unknown appraisals" (328), sums up in a dramatic way the feeling that one must have in the presence of others, according to his philosophy. It is a feeling of bafflement, mistrust, and deep apprehension. I never know quite how I am being appraised by the other, or how I am going to be treated by him, now or in the future. His gaze shakes the foundations of my world and undermines my security and self-esteem. As Desan says, "there may be an enormous difference between what the Other thinks of me and what I think of myself" (1960:69, n. 24). There may be, but of course there also may not. I cannot really know how the other, in his radical freedom, is regarding me, or will regard me, at any time. This means that an atmosphere of mystery and unpredictability shrouds him, and that I am forever confused and off guard in my relations to him. Human relationships give no basis for mutual confidence or understanding.

It is just this pervasive mood of suspicion and distrust among human beings, and the ways in which they continually frustrate and bewilder one another even at the level of the most ordinary transactions, that Kafka gives such a powerful account of in his works, particularly in the novel *The Castle*. Sartre sees Kafka's portrayal of human relations as closely in tune with his own, although he thinks that the principal theme Kafka broods upon in his novels is that we are continually kept in the dark about the appraisal of ourselves and our actions given by the ultimate Other, God. Thus, we are doomed to perpetual ignorance of what Kafka apparently takes to be the objective "truth" about our intentions and acts (Sartre 1966:325-326). There is much to be said for this interpretation, which reminds us of the extreme religious scrupulousness, guilt, and dread which seem to suffuse Kafka's writings; but my present interest is in his portrayal of strictly human interactions in *The Castle*.

Although Kafka's outlook on human relations is not explicitly tied to a doctrine of radical freedom, it is so much like Sartre's in other ways that discussion of it can help spell out in more concrete detail the general thrust of this fifth argument and the overriding theme of this entire section. After reflecting on the despairing view of community that emerges from *The Castle*, I bring the section to a close by noting nihilistic consequences of the view that there is no basis for experience of authentic community among humans, and that the only alternative to cringing uncertainty and fear in the presence of others is a constant striving to nullify the threat of their freedom by converting them into instruments for one's private projects and concerns.

Several themes germane to our topic stand out in *The Castle*. The first one is the isolation and loneliness of the main character, K., and his failure throughout the novel to find any trustworthy, satisfying relations with others. Ostensibly brought to a village to be hired as a Land Surveyor, he is unable, despite all his efforts, to confirm his hiring or to begin his work. The officials at the Castle are remote and inacessible, and he is never able to break through the layers of documents, procedures, or bureaucratic officialdom to find out exactly why he has been brought to the village or what he should do now that he is there. He cannot get anyone in the bureaucracy to take up his cause or to make the slightest admission of a mistake, or even of the possibility of a mistake, in his summoning. This is in spite of the fact that the mayor frankly informs him that there is no work for a surveyor in the village.

K.'s relations to the villagers are perplexing; he is plagued by the feeling that he is a stranger, a nuisance, in everyone's way, and that he is caught up in machinations quite beyond his comprehension. As the novel progresses, he feels more and more isolated, frustrated, and exploited, because of the bizzare, unpredicatable responses of those about him. People make promises they do not keep and provide contradictory information. He cannot be sure that some are what they claim to be. His pleas for help are often met with resentment, fear, faint amusement, or indifference. He can find no one to trust. The villagers as a whole seem to be buffeted about "like the wind, according to strange and remote behests that one could never guess at" (Kafka 1969:153). Instead of being welcomed and assisted to find a meaningful place within the life of a community, he seems to be living through a bad dream that only gets worse as it progresses. He tries to be persistent, to draw upon his own resources, and to get through to the Castle at last in spite of the formidable obstacles he encounters on every hand. But his efforts have no effect.

A second theme is the complete domination of the villagers by the officials of the Castle and the shame of their unquestioning acceptance of this domination. This theme reminds us of the two basic courses available to us in our relations with others, according to Sartre. The theme is constantly alluded to in Kafka's novel, but it is especially prominent in the story of a young girl, Amalia, who is summoned to a sexual liason by an official of the Castle by a letter. The letter is couched in the vilest kind of language, with no suggestion of tenderness. It is not in any sense a request or a plea, but a peremptory command. Amalia refuses to go, and the consequence of her act of dignity and pride is that her father loses his business and his status within the village. Her family is ostracized by everyone, because everyone instinctively takes the side of the bureaucrats of the Castle. The swiftness with which the villagers turn against a family in their midst, and their readiness to give unqualified support to the most flagrant injustices of the officials of the Castle, demonstrate the depth of their shame and the complete absence of any spirit of true community among them.

Even Amalia's family finally succumbs to the shame, petitioning the Castle for its "forgiveness," as though Amalia had been in the wrong. The Castle turns a deaf ear to the family's pleas, pretending to have no awareness of, or complicity in, what has taken place. It can be aloof and indifferent, as ever, because in the eyes of the villagers it "always has the advantage" (274). No one will take the risk of questioning its prerogatives or authority. Their toadying attitude toward authority makes any sense of community among the villagers impossible; when it means going against the Castle, no individual will dare to give support to another or to take any chances on his behalf. The villagers' humiliation in bowing docilely to external authority is complete. This means that no one can trust anyone else and that all must live in a constant state of wariness and fear.

A third theme is the marked resemblance between the form of life of the villagers and that of the bureaucrats themselves. As someone remarks early in the novel, "There is no difference between the peasantry and the Castle" (14). Every department at the Castle is separated from the others, making its plans and decisions in secret, swiftly concealing its mistakes, and jealously guarding its prerogatives. Hostility, confusion, and jockeying for power are rampant, although never made obvious. Each remote bureaucrat is shielded from the others by inviolable rankings and procedures, and by mountains of papers and reports. Here, too, no sense of community or cooperation for a common cause is found; only competition, suspicion, and mistrust, each bureaucrat being constantly burdened with the sense of being subject to the other's hidden judgements and enigmatic designs. In addition, an accepted attitude of studied indifference and contempt toward those lower than oneself in the bureaucratic scale is evidenced. But it is also true no one dares to step out of line or to give any indication of independence of thought or action. Every decision or exercise of power is kept subtle and submerged, so that responsibility for it is difficult, if not impossible, to assess. The real leaders, if any exist in this vast bureaucratic machine, keep (as we would say today) and extremely "low profile."

Clearly, therefore, officials of the Castle and villagers alike exist in a state of atomistic competition, mutual hostility and distrust, and virtual enslavement to a system that represents the exact opposite of sustaining human community. The only possible exception to the enslavement of each by all is the power wielded by those at the top of the bureaucratic hierarchy, but even their dominance cannot be overtly expressed. The strong similarity between the lives of the bureaucrats and those of the villagers is evident throughout the novel, despite the fact that the Castle a whole retains the upper hand. Kafka can be interpreted as saying that the dismal pattern of life in which the villagers and their leaders are embroiled is not a local aberration but the actual state of human relationships.

Finally, there is the theme of the failure of love between man and woman. Not even this powerful force can forge the bonds of genuine community between human beings. K. falls in love with a barmaid, Frieda, and it seems that she is deeply in love with him. But as their relationship develops, it is increasingly eroded by misrust. Each is frustrated and puzzled by certain statements or actions of the other, and comes to suspect that he or she is being exploited by the other in mysterious ways. Frieda was formerly the mistress of Klamm, a high Castle official with whom K. has been desperately trying to establish contact. She tells K. at one point that she is beginning to believe that he has sought to possess her in order to make use of her as a conduit to Klamm. When this attempt fails, as surely it will, she predicts that he will come to despise her. Later, another barmaid, Pepi, tries to convince K. that Frieda became his lover for purely selfish reasons—to call attention to herself, to make Klamm jealous, or to gain some other advantage—and that this is the only reasonable explanation for her entering into a relation with K., whom everybody in the village regards as a pathetic nonentity, even lower in status than a lowly barmaid. K. has already come to suspect that Frieda and the bungling assistants who have been assigned to him are somehow in league, and that they might all be tools or spies of the Castle. His suspicion is reinforced when he learns that it was Frieda who first spread the word about Amalia's having broken the taboo which prohibited any villager from ignoring commands from officials at the Castle. Does this suggest that she is in the employ of the Castle, charged with keeping careful watch on everything that goes on in the village?

K. is sometimes overwhelmed with the feeling that everybody in the village, including Frieda, is merely playing with him, treating him in a manner secretly engineered by the Castle, for reasons known only to itself. His relationship with Frieda deteriorates and finally ends in failure, foundering on her doubts about his sincerity and on his inability to put to rest the suspicion that he is being made an instrument of her manipulations and deceit. Their love (if it ever was that; even this is not made clear by Kafka) has the same overtones of mistrust, manipulation (whether actual or only imagined), and pervasive uncertainty and ambiguity that destroy any hope for community in other aspects of the life of the village and its rulers. One gains the impression once again that in his portrayal of the relationship between K. and Frieda, Kafka is not just describing the vicissitudes of a particular love but is trying rather to symbolize a wider truth: that all attempts at community among human beings are doomed to defeat.

Kafka's treatment of the breakdown of K.'s and Frieda's love brings to mind Sartre's insistence that the failure of love is unavoidable, because the ideal of love is rooted in a contradiction. The contradiction is that, on the one hand, one wants to be loved by a freedom, to be freely chosen and cherished, brought into the center of the other's orbit of commitments and concerns. No satisfaction is derived from making love to a puppet! On the other hand, one aspires to achieve such complete control over the other's freedom as to eliminate from it every aspect of unpredictability or ambiguity, every ground of possible suspicion or threat. One wants to possess the other heart and soul. Thus, to be in love is to want to become subject to the impenetrable mystery of the beloved's freedom, while at the same time wanting to reduce the beloved to the status of an object wholly at the mercy of one's own calculations and will. One dreams of being the center of the other's world, and thus subject to the other's freedom, but also of bringing the other into the center of one's own world. Sartre states the contradiction which makes forever unrealizable the ideal of unity with the other in love: "the assimilation of the for-itself and the Other in a single transcedence would necessarily involve the disappearance of the characteristic of otherness in the Other." Fatal conflict and inevitable dissolution (and thus disillusionment) are built into the love relation from the start (1966:447-449). There is no more basis for genuine community here than anywhere else in human experience.

This section's theme is denial of the possibility of human community; we have now looked at five ways of arguing for it. Our next task is to trace connections between this theme and despair of the meaning of life. Three connections will be noted, each emphasizing some fundamental deprivation or absurdity in human existence (or at least in the situation and prospects of the bulk of humanity) that seems to follow from the premise that achievement of community among human beings is an impossibility.

The first connection is brought into focus by Britton when he states that it is essential to a meaningful life "that people matter or may matter to each other" (1969:184). This is the third of his four criteria for a meaningful life (I referred earlier to the other three). This section claims that Britton's third criterion cannot be fulfilled. If he is right in insisting on this criterion as a necessary one for assessing the meaning of life, it follows from the arguments considered here that it is impossible for life to have meaning. Britton does not just leave us with a terse statement of his criterion; he elaborates upon it and argues for it in a concise but persuasive way, showing how little sense it would make to call a life meaningful that failed to incorporate, or could never incorporate, any sort of mutual, sustaining interactions with other human beings:

> One of the great 'injustices' of life is that some people fail to achieve the most important mutual relationships.... Nevertheless the possibility of positive mutual concern seems to be fundamental. It is a fact of life that all the higher animals enjoy each other's society in one direction or another: the existence of life in mammalian species depends upon it; in human society the existence of speech depends on it. In man the relationship is apprehended and valued for itself. It is a fact that a meal unshared loses much of its value...(1969:185).

Dewey hints at this same criterion of existential meaning when he asserts that "[s]hared experience is the greatest of human goods" (1958:202), for this suggests that a life completely deprived of such shared experience would be deprived of something of profound value.

Both Dewey and Britton speak in the spirit of Aristotle, who observed long ago in the *Nichomachean Ethics* that it was extremely implausible to say, as some philosophers had wanted to, that those who are supremely happy have no need of friends, because they are entirely sufficient in themselves. Aristotle's own view is that friends are the greatest of all external goods. He insists that "no one would choose the whole world on condition of being alone, since man is a political creature and one whose nature is to live with others.... Therefore the happy man needs friends." (Aristotle 1941:1088 [1169b]). Aristotle also argues that the highest and most enduring type of friendship is that among persons who are virtuous by nature and who therefore wish well to their friends for their friends' sake, and not merely for something they themselves can gain from the relationship. Such friendships are admittedly rare, but they impart a quality to life without which it could not be said to have attained the ideal of *eudaimonia* or "living well" (1941:1060-1061 [1156a-1156b]). What Aristotle says about friendship could also apply to love between a man and a woman, or between a parent and a child.

According to the arguments of this section, however, the reciprocal caring and concern on the part of human beings which Aristotle so fondly recommends are impossible. This means that there can be no hope of having friends or loved ones who can be cherished for their own sakes, or for being cherished by others in this way. It is either exploit or be exploited. Each person is condemned, as we have seen, to a state of radical separation from others or to an unending struggle for purely personal advantage from which there can be no respite. If this is the true account of the human situation, then by the reasoning of Aristotle, Dewey, and Britton, we can only conclude that our lives lack an essential dimension of meaning, and that we must somehow resign ourselves to being forever deprived of what has long been thought to be one of the most elemental goals of existence and essential sources of happiness and fulfillment. But because community with others is such an instinctive need and compelling good, it is unlikely that we will be able to cease yearning for it. So we will continue to seek for it in vain, and set ourselves up again and again for frustration and disappointment. Our situation will be much like that of K., in Kafka's *The Castle*, the image of a life doomed to pointless pursuits.

A second connection between the denial of community and despair of the meaning of life becomes apparent when we reflect on the fact that most of civilized existence rests on the assumption that community can be achieved. If this assumption has no foundation, then what parades as civilization turns out on closer inspection to be a mockery and a delusion. The forms and institutions of civilized life—language, tradition, family, morality, art, education, industry, sworn agreements, laws, and the like—give every indication of being grounded in, and facilitating the realization of, mutual interests, values, and aims. But by the reasoning of this section these forms and institutions are mere stage props; behind the scenes, there is no such thing as cooperation, trust, mutual enjoyment, or sharing, only relentless struggles for dominance and power waged by completely isolated and totally self-centered persons. Civilization is founded on a lie, and all its structures are instrumentalities of that lie.

This lie at the heart of civilization strikes to the core of our individual existence. For each of us, by being required to maintain the postures of a civilized person in a thousand ways every day, is enmeshed in the lie and gives constant tacit endorsement to it. The lie is so cleverly conveyed by the trappings of civilization that we are in constant danger of falling prey to the illusion that there is, or can be, something like community among human beings. But to succumb to this illusion is to be made easy victim to the schemings of those who know better, and who are quick to take advantage of the naive ignorance and trust of others. To live the life of civilized society, therefore, is to be caught in a web of fraudulence, seduction, manipulation, and danger from which escape appears impossible.

Even if this or that individual is able to travel to some place far from civilization, she cannot escape her language or the effects of her acculturation and upbringing; nor can she hope to avoid many other consequences and influences of civilization in this shrunken world. Moreover, this kind of flight is an alternative available only to a privileged few. Most of us, therefore, and probably all of us, will be forced to endure the built-in contradictions and deceptions of civilized existence as long as we live. According to the arguments of this section, to be a civilized being is to live in the midst of an all-encompassing absurdity; it means being condemned to a life of elaborately disguised pretense and bad faith, a life at perpetual cross-purposes with the truth.

In the third place, if there can be no such thing as community, and if life is a struggle of each against all, some may win, but most will lose. In a deeper sense all must lose. Kafka's *The Castle* brings this truth home to us in no uncertain terms. We saw that only a few bureaucrats at the pinnacle of the hierarchy are able to achieve anything like positions of clear dominance over others; all the rest, other members of the Castle bureaucracy as well as the villagers, are consigned to lives of utter dependency and humiliation, with nothing about their lives they can call their own and with no sense of autonomy or self-worth. Their lives are completely at the beck and call of others; their role is that of slaves—timid, cautious, forever worried about causing even the slightest offense to those who wield power over them. By the arguments of this section, this predicament is what most human lives are reduced to. Only the few very strong will be able to prevail; the rest must forfeit their freedom, and thus their dignity, to others. They must become acustomed to weakness, embarrassment, and shame. In the struggle between power and fear, most will be made captive to fear.

Even those who win do so at a very high price. They will have no friends or loved ones; they will be able to trust no one, nor can anyone trust them. They will always be in danger of having their power usurped and overthrown. The extent of their success will be the extent to which they can reduce those around them from the status of persons to the status of automata. Those who do their bidding will not do so out of admiration, love, or mutuality of care and concern, but simply out of craven fear. Obviously, nothing is satisfying about being a slave, totally subservient to the will of others. But a life of aloof and precarious domination, devoid of friendship, trust, or love, also leaves little to be commended or desired. If these are the only alternatives, the conclusion is inescapable that human existence is a cruel and fatuous charade, with no place to turn for anything of substance or enduring value.

4. A LOOK AHEAD

In this and the preceding chapter, using seven main headings, I have presented some principal arguments for the nihilistic position. With this task completed, I am now ready to tease out certain ruling assumptions lying behind these arguments and to begin critically examining these assumptions in their historical setting. I do so in the spirit of Dewey's suggestion that the most promising way out of the "snarl" of any complex problem "is a reconsideration of the conceptions in virtue of which the problem exists," for these conceptions enter tacitly into the formulations of the problem itself (1958:252).

By placing these assumptions in the context of their origins, developments, and past employments, I intend to show where we are today in the light of processes of intellectual history that have helped to bring us to this time. Had the sources and evolvings of those processes been different, we ourselves might have been quite different, and our problems might have been of a different character or have been seen in a different light. Becoming more fully aware that other possibilities of conceptual development existed in the past, and that these possibilities are still available to us today, can enable us to gain critical perspective on the problem of nihilism in the modern world by reminding us of alternatives to our accustomed and often unexamined ways of thinking.

I need to put the task of this book in broader context, however, by noting that the nihilistic outlook is not arrived at solely on the basis of intellectual arguments, despite my preoccupation with such arguments in the last two chapters. It also results from visceral and ill-defined intimations that are sometimes overpowering in their effects. Sartre's vivid descriptions of Roquentin's repeated attacks of "nausea" help to bring this fact home. The malady of nihilism can creep up on us and seize us unawares, through a sequence of what might be termed "negative revelations" whose cumulative impact is that of transforming (or more accurately, undermining) our lives and converting us to a radically different viewpoint. Such experiences can engender a pervading temper of dread and despair that usurps the place of the confidence and hope that formerly sustained us. Then, just as religious faith seeks understanding through philosophical reflection, so may these experiences of negation seek confirmation in arguments, some of which will bear a close resemblance to those discussed in these two chapters. This is not to say that such arguments are merely tacked on as a kind of afterthought, but that they are often given impetus and plausibility by an already emerging or existing nihilistic consciousness.

Thus, it is not only the case that such arguments contain historically inherited assumptions that must be critically analyzed. Whatever propensity we may have to succumb to the nihilistic conclusions of these arguments also needs to be studied in relation to our formative experiences, including the social experiences of this century. The combination of conditioned susceptibility and seeming plausibility of argument can make the nihilistic position appear unassailable to some and cause it to loom as a profound threat to others.

The formative social experiences to which I allude—such things as the devastations of World Wars I and II; a shattering economic depression in the third decade of this century and present threats of collapse of a fragile and ever more interdependent world economy; the "final solution" directed against the Jewish people, with its nightmare images of grotesque, wholly gratuitous inflictions of widespread suffering and death; the development of weapons capable of killing millions in an instant, of wreaking genetic havoc on the descendants of those who survive, and of possibly inflicting irreparable damage upon our planetary ecosystem; the experience of having the promise of boundless scientific progress turn into a perception of technology out of control, threatening wholesale military and/or environmental disaster; bewildering encounters with radically different cultures of the world, no longer shielded from us by geographic remoteness or insufficiency of information; daily exposure to strife and mayhem across the globe in our living rooms each evening (and in living color); the loneliness and sense of impotence or remoteness from the centers of power created by an increasingly mobile, urbanized, and bureaucratized civilization—are fit subject matters for inquiry, highly relevant for trying to understand the advent of nihilism in our time. But they are topics for another study; too complex and involved to be treated here with anything like the adequacy they deserve. Thus, I make no claim to be offering a comprehensive analysis of the sources of modern nihilism. Instead, I restrict my discussion in Parts Three and Four to entrenched religious and philosophical assumptions that seem especially pertinent for placing nihilism in the context of our intellectual history.

Finally, nihilism should not just be viewed as a position or mood peculiar to modern thought, explicable only against the background of the intellectual and social history of the West. It is, as Stanley Rosen says, "a perennial human danger;" one that "cannot be 'solved' without the dissolution of human nature" (1969:xx). The Book of Ecclesiastes in the Hebrew Bible makes the truth of this observation abundantly clear, because its nihilistic themes predate by two millennia the emergence of the modern mind. I will give explicit attention, especially in Part Five, to some factors in the human condition that help to explain why nihilism is a perennial threat; I will also suggest ways of profiting from its significant disclosures of truth without being swept away by its rampant negations.

PART THREE

A Critical Look at Religious Sources of Nihilism

Chapter 5

Anthropocentrism, Externality of Value, and Religion As Theism

Is what is holy holy because the gods approve it, or do they approve it because it is holy?
—*Plato (1973:178)*

One way to understand the phenomenon of nihilism, as that has come to the fore in the Western world over the past one and one-half centuries, is against the background of the prevailing religious tradition of the West: Christianity. It is no secret that this tradition, which has long held sway over the thinking and practices of vast numbers of people, has suffered a sharp recent decline in its credibility and influence, giving way to an increasingly secular outlook. Bernard Meland and many others have traced the origins of this secular outlook to the latter part of the seventeenth century, the time of the scientific revolution. In that century, says Meland, we can witness the emergence of "a new community of mind ... centering around new disciplines and forms of inquiry that were to challenge, and eventually to supersede, this prevailing Christian consensus in major centers of learning and scholarship." These new disciplines and forms of inquiry soon began to merge "with the technical demands of industry until science, together with industry, laid the ground for a new technological civilization in the West." The outcome was "a full-blown modernistic consciousness that had all but cut its ties with the historical legacy of past centuries." The full impact of this process of secularization is only now being acutely felt in the West, despite the fact that it has been underway for three centuries and was already, as Meland puts it, "steadily recognizable and definable" in Europe and the United States by the close of the nineteenth century (Meland 1966:16-17).

Whatever we may think of the Christian tradition as such, it clearly provides a unifying vision and sustaining worldview in which human life holds a place of special dignity and importance. It is not surprising, therefore, that its decline and increasing supplantation by the secular mindset of technological civilization has left a void of existential meaning for many in the West, exposing them to the ravages of the nihilistic mood.

But there are religious sources of nihilism in the West that are more subtle and easier to overlook: certain basic assumptions carried over relatively unchanged and unchallenged from the heritage of religious thought into modern consciousness, or ones which have given way to closely analogous secular substitutes. I want to characterize and criticize these assumptions.

I begin with a sketch of some salient features of the classical Christian vision, in order to emphasize the gaping hole that can be torn in the fabric of social and individual existence when that vision ceases to convince or compel, and nothing else seems able to take its place. I will then identify some key assumptions of the Western religious tradition that have continued to inform modern consciousness or have been transmuted into closely resembling secular beliefs, and try to see how these relate to the nihilistic mood. I will also criticize these assumptions, or at least their religious aspect, in the case of ones that are not exclusively religious in background or character. Further critical analysis of assumptions of this second type will be presented later. In this way, I begin the task of making a case against the philosophy of nihilism, a task that will come increasingly to the center of our attention in this and the next part, and be brought to its final development in Part Five.

1. THE CHRISTIAN WORLDVIEW AS AN ANTIDOTE TO NIHILISM

The traditional Christian worldview can be sketched under six main headings: (a) belief in a personal God; (b) belief in the meaningfulness of history; (c) belief in special revelation; (d) belief in nature's subservience to human beings; (e) belief in an objective moral order, rooted in the will and purpose of God; and (f) belief in an afterlife. Some of these beliefs, as we will note, stand in direct opposition to particular types of nihilism discussed in Chapter Two. The whole cluster of beliefs and the way of life it represents constitute a confident affirmation of existential meaning, thereby countering the type of nihilism that is the main focus of this book.

(a) Belief in a personal God. This belief means that at the heart of reality is something much like human persons, a Being with consciousness and intentionality who created the world and sustains it. So personality is not a chance by-product of an essentially impersonal cosmic process. It is the ultimate order of existence, the source and explanation of all else. This God also enters into "I-Thou" relations with human individuals and groups, responds to their prayers, and performs providential acts on their behalf. These ideas cannot help but enhance the importance of human personality. This importance is further emphasized by the Christian belief that the climactic historical manifestation of God's purpose and nature is his incarnation in a human being, Jesus Christ.

(b) Belief in the meaningfulness of history. History for the Christian is not a round of endless repetitions, nor is it a collection of basically disconnected, whimsical events. It has a definite beginning and will come to a definite end, for it is given its beginning by God in order that it may attain the end he has appointed for it. There is continuity, coherence, and abiding significance in the historical process.

In the Christian view, history unfolds like a drama. Nature is its stage and provides its props, while human beings are its actors. The Author and Director is God. The human actors may introduce improvisations into the drama from time to time, and on some occasions they may even deviate badly from the script. But so forceful and ingenious is the Director that these improvisations and deviations do not detract seriously from the play. It still develops mainly as he intends and will be brought eventually to the dramatic end he has envisioned for it. To the extent that human beings accept their role in the drama, to that extent their lives become meaningful. For they are now cooperating with their Creator to realize the purpose of their lives, the purpose of human history, and the purpose of the created universe as a whole.

(c) Belief in special revelation. The problem remains of how the actors find out about the script and gain access to it. Some intimation of the script is given in their everyday experiences, or perhaps in the inner recesses of their minds, and other clues to the broad outlines of the play are provided by the markings on the stage and arrangement of the props in the natural order. But these are all bare hints at best and cannot substitute for the details of the script itself.

The full script is given out by God over a portion of history which may be termed the *revelational epoch*. The mode of this disclosure is often called *special revelation*, which is so absolute and final that it transcends the relativities of history and of cultures. Other epochs and civilizations may have their own ideas about what the meaning of human life is and what significance, if any, history has. But to the extent that these accounts depart from the special revelation attested to in the Christian Bible, they are flatly false and should be dismissed.

Unaided human reason may have difficulty comprehending or accepting some things about this special revelation. But that is just so much the worse for unaided human reason. There is only one truth for all times, for all places, and for all peoples. That is the truth of the Christian revelation, which reaches its climax in the life, teachings, redemptive death, and resurrection of Jesus

Christ. Reason's hesitation serves only to give evidence of its limitations. There is no room here for skeptical doubt or suspension of judgment in the face of other likely alternatives. The revelation has been given and has only to be accepted to bestow upon human life a full and complete significance.

(d) Belief in nature's subservience to human beings. This article of belief has already been alluded to in our use of the metaphor of nature as the stage for the acting out of the historical drama. But a little more can be said about it. In the classical Christian view, nature and the human species are created at the same time and will come to an end at the same time (or at least, the existence of the human species on this earth in its present form will come to an end; as we note below, it continues on in another order of existence, or perhaps on a new earth, for all eternity). This leaves little doubt that nature exists primarily, if not solely, to serve as the platform for human history.

Moreover, nature is fitted to serve this role by its character. It is qualitative in character, no different in its essential nature from the way human beings perceive it and relate to it. Again, just as its time span is relatively brief, corresponding to the time span of the human species on earth, so its spatial dimensions are relatively small. The earth is at the center of things, and the stars, the sun, and the planets are ranged neatly around it. Somewhere up in the rarified stellar realm is heaven, and below the surface of the earth is hell.

Within these relatively confined spatial and temporal dimensions the whole cosmic drama is enacted. The angels of heaven and the demons of hell are participants in this drama and often act out roles on the earthly stage, insinuating themselves for good or ill into the lives of human beings. Miracles are relatively commonplace, for nature is suffused with spiritual significance and subject to frequent interventions of divine providence. Because nature exists mainly to subserve human destiny, human beings are at home in it, or at least as much as they need to be in order to use it as a springboard to a better and more abiding life beyond the grave and beyond the vicissitudes of human history.

The picture of nature I am presenting here is that of the ancient and medieval Christian, at least in some of its detail. It is not one which would be espoused in its entirety by most Christians today. But the felt mandate to abandon this cozy picture of the cosmos, so neatly circumscribed by space and time, is one of the forces which has introduced strain into the credibility of the Christian worldview in modern times.

Points (a) and (b) together constitute important ingredients of Christianity's way of countering existential nihilism: the first, because it gives central dignity and value to human personality and affirms an intimate relation between the Lord of the universe and the humans he has made in his likeness; the second, because it means that human life has point and purpose, both at the individual level and at the level of the historical experiences of the human species as a whole.

Implicit in points (c) and (d) is Christianity's answer to the radical intellectual skepticism we have seen to be one of the meanings of the term *nihilism*. That answer is as follows. Nature is largely knowable by human reason, because it was created with a character and proportion enabling it to be understood and used by human beings; and they were created with the ability to know and use it. In general, human reason is reliable, within its limitations. When it reaches its limits, it is providentially supplemented by special revelation. Point (d) also serves as an obvious counter to another type of nihilism: *cosmic nihilism*.

(e) Belief in an objective moral order, rooted in the will and purpose of God. We come next to Christianity's answer to the radical moral skepticism which constitutes another form of nihilism. Christians believe that knowledge about what is objectively and universally right and wrong in the moral sphere is clearly given in special revelation, and at least powerfully adumbrated in nature and human experience. Morality has an objective, universal basis because it is rooted in the will and purpose of God, as definitively made known in such things as the Ten Commandments and other precepts of the Jewish Law, the example and teachings of Jesus in the Gospels, and the moral injunctions of the Pauline Letters.

Furthermore, Christianity gives assurance of the capacity of human beings to act on this knowledge, i.e., to be moral and to enter into moral relationships. Moral living is a central part of Christian living, and gaining the power to live a moral life is a crucial aspect of what it means to be redeemed. This includes gaining the wisdom and power to act altruistically instead of being governed by one's selfish impulses. Furthermore, it means the ability to establish and maintain genuine community, both within religious institutions and outside them: in the social, political, and economic orders. Actualization of this capacity to live a moral life is not easy, but it is possible, a possibility guaranteed by the redemptive work of Christ and the constant availability of divine guidance and power. (Also implicit here is Christianity's response to political nihilism. Destruction for its own sake can have no justification, because it is rooted in a hopeless desperation that ignores the sovereignty of God and the power of creative transformation his historical acts and continuing presence afford to human beings.)

(f) Belief in an afterlife. The Christian affirmation of the meaningfulness of human existence is completed by belief in an afterlife of untroubled bliss for those who have found salvation through their faith in Christ. This means that no tragedy or atrocity occurring on this earth need be considered final. Good people may suffer or be killed, whether by crime, the fortunes of war, political persecution, accident, or disease. All human beings will have to face the last great enemy, death. But none of these things are more than passing incidents when gauged against the assurance of eternal life. For in the life beyond, the beloved of God will be brought forever into his presence. "[H]e will wipe every tear from their eyes, and death shall be no more, neither shall there be mourning nor crying nor pain any more, for the former things have passed away" (Revelation 21:4; Revised Standard Version).

The diminishing hold of the Christian worldview, which I have tried to summarize (all too inadequately) in these six beliefs, can be deeply disturbing for those whom it affects. It has provided what in many ways must be recognized as a richly satisfying and comforting vision of human existence, one that has exerted a profound, long-lasting influence on the Western world. Its decline is bound to force the question of whether anything comparable can be found to put in its place. To the extent that one concludes that the answer is "No," one tends in the direction of nihilism, in the sense of having no alternative pattern of commitment and belief from whose perspective the meaningfulness of human life can be confidently affirmed. In this sense the fading of Christian conviction in the West must be seen as a major historical root of modern nihilism.

We must do more, however, than take account of the profoundly unsettling effects of the marked decline in the persuasive power of explicit convictions such as those listed above if we are to comprehend the religious roots of Western nihilism. We must also ferret out certain assumptions which can be connected, at least in part, with traditional Western religious thought and whose persistence, rather than diminution, of influence has also played an important role in the emergence of the philosophy of nihilism.

I do not claim that these assumptions have been operative in exactly this form in the thinking of every person in the West, or that my characterizations of them do justice in every case to the most sophisticated thinking of Christians themselves, either now or in the past. Therefore, my criticisms of them should not be regarded as an attack on Christianity itself—a complex tradition that can be variously interpreted. My claim is rather that the particular assumptions to follow have figured prominently in Western thought in general and contributed in crucial ways to the development of nihilism. My principal interest is showing how the religious assumptions discussed here and the philosophical ones discussed in Part Four enter into the arguments for nihilism presented previously, especially in Part Two. In this way, the assumptions will be revealed as significant sources of nihilism and criticized as such.

2. ANTHROPOCENTRISM: THE SUBSERVIENCE OF NATURE TO HUMAN BEINGS

The first of the religious assumptions is that either nature is presided over by a cosmic Personality closely akin to our own, a Personality who created the world as a whole with the express purpose of using it as the theater for the drama of our nurture and redemption, or we are hopelessly adrift in an alien universe barren of value and completely inhospitable to our deepest aspirations. Without such a personality lying at the heart of the world, imparting to it a "human face" and exercising deliberate control over it primarily for our benefit, the world dissolves into a chaos without a center. A less expressly theological version of the same assumption is that we humans are either at the pinnacle of a nature regarded as subservient to our needs and concerns, or we are *nowhere*. Everything in the universe must focus mainly on us and the problems and prospects of our personal existence, or else the universe is meaningless and our lives are drained of purpose. This assumption, or something similar to it, figures prominently in the first argument linking atheism to nihilism presented in Chapter Three, Section 1. It is also a persistent undercurrent in some of the other arguments of the preceding chapters.

If we discover, or come strongly to suspect, that we are not the principal *raison d'être* of the universe, then this binary assumption leaves but one remaining alternative: the utter absurdity of our situation in the world. We have long taken for granted, as Stuart Hampshire expresses it, that "we are in nature as in our own garden made for our use and pleasure," and that everything in the universe is "arranged for the benefit of human beings" (1983:19). When we find it no longer possible to refrain from casting doubt on this deeply ingrained belief, as was the case with Camus, and find that there is much about the experienced world which does not fit neatly within any particular human scheme of interpretation, or that the world is perhaps not as wholly subordinated to our purposes and needs as we had formerly thought, then we despair. For we think that we must either have lucid comprehensiveness of understanding and undisturbed confidence in our central importance in the universe or be left with nothing (see the discussion of Camus in the last section of Chapter Two).

Walter Kaufmann assists us further in understanding the connection between this first assumption and the phenomenon of nihilism in the West when he reminds us that Copernicus and Darwin would probably have come as no particular shock or surprise to people reared as Buddhists or in some other Oriental religious tradition (1963:375-376). Yet the work of these men has had an excrutiatingly unsettling and disorienting effect on the culture of the West. Why the radical difference? One important reason is that the religious thinking of the East tends to be much less anthropocentric than that of the West. Eastern people have not been taught to believe that the whole universe is designed to serve human beings, or that nature is nothing more than a temporary theater for playing out a divinely directed drama in a narrowly circumscribed time-frame of human history. Nor have they learned to assume without question that the ultimate meaning of the universe, if there is such a meaning, must reside in a personal Deity whose nature closely resembles that of a human being and who acts with conscious purpose and design. This contrast of cultures suggested by Kaufman is highly instructive, because it helps to make us more keenly aware of the critical importance this first assumption has had in shaping the worldview of the West.[1]

But note how presumptuously anthropocentric and even narcissistic this assumption is, and how much it continues to reflect the type of hierarchical thinking characteristic of the religion and philosophy of the Middle Ages. When our developing perceptions of nature fail to accomodate to our comfortable anthropocentric expectations and demands, the shock of our disappointment is registered in an anguish of homelessness and despair. Nietzsche is correct when he claims that the anthropomorphic assumption is a fundamental cause of nihilism. "We have measured the value of the world," he says, "according to the categories *that refer to a purely fictitious world* . . . . What we find here is still the *hyperbolic naïveté* of man: positing himself as the meaning and measure of the value of things" (1968:13-14). The form of nihilism which turns on this assumption is therefore an old way of thinking in a modern guise, showing that we have not departed as radically from the traditional Christian outlook as has been commonly believed.[2]

Instead of succumbing to the nihilistic conclusion to which this assumption leads us, however, should we not challenge the assumption itself? The discovery of countless galactic worlds millions of light years from our own, and of eons of time predating the arrival of the human species on this earth, should cause us to call into question our rather astounding, if not even vulgar (Hampshire 1983:19), belief that the whole vast universe centers on us. If we have learned anything from Charles Darwin's discovery, stated in his 1837-1838 *Notebook* (excerpted Appleman 1970:73-78, p. 78), that "we may be all netted together," i.e., that humans, animals, and plants alike have a common origin in the astonishingly fecund powers of nature; or from contemporary ecological perspectives on the interconnected patterns of organic existence—it is that human beings are but one aspect of a dynamic, continually evolving cosmos which can no longer be conceived in terms of subordination to a single species, but must rather be seen as a delicate, intricately woven web of mutual dependencies.

One effect of this new vision is admittedly unsettling. It dethrones us from our former position of dominance; we can no longer think of ourselves as the focal point of the natural order. But another effect is more heartening. We are, if anything, more at home on the earth than ever before, bone of its bone and flesh of its flesh; and all species of life which dwell in it are in close community with us as our neighbors and kin. We rely upon them for the support of our life and enrichment of our experience. Their continuing viability in this technological age depends crucially upon our responsible concern. In this more recent vision, the natural world is no longer seen as a hierarchy with human beings at its apex, but as what Lynn White, Jr., has appropriately termed a "democracy" of creatures.[3] He suggests that St. Francis of Assisi was one thinker of the Christian West who anticipated this aspect of the new world picture (1971:91-94).

The theist (or one who sees no alternative to theism but nihilism) might object that this is all very well, but if there if no God, then the universe can no longer be seen as the outcome of creative design or as the object of ongoing providential care, and it thereby becomes meaningless and empty of value. Hence, it is of little comfort to learn that the human species shares with all other forms of life in relations of mutual dependency. Intentional beings like ourselves can hardly be said to be at home in a world stripped of all meaning and value. A system of purely contingent, absurd existents is not made any less absurd when viewed as a "democracy." This objection exposes a second religiously based assumption that demands critical attention.

3. THE EXTERNALITY OF VALUE

The assumption is that nature can have value only when value is conferred on it from without, and that the only conceivable basis of value is acts of deliberate creation or conscious intention. Many theists (and even some non-theists, such as Nietzsche, Camus, and Sartre) seem to have pushed this assumption to the point of thinking that only two possible perspectives on the world are available. Either believers in God such as the eleventh-century Muslim theologian Avicenna are right in saying that "there is nothing purposeless in nature" (Hyman and Walsh 1980:259), because everything that is has been created by, and is subject to, the rule of God; or we are left with a universe which is purely "contingent" and thus without justification or value. We saw that Sartre's character Roquentin reasons this way in *Nausea*, and that Küng, pursuing a similar line of thought, connects cosmic and existential nihilism with denial of God's existence, claiming that such a denial implies the worthlessness and hollowness of reality as a whole (see the discussion of the first argument tying nihilism to atheism in Chapter Three). One of Dostoevsky's characters in *The Possessed* comes to the same kind of conclusion, asserting that in a universe without God there can be no other principle than an absurd struggle for existence (1931:517).

But why must we give assent to the dogmatic either/or of this second assumption? One thing we should note by way of beginning to call it into question is the thinly veiled contempt for nature in the idea that it has no value apart from God. This idea requires that we deny that nature has, or can have, and *intrinsic* significance; it supposes that the only value or importance it may have is that which is externally bestowed.[4] It is but a step from the theological anthropocentrism of which we have already spoken, and from this disavowal of intrinsic value in nature, to the attitude, tragically prevalent in our time, that nature is nothing but brute "raw material" or "resource" subject to our every technological whim. (White makes a point similar to this; see his 1971:90.)

Furthermore, to acquiesce in the dichotomy posed by this second assumption is to be oblivious to other alternatives in the history of human thought, alternatives such as the naturalistic worldviews (Taoism is one example; Dewey's philosophy of nature, as laid out in his *Experience and Nature*, is another) which hold that while there is purpose in the universe, its role should not be exaggerated. Neither of these perspectives regards the universe as having been created by a God, so they do not think in terms of a purpose of the universe as a whole. But this does not mean that they must therefore judge the universe to be contingent and without value, for they feel no need to restrict value or importance to the products of conscious purpose and design.

Is the mountain or the rose suddenly deprived of sublimity or exquisite beauty when we attribute its existence, not to God, but to immanent natural principles and powers such as those in theories of geological or biological evolution? Does our enjoyment of loved ones and friends suddenly cease to have meaning when we no longer ground the existence of human beings in purposive acts of divine creation? Religious or philosophical naturalists see no compelling reason to draw either of these conclusions. They also experience no anxiety in not being able to give an answer to that favorite question of Western theologians and philosophers, "Why is there something rather than nothing?" For them, nature is simply accepted as given, as the unquestioned background or context for all interpretation and meaning. Their view does not deny purpose in human life and experience; it merely rejects the idea that something like human purpose is required to justify everything in the universe.

When we stop to think about it, why should it be required? Why should everything be modeled on us? To assume that it must is a form of reductionism as implausible as the reduction of nature to a mathematical calculus or a machine. Nature can be viewed as a pluralism of many different orders and perspectives. We have a place within it, but it is one of inclusion within a more encompassing complexity, not a place of simple dominance.

There is no obvious demand for the vastness of the world to be brought down to a single ordering principle such as God, or for it to be reduced in its every aspect to the dimensions of human, or human-like intelligibility, purpose, and value.

In fact, as Barrett suggests (in discussing Martin Heidegger's philosophy), abandoning traditional theism can have the positive effect of allowing the mystery of Being to be perceived as enveloping and present, rather than having it thrust "away from us into the remote and hidden region of the divine nature." Consequently, we can be better prepared to discover how sacred and sustaining the natural world can be in its own right, a discovery already made by the peoples of many other cultures, and one not entirely foreign to our own (see Barrett 1979:169). This discovery might mean that we no longer expect or demand that the mysteries of nature be made explicable through some divinely-grounded "principle of sufficient reason," or that its existence find justification in a realm outside itself.[5] We could come to have a reverence, respect, and reserve in the presence of an all-surrounding nature formerly restricted to God.

We can take issue with this second assumption in another way: by calling attention to a belief (or it could be termed a *sub-assumption*) implicit in it, and showing the untenability of this belief. The belief is that if God exists, and if he has a purpose in creating or sustaining something, then that purpose will necessarily have meaning and value for us. To question this supposition is to challenge the allegation that in the absence of God values are left without any basis or support. Let us try to see why this is so.

Plato is one thinker who questions this supposition, at least by implication. He asks in his dialogue *Euthyphro*: Is the holy holy for the reason that the gods approve it, or do they approve it because it is holy? The first possibility would imply that anything the gods command is made good simply by their fiat, while the second sees the gods as giving recognition to that which is good in its own right. But it is at least conceivable that the gods could command something which we would not be able to recognize as good, in terms of our own experience or reflection. In such a case, it would not be good for us, in any meaningful sense of "good," no matter how insistent the gods might be upon our accepting it as such. They might punish us terribly for violating or failing to respect their commands, but no amount of punishment in itself could convince us that the commands were good, except in the purely instrumental sense that obedience to them might safeguard us against punishment.

In other words, thinking that we could be *commanded from without to be convinced* that something is good makes no sense. We can only be convinced by our experience and reflection; we can only learn about its goodness from within (on this see Britton 1969:16-17, 198-200). If this is so, it is illogical to claim that values, moral or otherwise, must be grounded in divine purpose if they are to have any objective meaning or obligatory force. A deity might help to sensitize us to value, but it cannot create value for us by mere choice. The reason, once again, is that the deity's choices could conceivably appear, from our standpoint, to be arbitrary or unjust, in which case they would not be recognizably good to us.

The idea that something could be made valuable for us simply by divine decree is not only illogical in the sense indicated above. It is also extremely dangerous because it suggests that we ought to give assent to, and act upon, principles that find no confirmation in our experience or reason, simply because it is claimed that these principles are based in divine authority. But this means, in turn, that there need be no moral check on such claims; we now have no moral basis on which to "test the spirits to see whether they are of God" (I John 4:1; Revised Standard Version). This is a recipe for obscurantism and unbridled fanaticism which can have, has had, and is having today disastrous consequences both for societies and individuals.

The other possibility posed by Plato's question also blocks the assumption that values can be obligatory only if rooted in the purposes of God, for it implies that values are valuable already, independently of God, and they are simply acknowledged as such by deity. Thus, if the existence of a deity or deities were to be denied, *the values would still remain*. The upshot of this brief consideration of the two alternatives posed by Plato is that not only is the existence of God not needed to make things valuable; it is not even clear how it could *help* to give value to anything which is not already at least potentially recognizable by us as valuable on the basis of our own immanent experiences and reasoning. Therefore, the presence of values in the world cannot meaningfully be said to require the existence of God, in the sense of this second religiously based assumption.[6]

4. THE IDENTIFICATION OF RELIGION WITH THEISM

A third assumption rooted in Western religious thought is that religion and theism are one and the same, and therefore that to lose faith in God is to lose any possibility of satisfying our deepest religious aspirations and needs. This assumption is explicit in Nietzsche's lament in *The Gay Science*, quoted in connection with the third argument linking atheism with nihilism in Chapter Three. The third assumption is also at least implicit in the thinking of Dostoevsky and Tolstoy; for they both, as we have already seen, seem to think that the religious needs of individuals and societies can only be fulfilled through belief in God. But to make this assumption is to forget the varieties of religious experience, and the diversity of religious traditions that have emerged in the course of human history and will in all probability continue to emerge as history unfolds.

We have already mentioned Taoism as a nontheistic religious tradition whose focus is on the immanent powers and mysteries of nature. Other forms of religious naturalism could be cited as well: Stoicism, Spinozism, Bergsonianism, Albert Einstein's religious outlook (which is closely akin to that of Spinoza), and the religious aspects or implications of Dewey's philosophy of nature. And, of course, theism and religious naturalism in their various forms do not begin to exhaust the relevant religious alternatives.

So Nietzsche's conviction, apparently shared by Dostoevsky and Tolstoy, that to turn away from belief in the God of monotheism is to turn away from any possibility of religious hope or fulfillment, must be called into serious question. Millions have been nurtured, and continue to be nurtured, by religions or religious orientations that do not belong to the family of monotheistic traditions. We should be well aware in our time, even if Nietzsche seemed not to be in his, that religion and belief in God are not synonymous.[7]

Spengler and others might respond to this observation by saying that while this talk of religious alternatives to theism is true enough on a purely theoretical level, it is nonetheless the case that belief in God is embedded so deeply in the history and culture of the West that it is virtually synonymous with religion here. Thus, no *practical* religious alternative to theism can be found in the Western world. This way of thinking is bolstered by the idea that a culture, any culture, is something which is at bottom monolithic and irrevocable, something which can be defined by an unchanging "essence" that persists throughout all its historical evolvings (see our discussion of Spengler's claims to this effect in Chapter Three, Section 1).

But why must we view cultures in such a monistic, static, and substantialist manner—especially when modern Western societies are so notably pluralistic and dynamic, and when we bear in mind that other societies, such as that in India, have had to find ways to live in the face of religious pluralism for many centuries? Why must we assume that the crisis of faith in the West is a dead end? Could it not also be viewed as a point of departure for encouraging new directions of growth and transformation that are perhaps already underway?

In *Irrational Man*, Barrett suggests that this is indeed the case. He argues that the recent history of art in the West shows a strong movement away from the once dominant view, enshrined in classicism, "that the whole of reality is a system in which each detail providentially and rationally is subordinated to others and ultimately to the whole itself..." (1958:45). (Barrett's statement of this view could be interpreted as one expression of the principle of sufficient reason, referred to in the previous section.) Modern painting, literature, and other art forms in the West have broken with this view of the universe, says Barrett. Western art is becoming, in at least some important respects, more like the art of the East, i.e., less hierarchical, tidy, and linear, and more "formless, organic, and sprawling" (1958:48). This development need not be viewed as a disaster; it can be seen as holding the promise of leading "us to a more complete and less artificial celebration of the world" (Barrett 1958:51). It can also conduce to greater intellectual and spiritual rapproachment with the sensibilities of the East. The peoples of the East, in their turn, may well have much to learn from us, and their cultures may change accordingly; but again without any necessity of cataclysmic results.

What could be more important or natural on a rapidly shrinking earth than these recent experiences of interpenetration of formerly isolated cultures? Such experiences no doubt contain elements of existential and sociological danger which ought to be taken seriously. But we should not be blind to their ingredients of creativity and hope.

Before Darwin, we in the West tended to regard biological forms and other structures of nature as being permanent and fixed, but now we have learned to alter our perspective. Why, then, can we not also come to see cultures as always in process, and to learn to resist the impulse to foreclose in advance their potentialities for creative interaction and change? Awareness of fundamental transformations in our culture, and of having to allow to become less central what is no longer convincing or relevant to many, need not be reason for despair. Such awareness can point us away from the outmoded certainties and securities of a receding past toward the challenges and adventures of a beckoning future.

No one of us is really in a position confidently to project the directions which the religious developments of the West (or for that matter, of the East) may take. To think that the decline of traditional theism can only culminate in nihilistic malaise is to pretend to an exact knowledge of the future that none of us can have. Also, this way of thinking betrays a fatalistic attitude which does too little justice to human resourcefulness and inventiveness, to say nothing of the resiliency and adaptiveness of cultures themselves.

I hope that what has been said by way of criticizing the three religiously based assumptions discussed thus far will not be misunderstood. It is true that faith in God and commitment to Christian teachings have provided, and continue to provide, a comprehensive framework within which countless numbers of people have found orientation and direction for their lives, and that loss of this framework can be extremely traumatic for such persons. This is not being denied. What I am calling into question is the allegation that the loss of this faith must in itself consign them, or any human being, to a state of desolation by depriving them of any basis of value and meaning.

My arguments thus far have intended to show that nihilistic despair of the meaning of life does not follow directly or necessarily from failure to affirm the existence of God or to adhere to traditional Christian teachings. It does not follow for humankind as a whole, because the arguments do not succeed in exhibiting any necessary connection between belief in God and these teachings, on the one hand, and the meaning of life, on the other. Nor does there seem to be any overwhelmingly convincing reason to think that it must follow historically or culturally for the people of the West.[8]

Chapter 6

God's All-Seeing Eye, Search for Certainty, and Deprecation of the World

... in a universe suddenly divested of illusions and lights, man feels an alien, a stranger. His exile is without remedy since he is deprived of the memory of a lost home or the hope of a promised land. This divorce between man and his life, the actor and his setting, is properly the feeling of absurdity.
—*Albert Camus (1955:6)*

1. THE GOD'S EYE VIEW OF THE WORLD

The fourth religiously based assumption is suggested by Britton's statement that religious belief "seems to demand a view of the world *from without*" (1969:197). This tends to be true of theistic religious belief, at least, so we need not worry here about whether it is true of religious belief in general. The assumption to which I refer is a conception of what can count as adequate knowledge of the world, namely, that to know the world as it really is, in and of itself, requires that we be able to take a "God's-eye" view of it. In order to see what this means, we need to remind ourselves of two aspects of the traditional belief in God which give this assumption a religious basis. (The assumption, or a closely related version of it, also has important philosophical rootage to be considered later.) These two aspects are that God created the world in its entirety "out of nothing," and that he knows his world with omniscient clarity and completeness.

Because the world in this view has been deliberately created in its entirety by a God of infinite intelligence and wisdom, we can expect that it will be an artifact of astounding design and exquisite intelligibility. Nothing in it will be superfluous or out of place; its every aspect will flow elegantly from an economy of powerful first principles. It will be rational through and through, in both its conception and its construction. It goes without saying that God will have an exact knowledge of the principles on which his world is patterned. As sovereign Creator-Designer of the world, his knowledge will extend not only to its fundamental structures but also to its finest details.

But more than his role as Creator-Designer will be relevant to our being able to grasp the character of God's knowledge. He must also radically transcend the universe he has made. Because he has created it "out of nothing," it is in no sense a part of his substance or being. He can therefore contemplate created reality from a vantage point completely "outside" it, enabling him to know it in a wholly detached and comprehensive manner. God's radical transcendence of the world has also generally been thought to entail that he does not occupy time or space. He transcends finite temporal perspectives and exists in a kind of eternal "now." Therefore, his knowledge is not restricted by any forgetfulness of the past or uncertainty about the future. And his nonspatial, nonmaterial nature enables him to be everywhere at once, and thus to know synoptically and immediately what transpires at each and every spatial locus. Finally, because God is pure Spirit and has no bodily aspect, his knowledge does not depend on the contingency of having only five senses, or upon the notorious vagueness and variability of sensate experience. Thus, God's knowledge of the world is exact, complete, and unmediated; in other words, it is objective, all-inclusive, and non-perspectival.

My thesis here is that these interrelated beliefs about the nature of the world as created by God and about the way in which he knows the world have given considerable plausibility and force to what Blocker terms "the naive objectivist view of meaning and reality" (1974:73; see also ch. 2 *passim*). According to this view, meaning is inherent in reality itself and is constituted by the essential attributes or real natures of things. These intelligible characteristics exist "out there" as objective traits of reality, quite apart from human experiences or interpretations.[1] If we are to attain adequate knowledge of this world, our beliefs and assertions about it must precisely correspond to its objective meanings.

Furthermore, we must be able to demonstrate this correspondence by exhibiting the rationality of the world's structures and principles, and the inner logic of their relationships, in a manner suited to command the consensus of competent persons at any place or time. This requires, in turn, that we rid our beliefs and assertions of the refracting influences of all contingent human perspectives. We must strip away the distortions and limitations of such things as the biasing effects of our emotional interests and involvements, the pressing demands of practical life, the inexactitude and tendency to mislead of ordinary sensate experiences, the relativities of particular persons, places, times, cultures—anything that might distract from our ability to take account of the world as it exists in and of itself. We should note the similarity between this conception of meaning and reality and that championed by advocates of the scientific worldview, whose position was elaborated in Chapter Three, Section 2.

To have adequate knowledge, according to the present argument, is to see reality as God has long been supposed to see it in the theological tradition of the West: with a lucid transparency and comprehensiveness of vision that is independent of perspectives and focuses directly on the meanings which lie out there in the world waiting to be known. Hence, as Blocker states, "The idea persists that one should not settle for less than the absolute truth, i.e., a direct intellectual grasp of the real nature of the thing itself" (1974:62). I will not be able to give a full rendering of the background and significance of this idea (which simply restates the fourth assumption now under discussion, although with no mention of the religious basis we are attributing to it) until the next chapter, where I inquire into its philosophical parentage. But I am now in a position to reflect critically on its religious background.

I begin to do so by trying to make more explicit than I have so far two connections which could be alleged between belief in God and the possibility of objective meaning and truth, and to see whether these connections can withstand critical scrutiny. Perhaps the best way to understand these putative connections is to consider what would follow, according to those who claim them, from abandonment of belief in God.

The concept of a meaningful world under discussion is that the world's meaning is completely objective, i.e., something already out there awaiting our discovery and apprehension. Adequate knowledge will consist, therefore, in beliefs and statements that picture, represent, or correspond to the essential properties of the world and those intelligible relationships which bind them into a coherent rational order. If we view the world as an artifact of God, in the manner already described, this idea seems to make eminent good sense; but without belief in God as Creator, the idea seems to come unravelled. For with this belief, we can conceive of nature as a system of evidences and signs that contain everywhere the marks of God's intentionality and purpose and the traits of his workmanship. We can think of it as a kind of "book," lying open for our inspection and deciphering; view it in the manner of a marvelously intricate work of manufacture whose design and function we can aspire to understand; or construe it as a vast puzzle whose solution depends on our discovery of its root concepts and ruling axioms.

To represent such a world adequately, then, is simply "to think God's thoughts after him," to use the seventeenth-century astronomer Johannes Kepler's apt phrase. The point is that the meanings are all there independent of us, as fixed properties of the objective world, because they have been put there by God. In *A Pluralistic Universe*, William James gives us a concise summation of this idea, although he does not endorse it, when he says that, according to it, "truth exists *per se* and absolutely, by God's grace and decree, no matter who of us knows it or is ignorant, and it would continue to exist unaltered, even though we finite knowers were all annihilated" (1967:II, 28).

If we find ourselves no longer able to believe in God (or more precisely, in the conception of God now being discussed), it becomes much less easy to think of the world as endowed with this kind of intelligibility and meaning. One reason is that we cannot now think of it as possessing meanings bestowed upon it from without, by deliberate intention and design. There is also a second reason. The world is not only deprived of created purpose and intelligibility when we no longer believe in God; it also ceases to be a world timelessly and exhaustively known from a completely external, all-inclusive vantage point. As long as we can believe that it is *known* in this way, we can have unperturbed confidence in its *knowability*. It will be natural to assume that it possesses inherently knowable properties and relations which can be depicted by legitimate claims to truth, and that the quest for knowledge is the search for an accurate representation of these objective properties and relations. Belief in God's existence provides, therefore, two important assurances of the world's possession of intrinsic meaning. Without such belief, so the argument runs, the assurance is placed in jeopardy and appears to be left with no foundation.

In the absence of the assumption of a creative, all-knowing God, we seem to have no alternative but to think of reality as devoid of inherent significance, as a dense and featureless chaos upon which we must impose our merely human interpretations and projections. We are led to conclude that reality in itself is purely contingent and absurd, and that meaning is nothing more than an arbitrary and artificial human construct. Now there seems to be no such thing as truth that can be discovered; there is no objective nature of things to which our claims may or may not correspond. Reality just is: bleak, vacuous, empty of meaning. Claims to truth are reduced to baseless, purely subjective inventions.

More than cosmic or epistemological nihilism is involved in this scenario, because a world without God, a world which by this argument must be totally devoid of intrinsic meaning, is also one incapable of providing any answers to our urgent questions about fundamental values and the significance of our lives. C. S. Lewis seems to have something in mind similar to these alleged connections between belief in God and the possibility of veridical knowledge, including knowledge of universal values, when he recounts his sudden realization, at a point in his life prior to his conversion to Christianity, that any satisfactory theory of knowledge demanded that we "admit that mind was no late-come epiphenomenon, that the whole universe was, in the last resort, mental; that our logic was participation in a cosmic *Logos*." If a cosmic *Logos* such as that acclaimed in theism cannot be affirmed, Lewis declares, then we must give up our belief in objective, "indisputable truth" to which abstract logical thought can correspond, and we must lose confidence in the possibility of universally valid moral judgments (1955:208-209).

The connections between belief in God and trust in a meaningful world we have just sketched sound convincing at first. But if we stand back from them and begin to reflect critically upon them, they begin to lose much of their initial plausibility. For one thing, the idea of an all-comprehending God able to view the universe in a completely detached, objective manner can work to the *detriment* of confidence in our ability to attain adequate knowledge, rather than giving support to that confidence. Isaac Newton, for example, claimed that "God only can see objects themselves." As a "being incorporeal, living, intelligent, omnipresent," and existing in "infinite space," he "sees the things themselves intimately, and thoroughly perceives them; and comprehends them wholly by their immediate presence to himself." Human beings, by contrast, are imprisoned in their senses and can know the world only in a mediated and distorted way, as it presents itself to them through the images and manifestations of sensate experience (1721:344-345, 379; cited Burtt 1954:234, 287).

While Newton sometimes expressed and assumed the realist view that knowledge of the actual properties and relations of the world can be attained through the methods and techniques of the new science, he was at other times so keenly aware of a yawning gap between the knowledge of which humans are capable and that possessed by God that he was driven to the positivistic conclusion that we can only know the world as it appears.[2] This apparent world we can mathematically calculate and describe, but the world as it is in and of itself, the world as seen directly and intuitively by God, is forever inaccessible to us.

The Enlightenment philosopher Immanuel Kant, who stood in great awe of Newton's achievements, came to a similar conclusion in his *Critique of Pure Reason*. We are locked into our sensible intuitions of space and time, Kant taught, and can only organize and conceptualize the world in terms of the ingrained categories of our finite human understanding. Thus, a God's-eye view of the world, knowledge of the "thing-itself" as Kant assumed God to be capable of apprehending it (although he denied that the assumption could admit of any kind of theoretical proof), is denied to us (see Kant 1958:89-90 [B70-B71]). The dream of transcending merely human perspectives and attaining God's direct, nonperspectival way of seeing is a dream which it is pointless to pursue. What the world is like in itself, as known by God, we can never hope to learn. We can only know the structures and content of our own experience.

As these two examples show, belief in an all-knowing God can have the effect of making the character of the world seem remote and inaccessible, its real traits forever hidden from our eyes and impossible to penetrate with even our most sustained observations and carefully developed theories. Thus, far from averting skepticism about our prospects for knowing the world, this belief can give strong impetus to skepticism by destroying our hope of ever attaining to propositions adequately portraying the objective truths and meanings of the world. It can also produce a deeply disturbing sense of alienation from the real world, a world which, because of its inaccessibility, must remain forever foreign to us. The fact that belief in God can function, and has functioned, in this negative way makes doubtful the alleged necessary connections between this belief and confidence in the possibility of objective knowledge. It also calls into question the assumption about what would constitute adequate knowledge that has been preoccupying us in this section, because it implies the impossibility of such knowledge for human beings.

A second problem with this assumption bears on the intelligibility of the concept of divine knowledge by which it is informed. I will argue that this concept is not intelligible because it is shot through with internal contradictions and confusions. Therefore, the ideal of knowledge and the view of the world now before us, to the extent that they turn on this concept of divine knowledge, are obscure and unhelpful, and it makes no sense to assume them. In fact, when followed through to their logical conclusion, they give support to nihilism and constitute one of its important sources. Discussion of this second line of criticism will occupy us for some time, because it involves a number of subtle ramifications that must be carefully explored.

The concept of divine knowledge we have been working with is that of a God whose knowledge is assumed to be all-encompassing and yet completely objective and detached, and who is said to grasp the world just as it is, directly and immediately, in total independence of any limiting perspectives. Now if God's knowledge is thought to encompass everything the world is, then it must also encompass all finite perspectives, because these are presumably part of the reality of the world. He must enter intimately into each and every perspective, no matter how partial, distorted, or minute, and experience the world from that point of view. But then the limiting conditions of that perspective will have to affect his understanding. Hence, his knowledge must be both restricted and all-inclusive, perspectival and non-perspectival, which is a patent contradiction. The contradiction becomes especially apparent when we reflect that a God outside space and time and without senses must yet be able to enter into each and every spatio-temporal, sensate perspective (i.e., actually experience the world under its "limitations" of space, time, and sensation) in order to bring the concrete reality of these perspectives within the compass of his omniscient understanding.

Furthermore, if God is able really to enter into each finite perspective, then we can no longer speak of him as being radically transcendent over, or completely detached from, the world. For now he must be, or at least be capable of becoming, radically immanent within the world. So his transcendence of his finite creation, which was touted as the reason for his being able to comprehend it just as it is, from a purely detached vantage point, becomes severely compromised. Or at least we are left with no clear way of reconciling this transcendence with the immanence now required. If in response to this difficulty we make the move of denying to these finite perspectives their claim to be a part of the world, and in that way argue that they need not be included in God's all-inclusive knowledge of the world, then finite experiences and apprehensions such as those constantly undergone by human beings and other creatures would lose ontological status. We would be well on the way to eliminating the finite in favor of the infinite, to absorbing the created world's reality wholly into the reality of God. This would jeopardize his transcendence of the world in yet another way.

We cannot solve this problem by simply claiming that God's vision is the totality of all finite perspectives and more,[3] because the notion of a totality of perspectives does not make sense. Finite perspectives are at least partly incommensurable with one another. To experience the world at one place and time precludes our directly and simultaneously experiencing it at another. To come to it from one historical-cultural background, fund of memories, pattern of expectations, or similar conditions of awareness, restricts our ability to comprehend it from others. This strongly suggests that there can be no such thing as a nonperspectival knowledge. God's knowledge might include much more than any finite perspective could, but it is also invariably "finite" in the sense of excluding, and being excluded by, other perspectives. To know the world in the way that God is purported to know it is ineliminably different from knowing or experiencing it as a lion, a porpoise, or a human being does. Each has its own perspective or point of view. When we speak of God as knowing the world from a "vantage point outside it," we tacitly admit that his is one perspective among others.

This idea of God's being completely outside the world suggests still another unintelligible aspect of the present concept of how he knows the world. Knowledge requires a tension between participation and detachment; emphasis on either to the exclusion of the other makes knowledge impossible. This seems as true for God as it is for us. Without some distance or detachment, the knower would collapse into the known and lose its function and status as knower. Such a collapse is implicit in the notion that God could completely comprehend all the world's perspectives, i.e., participate fully in their own points of view. As already seen, this requires that God be radically immanent in the world and seems to eliminate any real distinction between God and the world. On the other hand, without participation or involvement in the world, God is unaffected and unaffectable by it. It is then impossible for him to take any account of the world's perspectives, singly or collectively, or for him to know the world in any way. We noted in Chapter Three, Section 2, how this difficulty plagues mind-body dualism; it applies no less severely to a view of God and the world in which the two are relegated to completely separate domains. Thus the concept of God's radical transcendence over the world is just as incompatible with his being able to know it as is that of his total immanence within it. Neither total detachment nor total immersion can allow for a meaningful concept of knowledge, divine or otherwise.

The only way the required tension between distance and participation can be maintained is to insist that all knowledge, whether divine or human, must be perspectival, a knowing of the "there" from the standpoint of "here." If this is so, then something of the "there" must be reserved to it as uniquely its own, as distinctive to its own internal perspective. Thus, nonperspectival knowledge cannot exist. Nor can there be a knowledge that includes everything there is, in its full concreteness and specificity of detail. To conceive of a God having such knowledge, or to aspire toward such knowledge as an ideal, is to build castles in the air.

In *Perspective in Whitehead's Metaphysics*, Ross makes a similar point about the tension between participation and detachment in knowledge when he reminds us that "a consciousness without significant perspectival limitations is no consciousness at all." Such a consciousness would lack "focal attention." Knowing everything, it could attend to nothing, because attention requires exclusion. Hence, it could not be said to be conscious of anything. Ross draws the clear implication for divine knowledge in another place: "All perspectives and orders, including God, are selective and qualified, exclusive and restrictive" (1983:251, 272).

Sartre forcibly draws our attention to the contradiction inherent in the ideal of an all-comprehending, nonperspectival, wholly objective knowledge by suggesting that a being capable of knowing the world in this way would have to enter exhaustively into all finite perspectives, thereby becoming indistinguishable from the world. Such a being would be a for-itself which is also an in-itself. But this is a contradictory idea, because it merges the nihilating acts required by knowledge, as Sartre understands knowledge, with the density or compactness of being. And because, on his account, the nihilations of knowing require freedom, such an idea also illogically combines the notions of a being whose nature is at once wholly determined and fixed, because identical with or completely circumscribed by what is, and yet open to the future and free. On Sartre's reckoning, as Macintyre phrases it, an all-knowing being (such as God is held to be by the assumption being discussed in this section) "must have the freedom of a person and the fulness of a thing" (Warnock 1971:28). Or to put it in our parlance, such a being needs the critical detachment of a knower and yet an unqualified union with the world which it knows, which is an impossibility.

Sartre states this impossibility in a passage that demonstrates his own commitment to a perspectival theory of knowing:

> The point of view of pure knowledge is contradictory; there is only the point of view of engaged knowledge.... A pure knowledge in fact would be a knowledge without a point of view; therefore a knowledge of the world but on principle located outside the world. But this makes no sense; the knowing being would be only knowledge since he would be defined by his object and since his object would disappear in the total indistinction of reciprocal relations. Thus knowledge can be only an engaged upsurge in a determined point of view... (1966:377).

Still another way in which Sartre calls attention to the unavoidable perspectivity and conditioned character of knowing, and thus to the impossibility of such a thing as an all-knowing God, is to note that the possible perspectives are limitless and therefore inexhaustible by *any* consciousness, however vast its scope. A simple way of seeing this inexhaustibility of perspectives is to reflect that a being which is said to comprehend everything could always add another point of view to its comprehension, namely, its awareness of itself being aware of those objects of consciousness, and then its awareness of itself as possessed of that additional content of consciousness, and so on, *ad infinitum* (1966:764).

The impossibility of nonperspectival knowing also makes untenable the idea of wholly objective states of affairs, meanings, or truths existing independently of all perspectives. It makes no sense to talk of the thing-itself, the world-itself, reality-itself, meaning-itself, truth-itself, or any such locution. None of these notions has meaning because each one implies the possibility of something being real, meaningful, true, etc. apart from all perspectives. But the world is not actually meaningful in itself; indeed, there can be no world in itself. The world is only potentially meaningful; it becomes meaningful *only in relation*, and this from some perspective or other. Even this way of putting the matter is misleading, for there is no "it" prior to the act of apprehension, because individuation or recognition of anything, including the world itself, is a kind of meaning. Because meaning is a relational concept, it follows that nonperspectival meaning cannot exist. Thus, the world is meaningful, true, real, etc. to this or that knower or experiencer, from this or that perspective, in this or that way, depending on the "angle" of the perspective. By *angle* I mean the conditions and means of knowing that enter into that perspective.

Because the world could never be comprehended in its totality, given the exclusivity and inexhaustibility of the various perspectives from whose standpoint it can be known, and because meaning and truth are relational concepts, the notion of its having a totality of fixed and inherent meanings or truths is nonsensical. Meanings and truths exist or come into being in specific relations of knower and known; they cannot lie on the side of the known taken by itself. Thus, as Blocker emphasizes, to conceive of, or to search after, traits of the world that are "absolute" or wholly objective, in the sense of being nonrelational or nonperspectival, and free of the constraints of particular conditions or concerns, is to long for "an interpretation which is not interpretive." It is to yearn for the realization of a logical contradiction (see Blocker 1974:61, 116). Because meaning-itself is a meaningless notion, it makes no sense to assume, as does the ideal of knowledge now under discussion, that our claims to knowledge are adequate just to the extent that they accurately represent properties and relations of the world as created and envisioned by God, i.e., ones which exist absolutely and externally, quite apart from relations to finite knowers or would-be knowers.

One could object at this point that the world does have meanings independent of any relations to finite knowers because it is timelessly known by God. Hence, it is meaningful in a purely objective sense. But this way of looking at the matter poses a situation similar to the one discussed in Chapter Five, Section 3. There we saw that certain choices might have meaning and value to God, but not to us, because they are not recognizably meaningful or valuable to us in terms of our own reasoning and experience. The same thing holds for a world said to be objectively meaningful because God timelessly knows it. This allows for the world being meaningful for God, but it can in no way guarantee that it will be meaningful for us, from our human perspectives. It will be meaningful only if we discover it to be so within the immanent conditions and circumstances of our own lives. And for this there *cannot be*, and hence *need not be*, any kind of external guarantee! So once again, meaning is not the sort of thing that can exist "out there" in complete independence of perspectives or interpretations. There is no such thing as a purely "objective" meaning, in this sense of that term. Nor could there be.

The existence or nonexistence of God makes no difference to this conclusion, contrary to those (some nihilists among them) who argue that it makes a profound difference. Just as it would be senseless to aspire toward objective meaning of this sort, so it would be senseless to be consumed with anxiety on account of its unattainability by human beings, or to be reduced to despair by a supposed unbridgeable gap between the world as it is in and of itself and the world as we experience it. Yet some versions of nihilism seem to have been based, at least in part, on just this kind of illogical anxiety and despair. Sartre's character Roquentin, for example, is overcome with "nausea" at the realization that "the world of [human] explanations and reasons is not the world of existence" (1964:174), thus betraying his assumption of an ineradicable and horrifying hiatus between the world as it appears to human conception and experience and the world as it objectively is.

The same hiatus haunts the whole of Sartre's *Being and Nothingness*, despite his commitment to a perspectival theory of knowing. Here, as we have already seen, the author stresses the logical impossibility of uniting the for-itself of consciousness and awareness with the in-itself of brute, uninterpreted reality. With that we can agree. But he goes on to insist that our most fundamental desire as human beings is to attain this kind of union, an ideal he identifies with the concept of God (1966:694, 762). This identification is significant for our purposes, because it highlights the historical connection between belief in God and the concept of adequate knowledge we have been discussing. If Sartre is right and human beings are, by nature, relentlessly driven by the pursuit of meanings and truths significant for them and yet completely objective, in the sense of being independent of human perspectives, then he is also right in his conclusion that human life is a "useless passion" (1966:754). For it is obsessed with the pursuit of that which, by his own analysis as well as our own, is impossible. But having said this, his gloomy judgment about human life must come as a surprise, because it seems to rest on the supposition of an inflexible human nature he takes pains elsewhere to deny.

The trouble with Sartre's position lies deeper than this. It lies in his assumption that there is such a thing as an in-itself that "has no need of the for-itself in order to be" (1966:761). It is true that he denies meaning to this in-itself, as indeed he must, because it is by definition outside any knowing relation. But his positing of it and giving such a pivotal role to it in his system attributes to it a calamitous status and significance. It is that which we aspire to know but must despair of ever being able to know. Once having made this move, then reality-itself, the supposed true state of affairs beyond our human inventions, comes to be seen as a dumb, intractable realm which must forever frustrate the human need to know the world and to find meaning in it. The tragic truth of the world is then thought to be that there is no "real" truth or meaning; all is merely contingent and absurd. Having made the fatal move of positing this kind of world in-itself, a move all too commonplace throughout history of Western thought, Sartre is locked into a dualism from which there can be no escape and whose unavoidable outcome is conviction of the absurdity of the cosmos and the futility of human existence.[4]

It might still seem that rejection of the kind of objective meaning we have been discussing, whether or not we posit a world in-itself, has to result in a radical subjectivizing of all claims to truth or propositions about value, and thus in capitulation to nihilism. But repudiation of a nonperspectivist,

nonrelational concept of objective meaning need not have this effect. In order
to show why not, I will introduce in Chapter Nine an alternative concept of
adequate knowledge to the one we have been considering here, an alternative
not bound to a representational theory of truth or absolutist view of meaning.
I will also distinguish there the idea of an inevitable plurality of perspectives,
and thus of a pluralistic conception of truth and value, from a merely
relativistic conception.

My third and final criticism of the fourth religiously based assumption
calls attention to its implication for the status of space and time, and thus for
the place and significance of human beings in the world. Because God's way of
·knowing is said to be privileged, and he is believed not to occupy, or to be in
any way dependent upon, space or time, it follows that genuine knowledge is
oblivious to space and time. This means, in turn, that space and time are
unimportant and unreal. Because our lives are pervaded by spatio-temporal
restrictions and challenges, then they must also be, from God's ultimate
standpoint, unimportant and unreal. Or at least those aspects of our lives that
seem to presuppose space and time must be so. Therefore much, if not all, of·
human life becomes a pointless illusion.

Understanding what this means for our temporal existence is
particularly important. If God is able to comprehend everything that
transpires—past, present, and future—with an eternally present, all-seeing
eye, then an open future really does not exist. If there is no open future, there
is no distinction between the past and the future, and time becomes unreal. To
conceive of objectivity along the line of God's timeless vision of the world is to
opt for a static world, a world in which nothing ever truly changes, a world in
which we are left with no reason to strive for the actualization or preservation
of value, simply because nothing ever happens and all the value that will ever
exist has already been achieved.

In such a world, there can be no such thing as human responsibility or
freedom, nor can there be any point to human life or human activity. Nothing
that human beings do could ever make a difference. Even the idea of their
being able to "do" anything is made nonsensical. Thus we are brought, by a
different route, to an outcome similar to that discussed in connection with the
reductionistic version of the scientific worldview (Chapter Three, Section 2),
which also denigrates human freedom and value in its drive to attain a purely
objective view of the universe.

If this is the ultimate truth about the world, despair of the meaning of life
seems to be a foregone conclusion. To conceive of God as capable of knowing
the truth of the world in a manner independent of all perspectives, including
spatio-temporal perspectives, is to make a mockery of human existence.
Recognition of this consequence gives us one more reason to reject the
assumption about the nature of adequate knowledge we have been

considering. It is ironic that an idea of God which has been supposed by many to stand as a mighty bulwark against nihilism can lead so directly to nihilistic consequences such as this one and the others we have brought into view. We should emphasize that these consequences flow from the specific conception of God we have focused upon; we have not been given reason to suppose that they follow from all conceptions of God. But this is a conception that has persistently and powerfully influenced the thought of the West, although often subconsciously.

The ideal of non-perspectival knowing and its related belief in an absolute reality and meaning independent of all perspectives and relationships, both of which are here associated with a prevalent concept of God, have given impetus to the conviction that genuine truth must be something universal and unchanging, i.e., unconditioned by the relativities of place and circumstance and unaltered by the passage of time. This conviction ties in with the fifth religiously based assumption, to be discussed in the next section. As we shall see, it is one of several religious facets of that assumption.

2. THE SEARCH FOR CERTAIN FOUNDATIONS

The fifth religiously influenced assumption is that claims to knowledge, to be confirmed as knowledge, must either be known with noninferential certainty to be true, or must be justified as true by being derived or derivable from a foundation of clear and exact propositions that are infallibly or certainly true. The method of their derivation, it is usually further assumed, must itself be necessary and indubitable.

This assumption about the test of genuine knowledge, and especially its concept of what is required for non-certain propositions to be justified as true, is commonly referred to as *foundationalism*. Nicholas Wolterstorff indicates its widespread assumption in both the religious and philosophical thinking of the West:

> Foundationalism has been the reigning theory of theories in the West since the high Middle Ages. It can be traced back as far as Aristotle, and since the Middle Ages vast amounts of philosophical thought have been devoted to elaborating and defending it. It has been the dominant tradition among Christians as well as non-Christians. It has been presupposed in attacks on Christianity and on the possibility of Christian scholarship, and in defenses of Christianity and of the possibility of Christian scholarship. Aquinas, Descartes, Leibniz, Berkeley, the logical positivists—all of them and many more have been foundationalists (1984:30).

We saw in the opening section of Chapter Four that both Lehrer and Unger give pivotal importance to the requirement that reliable claims to knowledge must either be certain or be reducible to a base of certitude in arguing for their skeptical dismissal of the possibility of knowledge. Camus also seems to be assuming something like the foundationalist theory when he laments the futile history of human attempts to attain objective knowledge, by which he means certainty and comprehensiveness of understanding. For him it is either that or nothing (see Chapter Two, Section 5).

The question of the philosophical background of foundationalism is set aside in this section in order to concentrate on its religious background. Its philosophical basis and expression will be critically discussed later. Two important aspects of the religious background of the foundationalist assumption were adumbrated in the previous section, and a third was mentioned in Chapter Five, Section 1, as part of our outline of the classical Christian worldview.

In the first place, it was stated that in order to attain, or at least to approximate, the God's-eye vision of the world, we must strip away all of the biasing influences of cultural inheritance, emotional predilection, immediate practical involvement, uncriticized sensate experiences, and the like, and seek claims to knowledge that can command the consensus of competent persons at any place or time, under any conceivable set of circumstances. Genuine knowledge will consist, this is to say, of universal, necessary truths which emulate the timeless immutability of God's all-seeing eye. Possession of it will enable us to surmount the relativities and contingencies of our life in this world and to grasp reality as it objectively is, undistorted by fallible preconceptions, prejudices, or conjectures.

There would seem to be no other way to gain assurance that we have indeed attained such knowledge than to confine our claims to truth to those which are either intuitively certain or deducible from a foundation of certain or infallible propositions. Only in this way can we render our claims immune to objection now or in the future and make them acceptable to all persons everywhere who are competent to judge, thus imparting to them the timeless universality deemed to be the hallmark of truth. Viewed in this light, the foundationalist theory can be seen to fit naturally with the concept of adequate knowledge already discussed; it appears to provide the only conceivable method whereby the attainment of a nonperspectival, God's-eye view of the world can be convincingly demonstrated and guaranteed. The first factor in the religious background of the foundationalist assumption, therefore, is its intimate connection with the concept of God and God's way of knowing the world elaborated in the previous section.

The second kind of religious influence behind this fifth assumption was also alluded to in the preceding section when we made note of the fact that it is not only our desire for theoretical understanding that is at stake when we weigh our prospects for attaining adequate knowledge. Also involved is the matter of our ability to find answers to pressing questions about moral value and existential meaning. Similarly, what is at stake for Christians and other theists in confronting the problem of knowledge is much more than satisfaction of their theoretical curiosity about ultimate questions. It is the urgent need to acquire understanding of the goals of human existence as these have been ordained by God, and fully to comprehend, so as rightly to put into practice, the means he has graciously provided for the realization of these goals. Succinctly stated, what is fundamentally at issue for such persons is the hope of their salvation.

On an issue this momentous, or so it has seemed to many, no uncertainty or ambiguity is tolerable, for such might easily delude us and lead us astray. Nor would it make sense to suppose that a loving God would provide his human creatures with anything less than the possession of, or the ability to attain, complete certitude with respect to those matters of faith and morals on which their salvation depends. It has been a common belief among Christians and other religious groups in the West, therefore, that God has made available to human beings, or at least to those whom he wills to save, the exact and indisputable knowledge of his holy will that is necessary if they are to set out upon the path of salvation he has laid down.

But just how is this certain knowledge made available? Most Christians have claimed that it is to be found in the Bible, believed by them to contain, or to testify to, God's special revelation. This claim constitutes a third important ingredient of the religious background of the foundationalist assumption. Many Christians have contended that certain knowledge can also be gained from human reason, or from a combination of human experience and reason. Still others have argued that there is no such thing as a certainty of ordinary reason or experience but have gone on to talk of a certitude of faith, which they have then related to scriptural teachings and rational investigations in different ways. In all these cases, we can witness variations on the theme of foundationalism. Indeed, the foundationalist assumption, with its requirement of a certain basis for all reliable claims to truth, had been deeply ingrained in Christian thinkers at least since the time of their religion's coming into ascendancy in the West.

In order to provide more detail on the ideas sketched in the previous paragraph, let us first turn to the idea that the Bible provides a foundation of certain truths from which other universal truths can be deduced: the third religious ingredient in the foundationalist assumption. The enduring Christian belief in special revelation has given significant impetus and support to this assumption in the thought of the West by implying the necessity for a set of authoritative truths, absolutely binding for all places and times, to serve as the basis of justified claims to knowledge.

Christians have long taken it for granted that the Bible portrays the nature and meaning of the objective world as God himself views it, and that it perspicuously conveys his purpose to humankind. Implicit in this idea is the duty of rejecting those claims to truth that are either not derived from the Bible as foundation, or which are inconsistent with its teachings. As is well known, some Christians have even gone so far as to insist that every single word of the Bible comes immediately from God, and therefore that every aspect of its content is made infallible or certainly true by divine authority. This notion of the literal inerrancy of the Scriptures is an especially strong version of the foundationalist idea in its religious context.

The foundationalist assumption has affected religious thinking in other ways as well. Augustine and Thomas Aquinas, to cite two brilliant shapers of the Christian tradition, unhesitatingly equated knowledge with certainty and insisted that foundational certainties are not only set forth authoritatively in the Bible but are also discoverable by human reason. Augustine was a believer in the verbal inerrancy of the Bible, but he was not content to base religious teachings only on that foundation or to have them accepted merely by unquestioning assent to its authority. He also stressed the ongoing role of divine illumination in the discovery of truths whose certitude is either recognizable by reason or can be rationally deduced, and he regarded the search for such truths as the solemn obligation of "faith seeking understanding." Thus, as Hyman and Walsh comment, "Augustine's writings were marked by a passionate quest for certain truth" (1980:15; see also Cochran 1944:400-405, 409). At one place in the most magisterial of his profuse writings Augustine draws a triumphant contrast between the "certainty of the Christian faith" and the debilitating skepticism of the New Academy which had disturbed him deeply earlier in his life (*The City of God* XIX, xiii; see Hyman and Walsh 1980:108).

Aquinas, for his part, conjoined indubitable propositions of reason with the data of human experience in order to construct independent proofs of many biblical doctrines and to erect a philosophical framework for the presentation and interpretation of those he judged not to be amenable to strict rational justification. Like Augustine, he saw no conflict between the authority of the biblical foundation and the foundational truths and their necessary implications that can be perceived throught the careful employment of human reason. Although he did acknowledge that some of the truths of the Bible cannot be rationally proved, he evidently believed that God and the blessed do know with rational certitude the truth of the particular propositions of the Bible which we here on earth have no alternative but to accept solely on its authority. So, from their exalted vantage point, the bibilical foundation and its entailments and the foundations and entailments of reason neatly coincide, showing that for Aquinas all biblical teachings are rationally certain in principle, even if not recognizable as such by us in this life (see *Summa Theologica* I, i, 2; cited Wolterstorff 1984:149).

Even so iconoclastic a figure as William of Ockham, who sharply challenged Aquinas's confidence in the competency of natural reason and experience to reach certainty about theological or other truths, showed no inclination to abandon the foundationalist assumption itself. Ockham held that reason or experience can only yield probabilistic conclusions. Because he assumed, with Augustine and Aquinas, that truth and certitude are one, he had to deny to these conclusions the character of knowledge, in the full sense of that term. Yet, so deep-seated in him was the foundationalist idea that genuine knowledge consists in that which is either known *per se* or can be demonstrated from *per se* propositions (see Klocker 1983:41-42), and so concerned was he to accord to Christian teachings the status of firm knowledge, that he gave a pivotal role in his epistemology to what he called "the certitude of faith." By firm adherence to what is revealed in the Bible, he claimed, and through pious development of the faith infused in them by their baptisms, Christians can come to have an awareness of certain truth transcending all the probabilities and susceptibilities to error built into the deliverances of ordinary reason and experience. In that way, they can attain solid knowledge of the specific teachings of their religion and of many other truths as well. Such knowledge is based, not simply in heteronomous acquiescence to the Bible's authority, or in the pale probabilities of natural reason or experience which are always open to doubt, but in a clear and untroubled sense of personal certitude, grounded in faith. This personal certitude is an opening of our eyes to objective certainties that, in the absence of faith, we would never have been able to recognize or comprehend (see Klocker 1983 for citations and discussions of relevant writings of Ockham on these themes).

Despite their many differences from one another, therefore, Augustine, Aquinas, and Ockham obviously shared the foundationalist theory of knowledge, which is our current topic. As already indicated, all Christians who appeal to the Bible as the absolutely authoritative basis of religious belief tacitly subscribe to one version of the theory. The rallying cry of the Protestant Reformation, "*Sola Scriptura!*", was an impassioned plea for a return to the biblical foundations as the final arbiter of Christian truth. These few examples will have to suffice to illustrate the commitment to the foundationalist assumption running through the long history of religious thought in the West. Now that I have placed this assumption in its religious context and identified three important aspects of its religious background, I can begin to reflect critically on each aspect.

One aspect of this religious background is the intimate connection between the ideal of trying to approximate as closely as possible to the timeless immutability and nonperspectivity of God's vision of the world, on the one hand, and the search for certain foundations and their logical entailments, on the other—a connection in which the first is conceived as the end of knowledge, and the second as the means most suited to the attainment of that end. My reasons for rejecting this ideal of knowledge, presented in the previous section, also bear on the assumed necessity of searching for certain foundations, to the extent that this assumption is tied to the pursuit of that ideal. When we find ourselves no longer able to accept this concept of the goal of adequate knowledge, we also need no longer be concerned with the problem of how such knowledge can supposedly be certified or guaranteed.

But more than this needs to be said by way of criticism of this first element in the religious background of foundationalism. The search for a certain basis for claims to truth also founders on the fact that what are regarded as indubitable certainties of religious or other modes of thought by one age often turn out to be dubious conjectures for another. The alleged certainties which meant so much to Augustine and Aquinas, for example, often do not seem certain to us. Blaming this fact on our lack of faith, as Augustine and Ockham tend to do, or on our failure to reflect with sufficiently focused rational attention on the putative starting points and entailments which appeared so perspicuous to Aquinas, borders on *ad hominem* argument or comes close to simply begging the question. In any event, it fails to persuade or convince. For try as we may, many of us living today cannot render certain (or, in some cases, even very plausible) to ourselves many of the premises and arguments which to thinkers like Augustine and Aquinas were true or convincing beyond question.

To cite a familiar theological example, Aquinas thought he could convince anyone that there must be some transcendent explanation for the continuing existence of the universe from one moment to the next, and thus that the existence of God can be deduced with lucid certainty. His argument evidently had great persuasive force in his day. But the same argument is wholly unconvincing to many able thinkers in our own time, even after they have taken the trouble carefully to study the systematic unity and inner logic of Aquinas's works, or have made every effort to enter sympathetically into the thought patterns of the Middle Ages.

The same point can be supported by a telling example from philosophy. Immanuel Kant cited as illustrations of systems whose fundamental principles were, to his mind, secure, certain, and complete, three schemes of thought already developed by his time: Euclidian geometry, Aristotelian logic, and Newtonian physics. He was convinced that he had achieved a like certainty and finality in the "critical philosophy" laid out in his own *Critique of Pure Reason* (see especially Kant's two "Prefaces" to that work). Yet, not one of these four systems has survived as a credible claimant to final truth to our day; distinct and eminently reasonable alternatives to each of them have been conceived.

The clear implication is that the passage of time does make fundamental differences in our ways of thinking and reasoning, no matter how independent of time they might seem to us. This is as true in the domain of religious thought as it is in other domains. We are not free-floating intellects, nor are we capable of becoming such. As creatures of time, we invariably reason, discover, create, value, plan, and act within the context of our historical and cultural situations. Even the form of the questions we raise is conditioned by the cultures and times in which we live. Philip Wheelwright makes this clear when talking about attempts on the part of the pre-Socratic philosophers to find an answer to the question, What is the nature of nature (*phusis*)?

> The general ontological question of 'What' is never a pure question: it rests upon certain assumptions as to the kinds of answer that are possible or acceptable; and since the assumptions take different forms in different ages and different climates of opinion, the precise meaning of a question will vary accordingly. A question takes its rise within some human frame of reference in which there is a natural expectation of certain alternative answers, or at any rate of certain general kinds of answers (1960:10).

Having made this general observation, Wheelwright launches into a discussion of specific beliefs and expectations that were axiomatic and indisputable to the Greeks in the time before Socrates but that seem quaint and far-fetched today.

This is not to say that we are complete slaves to our cultural heritage. For one thing, we have the ability to understand, appreciate, and learn from many aspects of cultures other than our own. For another, our own heritage provides opportunity as well as limit for our endeavors, and we are collectively capable of transforming it, over time, in far-reaching ways. Indeed, we cannot help transforming it as we draw upon it in responding to new problems, challenges, and opportunities as they arise. This dynamism and plasticity of cultures is clearly exhibited in the history of Western culture; we are living through an especially volatile phase of its history right now. The main point I want to establish here, though, is that we are profoundly influenced and shaped by culture, and that it provides the ineluctable environment within which we must conduct our inquiries and reach our conclusions. We do not think in a vacuum; whatever creativity we are capable of involves our producing new twists and directions in that which is already given to us. The pervasive influence of culture and tradition on our thought is a critical factor in that unavoidable perspectivity of knowledge on which we laid so much stress in the previous section.

These differences of perspective which develop over the history of a culture are not absolute; threads of continuity and commonality can still be traced. But the differences are significant enough to cast at least some doubt on the assumption that there is a residue of unalterable certainty which is immune to all the evolvings of a given culture, to say nothing of transcending all the varieties of human cultures throughout the histories of their development, and at all the distinct locales where different patterns of development may occur. Even if there were such a residue, its mere survival would be no guarantee of its truth. Moreover, it would perhaps be too vague and abstract to be of much use for dealing concretely with the pressing questions and problems which are the concern of religion. Still more to the point, suppose that we could succeed in somehow establishing the existence of a residue of important certainties in the history of all cultures up to the present moment. How could we ever be *sure* that it would survive future transformations of time and space?

This searching question forces us to recognize the difference between certainty as a psychological state and what might be called "warranted certainty." How can we ever be completely sure that a given mental state of certainty is warranted, in the sense of providing an indelible mark of truth? We have all had the experience of being certain about something we claim to remember, and then later finding out that we were mistaken. In this case, our certainty, however vivid and forceful it may have been to us at the time, was, we would now have to admit, unwarranted. Just so, the indubitables of one time have become the dubitables of another, and there can be no absolute guarantee that the same thing will not happen to the candidates for universal certainty of any particular place or time.

The general thrust of this argument against the possibility of grounding our claims to knowledge on a foundation of absolute certitude can also be found in Unger's defense of skepticism, discussed in Chapter Four, Section 1. What also needs to be questioned, however, is Unger's (and Lehrer's) assumption that without a foundation of certitude there can be no such thing as knowledge, for that is to assume without argument the foundationalist theory of knowledge. I will have more to say about this topic later. Enough has been said by now, however, to bring into serious dispute the idea that we ought to strive to emulate the supposed timeless immutability and absoluteness of God's vision of the world by searching for a bedrock of certainty on which to build an impregnable fortress of truth.

But what of the hope and surety of salvation, that urgent concern which lies at the core of every religion? Are not certain foundations or a basis of solid, irrefutable truth essential at least with respect to those matters directly relating to this concern? This question shifts our attention to the second part of the religious background of foundationalism. It seems to make a perceptive point, one which anyone who takes religion at all seriously would have to acknowledge. But I think that it will have to be recognized that arguments similar to those already advanced against the first kind of religious impetus toward the foundationalist assumption apply here as well.

Despite the momentous seriousness of the topic of salvation, there can be no absolute guarantee that propositions about it commanding our unquestioning assent at one time in our lives will continue to do so at another. Conversions from one religion to another do occur. People have been known to abandon or substantially change their most ardent religious beliefs, sometimes under the pressure of experiences later in life whose occurrence they had not anticipated or whose actual effects proved more unsettling than they could earlier have conceived. John Beversluis argues, for example, that C. S. Lewis's concept of the goodness of God, one he had taken for granted and strenuously defended in earlier books, was radically altered by the experience of the death of his beloved wife, an experience Lewis describes and struggles to make theological sense out of in his book *A Grief Observed* (see Beversluis 1985, chs. 9, 10).

Nor can there be any guarantees that religious propositions seemingly beyond doubt to one person will appear so to others. Our personal sense of certainty about a given set of soteriological claims does not in itself ensure the universality of those claims. Given the plurality of religions in the world, each with its own earnestly recommended path of salvation, it is plain that profound disagreements about the nature of salvation currently exist. They exist among persons whose lives show every outward sign of exemplary piety and faith. They exist not only among, but also within, religious traditions. No evidence indicates that this religious pluralism will be appreciably different in the foreseeable future.

It remains true however, that a kind of certitude exists among people of genuine religious conviction, whatever their particular religious persuasion. As already suggested, this certitude attaches particularly to their religions' teachings about the hope and means of salvation, and it is important that we do justice to it. But an adequate recognition and explication of the fact of this certitude can be given without recourse to foundationalism. Indeed, insistence on the foundationalist theory of knowledge only obscures its true character, as I will now try to show.

Behind our strong tendency to think that confidence in salvation requires a foundation of cognitive certainty, is a confusion of two types of certitude that are really quite distinct. Religious thinkers in the West have been particularly susceptible to this confusion. It muddled the thinking of Augustine, Aquinas, and Ockham, leading each to endorse a version of the foundationalist theory of knowledge when he really had no compelling religious reason to do so. One Christian theologian of our time who has insisted on the importance of distinguishing between these two types of certitude, and who has devoted a great deal of thought to tracing out the implications of the distinction, is Paul Tillich.

The two types of certitude to which I allude have been given various labels; Tillich refers to them as *theoretical certitude* and *existential certitude* (1957, Chs. I, II, esp. 33-35; see also 1951:22-23, 94-105, and my discussion in 1981:205-210). The first, he tells us, is a certitude of belief, and the second, a certitude of faith. *Theoretical certitude* means giving cognitive assent to propositions whose claim to truth we find it impossible to doubt or deny. The search for such certitude requires critical detachment and distance, or a mood of "objectivity." The reason for this requirement is that our interest is in propositions which will be certainly true not just for ourselves, but for any rational person at any place or time. Therefore, we try as much as possible to keep our investigations into such propositions from being in any way affected by our private needs, emotions, or preferences, or by personal or practical considerations of any kind. We seek to identify these propositions and to study their logical consequences and interrelations for the sake of theoretical understanding and for no other reason.

Possible examples of propositions of this type would be axioms or theorems in mathematics or logic, root principles of philosophical or scientific theorizing, or perhaps statements making reference to the immediate data of sensation and considered apart from corrigible inferences we might make from such data. I am not concerned at the moment with the question whether any theoretical certainties exist that can give us knowledge about reality (i.e., whose truth is not only certain but also nontautologous and nontrivial), but only to explain what such certainties would be like and how we might come to recognize them. I should note, however, that a negative answer to this question is implied by my earlier criticisms of the possibility of nonperspectival knowing and of the hope of gaining absolute knowledge guaranteed to be immune to all temporal or cultural variations.[5]

By contrast with the mood of critical detachment Tillich associates with theoretical certitude, existential certitude (or the certitude of faith) connotes for him an intensity of passion and involvement in the object of its concern. It reflects one's total life posture, evidences that which gives integration, purpose, and meaning to one's existence at its deepest level, and expresses "the promise of ultimate fulfilment" (1957:2). It is not merely cognitive in the way that theoretical certitude is, but grows out of a "total and centered act of the personal self" in which cognition, emotion, volition, and the springs of action are fused (1957:8).

This centered act is for Tillich the act of faith, and its "certitude" stems from the pervasive importance and integrating power it has for every aspect of one's life. Because one's faith is the linchpin, core, or fundamental orientation and commitment of one's existence, it follows that nothing could be more basic or unquestioned than it is. We can even say that one's faith is "foundational," as long as we remember that it is such in an existential, not a theoretical, sense. In Tillich's own parlance, existential certitude is that "restful affirmative confidence" or "courageous affirmation of oneself in the state of ultimate concern," which is of the essence of faith (1957:21).[6] The role Tillich accords to faith and its accompanying existential certitude is very close to that given by Sartre to one's "original project," or by Ludwig Wittgenstein to one's "form of life" or "way of living as a human being" (see Chapter Four, Section 2 above; also High 1981:257-258, 264).[7]

Because of this stance of existential certitude, particular propositions, especially those relating to the most basic hopes and aims of our lives, can acquire a surety and depth of conviction that makes it unthinkable that they be false. The following statement by Malcolm Muggeridge shows with exceptional clarity how theoretical doubt can exist in one's mind alongside existential certitude: "God, of course, cannot die. He might not exist at all, though I am more certain he does exist than I am of my own existence" (1980:12). We are not content to regard such propositions as merely certainly true for us, or for those who stand within our own circle of faith. We cannot help but consider them true for everyone, under all circumstances. There is thus a universality of intent in our attitude toward such propositions, despite the fact that we can give no knockdown foundationalist proof of their claim to universal truth. Accordingly, we can say, with Wittgenstein, "I act with *complete* certainty, but this certainty is my own," and yet go on to add, "There is something universal here; not just something personal" (Wittgenstein 1969:174, 440; quoted High 1981:258). We can be well aware that we are speaking from a perspective. We can understand that others may not share that perspective, and thus that they may not even accept as true, to say nothing of certainly true, what informs all our beliefs and actions and gives focus and integrity to our lives. We therefore need be under no illusions about winning universal assent to our religious propositions through the strategy of trying to convince others that they are objective certainties or that they can be derived from a foundation of objective certainties.

Dallas High refers to the kind of beliefs we are discussing as "indwelt beliefs." The following statement he makes about them is a lucid summary of the distinction between theoretical and existential certitude we have been trying to explicate, and it helps to make clear the negative implications of this distinction for the foundationalist assumption in its religious guise.

Indwelt beliefs, including religious beliefs and the attending comfortable certainty, (1) are not first premises of a logical chain of argument, and (2) are not defenseless or beyond all justification. On the latter they attain that appearance only against the paradigm that justification must consist of prescribed steps of reasoning, testing, and evidence. Regarding the first, what needs to be seen is that, if indwelt beliefs or activities are treated as first premises or presuppositions, then they cannot serve as grounds or the grounding since they can always be given a regressive push. But these beliefs are like grounds or serve as grounds if they are and are seen as the way we act and live. Religious believing, therefore, is not a matter of opting for a premise, citing a logical chain of evidence, and then making up one's mind to believe, as if to have found the argument sound, with a premise which is indubitable, or to have found that it all coheres (1981:262-263).[8]

This insistence on the pivotal role of existential certitude or indwelt belief, as expressive of "the way we act and live," makes evident the sense in which Augustine and Ockham are right to claim that particular religious propositions come to be seen as certainly true under the impetus of faith. In this sense, and only in this sense, is it correct to say that there can be, and indeed must be, certainty about the central salvific claims of a religious tradition around which one orders the whole course of one's life. But all this had nothing to do with the foundationalist assumption in its theoretical form.

The third part of the religious background of foundationalism, the appeal to a divine revelation assumed to be absolutely authoritative for all human beings everywhere, is open to a number of criticisms, only a few of which need be indicated here. The first and perhaps the most obvious problem with this appeal is the simple fact that many alleged revelations or authoritative scriptures are found among the religions of the world. The Christian Bible is only one of these. So to rely on it for religious truth is not to have come down to a bedrock of incontrovertible authority. The question of why someone depends on this particular body of scriptures, rather than some other one, remains to be answered. If this question is met with the claim that only these scriptures have actually been given by God, it can then be asked how we can be sure that the claim is true. There seems to be no way for us to be sure, in the strictly theoretical sense of "sure" required by foundationalism.

A serious Christian could be expected to be existentially sure of the Bible's truth, and presumably, of its superiority to the scriptures of other world religions. But as we have already seen, this kind of surety, for all its serene confidence and universality of intent, cannot finally ignore the problem posed by the plurality of religious traditions. Each of these traditions has its own sacred texts, and these texts are usually assumed by those who stand within a tradition to give normative expression to the character of their own existential certitude or faith. Clearly, then, appeal to an authoritative revelation cannot provide a foundation of theoretical certainty from which to derive a certainly true content of religious belief.

Suppose, however, that it was self-evident to everyone that the Christian Bible is God's definitive revelation to humankind, or that we could somehow show conclusively that this is the case. We would still have the uncertainty of not being able to tell beyond the shade of doubt what the Bible's teachings are or what the revelation means. This would be the case even if every proposition of the Bible in its original form were infallibly true (whatever that might mean). For one thing, we do not possess the original manuscripts of the Bible; we only have copies, and these copies do not always agree. Secondly, these copies are the products of ancient cultures and are written in ancient languages, which scholars living today have to interpret in order to try to understand or translate. These scholars do not always agree, and even if they did, we could not be absolutely confident that they were not unconsciously smuggling in assumptions from their own history or period into the documents. Third, the Bible itself came into being over many hundreds of years and contains a large number of distinct books, of many different types, written or edited by various persons or groups with varied backgrounds. To find a unitary message in this collection of books requires principles of selection and interpretation about which there can be, and has been, much honest disagreement.

Fourth, the Bible does not have the prosaic exactitude and literalness of a theoretical treatise but is often highly symbolical, metaphorical, poetical, or allusive in its language and tone, meaning that it allows considerable room for differences of interpretation. Fifth, what is sometimes assumed to be just what the Bible is saying, literally on on its face, turns out upon examination to be a long-standing interpretation, so familiar as to be thought undebatable. The doctrine of the Trinity is one good example; one can make a case for its being taught in the Bible, but the case is far from being beyond dispute. Finally, the history of Christianity exhibits the many different ways in which the Bible can be interpreted and the many profound disagreements which have been engendered precisely by appeal to its authority. Wolterstorff neatly sums up this second major way in which we must question the foundationalist assumption as it applies to the Bible: "even if the Bible were a book of indubitables, of what benefit would it be if we cannot indubitably apprehend them?" (1984:61).

Nothing said so far is meant in any way to deny that the Bible is authoritative for Christians or that it has revelatory force and import for them. We are questioning only the foundationalist conception of the nature of its authority. Many Christians in recent years have also criticized this conception. Nicholas Wolterstorff, quoted twice above, is a good example of such a Christian, and I have drawn upon his excellent book *Reason Within the Bounds of Religion* in developing some of the points made in this section.

The foundationalist conception of scriptural authority is similar to the assumption of meaning-itself or truth-itself criticized earlier, because it tends to think of the Bible as having an authority that is absolute and external, entirely independent of changing human interpretations, perspectives, or relations. For a religion which gives as much importance to history as Christianity does, it is ironic that some of its most vocal proponents have insisted that the Bible's authority be understood in a completely nonhistorical manner. They have held, in effect, that it was dictated by God to passive secretaries, so that no element of fallible human interpretation or variable historical consciousness could enter into its composition. They have forced its rich diversity of types and styles of writings, written for different purposes, by different persons, and under different historical circumstances, into a straitjacket of doctrinal uniformity. They have insisted that its meaning must be precisely the same for all generations, seeing it as a compendium of frozen doctrines to be rigidly conformed to, rather than finding it greatness to consist in its having a fluidity of meaning which can and must be adapted with creative ingenuity to different situations and times.[9]

In short, these interpreters (and note that they also cannot escape being interpreters) have so emphasized the Bible's objective indubitability and binding authority as to lose sight of the fact that it will be revelatory only for those whose lives it continues to enrich and transform, meaning that its authority, like the certitude of faith, is existential, not theoretical. This is to say that it, like any other sacred scripture, must find new confirmation and significance in each individual life, and for each community of believers. It is to argue that instead of thinking of the Bible as a foundation of infallibly true propositions, it makes more sense to conceive of it as a book (or, more properly, a collection of books) whose authority consists in its power to inspire and renew, to give coherence and purpose to life, and to speak relevantly and forcefully to the deepest religious aspirations and needs of human beings. Its claim to this power is not something that can be guaranteed once and for all, but something that must be continually tested amid the challenges and struggles of everyday life, in each new period of history, and in the face of new problems and experiences as they arise. For this task, antecedent theoretical certainties would be of no avail, even if they could be attained. They are simply irrelevant.

I have identified in this section three kinds of religious influence upon the foundationalist assumption and have argued against each kind. Because I have shown foundationalism to be intimately connected with the conceptions of adequate knowledge and objective meaning which I have also critically discussed, and because some versions of nihilism rest squarely on those very conceptions, the discussions here and in the previous section have important implications for the criticism of nihilism itself. By initiating a challenge to the belicf that the only reliable claims to truth, value, and meaning are those which can be shown to be universal, timeless, and exclusive, and that the only way conclusively to demonstrate these traits is to be able to anchor our claims in a foundation of absolute certainty, I have also begun to take issue with one of the basic premises of nihilism. For many nihilists (as well as critics of nihilism) have taken it for granted that if these goals are unattainable, then our beliefs and value commitments lose all legitimacy and we are left with the sole alternative of complete relativism and subjectivism—in other words, a situation of pervasive arbitrariness and absurdity. I will pursue this matter further later on, arguing that these are not the only available alternatives.

In the last section of this chapter, I consider one other principal religious source of nihilism: the tendency on the part of a culture informed by the Christian vision to deprecate this world in favor of another world believed to await us beyond the grave and beyond the ordeals and frustrations of earthly existence.

3. THE DEPRECATION OF THIS WORLD

Muggeridge considers "the basic nature of a religious faith" to be "that in this world I am a strangcr. I don't belong here. I am staying here for a bit and it's a very nice place, an interesting place, but I don't belong here" (1980:29). His statement suggests a sixth religiously based assumption that, for reasons presented in this section, can be regarded as a source of the nihilistic outlook. This is the idea that this world is not our true home, and that in comparison with the world to come, what it has to offer is at best preliminary, meager, unsatisfying, and incomplete. This assumption has already been hinted at in the sixth trait of the Christian worldview, sketched in Chapter Five. The assumption plants a seed of nihilism because it establishes such a sharp and unfavorable comparison between this world and the coming world, that if we find ourselves without the hope of an afterlife, or without what we consider to be adequate support for that hope, we are apt to lose confidence in the meaning of our lives.

Let me first indicate some of the ways in which the promised paradise of the other world contrasts with life here and now. Generally, that paradise is believed to be perfect in every conceivable way, compared to the perceived imperfections of this world. We can spell out this contrast in more specific terms. For one thing, there is no death or threat of dying, for ourselves, our loved ones, our friends, in the world to come. Second, there is no fleeting evanescence of time or risk of lost opportunities in a brief span of life; one's new existence opens out into all eternity. Third, there is no sin or moral evil, no weakness of will or moral inadequacy. Fourth, there is no animosity or hostility among human beings, no exploitation of the weak by the strong, no competition, envy, or crushing loneliness. Instead, there is perfect community. Fifth, there is no ignorance or incompleteness of knowledge; the ideal of absolute certitude and comprehensiveness of understanding has at last been achieved.[10]

Sixth, there is no disease, old age, ugliness or disfigurement, impairment of mind, threat of accident or natural disaster, or need to secure our living by the sweat of our brows. In other words, there is no kind of "physical" (nonmoral) evil. Hence, there is no anguish of living in, or being at the mercy of, an indifferent, capricious natural environment. Seventh, all injustices perpetrated on earth are put to rights. Appropriate punishments are meted out to evil doers, either in a rehabilitory purgatory or in a retributive everlasting hell, and just compensation or reward is given to the innocent and the doers of good. Eighth, there is no sorrow, disappointment, guilt, regret about the past, anxious uncertainty about the future, anger, frustration, or any of the negative, deeply disturbing emotions that plague our lives on earth. Finally, and most important, there is no sense of separation or distance from God; in joyous, inviolable fellowship with him, his human creatures find at last their utter fulfilment and peace.

One consequence of this belief in an afterlife of serene contentment has been emphasized by Kurt Baier: a strong inclination to view this present world as a dreary vale of tears, full of trouble, torment, and uncertainty, vapid and pointless in itself and capable of being endured only when viewed instrumentally, as trial and preparation for the better life to come. To many Christians of the traditional mold, says Baier,

> The stretch on earth is only a short interlude, a temporary incarceration of the soul in the prison of the body, a brief trial and test, fated to end in death, the release from pain and suffering. What really matters, is the life after the death of the body. One's existence acquires meaning not by gaining what this life can offer but by saving one's immortal soul from death and eternal torture, by gaining eternal life and everlasting bliss (Baier, in Sanders and Cheney 1980:48).

This embedded Christian view, which "adopts as its standard of judgment the perfect life, dismissing as inadequate anything that falls short of it"— combined with a sharply diminished confidence in immortality among moderns which Baier attributes primarily to the influence of science—he sees as one of the most important roots of contemporary nihilism (Baier, in Sanders and Cheney 1980:60).

I think that Baier is right in this assessment, and that a major impulse toward nihilism in the West is the long-established tendency of many Christians, and of others influenced by Christian belief in the afterlife, severely to depreciate the value and importance of life in this world by applying to it a standard of perfection grounded in the hope of an ideal world beyond death.[11] When that hope of immortality grows dim and uncertain, as it has among many people living in the West today, the disparaging attitude toward the world often persists. We still assume (whether consciously or unconsciously) this prevalent standard of judgment of our earthly existence, although we may no longer find it possible to accept the compensating Christian hope of an afterlife. The consequent harsh view we take of our present lives pushes us toward the brink of nihilism. Thus, while Nietzsche (in Kaufmann's words) "sought the roots of otherworldliness in a resentment against this world" (Kaufmann, in Edwards 1967:V, 512), his analysis can also be turned around: we can find roots of resentment against this world in a form of Christian otherworldliness.

A second, closely related concomitant of this long-standing belief in an afterlife is a completely derogatory attitude toward death. We in the West have long-tended to view human death not as a normal, constituent part of life, but as an unnatural curse whose terrible power over us can be broken only by assurance of a coming resurrection. When we no longer have this assurance, the curse of death (for such it is often still assumed to be) stretches a pall of hopelessness over the whole of life. The prospect of death is now seen as a wholesale indictment of life itself, the climactic revelation of its unrelieved tragedy and futility. A 1965 *Time* essay on death concisely characterizes this attitude, saying that it views death as "a trap door to nothingness" for which all of life is only the pointless prelude ("On Death as a Constant Companion":53).

When the hope of resurrection can no longer be comfortably assumed or instinctively believed, our feelings of abandonment and bitter disappointment can cause us to regard death as a topic of inexpressible dread, to be put out of mind in any way possible, to be plastered over with euphemisms and evasions of every conceivable kind. To think of our deaths is now intolerable because it means being forced to acknowledge the emptiness of an existence with no hope of culmination in a perfect afterlife. We recoil from the thought of death as we would from a messenger whom we surmise to be carrying the news of some unspeakably horrible catastrophe; we cannot bear to face the truth about human life we think it conveys. But what can be more universal or impossible to ignore in this world than the fact of death? With the hope of immortality shattered, we encounter evidence on every side of what we now conceive to be an all-consuming nothingness, a black hole of the spirit that sucks everything into its darkness.

Finally, the Christian dream of a perfect paradise beyond the grave can incline us to think of finitude itself as something opprobrious and evil, something we must have assurance of being able to transcend if our lives are to have meaning. I spoke earlier, for example, of the idea that in the afterlife there will be no limitations to our knowledge. All that can be known will be known, and with complete certainty. Aquinas gives expression to this idea when he states that "final and perfect happiness" for human beings can be attained only when they have found the completeness of knowledge made possible by "the vision of the Divine Essence," i.e., of the essence of the ultimate cause of everything that is; and have thereby ceased to long to know anything. Because he believes the state of the blessed in the life to come to be one of perfect happiness, he concludes that the gnawing drive of curiosity and wonder, spoken of by Aristotle in the beginning of the *Metaphysics*, will have been fully satisfied in the new life (*Summa Theologica* II, I, ii, 8; see Hyman and Walsh 1980:521).

What holds for the finitude of knowledge also holds for other kinds of incompleteness and limitation marking our lives in this world. According to traditional Christian teaching, we have every right to expect that all sense of inadequacy, yearning, want, struggle, and need will have been eliminated when we come into the eternal paradise. But once again, if the hope of immortality pales, its accompanying denigration of finite existence is apt to stay fixed in our minds, so that we feel condemned to lives of wrenching frustration and disappointment. We once had the fair hope of God-like perfection; now we must resign ourselves to the dismal prospects of a puny earth-bound life. The contrast seems too stark and painful to endure, and we are tempted to despair.

Is belief in an afterlife of endless bliss really necessary to meaning in this life? Would we be right in concluding that this life is worthless if we could no longer think of it as preparatory to a perfect life awaiting us on the other side of death? One good reason for answering these questions in the negative is presented by Baier. He contends that the "Christian evaluation of earthly lives is misguided because it adopts a quite unjustifiably high standard." Assumption of this standard "is as illegitimate as if I were to refuse to call anything tall unless it is infinitely tall, or anything beautiful unless it is perfectly flawless, or any one strong unless he is omnipotent." Baier goes on to assert, "Even if it were true that there is available to us an after-life which is flawless and perfect, it would still not be legitimate to judge our earthly lives by this standard." This would be like rejecting every candidate for a degree who does not have the intellect or creative genius of an Albert Einstein (Baier, in Sanders and Cheney 1980:60-61).

What follows from this reasoning is that we should judge this world by the ordinary standards of our experience within it, not by the extraordinary conditions of another world alleged to be faultless in every way. We are not entitled to condemn all qualified or limited mundane goods simply because they fall short of perfection. We can make immanent evaluations of our experiences in the world quite independently of our particular attitude toward the Christian promise of another world. Baier makes an excellent point. His careful examination of the logic of the alleged connection between affirmation of meaning in this life and expectation of a life to come shows that the connection is not as tight or convincing as we might have supposed. Loss of belief in a perfect afterlife is not a sufficient reason to despair of this life. We need to be persuaded on grounds other than comparison with the ideal of such a life to be justified in concluding that this life is not worthwhile.

A second line of criticism of this sixth religious source of nihilism questions the concept of perfection implicit in the traditional Christian view of the afterlife. The criticism is suggested by Schopenhauer's observation (cited in Chapter Three, Section 4) that boredom is a worse scourge than struggle or pain, and that it hovers over us like a bird of prey, ready to attack whenever it finds us secure from want or need. His observation forces us to raise this probing question: Is it conceivable that beings such as we are could be genuinely happy in a state of existence with no risk, no uncertainty, no mystery, no challenge or adventure, with nothing for which to strive and nothing that invites improvement or change? We need not ponder this question very long before we begin to think it highly unlikely that a static life of this kind would be experienced as perfect by us, or that it could give us lasting contentment. Schopenhauer's insight points in just the opposite direction, implying that such a life would soon become so insufferably monotonous as to feel like an endless hell rather than a paradise; so much so that we would probably be willing to pay any price for our annihilation, or for a return to our former earthly state, with all its uncertainty and susceptibility to pain.

It does little good to argue that we will be so fundamentally transformed in the afterlife that concerns such as these will lose their point. For I do not think that we can conceive of how a change as radical as the one required could still allow for continuity or identification with the kind of beings we are on earth. It could not be *we* who survived and found fulfilment in such an afterlife, but beings of a wholly different sort. It could not be *our* resurrection into newness of life which had occurred; what would have to happen instead would be something like a creation from scratch of beings totally unlike ourselves. Accordingly, the promise of completion and fulfilment in such a life seems irrelevant to who and what we are.

As I write these words, I try to imagine what it would mean to live in a state of perfection in which there would be no labor of thinking, nothing to puzzle over, no need to probe more deeply or to try to express myself more clearly, no reason ever to rethink or revise my ideas. What would it be like, in other words, for me to have ceased to long to know anything, the state Aquinas thinks to be so essential to happiness in the life to come? Would this not be analogous to my leaving my desk in the evening and coming back the next morning to find that elves had written this chapter while I slept, and written it far better than I ever could? What if all my endeavors, and the endeavors of every person in paradise, were to be useless in this same degree, as they presumably would have to be in a state where nothing remains to be done? What point or purpose would there be our lives? How could we escape feelings of aimlessness and boredom?

It is said that in an afterlife of the kind we are discussing all good is timelessly realized. But it seems logically impossible that this could be, because some goods requiring the flux of time and playing a pivotal role in our present lives would be notably absent. One is the good of the zest and challenge built into the very process of having to work for the achievement of goals as yet unattained, whether in the domain of theory or that of practice. Another is the good of freedom. In a static world secure against even the slightest degree of risk, uncertainty, or possibility of mistake, an open future posing options for real choice would not exist. The reason is simple: there could not be the slightest likelihood of choosing a lesser over a greater good; choice of the greatest good in every situation would be guaranteed. And "choices" guaranteed in advance to always turn our in only one way would not be choices at all. Nor could we have anything like a sense of responsibility for helping to direct the course of the future, because the present would be perfect and needing no improvement, and its unaltered continuation into the remotest future would be completely assured. In such an afterlife, we would have attained the good of absolute safety, but at the price of losing the goods of adventure and freedom. Perfection of the first entails the extinction of the other two.

Ninian Smart has pointed out that in a utopia of the sort Christians have commonly assumed heaven to be,[12] many other things that we now regard as exemplary goods or virtues would also be missing. No situations would call for generosity or self-sacrifice, for example, because no one would lack anything. Because no danger would exist in the afterlife and thus no need to confront and overcome fear, the virtue of courage could have no place. The virtue of resisting temptations and developing one's moral character and capacity for good in the face of obstacles would be absent because there would be no temptations or obstacles (Smart, in Pike 1965:108-109).

The goods of this life are dialectical, elusive, and complex. We are not always sure how to conceive them; they often come into conflict even when clearly conceived; it is not always easy to judge how best to put them into practice in specific situations; and we often confront substantial obstacles to their realization. But for these very reasons they challenge our ingenuity, require the risk and responsibility of our freedom, and make possible the expression and development of virtues such as the ones we have just described. By comparison, the promised perfections of the life to come seem flat, one-sided, and curiously unappealing.

In the context of reflections such as these, I have to agree with the familiar statement of Gotthold Ephraim Lessing, who saw fit to choose the limitations of a human being as over against the limitless knowledge it is customary to attribute to God:

> If God held all truth concealed in his right hand, and in his left hand the persistent striving for the truth, and while warning me against eternal error, should say, Choose! I should humbly bow before his left hand, and say, 'Father, give thy gift; the pure truth is for thee alone' (*Werke,* X, 53; quoted in Kierkegaard 1951:195).

To be limited and incomplete, to be required to strive and struggle, often at the expense of doubt, frustration, and pain, seems to me—as it apparently did to Lessing—to be an essential part of what it means to be a human being. I cannot conceive of this situation being fundamentally different and our still being able to find happiness.

Happiness in a state of static perfection may be possible for beings other than we are, if there be such. But I cannot think how it would be possible for us. This is not to say that all conceptions of an afterlife must be equally unappealing; it is the ideal of an endless state of static perfection that we have good reason to reject. Although in a less reflective mood I can feel the lure of many of the perfections of the traditional Christian picture of the afterlife (who of us does not sometimes long for complete understanding or absolute safety?), I think we must finally judge them to be not only incomprehensible to beings such as ourselves, but also wholly inappropriate and undesirable. This conclusion stands in pronounced opposition to the two main strands of the assumption we have been treating as a sixth religious source of nihilism: that in comparison with the hope of a perfect life to come this life is shallow, unsatisfying, and incomplete; and that this hope, and it alone, can give meaning to our lives.

Even if we put these two criticisms aside, there is a third criticism that is equally damaging to at least the second strain of this assumption. The two criticisms already presented argue against the notion that without the hope of a perfect afterlife this life must be branded as meaningless. This third criticism seeks to show that belief in a perfect afterlife can itself work strongly against the affirmation of meaning in this life. It does so by raising the question of why God should have put us here on earth when he could have put us in heaven in the first place. If the afterlife is such a perfect fulfilment of our lives here and now, and if these lives can only be seen as fragmentary and incomplete in comparison with it, why should we have to suffer the ordeals of earthly existence at all?

An answer to this question that has an initial ring of plausibility can be traced back at least as far as Irenaeus in the second century A.D., and has been presented by John Hick and others in our own time. The answer is that we need to undergo the trials and tribulations of this life in order to develop our characters. This world was not created by God as a hedonistic paradise, but as a vale of soul-making. God wants to enter into relation with free beings who are given the opportunity to choose for or against fellowship with him. He desires to relate to persons, not to mere puppets or automata who cannot help adoring him and obeying him in every way. Moreover, we could never come to understand the nature and extent of our creaturely dependence on God if he made us impervious from birth to all want or need (see Hick 1963:40-46).

But this answer is open to objections that, when taken together, seriously erode its plausibility. For one thing, as Hick himself points out, it appears that the tribulation of this present life has "crushed the human spirit as often as it has developed it, and that men have collapsed before life's challenges and opportunities as often as they have risen triumphantly to meet them" (Hick, in Edwards 1967:III, 139). The fact that the alleged process of earthly education seems so often to fail to achieve its divinely appointed aim, and for reasons other than stubborn pride or malice on the part of human beings, weakens the attempt to justify the sufferings of life on the basis of that aim.

Secondly, very few, if any, persons in this life seem to have learned its putative lessons so well by the time of their deaths that they are no longer susceptible to sin in even the slightest degree. But it is believed that in the afterlife humans will no longer have any inclination to sin. So once again, a glaring gap is implied for even the best among us between the beings we are on earth and the beings we will become in heaven, and the problem of continuity or identity between our natures here and our natures in the next world is once again posed. Something radically discontinuous and new must be added to the earthly process of education and development of character if human beings are to be made fit for a perfect paradise, namely instillment of a practical incapacity to sin. In view of the fact that the struggles of our earthly lives generally prove incapable of producing it in us, and that and it must finally be granted to us as a miracle or gift, why could not this total disinclination to sin be instilled in us at the very outset?

This question becomes even more pressing when put in the context of the belief of many Christians, including that of such revered teachers as Augustine and Martin Luther, that eternal salvation is not based on any human achievement or incremental process of development, but solely on the grace of God. Why could God not simply infuse in us by grace the sense of complete dependence on him that is required, and put us in heaven right away? As Augustine has said, "My weight is my love; thereby I am borne whithersoever I am borne," i.e., we inevitably decide in accordance with those loves or inclinations we find already within ourselves (*Confessions* xiii, ix, 10; quoted Cochrane 1944:445). Why then does God not tip the scales entirely toward love of him in the case of all his human creatures, and away from the distortions and corruptions of lesser loves?

Third, we can readily turn Hick's indictment of the idea of a hedonistic paradise on earth against the idea of a perfect heaven. Even if our experiences did succeed in educating us to the point of complete lack of interest in sin (which they rarely, if ever, do), in the state of heavenly bliss we would seemingly have an eternity in which growing complacent or rebellious and forgetting the lessons about responsibility and dependence on God we have learned in this life are possible. If we are somehow to be made completely immune to this possibility in the afterlife, then we will no longer be truly free, and God will be relating throughout all eternity to puppets or automata. Only for the short span of a human life will he have been able to relate to any of his human creatures as free and responsible persons (assuming that we put aside for the moment the Augustinian doctrine of divine predestination of the course of every earthly life). For the rest of the time, he will have inducted beings now wholly insulated against the risks of genuine freedom into what has every appearance of a hedonistic paradise. If this state is good enough for all eternity, why was it not good enough for earth as well? Or if this is how it is best to end up anyway, why not just start there?

What is the point, in other words, of having freedom in the first place, with all its susceptibility to evil and pain, both for the individual and others affected by his choices (think of the Nazi holocaust, for example) if we are going to end up without it anyway, as we would have to in a perfect paradise where it is impossible for evil or pain to occur? This question becomes especially poignant when we reflect that according to standard Christian teaching, many human beings incur the guilt of flagrant misuse of their freedom on earth, and instead of attaining the perfection of a heavenly afterlife are condemned to the torments of an eternal punitive hell. It is not as though God could have been surprised at, or unprepared for, the amount of eternally punishable evil and everlasting suffering that his creation of free human beings would bring into the universe. He is commonly supposed by Christians, as noted earlier in this chapter, to be above time and to see all temporal unfoldings with an eternally present immediacy and comprehensiveness of vision. But even without such omniscience, knowing the nature and inclination of his creatures, could he not have predicted that they would misuse their freedom, and on a catastrophic scale? Is the bestowal of a transitory freedom, soon to be colossally oughtweighed by an eternity in which neither the blessed or the damned are free to alter their outlook or actions in even the slightest degree, really worth the horrible price of eternal perdition for so many of God's creatures?[13]

The main conclusion I am leading up to is that the Christian conception of heaven (especially of a heaven restricted to only some humans) can make this life seem more pointless and futile than it would otherwise seem, because it implies that we are subject to a God who allows all the evils flowing from human freedom to occur for no finally defensible reason. What has been said of the moral evils of this world must also be said of its physical evils, because the belief in heaven implies that God is capable of creating a kind of existence without those as well, and that he does create it for the blessed in the afterlife. Here on earth we can sometimes find ways of preventing particular physical evils, such as diseases for which we eventually discover a cure. Why does God not prevent them to begin with? Why does he create them at all? Is it really conceivable that a loving God would allow innocent children to be ravaged by terrible diseases just to make their parents or others about them more acutely aware of their dependence of him? Would we not have to call the meaning of life much more seriously into question if we thought that the suffering and death of an innocent child on account of a preventable disease was somehow willed or allowed by God for an ulterior end, than if we simply attributed it to blind chance? (See McCloskey in Burr and Goldinger 1976:135-136.) According to this third criticism, then, the very prospect of a perfect afterlife can make our existence on this earth seem scandalous and absurd.

I do not have space here to enter into all aspects of the concept of a perfect afterlife, or into alternative views of life beyond the grave which some Christians today might be more comfortable in defending. Nor have I responded to possible objections to the three lines of criticism. However, enough questions have been raised about the sixth religiously based assumption to exhibit its dubiousness and to show that arguments for nihilism that grow out of it can be countered in important ways. In Part Five I will return to the question of whether the extent of suffering in the world or the fact of death, quite apart from any conception of heaven or God, entails the meaninglessness of human life. But my next task is a critical inquiry into some principal philosophical sources of nihilism.

PART FOUR

A Critical Look at
Philosophical Sources of Nihilism

Chapter 7

Correspondence-Substance and the Hegemony of Science

... we conclude the least particles of all bodies to be ... all extended, and hard and impenetrable, and movable, and endowed with their proper inertia. And this is the foundation of all philosophy.
—*Isaac Newton (1953:4)*

We saw earlier that the philosophy of nihilism began to emerge as a distinct movement in the West during the mid-nineteenth century. But just as the scientific revolution of the sixteenth and seventeenth centuries did not spring from a vacuum but had antecedents reaching back into the Renaissance and the Late Middle Ages, so the nihilistic outlook which has crystallized in recent years can be viewed, at least in part, as the climax of trends of philosophical thought whose origins can be traced to the beginnings of the modern era or earlier. I do not have space in four chapters to elaborate these trends in extensive detail, or even to note all of them, but I will try to highlight some of the more important ones, employing again the strategy of the preceding part, where we sought to understand some key religious, or religiously influenced, assumptions underlying the nihilistic view. In the chapters of this part, I identify and criticize certain philosophical assumptions that also can be seen to play a prominent, though not always expressly recognized, role in the articulation of nihilistic thought. In addition, I note linkages between the religious and the philosophical assumptions which remind us that the two types of assumption cannot always be kept completely distinct but sometimes merge in significant ways.

1. CORRESPONDENCE AND SUBSTANCE

The first philosophical source of nihilism is assumption of the correspondence conception of truth in the context of traditional substance-attribute metaphysics and the new application of that metaphysics to the idea of matter in the modern period. I use the term "conception," rather than "theory," because this view of truth has only recently come to be clearly recognized as one theory among other possible theories; it was long taken for granted as the sole obvious meaning of truth, and continues to be taken for granted by many today, despite the enormous difficulties that soon become apparent when it is subjected to careful examination.

I will first explain the correspondence conception of truth, exploring in the process its close ties to the substance-attribute metaphysics with which it has long been associated, and emphasizing a crucial new development in that metaphysics pertaining to the idea of matter. Next, I will bring out some of the difficulties with this conception of truth in general and show how these difficulties are made even more acute by the new notion of substantial matter which becomes widespread in the early modern era. I will also indicate how these difficulties relate to nihilism. Finally, I will discuss a trenchant criticism of the correspondence assumption that demonstrates in a simple but cogent manner the need to question this assumption and to opt for a different theory of truth. Later in the book I will discuss an alternative theory that avoids many problems of the correspondence view. At various points in this chapter, including this first section, I will draw on observations and arguments contained in earlier chapters.

What, then, is the correspondence conception of truth? Aristotle presented a version of it in the fourth century B.C.: "to say of what is that it is not, or of what is not that it is, is false, while to say of what is that it is, and of what is not that it is not, is true..." (*Metaphysics* 1011b26; see Aristotle 1941:749). In other words, a statement is true if it depicts or describes an existing fact or state of affairs; false, if it claims something to exist which does not exist. What makes a belief or sentence true or false is its correspondence, or lack of correspondence, to reality. A formulation used often by Aquinas to express this idea says that truth is a relation of adequation between things and the intellect. There have been many exponents of this conception of truth in various forms, ranging from Aristotle and his teacher Plato, through the Stoics in the Hellenistic period and Aquinas in the High Middle Ages, to prominent twentieth-century philosophers such as G. E. Moore, Russell, Wittgenstein (in his early period), and Alfred Tarski (see Prior, in Edwards 1967:II, 223-232). This conception of truth is also the view generally assumed by "the man [or woman] in the street."

We can take as our main example of this conception a thinker of the early modern period who devoted a treatise called *De Veritate* (published 1624) to its elaboration. The thinker is Edward, Lord Herbert of Cherbury; his treatise is discussed by Richard Popkin, in the latter's *The History of Scepticism from Erasmus to Spinoza*. Herbert's commitment to the correspondence idea is made clear in his presentation of what truth is and how it can be attained. There are four kinds of truths, he tells us. The first is "the thing as it is" (*veritas rei*); it is this that we seek to know by means of the other kinds of truths, which are related to the knower rather than to the object itself.

The other three kinds of truth are the truth of things as they appear to us, the truth of concepts, and the truth of what Herbert terms "Common Notions"—something like innate truths, confirmed as such not only by their self-evidence to the individual but also by their being universally admitted to be true by all rational beings or normal, mature persons. He proposes that the last type of truth be used as the principal criterion of when our subjective appearances or concepts do or do not conform to the truth of things in themselves, though he also stresses the importance of making sure that proper conditions of perception and concept formation have been met, carefully explaining how this can be done. In this way, he seeks to meet the crisis of a newly revived Pyrrhonian skepticism, given expression in the sixteenth century by various thinkers, but most notably by Michel de Montaigne (see Popkin 1979:151-156).

Our interest in Herbert is not in the details of his system but in what it typifies of the age. First, it shows unquestioning acceptance of the correspondence conception of truth, a conception not challenged by his critics, despite the incisive character of many of their criticisms. Pierre Gassendi, for example, charges in a letter to Herbert and one addressed to their common friend, Elie Diodati, that Herbert has not solved the problem of showing us how to bridge the gap between the truth of things-in-themselves and the subjective conditions of conceptualization and experience, because no universal agreement has been reached on what are the so-called Common Notions. Notions that are indubitable to some are dubious to others. So we are left where we started, with a situation in which only God knows the real nature of things. At best, Herbert has explained more about the nature of those conditions whereby we comprehend our own experience; he has not elucidated a basis for understanding the unconditioned *veritas rei* (Gassendi 1658:III, 411 ff.; Mersenne 1955:336 ff.; cited and discussed in Popkin 1979:158-159). Gassendi makes no explicit criticism of the conception of truth presupposed by Herbert; he argues only that in the context of this conception Herbert has failed to achieve his end.

A second important thing to notice about Herbert's program is his appeal to certitude as a way out of the impasse of skepticism. Sensate experience, he states, does not enable us to "pierce beyond the outer shell of things." But, with the Common Notions, we are able to arrive at certainty, thereby establishing a firm basis for deciding when "our subjective faculties have accurate knowledge of the facts," or when a given subjective appearance is "in a precise external conformity with its original" (Herbert 1937:135, 105-

106, 101; quoted Popkin 1979:156, 154, 153). Gassendi's criticism, as noted, is that the Common Notions, so meticulously detailed and codified in Herbert's treatise, do not command universal acceptance. To this criticism can be added René Descarte's observation that because few people even try to control their reasoning by the "natural light" of genuine innate truths, the appeal to universal consent is itself useless as a criterion of truth (Descartes 1897-1910:II, 597-598; see Popkin 1979:161).

The problem, therefore, was to find a kind of certainty that could serve as a sure criterion of truth in the face of what Gassendi called "the great contrariety of opinions that are found on almost every subject" (Letter to Diodate, in Mersenne 1955:337; quoted Popkin 1979:158). This sense of baffling, widespread disagreement was symptomatic of the final breakdown of the Medieval consensus, and as Popkins shows, that breakdown was both exhibited and greatly exacerbated by such movements as the Protestant Reformation and the new attention given to the arguments of the ancient skeptics. It was typical for thinkers of the early modern era to seek a new basis for consensus in the appeal to certainty, either through Herbert's Common Notions, i.e., innate truths, or through putting all claims to knowledge to the test of their reducibility to alleged pure givens of sensate experience. In either of these approaches or in some combination of them, it was believed, we can find the avenue to knowledge of reality-itself. I will return to these two ways of seeking confirmed knowledge as the discussion develops. We can note at this point, however, that each is a version of the foundationalist idea discussed and criticized in the preceding chapter.

An important concomitant of the assumption of the correspondence conception of truth is the substance-attribute metaphysics, widely adhered to in the philosophy of the seventeenth and eighteenth centuries and constituting its basic notion of what Herbert called the *veritas rei*. According to the classical concept of substance developed by Aristotle, reality consists of a plurality of substances, most of which (exceptions are non-material beings such as the astronomical intelligences and the Unmoved Mover) are unifications of four factors: a material substrate; a defining essence or substantial form; a variety of accidental properties that can undergo change through time without the substantial entity itself, as defined by its essential attribute, undergoing change; and a privation or potentiality of accidental changes appropriate to that type of substance. Because knowledge is of universals, the forms, both essential and accidental, are the knowable aspects of things; we cannot attain knowledge of the underlying material substrate as such. It is not an actuality but a potentiality, some of whose manifold possibilities are actualized at any given time by a particular set of forms (see *Metaphysics*, VII, in Aristotle 1941:783-811).

Christian thinkers had long been accustomed to thinking that human beings possess an immortal, self-subsistent soul, an idea influenced not only by Christian belief in an afterlife but also by Platonism. With the revival of Aristotelianism in the thirteenth century, the human soul was claimed by such Christian Aristotelians as Aquinas to be one of the types of non-material substances spoken of by Aristotle. In this life it can be conceived as "the form of a certain matter," but unlike animal souls, it is incorruptible and self-subsistent and will, therefore, survive the dissolution of the body (*Summa Theologica* I, lxxv, 6; I, lxxi, 2; see Hyman and Walsh 1980:500-505). Aristotle, by contrast, had conceived of the "soul" or rational life-principle of human beings as the distinctive actuality or essential form of the organized human body, and as inseparable from the body. The Christian idea was carried into the modern period by such philosophical thinkers as Descartes and John Locke, both taking the position that the human soul is a substance in its own right, with its own defining form and distinctive types of accidental properties.

Another crucial departure from the Aristoleian doctrine of substance further widened the gap between mind and body already implicit in the Christian doctrine of an immortal self-subsistent soul. This breach with Aristotle, which came into dominance in the seventeenth century, conceived of matter as a type of substance existing in its own right, with its own essential property or properties, and with types of accidental traits appropriate to it. This idea contrasts with the Aristotelian view that matter is but one aspect of material substances, i.e., the element of potentiality susceptible to actualization by, or in terms of, various forms. Ivor Leclerc argues that this sea change in the concept of matter was greatly influenced by the work *Philosophia Naturalis* (1621), whose author was a medical man, Sebastian Basso. Leclerc shows how the new outlook toward matter espoused by Basso and other thinkers of the sixteenth and early seventeenth centuries, many of them students of medicine concerned with the theory of material elements and their chemical combination, captivated the thought of such luminaries as Descartes, Gassendi, Galileo, and Newton (see Leclerc 1972:34-35, 143-148, 184, 232).[1]

Now if we critically assess the correspondence conception of truth in its relation to the doctrine of substance laid out by Aristotle, and with respect to the two modifications of that doctrine just mentioned, what is the result? Five problems posed by this combination of factors stand in sharp relief. The first is the difficulty of knowing how to go about assessing the degree of correspondence between the qualities of the knower and the qualities of the known. Must not the skeptic always win the argument when he challenges us, within the context of the correspondence conception of truth, to prove conclusively that particular experiences or claims do in fact correspond to the structures of a purely objective world? Giving such proof seems impossible because, as Richard Rorty reminds us, we have no "transcendental standpoint outside our present set of representations from which we can inspect the relations between those representations and their object" (1979:293). The best for which we can hope, as suggested by Gassendi's criticism of Herbert, is to become clearer about such things as the patterns of our experience, our characteristic modes of conceptualization, or the contours and commitments of our language; we can never expect to demonstrate anything like a one-to-one correspondence between those things and features of a supposedly completely independent, uninterpreted world. If truth requires such a demonstration, then truth is impossible and epistemological nihilism is confirmed.

Kant's *Critique of Pure Reason* makes it abundantly clear that this would be so even if we could attain complete certainty about specific beliefs or claims. For there would be no way to give conclusive evidence that the certainty is not merely intersubjective, reflecting commonalities of our make-up as human beings (as Kant believed) or perhaps pervasive traits of our particular culture, rather than giving us priviledged access to reality-itself. The upshot of an insistence that truth must mean correspondence is that we seem to eliminate at the outset any possibility of gaining assurance of truth's attainment; we forfeit the race to the epistemological nihilist before it has begun. Indicated elsewhere are some of the close connections between epistemological and existential nihilism (e.g., the opening sections of Chapters Four and Six).

The second thing to notice about the correspondence conception of truth is that it rests upon the absolutist, non-perspectivist view of truth and meaning criticized in the first section of the previous chapter. The implication becomes particularly obvious when we conjoin this conception of truth with the classical concept of substance. According to the concept of substance, reality is comprised of substantial entities which have status and meaning quite apart from any relations to things beyond themselves. As Elizabeth Kraus points out, the classical view of substance "exalts the categories of quality and quantity over the category of relation, failing to realize that the former themselves are relational in that they express the ways in which substances *are for* other substances, and are not attributes of isolated substances." She illustrates her point with the example of fire, saying that "'hot' *is* the fire as appropriated by a hand—*is* the modal existence of the fire for the hand—and not an accident *through* which an underlying reality is grasped." Similarly, "crackling" is the fire for the ear, and "red," the fire for the eye (1979:2, 53). The view she attacks is that of a nonperspectival reality-itself, meaning-itself, truth-itself: precisely what Herbert called *veritas rei*.

In the substantialist version of this view, substances are what they are and mean what they mean independently of specific contexts of experience or construal; the attributes they possess are thought to be possessed by them in complete autonomy, apart from any perspectives or relations. The task of knowledge is then to capture those independently existing meanings or truths of substances, making sure that our claims to knowledge are not tainted by anything contributed by ourselves as knowing subjects. The conception is similar to that earlier associated with the ideal of trying attain a God's-eye view of the world. The combined doctrines of correspondence and substance thus endorse from a philosophical direction notions of adequate knowledge and objective meaning earlier traced to religious sources. We have indicated the connections of these notions with nihilism and sought to expose their inherent untenability.

This brings us to a third problem with the concept of reliable knowledge as the adequation of thought and thing. If the thing is conceived in substantialist terms, an aspect of it must always elude our understanding. As Aristotle taught, the material substratum cannot be known; only the substance's display of properties can be known. But it is natural to want to penetrate beneath the veil of properties to the thing-itself, or to comprehend the thing-itself in all its fulness. Otherwise, we have no way of knowing whether the properties we perceive or conceive are properties really attributable to that substance. Might not some of them be secondary effects of the substantial reality on the percipient or knower, and not primary attributes of the substance itself? Or even more disturbing: might not all of these properties be mere traits of the mind, or sheer unanalyzable givens that cannot be connected with any underlying substance, mental or physical, because none of them can afford us the confident privileged access to reality-itself we think we must have in order to have truth?

This problem perplexed John Locke, forcing him to confess that the substance underlying its play of properties was a "*something, he knew not what*" (1959:I, 391-392). That is to say, he was led by the classical substantialist doctrine to posit external substances but forced to admit as an empiricist that he had no idea, nor could he have, of what they might be outside all contexts of experience or relation. The thing-itself was devoid of meaning in a manner analogous to Sartre's being-in-itself. Yet, it is just that thing-itself to which, according to the correspondence conception of truth, our veridical beliefs and claims are supposed to correspond! The correspondence conception of truth and the doctrine of substance have gravitations toward idealism and, finally, skepticism that Locke only vaguely defined, but that were soon to be made painfully explicit by his fellow empiricists George Berkeley and David Hume.

Of course, Sartre does not endorse the metaphysics of substance-attribute, and he is no British empiricist. But his notion of an objective reality of meaningless facticity from which we must be forever estranged is notably akin to Locke's "something, he knew not what," suggesting a common philosophical (and perhaps religious, as argued in the previous chapter) parentage of the two points of view. At any rate, in their common fascination with the idea of bare, uninterpreted, purely objective reality, both Locke and Sartre are led to imagine an impassable gulf between themselves and the world as it really is, and thus to feel the shudder (though in markedly different degrees) of chill winds of the absurd from that opposing shore.[2]

A fourth problem relates to the status of values. While it perhaps makes some sense to think of true beliefs as ones which correspond to existing facts, what it would mean for beliefs about values to be made true by their conformity to such facts is not at all clear. One basic reason is that facts and values are often in conflict; there is the frequent awareness of obligation to change the facts in accordance with the values. Another reason is that even when certain values have been realized, e.g., in individual life or social institutions, we cannot simply rest content with the fact of their realization but must continue to work for their preservation or improvement. While the correspondence conception in its classical form inclines us to conceive of facts as properties of antecedently existing substantial entities, values seem to require an orientation to the future and to involve elements of anticipation, purpose, and will with which the idea of truth as correspondence does not accord. When Abraham Lincoln spoke of the American nation as the "last best hope for mankind," for example, he was not simply referring to existing facts but stating a responsibility for the future. And it seems to make sense to say that he was claiming an important truth in his statement.

A correspondence theorist might respond to this objection by saying that Lincoln's comment gains its element of truth by its calling attention to a potentiality in an existing state of affairs, a potentiality that is "really there." But this response does not get at the thrust of the objection, because it is not the potentiality as such that is central in the statement (though it has admitted relevance for an assessment of its truth) but the obligation to try to bring about one potentiality among others in the existing situation. It is the statement of this obligation that we can judge to be making an important claim to truth, a claim not merely dependent for its truth on its implicit reference to a real possibility. Similarly, to say, "This vitamin is good for us," is not simply to predict biological effects of its regular use—and therefore to take notice of established probabilities—but to state that these predictable effects are worth pursuing.

The correspondence conception, if taken as the very meaning of objectivity and truth, can have the result of denying cognitive status to, and radically subjectivizing, valuational claims. Dewey analyzes this consequence in detail, summarizing it as follows: "When real objects are identified, point for point, with knowledge-objects, all affectional and volitional objects are inevitably excluded from the 'real' world, and are compelled to find refuge in the privacy of an experiencing subject or mind" (1958:24). This complete privatizing of values renders the choices, values, and aims of any given course of life indefensible or unarguable, and therefore purely arbitrary and absurd. Both moral and existential nihilism are the result.

The fifth negative implication of the combination of factors we have been discussing relates particularly to the new concept of matter as a substantial entity in its own right. The implication is that the human self, conceived as spiritual substance, is now alienated from its own body as something purely material, to say nothing of being distanced from nature, which now comes increasingly to be conceived as nothing more than a concatenation of material substances. This makes it inconceivable that the properties or functionings of mind could have anything to do with the properties or functionings of matter, and thus that the demand of truth as correspondence between thought and thing could ever be realized. Soul and body, human being and nature, now seem to have nothing whatever in common. Each is a distinctive type of being, a class of finally real substantial entities whose relations to the other class of entities are left murky and inexplicable. The relation between subject and object has been stretched to the breaking point.

Dewey brings our attention to the incoherence of this position when he takes account of the assumption (widespread in the seventeenth and eighteenth centuries) that mental phenomena have their basis or cause in physical events and shows how inconsistent this is with the separation of reality into two radically different types of substances:

> The notion that the universe is split into two separate and disconnected realms of experience, one psychical and the other physical, and then that these two realms of being, in spite of their total disjunction, specifically and minutely correspond to each other—as a serial order of numbered vibrations corresponds to the immediately felt qualities of vision of the prismatic spectrum—represents the acme of incredibility (1958:267-268).

It also makes no sense, as Dewey notes elsewhere, radically to separate mind from the world and yet to continue to think that mind's acts can have effects on the world. He laments that we somehow "find it easier to make a problem out of the conjunction of the two inconsistent premises than to rethink our premises" (1958:286).

Problems similar to these referred to by Dewey arise when we try to reconcile the correspondence conception of truth with the sundering of reality into fundamentally different substances with fundamentally different properties. Berkeley raised a fair question when he wondered how the properties of autonomous mental substances can be thought to resemble or represent properties of wholly distinct physical substances (*The Principles of Human Knowledge*, Section 9, in Berkeley 1965). How, in other words, can any possible connection or relation exist between the two entirely separate realms of being entailed by the new concept of matter and the older concept of soul?

It is no wonder that a tendency was set in motion early in the modern era to construe the world along the lines of one of the sundered factors to the complete exclusion of the other, and in that way to try to resolve the crisis of radical incoherence that follows hard on the heels of the new view of matter. I discussed both the incoherence and the tendency toward materialistic reductionism in some detail in Chapter Three, in connection with the descriptions of nature emerging from the methods and findings of natural science. Modern science was long-committed to a substantialist conception of matter, in the form of the material atomism which reigned until the end of the nineteenth century. Leclerc argues that a semblance of this commitment still haunts the revolutionary new science of today in its talk of, and continuing search for, "elementary particles" (1972:242, 286, 314-315).

I will have more to say later about the role of natural science in the creation of the above-mentioned crisis of the modern mind. But the tendencies toward materialistic reductionism, on the one hand, and mentalistic reductionism (e.g., the subjective idealism of Berkeley, which reached its logical culmination in the skeptical phenomenalism of Hume), on the other, as ways of trying to resolve that crisis, are no less prone to be nihilistic in their final result than the polarizations of dualism. And we seem to be left with no other options. I think that this will remain the case as long as we persist in assuming the correspondence conception of truth in the context of the other factors I have been elucidating.

I have questioned this conception in its modern setting by pointing out five negative consequences or central problems stemming from it. Some of these problems were anticipated in the previous chapter, where they were discussed in a religious context. Additional critical perspective on the correspondence conception of truth will be gained when I contrast it later with another, more tenable view of truth. But before ending this section, I want to present a particularly devastating criticism of the correspondence view, treated here as the principal feature of this first philosophical source of nihilism. Taking account of this criticism makes us even more aware of the necessity for finding an alternative less generative of insurmountable paradoxes and problems and less likely to lead to a nihilistic outcome.

The thrust of this criticism is that the correspondence conception not only establishes a goal impossible to attain (a point already made), but also supports an ideal completely irrelevant to any genuine problem of knowledge. A philosopher who makes this second point with admirable clarity is O. K.

Bouwsma, in a now-classic essay entitled "Descartes' Evil Genius" (first published in 1949 and reprinted in Sesonske and Fleming 1966). Before discussing Bouwsma's essay, I must note a distinction Descartes makes in his *Meditations on First Philosophy* that demonstrates his unquestioning commitment to the correspondence conception of truth. This commitment, in turn, gives shape and direction to the main problem of the *Meditations*: how to avoid the paralysis of total skepticism.

The distinction Descartes draws is between "the objective reality of an idea" and its "formal reality." The *objective reality* is simply the reality of the idea *qua* idea, taken apart from any reference beyond itself. An idea has *formal reality*, on the other hand, if it refers or corresponds to some fact in the world. Descartes's problem is precisely this: how do I know that any of my ideas have formal reality? Can I at least be sure that those ideas which are clear and distinct, i.e., unequivocal and indubitable, correspond to the fundamental entities and structures of the world? No, I cannot, says Descartes, because it is at least conceivable that a deceiving demon or evil genius exists who creates in me an unassailable confidence that certain of my idea resemble or correspond to existing reality when, in fact, none of them do. Thus Descartes introduces the skeptical possibility in what seems to him to be its most radical form, the form of total deception about the correspondence to reality, and thus the truth, of his deepest commitments and beliefs.

Bouwsma's thesis, as I interpret it, is that this hypothesis of total deception, which is made perfectly plausible by the correspondence conception of truth and precisely along the lines Descartes has sketched, is complete nonsense. Because it is nonsense, we must, in throwing out the hypothesis, also abandon the correspondence conception of truth as equally pointless and irrelevant. Bouwsma brings us to this conclusion by establishing two scenarios of deception, both engineered by a deceiving demon.

In the first scenario, the demon creates a situation of partial deception in which the world of the hero of Bouwsma's article, Tom, is changed in one fundamental respect but not in others. The demon changes all forms of matter into paper. But Tom soon sees through this deception by such normal tests of delusionary experience as we use when we decide that the "room" which seems to exist behind a mirror is, in fact, only the reflected image of the room in which we are standing. Similarly, Tom soon comes to realize, by close inspection, touching, listening, sniffing, etc., that his girlfriend Milly has been changed from flesh to paper by the evil genius, and that the flowers on the piano in the room where he greets her, and the piano itself, have been altered in the same way.

Tom's ability to see through the situation of partial deception infuriates the demon, and he decides to transform everything in the universe in such a way that it is totally unlike the way in which Tom thinks he perceives it. Tom is, of course, now completely unaware that any deception is taking place, and he confidently lives his life and arrives at his judgments as before. The devil is extremely frustrated, because Tom is being totally deceived and yet has no awareness of it. So the devil suffuses himself into Tom's mind and whispers to him that he is being totally deceived. This is analogous to Descartes's suspicion that none of his ideas or beliefs, however indisputable they might seem, corresponds to the world as it truly is. The devil explains to Tom that he, the devil, has a sixth sense with which he is able to perceive the true nature of things, and on the basis of that sixth sense he can assure Tom that nothing he perceives is as he thinks it is to be, i.e., none of his beliefs corresponds to the existing facts of the world.

But Tom surprises him by being completely unimpressed by this information. He is unimpressed because he is unconvinced that what the devil is telling him is true. He is unconvinced because no basis on which the devil can persuade him of the truth of his claim is available to him. Everything in his universe is exactly as before, unlike the first scenario in which only some things were altered. The devil may claim that he has a sixth sense showing that none of Tom's beliefs corresponds to reality, but Tom is left in a situation in which he can only take the devil's word for his claim, because he has no evidence available to him that could give the claim independent support. And Tom chooses not to take the devil's word for it.

Tom chooses, in other words, to ignore the possibility of total deception or complete skepticism which so profoundly threatened Descartes's peace of mind. Bouwsma's point is that Tom is perfectly within his rights to do so. A situation of total deception makes no sense, because it allows for no contrasting veridical experiences (such as we might have when we walk behind the mirror and find no room, or touch Milly's hair and find that it has the texture and sound of crepe paper).

Whether our concepts and experiences do or do not correspond to the world as it "really is, in and of itself," is irrelevant and unimportant in exactly the same way. The best criteria we can find or use to separate the truth from error (e.g., consistency, simplicity, coherence, adequacy to experience past and future, fruitfulness) have nothing to do, in the final analysis, with the idea of correspondence, because if they are satisfied, it can make no conceivable difference to us whether the beliefs or claims we have put to their test conform to a supposedly independent, unexperienced, uninterpreted reality. Therefore, we can safely ignore any nihilistic conclusions that seem to follow from assumption of the correspondence conception of truth. What looked like a daunting problem of momentous import to Descartes and others of his time turns out, on Bouwsma's analysis, to be a mere pseudo-problem.[3]

2. THE HEGEMONY OF SCIENCE

I have given the label the *hegemony of science* to the next philosophical assumption to be analyzed and criticized as a source of nihilism. By this phrase, I mean a strong propensity among modern philosophers to accord to the methods and claims of natural science an authority and finality in relation to other domains of thought not very different from that accorded to theology in the Middle Ages. This tendency is especially manifest in three closely related beliefs.

The first belief is that natural science alone is qualified to give an account of the principles and properties of nature. This means that philosophy and other intellectual disciplines have no competency to question the findings of science regarding the natural order but must work entirely within the framework of these findings in conducting their investigations and supporting their conclusions. Whenever these conclusions come into conflict with the claims of science, they must be set aside in favor of views consistent with those of science. Science, by contrast, has no corresponding obligation to attend to the problems, concerns, or findings of philosophy or any other discipline in developing its interpretations of nature.

This conviction that science is entitled to hold a monopoly over the study of nature is undergirded by another belief, discussed in Chapter Three, Section 2: the idea that the methods of natural science are completely impersonal and objective, free of human biases or preconceptions, and wholly uninfluenced by human purposes and values. Thus, the descriptions of nature resulting from the proper employment of these methods are assumed to portray nature as it is in itself, nature as it would remain if humans were entirely removed from the scene. At least as far as physical nature is concerned, according to the general assumption now under discussion, science alone is capable of providing us with reliable descriptions of what Herbert termed the *veritas rei*, or with the closest possible approximations to what we spoke of in the last chapter as the God's-eye view of the world. It is thought to do so with a steadily accumulating fund of theoretical discoveries, progressively revealing the long-hidden secrets of nature and bringing us ever closer to a complete understanding of its fundamental constituents, traits, patterns, and laws.

The third belief that gives expression to the hegemony of science in the modern era is that scientific thinking sets the norm for the proper use of reason. Because it is taken for granted that the methods of natural science constitute the most, if not the only, objective and reliable way of establishing truth, it is believed that philosophy and other disciplines aspiring to exact and well-founded systems of thought should try to emulate or approach science's methods as far as they can. This view soon became dominant in the philosophy of the modern era, and its influence continues to be pervasively felt.

I will focus on the first two of these interconnected beliefs in this section and devote the next chapter to the third one. While intimately linked to the hegemony of science, the third belief is sufficiently distinct, and has had such far-reaching consequences in its own right, as to warrant our treating it as a separate philosophical source of nihilism.

Let us begin with the belief that natural science alone is qualified to give an account of the traits and workings of the natural order. Leclerc connects the emergence of this belief with the new substantialist conception of matter discussed in the previous section. This conception gave legitimacy to the study of the properties and functions of material substance as a separate subject-matter, and helped to give rise to a dualism of matter and spirit explicitly endorsed by Basso and Galileo, systematically developed by Descartes, and carried forward into the outlook of Newton. Concurrent with the growing acceptance of this dualistic outlook, argues Leclerc, a consensus developed about the respective domains of science and philosophy.

The study of nature was now given over entirely to natural science. Science came to be seen as the final arbiter on all questions about the nature of nature. Philosophy, on the other hand, was restricted to what remained after natural science had done its work and reached its conclusions, i.e., the realm of mind or spirit, with a focus on such topics as the epistemological implications of scientific methodology, or the place left for mental activity by the taken-for-granted scientific descriptions of the physical world.

Leclerc notes that one result of this division of labor between science and philosophy was that the philosophy of nature, which had long been a significant subset of philosophy, ceased to exist as a field of investigation. Because science and philosophy each went its separate way, the one attending to matter and the other to spirit, no place was left for ongoing critical inquiry by philosophers into the root categories and assumptions, fundamental approaches, or general claims of natural science regarding the material realm, now viewed as the realm of nature. Instead of having philosophical investigations into the concept of nature as one of its fundamental areas of concern, the closest philosophy could now come to the study of nature was logical and epistemological inquiry into natural science and its methods, i.e., the philosophy of science (Leclerc 1973:159). Until quite recently, even this inquiry has been not so much critical as explicative, and often even obsequious. Science's monopoly over the study of nature meant that it was effectively shielded from fundamental philosophical criticism, including the kind of criticism that seeks to distinguish claims strictly amenable to scientific investigation and support from claims of a more philosophical character that might be assumed or set forth by scientists in the name of science.

A second result of this distribution of fields between science and philosophy, according to Leclerc's analysis, was that science's hegemony over the study of nature soon came to be extended to all topics of study and to all intellectual disciplines, including philosophy. He describes this result as follows:

> [S]cience has come to be accepted, explicitly or implicitly, as the primary and basic enterprise, that by virtue of which positive knowledge is attained— whence this enterprise has been called "science," that is, "knowledge"—and philosophy, in so far as it has retained any relevance to science, is a second-order enterprise, reflecting upon science (1972:351).

Thus, not only did philosophy forfeit responsibility for subjecting emerging scientific descriptions of nature, or the operating assumptions and sometimes sweeping pronouncements of natural scientists, to critical analyses of its own. It also came to acquiesce in a virtual veto power of science over its own type, and all other types, of intellectual endeavor (see Leclerc 1972:226-227, 350-351; 1973:159, 165). This acquiescence amounts to what was earlier called *scientism*, another name for assuming the unrestricted hegemony of science.

This second result indicated by Leclerc was a predictable outcome, for at least two reasons. The first is that the term *nature* can readily be interpreted to mean *the universe*, the all-surrounding context within which every sort of human enterprise, and the totality of cultural experience, occur. Nature construed in this sense comes close to being synonymous with reality, or at least with the most comprehensive way of thinking about reality.[4] The complete hegemony of science over all domains of thought is already implicit, therefore, in the notion that the study of nature is its exclusive prerogative.

I also submit that the allocation of the study of nature entirely to natural science, its accompanying insulation of scientific claims from philosophical criticism, and the expanding hegemony of natural science over all fields of theoretical inquiry was greatly reinforced by the growing conviction among philosophers and others early in the modern era, and continuing well into this century, that scientific methods are completely impersonal and objective and that they yield conclusive results beyond criticism or debate. These methods soon came to be prized as the climactic achievement of the age-old search for a route to veridical knowledge. The general assumption about the hegemony of science has been undergirded, therefore, not only by the substantialist conception of matter and the eclipse of the philosophy of nature Leclerc emphasizes, but also by the second basic belief implying that hegemony characterized earlier.

A good example of what we are talking about, as far as the early modern era is concerned, is Kant's work during his "critical" period. The second section of the previous chapter notes that Kant assumes the finality and completeness of Newtonian physics. On the basis of this assumption, he devotes his *Critique of Pure Reason* to the task, among others, of giving an elaborate philosophical explanation for the possibility of that physics, i.e., to showing the basis in human experience and conceptualization for what he unquestioningly assumes to be the universality and necessity of its root principles and laws. Despite the fact that the scientific descriptions of nature regnant in his own day create enormous problems for the status and significance of morality and freedom, topics of vital import for Kant, he does not think of criticizing the claims of science themselves but struggles with those problems as best he can within the accepted context of Newtonian physics and the concept of nature he believes it to require.

The best he can do is to establish a dualism of two fundamentally distinct kinds of reason and experience, the one appropriate to science and the other to morality and freedom—a strategy that leaves the theoretical study of nature entirely to science and allows to stand uncriticized the scientific picture of nature as a realm in which everything is causally determined and in which, therefore, human purpose or value has no place. We have already noted some of the nihilistic implications of dualistic approaches such as that of Kant, approaches that have the effect, among other things, of cutting off human beings and their cultural aims and values from the natural order and leaving them with no coherent account of their emergence from that order, or of their ability to act upon it or to be influenced by it (see Chapter Three, Section 2).

Russell, in our own time (at least in his two works examined earlier; see the second sections of Chapters Two and Three), operates with a dichotomous vision of the relations between nature and human life similar in important respects to Kant's vision. Like Kant, he assumes the complete hegemony of science over the study of nature and finds no room or sanction in scientific descriptions of nature for the goals and ideals that are of pervasive importance in human cultures. But while Kant gives to moral utterances the cognitive import of a distinct kind of reason he calls "practical reason," Russell denies to these utterances cognitive import of any kind. He also claims, as we saw, that knowledge can only be attained by the methods of science. We noted in previous chapters the cosmic and moral nihilism implicit in Russell's outlook, which is one contemporary version of the thesis of scientism.

Other recent thinkers such as Monod and Skinner also express an attitude toward science similar to that of Kant. But in a manner akin to Russell's allocation of the whole field of knowledge to the domain of science, they extend the hegemony of science beyond the realm of nature to the whole of life. Their strategy is that of trying to accomodate every aspect of human existence to methods and claims of natural science they regard as all-inclusive, nonnegotiable finalities. We noted previously some of the nihilistic consequences of Monod's and Skinner's respective brands of scientism, or unquestioning assumption of the complete hegemony of science.

To take issue with the second philosophical assumption, in the form of the two beliefs expressing it which we have just outlined and illustrated, is to call into question the general line of argument from the scientific conception of nature to nihilistic despair of the meaning of human life. That line of argument was developed in detail in the second section of Chapter Three. What can be said, then, by way of criticizing these two beliefs?

We should note at the outset that the first belief—that natural science alone is equipped to investigate the properties and principles of nature, implying that there is no longer any role or need for the philosophy of nature—is not entailed by recognition of, or proper respect for, the distinctive contributions of modern science. That scientific observations and theories are of critical importance for an understanding of the processes of nature is indisputable, but it is by no means obvious that science's methods of inquiry are the *only* dependable ones for attaining understanding of the nature of nature, or that they should be the *sole* determinants of our outlook on the place of human beings in nature. Even more to the point, the claim that they are cannot be evaluated on scientific grounds. It is not a scientific claim, but a claim about the range and competency of science itself.

The first belief expressive of the hegemony of science is methodological and metaphysical, not strictly scientific, because it makes an allegation about the methods of science taken in their entirety, and one which, if accepted, would wholly determine our concept of nature. This means that the belief is philosophical in character and ought to be assessed on philosophical grounds. It has no direct scientific warrant. There are other ways of viewing scientific method and the metaphysical implications of the claims of science than the view expressed in this belief. It should be emphasized that defense or rejection of this belief is not a defense or rejection of modern science, because the two are independent of one another. The arguments for nihilism based on scientific descriptions of nature are seriously weakened by their tendency to take this first belief for granted and to fail to recognize its debatability and need of defense in the context of relevant philosophical objections and alternatives; or by their tendency to assume without argument that this belief and fitting recognition of the contributions of modern science come down to the same thing.

Leclerc develops, at length, a second way of criticizing the first belief. The thrust of his criticism is that the separation of fields between science and philosophy, in the manner sketched above, has been an unmitigated disaster for both. For not only has philosophy failed to address the conceptual and metaphysical issues relating to nature that fall squarely within its competency; science has also been cut off from the kind of constructive criticisms of its central assumptions and categories that philosophy could provide. What is urgently needed, Leclerc contends, is restoration of the philosophy of nature to its former important position in the intellectual life of our culture, a position it had prior to the scientific revolution and continued to have up to the triumph of Newtonian physics in the eighteenth century (1972:31-32, 227).

Leclerc believes that the recent revolution in physics has produced a ferment of though in which this restoration can be accomplished, because it has brought about a decisive change in scientists' ways of conceiving such fundamental categories as continuity-discontinuity, matter, space, time, and motion, showing thereby that the content given to these categories by Newtonian physics was always debatable and should never have been thought to be immune to basic criticism or alternative conceptualizations. His book is an attempt to set the need for the restoration of the philosophy of nature, with its ongoing critical assessment of scientific descriptions of nature and their implications, in full historical perspective. He makes observations throughout about the logical and metaphysical inadequacy of certain key features of those descriptions, dominant in the science stretching from the period of Newton up to the end of the nineteenth century—features which continue to distort our thinking about nature today.

Furthermore, Leclerc presents an approach to a contemporary philosophy of nature that can not only take seriously into account the findings of recent science and analyze their critical implications for the descriptions of nature in classical science, but can also address the subject of nature with critical and constructive perspectives of its own. Thus, instead of thinking in terms of "two independent enterprises, science and philosophy," with only the first entitled to study nature, we can learn to think of one major enterprise, "the inquiry into nature, having two complementary and mutually dependent aspects" (Leclerc 1972:351). His volume is a sustained argument, persuasively developed in the context of the entire history of change and development in pivotal philosophical and scientific ideas about nature in the West, against the first belief expressing the deeply entrenched philosophical assumption of the hegemony of science, an assumption whose nihilistic consequences we examined earlier.

A third criticism of this first belief calls our attention to the deceptive ambiguity of the key term *nature* and challenges us to deal critically with this ambiguity and its consequences. The term can mean a number of different things, but three meanings are especially important for our purposes. One thing nature can mean is those aspects of experienced reality most amenable to study by the specific techniques of natural science. Another is the whole universe, excepting only human beings (and perhaps God and other spiritual beings, if one believes in such). If the hegemony of science over nature is assumed in connection with this second sense, a dualistic vision of the relation between human beings and a scientifically described nature is implied. A third thing nature can mean is all of reality, i.e., the universe and everything it contains. If nature in this third sense is considered the province solely of natural science, then implicit assent is given to the scientific reductionist view of the relations of humans to a scientifically described nature, the view earlier attributed to Monod and Skinner. I already alluded to the common tendency to assume something like the third sense of the term *nature* when I suggested it as one explanation for the expansion of the hegemony of science from its initial restriction to the study of physical nature to a dominance over all fields of inquiry, including philosophy.[5]

That the second and third meanings of nature are quite different from the first meaning, and that they do not follow from it, or at least not without additional premises, should be obvious. But the patent successes of science in investigating nature in the first sense of the term (especially as exhibited in the rapid technological advances its theories have helped to make possible)[6] have given subtle but powerful psychological impetus to a growing assumption of its hegemony over the study of nature in the second and third senses as well. I contend that failure to recognize and critically weigh the consequences of the ambiguity of the term *nature* has aided this process; therefore, it can be regarded as one important element in uncritical acquiescence in the hegemony of science on the part of philosophers and others. The fact that little argument is needed to defend science's entitlement to the study of nature in the first sense of the term does not mean that investigation of nature in the second or third senses must also be confined to science's special competency.

I want now to suggest, by way of further development of this third line of argument, that the most reasonable way of understanding the province of natural science is to associate it with the first sense of the term *nature*, and then explicitly to acknowledge that this first sense is partial or selective and does not encompass the usual, more extended meaning or meanings of that term. By restricting the province of science—though not the whole meaning of nature—in this way, we resist the marked tendency of our culture to assume the hegemony of science over the study of nature, while still giving the role and contributions of natural science their due. Furthermore, this approach places us in a position to see clearly that the dualism and reductionism we connected with the extension of the dominion of science to the two other meanings of nature are not the only options left to us by scientific descriptions of nature. The supposition that they are, which is implicit in the arguments from the scientific view of nature to nihilism discussed in Chapter Three, is then seen to be an offshoot of unanalyzed and implausible belief in the hegemony of science. Let us examine this third argument in more detail.

First, what part of nature, or what aspects of experienced reality, can we conclude to fall most particularly within the province of natural science, or to be most suitable for investigation by its special approaches and techniques? Because I have addressed an issue akin to this one elsewhere, I borrow from that work some statements about the types of phenomena that seem to fit this description most closely. Such phenomena will be "predictable and experimentally repeatable under controlled conditions," and "can be shown to be caused or grounded in some precise and regular way" or to "exhibit unvarying correlations with other specified phenomena." Moreover, such phenomena "can be made explicable by reference to a system of well established, highly general laws," or more ideally, their "occurrence in specified situations can be *deduced* as entailments of well established, highly general laws of nature . . . " (emphasis added). In addition, such phenomena will be those whose putatively regular and lawlike occurrences and correlations, as interpreted and predicted by scientific theories, can not only be confirmed in an exact empirical manner, but are also (again, ideally) open to decisive disconfirmation by conceivable empirical events clearly excluded by the predictions of the theories (Crosby 1983:247). The emphasis on deducibility, exactitude of formulation, and a high level of measurable accuracy in the predictions of scientific theories suggests that scientific analyses and explanations should be couched, whenever possible, in quantative or mathematical terms. In summary, the aspects of experienced reality most amenable to investigation by the special techniques of natural science will be those which exhibit (or can be shown to exhibit) exact lawlike regularity and predictability; those which can be made subject to confirmation or disconfirmation by precisely designed, carefully controlled experiments; and those which are exactly measurable and quantifiable.[7]

It is possible, of course, that this description applies not merely to a part of nature or experienced reality, but to everything. And there are those who claim that it does. But no conclusive evidence is available for the truth of this claim at present, and much in our experience seems to militate against it (more about this later). It seems eminently reasonable, therefore, to regard natural science as highly selective, in the sense of focusing on some aspects of experienced reality at the expense of others, and as gaining much of its exactitude, rigor, and success at the price of having to ignore crucial aspects or dimensions of that reality taken in its full complexity and concreteness. Morton Kaplan calls attention to the selectiveness of physics and notes the usefulness of this selectiveness when he muses, "The physicist would be hard put to intuit his universal laws if the physical entities he had to work with were contaminated by the operation of the large numbers of variables belonging to other disciplines" (1971:96). To view natural science in this way is to reject the claim to its hegemony over the study of nature in the second and third senses of that term indicated above. It is to deny to it the role of presenting the God's-eye view of the physical universe and to regard it instead as one perspective on nature among others, a restricted, partial view that needs to be complemented by other important angles of vision.

Further clarification and support for this thesis about the perspectival limitations of natural science can be garnered from another direction: by critical reflection on the second belief expressive of the hegemony of science. For the selectiveness of science can be seen not only in light of its restriction to particular aspects of nature, but also in light of the wider context its methods presuppose. My reflections on this topic can be considered a fourth argument against the hegemony of science. Once these reflections have been brought to view, I will return to the supposition that dualism or scientific reductionism are the only options left to us by scientific descriptions of nature and explain more fully why this supposition is mistaken.

This fourth argument relates most specifically to the second belief conveying the assumption of the hegemony of science: the belief that the methods of science are completely detached and impersonal, capable of interpreting the properties of nature in a purely objective manner, with no distortion of human preferences or values. The criticism is partly that this view is an unsupportable idealization of scientific method and of the results of scientific research. More fundamentally, it overlooks the fact that science is a human endeavor and, as such, the outcome of fallible and debatable human perspectives, commitments, and decisions. Any attempt to free science from this human basis amounts to an attempt to undermine science's own foundations.

This point could be defended in many ways. I will briefly indicate two ways of arguing for it here. I begin by noting a paradox implicit in Monod's restriction of reason to scientific reasoning (see Chapter Three, Section 2). His act of restriction implies a capacity of reason to reflect on its own scope and significance, a capacity of self-awareness and self-criticism to which Aristotle's phrase "thinking on thinking" could apply. But this reflexive power of reason, which Monod's plea for complete objectivity presupposes, belies his confinement of reason to strictly impersonal, formal modes of thought, because it is an informal power that encompasses and attributes significance to those very modes of thought.

Monod is aware of this paradox and tries to take it into account, but he does not resolve it. He recognizes that science is impossible without giving supreme *value* to the so-called postulate of objectivity. However, because he insists that values can have no rational character or defense (by which he means they can admit of no *scientific* justification), he is driven to conclude that science, for him the sole paradigm of objective rationality, is grounded in a completely subjective and nonrational commitment. And he is content to leave the matter there. Consequently, he does not so much resolve the paradox as cast in into bold relief. His inability to eliminate this paradox in his thinking should warn us that something is fundamentally wrong with the scientistic attempt to restrict reasoning to scientific reasoning and radically to separate fact from value. It should also alert us to the untenability of the claim that the methods and findings of science are completely detached and objective.

This paradox in Monod's explication and defense of scientism confirms Barrett's allegation that formal techniques of reasoning have significance only in wider contexts of human commitment, belief, action, and purpose, showing that they are not as detched, self-sufficient, or all-encompassing as scientism thinks them to be. Barrett comments that "every technique is put to use for some end, and this end is decided in the light of some philosophic outlook or other. The technique cannot produce the philosophy that directs it" (1979:117). Weil makes a similar observation when he remarks that science is "possible only in a structured and meaningful world," a world where purpose and value play a fundamental role. He goes on to insist that it "is an absurd wish to reduce understanding to science," because "science is a human activity in a world that man *understands* and *understood* before he tried to *know* it scientifically (1965:183, 185).

Scientific reasoning *per se* is as far from being all-inclusive as it is from being completely objective and detached, because it can do little justice to the larger contexts of significance, evaluation, and choice within which it operates and acquires its meaning. Those who regularly employ scientific reasoning need not concern themselves with its assumptional basis or raise any probing philosophical questions about its competency or scope. They can be content to take that basis for granted and to inquire into the selected aspects of experience that science's methods of inquiry are competent to illuminate, without having to concern themselves with the whole. By doing so, and accepting the trade-off of selectiveness for the sake of clarity and precision, scientists have enjoyed considerable success, both in the way of theoretical understanding and of technological innovation.

The implication of this first part of our argument against the second belief expressive of the hegemony of science, then, is that scientific methods and scientific knowledge are meaningless and inexplicable if taken by themselves; they presuppose the broader background of understanding of which Barrett and Weil speak, and which even Monod is forced reluctantly to acknowledge, an informal, valuative, and purposive background. To restrict the scope of reliable reason to detached, formal, "objective" modes of thought is fatal to science itself, because it deprives science of any rational basis. Henry James's statement about the proponents of scientism in his own time is highly pertinent, reminding us of the restricted scope of scientific reasoning: "the blunder of the savants was in fancying that science *contained* rather than *being contained*..." (paraphrased by Brooks 1932:176).

The second part of our present argument calls attention to the role of informal imagination and invention in the design and confirmation of scientific theories in and of themselves, quite apart from the wider contexts of significance just emphasized. We thus bring into question in another way the second belief expressing the assumption about the hegemony of science.

Fundamental theories of science are not simply "discovered" or read out of the world, nor are they typically arrived at on the basis of strict logic or formal algorithms. It is widely recognized today that such theories accord a central role to models, analogies, and conjectures that must be recognized as constructs of the creative imagination. Leon Brillouin states the point succinctly and well:

> As soon as we abandon the familiar ground of terrestrial experiments practiced on a human scale upon inanimate objects, our mind is suddenly faced with incomprehensible facts. The role of imagination then becomes preponderant: astronomy, geology, ultimate particles or nuclei, finally biology—in all these fields strict logic is no longer sufficient. Down-to-earth reasoning fails, and imagination rules (1964:45).

In fact, formal modes of reasoning, such as the various systems of mathematics, can be regarded as one type of model or imaginative construct, some versions of which have proved useful for interpreting certain aspects of experience. The invention of these mathematical models does not admit of formal derivation or explanation; it cannot be "objectively" accounted for.

Furthermore, because the network of theories believed to be true at any time helps to dictate the nature and significance of those "facts" called upon for their confirmation, not even the empirical confirmations of scientific theories can be said to be free from the coloration and influence of informal modes of reasoning. Operative here are not only the crucial imaginative factors in the theories themselves, but also the values, purposes, and decisions implicit in every phase of scientific theorizing. The putative facts, says Weil, depend "on the scientist's axioms, and the choice of these axioms is actually a choice, in other words, a value judgment." Hence, there is some deep sense in which "facts become relevant only through values." No theoretical choices "would be imaginable," he continues, "in a magma of facts, nor could there be choice under conditions of total value entropy" (1965:182-183). A moment's reflection should also convince us that facts can have significance only in the context of scientific inquiry taken as a purposive activity of human beings. Thus, not only are the confirmations of scientific theories to a significant extent theory-laden, they are also in some important sense value-laden.[8]

If we forget that science is partial or restricted in the ways described or assume that its methods and results can somehow escape the fallibility of all things human, we can be easily seduced by the notion that its descriptions of nature leave us with only two alternatives for understanding the relation of human beings to nature: dualism or scientific reductionism. We then either set human beings and their mental and cultural life in sharp opposition to a scientifically described nature, supposing that description to be comprehensive and final, or we try to bring human existence wholly within the compass of nature as scientifically described. In either event, we are well on the way to nihilism, because neither of these options, for reasons presented in Chapter Three, allows a meaningful place to human beings in the natural order.

It is essential to see that these two options fail as metaphysical interpretations, and not only because they lead to the *reductio ad absurdum* of nihilism. Another measure of their failure is that neither is able to account for the possibility of science itself. Dualism fails because it tries to pack everything left out of the scientific interpretation of nature into a completely distinct order of being. As a consequence of its dichotomizing of reality, it can give no explanation for the interactions between humans and nature that must be presupposed if we are to think ourselves capable of understanding anything about the natural order. Scientific reductionism fails because it can give no significant role to the purposes and values implicit in the very acts of scientific theorizing, a theorizing that makes sense only if it is the activity of beings who are free to weigh alternatives and to choose among them in light of reasons, or even more fundamentally, to value the process of free and rational inquiry.

Obviously, something has gone wrong when we think that dualism or scientific reductionism are the only two metaphysical possibilities left to us once science has done its work. This section's thesis is that the heart of the problem is a misperception of the competency of natural science. With Leclerc, we conclude that natural science cannot, by itself, give an adequate philosophy of nature, a field of study that must be understood as a major subdivision of the philosophical enterprise known as metaphysics.[9] In contrast with science, which I have argued to be selective and to gain its specific competency and success at the price of its selectiveness, metaphysics must aspire to encompass the full complexity, range, and depth of human experience and thought—not only the lawlike, mathematical, precisely testable aspects emphasized by natural science, but all the other aspects as well, aspects such as aesthetic insight and expression, the sense of moral value and responsibility, and the central existential challenges and concerns off human life.

Metaphysical visions are abstract in their own way, of course, but their kind of perspectivity is different from that of science. Metaphysicians search for schemes of interpretation that can be called *generically abstract* i.e., ones designed to provide highly general, unifying perspectives on the whole of our experience, in all its distinctive dimensions and varieties of cultural expression. The import of the arguments above is that natural science must be regarded as *selectively abstract*, in the sense of deliberately highlighting particular aspects of experience (such as those we mentioned) and paying little or no explicit attention to others.

It is an egregious mistake, therefore, to regard natural science, a discipline by its very method and approach selectively abstract, as constituting, or somehow substituting for, a comprehensive philosophy of nature and of the role of human beings in nature. Dewey correctly insists that all significant modes of experiencing, and not just those focused on by natural science, "are ways in which some genuine traits of nature come to manifest realization." He rightly warns us against the folly of categorically denying reality or importance to that which happens to be omitted because it "is not relevant to the particular problem and purpose" of a given selective emphasis, such as that of natural science (1958:24-25). Both dualism and scientific reductionism, each in its own way, fall prey to this mistake of confusing selective abstraction with generic comprehensiveness, because both assume the complete metaphysical adequacy of the scientific description of nature. This mistake has plagued the thinking and general outlook of Western culture from the time of the scientific revolution to the present.

Other metaphysical approaches are available that do greater justice to the possibility of science itself than either dualism or reductionism can. They also do a much better job of accounting for the place and significance of human life and experience within the natural order. For example, there is the organic, emergentist model of nature and of the status of human beings in nature developed by Whitehead in the 1920s and 1930s, principally in his cosmological essay, *Process and Reality*. Whitehead's model is neither dualistic nor reductionistic. The distinction between human beings and other aspects of nature is one of degree, rather than kind; yet it is a distinction allowing a fundamental role to consciousness, value, and freedom. It is both *panpsychist* and *panphysicalist* in its conception of nature and of the whole of reality, thus breaking down the hard-and-fast distinction between these two realms argued for by dualism. It posits no rigid separation of fact and value, causality and freedom, but seeks to illuminate the dialectical interplay of these factors in experience. It gives an important place to the findings of science in the construction of its theory of reality but regards those findings as only one important source of evidence. Thus it can draw extensively on the results of science without succumbing to scientism or making the mistake of assuming the unqualified hegemony of natural science.

Whitehead's metaphysical vision is not without its problems, but I would argue that it more closely approximates what a coherent and adequate metaphysical scheme would need to accomplish than does either dualism or reductionism. My purpose here, however, is not so much to defend the superiority of this scheme as to call attention to it as one important alternative that is overlooked when we assume that dualism or reductionism are the only two options made available to us by the scientific perspective on nature. Other metaphysical alternatives could also be discussed,[10] but mention of this one should suffice to make the point.

If we take seriously the debatability of some of the assumptions built into arguments from the methods and discoveries of modern science to the nihilistic outlook on human life—particularly the debatability of the assumption of the hegemony of science discussed in this section—then I think that much of the disruptive force of these arguments will be dissolved and that they will come to be seen in a different, more critical light. The generally unspoken and unexamined beliefs and predilections on which these arguments rest are by no means the only source of nihilism in our time, but they do represent one major source. For ours is not only an age of science; it tends to be an age of scientism as well.

Chapter 8

Truth Through Method and Seeds of Nihilism in the Thought of Descartes

. . . it were far better never to think of investigating truth at all than to do so without a method.

—René Descartes (1967:I,9)

In the last chapter I stated the third philosophical assumption which now will be analyzed as a major source of nihilism. One of three beliefs expressing the hegemony of science in the modern period, it is the conviction that philosophy and other disciplines aspiring to exact and well-founded systems of thought must employ to the fullest possible extent the methods of analysis and proof employed in natural science.

This belief has not only fundamentally affected the general strategies and specific contents of modern philosophy, it has also exerted a profound influence on developments in other disciplines and become one of the dominant themes of modern thought. Some of these other disciplines, such as sociology and psychology, are themselves relatively recent offshoots of philosophy (just as natural science had been earlier), and their emergence as separate fields of inquiry can be traced in significant measure to this third philosophical assumption. The strategies and contents of modern philosophy, and of modern thought as a whole, that have grown out of this assumption contain certain nihilistic tendencies that I will examine critically against the background of the arguments for nihilism discussed in earlier chapters.

The first section of this chapter considers some significant differences—and some important similarities—between the medieval method of inquiry and what in the modern period came to be understood as the scientific method. This discussion sets the stage for an examination, in the second section, of the concerted effort on the part of René Descartes to apply the method of natural science to his own research in philosophy.

I give considerable attention to Descartes because his thought bequeaths to his successors, or at least articulates with extraordinary clarity, the general context and problematic within which most modern philosophy (and much of modern Western culture as well) has developed. To adapt Whitehead's well-known statement about Plato, the history of modern philosophy to the present day can be regarded as a series of footnotes to Descartes. (Descartes is also a Platonist in many respects, but that is another story.) An examination of his philosophical system will uncover some implicit nihilistic themes that stand in marked contrast to its tone of confident rationalism. These themes stem to a significant extent, I argue, from Descrates's search for philosophical truth through scientific method, and they have loomed large in later thought. Some of the themes have already been anticipated; others are further elaborated in Chapters Nine and Ten, where they are discussed as additional philosophical sources of nihilism.

1. MEDIEVAL AND MODERN METHODS

I begin by noting three differences between the method of natural science, or what modern thinkers have generally considered that method to be, and the method for arriving at truth characteristic of the Middle Ages. A first important contrast turns on the fact that the medieval method sought to trace implications and connections of truths already accepted as such, and accepted largely on the basis of the teachings of the Bible and long-standing ecclesiastical tradition. Any claim to truth, in order to have a chance of acceptance by scholars of the day, had to be consistent with these two paramount sources of authority. There was also a strong tendency for the mantle of authority to be thrown over those philosophical approaches with which biblical interpretations and ecclesiastical traditions had come to be skillfully interwoven at various stages in the development of medieval thought, approaches such as those of Plato, Aristotle, and Plotinus.

The medieval method was, therefore, decidedly heteronomous in character. Its orientation was toward past authority, and it was intent upon systematically interpreting and clarifying the central claims of that authority with respect to all subject matters, including that of nature. This reliance on antecedent authority was pervasive in the Middle Ages, even though thinkers of the period did pay a modicum of attention to the evidence of the senses and to what were thought to be self-evident principles of reason.

Scientific method, on the other hand, was conceived from the time of its inception as a means for finding truths as yet unknown. Galileo, for example, contrasts this method with the method of Aristotelian logic, claiming that the latter is useful for assessing the consistency and validity of our reasoning, but not for making fresh discoveries (see Burtt 1954:76). The new method was assumed to be oriented toward the future rather than the past, and its essential spirit was seen as one of autonomous inquiry and new discovery rather than reliance on accepted authority.

After some of its striking initial successes, it was soon taken for granted that scientific method would overturn many of the entrenched beliefs of the past about the structures and workings of the natural order by putting these beliefs to the test of experiment and firsthand critical reflection. "[I]n the discussion of natural problems," says Galileo in a letter to the Grand Duchess Christina in 1615, "we ought not to begin at the authority of places of scripture, but at sensible experiments and necessary demonstrations" (quoted Burtt 1954:83).

A second notable difference between the two methods is one of focus. The focus of medieval method was upon issues of value, purpose, and existential fulfilment. John Herman Randall, Jr., says of one of the principal practitioners of this method, Thomas Aquinas, that the aim of his thought "was wisdom, a comprehension of the meaning and significance of things, above all of the chief end of man, the meaning of human life and of all creation as related to it; and hence its object was that which alone gave purpose to existence, God" (1976:98-99). By contrast with this preoccupation with values and ends, purposes and meanings—issues indispensably relevant to the daily lives of human beings—the emphasis of scientific method, as viewed at the dawn of the modern age, is on the properties of material substance and the workings of efficient causes; the discovery of highly general laws that can describe, predict, and explain the functionings of physical substances and the patterns of their causal interactions in an exact, comprehensive manner; the "how" rather than the "why" of nature's operations.

Thus, while the method of the Middle Ages was greatly concerned with human beings and little interested in the study of nature as a subject matter in its own right, the method of the new science fixed its gaze on physical nature and paid little attention to human life and its special problems and interests. The medieval method made the needs, purposes, and concerns of human beings the key to its interpretations of the universe; the scientific method tended to exclude human beings altogether from its concept of nature, thereby leaving the problem to philosophy of how to find a place for humans in, or in relation to, the natural order.

A third distinction between the two methods bears on the role of mathematics and the related issue of whether nature should be pluralistically or uniformly conceived. The medieval method paid slight attention to mathematical analysis or reasoning. Its concern was to understand the qualitative essences of things and the modes of interrelation of different types of substantial entities defined by their various qualitative essences. This method was informed by the assumption that these different types of substances taken as a whole constituted tier upon tier of irreducibly distinct levels of being and value, all of them ordered by and subservient to the highest Being, God. It took for granted, therefore, the twin notions that the universe was a domain of quality and value, and that it was a hierarchically ordered, pluralistic domain, consisting of fundamentally different levels or grades of being.

Scientific method, on the other hand, was generally considered to be mathematical to the core. Physical nature, regarded as this method's special topic of study, also came to be viewed as mathematical or quantitative in its essential character, a view related to the new notion of physical substances as existing in their own right, discussed earlier. Thus, Galileo can speak admiringly of nature as a "grand book... written in the language of mathematics, its characters... triangles, circles, and other geometrical figures without which it is humanly impossible to understand a single word of it..." (*Assayer*, 1623, quoted by Nelson, in Gingrich 1975:370-371, n. 10). Accordingly, the new method searched for mathematical principles of interpretation and explanation that would apply to the universe as a whole, from its tiniest terrestrial details to the most distant reaches of astral space. The guiding principle of this method was belief in the uniformity of a nature whose constitutive physical substances were everywhere the same: mathematical or quantitative in their essential character. This conviction implied the reducibility of all of nature's complexity, variety, and splendor to a small set of mathematically formulated, universally applicable principles and laws. To achieve this elegant and sweeping reduction was the basic task of scientific method.

These three differences are familiar and have been discussed widely. What is perhaps not so commonly recognized or taken into account is the point made by Randall that, despite such important and far-reaching differences, there are also some basic similarities in the two methods.

One context in which Randall makes this point is his noting the wonder and admiration that spread through the educated classes of Europe on learning of feats of science such as Newton's deduction of Kepler's inductive law of planetary motion from his own general principle of gravitation. These feats did not alter but instead gave new impetus to "the medieval Thomistic and Aristolelian ideal of a body of knowledge that could be deductive, universal, and infallible, one great logical system . . . ." Randall continues, saying that the new science

> had only, as in Descartes and Spinoza, changed its type from the syllogistic logic of Aristotle to the geometrical propositions of Euclid. Such a science must be founded, like geometry, upon a small number of definitely true

axioms, from which every law of nature will follow deductively; and it is characteristic of the eighteenth-century[1] scientific ideal that, however much it might turn to experience to suggest these axioms, and to formulate the specific laws governing phenomena, no law was regarded as conclusively established until it could be fitted into such a great universal deductive system (1976:261).

A good example of what Randall has in mind is Kepler's contention that of a number of likely hypotheses about experienced facts, that hypothesis is true which explains why these facts, which in the other hypotheses remain diverse and unrelated, are as they are through rational demonstration of their orderly mathematical connections. By this test, Kepler argues, the Copernican hypothesis has to be seen as true, in contrast to its Ptolemaic alternative (see Burtt 1954:65). One great similarity between the medieval and scientific methods, then, is that both aimed for systems of thought every aspect of which could be deductively derived from a foundation of complete certainty.

A second important similarity is that the correspondence conception of truth continued to be assumed, and with it, the ideal of attaining a nonperspectival, God's-eye view of the physical world—in the case of scientific method, by precise mathematical reasoning and exact experiential tests. Galileo gives expression to both the conception of truth and the ideal of knowledge when he states that whatever can be said of nature in the discourse of mathematics portrays its structures and functionings with objective certainty, in complete independence of fallible human judgments; and that God Himself can have no clearer knowledge of what mathematical analysis and demonstration enable us to comprehend. This is expected, because God, the great Geometrician, has created the entire world according to rigorous principles of mathematical necessity (see Randall 1976:237; Burtt 1954:75, 82). The only difference from the Middle Ages is that mathematics, not the Bible, ecclesiastical tradition, or reasoning from qualitative essences, is now the basis on which the search for absolute certainty and the God's-eye view of the world is fervently conducted. Even the idea of deducing the facts of experience from fundamental principles and laws is not entirely new; it is closely akin to Aristotle's concept of scientific demonstration, as set forth in his *Posterior Analytics*. But once again, it is the ideal of restricting these fundamental principles and laws to those which can be mathematically formulated or derived that is different.

Randall provides an apt statement of this second similarity when he says that scientists were trying, through their modern method of investigation, "to reach an absolute system of truth quite independent of any limitations of . . .[human] mental powers. . . ." Seeking "that complete and perfect understanding and explanation of the universe that only a God could possess . . . , [t]heir ideal was still a *system of revelation*, although they had abandoned the *method* of revelation" (1976:267). Therefore, from the side of modern science and of the modern philosophy with which it is intimately connected, we have continuing emphasis on the search for certain foundations, the objectivist conception of truth and meaning, and the ideal of attaining a God's-eye view of the world—themes which Chapter Six associated with the influence of religion.

With these contrasts and comparisons of the medieval and scientific methods in mind, let us try to formulate more concisely how the nature of scientific method was conceived by thinkers of the early modern period. Two components of the new method are fundamental; they stand out clearly in Galileo's insistence on "sensible experiments and necessary demonstrations" in seeking truths about nature. Thus, scientific method has an empirical side and a deductive side; these two aspects helped to inspire the two movements in modern philosophy that came to be known as empiricism and rationalism. Each movement was an attempt to apply what is regarded as the most important or usable aspect of the scientific method to the study of human beings and human institutions.

Two additional points must be made about the scientific method before discussing ways in which Descartes sought to apply or adapt this method to problems in his own field and considering some of the tendencies toward nihilism implicit in his procedure and its results. One of these points has to do with the role of reductive analysis. In a manner similar to Aristotle's notion that a basic step in scientific demonstration is resolution of substances under study to their essential properties or formal causes, both Galileo and Newton explicitly emphasize the need to reduce experienced phenomena to their mathematical properties or elements, so they can be brought within the realm of mathematical deductions and demonstrations. Only when our sensate experiences are resolved into their quantifiable aspects, Galileo insists, have we penetrated to their true essences, or to the "alphabet" of physical nature seen as a great book of mathematics (see Burtt 1954:78-81, 208-212, 220-221).

A second point is the emphasis placed by scientific method on the highest possible mathematical exactitude in the confirmation of hypotheses. Just as this method begins by reducing experienced phenomena to their mathematical aspects, so it concludes by testing its hypotheses by mathematiclly precise experiments. This way of testing hypotheses is an important point of difference from the medieval method for establishing truth. Kepler rejected his own splendid theory of the planet Mars, for example, on account of a small discrepancy of eight minutes between some of his conclusions and the exact empirical studies of Tycho Brahe on which he relied. As Burtt points out, no medieval thinker would have insisted on such strict confirmation of theory to observed facts (1954:61; see also 64). In summary, then, not only does the method of science combine deductive and empirical elements; its deductive aspect is mathematical, and its empirical aspect requires resolution of sensed phenomena into mathematical properties and the testing of hypotheses in accordance with extremely high standards of quantitative exactitude.

Why were modern philosophers so intent upon employing the method of science, or some close approximation of that method as they understood it, in their own discipline? Why did they acquiesce so easily in the the third philosophical assumption which is this chapter's topic? One reason is that science and philosophy were not as clearly separated as they later came to be. Only gradually were their provinces distinguished along the lines Leclerc describes and which were discussed in the preceding chapter. But this cannot be the complete explanation, because this third assumption continued to be made by seventeenth- and eighteenth-century philosophers after most of them had come to conceive of their field as that of mind or spirit rather than the study of physical nature, now restricted to natural science.

Some other explanations can be briefly indicated. One of them, no doubt, was the philosophers' desire to have their own discipline and their own constructive theories share in the certainty, progress, and prestige increasingly associated with the emerging physical science. Another was their need to find an authoritative method on whose basis they could develop and defend the new worldview that seemed to be demanded by the scientific revolution and counter the worldview of their medieval forebears. Philosophers also required a method for establishing truth with which they could respond to the threatening currents of a recently revived skepticism, a subject referred in the Chapter Seven. Also of critical importance were the social, political, and economic factors involved in the demise of feudalism and the emergence of the middle class, with its nationalistic sentiments, desire for free trade, and critical attitudes toward existing authorities and institutions. These factors stimulated the search among philosophers for new foundations for social theory and practice, and the method of science lay ready at hand for that purpose.

2. SEEDS OF NIHILISM IN DESCARTES

Rationalistic philosophers characteristically emphasize the mathematical or deductive side of scientific method when attempting to apply that method to problems in philosophy. Accordingly, they hold up the model of mathematical reasoning as the ideal to be aspired toward in philosophical reflection and argumentation. In the case of Descartes, the distinction between *philosophy* proper and *natural philosophy* (physical science) was not as clearly drawn as it came to be later, especially after the 1687 publication of Newton's *Philosophiae Naturalis Principia Mathematica*. Descartes was not simply a philosopher but a physicist in his own right and a mathematician of the highest rank. He applied the method of science, with principal stress on its deductive side, to problems in physics as well as to problems in epistemology, philosophy of mind, and metaphysics.

He believed that because this method had worked so well in its applications to physical nature, as could be seen in the spectacular discoveries of Copernicus, Kepler, and Galileo, it was only reasonable to believe that it would work as well in other domains. As Randall says, Descartes was the one "who formulated, generalized, and popularized Galileo's ideas." One result was that by the time of his death in 1650, Descartes "had spread the fame of the mathematical interpretation of nature through the length and breadth of Europe..." (Randall 1976:222, 240). Another result was that he had popularized Galileo's concept of scientific method (or at least his own interpretation of it), as well as winning many converts to his fervent conviction that this method should be applied throughout philosophy.

The first feature of this method, as Descartes construes it, is that it requires us to rid ourselves of reliance on custom, authority, or unanalyzed assumption and belief, by resolving to accept as true only that which cannot be doubted and to reject as false whatever admits of doubt even in the slightest degree. Because our senses sometimes deceive us, we must also resolve not to trust them until our reason gives us firm license to do so. We must raze the edifice of our former beliefs just as one levels a house in order to rebuild it when its underpinnings have been discovered to be dangerously insecure. Starting anew, we must build only on a foundation of absolute certainty, if we can find materials out of which to construct such a foundation (1967:I, 89). This first feature of Descartes's method recalls the spirit of the new science, which overturned so many cherished beliefs of the past about the natural order, challenged in many crucial respects what seemed to be the direct evidence of the senses, and set out boldly on its own to erect a radically different view of the universe on the basis of its innovative method of discovery and proof.

The second important trait of Descrates's method is that it is modeled on the mathematical aspect of the scientific approach to knowledge. It therefore eschews mere probability and demands a deductive mode of argumentation throughout. In his search for a method, says Descartes, "Most of all was I delighted with mathematics because of the certainty of its demonstrations and the evidence of its reasoning" (I, 85). Just as mathematical reasoning lay at the heart of the new science, Descartes makes it the guiding exemplar for the kind of reasoning he incorporates into his method. He views this method as capable of solving problems not only in the realms of geometry and physics, which it already had or was now beginning to do, but in every area of human conceptualization and experience.

Descartes had used his method with great success, he points out, in his invention of analytic geometry, with which he had achieved a remarkable synthesis of the formerly separate areas of geometry and algebra (I, 93-94). The ideal there exhibited, of making principles and truths of different domains conform "to the uniformity of a rational scheme" (I, 89), is his ideal of deductive demonstration and comprehensive deductive systems of knowledge modeled on mathematics. As we saw earlier, it was also the ideal assumed by Kepler, who argued on its basis for the conclusion that Copernicus's system was true and Ptolemy's, false.

A third important feature of Descartes's method is its movement from analysis to synthesis. Just as Galileo had insisted that we must resolve our sensate experiences into their quantitative aspects in order to make them amenable to mathematical deductions, so Descartes contends that we must resolve our thinking into its simplest constituents and then build deductively from these constituents the whole structure of knowledge in any field. Thus, in his view, a system of genuine knowledge can be broken down into discrete units and then put back together again, piece by piece—disassembled and reassembled as often as we wish, like a machine.

With regard to knowledge, the separate units are what Descartes calls "clear and distinct ideas," or those "certain germs of truth which are naturally existent in our souls" (1967:I, 121). Commencing with these objects that are "the most simple and easy to understand," we can then rise "little by little, or by degrees, to knowledge of the most complex," thus carrying on our reflections step-by-step and "in due order" until (as he expresses it in his *Principles of Philosophy*, first published in 1644) we "acquire in time a perfect knowledge of the whole of philosophy and attain to the highest degree of wisdom" (I, 92, 214).

One is again reminded of the analogy of a machine, although the metaphor most immediately in Descartes's mind seems to be that of mathematical systems such as Euclidian geometry or his own analytic geometry. These geometries and machines are examples of closed, formal systems such as that for which Descartes aimed in philosophical reasoning. Both require that there be an invariant progression or sequencing from simple parts and subroutines to more complex ones, and then to the final outcome: the entire complex of interlocking theorems in geometry and the smooth interworkings of the parts to produce the dependable running of the whole, in the case of a machine.[2]

But where in Descartes's thinking is the role of that other component of the method of science, the emphasis on exact empirical testing of hypotheses? He admits that the principles and relationships discoverable by his deductive method are highly general and that they cannot explain every particular fact of experience, in the sense of showing not merely why those facts *might* occur but why they *must* occur as they do, or why they could not be otherwise. To have knowledge of such particular facts we can only rely on our experience, but it is an experience that must be carefully controlled or purified by reason; we should not jump to conclusions, and the senses have a tendency to make us want to do that. Moreover, we should have always in mind the ideal of deducing as many facts of experience from first principles as we possibly can (I, 121). Our inability to derive every recognized fact from the innate potentialities of our minds is for Descartes a limitation of the human mind that we cannot overcome. It is a limitation because the ideal of knowledge for him, as we have seen, is inclusion of every truth in the taut coherence of a deductive scheme, i.e., its certain, unequivocal derivation from the first principles of that scheme.

The facts of experience that cannot be deductively derived are on a low level of truth for Descartes; he is somewhat embarrassed by them. He is much more interested in those "primary and most ordinary" (most pervasive and regular) experienced effects that can be deduced by proper employment of his method (I, 121). Experiencing the more particular facts can assist us in developing deductive schemes, however, by stimulating us to become aware of the mind's own innate principles. These particular facts can also provide approximate or rough tests of the results of those schemes in the sense that, because these particular experiences are possible (as is shown by their occurrence), the deductive scheme must be able to account for their possibility (though it cannot account for their actuality).

In conclusion, then, Descartes's ideal of knowledge is that of deduction and absolute certainty; he is little interested in mere probabilities. He speaks with disdain at one place in his *Discourse* of "those who do not know the force of mathematical demonstration and are unaccustomed to distinguish *true reasons* from merely probable reasons..." (I, 112; emphasis added). The medieval schoolmen had been content with showing how things might be (I, 86, 125); Descartes wanted to show, whenever humanly possible, how they must be. He saw this as the aim both of physics and of philosophy.[3]

Some consequences of Descartes's application of scientific method to metaphysical problems are my next concern. In this deparment of philosophy, he earnestly seeks for, and is firmly convinced that through patient application of his method he has achieved, a certainty that surpasses even the certainty to be found in geometry (I, 106, 135). Geometry has to rely on postulates whose truth, in the sense of correspondence to the real world, admit of at least some degree of doubt. The same disturbing degree of doubt attaches to mathematical physics. Descartes's boast as a physicist is, "Give me extension and motion, and I will construct the universe" (Randall 1976:241-242). But if the findings of physics are to be put on a ground of absolute certainty, an even more fundamental Archimedean point is required, an assurance that the compelling deductions of mathematics and mathematical physics are not merely reflective of the makeup of our minds but of the structures of the objective world.

In his major metaphysical treatise, *Meditations on the First Philosophy* (1641), Descartes asserts that he has found this Archimedean point in his inability to deny his own existence, no matter how strenuously he tries to detect at least some shadow of doubt in his belief in that existence. Doubt anything whatever as he will, implicit in this very act of doubting is the absolute assurance of the existence of that doing the doubting. From this bedrock certainty he goes on to exhibit the existence of a perfect God, and therefore, a God who cannot be a Deceiver, as well as the essential properties of mental and physical substance and the existence of the real world of matter physics purports to describe. By applying his method of radical doubt unflinchingly, he exults in having triumphed in the end. He has run the risk of losing the whole world, but has now richly regained it and made his most basic convictions immune to any further assault.

We cannot doubt the sincerity of Descartes's confidence in his achievements, achievements made possible, he believed, by his adaptation of the method of scientific investigation to his own researches in philosophy. But are his conclusions as firm and unassailable as he believed them to be? If the subsequent turbulent history of Western philosophy is any indication, they are not. However, we are more interested here in the seeds of nihilism planted by Descartes's metaphysical project and its results, seeds whose fruits we are perhaps only in this century in a position fully to comprehend. Much more is at stake than the sometimes arcane deliberations and debates of philosopers, for we witness in Descartes's cogitations the first outlines of a world in which we continue to live, even in these last decades of our century.

Perhaps the most obvious seed of nihilism in Descartes's project is its requirement of absolute certainty. His "method of systematic doubt," as it is sometimes called, is nothing else than a procedure for trying to dig down to certain foundations. He takes for granted that only in this way can he attain genuine knowledge, which he assumes to be universal, absolute, timeless, and indisputable. This view of knowledge has roots, as we have already seen, in the Western religious tradition, with its God's-eye conception of meaning and truth, and its accompanying foundationalist appeal to an infallible body of revealed scriptures and indubitable propositions of reason.

Classical philosophical thought in the West, or at least that part of it by which the medieval outlook was mainly informed, also conceived of knowledge in this way. For Plato, the attainment of knowledge meant apprehension of transcendent, immutable forms through a sustained process of dialectical reasoning. Anything less than comprehension of these eternal archetypes and their intricate patterns of mutual coherence and necessary connection is not knowledge, but mere opinion. Aristotle equated trustworthy knowledge of the world with certain intuitions of the essential forms in substances and with syllogistic deductions of regular facts of sensate experience from the logical interrelations of these forms. Plotinus made a similar deductivist assumption about the nature and possibility of knowledge, including knowledge of value: "Since there is a Soul which reasons upon the right and good—for reasoning is an inquiry into the rightness and goodness of this rather than that—there must exist some permanent Right, the source and foundation of this reasoning in our soul; how, else, could any such discussion be held?" (*Enneads* V, First Tractate, in Saunders 1966:260).

If we couple the influence of the paradigmatic religious and philosophical traditions of the West with Descarte's passion for demonstrative elegance and his glowing admiration for the accomplishments of mathematical physicists such as Copernicus, Kepler, and Galileo, it is no wonder that he equated knowledge with certainty. He was also propelled in this direction by his acute dissatisfaction with the philosophy of his time and his felt need to repudiate many features of the worldview it represented by erecting a distinctively different worldview, consistent with the emerging new physics, on a basis of unassailable certainty. Furthermore, he had been taught by the Renaissance revival of skepticism (see Descartes 1967:I, 99), as well as by the new science, radically to distrust the evidence of the senses uncorrected by the certitude of reason. This derogation of the senses, although sometimes proferred in defense of skepticism, is not alien to the spirit of Plato, who taught that no trust can be placed in conclusions drawn directly from sensate experience and that we can hope to find truth only through methodical reliance on the innate capacities and resources of the mind.

All of this makes Descartes's demand for absolute certainty and the unequivocal exactitude of deductive reasoning quite understandable. But we should not fail to notice that his vow to dismiss as completely false any metaphysical proposition which cannot be derived from a basis of absolute certainty, or which is not itself inherently certain, leaves him precious little room in which to maneuver and makes his philosophy easy prey to the objections already brought into view against the possibility of attaining certain knowledge (Chapter Six, Section 2). Because the only two alternatives envisioned by his method of systematic doubt are absolute certainty or complete skepticism, with no allowance for any middle ground, the explicit character and intent of his philosophy pushes it from the start perilously close to the brink of epistemological nihilism.

If Descartes cannot handle the formidable objections to the search for certain foundations already considered—and I do not find in his thought any convincing strategies by which he either does or can successfully fend off such objections—then his whole project and system of thought must, by his own admission, tumble into ruin. Is knowledge thereby shown to be impossible, as Lehrer, Unger, and others have alleged? Must we conclude that nothing can be known, including not only dependable interpretations of facts but knowledge of values and ends that might have enabled us to find meaning in our lives? This is one possibility. As long as we assume a model of knowledge like that endorsed by Descartes, the nihilistic conclusion seems inescapable. But we should not overlook another possibility: that the conception of knowledge on which this despairing conclusion rests may, despite its seeming plausibility and persistent enshrinement in our intellectual traditions,[4] be thoroughly wrong-headed and in need of radical rethinking. I will return to this second possibility later in this book.

Much more than the unattainability of absolute certitude needs to be taken into account, however, when we are trying to assess the seeds of nihilism contained in Descartes's program. His one Archimedean point of mathematical extension and measurable motion, taken as the criterion of what is real in the natural order, divests nature of most of the properties with which it presents itself to our sensate life, as well as depriving it of any of the value or significance it might be thought to possess when regarded from the standpoint of our religious, aesthetic, or moral sensibilities. As he sees it, the scientific method of reasoning teaches that all we can be certain of in the natural world, and hence all about it which can be truly known, is its mathematical or quantitative character (which for him meant, finally, its spatiality or geometric extensiveness). It is this alone that we are entitled to affirm as real in nature. Nature is the domain of primary mathematical properties; all else we may be inclined to attribute to it is mistakenly attributed, for all else is secondary, residing solely in us, in our human subjectivity.

At the time of his life when he was in the grip of this stern, hard-edged view of nature, says C. S. Lewis, "Nearly all that I loved I believed to be imaginary; nearly all that I believed to be real I thought grim and meaningless" (1955:170). F. H. Bradley characterizes the view in similar fashion: "Nature is, on the one hand, that show whose reality lies barely in primary qualities. It is, on the other hand, that endless world of sensible life which appeals to our sympathy and extorts our wonder. It is the object lived in by the poet and the observing naturalist" (1969:435). The qualitative, evaluative, affectional, informal, non-scientific ways of relating to the world to which Lewis and Bradley refer have no veridical significance, according to Descarte's first Archimedean point. They tell us nothing about nature as it objectively is and merely hold up a mirror to internal states of our subjective being.

Whatever value nature now has must be conferred upon it arbitrarily from without, as the imposition of human purpose and will. Descartes's conception of nature thus connects with the religious assumption about the externality of value discussed in Chapter Five. But because he counsels us on the futility of trying to comprehend by reason the purposes nature might have for God, and insists that we can only hope to understand the mechanical interworkings of its efficient causes, the sole source remaining in his metaphysics for the imposition of value on nature is human subjects (1967:I, 230-231). The heady sense of power implied by this notion of a world wholly compliant to human aims is conveyed by a passage in the *Discourse* where Descartes dreams of devising a "practical philosophy" whose probings of the forces and actions of matter will enable human beings to render themselves "the masters and possessors of nature" (I, 119). He fails to notice the nightmare that stalks the fringes of this happy dream.

The extent to which those under the sway of Descartes's portrayal of the physical universe can think themselves entitled to ignore their most elemental feelings about nature and to follow the dictates of a calculating reason informing them that nature is a system of blindly running causes and effects to be subjected at will to human ends, is epitomized by the Port-Royalist Cartesians who tacked living animals to the wall, split them open, calmly observed their writhings, and studied in a spirit of serene scientific objectivity the pumpings and palpitations of their internal organs before they died. These scientifically minded gentlemen saw no need to attend to any intrusive emotions of guilt or empathetic horror, because Descartes' method and reasoning gave every assurance that animals, despite all appearances to the contrary, are mere automata, part of the whirring machinery of the physical world (see Singer 1975:209).

Thus, Descartes's method, when applied resolutely to nature, not only rapes our senses, but brutally assaults our most instinctual responses and predilections. It condemns us to the barren, indifferent universe of the cosmic nihilist, slamming the door on what we in the West had long-regarded as the warmth and support of our natural home. This stark devaluation of the lived world of nature continues in fashion to the present day. Its seepage into the deepest levels of thought and awareness since Descartes and the early years of the scientific revolution goes a long way toward explaining our current vulnerability to the nihilistic mood.

The contrast between the medieval view of nature and the modern view set out so uncompromisingly in the philosophy of Descartes is tellingly conveyed by Antoine Roquentin's bitter musings on the sea in Sartre's *Nausea*. Roquentin contrasts his perception of the sea with that of a priest who walks nearby reading his breviary. The priest, with his medieval outlook, glances at the sea comfortably and approvingly, because for him the sea is "also a breviary." "Delicate colours, delicate perfumes, souls of spring," the sparkling greens and blues of the water, can all be taken at fact value. They speak not only of God, but of a nature resplendent with quality and value, nature as home for the human spirit. Whatever imperfections nature might exhibit need not worry us overmuch, because they will be compensated for in the everlating life to come. But for the modern Roquentin, the sea, emblematic of nature as a whole, is seen in an entirely different way: "The TRUE sea is cold and black, full of animals; it crawls under this thin green film made to deceive human beings" (Sartre 1964:167). Roquentin had earlier spoken of the deceptively placid surface of the sea as hiding monsters, giant carapaces, and "claws or fins labouring slowly in the slime" (108). Nature as it truly is, therefore, is not something to which we can relate with feelings of kinship, affection, and easy familiarity. Instead, it is hopeless aloof, creepy, and strange.

More than a hint of this same conclusion about nature is contained in Camus's conjoining of cosmic and existential nihilism in *The Myth of Sisyphus* (see the discussion in Chapter Two, Section 5). Camus does not talk of the scientific description of nature. We can surmise, however, that it lurks in the background of his sensibilities as a child of the modern age and that it helps to inform the sharp dualistic opposition both he and Sartre assume between the unrelieved absurdity of reality-itself, on the one hand, and human subjectivity, with its pitiful and yet comic cravings for objective value and meaning, on the other.

Descartes's second and purportedly more fundamental Archimedean point, that of the indubitability of his own existence, is a seed of nihilism no less disastrous in its outcome than the ones we have already discussed. To talk of *two* Archimedean points is admittedly odd, but it is one way of calling attention to the Janus-like character of Descartes's outlook—its facing in opposed, irreconcilable directions: the *objectivist* one of nature conceived according to formal principles of mathematical reasoning, geometrical and mechanical in its every detail; and the *subjectivist* one, with its insistence on the primacy of self-awareness and the derivative, problematic character of everything else. His outlook is also caught in the conflict of two discordant historical perspectives, the one facing forward to the new substantialist conception of matter and a nature viewed wholly in materialistic terms, and the other facing backward to the traditional belief in a spiritual soul not requiring the body for its existence, a soul which is the principal focus of value and importance in a divinely created world. When followed through to its logical conclusion, this second Cartesian fulcrum leaves us with a subjectivism so radical as to make doubtful in the extreme not only our relations to the world, including our fellow human beings, but even our relations to our own bodies, and to our own past and future.

What exactly is it that we find that we cannot possibly doubt when we fix our gaze on our own consciousness? According to Descartes, it is the existence of the individual soul as a substance radically distinct from the reality of physical nature, a substance defined by its essential attribute of thinking. Any act of thinking, such as the act of trying to think or affirm one's own nonexistence, gives certain proof of the existence of an individual soul-substance or *thinking entity* (*res cogitans*). However, Descartes's confident appeal to the existence of his own mental substance as the Archimedean point of his metaphysics proves but one thing: that he has not carried his method of systematic doubt far enough.

For example, he does not question for a moment the substance-attribute metaphysics implicit in this appeal and uncritically assumed in his day. Yet philosophers such as Hume, in the century after Descartes, and William James, Russell, Whitehead, and others in our own time have found plausible reasons for at least questioning the self-evidency of this metaphysical assumption, if not for rejecting it altogether. To make this kind of observation is admittedly to assess Descartes's thought with the wisdom of hindsight. But it is also to illustrate how inordinately difficult, if not impossible, it is to know when one has carried the method of systematic doubt far enought. Pregnable assumptions secreted in one's culture can all too easily be mistaken for indubitable certainties.

For another thing, all that we find with absolute certitude when we try to deny our existence is that we cannot deny it *at that very moment*. By strict application of Descartes's method, it would seem that we can doubt in at least some degree that we existed at any previous moment or that we will continue to exist at any future moment. Because he insists that we reject anything which cannot be shown to be true with indubitable certitude, he must, by the terms of his own method, reject his belief in his own existence over time. Because a substance is, by definition, something that endures unchangingly through at least a finite span of time, while its accidental properties (what Descartes calls *modes*) come and go, he must reject his substantial existence. What he is left with, therefore, if he sticks to his requirement of absolute certainty, is the existence of a momentary act of thinking: an Archimedean point shrunk to the vanishing point!

He opens himself to this line of criticism when he states that "all the course of my life may be divided into an infinite number of parts, none of which is in any way dependent on the other; and thus from the fact that I was in existence a short time ago it does not follow that I must be in existence now..." (1967:I, 168). He seems almost ready to acknowledge, in other words, that there is no certain basis in momentary awareness for concluding that there is an enduring substantial entity underlying and supporting that act of awareness as one of its properties or modes. We cannot even with certainty connect the discrete moments of awareness with one another, so as to give them continuity over time.[5]

One reason supporting this second conclusion, at least in the context of Descartes's own thinking, is his allegation that we can detect no principle of relatedness to the past or future in our present awareness. In the statement quoted just above, he claims that no moment of existence "is in any way dependent on another." He even goes so far as to suggest that human mental substances would not exist from one moment to the next did God not re-create them from scratch in each new instant. (I, 168).

Descartes's conception of soul-substance is analogous to his conception of physical motion. He identifies physical motion, and in fact, all physical change, with locomotion, or change of place. He further states that motion can be reduced to extension, the sole defining property of material substance, in the sense that all motion really amounts to is occupancy of first one extended region and then another. But he gives us no metaphysical explanation of the *process* of movement from the first to the second spatial region. Similarly, he can give us no account of any process of transition from one moment of awareness to another. Each moment, therefore, must be created by God fully actual and intact, with no inherent potentiality to allow for continuous development and change over time. Ironically, Descartes dismissed with ridicule the scholastic, Aristotelian concept of change as "the actualisation of what exists in potentiality, in so far as it is potential" (I, 46). This definition seems far more adequate to our experience of change and of the continuity of our selfhood over time than the point-instant conception he regards as so clear and distinct.

It is an odd kind of substance that has in itself no power of continuing existence, and which can be resolved into distinct, separately created units with no inherent connectedness to one another. Yet it is his existence as a substantial, and therefore (we would presume) *enduring*, soul that Descartes claims elsewhere in his *Meditations* to be beyond all possible doubt. What has happened to produce this paradoxical result? It is partly the outcome of his insistence on absolute certitude and his glimmering recognition that this can apply, if at all, only to the awareness of the present moment. His religious faith in the finite creation's dependence at every phase of its existence on God's sustaining power also plays an important role.

One suspects that also lurking behind Descartes's reasoning is an incoherent blending of his two Archimedean points. He has unconsciously geometricized change and time, treating them as though they could be infinitely subdivided into independent, fully actual units, like isolable segments of the geometrician's line. Furthermore, he is probably strongly influenced by the scientific approach to change and time, which renders them measurable, and thus mathematically quantifiable, by breaking them into calculable units. This is a convenient and necessary approach for mathematical physics, illustrating the method of quantitative analysis or resolution of which Galileo and Newton speak. Its adequacy as a metaphysical account of change and time is not nearly so obvious or compelling, but it seems to be all that can be left to us by Descartes's stubborn requirement of absolute certainty.

This point becomes clearer when we consider a second reason for the conclusion that, by Descartes's own reckoning, we cannot with certainty regard ourselves as continuing substances or enduring entities of any kind. In order to do so, we must rely on our memories. But memory, like the senses, can mislead or deceive and is therefore always open to doubt. In light of this consideration and the others brought into view, why does Descartes not abandon his claim to the pivotal certitude of his own substantial existence and lapse into complete skepticism? Why does he not end up with a view of the self akin to that of Schopenhauer and of Sartre's character Roquentin, both of whom despairingly conclude that only the present detached and ephemeral moment is real? Why does he not agree with Roquentin that the past is dead, and that any attempt to recapture it in recollection will in every likelihood distort it beyond all recognition? And why does he not concur with Roquentin's (and Hume's) contention that "anything can happen" in the future, because we have no basis in our radically disconnected present awareness for believing that the future will resemble the past? Why does reality not collapse for him, as it did for Nietzsche, into an unstructured chaos?

The answer to all these questions is that Descartes takes refuge in God. God, by his acts of constant re-creation, ensures the existence of the finite self over time, thereby giving continuity to that which has no power of continuity in itself. God guarantees the reliability of memory and the predictable order of the universe (see 1967:I, 183, 224). Did God not do these things, Descartes reasons, then God would be a Deceiver. He thinks that he has been able to show with absolute certitude not only that there is a God, but that this God cannot be a Deceiver. There are at least two fundamental difficulties, however, with this appeal to God in Descartes's thought (as well as a third difficulty we will note later, in connection with his concept of the will).

One is that it exposes the dubitability of the supposed Archimedean point of Descartes's Second Meditation, suggesting that it is the reality of God, not the awareness of his own substantial existence, that is in fact the one unassailable certainty of his system. This tends to throw the system into a muddle of contradiction and confusion, because Descartes's certitude about his own substantial existence is supposed to be the paradigmatic example of a clear and distinct (and therefore indubitably true) idea, and he expressly relies on this pivotal certitude in arguing for the existence of God. A second difficulty is that by Descartes's reasoning God *does* routinely deceive us because he leads us to assume that we are substantial selves existing, changing, and developing over time, when in fact (if Descartes's analysis is accepted) each of us is but a succession of fully actual, instantaneous pseudo-substances made to more or less resemble one another. Each element in this succession is then presumably endowed with a stock of ready-made memories which creates an *illusion* of the continuous existence of a single self-substance over time.

We cannot help but be reminded by this Cartesian model of the self of Sartre's conception of the ongoing self as a string of successive acts of nihilation, each "totally free" in its capacity radically to remake or transform at any given moment a past that is strangely passive and inert, far more pliable in principle to the sovereign powers of the will than we would seem to have basis in our experience to expect (see Chapter Four, Section 2). Sartre's successive, largely *de novo* acts of the nihilating will are not only akin to Descartes' disconnected moments of self; they are also suggestive of that majestic, wholly untrammeled power of will whereby God creates radically distinct human selves in every moment of time. What God does at each instant in Descartes's universe we humans have the capacity at any moment also to do, according to Sartre.

Still another resemblance between the two philosophers' respective views of the self is that the self is on either account, a "nothing." Descartes's infinitely divisible self, despite his claims to the contrary, is flagrantly *insubstantial*, in both the technical and non-technical senses of that term. Sartre's active self, on the other hand, is a momentary upsurge of nihilation whose derivation from the fixed, timeless reality of the in-itself is shrouded in mystery and whose continuity with the immediate past is either unexplained or accounted for entirely in terms of its own autonomous decisions (see especially Chapter Four, note 1).

The explicit source of Sartre's view of the self is, of course, different from the explicit source of Descartes's view. Sartre is not making a conscious attempt to apply the method of science in his philosophical deliberations. But Descartes's attempt to do just that drives a wedge between self and the world and leads him and his emulators in the modern period to try to justify or explain experiences of self and the world on the basis of detached items of subjective awareness (e.g., Locke's "simple ideas," Hume's "simple impressions," and the "sense data" or "sense contents" posited by epistemologists of our own century). Chapter Four stressed the considerable extent to which Sartre's philosophy continues in the vein of dualism, and I discussed there his conviction that repeated momentary acts of freedom are the source of what count for humans as the intelligible structures of the surrounding world. These considerations and others suggest that the resemblances between Descartes and Sartre are not merely coincidental but grow out of a common conceptuality, a conceptuality that—thanks largely to

Descartes himself—has become an integral part of the mentality of the modern age.

An existential outcome of the views of these two thinkers is the sense of being imprisoned in the present moment and tortured by the fickle ephemerality of time, with no basis for trusting our memories of the past or anticipations of the future. It is not even clear how our decisions of will can affect the future or be affected by the past, given the radical disconnections of self and time implied in both philosophers' systems of thought.[6]

If we cannot even be sure of our own existence over time, how can we know with certainty that we have physical bodies or that a physical world actually exists? And how can we know with certainty that there are other human beings in the world, that they are conscious beings like ourselves, or that they share with us in a common world? The burden of Descartes's second Archimedean point and its implied radically subjectivist turn is that we must somehow deduce the rest of the world from the assumed primacy of our individual self-awareness. But as we have just seen, we now appear to have no certainty of a continuing self but to be marooned in the solitude of the immediate present, with no basis for confident assertion of the existence of *anything* beyond or outside this fleeting instant.

Once again, Descartes calls upon God to save him from the metaphysical embarrassment to which he is inexorably led by the inner logic of his system, and he does so with unruffled confidence. He is already assured in his heart of God's reality and is therefore readily persuaded by arguments for God's existence he sets forth, arguments ingrained in the instinctive thought-patterns of his culture. For him, to think his own existence is at one and the same time to think God's. Is he not a finite creature who must depend on God for every moment for his being?

But what if we are unconvinced by his arguments for God's existence, partly because we suspect them of involving elements of circular reasoning;[7] partly because they do not carry the certain conviction for us that they did for him and others in his time (though not for all, even then); and perhaps more basically because they strike us as being too pat and convenient, too easy to fall back upon to resolve threats of incoherence in his system? In this event, then only the solipsism of the present moment remains, a tiny residue of certain knowledge salvaged from the concreteness of everyday experience. The method of systematic doubt will then have caused us to lose the world after all and our own souls in the process.

What for Descartes himself turns out so happily, with all that was formerly doubted now regained on a new basis of absolute certitude, we find, on more careful examination, to culminate in complete negation and absurdity. His use of the scientific method of investigation and reasoning can thus be seen as a source of nihilism, not only for him but for all those moderns who identify knowledge with certainty or with the results of exact scientific procedure and proof, who acquiesce in his exclusively mathematical or "objectivist" conception of nature, or who concur with his radically subjectivist approach to epistemological, axiological, and metaphysical problems.

Sartre's character Roquentin subscribes to a version of each of these three suppositions, suggesting that in these respects (as well as others) it would not be stretching things too far to see him as a Cartesian deprived of belief in God, or as a more consistent Cartesian than Descartes himself: a human being who lives through to their ultimate conclusion the covert tendencies and implications of Descartes's philosophy and finds the result to be sickening and unbearable. Roquentin despairs of knowledge because his experience and beliefs do not exhibit the certitude and precision of deductive reasoning[8] and because he has reluctantly to conclude that names, concepts, relations, descriptions, and explanations are locked up in his own head, with no correspondence to anything in the world. He is menaced by a horrifying nature of meaningless facticity, a nature that smirks at his deepest human yearnings. He is trapped in a subjectivity of the present moment, closed off not only from the world and other human beings but from his own past and future, and thus estranged from his own self.

Sartre does us a distinct service in *Nausea* by showing in excruciating detail what the Cartesian philosophy looks like when seen not merely as abstract theory but as applied to the concrete circumstances of a human life. In this way, although perhaps unwittingly, he helps to make us more fully aware of the seeds of nihilism contained in that philosophy—a philosophy giving trenchant expression to certain dominant themes of modernity that were taken up at their inception with an attitude of unbridled enthusiasm but have lately come to weigh heavily on the human spirit.

So far we have discussed three seeds of nihilism in Descartes's metaphysics: his requirement of absolute certainty, his divesting nature of everything but mathematical properties and mechanical functionings, and the radical subjectivist turn implicit in his appeal to the primacy and certainty of self-awareness. We have seen that each of these seeds is generated by his determination to utilize the method of physical science, as he interprets that method, for the solution of philosophical problems. Two other nihilistic trends in Descartes's metaphysics remain to be discussed. They too can be traced to his adulation of the method of scientific reasoning.

The fourth seed of nihilism in Descartes's philosophy relates to those elements of culture that cannot be brought down to a basis of certitude, or whose status in relation to his method he leaves obscure. The elements I will discuss are tradition, the arts, religion, and morality. The distinction among these categories of culture is somewhat artificial, because they interpenetrate one another in important ways, but it will do for our purposes. The fifth and final seed of nihilism is related to conflicting tendencies in Descartes's conception of the nature and role of the human will. Once these last two nihilistic trends in Cartesianism are explicated, I will conclude this chapter with some general critical comments on the methodological assumption identified as a third philosophical source of nihilism.

What implications for culture and its role in human experience can we draw from Descartes's stern methodological "resolve to strip oneself of all opinions and beliefs formerly received" (1967:I, 90), and to raze to the ground all that does not rest upon certain foundations? Let us look first at what we are calling *tradition*. In his *Discourse*, Descartes warns that a culture's cherished accounts of events of the past and of the teachings and accomplishments of exemplary ancestors usually combine fancy with fact, inhibit reason with emotion, and tend toward gross exaggeration; so we must resist their influence. Social customs and practices vary widely from place to place, and their origins are hidden in the mists of time, so they can have little interest for the inquiring mind intent upon absolute clarity and universal truth (I, 84-85, 87, 91). By a similar process of reasoning, the formative images, stories, myths, and rites from which the members of a culture get their bearings and steer their collective course through time might have their place, especially for the unlearned. But because these aspects of tradition are notoriously multifarious and inexplicit in their significance, it seems that they cannot be trusted as sources of truth. Only to the extent that lessons of tradition can be pinned down to single meanings, resolved into clear and distinct propositions, and incorporated into the uniformity of deductive schemes can they be said to qualify as knowledge.

In this aspect of his method, perhaps more than any other, Descartes shows himself to be (in MacIntyre's words) the "lonely epistemological hero" (see Warnock 1971:57), bringing the accumulated experience and lore of his culture to the magisterial test of his individual powers of reason. It was from the day that he decided to turn away from example and custom, to make himself his principal object of study, and to employ all the strength of his individual mind, he informs us, that he began at last to make progress in his thinking (1967:I, 87). Here, Descartes also shows himself to be a true representative of the modern age, which gives so much credence and emphasis to the thought and experience of the individual subject, a concept that reaches its definitive form in the outlook of later moderns such as Stirner, Mauthner, Nietzsche, and at least the early Sartre. I examine this concept in greater detail in the next chapter, where it is treated as another major philosophical source of nihilism.

Also decidedly modern, as MacIntyre again points out and as we saw above when contrasting the medieval and modern methods of reasoning, is the notion that authority and reason are at odds with one another, and that it is irrational to trust in authority of any kind, including the authority of one's cultural traditions (MacIntyre 1981:41). Descartes's ideal of reasoning thus goes to the other extreme from the ideal of the Middle Ages: where the latter tended to depend excessively on the past, he refuses to put any trust in the past at all! He wants to make a clean break with it and to orient himself exclusively toward the future, erecting a bold new system of knowledge from the inner resources of his own mind.

Implicit in these two closely connected, typically modern conceptions is the conviction not only that it is *highly desirable* to keep one's cultural traditions at a distance, but also that it is *possible* to completely resist their influence, to stand outside them and evaluate them in a detached, purely analytic manner. This conviction is one of the guiding principles of the hero of Skinner's *Walden Two*, who prides himself on his decisive rejection of a past he sees as a melange of distortions and misconceptions. "Nothing confuses our evaluation of the present more than a sense of history," says Walden Two's founder, the behavioral psychologist Frazier. He goes on to proclaim, "What we give our young people ... is a grasp of the *current* forces which a culture must deal with. None of your myths, none of your heroes—no history, no destiny—simply the *Now*! The present is the thing. It's the only thing we can deal with anyway, in a scientific way" (Skinner 1948:239).

The lonely epistemological hero seeks to rid himself of the trappings of tradition and the constraints of his particular historical circumstances, and to stand with pristine receptivity before the tribunal of his own reason. If one of his present-day counterparts is Skinner, an earlier analogue is the religious hero, Martin Luther, who assumed that it was both possible and necessary to recover the Bible's original meanings on his own, with a mind rid of the encumbrances of centuries of Christian interpretation. Girded with this assumption, he dared to challenge and rethink the religious traditions, practices, and institutions of his time from his critical vantage point as a solitary man of faith. Luther's announced tribunal was the guidance of the Holy Spirit rather than the spirit of scientific reason, but the keynote of heroic individualism still sounds loud and clear.

An important difference that still separates Luther from Descartes and Skinner is the religious reformer's insistence that the inquiring individual must continue to work from a basis of historical authority and inherited tradition: that which is contained in the Bible itself. Luther's sharp criticism of the recent past in the name of a more remote past shows him to be a transitional figure, more representative of the characteristic approach of the Renaissance than a full-blown exemplar of the modern mind. Descartes and Skinner, by contrast, insist on the necessity of starting without cultural presuppositions of any kind, with a polished slate wiped clean of all the clutter of traditional attitude and belief.[9]

Even a cursory examination of Descartes's thought shows, however, that he does not succeed in detaching himself from his traditions and historical conditioning or in building his metaphysics from scratch. Instead, he continues to accept without question or defense much that he inherits from his past. We have already noted his uncritical assumption of the correspondence theory of truth, of foundationalism and deductivism as the only reliable methods of reasoning, of the doctrine of substance and attribute, of the reality of God, and of the idea that "all that is in us issues from Him," including every moment of our mental existence (1967:I, 105). This list of examples is by no means complete, but it implies the impossibility of sweeping away one's past or of being anything other than a socialized, historical being, no matter how resolute one's sense of individuality.

But what if Descartes had implemented his program literally and completely? Then its outcome would have been quite different. To see why this is so we must recognize that it is just those aspects of tradition that cannot be made certain or fully explicit or that cannot be conclusively proved, which provide the indispensable background of understanding within which both our theoretical and practical endeavors take place. As Marjorie Grene observes, we are always, as human beings, "caught in the ambiguity of our finitude between the explicit surface of our knowledge, the formulable, impersonal aspect of it, and the tacit, often even unknown clues to it in reliance on which we attend to that explicit core" (1966:33). So insistent on our finitude in other ways, Descartes seems completely oblivious to it in this one.

The indistinct and yet indispensable clues upon which we must constantly rely in order to have a context or field within which "explicit questioning and explicit answering can grow" (Grene 1966:32); the broad, mostly unarticulated vision of the world (including our unspoken convictions about what is valuable and important in that world) within which all our reasoning takes place; and the implicit hypotheses or expectations we bring to every investigation—these are largely the contributions of our inherited tradition. Language itself is perhaps the clearest example of the tacit, socialized background whose patterns of meaning have to be taken for granted in order for us to conduct our investigations or communicate and defend their results. Our modes of education also play an essential role in shaping our general outlook, as do the culturally acquired attitudes and responses—most of them operating below the threshold of conscious awareness—that regulate our daily interactions with human individuals and groups and with other aspects of the world.

Descartes's insistence that all but the clear and distant be cast aside denies to these inexplicit dimensions of understanding their crucial role, so that the outcome of his method, if literally applied, cannot be a system of confident assertions but must be the defeat and futility of total silence! His blithe unawareness of the intimate dependence of the explicit on the inexplicit blinds him to this calamitous consequence of his own method. In this aspect of the method, if in no other, we can recognize that it offers us, not so much the guarantee of an all-inclusive, God's-eye view of ourselves and the world as the one-eyed squint of an abstracting rationalism that fatally underestimates what it means to know. If faithfully carried out, such rationalism would make it impossible to know anything.

The ineliminable context of the quest for knowledge and of the reasoned defense of claims to knowledge about which we have just spoken cannot be generated by the method of appeal to the clear and distinct, nor can it be justified by it, because aspects of it must be at every point *presupposed*. Progress in knowledge can only result, therefore, from a continuing dialectic of historical and social context, on the one hand, and individual experience, insight, and reason, on the other—a dialectic in which the tacit influences of tradition can never be set aside but must always be given their due. A clean break with the past and an insistence that everything which can be truly known must be brought down to an absolute starting-point of clear and distinct ideas leaves us with nothing to know because no assumed context of understanding exists within which the search for confirmed knowledge can take place. Applied literally, Descartes's method would soon consume itself and reveal the impossibility of its own implementation. In the previous chapter, a similar criticism of belief in the complete objectivity and detachment of science was mounted, which belief is but another expression of Descartes's unbridled but unwarranted trust in the exclusive competency of explicit method.

Descartes's method not only fails to take account of the informal, inexplicit, culturally transmitted contexts of theoretical investigation and the essential role they play in the quest for knowledge. It must also deny cognitive import to, and thus make peripheral and generally insignificant, those aspects of the arts, religion, and morality that cannot be distilled into a system of clear and distinct ideas. Yet it is just these aspects that, along with tradition itself, are the principal conduits and expressions of existential value and meaning for any people. What Barbara Thompson says about the role of tradition for the Hindu children of India in the last years of the British Raj—tradition that subtly interweaves elements of art, religion, and morality—has application to persons of every time and place:

[A] child learns the way he is to live his life and face his death in the same way that he learns to walk or talk: by the loving encouragement of his family, and by significant play, much of it inspired by the myths, fairy tales, legends, and fables passed down for generations within the family (1985:33).

I will discuss the implications of Descartes's method for religion and morality in a moment, but first I want to say something about its implications for the arts.

Descartes tells us that poetry, eloquence (and presumably all of the arts, as he views them) can be greatly admired for their displays of inventive genius and technical skill, as well as for their emotive and persuasive power, but that their contributions to knowledge are minimal at best and do not begin to compare with what can be established and made known throught the solid discipline of mathematical reasoning (1967:I, 84-85). We can briefly assess the implications of his view of the arts by considering one example of literary art, the novel. Choosing this particular example seems fitting, because the now-familiar literary form of the novel was born in the same century as that in which Descartes sought to put philosophy on a new footing.[10]

The glory of the novel, says one of its contemporary masters, Milan Kundera, is that it is equipped to express and convey a certain kind of essential truth that the methods of analytic rationalism are forced to ignore. This essential truth he characterizes as "the wisdom of uncertainty" and the inescapable "relativity and ambiguity of human affairs." Because the novel's essence is not clarity and simplicity but ambiguity and complexity, "[e]very novel says to the reader: 'things are not as simple as you think'," and it is just here that we come upon "the novel's eternal truth." Another thing that lies close to the heart of the novel as an art form, according to Kundera, is its ability to establish a sense of continuity with the past, of ongoing dialogue with what has gone before: "Each work is an answer to preceding ones, each work contains all the anterior experience of the novel." Its determination to be "a thing made to last, to connect the past with the future" is a fundamental distinction between the genuine novel and those forms of pseudo-art that push "the past over the horizon" and reduce "time to the present minute alone." Finally, as over against a scientifically dominated modernity that has "propelled man into the tunnels of specialized knowledge," the novel at its best enables us to see ourselves and the world as a whole (1984:15, 17-19).

Kundera's vision of the novel's function in civilized life (and, by extension, that of art in general) is similar to the view of Edward C. Aswell, who writes the following with regard to the American novelist Thomas Wolfe:

Tom believed with all his soul that the most that could be expected of a writer, or of any other artist for that matter, was that he observe life closely and see it as it really is—not just the surface, but the inner reality as well—

and then that he depict it in all its lights and shadows just as he sees it, and do so faithfully, in such exact colors, that even those of us who go from cradle to grave half-blind (which means most of us) cannot fail to see it also.

Perhaps some may think that this creed has as much of the scientist as of the artist in it, but such verbal distinctions lose their meaning when we are confronted with greatness. The true scientist of human nature *is* the artist. He is the only one whose vision takes in the whole man (see Wolfe 1941:362).

Art's preoccupation with the wholeness of life, with the "lights and shadows," and not just the clear and distinct surface features of thought and experience, places it outside the scope of Descartes's method, with its love of sharp distinctions and neat categorizations and its confinement to univocal statement and deductive proof.

However, it is just by virtue of their being outside the scope and competence of that method that works of art such as the novel can begin to do justice to the inexhaustible complexity of human existence. Their kind of truth can draw from the deepest springs and resources of the past and give expression to what is of most enduring importance in our common experience and shared cultural heritage. In contrast with Descartes's method, with its mistrust of ambiguity and rejection of any cognitive claim for imagination or feeling, the arts are free to explore, and to take fully into account, every aspect of human experience, no matter how elusive or indistinct, thereby providing us with an indispensable way of understanding and knowing. Following Descartes, we tend in today's culture to think of such modes of awareness as secondary and suspect, because they lack scientific "objectivity." But this is because we confuse objectivity with exactitude and certainty, failing to see that another, far more important kind of objectivity is directly concerned with comprehensiveness and depth.

A culture without this second type of objectivity, and also individual human beings who lack it, are doomed to skate over the surface of life, with no source of courage and perspective in the face of its ambiguities, uncertainties, and risks. The arts can shed light on the challenges and mysteries of human existence in a way that the method of systematic doubt cannot. Yet Descartes's method would exclude them, or at least their most central contributions, from any claim to knowledge and truth. Here we witness a foreshadowing of the nihilism of a later time, of the "abyss of darkness" and "profound ache" of misgiving and regret which Monod and many others in our day think we must learn to accept as the heavy price of scientific precision and objectivity (Chapter Three, Section 2).

Much in the religious heritage of a culture accords with the above description of the arts. Strip away from this heritage all but that which is clear and distinct, or all but that which can be certainly proved, and the most essential parts of its meaning and importance will be lost. The sustaining power of a religious tradition resides not simply in its overt pronouncements and proofs but in its attunements to pervasive mystery and its symbolic evocations of intuitions of continuity, cohesion, conviction, and hope in the presence of that mystery. This power resides also in those ritual enactments and religiously sanctioned duties of everyday life that are an intricate symbolism of practice: prescribed performances and deeds that act out inexplicit but profound meanings that cannot even be reduced to verbal statement, much less rendered into a system of clear and distinct propositional claims.

As discussed in Chapter Six, what is primarily at stake in the religious realm is existential certitude, the source and support of a whole way of life, not the distinct theoretical certainties called for in Descartes's method. Tradition must play a fundamental role here, for none of us is capable of creating a religion or a system of sustaining religious symbols out of thin air.[11] For the explication and development of this kind of existential assurance Descartes's method appears peculiarly unfit. Must we then deny to this assurance, and to the religious traditions that give it form and expression, the name of knowledge? Must we conclude that religion is suited only to stir the spirit and that it can have nothing to do with enlightening the mind? Such seems the clear import of Descartes's announced program. We can discern in this implication of his method a first faint stirring of the later positivistic outlook that consigns religion (and art and morality, as well) wholly to the province of vague, unanalyzable emotions, denying to it any cognitive significance.

But once more, Descartes fails to carry his program through to its logical conclusion. When he touches on religion, he sounds more like a spokesman for the Middle Ages than the harbinger of a new outlook that calls for freeing the mind of all that cannot be made clear and distinct. He explains, for example, that God's revelation, set forth in the Bible, supplements what the unaided mind cannot hope to discover or understand. He asserts, in an implied contrast with his method, that revelation "does not lead us by degrees, but raises us at a stroke to an infallible belief." And he cheerfully endorses the view that "theology points out the way to heaven," despite his adamant strictures against scholastic thought (1967:I, 229, 438-439, 205-206, 84).[12] Such sentiments are hardly consistent with his plea for a decisive break with the past!

That considerations of prudence partly inform these statements is possible, of course, although we have no reason to question their basic sincerity. An issue of more direct importance to us is that Descartes's explicit and unquestioning endorsement of the religious traditions of his own culture further insulates him and his readers from the nihilistic consequences of his approach to knowledge. He does not overthrow everything in his cultural inheritance that cannot be made clear and distinct. This means, among other things, that he does not jettison the principal source of the meaning of life in his time, despite its seeming inability to measure up to the requirements of his method of reasoning.

I have talked about the implications of Descartes's method for the artistic and religious aspects of culture but have said nothing specific so far about its bearing on morality. Throughout his *Meditations*, which purports to be a study of basic metaphysical questions or "first philosophy," he is strangely silent on the whole issue of values—whether aesthetic, religious, or moral values. With respect to moral values in particular, he tells us in his *Discourse* that he resolved to adhere to a kind of interim ethic while embarked on his search for truth. This meant such things as obeying the laws and customs of his own country, especially those set forth in the religious teachings by which he had been instructed since childhood; trying to find the most moderate course of action whenever he could, and not going to extremes; following those opinions about the actions of life which seemed to him most probable; and seeking to conquer himself rather than fortune (I, 95-98). But he gives us little information in the developed metaphysical system of his *Meditations* or, for that matter, in his other important metaphysical treatise, *The Principles of Philosophy*, on whether or how morality can be brought down to a base of clear and distinct ideas, or on how issues of value in general can be treated, or should be treated, by his method.[13]

He does assert in the "Author's Letter" appended to the *Principles* that "the highest and most perfect moral science," which presupposes "a complete knowledge of the other sciences, is the last degree of wisdom" (I, 211). This implies that he believes that his method is competent to generate a complete moral system. However, he never worked out this perfect moral science, presumably because he thought it required a detailed science of human nature that he did not pretend to have established. All we have in his philosophical writings are vague hints and sketches on moral themes (see Copleston 1963:150-156). Thus, he leaves us with only with a promissory note, so far as the relation of his method to moral values is concerned.

Three points relevant to the theme of this book are suggested by Descartes's treatment (or nontreatment) of the problem of the status and content of moral values. First, he fails to *show* that an adequate system of morality can be derived from his method. He postpones indefinitely rather than confronts head-on this central problem. His strategy of a provisional ethic, with its quiet affirmation of traditional moral values, like his fervent appeals to the authority of the Christian religious tradition and his tacit reliance on unanalyzed assumptions of his culture, tend to blunt the incipient nihilistic tendencies of his method, or to leave unanswered the critical question of existential value and meaning it poses. However, these problems did not go away. They soon surfaced in the thinking of those who endeavored to carry out his program more fully than he himself had done.

Second, Descartes evidently assumes that questions of metaphysical fact can be addressed in complete independence of questions of value. Rather than taking valuative experience, or the valuative dimensions of all thought and experience, as fundamental data to be brought into consideration at the very outset by a metaphysical system, Descartes thinks that he can bracket the entire question of values until the metaphysical questions have been wholly, or for the most part, resolved. The implied radical separation of metaphysics and morals, of questions of fact from those of value, is utterly foreign to the metaphysical systems of Plato, Aristotle, Plotinus, and the thinkers of the Middle Ages. But it was to become a fundamental feature of later thought, one with dire consequences. It can be regarded as one of the most important sources of nihilism in the modern period, and I will return to it in Chapter Ten.

Third, Descartes's dream of an exact science of moral values, rooted in a comprehensive science of human nature, foreshadows the concerted attempts on the part of later philosophers to derive moral values from the intuitions or experiences of the individual subject. They, like Descartes, believed that this could be done as one aspect of an investigation of the fundamental principles of human nature and human understanding. A major undertaking of the philosophy of the early modern period was the attempt to explicate these principles, together with their moral consequences. The hope of these philosophers, as apparently that of Descartes himself, was that moral values can be spun out from the subjectivity of the isolated individual just as the spider draws the filaments of its web from its own substance,[14] in complete independence of the individual's historical and social setting, and with no need to rely upon the guidance of the past or the authority of tradition. This brings us once again, therefore, to the theme of the subjectivist turn, a source of nihilism mentioned earlier and one to be examined more fully in the next chapter.

The last seed of nihilism in Descartes's metaphysics is connected primarily with his concept of the human will, but I want to make some reference to his view of the divine will as well. As will be seen, this concept pulls in two opposing directions, anticipating the two extreme nihilistic positions with respect to the will discussed in Chapter Four. On the one hand, some elements of Descartes' thought move in the direction of a causal determinism as thoroughgoing as that of a Schopenhauer, Freud, or Skinner.

On the other hand, certain elements point toward a doctrine of human freedom every bit as sweeping and radical as that of a Stirner, Sartre, or Camus.

Let us take first the deterministic tendencies. The most obvious of these is Descartes's unswerving commitment to the idea that "the laws of Mechanics . . . are identical with those of Nature" (1967:I, 115). The physical nature that invites comprehensive understanding by the scientific method of reasoning is a deterministic system through and through. There is no element of novelty or place for freedom within it and no discernible operation of anything like Aristotle's final causes. Its every feature and occurrence can be explained (at least in principle) by knowledge of its most general structures and of the interworkings of its efficient causes, just as the entire set of theorems in Euclidian geometry can be deduced from that system's axioms, rules, and fundamental definitions. The mathematical and the physical are one and the same, and the relation of causes and effects is exactly like that between premises and conclusions in a formal calculus. Everywhere in the realm of nature necessity reigns. The physical universe is a mirror image of the mathematically inspired method of deductive reasoning.

A second deterministic tendency is tied to Descartes's conception of God. His method yields the certain deduction that God must be infinite or perfect in every aspect. Two closely connected things this conclusion means to Descartes are that God's knowledge is all-embracing, extending even into the remote future, and that his power is absolute. God "has not only known from all eternity that which is or can be," says Descartes, "but also willed and preordained it . . . " (I, 235). Alongside this certain knowledge of God's omniscience and omnipotence is the self-evidency of our own freedom, but because our knowledge is finite and God's infinite, Descartes informs us that we cannot hope to be able to reconcile the seeming contradiction of these twin certainties. (I, 234-235).

Thus, human beings are hemmed in on the one side by a causally determined nature and on the other side by an all-knowing, all-controlling God; and Descartes's insistence on the reality and importance of human freedom—to be discussed in a moment—begins to take on the appearance of a desperate and precarious incoherence. The actual result of his application of his method, here as in so many other places in his developed metaphysics, is something jarringly different from his grand dream of the "uniformity of a rational scheme."

His metaphysics is pulled in a deterministic direction not only by his conceptions of nature and God, but also by his view of the human self. We have already seen how his method, with its requirement of absolute certainty, convinces him that no inherent power of continuity is found from one moment of the self's existence to the next, and therefore that the self must be constantly re-created by God. But if every moment of the self is created *in toto* by God, how could there be any such thing as human freedom? The whole course of the life of every human being must be attributed directly and unqualifiedly to successive acts of God. Viewed in this way, Descartes's concept of the self makes no provision for anything other than the full actuality of each detached segment of momentary awareness. It makes no allowance for an aspect of potentiality in immediate experience that could permit selection from alternative futures or the deliberate pursuit and realization of intended goals. Just as there can be no genuine continuity with the past in Descartes's concept of the self, so there can be no justified sense of one's ability to exercise any degree of control over the future. Each person's future appears to be entirely in God's hands.

When we weigh these pronounced deterministic tendencies in Descartes's thought and see how far from being clear and distinct are their relations to his continuing insistence on human freedom, it is little wonder that a thinker such as Spinoza should have sought to employ Descartes's method of geometrical reasoning in such a way as to eliminate all talk of human freedom. Spinoza collapses human life into the determined order of nature; he eliminates any conflict or tension between the determining power of natural processes and the freedom of a transcendent God by simply identifying God with nature; and he boldly proclaims that because only Divine Nature has in itself the capacity to continue in being without dependence on anything beyond itself, it must be regarded as the sole substantial reality in the universe. In this way, he uncompromisingly reduces everything to one formal system, aiming to satisfy the rigorous demands of the new method more fully than Descartes had, and seeking coherence at the price of a highly significant trade-off: the total eclipse of human freedom. It is but a step from the deterministic philosophy of Spinoza to the gloomy, resigned, despairing fatalism of Schopenhauer, both philosophers bringing to fruit, each in his own way, a seed of nihilism contained in the Cartesian metaphysics and in the emerging worldview for which that metaphysics provides one of the earliest, and also one of the most provocative and prophetic, systematic expressions. (Some of the links between determinism and nihilism are examined in the second sections of Chapters Three and Four.)

Despite these deterministic tendencies in his scheme, however, freedom of the human will is a crucial ingredient in Descartes's epistemology, because it provides him with an explanation of our susceptibility to mistakes in our thinking which is consistent with his rationalistic belief in the availability of clear and distinct ideas, and with his unshakable conviction of the goodness of God. We go awry in our thinking, he contends, when we willingly affirm as true, propositions we have not bothered to justify on the basis of clear and distinct ideas. "[T]he will is much wider in its range and compass than the understanding," and this explains its ability to affirm mistaken propositions as well as true ones (I, 175). When we willingly affirm false propositions, however, the fault is ours alone, and not God's, just as it is when we will ourselves into moral error or sin.

The importance of freedom to Descartes is also seen in his claim that it is freedom of the will, more than any other trait of human beings, which gives evidence of their bearing "the image and similitude of God." Compared with the vast power within us "of choosing to do a thing or choosing not to do it (that is, to affirm or deny, to pursue or to shun it)," our other faculties, such as those of remembering or imagining, or even the faculty of understanding, seem of "small extent and extremely limited." We are immediately aware, says Descartes, "of a will so extended as to be subject to no limits," and when we freely choose, "we are unconscious that any outside force constrains us in doing so." While he duly notes that the capacity of will in God "is incomparably greater" than it is in us, he also observes that when our wills are considered "formally and precisely" in themselves, they do not *seem* any less free than the will of God (I, 174-175). Descartes is obviously deeply impressed with the power of will in human beings; this fact, combined with the role he assigns to the will in accounting for our vulnerability to epistemological mistakes, explains his disinclination to let freedom go by the board (as does Spinoza) in order to eliminate paradox or incoherence in his system.

There is another way of viewing Descartes' concepts of nature, self, and God, which, when combined with his stress on the central role and vast extent of our power of will, pulls toward the opposite extreme from determinism, toward the ideas of a totally unconstrained human freedom and an ultimate arbitrariness of the will. This approach to these three topics, like the one used to explicate the deterministic themes in Descartes's philosophy, is also in keeping with certain consequences of his application of his method.

While it is true that for Descartes nature is a deterministic system, it is also true that the human self is not part of nature but a separate kind of substance or reality. The sharp distinction between physical nature and the human soul is one of the indubitable conclusions to which he thinks his method brings us. This dualistic position has the potential greatly to enhance the role of human freedom in at least two respects. The first is that nature now presents itself as a colossal machine, devoid of any intrinsic worth or importance and, thus, as amenable to prediction, utilization, and dominance by scientifically minded human beings in any ways they see fit. In this vision, the orderly processes of nature are completely subject to human beings and their freely chosen ends. The second respect is that it is by no means clear how the causal processes of nature could have any determining effect on the sublime autonomy of human subjects, suspended as they are above and outside the natural order.

This suggestion of the self's capacity to act in aloof independence of causes is fleshed out further when we consider again the disconnectedness of the self's manifestations through time, but from a different angle than that above. If there is no continuity of transition from the past, through the present, and on into the future, then there is an important sense in which each present moment can be regarded as radically free, because it has no constraining influence from the past. If this line of thought were pursued to its ultimate conclusion, we would have a picture of the sovereignty of the individual will analogous to that of Stirner—a will with the capability of constructing its own truths and values moment by moment, exclusively by its free choices. We would also have a doctrine of the pervasive power and importance of human freedom strikingly similar to that of Sartre.

The link with Stirner and Sartre is carried another step when we reflect on certain aspects of Descartes's concept of divine freedom. A necessary implication of the infinitude or perfection of God for Descartes is, as already noted, that God's power must be absolute. He pushes this notion to the extreme when he contends that God's power is so unrestricted that he cannot be said to be bound even by the very laws of logic themselves. God freely creates these laws, and if he had wanted to make it possible for there to be mountains without valleys, for two times four to equal seven, for a circle to have unequal radii, for triangles to have angles whose sum is not two right angles, etc., he could easily have done so.

This means that behind the certainty and necessary relations of the clear and distinct ideas an ultimate contingency and arbitrariness exists—that of a wholly unconstrained divine will. What holds for the truths of logic also holds for moral values; these, too, could have been quite different than they are, had God chosen to create them differently (II, 248, 250-251). Descartes would presumably agree with Ockham's claim that God could command the human will to hate him, and the will could obey; in so doing, it would be acting rightly, both in this life and in the life to come, for it would simply be affirming and carrying into practice that which makes any human act good, i.e., its accordance with whatever God commands (see Leff 1975:506). Hence, Descartes leaves no doubt as to which side of the dilemma posed in Plato's *Euthyphro* he himself would want to affirm (see the discussion of that dilemma in Chapter Five, Section 3).

Stirner's and Sartre's views of the power and role of the human will are noticeably similar to Descartes's view of the will of God. In all three cases, it is acts of the will which create intelligibility and value, and these acts are, in the final analysis, arbitrary. Truth is truth and goodness, goodness, because

God—or human beings—arbitrarily decide it shall be so. The subordination of intellect to will, or of truth and value to radical freedom, and the reign of ultimate contingency in the universe and human life are the same in both cases. What is different is that Stirner and Sartre locate the soverign power of will in human individuals, whereas Descartes locates it in God. One consequence of their atheism was that they tended to load upon the human individual many of the roles traditionally allocated to God, and this idea of the ultimate absurdity of God's decisions and decrees was transferred to individual human beings. That absurdity already existed in certain aspects of the theological tradition of the West, especially in the nominalistic theology of the late Middle Ages for which Ockham is a principal spokesman. But it somehow became more glaringly evident and deeply disturbing when brought down to earth and reposed in human beings. This is due, perhaps, to the lingering hope among theists of Ockham's and Descartes's persuasion that God has *some reasons* for making the decisions he does, even though we cannot comprehend those reasons. Any such reasons, however, seem to compromise that "supreme indifference" in God on which Descartes so strongly insists (see below).

Thus, a fundamental tendency toward irrationalism or criterionless volitionalism in Descartes's system is unmistakable. This is highly ironic, given its reputation as a paragon of rationalism. The method itself leads to this surprising result, because Descartes takes it to be a clear and distinct truth that God's infinitude entails his total freedom of will. Not only does this proposition, as he spells it out, carry the troubling implication that God has constructed our minds in such a way that we cannot conceive alternatives to clear and distinct ideas, while he himself easily can—meaning that God and human beings "are not aware of the same thing" when they " apprehend what is supposed to be the same truth," and thus that God, in some fundamental sense, constantly deceives us (Miller, in Sesonske and Fleming 1966:48).[15] Also implied is that will, and not reason, lies at the basis of truth and value, and that these latter have no status in their own right but derive their entire significance from capricious acts of will.

God can at any time cause to be possible what we had thought to be impossible because to us inconceivable, to be true what we had thought to be certainly false, or to be good what we had thought to be flagrantly evil. If we are tempted to say that he would never do such a thing, the obvious response is that he is under no obligation to be consistent with himself or faithful to us. Nothing whatsoever is incumbent on God; nothing whatsoever can constrain the absolute authority of his will. Descartes concedes as much when he speaks of "that supreme indifference in God" which he takes to be "the supreme proof of his omnipotence." If any reasons had preceded his ordinations of what is possible, true, or good, they would have determined him toward some options rather than others and abridged his freedom (1967:II, 248, 250-251).[16]

We are strongly reminded here not only of the voluntaristic subjectivism of Stirner, Sartre, and Camus, in which there is no appeal beyond arbitrary acts of the will, but also of Nietzsche's idea of the will to power as the root principle of the universe and latent basis for all manifest claims to truth and value. In Chapter Ten, I will trace further the tendency, already discernible in the metaphysics of Descartes, toward the ascendancy of will at the expense of reason, a tendency that can be counted as yet another principal philosophical source of nihilism.

I have argued throughout this section that the seeds of nihilism in Descartes's metaphysics can be traced, at least to a significant degree, to his attempt to apply a method based on the techniques of mathematical physics to problems in philosophy. The assumption that we should extend the method of science to all domains of thought and experience, and that this method provides us with the only reliable route to genuine understanding, became commonplace in Descartes's own century and in the centuries to follow, even though it was seldom conceived or applied in exactly Descartes's manner and usually produced different results from his own.

Randall notes that Descartes paved the way for Newton, "who may almost be called the greatest of the Cartesians..." (1976:240). Newton's achievements, in their turn, gave powerful impetus to the universalization of the method of physics proclaimed in Descartes's philosophy:

Isaac Newton effected so successful a synthesis of the mathematical principles of nature that he stamped the mathematical ideal of science, and the identification of the natural with the rational, upon the entire field of thought. Under the inspriation of Locke, the attempt was made to discover and formulate a science of human nature and human society, and to criticize existing religious and social traditions in the light of what seemed rational and reasonable. The two leading ideas of the eighteenth century, Nature and Reason, . . . derived their meaning from the natural sciences, and, carried over to man, led to the attempt to discover a social physics. Man and his institutions were included in the order of nature and the scope of the recognized scientific method, and in all things the newly invented social sciences were assimilated to the physical sciences (1976:255).

I do not have space here to go into the specific details of this process of assimilation. Suffice it to say that Descarte's conviction of the omnicompetence of a method of inquiry and proof based on the method of physical science has been held by such diverse figures in the history of modern thought as Thomas Hobbes, Spinoza, Locke, Bernard de Fontenelle, Hume, Kant, Claude-Henry Saint-Simon, August Comte,[17] John Watson, Rudolf Carnap, and Otto Neurath.

Carnap, for example, took the position in 1932 that "science is a unity, that all empirical statements can be expressed in a single language, all states of affairs are of the one kind and are known by the same method." This fundamental language, he argued, is the language of physics. Neurath, in a publication that same year, also claimed that all empirical statements can be expressed in the language of physics, and that whatever cannot be so expressed is either tautologous of nonsensical. Furthermore, all the sciences form a unity and are equally "natural," meaning that their significant statements are reducible to those of physics. There is no separate realm of "spiritual" sciences, with their own distinctive subject matters or methods (see Passmore 1966:379-380).[18] Among the statements deemed nonsensical by this view, presumably, are answers proposed for such questions as "What is the meaning of life?" because no way can be found to decide among such answers scientifically (see Passmore 1966:375).

The spirit of Descartes's unbridled adulation of natural science and its method which lies behind the allegations of Carnap and Neurath also informs those statements we read in the newspapers and hear over television and radio almost every day (usually announced in an oracular tone): statements such as "Science says...," "Science has learned...," or "Science will soon be able...," as though science were not the work of particular fallible human beings, or not merely one set of selective techniques or approaches among others, but a kind of Supermind, the sole dispenser of all wisdom and truth, the final authority for deciding every kind of disputed question or for determining what kinds of questions admit of significant answers and what kinds do not. Practitioners of academic disciplines such as psychology, sociology, economics, and even history often seem desperately intent on convincing us that they can qualify as fully for the sacred name "science" as can physics or chemistry, proudly claiming as their own what they conceive as the method of natural science. Somehow lost on such persons is the eminent good sense of the plea of the eighteenth-century naturalist, Georges Buffon, for a plurality of methods, even *within* the natural sciences (see Cassirer 1961:77-80).

Thus, Russell, Skinner, and Monod do not stand alone in their scientistic outlook, nor does that outlook—pregnant as we have shown it to be with nihilistic implications—belong exclusively or even primarily to our own century. These three thinkers are part of a steady and ever-enlarging stream of thought running from the seventeenth century to the present, a stream whose headwaters lie in the philosophy of Descartes and in that overall perspective and problematic of the modern era that he was the first to set forth in a throughgoing way.

If I have spent a considerable amount of time tracing seeds of nihilism in this philosophy, it is because I agree with Barrett that Cartesianism is "[f]ar more than a passing episode in the history of philosophy." It "is in fact the secret history of Western civilization during the last three hundred years" (Barrett and Aiken 1962:I, 36). This is true in respects other than Descartes's demand for extending the method of natural science to the study of the whole of experienced reality and his claiming that it alone is competent to produce dependable knowledge. But those other respects can be traced to a large extent to this one, as I have tried to show. If Barrett is right in his judgment, and if I am correct in bringing it to bear on this book's central theme, we stand to learn a great deal about own situation and the nihilistic tendencies of our time when we look carefully and critically at the paradigmatic content and formative influence of Descartes's thinking. Additional evidence for these statements will be marshalled in the next two chapters.

I conclude this chapter with a some critical summary remarks about the assumption that has been its theme. In so doing, I also bring into question the nihilistic conclusions to which this assumption has tended, not only in Descartes's thought, but in the thinking of those who share his conviction that the method of natural science should be made normative for all reasoning and for all domains of thought and experience. I briefly note three points of criticism, each of them implicit in the discussions of this section: the unacknowledged abstractness of the approach to understanding endorsed by this assumption, the glaring anomalies the approach generates, and its thinly veiled arrogance.

The abstractness of Descartes's methodological approach has been noted in a number of ways. It leaves out all that cannot be made certain of deductively derived. It excludes everything in nature and our relations to nature which cannot be reduced to extension and number. It restricts consciousness to the solipsism of the present moment. It denies any role to tradition or communal experience, as far as knowledge is concerned, and it excludes the arts from making any significant contributions to our understanding. It claims to have been able to address a series of fundamental metaphysical questions without giving any explicit attention to the moral dimension of our thought and experience. It denies, by implication, the contributions of story, myth, symbol, and rite to our comprehension of the world. If applied uncompromisingly, the method of systematic doubt requires that most of what gives religious traditions (or systems of secular faith) their evocative power and relevance be denied the name of knowledge.

Descartes's positing of the durationless moment, which he thinks to be required by his method's demand for unequivocal certainty, is perhaps the most telling example of the way in which he allows his method to blind him to obvious features of our experience. Durational moments, involving as they do overtones of memory and anticipation, and thus laden with an ineliminable vagueness and certainty, lack the clarity and exactitude of knife-edge instants, complete in themselves. His inclination to break down the physical as well as the mental world into static moments reveals the tendency of a method modeled on mathematical physics, and one which requires certainty above all else, to replace the elusive complexities of lived experience with tidy, more manageable abstractions.

Descarte's thought bears out Dostoevsky's observation that "[m]an has such a predilection for systems and abstract deductions that he is ready to distort the truth intentionally, he is ready to deny the evidence of his senses only to justify his logic" (*Notes From Underground*, in Kaufmann 1956:68). It is ironic that such intense preoccupation with logic should lead to nihilistic absurdity, but this is what happens when logic, in the form of exclusive attention to a single method of reasoning, is given tyrannical sway over the whole of life and allowed to run roughshod over everything that cannot be made subject to its narrow decrees.

I have also noted that Descartes's method gives rise to fundamental anomalies and contradictions. For example, we are said to affect and to be affected by the physical world, despite the fact that we are not, as pure mental substances, in any way related to that world. We are said to be certain about our substantial existence as mental beings; yet we are also told that the only thing we can really be certain about is the isolated consciousness of the fleeting moment. We are informed that God foreknows and foreordains everything but also that we are free; and that the physical universe is a deterministic system and yet somehow responsive to our free acts, operating upon it from without. We are advised that nothing can count as reliable knowledge that cannot meet the requirements of the method of systematic doubt but also assured that relying on the unquestioned authority of divine revelation is appropriate. Descartes claims that he will doubt everything, but he carries many key assumptions into his thinking which he never bothers to question or defend.

These anomalies give an air of comprehensiveness to his system that it would otherwise lack. They help to shield him from the full implications of his method, implications which, if more coherently traced, would glaringly expose its nihilistic tendencies and even, as argued, force him finally to replace his confident rationalism with total silence. Had he traced these implications more consistently, he would perhaps have been compelled to rethink his commitment to the exclusive competency of scientific method, for it is that commitment, more than anything else, that generates the anomalies infecting his system at almost every turn.

Finally, a thinly veiled arrogance can be discerned in Descartes's method of inquiry. It is the arrogance of pretended neutrality, of claiming to be able with the right method to approach all problems without coloration of bias or debatable valuational commitments. But Descartes is obviously biased in favor of the new science rather than Aristotelian physics; the dictates of reason rather than the evidence of the senses; deductive modes of reasoning rather than other modes; the scientific method rather than other methods; theoretical detachment rather than existential involvement;[19] a static philosophy of being rather than a dynamic philosophy of becoming; certain basic Christian beliefs rather than beliefs of other religious traditions; and so on. His purported "objectivity" must therefore be called fundamentally into question; he is a child of his own age, despite his undeniable originality and genius. He no more starts from scratch or reasons without valuation or bias than anyone else can. The dream of complete detachment and objectivity, the dream of resolute, heroic individualism, is not realized by Descartes, nor will it ever be by any finite human being.

However, it is not so much Descartes's latent biases and commitments that are at issue here, for these are unavoidable in any thinker. It is the pretense of total objectivity in his philosophy and the illusion of total objectivity in the method of science he tries to foist upon us, just as it has been foisted upon him, which is the thrust of our criticism. For this illusion accounts for much of the nihilistic malaise of our time, a malaise rooted in the perception that the world of science, the world as it "really is," is remote from our most distinctive human interests, endeavors, and concerns.

A gulf between existence and value is thus established. A consequence of our modern tendency to idolize science—to set it "on an altar in a temple remote from the arts of life" (Dewey 1958:382), as though it were not itself one such art, replete with its own assumptions, values, and constructs of finite, historically informed sensibility and imagination—is that values come to be seen as arbitrary, subjective, and somehow unreal. "[C]riticism of values, whether moral or esthetic," says Dewey (and we could add, "or existential"), "becomes pedantic or effeminate, expressing either personal likes and dislikes, or building up a cumbrous array of rules and authorities" (1958:383). Dismissed from the realm of objective (i.e., scientific) knowledge, all-important questions of value are either left to the vagaries of personal inclination and private choice or consigned to the capricious rulings of some external authority.

The dangerous arrogance in the illusion of having a method of reasoning free of all bias and valuational commitment and equipped to describe the world as it objectively is—nothing more, nothing less—was brought home vividly to me by an experience of one of my graduate students. He was doing a thesis on the ethics of consulting, and part of his research was interviewing faculty and administrators on our campus to find out what kinds of consulting were taking place, what ethical problems might be involved, and what attitudes people had toward these problems. An administrator in one of the technical colleges of the University told him that he had nothing to investigate, that his thesis project was focused on a bogus topic. Why did the administrator think that? Because, he explained, everyone knows that ethics is purely a matter of personal opinion; it has no "objective" status or relevance. Because ethical questions cannot be resolved scientifically, they are unresolvable. When the student told me about this conversation, I was reminded of the place in Plato's *Apology* where Socrates says of the skilled craftsmen of his time: "on the strength of their technical proficiency they claimed a perfect understanding of every other subject, however important, and I felt that this error more than outweighed their positive wisdom" (*Apology* 22d, Hamilton and Cairns 1973:8-9).

If such arrogance is not seen through, it is all too easy to acquiesce in the hegomony of science and the restrictive tyranny of a single acknowledged mode of reasoning, as though the assumption of such things did not point to a contingent and in many ways deplorable feature of our present culture but to an eternal truth. With that acquiescence, our susceptibility to nihilism is made especially acute. The tragedy of our times, as Gregory observes, is not so much that the advance of science has been perceived as invalidating the Christian worldview; it is that this advance has been perceived as invalidating any non-scientific worldview (see Gregory, in Brock 1984:17). We are thus left with the choice, either of a worldview that is patently inadequate to illuminate the central questions of value and meaning with which we must contend every day of our lives, or nothing. But this is really a choice between two nothings, for at the heart of the scientific worldview (or what I have termed scientism) is the nothingness of nihilism, the specter of the absurd's hollow stare that turns everything to stone.

Chapter 9

The Subjectivist Turn in Epistemology, Philosophy of Language, and Ethics

The individual subject of experience has been substituted for the total drama of all reality. Luther asked, 'How am I justified?'; modern philosophers have asked, 'How do I have knowledge?' The emphasis lies upon the subject of experience.

—*A. N. Whitehead (1948:127)*

In Chapters Seven and Eight, I discussed three assumptions found to be philosophical sources of the nihilistic outlook of the last one and one-half centuries: the correspondence conception of truth, in connection with the classical doctrine of substance and the modern doctrine of material substance; the hegemony of science, especially as that bears on the concept of nature; and the idea that reliable truth can best be attained through applying the method of natural science to philosophy and other disciplines. We saw how the last assumption generated seeds of nihilism in Descartes's philosophy. Some of these seeds related to assumptions we have examined earlier, while others anticipated the philosophical sources of nihilism to be highlighted in this and the next chapter.

The assumption to be examined in this chapter is the subjectivist orientation of modern philosophy. By this I mean the emphasis that philosophy has placed on the individual self, conceived as prior to and independent of all that supposedly lies outside it: the natural world, other human beings, social institutions, socially prescribed roles and responsibilities, cultural meanings and values, traditions and historical contexts. "The self of contemporary man," says Nishitani, "is an ego of the Cartesian type, constituted self-consciously as something standing over against the world and all the things that are in it" (1982:13). His statement correctly identifies Descartes's philosophy as the fountainhead of this assumption, because it finds there its first definitive expression and support.

I will explore three areas of modern philosophy where this fourth assumption operates: epistemology, philosophy of language, and ethics, critically analyzing its relations to nihilism. As the capstone of my critical discussion I will outline an alternative view of knowledge, communication, and value less prone to the nihilistic denouement of the general approach to these topics dominating thought in the modern era—an approach instinctively assigning primacy to an assumedly detached and autonomous self.

1. EPISTEMOLOGY

C. D. Rollins points to the Cartesian roots of this pronounced subjectivist tendency in modern philosophy, particularly in epistemology, when he states that "Descartes must be considered responsible for the introduction of solipsism as a recognized problem" in philosophy (see Edwards 1967:VII, 488). There is more than a hint of solipsism—the doctrine that I alone exist and that everything in the universe that seems to be distinct from me actually exists merely in my own mind—in Descartes's contention that he can certainly and directly know only himself and that the existence of anything else is problematic, needing somehow to be deduced from this axiomatic self-awareness. The solipsistic trend is also implicit in his emphasis on the difference between the "objective" and the "formal" reality of an idea. We can, he says, be certain of an idea's "objective" reality, because it is part of the content of our own minds, about whose existence we are certain. But whether any of our ideas give us information about a reality beyond ourselves is again highly problematic.

The drift toward solipsism in Descartes's philosophy is discernible as well in the sharp distinction he draws between mental and physical substances, because this distinction implies an isolation and separateness from a world completely unlike oneself, a foreign "external" world that encompasses even one's own body. How can such a totally distinct world be experienced or known? This in-itself world soon becomes, with Kant, a mere postulate, leaving only sensory impressions and their ordered relations in the mind as the objects of knowledge. Furthermore, the requirement of Descartes's method that we overthrow everything from the past about which we cannot attain absolute certainty sets the individual self against communal beliefs and practices, giving to it alone the authority to decide what, if anything, is legitimate among those beliefs and practices. Descartes also constantly harps on the unreliability of the senses and on the need to judge and correct them by the sovereign dictates of his own internal processes of reasoning, thereby making tenuous still another line of connection between self and the world which had long been taken for granted.

Finally, even Descartes's formal definition of "substance" as "a thing which so exists that it needs no other thing in order to exist" (1967:I, 239) adds to the sense that one's individual mental substance is something existing autonomously, in self-contained isolation from the rest of the universe. He hastens to tell us that this definition applies univocally only to God. But as Whitehead notes (1978:50), there is an important respect in which the definition applies to every substantial existent, because by definition substances themselves cannot directly interrelate. As Aristotle phrases it, substances cannot be "predicable of" or "present in" one another, but can affect one another only through their respective attributes (*Categories*, 2a; see Aristotle 1941:9). As noted in Chapter Seven, Section 1, the notion that substance must always remain concealed behind its veil of attributes led Locke to characterize it (with considerable frustration) as a "something, he knew not what." This means that I cannot directly know substances beyond myself, whether mental or physical, but only their putative effects on my mind, i.e., ideas in my mind.

But how can I be sure that these ideas are not attributes of my own substance merely; how can I *know* that they are caused by other substances or that any of them correspond to real traits of those substances? This problem is exacerbated by Descartes's contention (readily accepted by Locke) that many of my ideas have no reference beyond the mind and that only specific ones of them—termed by Locke the ideas of "primary qualities"—correspond to properties of the physical world. It was relatively easy for subsequent thinkers such as Leibniz, Berkeley, and Hume to show that arguments similar to those purporting to demonstrate that some of our ideas are only secondary or purely mental in their reference can be used with equal effect on all of our ideas, thereby eroding the conviction that at least some of them are primary or representative of the natural world. Once again, everything beyond myself is left uncertain.

As we saw, Descartes is even led to the paradoxical conclusion that he cannot know his own substantial self as existing throughout time; all he can know are momentary experiences which he is entitled to regard as properties of an ongoing self only through appealing to the existence of God. But the best that belief in God can do is to assure him of a continuing process of re-creation of resembling mental "substances," with no internal relatedness to one another. Here is a self that is isolated and cut off in the extreme, a minute islet of certitude awash in a sea of doubt stretching to every horizon.

The subjectivism and self-centeredness of Descartes's philosophy, or at least of those aspects of it just enumerated, have by no means remained peculiar to him but have left an indelible stamp on most subsequent philosophy. As Robert C. Solomon comments,

> From the time of Descartes until the present, the mainstream of philosophy has been defined by this subjective standpoint, the view that it is *my* thinking, *my* experience, *my* reasoning, *my* moral prejudices and principles, that form the foundation of all human knowledge and value. (It is not always clear to what extent these first-person singular *I's* and *my's* might be replaced by first-person plural *we's* and *our's*; what is essential is the 'first person'.) (1983:58).

Evidences of the subjectivist bias in modern epistemology are available on every hand and do not require extensive elaboration. I will cite a few examples (including examples from our previous discussions), to indicate its pervasive presence and effect.

The subjectivist stance explicit in Descartes's statement, "I see clearly that there is nothing which is easier for me to know than my mind" (1967:I, 157), is also assumed by Locke, who asserts in his *Essay Concerning Human Understanding* not only that we know our own existence with an "internal infallible perception" unattainable for beliefs about the natural world, but also that all "our knowledge is founded on and employed about our ideas only" (1959:II, 304-305, 188). Just as Descartes's rendition of the method of natural science led him to analyze reason into the fundamental building blocks of clear and distinct ideas, so Locke's employment of a similar reductive method leads him to take it for granted that experience—his own announced ultimate court of appeal—can be resolved into simple ideas of sensation and what he terms simple ideas of *reflection*, i.e., ideas of the mind's elementary responses to, and operations upon, the ideas of sensation. He then proceeds to try to build from these empirical simples, as Descartes had sought to do with his simples of reason, a new structure of knowledge, firmly grounded in his own introspective investigations.

Locke trumpets his ability, on the basis of this method, to develop, or at least begin to develop, a theory of human nature that can accomplish in that sphere what Robert Boyle, Christian Huyghens, Newton, and other "master-builders" of natural science had accomplished in the field of physical nature (1959:I, 14). The first book of his *Essays* is a sustained argument for the rejection of "innate ideas," by which Locke seems mainly to mean beliefs accepted on the basis of authority or tradition, or those simply taken for granted and not brought to the test of the proper method of inquiry. These inherited, unanalyzed, uncriticized ideas or beliefs he regards as so much "rubbish that lies in the way to knowledge," a kind of thick "underbrush" that pathfinders such as himself, possessed of the new method, can now clear away (I, 14).

Hence Locke, the champion of empiricism, holds up essentially the same banner of resolute, firsthand, method-guided inquiry as does Descartes, the champion of rationalism. For both philosophers the starting point of all reliable knowledge lies in the content of each person's own mind. It is this content alone that the self can directly and certainly know. To it as the foundation of all truth the technique of philosophical reasoning modeled on the method of natural science inexorably leads us (exhibiting a point of intersection of the third and fourth philosophical sources of nihilism).[1]

The existence of anything outside the individual mind must be inferred, because it cannot be immediately known or experienced. An external world must be deduced from ideas that are traits or properties of the particular knowing subject (see Locke 1959:II, 186). Especially problematic for Locke is the status of beliefs about the past or expectations of the future, because there is no "necessary connection" of ideas entertained in the present moment with anything beyond that moment. Here we are reminded both of Descartes and Hume. Like Descartes, Locke appeals to the assurance his belief in God gives him that a real world (and by implication, a substantial self) exists through time independently of the ideas ingredient in his present awareness (1959:II, 325-328, 334).

Ernst Cassirer's statement about what, for Thomas Hobbes, qualifies as knowledge applies equally well to the methodological commitment and subjectivist stance of Descartes and Locke—as it does to the great majority of modern philosophers:

> We understand only what we can cause to develop under our observation.... If one wants to 'know' something, he must constitute it himself; he must cause it to develop from its individual elements. All science, the science of the corporeal world as well as that of the intellectual world, must be centered around this act of producing the object of knowledge (1961:254).

The act of which Cassirer speaks is an act of the isolated individual, probing the depths of his own subjective thought and experience and expecting to find there the raw materials for a pristine derivation of the essential content and ruling principles of nature, human nature, society, and religion.[2]

The logical culmination of both the rationalist and the empiricist programs, however, turns out to be radical skepticism or epistemological nihilism, showing the inability of either approach to break out of the predicament it poses for itself with its initial assumption of the absolute primacy of self-awareness.

On the side of rationalism, the latent skepticism comes to the surface in the philosophy of Kant, who despairs of our ability to know the world in itself or to obtain any metaphysical knowledge on the basis of theoretical reason. All we can know are the data of sensation organized by the innate intuitions of the sensibility and categories of the understanding. This is the central theme of Kant's first *Critique*, which he characterizes as "a treatise on the method" or "whole plan" of pure speculative reason (1958:25), exhibiting once more the preoccupation with method typical of modern philosophy. In Kant's case, it is a method designed to explain once and for all, on philosophical grounds, the possibility of Newtonian physics, with its intricate interweavings of empirical and strictly rational (especially mathematical) modes of thinking.

Comparing his own method with the radical alteration of vantage point inaugurated by Copernican astronomy, Kant indicates that his treatise will bid us no longer to try to determine whether, or to what extent, our minds relate to external objects, but how the objects of experience must conform to the subjective conditions of our knowing—showing how decisively the center of balance in philosophy has shifted from the public world toward the private world of the individual knower (Kant 1958:22-26). In a statement echoing Cassirer's characterization of Hobbes, Kant writes (in his *Critique of Judgment*, published in 1790) that "we see into a thing completely only so far as we can make it in accordance with our concepts and bring it to completion" (1951:231). What we assuredly know, therefore, is the contents and constructions of our own minds; all else is shrouded in darkness.

However, Kant assumes without argument that the basic character of his own thought and experience is shared with that of other human beings, and thus (as Solomon put it) that he can move easily from "I" to "we," or from conclusions about his own particular nature to conclusions about human nature in general. Because he takes for granted that he has succeeded in deducing and explicating a common structure for all human minds, he thinks he has demonstrated an intersubjective objectivity despite his claim of the inaccessibility of the in-itself world. But included in that world from which his "critical" or "transcendental" idealism forever separates him must be both the independent existence and the in-itself character of any other human being; he is left with no basis in the system of *The Critique of Pure Reason* for assuming the reality of other persons, much less the commonality of their mental processes with his own. Despite his intent, therefore, he is not able to present a convincing case for his claim to have found a firm middle ground between the problem-ridden epistemological realism of Descartes and Locke, on the one hand, and the skeptical-tending phenomenalism of Berkeley and Hume, on the other.

On the side of empiricism, the implicit skepticism of the subjectivist turn is made glaringly evident in Hume's work. The Scottish philosopher contends that we can know only our private impressions, which have a character and role in his system similar to the simple ideas of sensation and reflection posited by Locke. The principle of causality, which represents for Hume our only possible way of moving beyond fleeting impressions to an enduring world to which they might be thought to correspond, is itself reducible without remainder into simple impressions which have (as Locke himself had noted) no "necessary connections" to one another.[3] Consequently, an appeal to this principle to give ontological reference to our impressions is circular and futile. This point applies as much to the mental substances (including God) assumed in Berkeley's idealism as it does to physical substances.

As far as our inductive reasonings about the future are concerned, Hume contends that they lack the empirical support of our impressions, because we can discover no necessary connections between or among any of our impressions, and only such a discovery would warrant our instinctive confidence that the future will exhibit continuity with the past. A similar problem is posed for the reliability of our memories. Hume distinguishes between memory and imagination partly on the basis of the force and vivacity of their presentations to the mind, an analysis that may explain in psychological terms our tendency to trust our memories but does nothing to tell us whether or to what extent this tendency admits of epistemological justification. Even more to the point, the radical disconnectedness of our impressions makes our memories highly suspect. There is no inherence of past impressions in present ones, and, thus, no continuity of passage from the one to the other.

Hume does not dispute our strong propensity to believe in an abiding external world and in a predictable future that flows from a knowable past. He offers us psychological explanations for this propensity that go beyond mere contrasts of the force or vividness of some impressions as compared with others, basing his explanations on three principles of association whose power of "attraction" he relates to the principle of gravitation in physical science (1980:12-13).[4] However, he can discover no rational justification for the aforementioned beliefs. The sole objects of dependable knowledge for him are impressions, each of which is distinct and separable, exhibiting no essential relatedness to one another (233). These are the correlates in his philosophy of those fragments of fleeting awareness that constitute, as we have seen, the final residue of certainty in Descartes's epistemology. They are also comparable to the physical atoms of Newtonian science, which are fully actual and sufficient to themselves, exhibit no internal principles of relatedness, and can be brought into relation only by externally imposed forces.

Because each impression may be considered as distinct from all others, may exist separately, and has no need of anything else to support its existence, says Hume, we may conclude that impressions are "substances," as far as this definition explains a substance (233). He thus espouses an atomistic or thoroughly nominalistic epistemology, the discrete units of which are usually brought into patterns of relation by the "gentle force," exercised upon them entirely from without, of the psychological propensities of association (10). The whole machinery of this epistemology is closed in upon itself, unable to provide justification (although it does offer explanation) for belief in a world beyond the detached data of present experience. With Hume, as with Descartes, even the continuity of the human subject over time collapses into instantaneous, unrelated impressions. Neither philosophy leaves us with anything to be confidently affirmed other than the ephemeral content of each distinct moment of subjective awareness.

Locke, himself no skeptic but a confident representative realist, speaks in one place of the human understanding as being "not unlike a closet wholly shut from light, with only some little openings left, to let in external visible resemblances, or ideas of things without...." These little openings or windows are the senses, and by them alone is some small amount of light "let into this *dark room*" (1959:I, 212). Reasoning from Locke's own subjectivist standpoint—made so evident by this telling metaphor of the dark room— Hume reluctantly concludes that for all we can know, the so-called windows of the senses may only be panes of silvered glass reflecting and re-reflecting myriad angles and aspects of the closeted human subject back upon itself.

The subjectivist bias and orientation of the epistemological thinking of the seventeenth and eighteenth centuries is carried over into that of the ensuing two centuries. The trend of rationalistic philosophy rooted in Descartes and given its "Copernican" twist by Kant is developed in one direction by the absolute idealism of the nineteenth century and in another by the phenomenological philosophy of the twentieth century (especially the earlier stages of that philosophy). From there it finds its way into existentialism. Epistemological systems in the vein of Locke's empiricism (but also informed in significant respects by Descartes) continue to be worked out in the nineteenth and twentieth centuries, as empirical-minded philosophers struggle with the skeptical tendencies in Locke's scheme made explicit by Hume, while retaining most of the assumptional and methodological framework common to the two British thinkers. I do not have space to go into detail about these developments, but I will make a few points in passing about them, showing their relation to the philosophical source of nihilism now under discussion. My remarks on the empiricist philosophies subsequent to the eighteenth century can be most conveniently presented in the context of the discussion of the second main topic of this chapter: the subjectivist turn in philosophy of language.

At the risk of grossly oversimplifying a complex movement in the history of Western philosophy, I suggest that we can interpret absolute idealism as a response to two basic problems posed by Descartes and Kant. Both of these philosophers assumed that the natural world is entirely independent of mind, and that mind is entirely independent of the natural world. In other words, both were mind-body dualists. However, the mind's access to the nonmental world is imperiled by certain incoherencies in Descartes's dualism noted in various places herein; it is made even more precarious when key arguments for the crucial distinction between primary and secondary qualities are shown by later philosophers to be untenable. Kant, like Descartes, assumes the reality of a mind-independent world but insists that it is unknowable in principle by theoretical reason. In this first case, where the individual mind is set against an inaccessible in-itself world, it is pushed relentlessly in the direction of solipsism. All it can hope to "know" are its own subjective states.

Absolute idealists in the post-Kantian tradition—Johann Gottlieb Fichte, Friedrich Wilhelm Schelling, and George Wilhelm Hegel—seek to resolve this first problem of the knowability of the world by rejecting mind-body dualism and, more particularly, Kant's notion of the nonmental, thing-in-itself world, and claiming that reality as a whole is nothing but mind or manifestations of mind. Theirs is a version of the mentalistic reductionism mentioned in Chapter Seven, Section 1. But this move immediately poses the threat of solipsism from another direction, because it suggests that the "world" has no integrity or status in its own right but is simply the construction of the individual mind. The absolute idealist's solution to this second problem is to argue that while the world is nothing but mind, it is not the content or creation merely of my mind or your mind but of cosmic mind. By these two moves, then, absolute idealism seeks to secure, first, the knowability of reality, because it is in no way distinct from mind but is mental through and through, and second, reality's independence of the individual mind.

However, this proposed solution of the problem of solipsism posed by the subjectivist orientation of the epistemologies of Descartes, Kant, and other philosophers of the seventeenth and eighteenth centuries is not without its own profound difficulties. I will briefly indicate three of these. One is that the absolute idealists continue to take for granted Kant's assumption of intersubjective objectivity, which we have already criticized as begging the question of solipsism. In the philosophy of absolute idealism, I must still start from my subjectivity as the primary given, exactly as Descartes and Kant did. But now, instead of merely assuming the existence of other minds and attributing to them the forms and principles I believe to operate in my own awareness, I must make the even greater leap of supposing that reality as a whole is ideal and patterned after the putative structures of my mind.

Rather than resolving the question of solipsism, therefore, this philosophy simply throws up a metaphysical storey over the already rickety epistemological ground floor of a Kantian intersubjective objectivity inconsistently substituted for an unknowable metaphysical reality, and itself perched on the insecure footings of Cartesian subjectivity. This first difficulty with post-Kantian idealism lies deeper than its questionable anthropomorphism, its transference of allegedly universal structures of human consciousness to reality as a whole (on this see Copleston 1985:VII, 24). It lies in the yawning gap between individual subjectivity taken as primary and the positing of supposedly objective conditions of human awareness in general, as well as between these conditions and the characterization of all reality as purely mental or ideal and as constructed on the same epistemological conditions, now converted into metaphysical principles.

A second difficulty with the absolute idealist approach is that it simply replaces one of Kant's unknowables with another of his unknowables. The cosmic mind posited by absolute idealism as the fundamental reality of which everything in the universe is a mode or manifestation, is a deliberate projection of Kant's "transcendental unity of apperception," now also accorded metaphysical rather than mere epistemological status. Kant had argued that we must assume the role of the transcendental unity of apperception because without it our experience would suffer from chaotic disunity. There would be no unified field of awareness within which knowing could take place, no systematic organization of the discrete data of the sensible manifold (an assumption about the character of the raw data of experience carried over from Hume), or central coordination of the intuitions of sensibility and categories of the understanding. But because the unity of apperception is prior to, and presupposed by, all phenomenal awareness, none of the distinctions, discriminations, or chacterizations presented in experience can be applied to it. As with Locke's material and mental substances, we can know only *that* it is (i.e., that it is required for all knowledge); we cannot hope to comprehend *what* it is (see Kant 1958:136-138).

When converted into the underlying cosmic reality, the transcendental unity of apperception retains its unknowability, at least in the philosophies of Fichte and Schelling. So it is not clear that absolute idealism offers a solution to the problem with the dualistic philosophies of Descartes and Kant we indicated above, namely, the inaccessibility of reality-itself to human apprehension. Fichte claims that the world is the image or scheme of the divine life. This divine life, which is the underlying reality in his philosophy, transcends the reach of the human mind and can only present itself in images and pictures. It is these that we know, not the reality in itself. Similarly, Schelling regards the cosmic mind or absolute as pure identity, swallowing up in itself all differences between subjectivity and objectivity. This distinction and all others are outside the absolute, meaning that it is radically unknowable by human beings. We have to be content with knowing its appearance only, not what it is in itself (see Copleston 1985:VII, 85-87, 123-

125). We are bound to wonder whether these views have any great advantage over the dualisms of Descartes and Kant, as far as the problem of comprehending reality-itself is concerned.

It is true that Hegel, the third in our triad of idealists, lays great stress on the absolute spirit's knowability, holding that it is moving steadily toward a self-knowledge exhibited in the expanding awareness of human beings as history unfolds. But a subjectivist bias and solipsistic tendency are secreted in this brand of absolute idealism as well, despite Hegel's protestations to the contrary. This bias and tendency come most clearly (and ironically) to the surface in his serene confidence that the absolute has reached its highest degree of self-awareness to date in absolute idealism, and more particularly, in his own version of absolute idealism (see Copleston 1985:VII, 179, 243-244). To understand Hegel is thus at one and the same time to understand the most recent stage (as well as all previous stages) in the progressive self-disclosure of absolute reality or the absolute spirit. That spirit knows itself best and can be most fully comprehended—at least at this point in history[5]—in the system of philosophy that is the outgrowth of Hegel's own reflections.

I am speaking of a latent bias and tendency in absolute idealism, not of the overt intention of the absolute idealists themselves. Hegel, for example, takes Kant to task for claiming that "the things we know about are to us appearances only" whose "essential nature belongs to another world which we can never approach," and he goes on to decry Kant's "subjective idealism with its reduction of the facts of consciousness to a purely personal world, created by ourselves alone." He further states that the proper interpretation of things "is to have their existence founded not in themselves but in the universal divine Idea." It is true that this latter view, the one which he himself espouses, is "as idealist as Kant's; but in contradistinction to the subjective idealism of the critical philosopher," it "should be termed absolute idealism" (*The Logic of Hegel*, trans. W. Wallace (1892), 93-94; quoted in Friedrich's Introduction to Hegel 1954:xxxii).

The point I am stressing, however, is that the "universal divine Idea" turns out to be all too remarkably (and conveniently) identical, at least in its present stage of manifestation, with the particular ideas of Hegel himself. He is not the first to announce, "I think God's thoughts after him." Hegel's philosophy is but another version of that ancient dream of being able at last to peer at the world and the whole of human history through God's transparent eyeball. But the proclamation of the long-sought realization of that dream sounds no more persuasive, or any less presumptuous, on his lips than it does on that of his predecessors[6]—and this despite the undeniable subtlety and grandeur of many aspects of his philosophical system, a system with few rivals in either depth of insight or extent of influence on subsequent thought.

Copleston makes an important observation about the continuity of

Hegel's thought with that of Kant, and, by implication, about Hegel's and the other absolute idealists' failure to resolve, *except by metaphysical fiat*, the problem of the subjective idealism that Hegel attributes to Kant. He ventures the "paradoxical statement" that

> the closer idealism kept to Kant's idea of the only possible form of scientific metaphysics,[7] the greater was its confidence in the power and scope of philosophy. For if we assume that philosophy is thought's reflective awareness of its own spontaneous activity, and if we substitute a context of idealist metaphysics for the context of Kant's theory of human knowledge and experience, we then have the idea of the rational process, which is reality, becoming aware of itself in and through the mind of man. And philosophy can be interpreted as the self-knowledge of the Absolute (1985:VII, 10).

But philosophy now can be also interpreted—in light of the critical comments about Kant's program and its appropriations by the absolute idealists we have already made—as an arbitrary identification of the reveries of the individual philosopher with the cognitations of the absolute. If this identification is at bottom arbitrary or groundless, all we have remaining is the isolated and now absolutized particular subject with its idiosyncratic creations and "possessions."[8] This is precisely the view of one so-called young or left Hegelian of our acquaintance, Max Stirner.

A final difficulty with absolute idealism is that in its very zeal to avoid the skeptical atomization of solipsistic or relativistic individualism, it moves relentlessly toward high-flown abstractions (most notably, in its claims about an all-pervading cosmic mind of which individual minds are mere aspects or moments) and sweeping generalizations about inevitable historical progressions and the ruling traits and "spirits" of entire epochs and peoples. It moves so far in this direction, in fact, as to threaten to leave far behind the experienced particularity and stubborn diversity of things, including the distinctive awareness and activity of individual human beings. In opting so forcefully for one extreme, it invites equally extreme reactions in defense of what it leaves out of account. But the extreme positions on either side tend to be held within the orbit of the subjectivist turn.

Setting forth his own philosophy as the science of the inexorable workings of the absolute spirit, Hegel states in his *Phenomenology of Mind* that "it is in the nature of truth to force its way to recognition when its time has come," and that a particular thinker such as himself, possessed of such truth, need not worry when his system does not meet with immediate universal endorsement and acclaim, especially on the part of those who arrogate to themselves the role of being the public's "representatives and spokesmen." It is the power of truth persistently making its way in the world that transforms what at present may be regarded as no more than the viewpoint of the philosopher "himself singly and alone" into "something universal," and that will lead to its eventual public acceptance (Hegel 1929:66).

The individual, therefore, does not matter so much; an individual such as Hegel matters only to the extent that his thought comes to be recognized as the medium or vehicle of the mind of the absolute.

> [A]t a time when the universal nature of spiritual life has become so very much emphasized and strengthened, and the mere individual aspect has become, as it should be, correspondingly a matter of indifference, when, too, that universal aspect holds, by the entire range of its substance, the full measure of the wealth it has built up, and lays claim to it all, the share in the total work of mind that falls to the activity of any particular individual can only be very small. Because this is so, the individual must all the more forget himself, as in fact the very nature of science implies and requires that he should; and he must, moreover, become and do what he can (Hegel 1929:67).

It is just this brazen mixture of humility and arrogance in Hegel, with its claim to the submergence of mere individuals in the onrush of the absolute—but in a manner which this one individual, Hegel, assumes himself to have been given most fully to understand—that so deeply offends such emphasizers of the concrete life, experience, and outlook of the particular person as Stirner, himself a vehement critic of absolute idealism in its Hegelian form.

Stirner is in the grip of the radical subjectivist tendencies that infect the philosophies of Descartes, Locke, Hume, Kant, and the absolute idealists themselves. He follows these tendencies throught to their absurd conclusion with a stubborn clarity and persistence, the closest approximation to which, among the philosophies mentioned above, is the phenomenalistic skepticism of Hume.

A way of seeing the point of this third difficulty with the philosophy of absolute idealism is to note that Hegel and Stirner are not as far apart as they might initially seem to be. Both share in the subjectivist orientation of modern thought but move within it in different ways. It is ironic but predictable that the high abstractions about the workings of the cosmic Self with which Hegel sought to nullify the peril of solipsism lurking beneath the surface of Kantian idealism, and yet to persist in an idealistic framework of his own, would invite a reaction like that of Stirner. The latter is willing to run the risk of solipsism in order to avoid what he sees as the far greater Hegelian evil: an eclipse of the concrete, here-now, irreducibly particular self. This self he sees as the beginning and end of any adequate epistemological, moral, or metaphysical theory. His defense of this self at all costs is one way of trying to keep the Cartesian flame, while Hegel's defense of the absolute spirit is another. Each extreme position clouds the issue of the proper status and role of the individual person.

I turn finally to another offshoot of the rationalistic philosophies of Descartes and Kant, the thought of Edmund Husserl. In Husserl's phenomenology, especially as set forth in his *Cartesian Meditations* (first published in French in 1931), we can witness the persistence into our own century of a version of the subjectivist orientation in epistemology which we have been discussing. Husserl's *Cartesian Meditations* is aptly titled, for in it he carries forward several assumptions already associated with Descartes. One is the ideal of an altogether disinterested or purely objective knowledge, made possible by a well-developed method, which in Husserl's case is the method of "transcendental reflection" (Husserl 1960:35). A second is the insistence on grounding this knowledge in apodictic certainty. As with Descartes, philosophy must be conceived as "an all-embracing science erected on an absolute foundation" (1960:152).

A third Cartesian assumption embraced by Husserl (and the one most germane to the topic now under discussion: the subjectivist turn in epistemology) is that self-awareness must be viewed as the primary given and fundamental starting point of all knowledge. Husserl asserts that the *ego cogito* is, as Descartes saw, "the ultimate and apodictically certain basis for judgments, the basis on which any radical philosophy must be grounded." It is "the only thing I can posit in absolute apodicity as existing" (1960:18, 139). By the strategy of the "phenomenological epoché," a "parenthesizing" of all questions or problems about the objective world (the world of other egos and the social and cultural world, as well as the world of nature), I am left with the indubitable foundation of "my pure living, with all the pure subjective processes making this up." This also includes everything meant in (or intended by) these processes, "*purely* as meant in them: the universe of 'phenomena'." In other words, the strategy of epoché requires me to "apprehend myself purely: as Ego, and with my pure conscious life, in and by which the entire Objective world exists for me and is precisely as it is for me" (20-21). Or as Husserl states toward the end of his book, "everything existing for me must derive its existential sense exclusively from me myself, from my sphere of consciousness . . ." (150).

Husserl is well aware of the crucial difficulty this third assumption poses for philosophy: if philosophy must begin with "a pure egology," is it not then a science that "condemns us to a solipsism?" (30). The only escape from this devastating conclusion he can envision is the possibility of establishing an intersubjective objectivity, i.e., showing the reality of other egos structured as my own ego is, and thereby bringing into view a world which is not merely phenomenal for my subjectivity but phenomenal to other subjectivities like my own: a world present in common and patterned alike for all experiencing human beings (30, 130).

Husserl brands as "absurd" Descartes's attempt to establish a representational realism from a basis of the primacy of self-awareness. Descartes was within a hair of discovering the only approach with any promise, that of the transcendental idealism of Kant, but he failed to pass through the gateway that was open before him. Accordingly, he remained mired in the egocentric predicament that Husserl characterizes as "the whole problem of traditional [early modern] theory of knowledge" (24-25, 82). A remnant of this untenable Cartesian realism clings even to the shoes of Kant, in the form of Kant's distinction between the phenomenal and the noumenal worlds, the latter conceived as "the universe of true beings . . . something lying outside the universe of possible consciousness, possible knowledge, possible evidence . . . ." Such a universe of pure being is, for Husserl, "nonsensical" and patently inconsistent with the whole inclination and significance of Kant's own philosophy (84).

Although he rejects Kant's positing of a thing-in-itself world, Husserl includes as a basic feature of his own philosophy Kant's pivotal distinction between the empirical self and the transcendental unity of apperception, or as Husserl prefers to call it, the transcendental ego. This latter is "prior in the order of knowledge to all objective being," including the being of the self as an object of knowledge (Husserl 1960:26; see also Kant 1958:336-337). It is not Descartes's supposed substantial self with which philosophy must begin, therefore, but with the transcendental self, the field of awareness presupposed in every act of consciousness. And as did Kant, Husserl assumes that there is a set of universal and necessary "structural types" or "eidetic laws" (the terms are Husserl's) that constitute the forms of any possible experience. These principles insure that experience will not be merely chaotic or Heraclitean; their operation also entails that every object of experience, including the empirical self, must be regarded as the "constituted product" of the transcendental ego (49; 74; 52, n. 1; 85). The task of uncovering the apodictic constitutive principles of the transcendental ego is the principal task of philosophy, according to Husserl, and its possibility is what gives promise of philosophy becoming an "all-embracing science, grounded with absolute strictness" (72).

However, Husserl is not content, as Kant had tended to be, with merely assuming that the structures implicit in the operations of the transcendental ego are the same for all persons. Nor is he willing to follow the absolute idealists, who converted the transcendental unity of apperception into one overarching cosmic principle or absolute spirit. He sets himself the task of trying to *prove* that there is a plurality of concrete and particular transcendental egos that he designates with the Leibnizian term *monads* (67-68). The problem then becomes that of how to move from the apodictic structures of my own constitutive consciousness to those of other subjects, how to provide some basis for "experiencing someone else," in order to counter "the objection that phenomenology entails solipsism" (88). Or as Solomon phrased it, the problem is how to move from the first person singular to the first person plural, from "I" to "we."

It is of obvious importance that I be able to find some basis whereby others become not just objects constituted by my own consciousness but self-constituting subjects in their own right. Of further importance is that I be able to give reasons for thinking that these other monadic egos operate with necessary and universal principles or eidetic laws like those which structure my own awareness. Were I to fail in this combined task, then there would be no demonstration of a world common to me and to others, and hence, no basis of intersubjective objectivity (which Husserl also calls a "communalization of constitutive intentionality" or "a harmony of the monads") (107-108). Phenomenology would then have given way to phenomenalism; transcendental idealism would have collapsed into a subjective idealism that tilts perilously toward solipsism.

Does Husserl succeed in averting this disaster, of whose imminent threat he is so keenly aware? His reasoning on the matter, while suggestive, falls far short of the apodictic certainty he holds to be necessary to philosophy conceived as a strict science. This reasoning consists of two main steps. The first is the observation that among the bodies belonging to the "nature" intended by my experiences, one is uniquely singled out as belonging peculiarly to me. This body, in contrast to all others, is "not just a body but precisely an animate organism" to which "I ascribe *fields of sensation.*" It is the only bodily object "'in' which I '*rule and govern' immediately*, governing particularly in each of its 'organs'" (97). However, it frequently happens that another body presents itself with traits and modes of behavior remarkably similar to mine. Even though none of its seemingly animate characteristics "can become actualized originarily in my primordial sphere," by a process of "association," "appreciation," or "analogizing apprehension" I can come to recognize it as another animate organism—animate, that is to say, for another ego (113, 111). This recognition is then continually reinforced by the harmonious behavior of the other body, by the fact that its behavior is in no way discordant with the modes of behavior, or anticipations of behavior, I associate with my own lived body (114).

Husserl hastens to add, however, that the movement from the perceived analogy between my animate body and certain other bodies to the conviction that other egos exist, as the subjects of those bodies, is not a matter of conscious inference. Such "apperception" is no more a thinking act than is the apperception of "the already-given everyday world," with its "horizons" of possibility and expectation within which we live and act (111). We quite naturally believe, then, that other animate organisms exist similar to our own, and that at their centers are egos similar to our own.

The second step in Husserl's attempt to prove that there are other egos, or more specifically, that given in my experience is the experience of egos not merely constituted as such by me but having their own constitutive powers, is his discussion of the idea of "pairing." I apprehend my animate body from "here," but there is another body entering into a pairing association with my body "here." This other body is "there," and it becomes natural to assume, given the similarities of its behavior with my own, that it has a center of "primordial ownness," with a "world" oriented around it and experienced from its perspective, which is as proper to it as my world is to me, experienced from "here." That world from "there" is the same world, I then further assume, which would be apparent to me, were I to shift from "here" to "there" (118-119).

Such an apperception is strikingly similar, Husserl maintains, to the one whereby I attach an "identifying synthesis" to separate moments of awareness, thereby acquiring the sense of the connectedness of my self through time. The "here" of the present is thereby connected with the "there" of some point in the past, and I can conceive myself as returning to that point in the past with the same centering consciousness I experience in the present moment. Just as in this example, "two" egos or centers of awareness become "one," connected through time, so we apprehend the "two" worlds present to my own centering ego and to an alien ego as "one" world seen from different vantage points, a world whose space and time are common to us both (1960:126-128).

Has Husserl really shown anything by these processes of analysis other than that it is *natural for me to believe* in the existence of other egos and to think that the worlds "constituted" by them resemble the world of my own experience? This much would readily be conceded by the most dyed-in-the-wool phenomenalist or subjective idealist. The critical question is whether these beliefs can be justified. Even if we were to grant at least some initial plausibility to the two stages of Husserl's attempt to demonstrate an intersubjective objectivity, mere plausibility is far from the apodictic certainty that his announced method requires. The specter of solipsism still hovers over the whole of the *Cartesian Meditations*, despite its writer's confidence, stated toward the book's end, that this threat or "illusion" has now been "dissolved." This is so, he assures us, "*even though* the proposition that everything existing for me must derive its existential sense exclusively from me myself, from my sphere of consciousness[,] retains its validity and fundamental importance" (150).

This pervasive theme of the absolute primacy of self-awareness or of the necessity for starting out from the perspectivity of the isolated individual—

especially when conjoined with the uncompromising demand of the *Cartesian Meditations* for pure presuppositionless descriptions grounded in apodictic certainty—establishes a barrier to the solution of the solipsistic enigma that Husserl no more succeeds in surmounting than did Descartes or Kant. His failure hearkens back to the extreme epistemological relativisms of Stirner, Nietzsche, and Mauthner, each taking for granted the primacy of self-awareness and doomed, like Husserl, to wander endlessly in the labyrinth of the Cartesian *cogito* with no mode of access to a shared world.

Husserl's failure to find a way out of solipsism also points forward in time to the Sartrean conclusion that separate worlds of meaning and value are constituted *de novo* and with absolute freedom by each particular human subject, implying what we earlier termed "the ideality or ultimate subjectivism and arbitrariness of everything" (Chapter Four, Section 2). The drive toward existential nihilism contained in the radical subjectivist stance of Sartre and his philosophical predecessors is made glaringly evident in the life and outlook of Sartre's character Roquentin. Throughout *Nausea*, Roquentin is swaddled in an intense, cloying self-preoccupation, consigned to an abject isolation and loneliness from which no escape seems possible. He has no vocation, no friends, no sense of rootage in his culture or its past, no feeling of responsibility to anything or anyone; and the world of nature, including his own body, is remote and terrifying to him. Everything beyond his immediate self-awareness is alien and unapproachable. His only recourse is to try to create a personal world of significance and worth by sheer acts of will. This is what it means to be condemned to be free. Roquentin's solipsistic self-centeredness and absurd freedom is the logical outcome of the subjectivist turn.

2. PHILOSOPHY OF LANGUAGE

When we turn to the philosophy of language of the early modern period, especially that promulgated by those of the empiricist persuasion, the subjectivist orientation is equally persistent and widespread. Hence, patterns and problems similar to those already sketched in connection with epistemology are much in evidence. For example, Hobbes and Locke, as a part of their passionate plea for thoroughgoing methodological reform, stress the importance of precise definitions of key terms, arguing that such terms are meaningful just to the extent that they can be resolved into explicit references to the simple units of experience, i.e., *sensations* in the case of Hobbes, and *ideas of sensation* and *reflection* in Locke's case. By "experience" is meant the content and character of immediate personal awareness, brought into focus by persistent introspective self-analysis (see Hobbes, *Leviathan*, Pt. I, Chs. IV-V, in Burtt 1939:140-148; Locke 1959:II, 8-13, 148-164).

Locke tells us that "words, in their primary or immediate signification, stand for nothing but *the ideas in the mind of him that uses them,*" and that "the end of speech is, that those [verbal] sounds, as marks, may make known his ideas to the hearer." He continues, saying that "words are the marks of ... the ideas of the speaker: nor can any one apply them as marks, immediately, to anything else but the ideas that he himself hath ...." Because the proper and direct signification of linguistic terms is ideas in the mind of the person making use of them, only in a secondary and derivative sense can they be regarded as having reference to conceptions in the minds of other persons or to "the reality of things" (1959:II, 9-11).

Language in its essential character is therefore private, and the problem is posed of how any given speaker can cause, or know herself to have caused, other persons to have the same or similar ideas in their minds as she holds in her own mind. There is also the problem of whether and to what extent the private mental phenomena directly designated by the terms of language correspond to things in a publicly accessible world, and thus of whether and to what extent language can refer or be known to refer, at least indirectly, to that world.

These problems are compounded by Locke's contention that words signify ideas, including ideas in the mind of the person currently using them, only by an "arbitrary imposition" of meaning that is subject to change at any time. Because "every man has so inviolable a liberty to make words stand for what ideas he pleases," it follows that "no one hath the power to make others have the same ideas in their minds that he has, when they use the same words that he does." Not even the Emperor Augustus, for all his might, could guarantee such a result in the minds of his subjects (II, 12). Finally, Locke teaches that individuals determine the meanings attached to universal terms on the basis of their own experiences; and any two individuals may frame them differently, to the extent that their experiences are different (see 1959:II, Bk. III, Ch. VI; also Aaron 1965:205).

The degree of variability or indeterminability in the meanings of linguistic terms implied by these aspects of Locke's analysis—especially by his insistence on the private character of what is primarily designated by such terms—is thus potentially great, and an aura of doubt and uncertainty is created about our ability to communicate with one another through the use of language. This problem is deepened by a development of the empiricist epistemology such as that carried out by Hume, in which a fundamental distinction is made between particular impressions and the general ideas based upon, or derived from, those impressions.

Hume is an unflinching nominalist, while Locke vacillates between nominalism and a form of logical realism. We have seen this already in Hume's case, when I pointed out that each and every impression is, according to him, unique and unrepeatable, and that it is into such discrete impressions that all meaningful ideas, as well as all experiences, must be resolved. Any given linguistic term, according to Hume, can only refer to some specific image or impression, and it is only by custom that we are able to associate such a specific datum of our experience with data of past experience that "resemble" it in some way. This association is facilitated by the term itself, which becomes the carrier, as it were, of a semblance of generality that is lacking in the stubborn particularities of our experience (Hume 1980:20-21). Locke's ideas, on the other hand, are themselves the givens of experience and have, or sometimes have, an aspect of universality or generality attached to them as given (see Aaron's argument for three "strands" of Locke's view of the constituent ideas of experience in their relation to universal meanings; 1965:197-202). This universality of the ultimate data of experience in Locke's epistemology, and thus of the ultimate referents of linguistic terms, makes some allowance for shared meanings among the users of language.

However, if we combine Locke's view of language with Hume's nominalistic epistemology—an epistemology that at least has the advantage of overcoming the ambiguity of Locke's uses of the term "idea," with their confusing fluctuations between the particular image and the general conception—the price paid for this greater precision is extremely high. For the consequence of holding an "idea" to be just a pale reflection of an impression and as particular as the impression itself, is that no two impressions can have exactly the same significance for two or more persons or even, for that matter, for one person at two different times. And because such distinct impressions are now the ultimate referents of linguistic terms, it follows that each individual is consigned to a personal universe of discourse whose connections with the semantic universes of other persons are left obscure.

It is doubtful that even the most charitable or imaginative interpretations of such a Lockean-Humean linguistic theory could succeed in explaining how it would be possible for us to impart determinate meanings to one another through the use of language. Certainly Locke's own prescription for ensuring exact communication, when combined with Hume's epistemological analysis, namely, that the significations of all our terms be resolvable into explicit references to the simple data of each person's private experience, seems to give little promise of either facilitating successful communication or of resolving the mystery of how such communication could ever occur. Mauthner's severe reservations on this score, discussed in Chapter Two, can easily be seen to follow from a "worst possible scenario" construction of Locke's theory of language, one which gives a pivotal role (as Mauthner indeed does) to a radical nominalistic epistemology similar to that laid out by Hume.

If this is what language is like, then it is difficult to understand how people could make use of it to explore or make manifest a common world of meanings. It seems, rather, that each person must live and think, largely, if not entirely, within the cramped confines of her own linguistic world, a world that is the possession of that person alone. Such a purely private realm of idiosyncratic meanings must also, by the same process of reasoning, be a private realm of idiosyncratic values. So we are led along the path of Locke's linguistic theory to a denial of the possibility of commonly held or commonly understood standards of value, the denial that lies at the heart of Stirner's ethical egoism or, as it might also be termed *moral solipsism*. What holds for moral values must also hold for existential values, the purposes and goals that define a meaningful life.

Despite the many difficulties with Locke's theory of language, its main outlines have been widely assumed in the modern era, and its influence has continued well into the twentieth century. In all the variations of the theory, the presence of the subjectivist bias in modern philosophy can be readily discerned.[9] Passmore states, for example, that for the positivist philosopher Moritz Schlick, in the early 1930s.

'verifiability by experience' means verfiability by mental states *which I alone can experience*. There is in principle, it will follow, no way of determining whether a proposition is verifiable—or unverifiable—for anybody except myself. Since meaning and verifiability are identical, we are apparently forced to the odd conclusion that only I can know what a proposition means; indeed, to say of anybody else that 'he knows what that proposition means' will be meaningless (Passmore 1966:375-376).

In an attempt to avoid this startlingly "odd conclusion," Schlick distinguishes between the formal structures of assertions in physics, maintaining that these can be public or intersubjective, and the empirical content of such assertions, holding that these are incurably private. But he then goes on to acknowledge that the formal aspects of a scientific system must be given empirical meanings in order to become a science containing real knowledge. To the extent that scientific claims can be taken as claims to real knowledge, therefore, their meanings must remain ineffable, for each person must fill the formal (i.e., logical and mathematical) structures of natural science with an emprical content which is incommunicable and private. Passmore cannot resist remarking that this is a "strange conclusion for a positivist!" (1966:376). It is a conclusion similar to that to which Mauthner, earlier in the century, was forced from similar premises and one which had long been implicit in Locke's empiricist account of the workings of language.

The "logical atomism" of Russell, Wittgenstein, and A.J. Ayer in the early decades of the twentieth century also closely resembles the Lockean-Humean epistemology and philosophy of language. Like Schlick's positivistic theory of language, it implies a solipsistic outcome, thereby presenting yet another version of the spectacle of insular selves incapable of interacting with one another by means of a common medium of discourse. The main premises that lead to this outcome are the following (here I draw for the most part on J. O. Urmson's exposition in 1958:134-135; see also 192, 198). (1) All *propositions of language* are meaningful just to the extent that they are either atomic propositions or truth-functions of atomic propositions. (2) *Atomic propositions* are ones that name atomic facts and derive their own meaning or truth from such facts. (3) *Atomic facts* are objects of direct acquaintance. (4) *Objects of direct acquaintance* are particular sense data or particular relations of sense data. (5) *Sense data* are in principle private and immediate, i.e., accessible only to the person experiencing them then and there. The interlinked conclusions directly implied by these premises are three in number. (C1) No two people can ever both be acquainted with the same atomic fact or object of direct acquaintance. (C2) The totality of atomic propositions intelligible to me, and giving intelligibility to my language, is intelligible to no one else *but* me. (C3) Any communication among persons by means of language is theoretically impossible!

So, once more, an analysis of language rooted in assumptions of the empiricist epistemology of the seventeenth and eighteenth centuries brings us to a self detached and alone, with no bridge from its inner experiences and understandings to an outer world of public discourse and shared significances. Such a self is not only an isolated self; it is a nihilistic self, because denied access to the "rules in common" that, as Britton observes, are essential not only to a usable language but also to a meaningful life (1969:182; see our earlier reference to this aspect of Britton's discussion in Chapter Three, Section 1). As he points out elsewhere in his book, the question of the meaning of life is not just a question about myself, about my solitary apprehensions, choices, or desires. It is also a question about whether I can join with others in a common world of meanings and values found to be cogent and worthwhile in their own right and capable of guiding us in the living of our lives. Britton summarizes the point in this way: to say that life has a meaning if the individual wishes it had a meaning, or arbitrarily decides to confer a meaning upon it, "is nonsensical: it illustrates a form of inference which can at once be seen to be invalid (wishes are not horses and beggars do not ride). We are considering not a wish but a discovery" (13). Such discoveries are made highly problematic, if not impossible, by the descriptions of language discussed in this section. At the heart of these descriptions is the implicit nihilism of the subjectivist turn.

3. ETHICS

I mentioned earlier Descartes's dream of elucidating a rational system of ethics through application of his philosophical method, a method of introspective analysis assuming the primacy of individual self-awareness (Chapter Eight, Section 2). Influential thinkers such as the third Earl of Shaftsbury (Anthony Ashley Cooper), Francis Hutcheson, Hume, Adam Smith, Kant, and John Stuart Mill—each working with essentially the same methodological assumption, seek in their own times to give substance to this dream by erecting theories of altruistic ethics on the basis of elemental instincts, sentiments, intuitions, or principles each claims to have discerned in his own consciousness. Others, such as Hobbes, Bernard Mandeville, and Claude Helvetius arrive at versions of ethical egoism, and of theories of politics and society based on enlightened self-interest, by the same introspective technique.

Each philosopher takes as axiomatic that he not only can but must begin with himself in isolation—setting aside all preconceptions of culture or tradition and every inherited belief—and proceed to build from the absolute starting point of his private introspections and original ruminations an ethic applicable to all human beings, at all times and places. When considering whether any action, such as that of willful murder, is truly one of virtue or vice, observes Hume in Book III of *A Treatise of Human Nature*, each person has but one recourse. The vicious character of murder will never be discerned "till you turn your reflection into your own breast, and find a sentiment of disapprobation, which arises in you, towards this action." Thus "when you pronounce any action or character to be vicious, you mean nothing, but that from the constitution of your own nature you have a feeling or sentiment of blame from the contemplation of it" (1980:468-469). Hume's two statements neatly encapsulate the entire approach to ethics based on the subjectivist turn, whether the foundations of ethics claimed to be discoverable only in "your own breast" or exclusively in "the constitution of your own nature" are held to be those of reason or experience, or some combination of the two.

I will briefly examine two examples of such attempts to produce universal ethical theories from the consciousness of the solitary individual— the one example that of a rationalist and the other, that of an empiricist— showing in each case why the attempt failed and what we can learn about nihilism from these failures. The first example is Kant's ethical theory; the second is Mill's ethical theory.

In his *Fundamental Principles of the Metaphysics of Morals* (first published in 1785), Kant rejects any empiricist form of ethics, insisting that ethics must be founded purely on the dictates of reason. He assumes that if a law or principle is to have genuine moral force (i.e., be a wholly dependable basis of moral obligation), it must carry with it absolute necessity and universality, or be unconditionally valid. An unconditionally valid law or principle is one that is categorical rather than hypothetical, because it applies in all circumstances without exception and because it ascribes an inherent quality to moral acts rather than allowing them to be regarded merely as a means to some empirical end, such as happiness.[10] Laws or principles derived inductively from experience are only probabilistic at best, never certain, so they cannot have the universality and necessity essential to *bona fide* moral rules. Moreover, such empirical rules can only be hypothetical in character, never categorical, because we could at any time decide to give up the empirical end or ends to which they are merely a means. A categorical imperative, on the other hand, leaves the will with no such license to justify its suspension.

Kant also rejects the goal of happiness, often presented as the supreme moral end in empirical ethical theories, on the ground that it suffers from a fatal vagueness (he claims that conceptions of what count as true happiness vary widely among human beings), and on the further ground that even if we could agree on what happiness is, the problem of deciding how to secure it would still exist. This problem would involve us in deliberations about an appropriate art or technique, rather than in considerations of necessary and universal principles. The central question of morality, Kant also tells us, is not how to *attain* happiness but how to *become worthy* of happiness.

Finally, he argues that the empirical approach puts motives to virtue and vice in the same class, because it views the moral end as the object of some kind of fundamental impulse or desire. He believes that this does violence to the distinctive character of moral obligation and requires that we become involved in the vague and endlessly debatable enterprise of trying to decide what motives actually underlie any particular action or projected action. Because we can never be completely sure that an act is not performed from a motive of mere self-love, we might despair of the ideal of acting from duty altogether, did not reason issue its own inflexible moral demands.

When he turns to the processes of pure reasoning he believes inevitably to accompany his most thoughtful assessments of moral situations, Kant claims to have found there the categorical principles that must forever elude any kind of empirical inference. These principles are three in number and are actually but variations on, or interconnected statements of, one fundamental moral law. Kant also interprets them as expressions of the three categories of quantity laid out in his *Critique of Pure Reason*.

The form of the moral law, he tells us, is that of universality: we are subject to the categorical command to act only on maxims that we can will to become universal laws. This statement of the moral law implies the category of *unity*; there is but one form of the moral law, namely, its universality. The matter of the moral law expresses the category of *plurality*, for it stipulates that each and every human being (or, more inclusively, every rational being) must be treated as an end, and never merely as a means to an end. There are, thus, as many moral ends as there are rational beings. The complete characterization of the moral law makes it clear that all rational beings are obligated to act in such a way that the maxims underlying their actions can qualify them to be members in a universal kingdom of ends. Because such a kingdom comprises all rational beings and is the comprehensive system of their mutual relations, its concept implies the category of *totality*.

The universal kingdom of ends is analogous to the kingdom of nature, Kant informs us, because it is inescapably bound to the rule of law. But while the kingdom of nature operates by laws of efficient causes acting under necessitation from without (as had been shown so conclusively in the mathematical physics of Newton and others), and can therefore be viewed as a machine, the kingdom of ends operates by laws of freedom. These laws are not imposed from without but from within, as each rational being discovers through its autonomous uses of reason the laws that are fit to govern its moral behavior and realizes that it must freely choose to submit its actions to these laws. In such a kingdom of ends, rational beings are thus both subjects and sovereigns—responsible to the moral laws decreed by their own rational wills, laws which, in that crucial sense, they legislate for themselves.

Because Kant insists that human beings are free just to the extent that their wills are obedient to the moral laws made known by the exercise of their "practical reason," it follows that a totally free human act is as law-bound as any event or set of events in physical nature. But it is also just this capacity of autonomy, or rational self-legislation and responsible freedom in the domain of morals, which shows each person to be possessed of a unique, irreplaceable dignity. This dignity means that persons must always be accorded the respect of being regarded and treated as ends, and never simply as a means, i.e., never as we feel entitled to treat a physical object or some other feature of the natural world.[11] The kingdom of nature and the kingdom of ends are therefore analogous in some aspects but fundamentally different in others.

Admirable though it is in many respects, Kant's ethical theory is open to a number of criticisms, some of which indicate serious problems with the subjectivist approach it typifies. Two points of criticism anticipated in our previous discussions are suggested by Kant's claims, first, that objectivity in a system of ethics entails the universality and necessity of its basis principles; and second, that such principles can be readily produced despite the requirement of a subjectivist and presuppositionless starting point for the ethical theory. The first claim regards the search for certain foundations as the only route to absolute, nonperspectival truths and values, a pursuit and ideal already criticized at some length in other connections (see especially Chapter 6, Sections 1 and 2; Chapter 8, Section 2).

The second claim makes evident that Kant continues to assume, as he did in his examinations of the capacities and limitations of pure theoretical reason in the first *Critique*, that methodical exploration of his own detached subjectivity will produce the requisite certain, universally applicable principles. He simply takes it for granted, in other words, that what seems necessary and universal to him, in his solitary self-probings, will be so for all other human beings who rationally contemplate their own subjective consciousness. Hence, he makes the same unargued leap from subjectivity to intersubjectivity in developing his ethical theory that I noted and criticized when discussing his epistemology and the epistemologies of others who followed in his train, such as the absolute idealists. He does so without expressing any new reservations about the chasm between the phenomenal and the noumenal worlds, which is such a prominent feature of the epistemology of the first *Critique*, and which, by implication, makes forever unknowable the ontic reality and structural traits of other minds.[12]

A third problem is the hiatus between a determined nature and a free human nature that Kant supposes but also tries to surmount, at least to some extent, by his notion that both realms are bound by necessary and universal laws and that a kingdom of rational beings would be as law-like in its modes of ethical deportment as is every aspect of physical nature. This move does not explain, and Kant is well aware that it does not, how human beings can be at one and the same time immersed in a causally determined nature and wholly subject to its laws, and yet free, as they must be, in their moral lives.

The only solution he suggests is that free rational beings belong to the realm of noumenal reality, while a causally determined nature belongs to that realm of phenomena or mere appearance to which pure theoretical reason is restricted (1949:73-79). This solution is singularly *ad hoc* and unconvincing, and it leaves us with a depiction of two entirely different kinds of reason resident in the same human breast, each disclosing its necessary and universal laws to introspective analysis and each suggesting a view of the world contradicting the other. Moreover, why ontological priority must be assigned to the conclusions of practical reason, centering on the traits and duties of the moral will, as opposed to those of theoretical reason, focusing on mathematical and scientific reasoning, Kant is never able successfully to explain. But in this assumption we see a significant seed of the subject matter of the third section of the following chapter, which I term *the primacy of the will*.

Fourth, Kant's reasoning is not nearly as naked and presuppositionless, i.e., as independent of influences of his own historical situation and cultural surroundings, as he believes it to be, or as his subjectivist method dictates that it *must* be. This fact casts doubt on the alleged universality and necessity of his moral (as well as his theoretical) first principles. One obvious indication of such influence is the extent to which he takes for granted the idea of a mechanical, wholly mathematical nature that, due largely to Newton's genius, was enjoying widespread and generally uncritical acclaim in Kant's time. This idea is a crucial factor in the problematic, near-absolute distinction Kant feels compelled to draw between theoretical and practical reason, and it tends to embroil him in those conundrums of the dualistic outlook that had already perplexed Descartes, Locke, and others among his predecessors.

Two other indications of Kant's acculturated ways of seeing add further detail to this fourth line of criticism. The first is his assumption, nowhere questioned but essential to all his thinking, that the defining property of human beings is their possession of reason. The overriding significance of the moral law, he tells us at one place in his *Fundamental Principles*, is not merely that it interests us, which it admittedly does, "but that it interests us because it is valid for us as men, inasmuch as it had its source in our will as intelligences, in other words, in our proper self . . ." (78). This notion of the "proper self" as one which is eminently rational and guides its choices by the mandates of reason is conspicuously Aristotelian, and it has had long and tenacious influence in Western thought. If we question it, much of Kant's ethics, as well as other aspects of his philosophy, is cast in doubt.

Second, we must consider the effects of Kant's religious heritage on his philosophical reflections. In all his ethical thinking he stresses the austere purity and majesty of moral duty, or what he terms "the absolute value of the mere will, in which no account is taken of its utility" (i.e., of its relations to mere sensuous inclinations and desires) (12). This pivotal theme reflects the influence of a certain kind of duty-obsessed, pietistic Protestantism, prominent in the Prussia of his day (Kant's own parents were pietists), which was radically distrustful of the natural instincts whose seductive power it viewed as a sign of the fallen nature of human beings. This same pietism also adamantly insisted on the practical character of Christian faith, downplaying its intellectual content as well as attempts at rational defense of that content— an insistence that foreshadows Kant's distinction between theoretical and practical reason and that is implicit in his statement in the first *Critique* that he had "found it necessary to deny *knowledge*, in order to make room for *faith*" (1958:29). He is speaking here of showing the limits of theoretical reason in order to make room for practical reason, and for the morally grounded religious faith that he was convinced the latter could rationally affirm.

Kant's sharp distinction between moral duty and sensuous inclination also exhibits the persuasive power exerted by the Christian scriptures on his thinking. The fact that we are *commanded* in the New Testament to love our neighbor, even our enemy, shows clearly, he says, the complete independence of duty from inclination. We are obligated to love those toward whom we might have "a natural and unconquerable aversion." This is "a love which is seated in the will, and not in the propensions of sense—in principles of action and not of tender sympathy; and it is this love alone which can be commanded" (1949:17). What is true of the Christian duty of love, Kant reasons, must be true of moral duty in general.

The intricate connections he draws out in his later writings between moral freedom, on the one hand, and belief in God and immortality, on the other, and his elaborate discussions of the ways in which "morality leads ineluctably to religion" (1960:5), give further evidence of the close ties between Kant's religious heritage and his moral theorizing (see my 1981, Ch. 4). To grasp this connection more vividly, we only need imagine how different the outcome of such theorizing would probably have been had Kant been the product of a Buddhist, rather than a Christian, culture. Finally, the stress on the dignity and uniqueness of each person that plays so crucial a role in his ethics reminds us of the Christian idea that every soul is infinitely precious in the eyes of God.

Observations such as these make apparent how mistaken it is to view Kant's moral theory in the way he intends us to: as the result of his systematic refining of an ore of innate truth, extracted by introspective tunnelings into the virgin soil of his subjective consciousness. But if the path to a universal moral system cannot be laid out by self-contained, apodictic principles of reason in the manner envisioned by Kant, can it then be mapped by the data of experience? Can the individual philosopher, by probing into his subjectively experienced sentiments, impulses, and desires find there the basis for an ethic binding upon us all?

Among the philosophers who have given an affirmative answer to this question is Mill, whose brief work entitled *Utilitarianism* (first published in *Fraser's Magazine* in 1861) has had as resounding an impact on subsequent ethical theorizing as has Kant's equally concise *Fundamental Principles of the Metaphysics of Morals*. When Mill delves into his subjective experience, he claims to find but one elemental desire of which all other desires are either subsets or to which they are simply the means. That desire is the desire for happiness. Accordingly, he sets forth a version of ethical hedonism, interpreting all moral principles, such as the rights and duties associated with the concept of justice, and the obligations of beneficience, in terms of what he holds to be the universal and all-inclusive desire for happiness.

Three problems with such an ethic immediately present themselves, and Mill addresses himself specifically to each. How can a merely empirical ethic be given a foundation of proof sufficiently rigorous for it to be judged strictly and universally binding on the moral life? Whose happiness ought I to be most concerned with—my own, or that of others? And what exactly is meant by the term *happiness* conceived as the moral end? The first question recalls Kant's criticism of empirically grounded ethical theories, and the third one relates to Kant's claim that happiness is too vague a concept to serve as the basis and goal for an operative ethical theory. The second question asks whether, or how, having a hedonistic ethic collapse into ethical egoism can be avoided.

A fourth problem also has some importance. It can be tied to Kant's complaint that an empirical ethic requires that motives to virtue and motives to vice occupy the same class—the class of all experienced desires—and that such an ethic condemns us to be forever examining our motives in order to gain assurance that we are acting in accordance with those that impel us toward good rather than evil. But we can never be entirely sure, in Kant's judgment, so such an ethic cannot safeguard us against either the pitfall of rationalization or the abyss of moral despair. Mill also develops a reply to this complaint, as will be seen.

Mill's response to the first problem is that, while he does not claim to be able to offer anything like a proof in geometry for his ethical theory, and thus cannot hope to achieve for the theory apodictic or deductive certainty, he can provide arguments for it that are entirely adequate and persuasive. He firmly believes that a strong probabilistic basis is all that is needed to give his ethics universal scope and objective status. I do not have space here to go into detail about his argument for the claim that happiness is the supreme universal moral good. Suffice it to say that he tries to demonstrate, by a process of elimination, that our happiness is the only thing we humans desire and that asking whether we *ought* to desire that which alone we *can* desire, especially in view of the evident fact that our desires are the springs of all our actions, would be odd (see Chs. 1, 4 of *Utilitarianism*; also Lang and Stahl 1969).

As for the second problem, Mill expounds on what he calls *the ultimate sanction* of the utilitarian ethic. This turns on the interaction of two fundamental instincts of human nature: the instinct of self-preservation and the instinct of sympathy. The latter motivates us to sense in connection with the welfare of others something closely akin to the instinct for our own welfare, and in their suffering and pain, something similar to our desire to eliminate our own misery. So just as we naturally endeavor to achieve our own happiness and to avoid personal pain, we find ourselves desiring happiness and release from pain in the experience of others. The upshot is that we come to see ourselves as but one unit in a calculus of universal happiness, and arrive at the concept of the supreme moral good as the greatest happiness for the greatest number.

As a unit in that calculus, we do owe ourselves happiness, but we are not entitled to treat ourselves differently from others or to give any precedence to our happiness over that of other persons. Mill's argument, then, is that an instinct of sympathy, which he finds to be deeply rooted and powerfully effective in his own consciousness, provides the transition from an indeterminate hedonism to an altrustic ethics of binding obligation to seek the happiness of all human beings, and not just happiness for oneself. He also points out that this instinct is reinforced and strengthened by "all healthy growth of society," that leads the individual to identify his feelings more and more with the good of others and to take it as axiomatic that he should pay due regard to their well being (1957:41, see also 22-23).

Mill deals with the third problem by asserting that the happiness focused upon in his moral theory is not a state of existence marked by all-consuming ecstasy or unbroken rapture—for such a moral end would be patently unrealistic—but rather a life of general tranquility, contentment, and absence of pain. He also explains that the happiness of which he speaks is not simply a matter of quantity but, first and foremost, a matter of quality. We can easily find out what the higher qualities of pleasure are by asking those who have experienced the full range of pleasures attainable by human beings which ones they most desire. If we do so, Mill predicts, we will discover that such persons give clear and unequivocable preference to the pleasures of mind and spirit over mere physical gratifications. His hypothesis, which he invites us to put to the empirical test, is that it is in our very nature to prefer those qualities of happiness that we are uniquely capable, as human beings, of attaining. He presumably has in mind pleasures of education, friendship, social improvement, religious contemplation, aesthetic enjoyment, scientific and philosophic investigation, and the like.

Mill therefore concludes that much more unanimity, or potential for unanimity, exists among reflective and experienced persons about the meaning of happiness, taken as the moral ideal, than Kant thought possible. He also observes that the term *happiness*, especially when its meaning is carefully specified and examined as above, suffers from no greater, and arguably far less, vagueness of meaning than do the general ideals of other moral theories. The point would apply not only to such key terms as *virtue*, *justice*, *beneficence*, or *moderation*, but also to Kant's concept of an inherently *good will* and the several formulations of the categorical imperative Kant uses to define the nature of that good will.

Mill's way of speaking to the fourth problem is to distinguish three aspects of an action: its underlying motive or pattern of motives, its intended consequences, and its actual consequences; and to insist that the morality of any action lies squarely and exclusively in the second aspect. An action is moral if and only if the person or persons performing it intend for it to bring about the consequence of the greatest happiness for the greatest number.

The motives behind an action, writes Mill, are relevant only to assessment of the moral quality of the agent, not to an appraisal of the moral quality of the action itself. We can speculate that one of his reasons for saying this would be directly in line with Kant's point: knowing precisely what the motives for any given action might be is extremely difficult. These are generally complex and difficult to determine, either by others or by the person whose motives they are. Mill does explicitly observe that we do not have to *feel* altruistic all the time in order to be practicing utilitarians; what is important is that we *intend* an altruistic outcome with our actions.

Finally, the actual consequences of an action, important though they be in other contexts, have nothing to do with the moral quality of the action. It is only essential that we carefully weigh all the possible consequences of the alternatives for choice available to us in a given situation, and that we choose that course of action we believe is likely to have the most utilitarian effect. Holding persons responsible for consequences of their actions that turn out to have been beyond their anticipation or control is foolish.

The shrewdness of these responses is undeniable and helps to explain why Mill's brand of utilitarianism has been so influential. But he does not succeed any more than Kant did in deriving an ethical theory from pure, presuppositionless introspection, or in setting forth a view of the foundations of morals immune to substantial objections. Four such objections can show the extent to which Mill's ethics fails to realize the Enlightenment dream of finding the basis for a scientific system of ethics, and one which will command universal acceptance, in the individual's own subjective awareness.

The first objection is that Mill's attempted proof (in the fourth chapter of *Utilitarianism*) for the assertion that the sole underlying incentive for all human action is the desire for happiness, tends to capitalize on just that vagueness of the term *happiness* of which Kant complained. One indication of this vagueness is that happiness can mean, and often does mean, simply the satisfaction of our desires. To say, therefore, that what we all most fundamentally desire is happiness, can easily turn out to signify nothing more than that what we all desire is the satisfaction of our desires (see 1957:59, where Mill seems to be asserting just this). In that event, the touted "proof" turns out to be the statement of a tautology rather than a carefully constructed empirical argument.

Second, Mill's argument—that our desires are the springs of our actions; that we have ultimately but one desire, that for happiness; and that therefore questioning whether we ought to act in accordance with that which alone impels us to act would be odd—seems to be in conflict with the distinction he draws elsewhere in *Utilitarianism* between motivation and intention. We have already called attention to the significance he attaches to this distinction, but it is also worth noting that in a footnote in the second edition (1864), he complains of "an oversight too common to be quite venial," i.e., that of confounding "the very different ideas of Motive and Intention" (1957:24, n.3). To draw a fundamental distinction between motive and intention seems to imply that at least two major springs of our actions are found, rather than just one; in which case it would not be at all odd to ask whether we ought always to act in accordance with our desires, or more particularly, with the putatively all-encompassing desire for happiness.

This second objection is given added force when we note that Mill is a determinist, because it is not at all clear how making a fundamental distinction between motives and intentions in a deterministic theory of human action is possible. In his *An Examination of Sir William Hamilton's Philosophy* (1865), Mill vigorously defends causal determinism, arguing for the view that we inevitably act in accord with our strongest desire in any particular circumstance (1884:II, 284-286, 299-302). If this is so, what role can be left to intention, as something distinct from motivation or desire? If Mill cannot make such a distinction in a manner consistent with his deterministic metaphysics, then he cannot consistently present the aforementioned response, pivoting on that distinction, to one of Kant's complaints about empirical ethical theories.

What exactly does Mill mean by the term *intention*? He says toward the end of the fourth chapter of *Utilitarianism* that the distinction between desire and will is "an authentic and highly important psychological fact" (1957:50). I interpret him to mean by *will* the same thing as he means by *intention*. The difference, he explains, is that between natural desires (all of which are variations on the theme of aversion to pain and attraction toward pleasure) and those habits of action that had their original source in natural desires but now constitute a kind of derivative motive or desire in their own right. There is no such thing as a will or intention capable of acting against the strongest desire in place at any given moment, but the strongest desire may have the form of habit, in which case it functions as will or intention. Thus, when Mill stresses the role of good intentions and claims that these, rather than good motives, are the basis for the morality of actions, he probably has in mind habits of practice that, as the outcome of the right kind of education and environmental conditioning, can be counted on to produce, or generally to produce, utilitarian choices (see 1957:50-51; 1884:II, 287-288).

By this analysis, motives and habits (the latter treated as one kind of motive but also construed as intentions) belong to the same class. So Kant's objection is not answered. We still have the problem of being able to ascertain whether, out of the welter of motives (including habits or intentions) which might have determined a decision, it was the morally right one which did in fact determine it. More fundamentally, Mill gives no assurance of having the kind of freedom Kant believes to be at issue in his criticisms of empirically grounded ethical systems: a freedom capable of acting in relative independence of motives in light of moral reasons, one that can be held morally responsible precisely because it is not captive to the strongest motive but is able freely to choose among alternative courses of action available to it in a single motivational context. The possession of such freedom implies an ability to act in accordance with a weaker motive, and thus to override the stronger motive.

Mill's intentions, however, for which he claims such great psychological and moral importance, do not allow for freedom of this kind. They are just one more type of efficient cause; so they cannot have the rationally adjudicative, purposive, telic significance the term *intention* ordinarily conveys. It is this assumed connotation that imparts to Mill's distinction between motive and intent most of its initial persuasiveness and that makes his response to Kant seem more deeply probing and decisive than it really is. To act on the basis of an intention, for Mill, is simply to play out the tape of our environmental conditioning. It is to behave "in character," in keeping with patterns of habit and disposition selected for us from without, by forces entirely beyond our control.

Mill does argue that our character "is in part amenable to our will," but his argument seems to assume a power of character-transcending choice inconsistent with his own deterministic theory. He concedes as much when, after saying that "we can, by employing the proper means, improve our character," he appends the qualification that we "shall not indeed do so unless we desire our improvement, and desire it more than we dislike the means which must be employed for the purpose" (1884:II, 299). Whether our desire for improvement outweighs our other desires, however, is a function of our previous environmental conditioning, and that conditioning, in turn, is the inevitable outcome of the causally determined character of reality as a whole, so there would not appear to be any way out of the circle.

Mill's problem with intentionality is an interesting reversal of a problem already discussed in connection with Kant. While the German philosopher is at a loss when it comes to explaining how free beings can possibly interact with a mechanistic kingdom of nature, the British thinker is beset with comparable difficulty in being able to defend a basic distinction between motives and intentions—or between efficient causes, on the one hand, and choices guided by reasons, on the other—given his subsumption of the whole of human life under what he and so many others of his time (and of Kant's time as well) regard as the unvarying cause-effect relations of the natural order (see Mill 1884:II, 280-281).

This polar opposition between Mill and Kant is one more illustration of the persistent supposition that dualism or reductionism are the sole metaphysical options, a belief criticized earlier and traced to the mesmerizing effect on the modern mind of its unquestioning submission to the hegemony of natural science (see the second sections of Chapters Three and Seven). We also have evidence here of a significant respect in which Mill's ethical thinking is shaped by the particular cultural environment within which he stands, contrary to his claim to be providing us with a detached, universal, strictly empirical account of the nature of moral obligation.

The third objection to Mill's theory discloses another way in which his thinking reflects aspects of his cultural environment.[13] This objection focuses on the distinction he makes between the quantities and qualities of pleasure, and on his insistence that we are morally obligated to prefer pleasures of higher quality over those of lower quality. The trouble with this part of his theory, as has been frequently observed, is that it inconsistently introduces a criterion of moral action other than that of sheer pleasure. As noted earlier, we can also view this aspect of his theory as attempt on Mill's part to reduce the vagueness and variability of the term *happiness* complained of by Kant; but it buys its measure of success at the price of incoherence.

It is not pleasure or happiness itself that we must now seek as the supreme moral end, but rather certain *kinds* of pleasure. How do we determine what the higher types of pleasure are? By asking those who have experienced the whole range of pleasures. But why should their preferences be obligatory for everyone else? Why should a small minority of what could be considered cultured aesthetes be allowed to override the great majority of other human beings? And how do we know that these few have not just been conditioned by the happenstances of their own particular environments to prefer certain pleasures over others? Mill's deterministic environmentalism is in apparent conflict with his appeal to a supposedly constant human nature, capable, when properly understood, of disclosing universal moral principles.

Moreover, we are given no indication that Mill has made any attempt to put his claim about the higher qualities of pleasure to an empirical test, in spite of his insistence on a precise empirical mode of inquiry; nor are we given any assurance such a test could even be devised that would yield the kind of uniform, unambiguous results needed to confirm the claim. Where are we going to find a set of persons who have explored in requisite depth the full range of pleasures and appraised their relative desirability in a cool and judicious manner? Given the fact that such candidates as would come immediately to mind have already devoted much of their time and attention to the so-called higher pleasures, would they not in all likelihood already be heavily biased toward those forms of pleasure? How could we be sure that they had ever given all the forms and intensities of the lower pleasures a fair and equal consideration? Mill suggests no experimental strategy for getting at these obvious problems; in fact, he does not even hint that such problems exist.

The immediate context in which Mill makes the distinction between quantities and qualities of pleasure is in response to the objection that utilitarianism is "a doctrine worthy only of swine" (1957:11). He introduces the distinction with the obvious intent of arriving at a conception of happiness peculiarly appropriate to human beings. But this means that his account of the moral *summum bonum* rests on a certain conception of human nature. That conception has not really been arrived at on the basis of detached scientific investigations into his own introspective experience, taken as typifying human experience in general, nor does it reflect any carefully designed scientific studies of the experience of others. Rather, it reflects Mill's own upbringing, and beyond that, the influence of Greco-Roman and Judaeo-Christian conceptions of human nature and human obligation. This is evident from the fact that he only mentions the distinction of quantity from quality of pleasure in passing and makes no attempt to give it detailed empirical support, despite its critical importance to his whole theory.

What began as a forthright hedonistic ethics becomes on further analysis, an ethics of obligation to fulfill the unique potentialities of human nature, an ethics not very different from Aristotle's. Were this not so, then we would be entirely right in concluding that Aldous Huxley's Brave New World is a fulfilment (and thus a telling indictment) of Mill's ethic (see especially Huxley 1958:ix, 119-120). As Huxley points out so dramatically and persuasively in the novel by that name, in order to achieve the higher pleasures of which Mill speaks, we must be willing to endure many anxieties and pains. If, by contrast, the maximum quantity of pleasure for the whole of society is all that is required, then the techniques of eugenics, behavioral conditioning, and drug-induced euphoria of the Brave New World can achieve that end eminently well. It is, to be sure, a static and conformist society, ruled in its every aspect by jaded despots; and the pleasures it offers are, by usual moral reckoning, deplorably low-grade. But what does that matter, given the enormous *amount* of pleasure it contains?

Would Mill have delighted in Huxley's portrayal of the Brave New World, regarding its universally accessible pleasures and pervasive sense of contentment and well-being as the achievement of his ethical ideal? Obviously not, as we can easily tell from his uncompromising insistence on the priority of the higher qualities of pleasure, notably absent in this society, as well as from Chapter Five of *Utilitarianism*, where he expounds a concept of social justice that stands in patent opposition to the ethos, institutions, and practices of Huxley's fictional society.[14] Totally lacking in the Brave New World, moreover, are the independence of thought and action, and the individuality and diversity of forms of life that Mill so enthusiastically recommends in his essay *On Liberty*, published just two years before the appearance of *Utilitarianism*.

Mill's ethical theory is like an ellipse, with two independent foci. The one is the pleasure principle altruistically conceived, where the only relevant consideration can be that of the amount of pleasure, distributed as evenly as possible over the whole of society. The other is a vision of a distinct *telos* or fitting ideal of human fulfilment and excellence reminiscent of Aristotle, an ideal in which the quality of attainment has paramount value. Mill does not succeed in weaving these two principles into a unified moral theory, and this must be recognized as a central failure of his theory. His inherited moral assumptions are in conflict with his intention to produce a purely scientific or empirical account of human obligation; and it is just these assumptions, smuggled into the theory at critical junctures, that impart to it an aura of plausibility and acceptibility it would otherwise lack.

The fourth criticism of Mill's ethic calls attention to another decisive moral premise on which it rests, a premise betraying the tacit influence of his culture and tradition rather than being derived from the detached self-examination his empirical method prescribes. The only basis Mill offers for opting for an altruistic rather than egoistic hedonism is his insistence on the fundamental role of the instinct of sympathy in channelling the root desire for happiness. But he nowhere shows why, in cases of conflict between the instinct of self-preservation and that of sympathy—cases that crop up repeatedly in our experience and constitute much of the challenge and difficulty of our moral life—we are obligated to favor the latter as over against the former. Yet the type of altruistic ethic Mill purports to defend requires that the second instinct outweigh the first one. Otherwise, by his own reasoning, we would routinely give, and be entitled to give, more importance to our own happiness than he contends it deserves.

The fact that Mill provides us with no argumentative analysis or defense for this basic feature of his ethical theory shows how natural and easy it is for him to assume an altruistic interpretation of morality and an altruistic view of human nature, as well as assuming unquestioning acceptance of his claims for them by at least the great majority of his readers. It shows in one more specific way that his theory is not built from the ground up by a patient amassing of unbiased data of introspective experience and a cumulative series of inductive proofs incorporating such data, but presupposes at nearly every stage of its construction a supporting framework of preexisting cultural attitude and belief. Descartes's myth of pure beginnings is exposed again for the delusion that it is.

Numerous similar attempts have been made to ground objective systems of ethics in the subjectivity of the isolated individual, attempts that presuppose both the possibility and necessity of penetrating into a universal core of human awareness untouched by the individual's specific cultural circumstances or concrete social relations. These attempts have had no more success in achieving their aim than do the ethical theories of Kant and Mill. It is not that all such attempts have been abject failures. Certainly this could not be said of the theories of Kant and Mill, which illuminate moral values and the moral life in many important ways. It is rather than they fail in what they centrally set out to accomplish.

Either the formulaters of such theories end up neglecting crucial problems or concerns of morality altogether—an example is Mill's failure to address coherently the problem of how to resolve conflicts between the two instincts of self-preservation and sympathy[15]—or they introduce and rely upon ethical principles not strictly derived by their theories as such but reflective instead of their own particular modes of acculturation—a factor perspicuously present in the theories of both Kant and Mill. Moreover, no theory of this kind has succeeded to date in realizing either Kant's ideal of a system of necessary and universal ethical principles that elicits the same degree of common consensus as mathematical physics did in his own time, or Mill's ideal of a theory of ethics rooted as firmly and unequivocally in simple givens of experience as he and most other nineteenth-century intellectuals perceived natural science to be.

We do not have to search very far to discover the basic reason for the repeated failures of this kind of ethical system. The reason is simply that there is no such thing as a core of human personality that is purely autonomous and self-contained, completely insulated from the influences of social institutions and commonly assumed social ends. And if there were, it could not be the source of the universal moral principles sought for in such systems. The human subject cut off from concrete patterns of cultural and social relatedness, and from all socially mediated systems of communication and meaning, would be as mute when it comes to fundamental ethical principles as I have already argued (Chapter Eight, Section 2) such a subject would have to be with respect to basic principles of knowledge and understanding.

The most we could expect from such a detached subject would be naked self-assertion and willfulness, devoid of context and constraint, and therefore devoid of moral significance. The self considered in complete isolation (assuming for the moment that there could be such) brings us not to universal moral (and existential) values, but to moral (and existential) nihilism. As Stirner, Nietzsche, Russell, Sartre, Monod, and others have discovered, the subjectivist turn in ethics, when carried out consistently to its end, can have but one outcome: radical *subjectivism*, the abandonment of all hope for an objective grounding of moral or other values. Their negative conclusion has persuasive force, however, only as long as we fail critically to examine the highly questionable premise on which it rests.

Why has the search for a foundation for moral rules in human subjectivity been so persistent from early modern times to the present day? I think it is largely because of a usually unspoken but generally assumed process of elimination. Reflection on this process can help us further understand and critically assess the connection between the subjectivist turn in ethics and the topic of nihilism. It has been widely supposed that the only possible sources of moral value, other than the reasonings or experiences of the isolated individual, are God, culture, and nature.

Modern thought has tended to eliminate God from consideration because it has wanted to find an immanent basis of moral values, one centered in human autonomy rather than in God's authority as putatively made known through the Scriptures or ecclesiastical doctrines. This desire lies at the very heart of the transition from medieval to modern times, as we saw in the preceding chapter when considering differences between medieval and modern methods of inquiry. As for existing social outlooks and customs, these have appeared too arbitrary, variable, and imprecise (as was illustrated by our discussion of Descartes's complaints to this effect). They have seemed to fall far short of the ideal of nonperspectivity, universality, and finality of results which for moderns is exemplified in the resounding successes of natural science. (This ideal was already firmly entrenched, as already indicated, in the theological and philosophical traditions predating the scientific revolution.) Also, reliance on customary beliefs and practices as the source of morality has not accorded with the modern ideal of starting our inquiries from scratch and facing boldly forward toward a progressive future rather than backward toward a past seen as stale and obsolete. Lastly , the concept of nature that has seemed to moderns to be necessitated by the scientific revolution has tended to eliminate nature from consideration as a source of moral or other values. Viewed from the Newtonian perspective, nature is without inherent ends or values; it is interpreted as nothing more than an efficient-causal mechanism.

The only viable approach that seems to remain, therefore, is to search for a basis of moral values in human subjectivity. When such sophisticated versions of this approach as those of Kant and Mill fail, and when it comes increasingly to be realized that all such attempts are foredoomed to failure, we are left with moral nihilism. This outcome is made to seem even more inevitable when we contrast the perceived successes of natural science with the collapse of the confident Enlightenment expectation of being able to match the achievements of natural science with an ethical science grounded in the universal traits of human nature discernible in each human breast—traits brought into clear light by a method of introspective analysis deliberately modeled on the method of natural science.

However, several key deficiencies are found in this process of elimination approach that brings us step-by-step to the outcome of nihilism. One is that it suffers from a misapprehension of the character of natural science and of the scope and finality of its results. Once this misapprehension is exposed, the contrast between scientific and moral principles is much less glaring than generally thought. The second deficiency is a failure to understand the need for a plurality of methods appropriate to different types of inquiry, coupled with a strong tendency to overestimate the importance of method itself. A third deficiency is overlooking an alternative not taken into account in the process of elimination approach. I will briefly examine each of these deficiencies.

Despite the tenacity of the modern view that the findings of natural science well up out of pure reason or pure experience, in complete disconnection from communally inherited valuations, assumptions, and commitments, a more astute analysis of scientific inquiry reveals that this is hardly the case. We have already alluded to this fact in calling attention to the valuative assumptions indispensable to scientific investigation and yet not themselves scientifically derivable or adjudicable; it is also implicit in our discussions of the ineliminable tacit, socially transmitted elements operative in all reasoning, including scientific reasoning. In what is probably the most influential and thought-provoking book on the nature of science in recent years, *The Structure of Scientific Revolutions* (first published in 1962; second, enlarged edition, 1970), Thomas Kuhn makes a detailed case for the decisive role of preexisting communal environment in the development and defense of scientific theories. He also presents persuasive arguments for the view that natural science is not so much a steadily accumulating body of finally verified theories as it is an active, ongoing program of paradigm-dependent research subject to revolutionary discontinuities.[16]

The process of elimination analysis presented above also misapprehends the scope of natural science. I argued in Chapter Seven that science by itself is not equipped to settle all questions relating to the philosophy of nature. The belief that there are no aspects of our experience of nature which can be drawn upon to address issues of value is highly debatable[17] and cannot be conclusively resolved on the basis of theories in science, especially the theories of a now outmoded Newtonian science.

As far as the requirement of a plurality of methods is concerned, we need only recall the by now well-documented failures of the logical positivist movement of the early twentieth century to confine all cognitive assertions to those which can be scientifically verified. Also relevant to recognition of this requirement is the fact that within science as practiced there is no single well-defined method, universally employed in every aspect or type of scientific investigation, but a striking variety of explanatory procedures (see Toulmin 1972:157-158). With regard to the modern tendency grossly to exaggerate the importance of method itself, a thoroughgoing exposure of this fallacy is contained in Barrett's appropriately titled book, *The Illusion of Technique*. I have also been critical of this tendency in discussions of the hegemony of science and the search for truth through method (Chapters Seven and Eight).

4. THE PLURALISTIC ALTERNATIVE

Finally and most importantly, there is the matter of an overlooked alternative in the process of elimination argument now under discussion. This alternative relates to the cultural and social dimensions of our knowing, including our knowledge of values. It has been widely assumed in modern thought that allowing any basic role to these dimensions would fatally compromise the objectivity of knowledge and value, making epistemic and valuative claims merely relative to some set of existing historical circumstances. Implicit in this assumption are two other suppositions. The first is that *objectivity* can only mean complete nonperspectivity and nontemporality of outlook. The second is that allowing a basic role to cultural and social influences on our thought and experience means that we are utterly captive to those influences, in the sense of having no capacity to transcend or criticize them, even in the slightest degree.

Each of these beliefs can be challenged, however, and challenging them will allow us to introduce the alternative not represented in the process of elimination approach above. Consideration of this alternative requires first that we take issue with the either-or manner in which that approach is presented, namely, that either the isolated individual, on the one hand, or the surrounding culture and society, on the other, must be regarded as a potential source of ethical values, and thus that both cannot be considered together or in relationship to one another.

What we must understand is that individual and society are correlative conceptions; only in abstraction can the one be contemplated apart from the other. Dewey gets at one side of this interdependent relationship when he asserts that

> the whole history of science, art and morals proves that the mind that appears *in* individuals is not as such individual mind. The former is in itself a system of belief, recognitions, and ignorances, of acceptances and rejections, of expectancies and appraisals of meanings which have been instituted under the influence of custom and tradition (1958:219).

It would be an equally egregious mistake, however, to conclude that there is no important distinction between individual thought and experience and patterns of societal belief and expectation.

Abstract notions, such as the individual considered apart from society, or society considered apart from individuals, are useful in many contexts. But it is fatal to confuse them with concrete fact, as we do when we search for a ground of objective truths and values in a supposed acultural substratum of individual subjectivity, or when we deny to individuals any distinctive creative insight or freedom, seeing them as nothing more than channels of environmental conditioning and social compulsion. The whole history of philosophy, science, art, morals, and religion, to echo Dewey, puts the lie as much to this second way of confounding the abstract and the concrete as it does to the first.

An individual-cum-society approach, in which each is seen as being in dialectical tension with the other, each as capable of shaping and influencing the other, is the neglected alternative to which I now refer. While not denying the decisive influences of culture on individual thought and awareness, we can still recognize the individual's capacity, especially in interaction with other individuals within a society, creatively to transform what is given in that society. Thus, while the individual cannot work effectively in a vacuum, but only in concert with others and only with the resources provided by existing cultures—her own in particular, but others as well—she is no mere pawn or plaything of social influences.[18] Recognition of the dialectical relationship of individual and culture can provide us with all the objective perspective required to develop and assess ethical claims, and to avoid the subjectivist conclusions of moral nihilism. The same approach and line of argument can hold against nihilistic claims about factual knowledge and linguistic meaning; it thereby gives us much needed critical focus on the confluence of these three tributaries into the mainstream of existential nihilism.

It could be objected at this point that because distinct cultural traditions do not always agree in their most fundamental convictions about fact, meaning, or value, and sometimes radically disagree, an individual-cum-society approach can only lead to a dead end of cultural relativism, which can afford no more opportunity for objective conclusions than does individual relativism. But this objection holds only if we make the unwarranted assumption that different cultures are hermetically sealed from one another and that, consequently, individuals within a given cultural setting have no capacity to enter sympathetically into, or to learn anything from, the assumptions and beliefs of cultures different from their own. If we refuse to acquiesce in this untenable assumption, then we are presented with a situation of cultural *pluralism* rather than one of mere *relativism*.

When we combine the individual-cum-society approach and a pluralistic view of differences among cultural systems, we have the makings of a new model of objective inquiry into questions of truth, meaning, and value. What we can expect to achieve with this model is not necessary, universal, or final conclusions; we must set aside any illusions about being able to arrive at a God's-eye view of the world. Objectivity in this view means the readiness to learn and the willingness to be critically informed by insights and discoveries gained through close interaction with other persons and the manifold resources of our own and other cultures. The barriers to such communication and interaction implied by the subjectivist turn no longer apply, because we no longer assume the primacy of individual self-awareness or perceive the isolated individual as the sole possible source of objective truth.

Such a vision of objective truth, meaning, and value is content to base its inquiries on cumulative, broadly based—albeit contingent—historical and social conceptualizations and experiences, rather than demanding absolute necessity in either its starting points or outcomes. It seeks to be as fully informed as it can by the diversity of human thought and experience, as manifested throughout human history and in the different cultures of the present day, but does not make pretentious claims to a universal point of view that settles or overrides important points of cultural difference. Objectivity does not require universality as much as it demands respect for the different ways in which human experience and basic factors in the human condition can be ordered and interpreted by cultural forms. This kind of objectivity safeguards us against cultural hubris and too narrow a view of the world in which we live. Finally, this vision of objectivity is open-ended and open-minded, rather than asserting or aspiring toward finality, because it realizes that it cannot predict what changes the future might bring, or what kind of revisions in present patterns of thinking, communicating, or valuing might be required by the deeper probings of an ongoing dialogical process.

In this vision, the legacy of our cultural past is not seen as a constraint but as an opportunity, offering us a wealth of materials, some perhaps long neglected or unnoticed, for present reappropriation and imaginative reconstruction. The diversity of cultures is viewed not as a threat but as a welcome invitation to widen our own understandings through encounters with novel ways of thinking and experiencing.

A provocative analysis of what this kind of intercultural dialogue could accomplish and come to mean in the field of religion is provided in the book by John B. Cobb, Jr., *Beyond Dialogue: Toward a Mutual Transformation of Christianity and Buddhism*. Cobb tries to show that Christianity and Buddhism have much to learn from dialogue with each other, both in the sense of each's being stimulated to reassess and bring into more comprehensive perspective its conventional ways of thinking, and in the sense of each's being encouraged to make creative use of aspects of its own cultural heritage that may not have been given the attention or emphasis they deserve, but that can now be seen in a fresh light. Thus the aim of religious dialogue, as viewed by Cobb, is not just mutual understanding of differences—which is where a relativistic approach would stop—but experiences of mutual challenge and growth such as those envisioned in the pluralistic approach to knowledge and value being outlined here. These experiences are not always pleasant, however; they can sometimes, particularly in their initial stages, be extremely disorienting and painful. But a readiness to undergo them in the interest of gaining a more adequate or inclusive understanding is an essential part of what is required by an objective approach to the world, in the sense of that term I am now advocating.

The following is an example of what Cobb has in mind. A Christian intensely concerned with her personal salvation finds it unsettling (to say the least) to be told by the Buddhist that there is no self to be saved. Her first reaction is to dismiss the claim as completely foreign to her own outlook and tradition. But by taking it seriously and endeavoring to learn from it, she gradually becomes aware of a certain one-sidedness and inadequacy in her religious vision—especially as that bears on the concept of the self—and of elements in her own tradition, hitherto unrecognized by her, which can serve as correctives to this distortion of vision. This need not mean that she becomes a convert to Buddhism, only that her understanding of Christianity is broadened, enriched, and altered in at least this one crucial respect by her encounter with Buddhism. Cobb tries to exhibit in some detail what such a transformed Christian conception of the self would be like. His analysis also has important implications for the concept of the self in general, suggesting that Westerners as a whole, and not just Christians, have much to learn from Buddhist views.

This approach to truth, meaning, and value can rightly be termed objective, because it orients outward toward the human experience in all its accumulated complexity, diversity, and depth, rather than focusing inward on the individual subject or narrowly restricting itself to what may seem obvious and indisputable only within a particular cultural context. Seen in this light, no incompatibility is evidenced between objectivity and perspectivity. We do not simply settle down into our own existing personal or cultural perspectives as we would be obliged to do in a relativistic approach, but aggressively seek their enrichment and transformation through continuing investigations of alternative possibilities in our own traditions, as well as by a sustained process of dialogical inquiry into what can be learned from the institutions, practices, and modes of interpretation, expression, and communication typical of other traditions. We cannot escape perspectivity by such an approach, because finite perspectives are all we have to work with, and we are always subject to the uncertainties of the future. But we can avoid having to do all our thinking within the confines of a single static point of view.

What of the world as it exists independently of our cultural perspectives? How can we have any hope of gaining access to that, if all our knowings and valuings are suffused with elements of our particular acculturation, or at most can be critically appraised only from the varied perspectives of cultural systems other than our own? Without the possibility of access to reality as it truly is, apart from us and our cultural systems, how can we judge any of our claims to be objective? The answer is that objectivity cannot be made to require this kind of access, because it is in the very nature of the case impossible.

The Kant of the first *Critique* was brilliantly right in saying that it makes no sense to yearn for a knowledge that transcends the very conditions making knowledge possible. His discovery of this principle is perhaps his greatest and most enduring contribution to human thought. My present interpretation of the concept of objectivity concurs with his insistence on this fundamental principle. My main differences from Kant, however, are the following: the stress on the role of culture in laying down the basic categories of thought and analysis, the allowance for significant variability in the assumed nature of such categories from one culture or historical period to another, and the rejection of Kant's felt need to uncover some unadulturated core of human subjectivity that can put us in touch with immutable principles of theoretical and moral reason.

Hence, "the world" is never the world as it might exist in and of itself; it is always the world as it exists *for us*, in our thought and experience. As such, it is a phenomenon of culture, just as everything which can come within the orbit of individual knowledge and awareness must be. As we have argued before, there is no world of bare facticity or in-itself reality that need concern us. There is for us only the world of human apprehension and meaning, the world as seen from our human perspectives.

These perspectives can be challenged and enriched by our continuing experiences of nature. However, such experiences are never pristine but always take place within the matrix of cultures. We do not come at nature "bare." This view of our situation is similar to the view of scientific theorizing taken by Israel Scheffler. Scheffler argues that observation statements in science "are not isolated certainties, but must be accomodated with other beliefs in a process during which they themselves may be overridden" (1967:119). Thus, even though such statements are usually (and rightly) accorded priority in the testing of scientific theories, that priority is not absolute, mainly because no set of observation statements is free of the influence of antecedent theoretical assumptions.

Harold Brown assists our understanding of this idea when he notes a constant "interplay" or "transaction" between theory and observation in science, "where theory determines what observations are worth making and how they are to be understood, and observation provides challenges to accepted theoretical structures" (1979:167). Similarly, our encounters with nature can and do challenge certain of our cultural assumptions, but those encounters continue to be informed by other cultural assumptions. To use the familiar image, we can never reconstruct our culture "in drydock," i.e., by recourse to some set of absolute, culture-transcending truths or values. We can only repair a part of it "at sea," i.e., while continuing to rely on other aspects of it.

I have argued for a dialectical relation of individual and culture; the same dialectical relation applies to culture and nature. Neither can be cleanly separated from the other, even though the relative distinction between them is of undeniable utility and importance. The point can also be made from another direction when we recall that human beings and their cultures are expressions of potencies within nature, and intimately dependent on the context of nature regarded as a sustaining ecosystem. Thus, in a profound sense, we and our institutions are part and parcel of the natural order—a fact we neglect at our peril. I touched briefly on this idea in Chapter Five, Section 2. Its increasing acceptance today is an excellent example of how existing cultural assumptions can be transformed by encounters with nature, even though these encounters are themselves mediated by the deep-lying cultural assumptions that make possible continuing conceptual development and change.

But what about nature before the evolution of human beings? What was it like when there was no human culture? Surely we can meaningfully ask questions such as these! The answer is that we can and do have conceptions of nature prior to the advent of our species because we can postdict on the basis of our present experiences and cultural understandings what nature would have been like *had we been there to perceive and contemplate it*. It is not really nature "bare" that we envision, therefore, but nature viewed from our present experiential, assumptional, and theoretical perspectives.

Maurice Merleau-Ponty calls attention to this inescapable fact in a work published posthumously as *The Visible and the Invisible:*

> I am forever subjected to the centrifugal movement that makes a cognitive object exist for a thought, and there is no question of my quitting this position and examining what Being might be before being thought by me or (what amounts to the same thing) by another, or what the interworld (*l'intermonde*) might be like where our gazes cross and our perceptions overlap; there is no brute world, there is only an elaborated world; there is no intermundane space but only a significant 'world' (1968; quoted Dallmayr 1981:104).

An important phrase in this statement for our purposes is "what amounts to the same thing." For here Merleau-Ponty, himself a phenomenologist, expresses his departure from the subjectivist perspective of early, Husserlian phenomenology and alludes to his own analysis of intersubjective truth, meaning, and value as mediated in large measure by the commonalities of tradition and culture, particularly the commonalities of shared speech (on this see Dallmayr 1981:93, 96, 103). The lesson is that these commonalities are given for each of us in the deepest levels of our being. Our experiences of intersubjectivity do not, therefore, require some tortuous explanation in terms of a presumed more primary level of wholly subjective awareness or absolute being-for-itself.[19]

Is a continuing dialogical discussion or interaction between individual and individual, individual and culture, culture and culture, and culture and nature all we can expect in the way of objectivity? Are there no truths to be established forever and ever, no discoveries of meaning and value to be put at last beyond the pale of reasonable debate? Must every hard-sought achievement of consensus be subject to possible future unraveling, and are there some deep issues on which universal consensus may never be won, even for a period of time? The answer to all of these questions is yes, an answer that recognizes and expresses the fact of our finitude. To be in this kind of situation, one in which we must learn to live with our differences of perspective and conclusion, is part of what it means to be a human being. The fact of these differences need not reduce us to despair; it does so only if we continue to insist on the goals of necessity, universality, and finality so fondly sought in the modern period.

We can even learn to value these differences if we come to see them as expressing possibilities of apprehension and awareness which no single perspective can encompass, and thus as offering us complementary and mutually corrective visions of the enormity of the experienced world. Because we cannot think and act within all the possible perspectives at once, and cannot even comprehend what all those possibilities are, we can at least strive to make the particular ones within which we do operate as coherent, comprehensive, and complete as we can, partly by bringing them into tension and interaction with alternative points of view. There is much for us to do in this pluralistic model of objectivity and not the slightest warrant for allowing our inquiries to slacken or cease, despite our recognition that not even our best individual or collective efforts can be expected to bring us to a final resting place. We can give up this dream of a final resting place as soon as we recognize the unavoidable perspectivity or temporal and social situatedness of all of our conceptions of truth, meaning, and value. This is not to say that there is no such thing as objective truth, meaning, or value; it is simply to say that objectivity does not require that we be transported to some absolute vantage point beyond the changing, finite conditions of our concrete historical and cultural existence.[20]

Absolutists sometimes argue that the only alternative to their position is an indifferent relativism in which inquiry collapses, because there are no universal truths or values to be inquired into. There is a valid criticism of relativism here, one which helps to account for the continued attractiveness of the absolutist position. But absolutism is not the only alternative to relativism, as I am trying to show; and we do not have to believe in timeless truths or values for meaningful inquiry to take place.

There is also validity in the relativistic critique of absolutism, e.g., relativism's emphasis on the historical and cultural situatedness of our knowing, communicating, and valuing; its stress on the extreme difficulty of achieving genuine cross-cultural understanding, to say nothing of adjudications of questions of truth and value that do not just load the issues in favor of one cultural outlook; and its insistence that after even our best efforts profound differences will often remain. But the pluralistic alternative can take these points into consideration without endorsing the kind of relativistic position that forecloses in advance the hope of progress in cross-cultural communications or inquiry, or that regards individuals as nothing more than standardized products of a given cultural milieu.

To recognize the fact of an irreducible plurality of perspectives does not mean that we must assume that all existing perspectives are equally cogent or immune to criticism. For example, some will turn out on examination to be more coherent, inclusive, resilient, or creative than others. Furthermore, each perspective is subject to constructive change through sustained exploration of its points of intersection or difference with other perspectives and through critical discussions about its comparative strengths or weaknesses in relation to those other perspectives. We cannot completely transcend our perspectives, but we can find ways to modify and improve them, or perhaps even radically to transform them, as we open ourselves to dialogue with those who hold to different points of view.

Chapter 10

Social-Political Individualism, Fact-Value Dichotomy, and Primacy of Will

... I put for a general inclination of all mankind, a perpetual and restless desire of power after power, that ceaseth only in death.
—*Thomas Hobbes (Leviathan, Pt. I, Ch. XI, in Burtt 1939:158-159)*

1. INDIVIDUALISM IN MODERN SOCIAL PHILOSOPHY

The fifth philosophical assumption to be analyzed as a source of nihilism is closely related to the fourth source. Whereas the latter seeks to base knowledge, cognitive meaning, and moral value in the isolated subject, this fifth source takes an atomistic view of social and political institutions, holding the individual human being to be both ground and end of these institutions. This conception is not without its positive values; to these I will pay due regard. But it also contains certain nihilistic tendencies to which I will devote my attention.

Four salient ideas inform the dominant social philosophy of the modern period, usually termed the *philosophy of bourgeois liberalism*. Each idea epitomizes the extreme individualism characterizing this philosophy. The four ideas are the concept of social contract; its accompanying notion of a state of nature; an instrumentalist interpretation of political institutions; and a "negative" conception of political freedom, emphasizing "freedom from" rather than "freedom for."[1]

That the idea of social contract be regarded as something that actually happened at some point in the past is not crucial. The Dutch jurist, Hugo Grotius, and Locke think that such contracts did serve as the original sources for political institutions, for example, while Hobbes and Jean Jacques Rousseau do not. What is crucial to this idea is that existing governments and states are seen to have legitimacy only to the extent that they can be regarded as deriving from an implicit, if not explicit, agreement among their individual citizens, an agreement that serves those citizens' best interests or that is founded on the dictates of their autonomous experience or reason.

This idea of social contract is set in opposition to medieval appeals to tradition, hierarchical authority, and the divine will as the basis of political cohesion, and it comes to play a central role in modern attempts at radical reform of social and political institutions. As such, it marks a transition from the feudal past to the ascendancy of the middle class and tends to express the distinctive interests and aspirations of that class. Here, as in epistemology, a program is set in motion that seeks to raze the old structures and get down to the legitimate foundations of political institutions through a scientific study of the needs, wants, interests, and judgments of the solitary individual.

Intimately allied with the idea of social contract is the notion that the "natural" state of human life is one prior to political community and independent of social and political institutions. It is only by the creation of social institutions that essentially isolated individuals come to live together in community. Thus, the individual is prior to the community, and it is assumed that if we are to understand and explain the existence of communal structures and organizations, we must do so by tracing their genesis to characteristics of the persons comprising them.

Here we witness in another context the reductive, analytic phase of the accepted method of scientific explanation stemming from Galileo, now being consciously applied in the domain of social philosophy. The emphasis given to the idea of the state of nature is also one manifestation of the pronounced nominalistic drift of modern thought. We have already been made aware of this drift by our investigations of the epistemologies of Descartes, Locke, Hume, and Kant,[2] as well as by our discussions of Mauthner's linguistic philosophy and Stirner's moral theory. The nominalistic belief in the priority of individuals to relations and relational concepts is also implicit, of course, in the fourth philosophical source of nihilism, given the primacy it instinctively assigns to the thought or experience of the detached human subject.

The state of nature, which the act of social contract supposedly brings to an end, is variously viewed by modern thinkers, but in all cases the absolute priority of the individual to society stands out clearly. Hobbes sees this state as one of ceaseless war of every human against every other human—as a condition of naked, unbridled aggression and conflict. How could it be otherwise, if he is granted his claim that all human activity is rooted in "a perpetual and restless desire for power after power," an unrelenting egoistic striving for personal gratification, dominance, and glory? (*Leviathan*, Pt. I, Ch. XI; in Burtt 1939:159). In sharp opposition to Hobbes, Grotius views humans in the state of nature as possessing a compelling social instinct or "appetite," even while living completely apart from social and political institutions. This appetite finds its fulfillment in the emergence of communities whose contractual basis is the natural law inscribed in each human breast or, as Grotius puts it, "appropriate to the human intellect" (*De Jure Belli ac Pacis*, Prolegomena, Section 16; quoted Cassirer 1961:257).

Locke, for his part, views the state of nature as one of relative social harmony rather than unremitting conflict, thus tending to side with Grotius in this respect. He differs from the Dutch thinker, however, in his tendency to view social and political institutions in more utilitarian, and less strictly juristic terms, although he does give stress to the role of natural rights. He represents a kind of transition point from the ideas of social contract based on natural law and those based entirely on considerations of utility. In the late eighteenth century, Jeremy Bentham sets completely aside the tradition of natural law and offers a purely utilitarian analysis and justification of political institutions. Bentham rejects the theory of social contract as such, but he retains a strong individualistic bias in his political philosophy. I will say more about him in a moment, when I present the third major idea characterizing modern political philosophy.

Rousseau, himself, a celebrated champion of social contract, joins with Hobbes in viewing the state of nature in egoistic terms. However, for him this state is one in which individuals are not so much actively set against one another as withdrawn from, and completely indifferent to, each other: a kind of passive egoism. He flatly rejects any idea of an original social instinct that naturally drives humans together. Each person in the state of nature is wholly preoccupied with his own self-interest and self-preservation.

The basis of contract Rousseau advocates is human reason, which can enact for itself by a deliberate act of will the ground of social order Rousseau calls "the general will." This will, like Kant's "good will" which it anticipates, is legislated by, and therefore binding upon, each rational individual. Its establishment in social systems can bring individuals into a new social framework that eradicates the evils of past societies and provides for the perfect freedom of which Kant also speaks: the freedom of absolute commitment to rationally legislated moral law. Rousseau sees this freedom as concentrated upon the true self-interest of the individual because it enhances and develops the rational side of human nature.

What all of the above conceptions of the state of nature have in common is their assumption that the individual is prior to all forms of social organization, logically if not historically, and that political institutions can be adequately interpreted and explained only by a method of resolution into properties of their constituent members.

The political philosophy of the modern period has also tended increasingly toward a purely instrumentalist view of the state, its third basic trait. The state is entitled to exist, according to most modern thinkers, not because it has any inherent value or importance, not because it commands any allegiance or loyalty in its own right, but solely for the sake of its constituent individuals. It is true that Grotius and Hobbes insist on the absolute authority of the state, once established on its contractual basis, and allow for no right of rebellion by individuals. But while Grotius views the legitimate state as enshrining divinely ordained principles of natural law, and thus as having a kind of inherent majesty and incontestible authority for that reason,[3] Hobbes views the absolute power of the state (embodied in its monarch) as the only effective antidote against the tendencies toward utter chaos and mutual violence and self-destruction inherent in an egoistic human nature. It is clearly in the long-range interest of each individual, therefore, that there be a state with absolute power to curb individual self-will. Realization of this long-range personal interest motivates people to enter the social contract in the first place. Thus, for Hobbes, the state is an instrument for each individual's protection against the aggressive, acquisitive tendencies of his neighbor; that is the sole justification for its existence. The individual is willing to put himself under its absolute sway, with no right of redress, simply because he is well aware that without the state his life would be "poor, nasty, brutish, and short" *(Leviathan,* Pt. I, Ch. XIII; in Burtt 1939:161).

Locke also tends to see the state in functional terms and is famous for giving primacy to its obligation to protect the right of individuals to accumulate and enjoy their private property, defined by him as those possessions which are the fruit of the individual's labor. "The great and chief end ... of men's uniting into commonwealths, and putting themselves under government," he proclaims in the second of his *Two Treatises of Civil Government,* published together in 1690, "is the preservation of their property, to which in the state of nature there are many things wanting" (Ch. IX; in Burtt 1939:453). Locke also puts great stake in the state's duty to insure the individual's right of personal freedom; I say more about this below.

Rousseau tends toward an instrumentalist view of the state as well when he traces its legitimacy solely to its incorporation of the "general will," i.e., to what each individual rationally wills for himself and thus consents, through contract, to make himself responsible to uphold under pain of legal sanction and restraint. He steers in the direction of Grotius and Hobbes when he argues that, once a state has been established on the basis of the general will, the individual must give up himself unreservedly to its authority and forfeit all rights of resistance. However, this total alienation of individual rights to the rights of the legitimate state which Rousseau advocates is inconsistent with his view that the state's sole claim to authority is the power delegated to it by the people, and with his admission that what may at one time be a valid system of government may at a later time be found to have failed in its obligation to live up to the mandate of the general will. There certainly is a sense, therefore, in which government for him is purely functional in relation to its citizens, as stated above. This sense is concisely conveyed in Cassirer's statement that for this French social theorist even a legitimate government's political authority has "merely administrative significance" (1961:264). Its only value and importance, that is to say, lies in its duty to carry out the moral will posited by each of its citizens.

Bentham minces no words in declaring the state's entire subservience to the needs, desires, and interests of the individual, thus bringing to climactic expression the instrumentalist conception of its nature and role that has come increasingly to be assumed in recent times.

> The community is a fictitious *body*, composed of the individual persons who are considered as constituting its *members*. The interest of the community then is—what? The sum of the interests of the members who compose it. It is in vain to talk of the interest of the community, without understanding what is the interest of the individual (*An Introduction to the Principles of Morals and Legislation*, Ch. I, Secs. iv and v; in Burtt 1939:792).

He gives further emphasis to this idea of the state in the same work when he declares that "the happiness of the individuals of whom a community is composed—that is, their pleasures and their security—is the end and the sole end which the legislator ought to have in view . . ." (Ch. III, Sec. i; Burtt 1939:800). The state is nothing in itself, then, but merely an aggregation of individuals; whatever value it has is simply the summation of their individual wishes and aspirations. Its entire purpose is to facilitate the maximum gratification of individual interests, which can all be brought down to an interest in avoiding personal pain and attaining personal happiness.

Nowhere else is the tendency of modern social philosophy to view social groups in purely individualistic and instrumental terms more clearly seen than in its largely negative conception of political freedom. This is the fourth general characteristic of this philosophy. What we are calling the "negative" idea of political freedom is, as noted previously, the idea of freedom from, rather than freedom for—freedom seen as the absence of governmental interference with individual liberty, except where such interference is clearly required for the protection of some individuals from encroachments by others upon their right to independence of thought and action.

Locke endorses this idea when he maintains that "the end of law is . . . to preserve and enlarge freedom," and proceeds to explain that the kind of freedom he has in mind is the individual's "liberty to dispose and order freely as he lists his person, actions, possessions, and his whole property within the allowance of those laws under which he is, and therein not to be subject to the arbitrary will of another, but freely follow his own" (second of *Two Treatises Concerning Civil Government*, Ch. VI, Sec. 57; in Burtt 1939:425). As noted earlier, Locke gives particular prominence to the individual's entitlement to acquire and make use of his material possessions in his own fashion. He contends that government is obligated to refrain from interfering with the economic activities of its citizens, except to the extent required to protect their right to economic freedom.

Mill makes the concept of negative freedom the linchpin of his essay *On Liberty*, as can be seen when he states that the essay's whole purpose is "to assert one very simple principle," namely, "that the sole end for which mankind are warranted, individually or collectively, in interfering with the liberty of action of any of their number, is self-protection." He puts the point even more strongly when he says that the "only freedom which deserves the name is that of pursuing our own good in our own way. . . ." It follows that "the only part of the conduct of anyone, for which he is amenable to society, is that which concerns others." This includes such things as sharing in the common defense, giving evidence in courts of justice, and guarding "the defenseless against ill-usage": all of which are ways of ensuring that the liberty of individuals within a society is not violated. In the part of his conduct "which merely concerns himself," Mill writes, the individual's "independence is, of right, absolute. Over himself, over his own body and mind, the individual is sovereign" (Burtt 1939:956, 958).

The particular individual freedoms that society has an obligation to protect and uphold, according to Mill, include such liberties as those of conscience, thought and feeling, expressing and publishing opinions, tastes and pursuits, "framing the plan of our life to suit our own character," and coming together "for any purpose not involving harm to others." He summarizes the ruling conviction that underlies this essentially negative conception of freedom when he says, "Mankind are greater gainers by suffering each other to live as seems good to themselves, than by compelling each to live as seems good to the rest" (Burtt 1939:958).

He states this conviction somewhat differently when he contends that it is in "proportion to the development of his individuality" that "each person becomes more valuable to himself, and is therefore capable of being more valuable to others."[4] Believing that encouraging individuality by governments and other social organizations "produces, or can produce, well-developed human beings," and that it will thereby bring about the salutary development of society itself (Burtt 1939:998-999), Mill leaves the distinct impression that persons or groups left free to pursue their own interests vigorously will automatically contribute to the social good. A version of this view was put forth earlier by his countryman Adam Smith and applied in the area of economics. It was also vigorously championed by the so-called Physiocrats in France.[5]

Thus, for Mill, who like Locke has been an extremely influential spokesmen for modern liberal social theory, society's good is simply the good of its constituent individuals. He argues that this good can be best achieved by leaving each person free to think, act, and set the course of his own life as he sees fit. Mill is, of course, a utilitarian, and continues to stress the positive obligation individuals have to be beneficent toward one another. His is not an individualism of mere self-seeking. But he recommends that this obligation of beneficence be undertaken by individuals on their own initiatives and through their own voluntary associations. It is not something he wants to entrust to government, especially in view of "the great evil" of adding unnecessarily to the government's power (Burtt 1939:1036-1037). As does Locke, he also stresses the importance of barring government from the economic affairs of individuals or groups. "Speaking generally," he says, "there is no one so fit to conduct any business, or to determine how or by whom it shall be conducted, as those who are personally interested in it" (Burtt 1939:1036). In this way, he adds his support to the liberal economic ideal of *laissez-faire*, echoing its unswerving commitment to the maximum independence of private property and private enterprise.

Many others have expressed and developed the concept of negative freedom. It has become one of the most widely acclaimed ideas in modern political thought and has insinuated itself deeply into political institutions of the West. Much good has resulted from this idea and, more generally, from the whole individualistic orientation and focus of modern social thought.[6] Whitehead notes that "this modern direction of attention emphasizes truths of the highest value. For example...it has abolished slavery, and has impressed upon the popular imagination the primary rights of mankind" (1948:127). Respect for the dignity and uniqueness of the individual person, for the zest and satisfaction of individual accomplishment, and for the equality of all persons under law—these are aspects of modern social theory to be rightly cherished.

Dallmayr reminds us that free individual scrutiny of ideas is essential to advances in knowledge and that "actions cannot properly be called moral in the absence of autonomous judgment" (1981:9). Kundera observes that genuine artistic creativity is possible only in those societies where there is fundamental regard for the distinction between the public and the private realms, so that the solitary reflections of the individual cannot be routinely "suppressed by the ubiquitous collectivity" (1981:17). The essential role of individuals in contributing to the transformation of cultures emphasized in the last chapter clearly would be made extremely difficult, if not impossible, without political guarantees of freedom of dissent and allowance for the dissemination of controversial ideas. In the absence of such guarantees, the pluralistic model of inquiry recommended there could hardly be implemented.

But the atomistic emphasis of modern social thought also has its darker side, expressive of yet another way in which the modern sensibility and outlook can be seen to have distinct tendencies in the direction of nihilism. We will look critically at three nihilistic tendencies implicit in liberal social philosophy.

The first of these is the disposition on the part of this philosophy, and of institutions based on it, to underwrite and inculcate the relativistic attitude toward values that we have frequently expounded upon and criticized in these pages as a species of nihilism. Berlin makes explicit the connection between the liberal doctrine of negative freedom and a relativism of values when he contends that the doctrine requires that "the frontiers between individuals and groups of men . . .be drawn solely with a view to preventing collisions between human purposes, all of which must be considered to be equally ultimate, uncriticizable ends in themselves" (1958:38 note; cited Strauss 1961:137). The last part of his statement is a clear declaration of relativism with respect to fundamental questions of value. The only exception to this relativism that Berlin and many other liberal social theorists will allow is their insistence that society must protect at all costs the absolute value of individual freedom.

In the classical liberal philosophy, then, government's role is conceived as that of efficiency of management, of treading a careful course among the varying value interests of individuals, trying to balance at best it can their contending claims and interests. Its central art is the art of compromise, not the art of moral leadership. Government's task is to be responsive, not directive, allowing for a diversity of value interests but making no attempt to work through that diversity toward some higher synthesis or larger social vision. Problems of value are left to the individual; the government's role is purely managerial. It sets policies as directed to do so by the majority of its citizens, or as needed to keep conflicts of interest among them to a minimum, with no attempt to appraise the moral quality of their varied expressions of will.

The typical stance of government in liberal social theory is not pluralistic (at least not in the sense of that term outlined in the previous chapter), although it is frequently claimed to be so. It is relativistic. People who grow up in the context of political and other institutions where relativism is the prevailing philosophy are encouraged to think of values as private and nonnegotiable. Formerly, under the aegis of the liberal doctrine of the separation of church and state, the church was expected to compensate for the valuative neutrality of the state. But the modern church is divided into a large number of denominations and groups that differ among themselves on fundamental valuative issues, so they have become just one more divided constituency for liberal governments to placate and manage. Moreover, many ecclesiastical organizations have themselves tended increasingly toward the accommodating, purely managerial style of leadership and conception of their institutional role we are attributing to liberal governments.

This pervasive outlook is something quite different from a pluralistic toleration and open-mindedness about differences of outlook, regarded as the necessary baseline for constructive, mutually transformative debate. I am speaking here of a relativistic view of such differences in which there is no anticipation that shared inquiry or focused dialogue can bring significant progress toward agreement on contested issues of value. Thus in liberal social theory, as practiced by liberal political institutions, official sanction is given to a radical relativism of values. Individuals within these institutions are routinely taught, mainly by unstated assumptions and attitudes underlying the practices of the institutions, to think of values in this nihilistic way.[7]

The effect of this kind of prolonged exposure to a relativistic outlook on values is illustrated by my experience as a university professor. When I ask my freshman students to give their perception of the difference between the natural sciences and the humanities, their answer is almost always that the sciences deal in concrete, publicly proven facts, while the humanities deal in emotions and personal opinions. If I press them to explain why they think this way, they usually answer to the effect that the humanities address vague problems of aesthetic and moral value, and pose unresolvable questions about the nature and meaning of human existence. These beginning students go on to argue that because it is well known that all claims to value and purpose are expressions of emotional preference and of particular kinds of upbringing, and are therefore relative to the individuals who make them, it is obvious that the humanities, where values are the central concern, must be as they describe them.

The majority of these students, in other words, take a positivistic view of values similar to that of Russell or Monod, although they usually know nothing about philosophical positivism. I have become increasingly convinced over the quarter of a century of my teaching career that they come to this conclusion in large measure because of the tacit influences of the social institutions that nurture them. To put the point more bluntly, I am asserting that they are routinely schooled in nihilism by governmental and other social organizations cast in the mold of the individualistic liberalism I have been discussing. Thus, they tend to confuse the virtue of toleration with an attitude of polite nonintereference in disputed questions of value, and they instinctively assume that the only alternative to a relativistic perspective on values is an unyielding absolutism they sense to be untenable in the kind of world in which we live.[8] When these young people do react against relativism—and some do so with a passion born of despair—they often opt for a type of religiously sanctioned, authoritarian absolutism similar to that of the student I talked about in Chapter One.

A second nihilistic implication of liberal social theory is that it imposes upon each individual the onerous and impossible burden of having to answer almost entirely by and for himself crucial questions such as: What is my freedom for? What are its positive responsibilities? What obligations do I have toward others and to society as a whole, beyond respecting the freedom of others to respond to such questions in their own particular ways? What do I do when my perceptions of these positive responsibilities come into conflict with the perceptions of others? How should I direct my life so as to find purpose and meaning in it? Where can I find help in doing so, and to what extent or in what ways should I seek to assist others in doing so?

The concept of negative freedom has the implication of assigning the resolution of such questions to the isolated individual, as already seen. This consequence is also implicit in the elusiveness and lack of specific content in such notions as "the general will," "the pursuit of happiness," "the greatest pleasure for the greatest number,"[9] or "the maximization of personal self-fulfillment," with which liberal theorists have at least made a stab at defining the positive significance of freedom. Further impetus is given to this outcome by the liberal notion that society has no value in its own right; it has value only to the extent that is subserves the needs, wishes, judgments, and decisions of its constituent individuals.

The citizen in modern liberal society is thus "condemned to be free" (in Sartre's words), with only negative guidelines for the exercise of that freedom. She is encouraged to think that the whole meaning of existence revolves around herself, or that she must somehow create that meaning for herself by her original reflections and introspections. She is given no positive context of values and commitments within which to stand, and discouraged from seeing herself as part of a sustaining tradition, culture, and community whose claim to value extends beyond the role of safeguarding her private interests and giving her latitude to direct her life in her own way.

Not only are persons taught by liberal social theory to regard their political institutions in this manner; they are also encouraged by the general outlook underlying this theory to think of all their social relationships as having only an instrumental significance. These are valuable to me to the extent that I can get something out of them. It follows that I have every right to abandon them when they no longer seem to serve my best interests, or when they are perceived as imposing unwanted restraints on my private freedom. Nothing can be of permanent value to me, in other words, but myself. Because others can be expected to look at their social relations in the same way, the implied situation is one in which each individual is intent upon making use of the others for his own benefit. I will return to this last point when I discuss the third nihilistic implication of liberal social theory.

The authors of a recent study of the effects of Western individualism, particularly as that has manifested itself in the United States, take as one of their focal issues the question of "whether an individualism in which the self has become the main form of reality can really be sustained." Their thesis is that it cannot, that the "quest for purely private fulfilment is illusory" and usually ends in emptiness (Bellah *et al.* 1985:143, 163). They speak of a deep-seated dissatisfaction among those they interviewed in preparation for their book, persons who have unconsciously absorbed and accepted the American ideal of rugged individualism. These people sense that something fundamental is missing in their lives. They yearn for sources of meaning beyond their own idiosyncratic preferences, and beyond the materialistic measures of success that loom so large in their society.

The authors remark that it is hard to find in any of these lives "the kind of story or narrative, as of a pilgrimage or quest, that many cultures have used to link private and public; present, past, and future; the life of the individual to the life of society and the meaning of the cosmos" (83). The highly individualized approach to problems of value and meaning implicitly recommended by classical liberal social theory is nihilistic because it has the effect of cutting off human beings from such communally transmitted and supported patterns of meaning, leaving them with no "objectifiable criteria of right and wrong, good or evil," consigning them to an untenable condition wherein "the self and its feelings" have become the "only moral guide" (76). This condition is recognized as untenable when we come to understand that we "find ourselves not independently of other people and institutions but through them. We never get to the bottom of our selves on our own" (84).

Thus, Bellah and his colleagues are brought by their empirical research and critical reflections to the conclusion that "only a larger whole, a community and a tradition" accorded value in their own right can sustain "genuine individuality" and nurture "both public and private life." Autonomy, far from being in conflict with social solidarity and a firm sense of social purpose, is only made possible by "a strong social group that respects individual differences." The individual is therefore not prior to, or merely subserved by, society and social institutions but is in reciprocal relation to them. Individual and society, private aspirations and larger public aims, must work together, each informing and enriching the other. Failure to perceive this truth is a central error of liberal social thought, one lying at the heart of the wistful, disoriented individualism of contemporary American life (307, 163).[10]

This book's case is convincingly made, and it is one with which I can readily concur. I presented arguments similar to it in response to Cartesian and other forms of the subjectivist turn, in Chapters Eight and Nine. In addition, I looked sympathetically in Chapter Four at the arguments Dostoevsky develops in his novels for his position that mere freedom is not enough, that personal autonomy and unrestricted self-assertion are pitifully inadequate when taken as the sole basis or standard for a meaningful life.

I also observed in Chapter Four that Sartre comes to much the same conclusion as do Bellah and his coauthors when he admits that his doctrine of radically individualized, contentless freedom is a doctrine of *absurd* freedom. It is absurd largely because Sartre's early philosophy, like liberal social theory, takes a highly abstract view of individual human beings, setting them adrift from the values and ends enshrined in their social environments, artificially separating them from the intricate network of their daily communal and cultural relations.[11] Thus for Sartre, as Dallmayr comments, the individual "does not derive his cues from, or own his self-conception to, environmental settings; rather the latter function merely as challenges or obstacles in relation to subjective-individual initiative" (1981:19).

Sartre's view of the individual in *Being and Nothingness* is notably akin to that of Stirner, as already indicated. This kinship of outlook can also be seen in Sidney Hook's exposition of Marx's criticisms of Stirner. Hook notes that Marx regarded Stirner's "ego" as "an even more monstrous abstraction" than the abstractions of "God" and "Man" that Stirner rejected. The isolated ego is an empty abstraction because it disregards "the temporal and social locus of ideals," and because it is oblivious to the fact that no self exists apart "from a whole complex of social relationships, of selves in relation." Contrary to Stirner (and Sartre), Marx saw personality as "a differentiation within a social continuum. It is not the precondition of social life but its most precious effect. Different social systems will give us different personalities and a different idea of personality" (Hook 1962:176-177). I am contending for a view of the self similar to this one, here and in other parts of this book. I defend it as an alternative to the concept of the self that is operative in liberal social theory, a concept that veers sharply in the direction of nihilism.

However, my view of the self as socially and historically situated does not mean—as a similar view has for some Marxists—that the individual person is just a construct of social factors beyond her control, or that she is swept pell-mell by forces of class consciousness and class conflict towards some foreordained historical outcome. It means, rather, that the individual's freedom, while genuine, is given specific, positive direction by her historical-cultural setting and by her character as a socialized being. As Ross puts the point, humans "grow and develop within social contexts which provide them with rational standards by which they can judge their own actions"

(1969:131). Humans conceived apart from these contexts and standards are bare abstractions, not the underlying concrete realities into which—according to liberal social theory—social systems and processes can be resolved.

My view of the self also implies that to regard relations with one's fellow citizens, family members, marriage partners, friends, occupational colleagues, etc., as having only an instrumental importance focused exclusively upon oneself is to strip human life of a major part of its potential value and meaning, and to make it prey to aimlessness and despair. Bellah and his coauthors trace this implication with forceful clarity, against a background of detailed empirical research. In the second general respect now under discussion, then, liberal social philosophy is an invitation to nihilism, to the loneliness and alienation of the narcissistic individual who radically underestimates the social dimensions of his own being, and whose horizon of concern is pinched in upon himself.

The third nihilistic tendency of this philosophy lies in its endorsement of the picture of social relations mentioned earlier: because nothing is of final or inherent value to me but myself, and because I have to anticipate that others will view their social relations in exactly the same way, I am locked into a competitive struggle in which I must strive to win out over others and to make maximum use of them for my own benefit. The motto of this philosophy is something like, "One for one, and none for all." By fostering an atmosphere of intense, self-seeking competition, liberal social theory in its classical form tends to give rise to a deep-seated distrust and mutual animosity among persons that is fundamentally destructive of human community, and thus of meaningful life.[12] It also opens the way, as we shall see, to a heavy-handed bureaucratic domination of public life and social institutions similar to that portrayed by Kafka in *The Castle*.

Of course, the doctrine of negative freedom forbids me from taking unfair advantage of others (i.e., it prohibits my deliberately interfering with any individual's right to freedom), but I am expected to take *fair* advantage of them in every way possible, and to procure for myself as many of the available material resources and as much status and satisfaction as I can. If each individual takes this as his aim, or so liberal social theory seems to assure us, then we will have a vigorous society in which all are given at least the maximum *opportunity* to thrive. Alfie Kohn gives us a concise statement of this aspect of the liberal creed when he notes the widespread assumption in Western societies that "[c]ompetition brings out the best in us. To compete is to strive for goals, to learn competence, to reach for success. Without competition, even minimal productivity, to say nothing of excellence, would disappear" (1986:22).

We can predict that many will be beaten out in the competitive battle, but that is the way of the world. This outcome is implicit in the very idea of competition: "making one person's success depend on another's failure" (22). If this sounds like a kind of social Darwinism, that is the point; the classical liberal theory as we are discussing—especially with regard to its purely instrumentalist view of society and its ideal of a "free for all" of individualistic purusits, with emphasis on unrestricted liberty to acquire and hold material possessions—easily lends itself to a "struggle for survival" and "survival of the fittest" interpretation of social relations.

Bellah and his coauthors point to this consequence as it applies to the star actors in liberal social theory: the middle class. Middle-class individuals in the United States, they note, are routinely taught to be self-reliant, to leave home in order to earn everything they get, to "accept no handouts or gifts," and to free themselves from their families of origin (1958:62). The authors also note that "[i]n the true sense of the term, the middle class is defined not merely by the desire for material betterment but by a conscious, calculating effort to move up the ladder of success." Assuming that "inequality of result is natural" in this process of upward striving, "[m]iddle-class individuals are ... motivated to enter a highly autonomous and demanding quest for achievement ... " (148-149).

Not all can successfully play this middle class game of social mobility; things such as abject family poverty, broken homes, racial and/or sexual discrimination, inadequate education, the perils of ghetto life, and physical or mental handicaps stand in the way of a significant proportion of the population. These people are the most obvious victims of a theory of society in which it is uncritically assumed that our optimal social choices are exactly equal to the sum of our individual choices (Dauer 1986). But even those who "succeed," according to the accepted norms of success, must continue to struggle to maintain their position, ever on guard against ambitious individuals like themselves who stand ready to take advantage of their slightest misstep or evidence of weakness.

There can be little serenity in this way of life for anyone, and no prospect of finding support in communities of mutual obligation and shared concern. Liberal social theory thus implicitly endorses a view of life with others not very different from the accounts of Sartre and Kafka, accounts that are thoroughly nihilistic. Central to all three views is the notion that society is a loose aggregation of wary, self-centered individuals, each seeking to protect his interests at all costs and intent upon finding ways to leapfrog over others so as to gain competitive advantage. Satisfied that this is the only realistic analysis of the individual's "being-for-others," Sartre concludes (see Chapter Four, Section 3) that insurmountable conflict and mutual objectification lie at the heart of all personal relations, and that each of us must resign himself to the pervasive anxiety of being "the unknown object of unknown appraisals" (1966:328).

What Sartre's analysis of human interactions means when translated into the daily affairs of a particular society is shown in chilling detail by Kafka. Rumor and suspicion are rife in the village of Kafka's novel *The Castle*. Each of its citizens is anxiously and exclusively preoccupied with his own interests, and there is no willingness among them to make any effort to support one another in the face of the machinations and gross injustices of the castle bureaucracy. The officialdom of the castle is itself riddled with secrecy, duplicity, and unremitting rivalry. As we saw, only a few at the very top of this highly competitive society have positions of any real significance or power, and their position is extremely isolated and perilous.

To connect liberal social theory with Kafka's nightmarish vision of a totally bureaucratized society might seem like a gross exaggeration. But a society of autonomous individuals, unrestrained by loyalty to family or any other group, ambitiously embarked upon a course of competitiveness and upward mobility, scorning the communal values of inherited tradition in their passion to be free,[13] is a society dangerously ripe for bureaucratic exploitation. It is made so in at least two ways.

One is that the "freedom to make private decisions is bought at the cost of turning over most public decisions to bureaucratic managers and experts" (Bellah *et al.* 1985:150; see also MacIntyre 1981:33). The point of this observation is that the commonly held positive values that in an earlier time were incumbent upon the leaders of a society can no longer be assumed in the highly individualized society of liberal theory. Questions of value are now left to the individual, and it is assumed that the responses to these questions will vary widely among individuals. With this relativizing of value, society loses its moral cohesion and becomes merely an arena of contending interests. The moral influence or constraint individuals might once have been able collectively to exert on the leaders of their social institutions is dissipated and rendered ineffectual.

Those leaders are accordingly left to their own devices, to order and regulate society as they see fit. Their standards for doing so, as we noted earlier, are not so much moral as expedient, for they are expected to respect the privatization of values as part of their respect for individual freedom. Leadership thus becomes a matter of avoiding conflicts or keeping them to a minimum, of ensuring the smooth running of the social machinery by tight organization and expert management and planning, of merely adjusting means to ends and not allowing fundamental moral appraisals of administrative goals to intrude, and most importantly, of jealously preserving the leaders' own positions and prerogatives. Within the administrative leadership there is an endless vying for positions of greater influence and power, the steady rise toward such positions being viewed as the ultimate criterion of success: a kind of administrative *summum bonum*. This view of administrative success is bolstered by the concept of social leadership as calling for the adroit manipulation of means, not for the weighing of moral ends—an attitude that tends over time to transform means into ends. The individuals putatively served by social institutions come to be seen as the most important type of means to be made pliable to administrative goals, and especially the goal of securing and maintaining the power of particular administrators.

Leadership, this is to say, takes on the style and mentality of a perverted bureaucracy. While ostensively based on a conception "of people as ends in themselves," societies based on liberal social theory gravitate in the manner described toward a conception of them "as means to organizational ends" (Bellah *et al.* 1985:125). As MacIntyre states, a society "in which the free and arbitrary choices of individuals are sovereign" turns out to have a marked partnership or affinity with "one in which the bureaucracy is sovereign." With the privatization of values, not only must organizational ends be taken as "given and ... not available for rational scrutiny"; administrators can also arrogate to themselves the function of employing "forms of collectivist control designed ... to limit the anarchy of self-interest" (1981:33).

Because an internal cohesion of communal values cannot be assumed in liberal social theory, the way is opened to the argument that cohesion must be externally imposed on social groups by the expedient stratagems of bureaucratic managers. The only response liberal theory can make to this argument is a restatement of its confidence that an "invisible hand" will somehow produce an orderly society out of vigorous competition and unrestrained pursuit of private interests. To the extent that this argument falls flat—and it is not so much an argument as a statement of belief—to that extent the bureaucratic position gains plausibility. Radical individualism and bureaucratic collectivism are thus, at least from this aspect, in a kind of collusion.[14]

This inherent tendency of liberal individualism toward a Kafkaesque society can also be seen from a second angle. Bellah and his cowriters allude to it when they observe that it is "isolation, not social involvement," that leads most commonly "to conformism and the larger danger of authoritarian manipulation" (1985:162). This spirit of conformism can stem from feelings of acute loneliness and of frustration with the staggering burden of personal autonomy in matters of positive value.[15] These factors may precipitate a desperate hunger for authentic community and cohesive social values—a hunger on which authoritarian groups feed (162). Isolated individuals are especially susceptible to the lure of radically centralized manipulation and control in times of extreme social stress, such as that which affected Germany in the period after World War I.

The shock of defeat, heavy postwar reparations and restraints, severe economic depression, seething resentment at being regarded as a pariah among nations, and other social ills both imagined and real, fueled in Germany a nostalgic longing for the cozy simplicities of a *Volk*-culture. Hitler and his confederates were able to capitalize on this longing. As Richard Rubenstein has shown, there had been in Germany for some time a yearning for *Gemeinschaft*: "an organic group which shared a genuine community of possession, morals, belief, and association," as over against mere *Gesellschaft*, "regarded as the rational and contractual association of isolated, self-seeking individuals bound by no such organic ties" (1966:28; see also Ch. 1).

This yearning, in the context of the shocks and strains of the postwar period, contributed to the disenchantment of many Germans with liberal individualism (clearly represented by the concept of *Gesellschaft*) and made them receptive to the thrilling new sense of national solidarity promised by submission to the absolute authority of the *Führer* and absorption in the collectivist rites and symbols of the Nazi regime. At last there seemed to be a way out of the alienating anonymity, confusion of values, competitiveness, and dissolution of close family and community ties following in the train of modern urban civilization, with its underlying philosophy of centrifugal individualism!

The ultimate result was disaster—especially for the Jews, who did not fit the image of a racially homogeneous *Volk*-culture and served as convenient scapegoats for perceived past ills—but also for the so-called Aryans themselves. Between Hitler's rise to power and the collapse of the Third Reich there came to prevail a ruthless bureaucracy of such monstrous proportions as to make even Kafka's worst nightmares seem like soothing dreams. Beneath its cloak of restored national dignity and inspiring communal ideals, allegedly rooted in ancient Teutonic tradition, it proceeded to develop a program of moral and spiritual nihilism that has had few (if any) parallels in the whole course of human history.[16]

My point is not that the deficiencies of bourgeois liberalism, as I have characterized it, can by themselves explain the rise of Nazism. Not only were there numerous contributing factors;[17] we must also acknowledge that an evil of this magnitude will probably forever elude rational explanation. The point is rather that the collectivist susceptibilities we have seen to be covertly contained in liberal social theory, and in the way of life endorsed by that theory, are made glaringly evident by the triumph of Nazism. The citizens of the Weimar Republic were right in sensing profound defects in the liberal view of social existence, but tragically wrong in precipitously concluding that Hitler's program pointed the way to a better outlook and a better life.

Now that we have explored these three nihilistic tendencies in liberal social theory, we can turn our attention to criticisms of the theory and, more fundamentally, of the individualistic assumption on which it rests. I have already discussed what are perhaps the two most basic mistakes of this theory. The first is supposing that there are or can be such things as concrete persons existing prior to, or apart from, cultural, communal, and historical settings. I have argued that the primordial, *tabula rasa* individual is an abstraction, not a concrete reality. It is that as much from the standpoint of social theory as it is from the standpoint of epistemology, philosophy of language, or ethics. The second mistake is thinking that human beings can find fulfilment in social institutions premised on self-centered, competitive individualism and privatization of values; or that they can flourish apart from communities of mutual support and in independence of communal traditions that define the nature of positive, and not merely negative, moral concern.

In addition to these criticisms, two fallacies and one flagrant contradiction implicit in liberal theory must be pointed out. Finally, an important empirical criticism of one aspect of the theory deserves notice. With these criticisms, I will further expose the untenability of the fifth philosophical assumption, and in that way complete the presentation of one more piece of evidence in my developing case against nihilism.

The first fallacy is the fallacy of composition: uncritically reasoning that the traits of the whole will be a simple aggregation of the traits of its parts. The fallacy is inherent in the liberal supposition, stated by Edward Dauer and mentioned earlier, that our optimal social choices are exactly equal to the sum of our individual choices. In a brief, perceptive article, Dauer discusses this fallacy in the context of economic law. "While some things are best managed by unregulated markets, other good things can only be achieved through collaborative strategies, such as legislation." It may be true, for example, that efficiency in resource use can best be attained by having society's resources "held by their highest-valuing users, and employed in their most productive way." And this end may be achieved by freely working markets and unrestricted private choices. But unregulated markets can also fail to produce the good of distributive fairness or other social goods that are not "capable of being priced and bought and sold." Such goods ought not to be ignored in arriving at legal decisions about economic matters, and their attainment sometimes requires legislation that restricts the competitive freedom of individuals or corporations, or that secures social services (e.g., public transportation or day-care centers) that individual market choices could not be expected to bring about (Dauer 1986).

The good of society, this is to say, is not just the adding together of private goods, and it is not always best attained by allowing maximum freedom to individuals. It may require sacrifice on the part of some or all individuals for the sake of larger, more enduring social ends, and this sacrifice may need to be legislated, not just left to individual good will. Such legislation will need to be based on positive moral principles that go beyond considerations of majority self-interest and that, while respecting the preservation of individual freedom as one extremely important good, do not hold it to be the sole overriding good in all circumstances.

There are dangers in restrictions of individual freedoms guided by visions of the social good, and it would be fatal to underestimate them. But acute dangers also lurk in the liberal philosophy, as we are trying to show. Some significant measure of risk is unavoidable in responsible moral choices, or in the legislation that may emanate from such choices. Despite such risks, a viable society cannot leave moral matters solely in the hands of isolated individuals, nor can it resolve urgent questions of public policy simply by counting noses or pursuing a goal of managerial efficiency. Such points are perhaps obvious when baldly stated, but they tend to be blurred by the exaggerated and fallacious individualism of liberal social theory.

This individualism continues to be uncritically assumed by many persons in contemporary society, persons who see encroachments on individual freedoms as the sole besetting danger. Such persons regard collectivist tendencies as the threat to be fended off at all costs, failing to perceive the subtle affinities that we have discussed between these tendencies and radical individualism. A society that could be completely resolved into atomic individuals or rightly regarded as nothing more than a loose-knit system of negative freedoms would be notoriously weak and fragmented—in fact, hardly a society at all. It would for that very reason be dangerously prey to the wiles of cynical public officials, demagogues, or authoritarian groups—all intent upon imposing a straightjacket of conformity from above.

In addition to the fallacy of composition, liberal social theory is prone to the either-or fallacy, a mode of reasoning that assumes but two extreme alternatives, overlooking other possibilities that may lie between these extremes. Bellah and his colleagues allude to this fallacy in liberal individualism when they comment that in American society, "[w]e deeply feel the emptiness of a life without sustaining social commitments. Yet we are hesitant to articulate our sense that we need one another as much as we need to stand alone, for fear that if we did we would lose our independence altogether" (1985:150). These authors make the same point later on, in talking of the dream "of living in a society that would really be worth living in."

> What we fear above all, and what keeps the new world powerless to be born, is that if we give up our dream of private success for a more genuinely integrated societal community, we will be abandoning our separation and individuation, collapsing into dependence and tyranny. What we find hard to see is the extreme fragmentation of the modern world that really threatens

our individuation; that what is best in our separation and individuation, our sense of dignity and autonomy as persons, requires a new integration if it is to be sustained (1985:285-286).

It is not a choice *either* of individuation *or* collectivization that we should be thinking of, therefore, but rather of ways of bringing the goods of personal autonomy and integrated community into a coherent, mutually supportive relationship. We do not have wholly to sacrifice one good for the sake of preserving the other, as liberal social theory encourages us to think.

Bellah and his colleagues also point to a fundamental contradiction in liberal social theory's advocacy of sustained interpersonal competition. The theory combines "a commitment to the equal right to dignity of every individual" with "an effort to justify inequality of reward, which, when extreme, may deprive people of dignity..." (1985:150). The contradiction is more flagrant than this statement suggests, however, because the very concept of competition, as already seen, makes one person's success depend on another's failure, and a series of such failures can be demoralizing in the extreme. Once again, we see the consequence of regarding the maintenance of negative freedoms as the sole social value. No sense of responsibility need even be felt for binding the wounds of the losers in the competitive battle, or for providing help and encouragement to them. It is every person for himself.

The competitive ideal of liberal social philosophy can also be criticized from another quarter, by questioning whether efficiency, creativity, and excellence do in fact result from intense competition. Many studies by social scientists indicate that they do not. On the contrary, these studies demonstrate an inverse relation between competitiveness and achievement. For example, a review of studies of the effects of cooperation in classroom situations, as compared with those of independent work, by David and Roger Johnson, professors of education at the University of Minnesota, and their colleagues, showed that cooperation produced higher achievement in 108 studies, while the reverse was true in 6, and 42 revealed no difference. Similarly, in two studies of problem-solving techniques, these professors found that "the discussion process in cooperative groups promotes the discovery and development of higher quality cognitive strategies for learning than does the individual reasoning found in competitive and individualistic learning situations" (quoted Kohn 1986:26).

Summarizing the results of his own survey of these and other reviews and studies of educational and other fields, in an article in *Psychology Today*, Kohn concludes that competition fails to achieve desirable outcomes because it (1) produces anxiety and loss of self-assurance, thereby deflecting energies away from the challenges at hand; (2) precludes the sharing of resources and skills by the members of groups, encouraging them instead to work at cross-purposes with one another; and (3) flies in the face of the fact that "trying to do well and trying to beat others simply are two different things." Kohn's investigations have also made him extremely skeptical about the general efficiency of such extrinsic motivators as money, fame, victory, or other fruits of competitive success, and brought him to the conclusion that intrinsic motivation must be foremost if high performance on complex tasks is to be realized. He cites evidence in support of the view that extrinsic motives may sometimes need to be minimized—especially for highly creative individuals—in order to allow the more effective intrinsic motives to develop and flourish. Finally, he contends that among extrinsic motivators, the sense of accountability to other people can be shown to be a much stronger inducement to peak accomplishment than a competitive arrangement in which "the only stake others have in your performance is a desire to see you fail" (27-28).

Liberal social theory is open to criticism on a number of fronts, therefore, including the empirical one surveyed in Kohn's article. To understand the necessity for searching criticism of the radical individualism that informs this theory is to defuse the nihilistic threats the individualistic assumption poses when left unanalyzed and unchallenged. It is also to make us aware of the need for conceptions of human society that comprehend the reciprocal dependencies and responsibilities of individuals and groups, rather than assigning unwarranted (and precarious) priority to assumedly detached, self-sufficient individuals.

2. THE DIVORCE OF FACT FROM VALUE

The sixth philosophical assumption I will examine as a source of nihilism is the radical disassociation of fact from value. We have witnessed the pivotal role played by this assumption in the outlooks of Russell and Monod, as well as in scientism in general, and traced some of its nihilistic implications in those contexts. We have also noted something akin to this assumption in the outlook of Descartes, given his apparent belief that he can develop a metaphysical system, descriptive of the most general sorts of things there are, without any sustained consideration of the problem of the nature and status of values, including moral values.

Kant too, as we have seen, sharply distinguishes between the questions of theoretical (e.g., scientific and mathematical) truth addressed in his first *Critique* and the issues of moral value discussed in the second *Critique* and other writings. He even associates radically different types of reason with the two kinds of inquiry. Kant differs from Descartes, however, in that he claims that practical reason gives us access to reality-itself, while theoretical reason is limited to the world of appearances. Practical reason is thus more fundamental for metaphysical purposes than theoretical reason, a view that seems to reverse Descartes's metaphysical priorities.

The fact-value dichotomy is also implicit in Kant's plea for the absolute separation of the moral will from natural motives (i.e., needs, desires, inclinations) on the one hand, and from probabilistic calculations of empirical consequences of human choices on the other. Only in the afterlife are we entitled to expect a joining of the demand of our moral nature to make ourselves worthy of happiness with the demand of our sensuous nature for actual happiness. In order to act morally in this life, we must focus exclusively on the first demand, but we can be sustained by the hope for the ultimate satisfaction of the second demand as well, a hope grounded in faith in God as righteous judge (Kant 1956:134-135; Crosby 1981:102-105). Thus, although the worlds of natural fact and moral value may coalesce into one world in the life to come, they must be kept rigorously separate in this present life.[18]

Locke also draws a basic distinction between moral and factual knowledge in his *Essay Concerning Human Understanding*. He contends that moral principles, like mathematical ones, can be deductively demonstrated, because they have to do with "nominal" rather than "real" essences, i.e., with ideas that do not make reference to "archetypes" beyond themselves but are their own archetypes. The principles of natural science and empirical claims in general, on the other hand, cannot have the certitude of deductive demonstration, because they require reference not merely to ideas and their relations, but to existing substances or matters of fact in the world (Locke 1959:II, 156, 208ff., 232ff., 347ff.).

Although he apparently planned to write a work on morals laying out this necessary system of moral principles and explaining its ontological status or applications, Locke never completed such a treatise. In that respect, he is similar to Descartes, who also failed to develop a projected science of morals. The hints at such a system in the *Essay* and Locke's other writings suffer from seemingly irreconcilable conflicts between empiricist and rationalist tendencies in his approch to morals, and from a pervasive vagueness that perhaps largely stems from these conflicting tendencies (see Aaron 1965:256, note 1; Pt. III, Ch. 1).[19]

Hume sets the scene for Kant's later distinction between theoretical and practical reason when, in the Third Book of *A Treatise of Human Nature*, he strenuously objects to attempts to derive moral principles from factual descriptions, on the ground that such attempts confuse two fundamentally different types of thinking.

> In every system of morality, which I have hitherto met with, I have always remark'd, that the author proceeds for some time in the ordinary way of reasoning, and establishes the being of a God, or makes observations

concerning human affairs; when of a sudden I am supriz'd to find, that instead of the usual copulations of propositions, *is* and *is not*, I meet with no proposition that is not connected with an *ought*, or an *ought not*. This change is imperceptible; but is, however, of the last consequence. For as this *ought*, or *ought not*, expresses some new relation or affirmation, 'tis necessary that it shou'd be observ'd and explain'd; and at the same time that a reason should be given, for what seems altogether inconceivable, how this new relation can be a deduction from others, which are entirely different from it (1980:469).

Hume not only contends that moral affirmations are wholly distinct from, and therefore underivable from, ordinary affirmations of fact; he also argues that they cannot be adequately construed as deductions grounded in relations of ideas (463-470).[20]

For Hume, the operations of human understanding (or reason) divide themselves either into assessments of the relations of ideas or judgments about matters of fact; consequently, moral distinctions do not have their basis in reason, but in sentiment or feeling. It also follows that actions, while they can be said to be laudable or blameable, cannot be said to be reasonable or unreasonable. A third result is that moral utterances are not expressions of truth or falsity (458).

One development of the early modern period that figures importantly in the sundering of fact from value is the mechanization and mathematicization of nature which attributes to it only the so-called primary qualities. This means that nature is no longer viewed as a system of final causes, as it had been for two thousand years, but as a realm of purely mathematical formal causes linked with material and efficient causes. A further implication is that nature must now be assumed to be devoid of any intrinsic value (or at least, devoid of any intrinsic value knowable to us, although its value is presumably known to God, if there is a God). The upshot is that values are relegated to the status of so-called secondary qualities, residing solely in the human mind. Thus, a wedge is driven between the facts of an objective nature and the subjective valuations of human beings—a split that would have seemed odd in the extreme to most ancient and medieval thinkers but that tends to be taken for granted by most moderns.[21]

Thinkers such as Hobbes and Mill try to heal this breach between nature and humans, facts and values, by arguing, each in his own way, that values are really only a species of natural fact. The approach represented by these two philosophers is implicitly resisted by Descartes, Locke, Hume, and Kant, who try to maintain the objectivity of values without reducing values to the bare facts of a scientifically conceived nature. In what follows, I will probe further into Hume's view of the origin and status of moral principles, contrasting it with the views of Hobbes and Mill. My purpose is to highlight the nihilistic consequences that can flow from the radical separation of fact from value, at least if that separation is interpreted—as it has often tended to be—along certain lines. Once I have traced these consequences, I will devote the remainder of this section to some basic criticisms of the sixth philosophical assumption.

Hobbe's moral theory is a prime example of the attempt to base values on the facts of a purely objective, scientifically interpreted nature. In his view, morality has to do solely with what is pleasant or unpleasant to humans, who possess desires not at all different from the desires of animals. This means that there is no special category of moral feelings and no "distinctively moral domain." Hobbes goes further in his reductionist, factually derived theory of morals, arguing that desires, whether human or animal, are simply ways in which each particular organism is driven to maintain its power of movement and to preserve itself in response to the buffetings of other bodies. Desires are thus a type of the impetus or pressure characteristic of all physical objects, and simply an aspect of nature viewed as a mechanical system (see Norton 1982:309, 22-24; Hobbes, *Leviathan*, Pt. I, Ch. 6; in Burtt 1939:148-156). Consequently, Hobbes's moral theory is relentlessly egoistic, and his ideal of the just society is one that can ensure the optimal satisfaction of personal desires.

While Hume bases his theory of morality on sentiments that are "natural" to human beings, his focus is on what he takes to be distinctively moral sentiments, not ordinary feelings of pleasure or pain. His theory is not only altruistic, in contrast to Hobbes's egoism; it is also nonreductionistic, in contrast to the theories of Hobbes, Bentham, and Mill. The "facts" or sentiments to which Hume finally appeals are not facts to be found anywhere in external nature, but only in the human breast. And they are not mere feelings of self-regard or adversions to pleasure and aversions from pain, such as can be found in all animals. Rather, they evidence the operations of a special moral sense or faculty in human beings.

It is true that Mill also tries to accord some distinctive character to human pleasures by arguing that they can be divided into higher and lower qualities, and that our obligation as human beings is to seek to maximize the higher pleasures in ourselves and others. But we have already noted that this argument introduces pervasive incoherence into his moral theory. Mill also contends, as we saw earlier, for a distinction between motives and intentions, insisting that the morality of an action depends, not on its natural motives, but on its intended consequences. However, because he also believes that intentions are a species of efficient causes, albeit ones that are socially conditioned or habituated, and denies any possibility of a "could have done otherwise freedom" (the causal circumstances remaining the same) to human beings, he in effect—like Hobbes—sees human life in its entirety as but one more expression of the inexorable mechanisms of a Newtonian universe. Finally, while Mill includes the instinct of *sympathy* in the class of basic desires, he provides us with no convincing empirical analysis of what we ought to do in cases of conflict between the instinct of sympathy and the instinct of self-preservation. He simply tells us that the instinct of sympathy needs to be reinforced by education and other kinds of social influence, and assures us that the *summum bonum* is not our own private happiness, but the greatest happiness for the greatest number of persons.

We can make an observation about Hobbes and Mill similar to that Weil makes concerning *historicism* (see Chapter Three, Section 2), namely, that both of these philosophers either assume that questions of value can be meaningfully addressed only by inquiries into the efficient causes of value commitments or (what is worse) that providing efficient causal explanations for persistent value commitments is the same thing as providing justifications for them. To the extent that it warns against this type of reductionism and confusion of disparate issues, the fact-value distinction merits respect. This distinction, however, can also lead in less salutary directions, as will be seen.

In his staunch opposition to the kind of reductionism just described, as well as by his belief in a type of direct, autonomous, and infallible ethical intuition, Hume shows himself to be much closer to Kant in his basic moral theory than he is to Hobbes, Bentham, or Mill.[22] This helps to explain why he is as adamant as Kant later was in insisting on a radical discontinuity between theorizing about matters of fact and thinking about moral values. Moreover, the central thesis of Norton's book on Hume (1982) is that Hume is a skeptic with regard to problems in speculative metaphysics but a confident realist in moral theory. If true, this is another close similarity between Hume and Kant. Their premises are quite different, but their conclusion is the same. Unfortunately, Hume's brand of moral realism rests on tenuous ground and is in imminent danger of caving in to that species of nihilism known as the emotivist theory of ethics. Kant's rationalistic defense of objectivity in ethical judgments has some nihilistic tendencies of its own, discussed in the previous chapter, as well as another notable drift in that direction that will be indicated in the next section. But our concern for the moment is with Hume, so let us examine his moral theory in more detail.

Hume does not deny that careful examinations of factual states of affairs or of the relations of ideas may be of crucial importance in paving the way for moral judgments. He only denies that such judgments can directly be implied by such examinations, or that they can be somehow reduced to them. Moral assessments turn on a certain distinctive class of feelings of pleasure or pain that we find ourselves experiencing in particular situations. These situations are ones in which we encounter actions that reveal the quality or character of a person or persons.

The actions themselves are not the cause or focus of our moral feelings, but rather the enduring traits of persons who perform those actions. "We are never to consider any single action in our enquiries concerning the origin of morals," Hume informs us, "but only the quality or character from which the action proceeded." He also asserts that "[i]f any *action* be either virtuous or vicious," then it "must depend upon durable principles of the mind, which extend over the whole conduct, and enter into the personal character" (1980:575). The character that shines through an action or pattern of actions elicits in us, quite automatically, feelings of approbation or disapprobation, and these feelings, in turn, inform us of the morality or immorality of the action itself. Thus, while Mill insists that the morality of an action must be kept strictly distinct from the morality of the actor, Hume is strongly inclined to assimilate the first to the second.[23]

Why must we trust these spontaneous feelings of moral approval or blame? Hume's answer in *An Enquiry Concerning the Principles of Morals* is that "nature" has provided us with "an internal sense or feeling" that is "universal in the whole species" (1975:172-173). Where Francis Hutcheson would have written "God," Hume simply writes "nature." That the faculty of moral feeling is universal and works to the same effect in all human beings is taken for granted. Hume does talk, as Mill does, of the importance of education and social conditioning in strengthening the resolve to act morally, particularly in the case of the so-called artificial virtues, chief among which is justice. But he does not believe that the basic content of morality is in any way dependent on such influences. Moreover, he holds that this content rests entirely on something in us, not on anything in the natural world. "Vice and virtue," he writes, "may be compar'd to sounds, colours, heat and cold, which, according to modern philosophy, are not qualities in objects but perceptions in the mind . . ." (1980:469). And while moral sentiments do have reference to something beyond the subjectivity of any one individual and correspond to reality in that sense, they refer only to the characters of other human beings, not to anything extramental.

Assuming that reason has prepared the way in providing the proper context and prior conditions for discerning with our sentiments the moral quality or character of any person (on this see Hume 1980:472, 581-583; also Norton 1982:129-131, 150-151), Hume confesses himself unable to comprehend how the judgments pronounced by our moral feelings could ever be mistaken. There is "such a uniformity in the *general* sentiments of mankind," he announces, as to give to the opinions of humans in moral matters "a peculiar authority" that renders them, "in a great measure, infallible" (1980:546-547 and note). This serene trust in our ability to have infallible moral intuitions is surprising for an empiricist, expecially for one with such skeptical leanings in his epistemological theory. It not only matches the unqualified ethical absolutism of Kant; it is a moral analogue of the confident metaphysical rationalism of Descartes.

But is Hume's theoretical account of the complete reliability of our moral sentiments warranted? It is not. On the contrary, his theory of morals inclines strongly toward nihilism. It does so largely because of his contention that reason is equipped to deal only with matters of fact or relations of ideas, and that it therefore has no competency to resolve basic questions of value. This means that answers to moral questions must be based on our emotions, and that those answers can have no cognitive, or rationally adjudicable, content.

Critical rationality may help to create the proper preconditions for our moral assessments, but the latter are based exclusively on the "gut feelings" evoked in us by the spectacle of persons acting in moral situations. Our moral appraisals of our own pending or past actions would also have to depend wholly on such nonrational feelings. Hume's ethics is perilously close, therefore to Russell's emotivist theory of ethics, to the view that when we exclaim, "This is morally right (or wrong)," we are merely giving vent to subjective feelings. Concerning such feelings, there would seem to be, as in all matters of purely subjective tastes, "no disputation." This last is Russell's gloss, at any rate, on the type of moral theory Hume seems on the verge of propounding.[24]

But does not Hume block such an interpretation of his theory by his insistence that the basic moral feelings of people do not vary but are everywhere the same? While he does counter Russell's brand of emotivistic relativism with persistent statement, he nowhere does so with effective argument. He merely assumes that "nature" had made us all alike, with identical moral instincts; and therefore that our responses to particular moral situations, under the proper conditions of assessment, will always concur.

It is exactly this putative universality of our emotional responses that Hume needs to prove, or at least to make as plausible a case for as he can. Such a claim surely cannot simply be taken for granted, especially in view of the basic moral disagreements among thoughtful persons, including those in Hume's own time. In the absence of such argument, there is nothing to prevent the slide of his moral theory toward a subjectivism as radical as that of Russell or the many other recent exponents of the emotivist view of ethics—a view that constitutes one of the main types of moral nihilism. Furthermore, because reason as Hume regards it has no competency to resolve questions of value in any form, existential values as well would have to depend solely on emotions and be swept down the same slope toward complete arbitrariness and relativism.

It is also important to note that Hume's basing moral appraisals on a distinctive type of moral sentiment, rather than seeing them as acts of reason, cannot really serve him in the way Norton thinks it can. I mentioned earlier the latter's allegation that Hume combines, or attempts to combine, a radical skepticism in epistemology and metaphysics with a confident realism in the field of ethics. The skepticism grows out of his distrust of reason, particularly to the extent that the factual claims based on reason assume reliance on causal necessity and induction. Because Hume can find no basis in experience for this reliance, he concludes that it has no empirical justification. Our moral feelings, by contrast, he asserts to be perfectly trustworthy and even infallible. Setting aside for the moment the objection to his utilization of the fact-value dichotomy that we have just made, Hume's assumption of this dichotomy seems to serve his ethics well in at least one respect, by providing him with a way of protecting ethical norms from the corrosive skepticism emanating from his critical analysis of claims to factual knowledge.

But this only *seems* to be the case, because if our judgments of fact are unreliable, so also must be our moral responses. The reason is that those responses, according to Hume's own account, *presuppose* the trustworthiness of claims to fact. "In moral deliberations," he writes,

> we must be acquainted beforehand with all the objects, and all their relations to each other; and from a comparison of the whole, fix our choice or approbation. No new fact to be ascertained; no new relation to be discovered. All the circumstances of the case are supposed to be laid before us, ere we can fix any sentence of blame or approbation. If any material circumstance be yet unknown or doubtful, we must first employ our inquiry or intellectual faculties to assure us of it; and must suspend for a time all moral decision or sentiment (1975:290).

If the relevant factual information must be completely in hand before any moral assessment can take place, and if moral feelings are to be viewed as responses to that information, then it seems obvious that the information must be reliable if we are to give any credence to the moral assessment. The point, therefore, is that Hume's insistence that ethical discernments are matters of emotion, and that they are to be arrived at only *after* issues of fact and other matters lying within the province of reason have been fully resolved, cannot save his moral theory from the destructive skepticism that characterizes his analysis of the operations of reason.[25]

It might seem that we have now reached an impasse. Attempts such as those of Hume and Kant to maintain a sharp distinction between factual judgments of the understanding and assessments of moral value, on the one hand, and attempts of thinkers such as Hobbes and Mill to resolve valuative claims into the factual descriptions of a scientifically envisioned nature, on the other, all tend toward nihilism. We found this to be true in the cases of Kant and Mill in the previous chapter,[26] and we have just seen it to be true in the case of Hume. As for Hobbes, his egoistic ethical theory is notably akin to that of Stirner. Chapter Two cited reasons for regarding Stirner's depiction of morality as a type of moral nihilism.

An earlier chapter showed, however, that dualism and reductionism are not the only available alternatives in conceiving the relations of human beings to nature. Similarly, a dualism of fact and value, on the one hand, or a reduction of value to fact (and more particularly, to scientific fact), on the other, are not the only alternatives. In order to demonstrate this, let me first attempt to sort out some of the ambiguity of the fact-value dichotomy by considering some of the different things it can mean.

This dichotomy might mean, first, that it is a mistake to confuse the issue of justifications of moral claims with that of giving efficient causal explanations of why individuals or groups are inclined to make such claims. To explain causally why Jones believes that stealing is wrong is not the same thing as showing that he is obligated not to steal.[27] Second, the separation of value from fact might be interpreted as calling attention to the strictly logical point that from a mere factual premise or set of premises we cannot validly deduce a conclusion about moral obligation (unless a suppressed valuative premise or commitment is somewhere implicit in our reasoning, in which case it would need to be made explicit to complete the argument). If either of these two meanings of the fact-value dichotomy were all that Hume and Kant had in mind, there would be no problem. Each meaning calls attention to a legitimate point, and the two points together constitute relevant criticisms of ethical theories such as those of Hobbes and Mill.

But Hume and Kant seem to have much more in mind. A third possible meaning of the fact-value distinction is that because no values are found in nature, as we learn from modern science, then values must be located exclusively in us. Nature as a realm of bare facts must be kept distinct from the valuative interests and aspirations of human beings. A fourth meaning is that questions of value cannot be resolved by reason, or at least not by reason in the strict sense of the term. Therefore, such questions can be addressed, if at all, only by means of some special type of cognition or through some nonrational faculty such as sentiment or feeling.

A fifth way of interpreting the rigid separation of fact from value is that, because investigations into facts can be conclusive only when carried out in a mood of objectivity or detachment, we should strive to conduct them in complete independence from our valuative concerns. Careful attention to fact and scrupulous value-neutrality go necessarily together. Implicit in each of these last three meanings is the supposition that our experiences or thought processes can be neatly compartmentalized into purely factual and purely valuative aspects, and thus that the one can be developed or analyzed in isolation from the other.

These last three meanings of the fact-value distinction, all of them assumed in the thought of Hume and Kant as well as in that of many others of their time and since, contain the thrust toward nihilism that is my concern in this section. But this nihilistic outcome is avoidable, because the austere dualisms from which it proceeds are highly questionable, and because the critique of such dualisms does not leave us with the sole alternative of trying to resolve values into efficient causal processes of a scientifically conceived nature.

Philosophers such as Hume and Kant assume the sundering of human beings from nature. To them it is obvious that nature is devoid of the qualities, ends, and values that permeate human affairs. These exist only in human subjectivity. This third version of the fact-value polarity is thus, from one aspect, an expression of cosmic nihilism. As in Russell's statement of that outlook, it sets the aims and values of human culture in opposition to a nature deemed to be without valuative import, a nature whose mechanical processes and mathematical laws would appear to have nothing to do with the moral and existential concerns of purposive beings.

Hume, Kant, and Russell are right in thinking that any attempt to find a place for values in a nature so conceived is futile and can result only in a hopeless obscuring, if not obliterating, of the all-important normative dimension of human life. But they fail to carry this reasoning one step further and to question the adequacy of the scientific depictions of nature current in their times. They uncritically assume what we earlier termed the hegemony of science with respect to the understanding of nature, and they fail to explain how the scientific portrayal of nature, if it is to be accepted as final and complete, can be so radically different from nature *as lived*.[28]

Nature as lived is a texture of interdependencies of which we experience ourselves to be an intimate part, rather than some alien system we come to from without and can only relate to from afar. In this nature, values are commonplace, and quality is as much at home as quantity. No philosopher of recent times has made us so acutely aware of this fact as does Dewey, in his masterful *Experience and Nature*.

In the nature we experience every day there is no mere endless churning of indifferent causes but the continuing manifestation of what Dewey calls "ends, terminals, arrests, enclosures" that can be entered into and enjoyed for their own sake (1958:97, 84). A friend told me recently of his teenager's reaction to the first snowfall of the season. "I love the snow," the boy exclaimed. "It is so beautiful in its white softness and in the way it drapes the bushes and trees. And I like the sharp feel of the cold!" He spoke these words as he bounded off into the outdoors, and he uttered them with the spontaneous enthusiasm of an immediate participant, not the bland detachment of a remote observer. In similar fashion, a farmer may exult in the fragrance of the handful of earth he scoops up in the spring. He does so, not just because the soil gives promise of causal regularities that can nurture his crops, secure the financial wellbeing of his family, or subserve other such purely human ends. He rejoices because the earthy odor gives him a sense of being a part of a larger whole, a whole that is awakening to life all around him and whose quickening pulse he feels within. It is a rejuvenation in which he shares, one to which he instinctively responds as a living organism and natural being.

Nature as lived has its destructive outcomes too, of course. The same farmer's fields may be swept by a late summer hail that brings to nothing his labor in that growing season. A virus may invade an animal or human body and produce grave illness. A lovely valley may be defaced by earthquake, flood, or fire. An overabundance of elk may severely damage a delicate ecosystem. But these culminations or ends also have valuative—albeit negative—significance. And some may enter into larger contexts of positive value later on, as when the shortage of browse reduces the number of elk to the point where the ecosystem can restore itself, or as when a new and more exquisite valley emerges from the destruction of the old one.

It is not as though any of these particular natural terminations or ends, whether good or ill, are consciously sought. A nature with valuative outcomes need not be thought of as the product of deliberate purpose or design. Nor need it be conceived as an ascending hierarchy of ends that culminates in some supreme, all-encompassing, timeless end. To recognize the presence of ends or values in nature we need not assume every aspect of the teleological outlook of the Middle Ages (on this see Dewey 1958:104-105).

But Dewey calls our attention to a measure of truth in the teleological view of nature, which finds it to be replete with ends, when he notes that

> [e]mpirically, the existence of objects of direct grasp, possession, use and enjoyment cannot be denied. Empirically, things are poignant, tragic, beautiful, humorous, settled, disturbed, comfortable, annoying, barren, harsh, consoling, splendid, fearful; are such immediately and in their own right and behalf (96).

Such naturally emerging ends cannot be separated from the causal factors in nature that produce them, but neither should the causal factors be arbitrarily separated from the ends they bring about.

Both are portions or aspects, as Dewey again reminds us, "of one and the same historic process, each having immediate or esthetic quality and each having efficacy, or serial connection." Thus, from the standpoint of nature in the concrete, nature as lived through in its fulness and completeness, it "is as much a part of the real being of atoms that they give rise in time, under increasing complication of relationships, to qualities of blue and sweet, pain and beauty, as that they have a cross-section of time extension, mass, or weight" (109-110). In the perspective of nature as lived, causes count no more than outcomes, quantities no more than qualities, facts no more than values. Our experiences of outcomes and qualities, and of the values or disvalues that may attach to them,[29] are therefore no illusion or mere subjective registration of processes that in themselves are barren and meaningless. They reliably inform us of the traits of lived nature, a nature of which we are a constitutive part.

Scientists may well want to abstract from this lived continuity of means and ends in order to study the system of means (or causes) in isolation, just as artists, for their own purposes, may want to preoccupy themselves with the achieved ends. Seen "[f]rom the standpoint of causal sequence, or the order with which science is concerned, qualities are superfluous, irrelevant and immaterial" (Dewey 1958:103). But the point is that each approach *is* an abstraction and should not be confused with the whole character or significance of the natural order. Hume, Kant, and many others have made the mistake of taking the useful abstraction for the concrete reality, with the result that they have been forced to locate ends and values exclusively in human subjects, and to establish an artificial dichotomy of natural fact and experienced value.

This dichotomy imparts a tone of disconnection, arbitrariness, and unreality to the domain of values that easily lends itself to nihilistic interpretations. We have a lesson here of the disastrous results that can follow when a single, partial perspective is assumed to tell the whole story, and when the contributions that could be made to understanding from other perspectives are thereby ignored. A more adequate philosophy of nature— one that does not assume the hegemony of science but takes scientific descriptions as but one aspect of a complete analysis of nature—can eliminate the need for a sundering of fact from value that was felt so acutely by Hume and Kant.

Saying this does not in itself resolve any moral problems, of course, nor does it give us a theory of morality. But it does help to disabuse us of the notion that if there is any basis at all for moral norms or existential meanings it must be dredged up from human subjectivity in complete disconnection from an allegedly purely factual nature. The mistake of Hobbes and Mill, on the other hand, is simply the other side of the coin from that of Hume and Kant, namely, the assumption that the only nature in which values can be sought is the nature described by the current physics. Both sides of the debate thus confuse an outcome of selective abstraction with the fulness of concrete experience.

Having said this, we should also recognize that not even strictly scientific descriptions of nature can any longer be regarded as eliminating such things as ends or values from the natural order. As far as ends themselves are concerned, when considered apart from questions of value, T. L. Short argues (1983) for the basic role of what he (following Charles Sanders Pierce) calls "finious processes" in such current scientific theories as statistical mechanics, chemical kinetics, and natural selection, as well as in scientific accounts of "teleonomic behavior" in organisms. In this last case, a concept of final causation is required to explain not only the tendency but also the initiation of a process. These finious processes require the cooperation of mechanical processes but are not reducible to them, just as Aristotle taught. Also as with Aristotle, the finious processes sketched by Short are not to be construed as purposes; i.e., they do not require a conscious agent.

But conscious purposes, whether animal or human, can be regarded as a type of finious process. And while the ends tended toward and regularly attained by finious processes need not be regarded as values, the presence of such ends, together with the idea of conscious purpose as a subset of end-oriented activity or behavior, helps to break down the sharp dichotomy between human beings and the natural order implied when nature is seen solely in terms of mechanical explanations and processes, i.e., as nothing but a welter of efficient causes.[30]

Furthermore, there is good reason to regard many of the natural ends, terminations, or closures described by science, together with the processes that subserve them, as values and even to see them as containing important implications for moral value. It makes sense, for example, for us to value the presence of life on earth, partly but not merely because life includes us. As Rolston points out, we have a *prima facie* obligation to preserve, or at least not wantonly to destroy, the numerous biological species on this planet:

> 'Ought species x to exist?' is a single increment in the collective question, 'Ought life on Earth to exist?' The answer to the question about one species is not always the same as the answer to the bigger question, but since life on Earth is an aggregate of many species, the two are sufficiently related that the burden of proof lies with those who wish deliberately to extinguish a species and simultaneously to care for life on Earth (1985:723).

To value the presence of life on earth, moreover, is also to value individual life, a valuation closely connected with the evidence indicating that each individual life form values itself. But we cannot value the life form, and it cannot value itself, without there being an implicit valuing of the instrumentalities in nature required to sustain and enrich its life.

This combination of intrinsic and instrumental value, as Rolston again instructs us, is not the whole account of natural value either, for in order to value the individual we must value the species of which it is a part, and in order to value the species we must value the ecosystem that gives rise to it and that continues to promote the arrival of new species over time. To intrinsic value and instrumental value we must therefore add what Rolston calls *systematic value* in nature. Each of these types of value is an appropriate object of moral concern, and not simply on account of satisfactions and pleasures it might produce for human beings. Although there is plausibility in regarding the highest and most concentrated intrinsic value of the system as "lofty individuality with its subjectivity," we should acknowledge that subjectivity is not confined to humans but extends to the higher animals as well. Furthermore, the "objective, systematic process" of the generating, nurturing, proliferating ecosystems must be seen as "an overriding value, not because it is indifferent to individuals, but because the process is both prior to and productive of individuality." In this process, "[s]ubjects count, but they do not count so much that they can degrade or shut down the system, though they count enough to have the right to flourish within the system" (Rolston, in Callicott 1987:269-272).

All of the kinds of natural value pointed to by Rolston figure prominently in what we today call the science of ecology. If so, and if his analysis of the presence of morally significant value in a scientifically described nature holds, then the rigid separation of fact from value, where we locate only the first in nature and speak of the second as residing exclusively in us, is no longer tenable (if it ever was), even from the standpoint of natural science itself. In so saying, we do not commit the so-called natualistic fallacy (most closely related to the second meaning of the fact-value dichotomy indicated above) because we reason, not from supposed bare facts of nature to human values, but from values found in nature to the imperative to see certain of these natural values as appropriate objects of moral concern. By the same process of reasoning, we can conclude that there is no yawning gulf between nature and human beings that needs somehow to be bridged, but a continuous passage from the valuative dimensions of the first to the valuative recognitions of the second, both being viewed as related aspects of the same general system. In this way we take strong issue with the third version of the fact-value dichotomy, and with its nihilistic tendencies.

The fourth meaning of the fact-value dichotomy argues the case for a special type of cognition or for some extrarational faculty to deal with issues of moral value, it being supposed that reason, strictly understood, can shed no light on the problems and concerns of the moral life. What is this strict sense of reason? The widespread assumption of the early modern period, and one taken for granted by many in our own time, is that this is scientific reason, reason which follows the methods and approaches of the current physics. The modern crisis of values is created to no small extent by this assumption about the strict sense of reason, because it calls into question the rational status or cognitive significance of valuative claims.

Hume breaks the task of this reason into two parts: investigation of matters of fact disclosed in experience, and analysis of the relations of ideas, the latter accounting for (among other things) the mathematical side of physics. While Locke had argued for the view that moral and mathematical reasoning are fundamentally alike in that both rest on the relations of ideas, Hume contends that moral inquiry cannot be comprehended within either of these two species of reasoning but must be relegated to another realm altogether, that of feeling—and, more specifically, to what he takes to be distinctive feelings of moral approval or blame. But the distinctiveness, as well as the alleged universality, of Hume's moral sentiments can readily be questioned;[31] and his attempt to protect the domain of morals from encroachments of the pervasive skepticism stemming from his critical analysis of reason is fatally flawed, as already observed.

Kant sees the inescapable outcome of theoretical or scientific reason as a portrayal of the world that leaves no room for morality because its unbroken causal connectedness does not allow for freedom. Another form of cognition must therefore be posited, namely, practical reason, which takes as its starting point, not the causal mechanisms and quantitative necessities that dominate Newtonian physics, but unquestioning faith in the freedom, dignity, and moral accountability of human beings. Try as he may, however, Kant is unable to provide any explanation of how the radically different perspectives and conclusions of these two forms of cognition can be reconciled or brought into coherent relation. He opts for the priority of practical reason, but at the price of leaving in metaphysical limbo the scientific analysis of nature. Thus, like Hume, he tries to set out an ethical realism rooted in a distinctive faculty of moral awareness, in the face of a systematic skepticism growing out of a critical study of scientific reason.

Both Hume and Kant posit a fundamental disunity in our experience and thought, therefore, and leave us straddling two seemingly incommensurable subject matters and points of view. This spliced, disjointed character of their respective systems already invites critical attack. But when they infer from their rigid separation of the basis of scientific understanding from that of moral judgment that we must choose between the two, and go on to urge the entire reliability of the latter at the expense of the former, these two philosophers become vulnerable to the additional criticisms that they have succumbed to mere wishful thinking and failed to be fully in tune with the modern scientific spirit. Behind this last criticism lies a commitment to the hegemony of science earlier identified as one of the root assumptions of modernity.[32]

It is understandable, then, that later thinkers should have sought for an interpretation of moral and other values that would not require the positing of a dichotomous view of reason like that of Kant and that would not jeopardize in any way the privileged status of scientific reasoning or its outcomes. Some of these thinkers, e.g., Bentham and Mill, develop the utilitarian strain already present in Hume's moral theory, interpreting moral values along the lines of scientific reductionism and seeking a straightforward way of deriving the moral "ought" from the scientific "is"—a way that would not end with Hobbesian egoism. Positivistic thinkers such as Russell, on the other hand, maintain the absoluteness of scientific reason by holding (as Bernstein phrases it) that whatever "cannot be assimilated, translated or reduced" to the "canons of scientific discourse" is to be "rejected as pseudo-knowledge." Because values, in this view, cannot be so assimilated, translated, or reduced, they are consigned to the status of "noncognitive emotional responses or private subjective preferences" (Bernstein 1983:48, 46).

In the first case efficient causal explanation takes the place of moral justification, leaving the most significant moral questions essentially unaddressed and, as long as we remain confined to this approach, *unaddressable*. In the second case, moral values are wholly subjectivized and relativized—carrying to its logical conclusion the emotivist tendency of the main body of Hume's ethics. Neither of these reductionistic theories is a satisfying alternative to the dualistic approaches of Hume and Kant. Both species of scientific reductionism lead us to the quagmire of a nihilism that either bypasses central questions of moral (and, by implication, existential) value in its obsession with the causal explanations assumed to be demanded by scientific reason, or that dismisses in advance as mere pseudo-knowledge all attempts to give rationally based responses to such questions.

What is called for, therefore, is a concept of valuative reasoning (as contrasted with mere feeling) that does not suffer from Kant's bifurcation of reason, on the one hand, and that does not make the mistake of simply equating the proper use of reason with assumptions and techniques associated with natural science, on the other. Kant's bifurcation is unacceptable because of the radical and implausible disunity it introduces into the life of the mind, needlessly hypostatizing and opposing two aspects of human rationality that cannot really be kept separate but interpenetrate at every point. Simply to identify reason with scientific reasoning is also unacceptable because it confuses a single legitimate employment of reason with reason itself, blinding us to reason's other important and intimately related uses. The nub of the problem with both approaches, moreover, is that each operates with a distorted notion of the objectivity or value-neutrality of scientific reasoning. I will take up these points in the context of the fifth meaning of the fact-value dichotomy.

The fifth meaning is that investigations into facts must be strictly separated from inquiries into values, because the former must be carried out in a mood of complete detachment or objectivity, uninfluenced by antecedent normative commitments or biases. An earlier chapter criticized this notion of scientific objectivity, pointing out that inquiry into facts and their explanations cannot be carried out in a vacuum but presupposes a larger context of commitment and purpose. This inquiry is an intentional activity and as such implies ends consciously sought. Ends consciously sought are valuations.

If scientists did not intensely value the end of gaining understanding of experienced facts and their interrelations, they would not even begin their scientific investigations. Nor would they devote such large parts of their lives to them or persist in them in the face of numerous setbacks and failures. If scientists regard it as good to stick to the facts, then facts become for them values, or at least objects of evaluation. Conversely, if there is no value in sticking to the facts, then why would anyone do it, or why should anyone do it? Rosen raises this question in the context of discussing the positivistic theory of values. He notes that the positivistic claim that truth and *ought* are incompatible" makes highly paradoxical the common assumption (which scientists certainly share) that "one ought to accept the truth." The paradox is compounded when we are told that *ought* utterances are purely emotive and can be given no reasonable defense, for this entails that "there is no *reason*, no *reasonable* reason, for believing the true rather than the false" (1969:70-71). If taken seriously, these claims would have to undermine the whole positivist program, leaving it without rational point or significance, because it is precisely their *devotion* to scientific truth that has led the positivists to be so insistent on the need to demarcate facts from values.

Implicit in all scientific investigation are such values as those of clarity; of accuracy; of consistency and coherence; of making fruitful contributions to the enterprise of science; of scrupulous honesty in reporting on the results of one's research; of elegance and parsimony in one's theoretical proposals; of staying in close communication with one's scientific colleagues, carefully attending to their work; of operating within the environment of established theories, taking issue with one or more of those theories only when one has strong grounds for doing so; of patience, reasonableness, and mutual respect in one's attempts to persuade; and, of course, the preeminent value of truth itself. If the status of such assumed values is somehow bogus or suspect, then so must be the status of the theories that grow out of those values. Or if values can only be defended on the basis of a mode of reasoning completely distinct from scientific reasoning, then the problem arises of explaining how the two modes, despite their alleged separateness, can be so intimately involved with one another. Even the passionate commitment to objectivity or value-neutrality is itself, paradoxically, a value—a paradox we highlighted earlier in criticizing Monod's scientistic worldview.

Perhaps it could be said that the kinds of value implicit in scientific theorizing are not moral values but methodological values, and that we should steer clear only of nonmethodological commitments in conducting our factual inquiries, in order to maintain their objectivity. If we say this, we have already attenuated the fifth version of the fact-value dichotomy to the extent of now having to claim that what is at stake in the pursuit of objectivity is not a form of inquiry that must be totally insulated from antecedent values but one in which we must choose certain values over others, one in which the selection of one type of values precludes commitment to another type.

However, even this analysis does not go far enough, although it does go some way, in criticizing the fact-value dichotomy. For some of the values mentioned above are, or at least strongly imply, moral values. One has the duty to be honest with one's fellow investigators so as to merit their trust; to be as clear and accurate as possible in reporting on the results of one's research because others may depend on it when conducting their own investigations; to refrain from stealing the ideas of others or misrepresenting their views; to follow the path of truth wherever it leads, even when it leads away from one's most cherished beliefs or expectations, or benefits someone other than oneself. In short, one has the duty to be a responsible member of the scientific community, with all the accompanying moral obligations that implies. Without the assumption of these moral values, this community could not survive, and the outcomes of scientific investigation would lose all credibility.

Has the fifth version of the fact-value dichotomy no significance at all, then? We certainly do not want to claim this. It warns us against those value commitments that may impede, rather than contribute positively to, our investigations into fact; or that may put us at cross purposes with others investigating in the same field. It reminds us that certain kinds of antecedent values can skew the results of our inquiries or close our minds to the truth that lies before us. What kinds of value (or, in this context, disvalue) are these? Preparing a list of them is not difficult. Such a list will include things like stubborn loyalty to past beliefs that makes it difficult for one to change those beliefs even when change is called for; an obsession with self that seriously inhibits one's ability to cooperate with, or to learn from, the work of others; a need for quick results that makes one impatient with the slow and often tedious process of careful investigation and testing of theories; or an overriding need to have the world conform to one's biases or wishes, rather than the resolve to do justice to the ways it presents itself in our experience. While it is true that in the total absence of values no inquiry would be possible, it is also true that some values are hurtful to constructive inquiry, while others are essential to it.

In saying this, we no longer dichotomize facts and values. We show rather that reliable claims to fact depend on certain kinds of values and argue for an understanding of reason, including scientific reasoning, that can illuminate this dependence in a dialectical, nuanced way that neither rigidly opposes facts and values nor simply treats values as another species of scientific fact. Neither of these latter approaches, the one representing the views of Hume, Kant, and Russell, and the other, the approaches of Hobbes, Bentham, and Mill, adequately interprets the complex interweavings of detachment and commitment, of theory and practice, of presumed fact and assumed value, that run through the whole life of the mind and characterize reason in all of its uses. We may separate out these elements for different emphasis in different contexts and for different purposes, and we may abstract from the one in order to attend more closely to the other; but we can never succeed in wholly detaching them from each other, or in simply reducing them to a single class. Nor should we want to, because each approach, in its own way, sets us needlessly on a path toward nihilism.

Claims to fact not only grow out of a matrix of purpose and value; they also express an outcome of value. This makes doubly fallacious this fifth meaning of the fact-value dichotomy, namely, the notion that we can conduct our inquiries into fact in complete independence of considerations of value. Drawing on the work of Heidegger, Sartre, and Gadamer, Rorty notes that what we take to be the received facts is dependent on the results of "normal" inquiry in the sciences and elsewhere. But we ought to be aware "that alternative descriptions are possible in addition to those offered by the results of normal inquiries." In addition, we need to realize "that to use one set of [putatively] true sentences to describe ourselves is already to choose an attitude toward ourselves, whereas to use another set of [putatively] true sentences is to adopt a contrary attitude" (Rorty 1980:363-364). What Rorty says concerning sentences about ourselves also applies to sentences about the world.

This being the case, supposing (as Hume and the positivists do) that we must *first* employ our reason to satisfy ourselves that all of the relevant facts are in hand and *only then* make some kind of noncognitive leap to assume an attitude of evaluation toward those settled facts is highly implausible. Quite to the contrary, valuational assumptions of the most far-reaching kind are already implicit in the way we come to conceive of the facts. The fact-value distinction, especially when conjoined with the belief that the natural sciences alone are competent to give us a reliable account of the facts, makes us oblivious to this intimate relation between description and evaluation. As a result, we unconsciously acquiesce in the tacit valuations contained in current theories in natural science and become too easily "convinced that we know both what we are and what we can be—not just how to predict and control our behavior, but the limits of that behavior (and, in particular, the limits of our significant speech)" (Rorty 1980:363).

As we did earlier, and as Thomas Kuhn, Gadamer, and others do, Rorty stresses the historical situatedness and variability of theories in science, denying to them absoluteness or finality. Alternative conceptions of scientific fact are possible, and with them, alternative conceptions of value, or of possibilities for attainment of value. Rorty argues, moreover, that confining our vision of value possibilities to what the natural scientists of any particular time hold to be the case is foolish. Scientific descriptions "are simply among the repertoire of self-descriptions at our disposal," to be included along with "the various alternative descriptions offered by poets, novelists, depth psychologists, sculptors, anthropologists, and mystics." Just because there is, at the moment, "more consensus in the sciences than in the arts" does not give to the former the status of "privileged representations"(362).

What Rorty says about the historical situatedness and nonprivileged character of current scientific descriptions is complemented by what Dewey says about morality. Dewey warns us against the illusion that reason either can or needs to generate out of its own substance a set of universally binding moral principles or an overarching *summum bonum*. Its task is not discovery of transcendent principles but criticism of the values already diffused in our experience, and of the assumed facts with which these values are associated. What is needed, therefore, is not so much a theory of values as a theory of rational criticism that can be applied not only to supposed facts but also to the values implicit in the various "beliefs, institutions, customs, [and] policies" of human culture. The knowing of value, like all knowing, must start "from some belief, some received and asserted meaning which is a deposit of prior experience, personal and communal." It can then proceed to put this received knowledge to the critical test, analyzing its relations to other claims to truth or value, and seeking to assess its consequences for experience and practice. Dewey argues convincingly for the idea that even the most fundamental moral problems are intelligible and resolvable only in specific contexts; they cannot be solved generally or for all time. The task of criticizing presumed values is, as a consequence, never ending (1958:408, 428, 431, 433; 1960:271-278).

A more inclusive and unitary view of reason than that allowed by the last three versions of the fact-value dichotomy we have been discussing, one that cedes to reason the competency to range over questions of both fact and value because it recognizes that the two cannot be sharply separated but are closely joined, can free us from the kind of myopic fixation on scientific descriptions Rorty criticizes—a fixation that goes a long way toward explaining the persistent appeal of the fact-value dichotomy in its last three versions. Understanding that any comprehensive picture of the facts is also a comprehensive statement about values, we are alerted to alternative and perhaps more adequate conceptions of ourselves and the world than those we had tended to take for granted in the past. Furthermore, recognizing that reason in all its manifestations, scientific or otherwise, is fallible and inescapably tied to history and culture can free us from the supposition, effectively countered by Dewey, that unless reason can arrive at timeless, universal principles in the realm of morals analogous to those believed to be permanently established by physical science, it is hopelessly bankrupt as a guide to ethical (and other) values.

There are good reasons, therefore, for us to think of reason itself as one, although its uses and applications are many. We dare not restrict its inquiries to the realm of fact if that means leaving the all-important questions of value to be resolved by uninterpreted feelings, no matter how compelling such feelings might seem in their immediacy. Nor need we assign these questions of value to some other kind of reason, distinct in kind from a reason competent to deal only with matters of fact. We can speak meaningfully of theoretical, practical, and technical uses of reason; or of scientific, moral, aesthetic, philosophical, or religious reason, as long as we do not allow these useful abstractions to fall apart into separate, reified faculties, forcing us to introduce artificial compartmentalizations into the concrete interdependencies of our mental life. To avoid this kind of artificiality is also to rid ourselves of the pernicious source of nihilism that has been the subject matter of this section.

3. THE PRIMACY OF WILL

The seventh philosophical source of nihilism, and the last I will assess, is an emphasis on the epistemological and metaphysical primacy of the will running through some significant sectors of modern thought. In this section, we witness an increasing tendency to see will, rather than reason, as holding the key to human action and awareness and even to the character of reality itself. As this trend develops, a mounting stress is placed on the radical independence of the power of will from rational constraints of any sort, including the constraint of intellectually grounded moral principles, or from empirical conditions.

The final stage of this development is the conclusion that all that is of significance and worth and all that counts as reality for any person are, at bottom, the arbitrary constructs (or acquiescences) of that person's will. We are brought, therefore, to the view of Stirner, Nietzsche, and Sartre, i.e., to their concept of absurd, normless volition as the ultimate basis of the beliefs and actions of individuals, and as the generative source of what individuals come to regard as the structures of the surrounding world. Meaning, truth, and value are not in any sense discovered, therefore, but can only be blindly posited or sheerly invented. This thesis was earlier associated with various types of nihilism, especially with existential nihilism.

Bernard den Ouden, in the second of his *Essays on Reason, Will, Creativity, and Time*, traces in brief compass some critical steps in the development of this seventh philosophical assumption. I am indebted to his work in what follows. However, den Ouden's discussion covers a narrower span of time than mine. He begins with Kant, works through some of the post-Kantian idealists (with side references to Romantic thinkers of the late eighteenth and nineteenth centuries), and culminates with Nietzsche.[33] I begin with Descartes and conclude with Camus and Sartre. I also place the theme of the ascendancy of the will in a broader conceptual framework than does den Ouden. For example, I note, as he does not, some important affinities between certain philosophers of the will who take their cue from Kant, and other philosophers (such as Hobbes and Hume) who sharply separate the human will from reason and view its decisions as but one more manifestation of the unbroken causal sequences of a scientifically conceived nature.

Toward the end of Chapter Eight I observed that the divine will is for Descartes absolute in its scope and power. Not only does he hold that God has brought the universe into being by a pure act of sovereign will, and that every finite thing depends for its existence from one moment to the next on the constancy of God's creative reenactments; he also contends that the axioms of reason and the basic principles of logical possibility, as well as the most fundamental moral and spiritual values, owe their status and significance solely to God's absolutely free decrees. What God has made and continues to make in all these domains he could unmake in a moment. There could be no legitimate objection to any new direction his choices might take, because his power is infinite and beyond any conceivable restriction. God's essence is will, not reason, and his will lies at the core of all reality. With his conception of God as absolute will Descartes anticipates those later philosophers, such as Schopenhauer, who claim that unbridled will is the fundamental principle of the universe.

Descartes also anticipates Kant and others of the modern period who see the will as the basic human faculty when he muses that our possession of freedom is our most God-like trait, and that compared with our expansive powers of will, our other capacities, such as that of understanding, seem small and limited. And Descartes exults, as we have seen, in the idea that a nature whose mechanical processes can be objectively known is a nature subject, in principle, to the mastery of our wills: a vision that at least suggests a construal of rational knowledge as a mere means to the end of power or dominance. Increasing emphasis after the seventeenth century on the empirical aspect of scientific knowledge, i.e., on the prediction and control of natural (or human) phenomena, and on the close relation of that knowledge to a burgeoning technology, supports this construal.

Descartes is unable to reconcile, however, his conviction of the all-controlling power of God with his direct awareness of his own freedom. He is also unable to explain how human freedom, which he claims to belong to the transcendent realm of spiritual substances, can have any influence upon a wholly determined, completely closed and self-contained system of nature. Finally, the central importance he assigns to the human will is in tension with his insistence that its wide-ranging powers must be kept strictly within the bounds of the clear and distinct ideas mandated by reason. Thus, while Descartes gives unrestricted primacy to the divine will, there are unresolved ambiguities in his view of the human will. Still, a tendency can be seen here as well to exalt the will over the understanding, a tendency that, like his theological volitionism, runs against the grain of his rationalism.

No such ambiguity attaches to Hobbe's view of the human will, and he is as adamant as Descartes in attributing unqualified primacy to the will of God God is entitled to reign over human beings, writes Hobbes, solely by his "*irresistible power*." From that power, and not from his being Creator or gracious, he gains his right to be worshipped and obeyed by humans and to afflict or to benefit them in any way he sees fit. This Hobbes regards as the clear teaching of the Bible, especially of the Book of Job. Because God is infinite and we are finite, we can have no idea of him save that his will is without bound and "effecteth everything." To say that God is "good, just, or holy" is not to ascribe attributes to him but to express our readiness to obey him and thus to acknowledge the absoluteness of his power in all things (*Leviathan* Pt. I, Ch. XXXI; in Burtt 1939:212-214, 216-217).

With respect to the human will, Hobbes contends that the ends of human life are dictated, not by reason, but by the will. The will, in turn, is nothing other than "the last appetite in deliberation"; and deliberation is simply "the whole sum of desires, aversions, hopes, and fears, continued till the thing be either done or thought impossible." To assert that we act freely, for Hobbes, means that we act from impulses or desires that are internal to us, or our own, and in "the absence of external impediments" (*Leviathan*, Pt. I, Chs. VI, XIV; in Burtt 1939:153-154, 163). His deterministic view of nature and his emphasis on the absolute power of God both require that our impulses or desires, and hence our choices, be viewed as internal effects of our bodies interacting with motions or forces in the universe external to us. These motions or forces produce first imagination, then appetites and aversions (Hobbes also calls them "endeavors" toward or away from something), and finally, actions. A free action is also a determined action, therefore, and Hobbes sees no incompatibility between the two conceptions. He even brands as "absurd, insignificant and nonsense" a concept of free action that would make such action in any sense or in any degree independent of efficient causes

(*Leviathan*, Pt. I, Chs. VI, XXI, V; in Burtt 1939:148-150, 196, 145).

Hobbes takes a basically relativistic view of moral values, explaining that "because the constitution of a man's body is in continual mutation, it is impossible that all the same things should always cause in him the same appetites and aversions." "Much less," he adds, "can all men consent in the desire of almost any one and the same object." Whatever anyone desires, asserts Hobbes, he calls "good," and whatever is the object of his aversion, he terms "evil." Such words "are ever used with respect to the person that uses them; there being nothing simply and absolutely so . . . ." Like everything else in the universe that is impelled to maintain itself in the presence of ubiquitous counter-forces, human beings are everywhere intent upon their own self-preservation and the maximization of their power, so as to satisfy their personal desires (*Leviathan*, Pt. I, Chs. VI, IX; in Burtt 1939:149-150, 158-159, 165).

What is the role of reason in all this? We have already noted that reason has nothing to do with determining the goals or ends of human action. These are dictated entirely by the will, and that stems from the passions of self-gratification, self-aggrandizement, and avoidance of harm, as automatically set in motion by the cause-effect processes of the encompassing world.[34] Reason can be at most a means to an end. Its function is prudential, analyzing the best ways to achieve the self-centered impulses Hobbes attributes to all human beings and, *mutatis mutandis*, to the whole of nature. Any altruistic justifications we might give for our actions, such as seeking to base them in an allegedly universal "voice of conscience," are mere rationalizing overlays for the insistent demands of our egoistic wills (*Leviathan*, Pt. I, Ch. VII; in Burtt 1939:157). There are no rationally grounded principles to give substantive moral quality to our decisions, only prudential rules such as those that give rise to social contracts and political system—the latter to be presided over, in Hobbes's altogether predictable prescription, by rulers whose power is so far-reaching and unconstrained as to mirror here on earth the absolute authority of God above. Only the awe of such power, he insists, can override the natural human condition "where every man is enemy to every man" and provide a peaceful context for an efficient net gratification of personal desires (*Leviathan*, Pt. I, Ch. XIII; in Burtt 1939:161). It is on the prudential ground of the self-interested will, therefore, and not on that of any rationally based moral principles, that humans come to live under the aegis of social and political institutions. Reason in all such matters is the servant, not the master, of the will.

Hume's well known statement, "Reason is, and ought only to be the slave of the passions, and can never pretend to any other office than to serve and obey them," is of a piece with this conclusion of Hobbes. Like Hobbes, Hume claims that our volitions are the expressions of our passions or emotions, and he contends that it is impossible for reason either to justify or condemn any given volition. He states the point as forcibly as possible when he says, " 'Tis not contrary to reason to prefer the destruction of the whole world to the scratching of my finger." The passions are, as it were, their own "reasons" or provide their own internal justifications. "Since a passion can never, in any sense, be call'd unreasonable, . . . 'tis impossible that reason and passion can ever oppose each other, or dispute for the government of the will and actions." Only another passion, never a reason, can alter or attenuate an original passion. And because our passions are in every case the causes of our volitions and, hence, of our actions, it is on them that the whole course of our life turns (1980:415-416).[35]

In contrast to Hobbes, Hume is not an ethical egoist. But he still maintains that the moral assessments and principles that ought to channel our actions are the fruit of sentiment, not of reason. It is by distinctively moral feelings of adversion or aversion, approbation or blame, that we determine the rightness or wrongness of an action; here, as in other contexts, it is passion or feeling that reigns, not reason. Reason is relevant to morality only when it tells us that the objects we desire (or approve with our moral sentiments) do not exist, or when it informs us that our chosen means are insufficient to attain our desired ends. Hume also remarks that, had we no ends in view, i.e., were there no prospect of pain or pleasure, we would never even bother to make deductive calculations or to inquire into relations of cause and effect. Because these are the only two functions he allows for reason, it follows that the directing ends are themselves immune to rational criticism. In this sense as well, reason is handmaid to the passions and, hence, to the will (1980:415). Hume's portrayal of the relation of reason to volition seems to make impossible the kind of restraint of the latter by the former recommended by Descartes.

Also like Hobbes, Hume is a determinist who can see no difference between our volitions and the workings of cause and effect in nature (1980:171-172). And again like Hobbes, he can envision no middle ground between determinism and absurdity with regard to the concept of human action. A freedom that exhibited any independence of antecedent causes would be a freedom for which no one could be held accountable, because it could give no evidence of passions or principles in the mind. It would allow for no judgment of the persons or character, but only of a wholly disconnected, transitory action. The distinction, so important in courts of law, between hasty and premeditated action—the latter testifying to culpable states of character—could therefore have no place. Hume concludes that it is "only upon the principles of [causal] necessity, that a person acquires any merit or demerit from his actions, however the common opinion may incline to the contrary." This same line of reasoning is suggested in another place in the *Treatise* where Hume states that it is "impossible to admit any medium betwixt chance and an absolute necessity." An act undetermined by causes would be a purely chance occurrence for which no one could be held responsible (410-412, 171).

Kant takes an exactly opposite tack from Hobbes and Hume on this last point, although he shares in their belief that no middle ground can exist between causal necessity and freedom. He also concurs with them in assuming the primacy of the will. Let us review Kant's rendition of the theme of this section, the primacy of the will; in so doing, we will also bring into view his either/or view of causality and freedom.

The moral will is, for Kant, the core of human dignity and importance, and it alone gives us access to the in-itself, noumenal world. In relation to its judgments, the findings of scientific or theoretical reasons have a decidedly subordinate role. While it is true that the moral will is held accountable to the norms of so-called practical reason in Kant's philosophy, these norms are in no sense external to the will but are posited autonomously by it. Thus, in a manner similar to the thinking of Hobbes and Hume, the will has its own reasons or provides its own inherent principles of operation. But in contrast to these two, who see human volitions as manifestations of the causal processes of nature, Kant contends that the will transcends these processes and that it can act in a morally responsible manner only when it functions in complete independence of them. Because possession of a causally independent moral will is the trademark of humanity, it follows (in den Ouden's words) that persons "become fully human when they separate themselves from nature" (1982:73). A "will" that is the mere creature of natural impulses or desires, or that allows its decisions to be swayed by them or any other kind of empirical circumstances or condition, cannot be the morally good will that Kant makes the basis of his concept of human nature, his ethics, his religious philosophy, and his constructive metaphysics.

Kant also, then, can see no middle ground with regard to conceiving of the human will. But for him this means that the will must either be completely free of causal constraints, and in that way morally responsible, or a mere pawn of the passions. If the latter, it is in no sense free and can have no moral significance. Nor can it put us in touch with noumenal reality, for it is then just one more aspect of the phenomenal world of all-encompassing efficient causes, a world describable to its every last detail by the iron laws of mathematical physics. A persistent theme of modern thought, from its earliest years to the present, is this dichotomous view of freedom, where it is assumed that the only alternative to actions that are completely caused is actions performed in total independence of causes. We see this dichotomy operating in the thought of Hobbes, Hume, and Kant, and we witnessed in Chapter Four the crucial role it plays in the philosophy of Sartre—a more recent proponent of the primacy of the will.

Hobbes's and Hume's version of what we term the seventh philosophical source of nihilism makes the will independent of, and prior to, reason, but not to causality, and insists that there can be no responsible freedom without complete causal determination. Kant, by contrast, makes the will totally independent of causality and of theoretical reason, though not of the norms of so-called practical reason. Sartre insists that a genuinely free will must be completely independent of causes and prior to reasons or norms of any kind, these latter having their source exclusively in the will's wholly untrammeled, "absurd" decisions. As we saw earlier, anything less than such "total and infinite" freedom, where only freedom can limit freedom, is for Sartre indistinguishable from slavery. Because he sees this doctrine of freedom as essential to his central idea of the "for-itself" as a sheer nothingness, he, like Kant, makes radical freedom the crux of human existence. An ancestor of Sartre's extreme view of freedom, therefore, is the idea of the primacy of the will in early modern philosophy, on both its deterministic and its indeterministic sides, especially when that idea is connected with the notion that actions of the will are self-authenticating, or that the will makes its own rules. Sartre also carries forth the pervasive notion that the will must be either radically determined or radically free, with no allowance for any kind of middle ground.

The degree to which Kant extends his entwined notions of an absolutely free will and of the disjunction of freedom from causality is at times no less startling than the extent to which Sartre drives his similar conceptions, although Sartre's view is, in the last analysis, more extreme. Kant not only argues that the decisions of the moral will should be made solely with respect to the austere demands of the moral law, with no consideration permitted either for antecedent circumstances of desire, aversion, character, or psychological or social influence, on the one hand, or for anticipated empirical consequences, on the other. He also contends, in the development of his idea of a purely moral or rational religion, that it would be a mistake to assume that any person, whether divine or human, could atone for the sins of another or even assist in the overcoming of someone else's tendencies toward evil-doing. Just as each of us has fallen into a state of sin through an "incomprehensible" act of freedom (i.e., one admitting no causal explanation, because a free act cannot be causally explained), so each must extricate himself from that state by his own wholly unaided efforts of will. Because this "must" is a moral "must," and "ought implies can," it follows that each individual is fully able so to extricate himself and to set out upon an entirely different course of life (Kant 1960:179, 133, 43).

Kant's conviction that we are free to reverse in a moment all of our past tendencies or traits of character (because any restraint from the past would be an unallowable causal restriction on our freedom), and that we are therefore totally responsible for the course of our own lives and fully capable by ourselves of directing them at any time or in any circumstance to good or ill, is very much like Sartre's doctrine of our being "condemned to be wholly responsible" for ourselves, with no excuse and no hope of help or forgiveness from another.[36] In Chapter Four, I traced some of the nihilistic implications of this doctrine. Kant and Sartre give expression in this context, not only to an assumption of the primacy of the human will, but also to the notion of the wholly isolated, completely autonomous individual that figures so prominently in the fourth and fifth philosophical sources of nihilism and in other aspects of the nihilistic outlook. In the philosophy of Stirner, in particular, we witness with extreme clarity the natural coalescence of these two themes.

We can now shift our attention to the emphasis on cosmic will in the thought of philosophers such as Fichte, Schelling, Schopenhauer, and Nietzsche. Pure will, unrestrained by any anterior principles of morality or reason, is made paramount in the cosmos by Descartes and Hobbes, with their nominalistic conception of God. Hobbes and Hume also see our human wills as continuous with the causal processes of nature, and Hobbes views these processes as a system of discrete forces or powers, each of which is bent upon its self-maintenance and self-aggrandizement in the face of an opposing tendency on the part of all the others. Nature is therefore a melange of assertive "wills," not unlike Nietzsche's vision of the universe as an arena of contending foci of the will to power. Or, because every aspect of the universe, including human beings, is believed by determinists to be steered by efficient causes and stringent natural laws, the workings of these causes and laws can be collectively characterized as a kind of all-encompassing cosmic "will," in the manner of Schopenhauer.

But it is not only with a nominalistic God or a deterministic concept of nature that will gains cosmic ascendancy in modern thought. Another important source of this idea is Kant's notion of the pure ego or noumenal self, as contrasted with the empirical or objective self. Kant realized, as Hume did not, that in order for there to be knowledge or awareness of any type, there must first be a unity of consciousness. This unity cannot be made derivative from discrete impressions but is prior to them. Were it not prior, no coherent experience of these impressions would be possible. The unity of which Kant speaks (the "transcendental unity of apperception," to which I referred in Chapter Nine) is that "self" or activity of self-awareness that must already be present when we think of ourselves as objects or contemplate any other type of object. The self *of* which we think is the empirical self, subject to categories of the understanding such as substance and causality. But the self *by* which we think transcends or stands apart from those categories. It is the precondition of all experience, not part of the stream of experiential data mediated by the intuitions of sensibility or the categories of the understanding. We have no basis, then, for conceiving of this *a priori* self, this self that is antecedent to all experience because it is the necessary precondition of that experience, as an individual substance entrenched in a spatio-temporal world of efficient causes. As *a priori*, it is "pure" and lies beyond the conditioned realm of things experienced.

Fichte converts this pure or transcendental ego of Kant into the basis of an idealistic system of metaphysics. He thereby comes to assert the cosmic ultimacy of pure will or pure activity, prior to all objects or representations, and thus prior to reason itself. Some of the steps in his thinking, as analyzed by Copleston, follow. First, Fichte determines that the only correct philosophy is an idealism based squarely on our awareness of freedom, because this type of philosophy alone can preserve the crucial sense of moral duty. He is convinced that if we take as the starting point of metaphysical inquiry the assumption of a thing-in-itself world, we must inevitably be led to a causal determinism in which moral responsibility is impossible. Accordingly, Fichte rejects that world and argues that the realm of objects and of particular subjects has no autonomous existence but is the production of the pure ego. Next, he continues Kant's line of reasoning that the transcendental ego must be prior to substantial being, and he concludes that it cannot be conceived of as a particular individual. Instead, it is pure and unlimited activity that expresses itself through, but cannot be confined to, finite selves.

Finally, because Fichte identifies this transcendental ego with the moral will that Kant held to be our link with noumenal reality, a will that is in no way conditioned by the realm of objects and yet requires a world of objects in which its free actions can be performed, he comes to conceive of it as dynamically creative cosmic will. This will gives rise to an intelligible world of finite subjects and objects, each reciprocally limiting the other, as its field of operation and as the objects of its awareness. In this way—in and through finite selves interacting with the finite world—the pure ego or cosmic will becomes conscious of its own freedom and strives ceaselessly toward moral self-realization (see Copleston 1985:VII, 38-48).

Schelling continues this notion of an absolute will that creatively strives toward moral ends, although in his later thought the ends come to be conceived of as more aesthetic than moral. He thus gradually shifts the emphasis of his philosophy of will, in effect, from Kant's second *Critique* to the third. He concisely states the theme of the cosmic primacy of the will when he contends that in the last instance there is no other kind of being than will. Will underlies not only human life but the entire natural order (see den Ouden 1982:79). In contrast with Kant and Fichte, who restricted freedom to human beings and denied it to nature, Schelling sees the whole of nature as pervaded by an inexhaustibly creative will, and on this basis rejects the mechanical conception of nature.

In works published in 1798 and 1799, Schelling expressly relates his view of nature to the idea of force, seeing mechanical, chemical, electrical, and vital forces as different expressions of the same underlying impetus or power. This latter he views, not merely as producing repetitive patterns of cause and effect, but as a source of emergent novelty that will never culminate in a state of static equilibrium. In this way, he seeks to break down even further than had Fichte the Kantian dualism of human beings and the material world and to make the ever-evolving ferment of a teleologically conceived nature an analogue or reflection of human freedom endlessly aspiring toward the unattainable ideal of moral perfection (see Margoshes 1967:306; Kant 1960:60).

By the time we get to Schopenhauer, the cosmic will is still regarded as "the prius of knowledge, the kernel of our true being" (Schopehnauer 1957:II, 293; quoted den Ouden 1982:82), and as the primal ground of the finite universe of particular persons and things. But as we saw in Chapter Two, this will has now lost its moral character and its connections with aesthetic creativity and degenerated into a blind fate not appreciably different from the mechanical operations of cause and effect in scientific determinism. As Schelling had before him, Schopenhauer tends to identify the cosmic will with the idea of force. The workings of this will he claims to be evident,

> not only [in] the voluntary actions of animals, but [in] the organic mechanism, nay even the shape and quality of their living body, the vegetation of plants and finally, even in inorganic nature, crystallization, and in general every primary force which manifests itself in physical and chemical phenomena, not excepting gravity (*On the Will in Nature*, trans. K. Hillebrand, London, 1888; quoted den Ouden 1982:81).

Schopenhauer views the cosmic will or elemental force of the universe in extremely negative terms, as the source of a sinister world of suffering and pain from which we must try to escape at all costs. It is ironic that a metaphysics of will originally rooted in Kant's optimistic confidence in unrestricted moral freedom comes to be conceived so deterministically and with such unrelieved pessimism. Nevertheless, Schopenhauer informs his readers that he considers himself to be Kant's "immediate successor" (1957:II, 5).

Schelling had sought to resolve Kant's alienation of human beings from nature by infusing into nature itself a creative, dynamically free will intent upon moral and aesthetic attainment and coming to its most distinctive focus in human life. Schopehnauer also breaks down the Kantian dualism of humans and nature, but only to make human beings and all sentient creatures the helpless victims of malignant natural forces that sweep everything in their path. His portrayal of the machinations of the cosmic will is echoed in Thomas Hardy's dour ruminations, early in the present century, on "the dreaming, dark, dumb Thing / That turns the handle of this idle show." Like Schopenhauer, the English poet-novelist bemoans "the Will's long travailings" and sadly wonders, "Why the All-mover, / Why the All-power / Ever urges on and measures out the chordless chime of Things" (*The Dynasts* [1919, originally published 1903-1908], 1,524; quoted Randall 1976:592).

But if Schopenhauer urges self-abnegation and ascetic escape from a delusionary, pain-riddled realm of individualizing representations spun out by a malicious cosmic will, Nietzsche counsels vigorous self-affirmation and endorsement of the opportunities of the here-and-now world. He couples his positive outlook with yet another version of the primacy of the will, the idea of the will to power. There is considerable ambiguity, however, in Nietzsche's portrayal of the nature and role of this primordial force, and of its meaning for human existence. This ambiguity, and the different faces the cosmic will assumes in the thinking of the other philosophers of the will already considered, reveal much about the theme of this section, as we will soon see.

Nietzsche often sets forth the will to power in the form of what den Ouden calls "creative potency" (1982:100). Here we have an aesthetic and even a moral rendering of the cosmic will, especially reminiscent of Schelling and showing a strong influence of Romanticism. In this guise, it is the power of creative transformation or Dionysian self-transcendence that suffuses the universe, expressing itself in the human sphere in the natural leadership of a far-sighted elite who point the way beyond stultifying, excessively Apollonian fixations on the past[37] to a future of as yet unrealized possibilities. In proclaiming the power and significance of this creative will in the context of his own culture, Nietzsche speaks in the spirit of the Genevan professor, philosopher, and critic, Henri-Frederic Amiel, who complained in 1851 that "the era of *mediocrity* in everything is at hand," and observed that "the mediocre freezes every desire. Equality engenders uniformity," sacrificing "the excellent, the remarkable, the extraordinary." In his increasingly "*egalitarian* century," predicted the professor, the time of "ideal individuals" would soon disappear and an "epoch of crowds" would take its place (Amiel, *Journal intime*, ed. Gagnebin and Monnier, I, 1063: quoted Gay 1984:62).

Nietzsche desperately wants to avoid such depressing mediocrity and uniformity, and he takes heart from his belief that a power in the universe is working to overcome it, a power that inspires creative innovation in every branch of human culture. His bold affirmation of this impetus toward radical criticism and change, and of the individual genius as its principal vehicle, reflects the romantic movement of the late eighteenth and early nineteenth centuries, as can be seen from Albert Hofstadter's characterization of that movement.

> Emphasis on the creativity of the imagination was associated with the developing romantic spirit... because one of the chief qualities of romanticism is its stress on individuality, subjectivity, the uniqueness of the individual, life, and freedom, and therefore departure from norms that constrict life within accepted schemes. Adherence to customary rule, conformity with habitual or accepted pattern and norm, is the opposite (for the romantics) to creativity, originality, spontaneity, breakthrough and discovery of the new—the making of something where there was nothing before.

Hofstadter goes on to compare the romantic view of art with that of the Enlightenment:

> Romanticism in this sense was a reaction against the neoclassical spirit of rule-conformity in the eighteenth-century period of Enlightenment. In contrast with the eighteenth-century stress on art as imitation, in which art imitates nature by copying actual reality, the romantics stressed art as creation, as imitating nature in her process of creation itself. The artist becomes godlike, participating in the divine action. In opposition to the artistic power of grasping and representing the outward form of nature, the romantics posed the priority of the artistic power of being creative like nature itself, the power of genius (1974:118-119).

The aspect of Nietzsche's will to power now under discussion extends this romantic view of art to every field of human endeavor. To be fully human (or to transcend the merely human, as represented by a torpid, levelling culture whose creative energies Nietzsche believed to be exhausted, as did Spengler after him), people of singular ability must dare to be iconoclasts and innovators, throwing over the religious, metaphysical, epistemological, moral, and aesthetic trappings of the past and courageously affirming an open-ended future of creativity and will.

This outlook is not wholly different from that of the Enlightenment, for Descartes had also proclaimed the need for radial new beginnings. But Descartes had premised his new departure mainly on the power of reason, while Nietzsche grounds it in the rule-defying power of the will.[38] Neither Descartes nor Nietzsche gives credit enough to the fact that history and tradition provide the essential materials for creative change, and that the resources they provide are therefore to be treasured rather than scorned. Still, there is much in Nietzsche's idea of the will to power as creative potency that we can applaud. Any individual or society that wants to continue to develop and grow, or even to sustain itself for long, must learn how to respond to the lure of future possibilities and not allow itself to become uncritically bound to what has already been conceived or instituted in the past. And individuals and groups must often look to the leadership of persons with exceptional daring and imagination to understand just what those possibilities are and how they might best be actualized.

On the other hand, Nietzsche's view of the workings of the will to power sounds its own somber notes of pessimism and nihilism. For example, his worldview is as rigidly deterministic, in the last analysis, as that of Hobbes or Schopenhauer, as can be seen in his interconnected themes of eternal recurrence and *amor fati*. And he sometimes presents the will to power as the incontrovertible and cosmically fated right of the strong and ruthless to rule over the weak, a right to dominance he thinks to be manifest in all of nature. In this guise, the will to power makes a mockery of moral considerations or restraint. Armed with it, or something very similar to it, Nietzsche can announce: " 'Exploitation' does not belong to a corrupt or imperfect and primitive society; it belongs to the nature of a noble soul" and "is justice itself." He can also tell us that the "essential characteristic of a good and healthy aristocracy" is "that it accepts with a good conscience the sacrifice of untold human beings who, *for its sake*, must be reduced and lowered to incomplete human beings, to slaves, to instruments" (1966:203, 215, 202; quoted Schutte 1984:156, 170-171).[39] Nietzsche seems to be thinking in the same general vein when he flatly insists that all claims to truth and value are, at bottom, only expressions of the will to power, and thus covert weapons of dominance wielded by individuals or groups. On the basis of this last claim in particular—perhaps his most characteristic wrinkle on the motif of the primacy of will—he develops the epistemological and moral nihilisms attributed to him in Chapter Two.

Can we not surmise that at least one of the significant explanations for this profound ambiguity in Nietzsche's expostulations on the meaning of the will to power, and for the degeneracy of the concept of the cosmic will that we come across in Schopenhauer, is the root concept of the will as anterior to reason, or as being held in check by no constraints except those it magisterially imposes upon itself? What assurance do we have that such an absolute power of will shall be benign rather than malignant, creative rather than destructive, liberating rather than oppressive? What entitles us to believe that it shall act with any semblance of consistency? Behind the post-Kantian vision of a universal cosmic will viewed as the producer of everything in the universe and human life, including all principles of rationality and morality, looms the daunting figure of the infinitely powerful and wholly capricious God of Descartes and Hobbes, as well as the all-controlling forces of a scientifically conceived nature. The latter create a mere simulacrum of reliance on reason and choices among freely deliberated ends, where in reality there are only the irresistible buffetings of indifferent causes.

Stirner, Sartre, and Camus bring the cosmic will down to earth once more, locating it exclusively in human subjectivity, where Kant had first found it. Here as well, arbitrary will is seen as the secret basis of all that is naively deemed rational or moral, and as poisoning with its patent absurdity the structures of value and meaning—personal or communal—it wantonly engenders. Stirner's program is a brash affirmation of unrestrained, purely egoistic will, without even the veneer of sociality endorsed by Hobbes. Sartre advises us to be content with having to choose in a vacuum, for only in that way can we learn how to live with "good faith," or without delusions, in the face of the absurd. And Camus's Sisyphus shouts his defiance of will across the abyss before putting his shoulder again to the burden of his futile existence.

In many political systems of modern times we observe deliberate embracings of the Hobbesian insistence on the absolute right of political leaders or state bureaucracies to dictate by decree of the will what shall be of value or importance to everyone (and thus to stand in the place of an omnipotent God whose decisions are assumed to be beyond all criticism), or methodical institutionalizations of the Nietzschian conviction that the few strong have the right of nature to exploit and enslave the meek, and to stamp out with merciless abandon all who dare to resist their will. The essence of this type of political thinking, and its connection with the theme of this section, is symbolized by the title of Leni Riefenstahl's hauntingly beautiful (but also diabolical) propaganda film about the exploits of Hitler and his Reich: "The Triumph of Will."

Only in recent years have we begun to be conscious of the wide-scale devastations already inflicted on our planet, and of even more pervasive dangers posed for it in the imminent future, by the glib assumption of many in our technological age that nature is devoid of inherent values or ends, that human beings somehow stand over against it rather than being a part of it, and that it can therefore be treated as a mere passive instrument for rampant manipulations of the human will. This assumption correlates with the Cartesian dream of gaining an objective knowledge of nature as the means to its complete mastery and control.[40] It also ties in with the Fichtean idea (as glossed by Max Horkheimer) that "the relationship between the ego and nature is one of tyranny," and that "the entire universe" is "a tool of the ego, although the ego has no substance or meaning except in its own boundless activity" (Horkheimer 1947:108; quoted Leiss 1974:152). Fichte had in mind, of course, the cosmic ego, but he saw that as having its fullest manifestation in the egos and volitions of human beings. In these and other ways, some of which we examined in earlier chapters, the assumption of absolute, unconstrained willfulness—whether cosmic or human, or focused on the personal, the societal, or the natural contexts of human life—is freighted with nihilistic threats and consequences.

Now that I have addressed the developments and various manifestations of this seventh philosophical assumption in the modern period, and commented on its nihilistic implications, it is time to present some specific criticisms of the assumption itself. The first criticism focuses on the polarized conception of determinism and free will that dominates the thinking of Hobbes and Hume, on the one hand, and thinkers such as Kant and Sartre, on the other. By "polarized conception" I mean the supposition that humans must be either wholly determined or wholly free, and that no middle ground can be found between the two extremes. We see seeds of this polarization already present in the philosophy of Descartes: each new moment of experience is entirely disconnected from each previous moment, and is in that sense radically "free" of the past; but each new moment is also said to be created *in toto* by God, and is therefore from that aspect completely determined. We should also not fail to notice that, despite his own deterministic stance, Hume espouses a point-instant view of experience and time closely resembling that of Descartes, thus showing a similar swing of the pendulum on this issue, from the one extreme to the other.

Hobbes and Hume treat as ludicrous or morally absurd the idea that human actions can exhibit any independence of efficient causes. They assign absolute primacy to the will in the sense of maintaining that reason can have no say with respect to the ends of our actions but can speak only to the means for their attainment. These ends are dictated solely by our volitions (or by what comes virtually to the same thing in the case of these two philosophers: our sentiments, passions, or desires), and all our volitions, in turn, are the inevitable outcomes of antecedent causes.

Why is Hobbes so adamant in equating free will with absurdity? One reason is that, for him, only one kind of explanation is feasible for any type of phenomenon, including the phenomenon of human choice: efficient causal explanation. Whatever cannot be sufficiently explained in these terms must be inexplicable and absurd. He also assumes that allowing any freedom for the will requires that the will be placed wholly outside the context of motives, character, or environment, so that the only alternative to a causal account of volition is a kind of acausal "chaoticism" that he rightly judges to be absurd.

Why does Hume take it to be self-evident that an action that cannot be explained in terms of antecedent causes is one for which no one could be held morally accountable? The basic answer is that he shares Hobbes's view that no middle ground can exist between explanation by efficient causes and total inexplicability and, thus, unaccountability. Accordingly, he reasons that any action that did not flow necessarily from a person's character would be a mere fluke or transitory episode for which there could be no praise or blame. We have also seen that the whole focus of Hume's ethical theory is on the character of the person acting, not on the action itself; hence, an action that did not express a character would be for him devoid of ethical import.

But if we once allow for explanations by reasons and not merely by causes, for the idea that the ends of our actions are not automatically determined by our volitions or desires but are criticizable and alterable in light of reasons, and for the possibility of character-transcending actions that still take place within, and are fundamentally affected by, a context of motivations or causes—then these particular objections of Hobbes and Hume to a nondeterministic view of free will cease to have point. As a further consequence, their particular case for the primacy of the volitions, which depends so heavily on a rigorously deterministic outlook, is made much less convincing. I will say more about these matters after commenting on the other side of the assumed gulf between determinism and free will, that represented in the views of Kant, Sartre, and other exponents of radical freedom.

Kant has a highly abstract conception of freedom. He contends for a will that can, and ought, to act in total independence of empirical circumstances and considerations. This view of the will suspends human beings above nature and above their bodies, and the radical freedom and responsibility for every action it insists upon makes each new action completely independent of motives and predispositions of character. This remains true even if these motives and predispositions are explained largely or entirely as the accumulated result of antecedent free choices. In fact, even the notion of such an "accumulated result" becomes highly problematical, just as we earlier saw it to be in the case of Sartre (Chapter Four, Section 3).

The extreme implausibility of Kant's version of the primacy of the will is partly concealed from us by two features of his thought. The first is the circumspection with which he develops his view. On the one hand, as seen earlier, he claims that the evil that arises from acts of freedom, and the radical renovation of life that can also stem from those acts, are wholly inexplicable because rooted in freedom. Here he plays into the hands of determinists such as Hobbes and Hume, who see as the only alternative to determinism an inexplicable chaoticism. But on the other hand, Kant gives strong empasis to factors in individuals' social environments that can profoundly influence them for evil or for good. This seems inconsistent. We cannot help wondering how a pristine will, all-competent at any given moment and possessing lucid understanding of its own self-imposed duties, could be in any way susceptible to, or dependent upon, such influences.

It is rare, in modern times, that a view of freedom is seriously entertained where the efficient causal factors are deemed to be necessary, but not sufficient, conditions for the performance of a genuinely free act: where it is assumed that choices can be made in light of reasons and sought ends that are not simply reducible to antecedent causes, but also that causal circumstances play a highly significant, if not wholly determinative, role in our decisions. Considerations of reason might induce us, for example, to choose a weaker motive over the stronger, but could not enable us to act with indifference to motives or the influences of our accumulated characters. Such a theory of action constitutes a middle ground between the two extremes represented by the philosophies of Hume and Kant. It is notable that while Hume holds that an action not wholly explainable in terms of efficient causes would have to be one empty of moral significance, Kant holds exactly the opposite. For Kant, an action done from freedom is, by definition, causally inexplicable, and only such an action can have moral import. This difference between the two philosophers places in bold relief the polarized view of determinism and free will that is our present concern.

Fig. 1: THE DETERMINISM—LIBERTARIANISM—CHAOTICISM SCALE

DETERMINISM

1. Everything that is, or will be, can be exhaustively explained in terms of antecedent causes and is completely predictable in principle, if not in practice.

2. *Freedom* means (a) absence of external constraint; (b) ability to do what one wants to do, i.e., to act in accord with one's strongest motive or pattern of motives.

LIBERTARIANISM

1. Although all things are constrained by a causal context, chance and/or free choice may also have a role in their occurrence. Not everything is completely predictable, even in principle.

2. In addition to (a) and (b) on the left, *freedom* means ability (c) to act purposefully, i.e., for the sake of ends, and not merely to be pushed from behind; (d) to select among alternative motives and actions in light of reasons; and thus (e) to have acted differently than one did act, even had all the causal conditions, including one's wants or motives and their relative strengths, remained the same.

CHAOTICISM

Some things can occur wholly unconstrained by causal contexts laid down by the past, namely, events of pure chance and free choices.

Fig. 2: DETERMINIST AND LIBERTARIAN MODELS OF ACTION

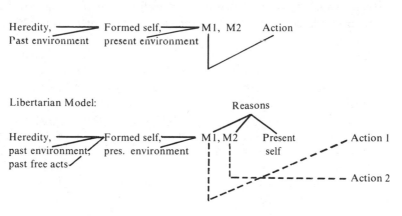

In Figures 1 and 2, I diagram an intermediate view of free choice that neither of our two groups of thinkers considered. Acceptance of it, or of some version of it, would have the effect of nullifying, or at least calling into fundamental question, the extreme position each takes, and, to that extent, each's way of arguing for the primacy of the will. Figure 1 shows clearly the intermediate character of what I call the *libertarian* position, and spells out its differences from *determinism* and *chaoticism*, the two extremes. Figure 2 gives past free acts a role, along with heredity and environment, in shaping the *formed self* (or character). This formed self determines what the strongest motive (M1) shall be in a given situation of choice, as well as determining the weaker motives (one of which is represented by M2). The present self is able to consult reasons for and against following the strongest motive in a given situation and may decide to act in accord with a weaker motive instead. It cannot ignore the motivational context altogether, or the circumstances of the present environment, but it can act with some degree of independence within the constraints these two factors lay down. Thus, it has available to it (in my over-simplified diagram), either Action 1, following from the strongest motive, or Action 2, following from a weaker motive. Both actions arise from motives and are, therefore, caused. But the present self has a say in selecting among the available causes and in this way influences the effect.[41]

Successive choices of weaker motives rather than the strongest one can, in time, produce changes in the formed self, showing how it can be progressively (but not instantaneously) altered by acts of freedom. Changes in the environment can also conduce to this process of change by helping to reinforce already existing motives that run counter to the strongest motive in the formed self, or by insinuating new motives into the complex of motives, both stronger and weaker, that characterize the formed self. Causal influences of the environment are accordingly given their due importance and place in libertarianism, contrary to Hume, who argues that only a doctrine of strict determinism can make sense out of the observations that "all human laws are founded on rewards and punishments," and that it is supposed on every hand "as a fundamental principle, that these motives have an influence on the mind, and both produce the good and prevent the evil actions" (1980:410).

The model of freedom set forth in these two diagrams also shows why human acts can be as predictable as we usually find them to be. It is entirely consistent with the model that the more we know about the hereditary dispositions, past choices, formed characters, and environmental circumstances, both past and present, of individuals, the more predictable their actions will be, because all these factors lay down "lines of least resistance" for present decisions. This predictability is further enhanced when we have insight into a person's intellectual and moral outlook, and, thus, into the kinds of reasons that are most likely to guide that person's choices in particular circumstances. Hence, the observed consistency of a person's actions can be explained partly in terms of causes and partly in terms of reasons.

But the model still allows for an element of openness in human choices— an unpredictability of principle, one that does not just result from lack of full knowledge of all the causal circumstances involved, and one that allows for rational justifications or appeals that may not have been entirely typical of that person in the past. Intellectual considerations and changes can, therefore, influence changes in action, meaning that the will is capable of working in concert with reasons rather than having to be viewed as prior to it, and that it can be seen as amenable to rational persuasion, not just causal motivation. This recognition of the respective roles of causal explanation and the weighing of reasons makes room for the all-important difference between explanation and justification that Kant highlights and that Hume in his own way (i.e., with his distinction between *is* and *ought*) also stresses. But it allows as well for the critical importance of efficient causes in the explanation for, and the shaping of, human actions that Hobbes and Hume so rightly emphasize.

Sartre, in particular, resolutely carries forward Kant's claim that a genuinely free will must be able to act in radical independence of the past, making the absurdist consequence of this claim apparent to an extent that Kant, with his inconsistent circumspections, did not. Our exposition of the libertarian view shows, however, that freedom does not require absolute independence of causal conditions; i.e., it does not require an absurd chaoticism. The dichotomy of determinism or chaoticism is a false dichotomy; the actions of genuinely free individuals can be partially, even if not completely, accounted for in causal terms. Neither Kant nor Sartre has recognized this, so they think they must jump from one extreme to the other. This results in their own versions of the primacy of the will, each turning on a vision of absolute freedom.

The second thing that tends to obscure the extreme implausibility of Kant's version of the primacy of the will is his claim that human freedom is responsibly exercised only when it is kept strictly within the bounds of the universal moral law, a law that the will itself, in the guise of "practical reason," lays down. This is reassuring because it purports to show a way to conceive both the primacy and the radical freedom of the will without giving license to moral nihilism. But the assurance is fragile and short-lived.

Philosophers of the will subsequent to Kant tend to follow the implications of his views more consistently than he himself did. We just cited the example of Sartre's tracing to its absurdist conclusion Kant's conviction that the will acts, or can act, in radical disassociation from the constraints of the past. Stirner, Nietzsche, and Sartre reason, further, that if the will is truly primary, as Kant held it to be, then it cannot be made beholden to any principles beyond itself, or to any principles that it does not posit arbitrarily at every instant of its self-actualization. This idea was already explicit in the nominalistic view of God. Kant's "categorical imperative" tries, in a sense, to have it both ways, i.e., to give primacy to particular acts of the will and yet to restrict the will's legitimate operations to unchanging norms of reason. The fact that Kant insists that it is a different kind of reason, said to flow autonomously from the will itself, does not blunt the point.

The later idea that each solitary individual lays down her own idiosyncratic principles for thought and action, and in that way gives expression to the absolute primacy of her will, is greatly influenced by a historical development discussed in Chapter Nine. The modern project of trying to derive universal epistemological and moral principles from the subjectivity of the isolated individual—a project of which Kant's first and second *Critiques* are outstanding examples—can be seen by the time of Nietzsche, and certainly by the time of Sartre, to have been a failure. One telling sign of its failure is that no consensus is even approached, much less achieved, among the project's most able advocates on just what these subjectively derived but universal principles are. The dream of discovering them fades, but not the subjectivist bias itself, and not the supposition, at least in some quarters, that the only conceivable alternative to timeless, absolute, and in that sense "objective" principles of thought and action, is purely subjective maxims legislated moment by moment by individual acts of will.[42]

In this way, we are thrown into a situation of epistemological, moral, and existential nihilism. In the case of Stirner, no common morality can exist, only egoistic will. In the case of Nietzsche, our truths follow from our values, and these, in turn, are the arbitrary constructs of our wills. We thereby manifest at the level of our individuality the cosmic principle of the will to power: Nietzsche's version of the nominalistic God, or his rendering of the post-Kantian noumenal will, viewed as the absolute source of all structures of meaning and value. In the case of Sartre, the whole intelligible world for each person is the free construct of that person's will. Thus, for all three of these philosophers, to choose is to make true and to endow with value; there is no other basis of meaning in the universe than an endlessly improvising will.

The free will side of the determinism—free will polarity that we are currently considering is notoriously time-phobic. It is so in one way because it takes freedom to require complete independence from the past, but it is so in another important respect, because it assumes that freedom can be meaningfully guided only by timeless norms, or that only such norms can have any "objective" significance for acts of the will. This second kind of time-phobia is at least as old as Plato, who believed that the only way to exorcise the demon of Sophistic relativism was to learn how to conform our thoughts and actions to the absolute standard of the eternal Forms. In that same spirit, Kant reasons that if there were no absolute moral law, discoverable within ourselves and transcending all cultures and times, moral obligation would cease to have meaning. Philosophers such as Stirner, Nietzsche, and Sartre continue to make this assumption and, finding no such universal law or set of moral principles, follow the assumption through to its nihilistic conclusion.

I have already criticized the first kind of time-phobia, showing its rootage in a false dichotomy. There is a way of allowing for the crucial role of the past in relation to present decisions without our having to view those decisions as the inexorable outcomes of efficient causal forces. My second main criticism of the seventh philosophical assumption is directed at the other type of time-phobia. Because this criticism has already been anticipated by my presentation of the pluralistic alternative in Chapter Nine, I need state it only briefly here to show how it applies to the present topic.

The point of this second criticism is simply that principles of intelligibility and worth are not suddenly made useless when shown to be dependent upon concrete, varying conditions of history, tradition, or culture. As noted above, one version of the assumption of the primacy of the will assigns it this primacy by forfeit; either the will is directed by universal, and therefore demonstrably *immutable* precepts, or it must be absurdly capricious, with no rational basis for its decisions. Because the alternative expressed by the first proposition turns out to be unattainable, we are supposedly left with only the second alternative.

But this is a false dichotomy, as patently false as the claim that the actions of the will must either be exhaustively explainable by efficient causes or be utterly inexplicable. I exhibited in some detail in the previous chapter the artificiality of the former dichotomy, arguing that perfectly serviceable and eminently reasonable truths and values can be found within the finite, time-bound conditions of cultural experience. We are not required to transcend these conditions in order to have a context of objective meaning for the exercise of our freedom, or to be able to assess in a rational manner the relative merits of options available for our choices.

I also noted in Chapter Nine that the historically inherited interpretive patterns and norms of a particular culture do not just mechanically structure our choices but are themselves subject to transformation over time, as we reflect critically on our cultural heritage, select out aspects of it for emphasis, explore the resources of other cultures and times, and enter into creative dialogue with those who envision the world in different ways than we do. Just as in the libertarian model of freedom the causal past influences but does not determine our choices, so does our culture provide both stable context and appreciable latitude for the expression of our freedom. Because this is the case, reason and the will can work together in codependent harmony. There is no desperate need for immutable principles to hold our freedom in check or to rescue us from blind caprice. Thus, the "forfeit" argument for the primacy of the will implicitly followed by thinkers such as Stirner, Nietzsche, and Sartre—but within the parameters laid down by Kant and other absolutists—fails. And with our recognition of its failure another part of the supporting structure for the philosophy of nihilism is eroded away.

5. THE JOURNEY SO FAR

Parts Three and Four of this book have been devoted to a critical investigation of thirteen assumptions—six of them religious, and seven, philosophical—that have played a dominant, although not always explicitly acknowledged, role in the development of nihilistic thought over the past two centuries. While this list is not meant to be exhaustive, I do claim that these assumptions are among the most important intellectual sources of modern nihilism. I have tried to show that bringing them under scrutiny can have the effect of exposing basic weaknesses in arguments for the nihilistic point of view: arguments such as those presented in Chapters Two, Three, and Four.

Although I have made considerable progress in the task of elaborating and critically evaluating the philosophy of nihilism, I am not yet at my journey's end. I must probe in more depth two categories of argument that strike to the heart of the nihilistic outlook, those relating to suffering and death. Much can also be gained from pondering the lessons of nihilism, so I need to indicate some of these lessons. Finally, I want to summarize the case against nihilism, showing why, despite the insights to be gained from attending to particular aspects of this philosophy, it remains a cramped and unpersuasive general account of human existence. I will address these remaining topics in Part Five.

PART FIVE

Final Appraisal

Chapter 11

The Case Against Nihilism: Lessons and Refutations

Man is that paradoxical being, unique so far as we know, who strives for a perfection which, if attained, would altogether deprive him of his nature.

—*Stanley Rosen (1969:214)*

1. SUFFERING AND DEATH

A man and his wife were returning to their home in separate cars. The husband arrived first and waited for his spouse, who had been some distance behind him. When he had waited much longer than he thought it would have taken for her to arrive, he got back in his car and anxiously retraced his path. He had not gone very far when he saw the scene of an accident before him, with the flashing lights of a police car, the glint of scattered glass in his headlights, and two smashed automobiles skewed across the road. He learned from police that his wife's car had been broadsided by another car running a red light and that the driver of that car was believed to have been drinking. His wife died soon after in the hospital. When reporters later sought the man's reaction to the accident, he could only respond: "What can you say? It's part of life and death. I don't have any great things to expound on. It hurts so bad" (Robinson and Kirksey 1987).

This experience, routinely reported in an urban newspaper, as are so many other events of its kind, can help set the mood for our meditations on suffering and death as they relate to the philosophy of nihilism. Not only does the experience show a close connection between suffering and death: some of our most grievous suffering is produced by the death or pending death of someone we love; it also strikes the right note of humility. For I also am afraid that I have nothing especially profound to say about these two solemn themes. But I do want to make some observations, the intent of which is to show that the facts of suffering and death, pervasive and deeply troubling though they be, need not finally bring us to a nihilistic conclusion.

The first observation is that a sizable amount of the suffering in the world can be traced to the free actions of human beings, and therefore need not be attributed to an indifferent or malignant cosmos, nor be seen as inevitable. With freedom comes responsibility, a responsibility that can either be shouldered or ignored, for good or ill. It is not logically possible for us to have freedom of choice and yet be immune to destructive misuses of our freedom. The carelessness, indifference, or vindictiveness of some can bring about the pain of others, as in the event cited above. An individual could have sought help for his alcoholism but did not; he could have taken prior steps to ensure that he did not drive while intoxicated, but did not. The result was tragedy. Others allow their fellow humans to suffer through indifference or neglect, a callous "passing by on the other side." Still others, letting themselves be driven by such motives as prejudice, resentment, greed, a passion for excitement, or a lust for power have trampled individuals or groups into the dust, willfully inflicting agony and death in order to gain their ends.

These and other abuses of freedom, although matters of utmost concern, need not reduce us to despair. For with the freedom to do evil there is also the freedom to do good. Although we cannot undo the tragedies of the past, we can work to find ways to motivate and assist one another toward more generous and caring relationships in the future. We can try to fashion and maintain institutions that procure greater protection and justice for the innocent against the guilty and that offer firm but constructive treatment for those who succumb—and not always simply through personal malice—to evil desires.

This is not to say that we can expect to eliminate altogether the perverse and destructive proclivities of the human spirit; these are a feature of our experience for which no one can convincingly claim to have adequate understanding or solutions. But we can strive to ameliorate these evil impulses in ourselves and others and to find ways to put more positive incentives in their place—through education, law, moral and religious influence, the transformative power of the arts, persistent psychological and social research, and institutional reforms. We are also free to work toward a more humane treatment of animals, toward creating a climate of concern in which we become more respectful of their needs and more sensitive to their capacity for pain. It is within our power as free beings, then, to reduce the amount of suffering in the world: this is a vision of hope, not of nihilistic despair. The obstacles are formidable and many, but the opportunities are genuine and far-ranging.

The second observation is that a considerable portion of human suffering is produced by the stable, predictable natural environment without which we could not implement our freedom. These orderly processes of the environment enable us to produce the automobiles that extend our freedom of movement, but that also constitute new sources of pain or death, as in the example above. The same can be said of many of the other technological inventions that enhance our freedom in today's world. But even without elaborate technologies, people can be hurt by the regularities of nature, as when someone tumbles from a cliff or is drowned in the sea. Where would we be without the pull of gravity or the properties of water, both of which usually sustain us but may on some occasions injure us or kill us? Could there be dependable regularities that work on our behalf and provide the necessary means for the expression of our freedom that would not also, in some circumstances, bring us to grief?

A nihilism that decries this ambiguity in an ordered universe appears to be demanding something that, in the very nature of the case, is impossible, at least if human freedom is to remain a reality. If there are alternatives to such ambiguity, they are by no means easy to conceive; furthermore, one would still have to show that they would be better overall. Here we are reminded of the critical discussions in Chapter Six of the seductive dream of a heavenly paradise. Despite the many elements of contingency and hazard in this world to which we all are consigned, the world also provides us with the protection and dependability necessary to life and freedom. Does it make any sense to demand the benefits and yet to expect to have none of the potential liabilities?

Third, our capacity for suffering is the necessary concomitant of our capacity for commitment, caring, and loving. Were we creatures of indifferent or dull sensibilities, our susceptibility to pain would be drastically reduced. But to be committed and to care and thus to feel deeply, is to be involved in relationships or ventures that do not always turn out in ways we hope for or expect. Such involvements can profoundly enrich our lives, but they also contain the seeds of disappointment and loss. To have persons and purposes for which to live and willingly to dedicate ourselves to them with intensity of concern, is also to run the risk of losing them or failing to attain them, or of getting hurt in the process of serving them. But only in this way can we hope to have things worth living for.[1]

Sometimes, in order to serve those commitments and values that make life worthwhile, we must sacrifice our own personal happiness or even endanger our lives. The "readiness to make such sacrifice," Mill asserts, "is the highest virtue which can be found in man." He adds that "in this condition of the world, the conscious ability to do without happiness gives the best prospect of realizing such [general] happiness as is attainable" (1957:21). Some of the most exemplary and meaningful lives on record fit this description. One thinks, for example, of the life of Mohandas K. Gandhi. Millions of people have been profoundly affected for the good, and much evil has been averted by this one man's sufferings, willingly undergone for the sake of others. Gandhi was finally assassinated, and his loved ones, friends, and followers were grief stricken by the senselessness of his death. But can one seriously claim that his life was not worthwhile, or that his sufferings or theirs canceled the incalculable good that he was able to accomplish? This good effect continues to the present day, in the inspiring example of loving involvement and concern Gandhi has set for us all, and in the great nation he helped to found.

Fourth, it would be a mistake to regard suffering as something entirely negative or merely instrumental, something itself devoid of value that must be risked or undergone as the price of commitment and caring, or of continuing to live. Suffering can often contribute positively to the quality of existence by teaching courage, compassion, sensitivity to the deeper issues of life, and the ability to cope with life's contingencies. This may result when the path of suffering is consciously chosen, as was the case for Gandhi, whose ordeals helped to mold him into the person of extraordinary vision, endurance, and spirituality he became. But it can also result when suffering descends on one unexpectedly, through no personal act of will. This was true of Franklin Delano Roosevelt, afflicted with poliomyelitis in his mid-life.

Many who knew Roosevelt were convinced that his struggles with this disease, which left him unable to walk without aid for the rest of his years, gave him humility, patience, a reflective capacity, and profound sympathy for the problems of humankind: traits of character for which he had not been noted before. These struggles helped to equip him for the burden of leadership he bore so long and well while president of the United States, during the trying years of the Great Depression and on into the time of World War II. Hence, not only did Roosevelt gain immeasurably from his own suffering; countless others gained as well (see Morgan 1985:258-262).

The examples of Gandhi and Roosevelt demonstrate that we should not approach the problem of suffering merely from the standpoint of the individual, though even there suffering can have creative power. We need also to see it from the standpoint of humanity as a whole, because the individual's sufferings may prove redemptive for the group and turn out to have positive significance for that reason. To confine our analysis of suffering to the scale of the individual is to continue the fallacy of thinking of particular persons as isolated, self-contained units, a fallacy I have criticized in other contexts.

We should also note that groups can benefit from their own sufferings and struggles, not merely from the sacrifices of their leaders. Ted Morgan cites the example of the American people during the Great Depression, arguing that just as out of Roosevelt's "pain came personal renewal, greater understanding, and surprising reserves of strength," so "[o]ut of the nation's pain" came "renewal, and the making of a more compassionate society" (1985:261). But we should not fail to note as well that while such corporate suffering can be a catalyst for renewal, this outcome is not automatic. It depends partly on how human beings, in their freedom, respond to their travails and opportunities. Germany in the late 1920s and early 1930s also experienced large-scale economic deprivation, but the historical outcome was tyranny and degradation, not renewal.[2]

It is possible for us to live meaningful lives, then, but not without the risk of suffering (and sometimes only through facing up to the near certainty of suffering, depending on what we dedicate ourselves to; Gandhi's life is a case in point). No guarantee is given that everyone's life will be equally meaningful, or that a life that is currently meaningful will always continue to be so to the same degree. And it is unfortunately true that the experience of suffering can sometimes be so shattering or all-consuming as to destroy a person's will to live, or to seem to cancel any possibility of a meaningful life for that person. Such sufferings must also be admitted, at least in some cases, to have had mostly negative impacts on a person's family, friends, or larger social group. In addition, whole groups can be exposed to sufferings so acute and senseless as severely to threaten the life-affirmations of many members of that group, as with certain American Indian tribes in the late nineteenth century or the Jews of the Holocaust.

These kinds of suffering, then, seem incurably tragic or without redeeming value. To acknowledge this fact is realistic, but it is not nihilistic, because the latter denies even the possibility of a meaningful life, dismissing any claim to such a life as based on delusion. The presence and prospect of suffering, and the fact that no guarantees of exemption from its most devastating effects are given, does not entail that meaningful lives cannot be achieved. Human life, like all kinds of life, is undoubtedly precarious. But this does not mean that it is hopeless or without point.

This last statement brings me to my fifth observation. Schopenhauer, Cioran, and others, who claim that but two states of human life exist, either deadening boredom or excruciating pain, are plainly wrong. This is a false disjunction. Most lives are lived on a middle ground somewhere between these extremes, showing experientially that life can be so lived. Cioran and Schopenhauer are guilty of gross exaggeration; they have fallen into what Charles Frankel calls "an operatic posture" or a case of "cosmic hypo-chondria" (1965:10-11). While true of some lives, and perhaps of their own, their analysis falls patently short of accurately describing all human life. Thus, their examination of existence, one that purports to be starkly realistic and to have peeled away the veneer from our usual, less probing perceptions, is actually histrionic and overblown. A similar point can be made about

Kafka's view (at least as interpreted by Ross) that because we find ourselves unable to live up entirely to our highest obligations and goals, we must forever be wracked by an anguish of self-loathing and guilt. Satisfaction can be gained from the relative attainment of high ideals, and our need continually to strive toward closer approximations to them can safeguard us against stultifying complacency and give sustained purpose to our lives. The fact that we fall short of these ideals need not, therefore, consign us to unremitting misery and frustration.

Having said all of the above, however, the fact remains that much suffering is a blight on existence that defies conceptual explanation or existential accommodation. While our lives are far from being entirely absurd, there are elements of the absurd in them, and inexplicable suffering is one of the most notable of these elements. We can account for it and give meaningful interpretations of it up to a certain point, as we have just tried to do. But Elie Wiesel is right in the last analysis when he says,

> Evil is in the world. The question is why innocent people are punished. There are no answers. I won't accept comfortable answers. If anyone would say there is an answer, I wouldn't believe it (Quoted Nellhaus 1985).

Rolston speaks similarly when he insists that much suffering is irremediably evil, and that to

> explain evil rationally is a contradiction in terms; this would be a religious equivalent to giving a scientific explanation for random events. Some events do not have causes, not at the point of their randomness. Some events do not have meanings, not at the point of their evilness (1987:287).

Suffering is part of the fabric of existence; it runs through the whole of human history and animal experience.[3] Its threads are often crooked and grotesque, refusing to blend with other aspects of experience, defying all analysis or moral resolution. To pretend otherwise is to succumb to sentimentality and mere wishful thinking.

Still, suffering is not the unmitigated bane and disaster Schopenhauer, Ciroan, and other nihilists have taken it to be. Its significance is mixed, not resoundingly absurd. Just as it cannot be explained to our final satisfaction, so it cannot be said to be totally beyond explanation or to lead to but one outcome, that of nihilism. We can face up to its reality and acknowledge its threatening mystery without despairing of the meaning of human life or without denouncing the universe in which it occurs. In order to do so, however, powerful symbolizations of the ever-present fact and possibility of suffering must be present, effective reminders that it is an aspect of existence over which we often do not have control, an aspect for which we must be constantly trying to prepare ourselves. The story of the cross in Christianity is one such symbolization, as is the figure of Shiva-Kali in Hinduism.

Although my own consciousness has been deeply molded by the story of the cross, which locates suffering in the heart of the universe, in its ultimate Source and Principle, and not merely in human consciousness, there seems to me to be something lacking in this symbolism that can be compensated for by the complementary Hindu perspective. The Christian symbolism portrays God as unqualifiedly good, as the innocent victim of sufferings for which he himself cannot be held accountable, and yet as finally triumphant over the evil effects of all sufferings. There is a sense in which this portrayal, for all of its evocative depth and power, remains too one-sided or unqualified in its optimism. It fails adequately to symbolize the impenetrable enigma of suffering, and to that extent does not prepare us to confront that enigma, meaning that the extent of our own or of the world's suffering may continue to come to us as more of an existential shock or bolt out of the blue than it should.

The traditional theistic problem of evil is a symptom of what I am trying to get at here: its assumed view of God as all-good and all-powerful, and as having calmly created evil (or the possibility of evil) for his own sovereign uses, does not quite ready us psychologically for the threat and presence of inexplicable suffering. Hindu symbolism, by contrast, portrays the Source and Principle of the universe as radically ambiguous, as containing in itself a serenity and creative energy that holds out the promise of bliss and salvation, but as also embodying a horrible destructive activity and potency. Shiva the serene and yet dynamic creator is at one and the same time black Kali the destroyer, with blood-drenched fangs and a garland of skulls, the wanton devourer of humans and animals.

The image of Shiva-Kali is in part an indication that creation and destruction must often go hand-in-hand, because destruction of the old is the frequent prelude or accompaniment to creation of the new. But more fundamentally, it serves as a stark reminder that the universe has a black side like a dark side of the moon, a side of shadowy menace and pain that can descend upon us at any moment. This is part of the universe's ultimate character: its aspect of unfathomable mystery.

It is significant that *Kali* is the femine form of *kala*, a Sanskrit word for time, suggesting the radical uncertainty of the future and the setbacks and deprivations the passage of time may force into our lives, as well as the unexpected opportunities for accomplishment and renewal the future may bring. To live realistically is to be acutely aware of this ambiguity of our temporal existence. This ambiguity must be clearly recognized as such; it cannot be simply resolved either into bouyant optimism or gloomy nihilism.

Such a recognition allows for confidence and hope, but only as tempered by compassionate awareness of the reality and extent of the sufferings of animals and human beings, and only as informed by a wary acknowledgment of the contingencies of all existence. These contingencies may bring suffering, but the same suffering will sometimes, although not always, have unforeseen transforming effects. Such an outlook, which can aptly be termed "the tragic sense of life," can also help prepare us for the sacrifices that we may be called upon to make as the price of our involvement in those commitments and pursuits that make life worthwhile and contribute to the world's betterment.

I turn now from the problem of suffering to that of death. Does the fact of death, or perhaps at least of untimely death, support a nihilistic conclusion? In opposition to the arguments of Chapter Three, Section 4, I contend that it does not—despite the wrenching agony of loss that is the frequent companion of death (especially the death of the young and unfulfilled), and despite the shock of incomprehension that can stagger us when a close relation or friend dies, or when we are brought against the rock-hard inevitability of our own death and the deaths of those we cherish.

It will help us to put the fact of death in perspective if we try to imagine what the earth or human society would be like if nothing ever died. Not only would there be no such thing as ecosystems or food chains in nature: those elaborate webs of interconnection in which ascendingly complex forms of life are sustained by the deaths of descendingly simple ones. There also could be no such thing as a course of evolution allowing the higher forms, including that of human life itself, to have emerged. Just as entropy is the price paid for the exchanges of energy that enable life, mind, and the universe to exist, so the death of individuals, and sometimes of whole species, is the price of the startling diversity of life-forms and the creative ongoingness of evolution. Thus, in the natural order, diversity and creativity fit hand-in-glove with impermanence and death, the one being made possible only through the other. To have contempt for the presence of death in nature, and to regard that presence as an unqualified evil and absurdity, is also to reject the entwined dependencies of an ecological earth and the workings of temporal processes that must destroy in order to sustain and to create: the very conditions of life as we know it.

According to the Hebrew Bible, the primordial temptation of human beings is their wanting to "be like God" (Genesis 3:5). We can apply this teaching to the theme of death by noting the tendency of our species throughout its history to be tormented by the dream of finding some way to nullify its earthbound, finite state and to escape the limiting conditions of life in the world. A desperate yearning to be something we are not constantly hounds us, tempting us to deny all that is satisfying and good in what we are and have the capacity to become.

The "curse" of this response of ingratitude and pride is perhaps not death itself, as in the more customary reading of Genesis 3:19, but rather an overweening anxiety about death, and unwillingness to come to terms with its necessary inclusion in limited, interdependent existence. Nihilism is symptomatic of this hubris in its unqualified rejection of the gift of a bounded life, based on the assumption that life cannot be meaningful unless it is everlasting. But the assumption itself seems absurd, as irrational as a child's stubborn refusal of a father's invitation to go to the circus simply because the child knows that it will last only for an evening and thus that its delights will not be experienced forever. Marcus Aurelius's contrasting outlook on death is appropriately sober but also eminently sane. He writes in his *Meditations* that he considers it "consistent with the character of a reflecting man" that he "be neither careless nor impatient nor contemptuous with respect to death," but that he "wait for it as one of the operations of nature" (1965:IX,3; quoted Meilaender 1986:11).

A similar conclusion can be drawn from an attempt to imagine what human society would be like if no human being ever died. First, a population problem would exist of such monumental proportions and madly accelerating pace as to make the present one seem trivial by comparison. In fact, the human race might well already have become extinct on account of its grossly outstripping the carrying capacity of the earth. Second, a massive inhibition of constructive change in society without death would probably be evidenced, a heavy weight of conservatism represented by all those who have already lived for hundreds or even thousands of years. The young, with their impulsively fresh approaches and ideas, would, in all likelihood, not even be given a chance. Their endeavors towards change would be squelched by an overpowering number of elders thoroughly set in their ways, firmly convinced that certain things can be accomplished only in the tried-and-true manner and that other things need not even be attempted because they simply "cannot be done." The delicate balance and tension between conservation and innovation that the cycles of birth and death now help to maintain in human society would be radically imperiled. The scales would be tipped toward deadening conformity and ever-increasing discouragement and alienation of the young. It is difficult to see how a society strained at every point with such unreconcilable polarization and conflict, and one rendered so intrinsically maladaptive to changes that would nevertheless be demanded by the passage of time, could long survive.

The mere fact that individuals die does not by itself guarantee a flourishing, adaptive society. But I am arguing that it makes its own kind of essential contribution to this end. In contrast to a purely individualistic outlook that deplores the passing of the particular person as something irremediably unjust and meaningless, the death of the individual can be seen as his gift to the future, his making way for others to transform his and his generation's contributions with their own fresh visions and enthusiasms. Seen in this light, the value of life does not depend fundamentally on its quantity but on its quality; not on what we each might hope to experience or receive for ourselves for all time, but on what we each can give to the world and to culture and society in the limited time allotted to us.

It can even be argued that we live fuller and more meaningful lives to the extent that we continue to remember that we are going to die. Our loves and friendships can be deepened and made more intense precisely through our being aware that they must someday be brought to an end. We can live with a zest to absorb and enjoy all that life has to offer, and with a focused effort to make our best contributions while there is still time to do so. Amos Wilder compares living with awareness of the boundary condition of death to the waves of the ocean crashing against a reef in the open sea. "It is against the cruel and adamant ledge" that these ocean currents "disclose their phosphorescence or break into iridescent foam and spray" (Wilder, in Scott 1967:25-26). Similarly, a peculiar iridescence and precious quality is imparted to our days by the knowledge that no life will last forever, that each must come to its limit at last on the "adamant ledge" of death. But this need not be a calamitous "shipwreck," as Schopenhauer claimed; it can be the fitting climax and fulfilment of a life well-lived.

But, of course, not all lives are well lived. Some are wasted. Tolstoy's title character in the short story, "The Death of Ivan Ilych" (1960:95-156) realized that his life had been squandered only when he learned that he was soon to die from what had at first appeared to be a minor injury. The central point of the story seems to be that this life did not have to be wasted, that it was wasted through a whole series of wrong choices and a kind of deliberate, prolonged insensitivity toward numerous opportunities to move in the direction of a meaningful life. Would living forever have changed the situation? There is no assurance that it would have, because the habits of insensitivity and neglect toward the deeper significance of life might well have been steadily reinforced as Ivan Ilych's life continued. The sheer length of life had nothing to do with its intrinsic meaning or lack of meaning in this case, as it has not in the case of so many others. It was only when he was forced to face his pending death that Ivan was brought to the realizations that his life could have been, and should have been, different—within the finite span of time that was his to live. He finally saw that life is made meaningful only when one learns to care for others and to give of oneself for others, rather than living solely for oneself. This lesson was embodied for him in the compassion of the servant-boy Gerasim, who tirelessly tended to Ivan's needs and talked frankly with him about his death (as no one of his family or friends had been willing to do) before he passed away.

Other lives, however, are neither wasted nor fulfilled, but interrupted by untimely death. Here there is no opportunity for a life well lived, at least not in the sense of having sufficient time to pursue one's own path and to find ways to make one's own distinctive contributions. Such lives are tragic in their lack of fulfilment and in the opportunities missed through no fault of the persons themselves. It would be callous in the extreme to speak of the deaths of such persons as "fitting." Here, as with some kinds of suffering, we must simply say that there is little or no redeeming significance, no kind of justification possible. There is even some sense, as we saw in Chapter Three, in which the end of any productive and creative life, no matter what its length, is untimely: the cases of Picasso and Gandhi come again to mind.[4] But this is not the same as a life snuffed out in youth, a life whose particular course and contribution have yet to be formed.

The fact that premature deaths do occur is a matter of profound regret, both for the individuals who die and for those who love them. But it is not sufficient reason to deny the meaning of life in general. Life can be meaningful; it contains this possibility. It is not a possibility that is actualized in every particular person's life, and it sometimes fails to be actualized because of deaths that occur before the fulness of time. This is a tragic truth, but it does not entail a sweeping indictment of life itself. Nevertheless, this truth should impart a somber urgency and sense of responsibility to all of us who are given a more normal length of life in which to find our way. This is one highly significant contribution that even those who die untimely deaths can make to those they leave behind.

It is sometimes claimed that because there is no way in which I can conceive of my own death, or that because my life must end in death and thus cease to have purposes and prospects lying before it, the whole of life is made absurd.[5] But there is a way in which I can conceive my own death. I find no great difficulty in contemplating or accepting the existence of the world prior to my birth. Is my death that much different? Will the world not continue to go on then as well? As Shakespeare writes, our lives do not merely *end* in oblivion but are "rounded with a sleep." We are for a period conscious participants in the world and can generally be grateful for being so, for being given the privilege to experience, even if only for a brief time, the world's inexhaustible fascination and mystery—its ineliminable, but at times still unaccountable, interlacings of joy and pain. The projects and relationships our lives afford need not continue forever for them to be worthwhile. They can be transitory but meaningful, assessed as such in terms of their particular character and donation, rather than being dismissed as absurd by a petulant demand for their infinite duration.

Finally, we need to recognize that there is a sense in which it is pointless to argue for or against the meaning of life in the presence of death. Most of us simply cannot help wanting to live, despite the uncertainties, perplexities, sorrows, and tragedies that confront us in life, including the ever-present fact and threat of unexpected deaths. The will to live is in the final analysis a wondrous gift. It cannot be created or destroyed by even the most sophisticated intellectual arguments. Something akin to this is true for all living creatures in whom, as Boethius remarks, "the desire to live comes not from the wishes of the will but from the principles of nature" (1962:68).

This ability in human beings to affirm life against all odds testifies, as Christians say, to the workings of a grace for which no one can claim credit and which no one is competent to explain.[6] Its absence in some is, by this same recognition, occasion not for moralizing blame but empathetic concern, for whatever encouragement and help the more fortunate might be able to provide, so as possibly to become conduits for the life-affirming power they unaccountably find within themselves. William James says of the paradoxes of Zeno that these are problems to be "solved livingly," ones that "ask no leave of logic." We resolve them by *doing* what Zeno claimed to be impossible, namely, by simply proceeding to move about in space (1967:II, 261, 255). In similar manner, the problem of the nay-sayings of nihilism is "solved livingly" in most of us: practically or existentially nullified by instinctive affirmations of our existence. There is something in us that justifies life in the face of suffering and death, something that insistently negates nihilism's negations, regardless of what even the most forceful nihilistic arguments may conclude.

2. LESSONS OF NIHILISM

I have devoted a considerable portion of this book to arguing against particular aspects of the nihilistic philosophy, and some further general observations and summary comments on the case against nihilism will be made in the next section. We should be careful not to dismiss this philosophy altogether, however, because it can teach us a great deal. Six important lessons of nihilism will be stressed in this section, thereby putting the arguments against it in more balanced perspective.

Perhaps the most important lesson of nihilism, or at any rate the one that has been given greatest emphasis in this book, is that it serves as a revealing *reductio ad absurdum* of certain basic assumptions that, despite their destructive and untenable character, have profoundly influenced modern thought. The nihilistic philosophies of this and the past century have pushed these root assumptions relentlessly toward their logical outcomes (although usually not with full awareness of doing so), thus enabling us to become more conscious of them and where they lead, and alerting us to the urgent need for their reappraisal.[7] I identified thirteen such assumptions in Parts Three and

Four, explained how they tend toward nihilism, and showed ways in which they can be criticized.

One especially striking fact about the assumptional framework of the modern Western mind is its strong tendency to think in terms of false dichotomies, binary options that commit us to one extreme position or the other with no recognition of alternatives that might lie in between. We have encountered in various places many examples of such dichotomies, but it might be clarifying to list here some important ones we have discussed: faith in God or existential despair, a human-centered world or a meaningless world, externality of value or no value, absolutism or relativism, complete certitude or total skepticism, personal immortality or futility, correspondence truth or no truth, the Christian worldview or the scientific worldview (scientism), objectivism or subjectivism, quantity or quality, reductionism or dualism, causal determinism or radical voluntarism, individualism or collec- tivism, fact or value, reason or sentiment, reason or will, boredom or suffering, unattainable ideals or no ideals.

This sad parade of bogus alternatives is enough to make one sometimes wish that Aristotle had never forumlated the Law of the Excluded Middle or labelled it a fundamental law of reason! Nihilistic arguments can often be seen to rest, at least in significant measure, on the supposition that if one of these extreme alternatives is rejected, the only recourse is to opt for the other one. This fact instructs us about certain persistent thought-patterns of modern Western civilization and warns of the necessity to break the spell of these uncritical and highly restrictive habits of thinking. For that we owe the philosophy of nihilism a debt of gratitude, even while having to admit the backhanded character of the compliment.

Frankel claims that "nihilism as it is experienced—the actual 'existential' sense of the meaninglessness and futility of life—is not the product of an intellectual theory, and it does not take a new theology or metaphysics to overcome it." Instead, it is the result of such things as "broken hopes, lost friends, impermanent commitments, and declining standards; and it may even be the symptom of a loss of intestinal fortitude" (1965:9). There is considerable truth in this assertion. It is the other side of what was said in the previous section about our instinctive overriding affirmations of life in the face of countervailing intellectual arguments. It also ties in with the distinction discussed in Chapter Six between theoretical and existential forms of certitude or doubt.

Nevertheless, Frankel's claim goes too far. It too cleanly divides experi- ence from thought, existential response from theoretical commitment, the contingencies of personal life from the pervasive commonalities of our intellectual heritage. The contention of this book is that not only much of the recent nihilistic philosophy, itself indisputably a movement of thought, but much of the nihilistic mood of contemporary life has been informed by certain long-held and too infrequently recognized (or challenged) intellectual assumptions.

These historically inherited, questionable assumptions have helped to mold our experience and to give added impetus to aspects of it that may already incline us in the direction of negation and despair. Trying to explain all the nihilistic susceptibilities of either the human spirit or modern culture on a purely intellectual basis would certainly be too facile. Nihilism has rootage in ineradicable facts of the human condition that sages of the world have brooded upon for thousands of years, and not merely in developments of Western intellectual history over the past few centuries. And we noted earlier that we cannot hope to gain comprehensive understanding of nihilism as a phenomenon of recent times without giving concerted attention to its social, in contrast to its more conceptual or theoretical, sources. When all of this has been acknowledged, however, we still have to give the intellectual sources their due, and we can be grateful to the philosophy of nihilism for casting them in bold relief and in that way exposing them to critical analysis. Alperowitz succinctly makes the point of this first lesson of nihilism when he states, in another connection, that "[h]onest pessimism has great value; it can be the first stage to a more fundamental reappraisal" (1986:64).

The second lesson is suggested by Tillich's statement that "the threat of nonbeing . . . opens up the mystery of being" (1953:67). By calling our attention to this threat in its many guises, the philosophy of nihilism can more deeply attune us to the stubborn ambiguities of our existence, to its myriad shadings of dark and light. In this way it can help us to understand and come to terms with life as it is, rather than overlaying it with naive delusions, oversimple interpretations, and unrealistic expectations. Heidegger rightly asserts that "the first and only fruitful step toward a transcending of nihilism" is to acknowledge its negations instead of blithely dismissing them, "to press inquiry into being explicitly to limits of nothingness," thus drawing "nothing ness into the question of being" (1961:170). To refuse to draw the threat of nothingness into our outlook on life is to refuse to recognize that tentativeness and insecurity are marks of our natural human state. It is to seek to live in a world of dreams, a world in which we pretend that our condition is something other than what it is.

However, nihilists are mistaken in thinking that the only alternative to such pretense is to conclude that life can have no value or meaning. To be fully aware of the precariousness of life need not doom us to the loneliness of despair. Such awareness can promote meaningful community, for example, by making us more responsive to the vulnerabilities and needs of others and more cognizant of our reciprocal dependencies on them, because no one individual can lay convincing claim to self-sufficiency or final wisdom when recognizing what Michael Novak terms the "emptiness, terror, and form-lessness at the center of human consciousness." Honest recognition of our insecure state can also create heightened sensitivity to life's challenges and joys, and to the "obscure coherences and often veiled beauty" (Novak 1971:115) that can be found to lie in, with, and under its elements of disruption and pain. This power of discernment not only opens up the mystery of being; it can also contribute powerfully to the courage to be. It affords a measure of understanding and strength that persons currently too sheltered against threats of finitude, fate, and death, or those marked by a shallow unquestioning optimism are in no position to attain.

I made observations similar to these in the previous section, although in the different context of arguing against the one-sidedness of the nihilistic outlook. There are, of course, depths of life that no mere philosophy can be expected to plumb. But the philosophy of nihilism goes farther than most in probing the menace of nothingness in its many forms, laying bare essential dimensions of experience that it would be foolish to try to minimize or ignore. This is the second important thing it has to teach us.

The third lesson of nihilism is its recognition of the perspectival nature of all knowledge, value, and meaning. It is not that nihilism makes a virtue out of this; rather, it tends to regard our inescapable situatedness in space and time and our consequent confinement to limited perspectives as a disaster. The reason for its conclusion is that nihilism tends to assume, with the thinkers of the Enlightenment, that the sole alternative to absolutes that utterly transcend the conditioning factors of tradition, or of social and personal outlook and experience, is a stultifying relativism that reveals epistemolog-ical, moral, and existential commitments to be glaringly arbitrary and therefore totally absurd.

But we have already seen that there is no reason to draw this extreme conclusion. To be finite and time-bound is no disaster but simply the character of our life in the world. The philosophy of nihilism can help us to acknowledge and accept our finite state by forcing us to give up the age-old dream of attaining a God's-eye view of things. But as against this nihilism, we must also cease assuming that the only alternative to this soaring dream is the fetid quicksands of relativism, with no place to stand and no place to build. To the contrary, the arguments of nihilism unwittingly show the way out of precipitous despair by making us realize that we need no longer aspire to the impossible. We can finally be free, for example, from such Cartesian requirements as those of infallible method; pure beginnings; indubitable foundations; a pristine, detached self unsullied by mundane social and historical biases; and a radically separate, in-itself world to which veridical beliefs must somehow exactly correspond.

We are not gods. We are born into particular families and communities and share in a particular heritage, as well as living at a specific time in the unfolding history of this heritage and the people it sustains. It is within such concrete contexts that we stand and on their basis that we learn to question, reflect, experiment, conclude, communicate, debate, choose, and build. What is so bad about that? We can take a positive view of such contingencies just because they cannot purport to provide us with anything absolute or unequivocal. By virtue of this fact, they give us room to breathe and latitude to find ways to make our own distinctive discoveries and contributions. Beyond our own culture and time there are others whose singular traits empower them to give creative stimulus to our imagination. Finally, in the life of each person there are experiences and realizations from which other persons have much to learn; these give further range for mutual testing and enlarging of finite points of view.

These historical, cultural, and personal perspectives are not completely sealed off from each other, as some would have us believe. Despite their sometimes substantial differences, these conditioned outlooks contain important points of intersection and commonality. Precisely because it is possible for us to "identify our presuppositions and thereby distinguish them from other presuppositions," as Rosen explains, "there must be a common environment of intelligibility within which this determination takes place" (1969:226). To become aware of our presuppositions and to be willing to expose them to the risk of dialogue with outlooks informed by different assumptions is not to settle for a bland, indifferent relativism but to engage in the type of objective, open-minded inquiry appropriate to finite beings. Through such process of inquiry, areas of overlap among finite perspectives can be explored and possibly expanded, and the perspectives themselves may be mutually challenged and transformed.

Still, we must recognize that different perspectives are not wholly commensurable either; so we should not expect to be able to reduce them to some single, more inclusive framework. This fact can serve as a constant reminder that there are ways of organizing and interpreting experience other than our own, and that the complexities of existence cannot be encompassed by any single perspective, including the one a particular society or individual finds most compelling. This can be a liberating and endlessly evocative realization, one that greatly enhances our sense of the glory and wonder of the world. Moreover, what the student in our first chapter, Camus, Cioran, and others have viewed as the bankruptcy of human thought—its failure to discover final, all-encompassing answers to ultimate questions and its tendency to crystallize into alternative points of view—can be seen in a quite different way: as proof of its irrepressible fecundity and power.

This same realization can also be a potent antidote to the fanatical close-mindedness that has been the bane of history and that afflicts or continually threatens present societies. To pretend that oneself or one's group or culture does not inhabit a finite perspective, that one's beliefs constitute absolute and final truth, is to preclude the possibility of learning from, or of having creative interactions with, any but a narrow coterie of "true believers." It is to settle for static reinforcement of existing attitude and conviction over the challenge of interacting with those who see things differently. This kind of ingrown mentality can have the psychological effect of tempting individuals and groups to become so haughty or protective about what they regard as the only possible point of view as to want to force everyone and everything into it. Such an attitude can give rise to radical evil, as the pages of history so plainly show, with their dolorous tales of ideological wars, inquisitions, crusades, pogroms, forced "conversions," colonial arrogance and repression, heavy-handed censorship and thought-control, and even genocide.

It is true that nihilism goes to the other extreme of asserting a debilitating relativism that, if followed through to its logical conclusion, would make all inquiry pointless and leave us with nothing to learn. It would also leave us with no binding moral standards. But at least nihilism's lucid exposure of the perspectival character of beliefs and commitments can have the good effect of warning against the fanatical delusion of thinking that individuals or groups can possess unconditioned and unquestionable truth. The positive moral significance of perspectivism is made explicit by Arthur M. Schlesinger, Jr.'s insistence that the beginning of an adequate state morality lies in "the assumption that other nations have legitimate traditions, interests, values and rights of their own" (*The Cycles of American History*, Houghton Mifflin; quoted Kennan 1986:4). This insightful comment about morality among nations also applies to morality among other kinds of institutions or social groups and among individuals. It points to a crucial aspect of nihilism's third lesson.[8]

The fourth lesson of nihilism is found in the insistence of thinkers such as Stirner, Nietzsche, and Sartre on the reality and critical importance of human freedom. Stirner pushes this theme to a ridiculous extreme, of course, as does Sartre. We have been highly critical of both for doing so. We have also seen that Nietzsche sometimes presents his concept of the will to power as an endorsement of tyranny of the strong over the weak, or as a wholly capricious willfulness, rather than as a recognition of a capacity of human beings to respond creatively to the concrete circumstances in which they find themselves—even though he also often assigns this commendable third meaning to that concept. In addition, Nietzsche is given to rhapsodies over the idea of eternal recurrence, an idea that if interpreted literally would make all human actions and the whole of human history instrumentalities of an irresistible cosmic will that moves everything in the universe, lap upon lap, over an immense circular course of time.[9]

Despite the exaggerations, inconsistencies, or questionable morality we may come across in the outlooks of Stirner, Nietzsche, or Sartre, something of great value is implicit in their common stress on the transformative power of human freedom. Each asserts that the social-historical settings into which we are born do not foredoom us to think and act only in certain set ways, because we have the freedom to alter those situations. Their position contains an urgently needed critique of the fatalistic attitude about such alarming current trends as an unchecked march of technology and its potentially disastrous effects, including devastation of the natural environment and global nuclear war—an attitude I earlier labelled "historical nihilism" (see Chapter Three, Section 3; Chapter Ten, note 40). This attitude, should it become widespread and deeply engrained among the peoples of the world, could easily take on the character of a self-fulfilling prophecy. People might simply resign themselves to destructive technological and other social-historical forces they have concluded to be wholly beyond their control or beyond any kind of human constraint.

While we do not have the limitless freedom that Stirner and Sartre often seem to think we have, the bold overstatements of their philosophies can help to jolt us into realizing that we have much more freedom than we usually credit ourselves with and hence, that our common future is significantly open, not fixed or foreordained. We should certainly not underestimate the accelerating momentum of sometimes mindless technological developments and applications, or the extent to which that momentum and other deleterious social trends are abetted by firmly entrenched and generally uncriticized beliefs and practices. We cannot exercise our freedom in a vacuum; to exercise it responsibly may require us to take arms against formidable odds. But we also should not underestimate our collective ability to reassess and redirect the intertial tendencies of our time.

What we have just said about social, political, and world-historical events also holds for the life of the individual. A surprising element of hope is found in the nihilistic philosophy, as long as we focus on its motif of freedom without going to the extreme of denying context or constraint to that freedom. "To refuse to acknowledge that I must discover meaning," writes Keen, "is to deny that my destiny is shaped by incarnation in a body and a historical situation," but "to refuse to accept responsibility for creating meaning is to deny my ability to transcend the givenness of my life" (1969:85). Stirner, Nietzsche, and Sartre, each in his own way, calls attention to this capacity for self-transcendence, meaning that we do not have to settle for what we already have become, give up because of past disappointments or failures, allow our self-estimation to be dictated by the responses of others, unthinkingly endorse the beliefs or values of our peers, or acquiesce in those psychological or sociological theories that would deny the considerable scope of personal freedom. This motif of nihilism also warns us against the dishonesty of simply blaming other people for our personal shortcomings or attributing them to circumstances we too facilely claim to be beyond our control.

We are not isolated individuals or totally free, and some are less free than others, but we are not totally determined either. We are appreciably free and to that extent responsible for how we deal with the given circumstances of our present lives, including those created by our own past choices. This is an optimistic message in which each of us can find challenge and inspiration, and it is an especially pertinent message for the world of today. Catalano states the fourth lesson of nihilism when he says of Sartre that "perhaps the most important aspect of [his] thought for our generation is its ability to unveil our self-deceptions and to oblige us to accept the free molding of our selfhood and our environment" (1980:xiii).[10] His statement has application to Stirner's and Nietzsche's views as well.

The fifth lesson of nihilism lies in its insistence on the uniqueness of the individual. Stirner, Mauthner, and Sartre are right to give crucial importance to the outlook and experience of the individual, as they are in their adamant refusal to swallow the concrete existence of free individuals into abstractions such as so-called principles of human nature or scientific laws of behavior. They are wrong, however (as we have seen), in their tendency to isolate individuals from one another; to assume them to be inevitably locked in conflict with one another; to abstract them from their historical, cultural, and natural surroundings; to conceive of them as the only important reality; and to make each individual a law or universe of meaning unto himself.

Bearing these qualifications in mind, profound truth is contained in the concentration on the particular person that is such a salient trait of nihilistic philosophy. We can gain fuller comprehension of this truth and its implications by approaching it from several different angles. First, we should remind ourselves in more explicit detail that each individual's life is irreducibly particular and unique. Nihilism is right in forcefully calling our attention to this fact. It errs, however, when it goes on to assume that uniqueness of personal outlook and experience precludes community with other human beings or having shared standards of meaning, truth, or value.

Bernard Loomer corrects this misconception when he asserts that the uniqueness of the individual human being consists not in its radical separateness or self-centeredness, but in its "self-creative subjective response to what it has relationally received from others." Thus, contrary to Stirner and Mauthner, no inconsistency exists in seeing the unique individual as a "communal individual . . . largely composed of its relations with the world" (Loomer, in Sibley and Gunter 1978:519). Despite having the same historical and cultural backgrounds, no two individuals have, or are capable of having, precisely the same perspective on things. People are intimately related to one another from birth by their joint inheritance of a common culture and common world, and each is shaped in profoundly similar ways by this inheritance. But people also differ from one another by ineliminable peculiarities of makeup, background, and experience, and thus in their specific modes of response to their culture and world. Each person is through and through social, but the perspective of each on the complex network of social relations is nevertheless unique. The distinctive character of their responses to the common environment is further enhanced to the extent that individuals become acutely conscious of their personal freedom, a theme of the nihilistic philosophy stressed above.

The legitimate emphasis of this philosophy on the distinctive character of personal experience also alerts us to a second truth, one that ought to be obvious, but one that is routinely ignored. This is the fact that no one else can live my life for me. I must live it at firsthand and discover its meaning, if any, for myself. There is no meaning of life in general, nor can the meaning of life be gathered up into a compendium of abstract instructions, rules, or norms. As Robert Ornstein expresses it, "There is no text in which the meaning of life is to be found" (1977:162). We can hope to discover it only through our own personal reflections and experiences, although this is not to deny that we may derive much insight from the experience and counsel of others.[11]

Existential nihilism rejects the possibility of a meaningful life, but this judgment itself is a glaringly abstract overgeneralization that fails to jibe with nihilism's insistence on the concreteness of individual existence. Countless individuals find their lives to be meaningful, and they do so without succumbing to self-delusion or bad faith. But the finding must be each person's own; it cannot be conferred upon, dictated to, or demanded of individuals from the outside. While the search for life's meaning will best be carried out in community and through conversation with others, it will be brought to satisfactory conclusion only at the deepest levels of each person's own being, in a manner suited to the irreducible particularities of each person's life. One's convictions about the meaning of life lie at the core of one's personal perspective on the world. There will, no doubt, be numerous intersections of this personal perspective with the standpoints of others, but no two such standpoints are ever exactly the same. It would be foolish to expect that they ever could be, or should be.[12]

Nihilism's stress on the uniqueness of persons, when properly qualified and when combined with its insistence on the reality and central importance of freedom, gives sanction, in the third place, to what Loomer terms "the virtues of an open society with its diversity, contrasts, and mobility" (Sibley and Gunter 1978:529). A society which has respect for the uniqueness and freedom of individuals will, at least in that important regard, be a just society, in contrast to one that tries to impose a deadening sameness of perspective on everyone, heeding the counsel of only a powerful few. It will also be a creative society, made so by its recognition and encouragement of individual uniqueness as a source of novel ideas and innovative energy of immense potential value for all.[13]

From its creativeness, such a society will gain adaptability to changing times and circumstances and have a better chance of moving with confidence into the future. By contrast, a conformist society will barely be able to hold its own in a constantly changing and increasingly complex world, because it is cast in the mold of a single static point of view. Furthermore, a society in the habit of seriously taking into account the diverse perspectives of its citizens, and of working continually to develop grounds of mutual understanding and enrichment among them, is also more likely to interact constructively with the different viewpoints of other societies. Thus, far from making other-directed morality or effective communication impossible, as Stirner and Mauthner believed, a stress on the uniqueness of individuals can give scope and flexibility to a society's moral consciousness and impart an ever-expanding subtlety and power to its modes of thought and means of expression. The two philosophers justifiably attend to the uniqueness of individuals, but the conclusions they draw from this important recognition are too narrowly conceived.

A last instructive aspect of nihilism's stress on the uniqueness of the individual is contained in Sartre's claim that there is no such thing as a fixed human nature,[14] and in his contention that we all, through our personal acts of freedom, contribute to a historically emerging conception of what it means to be a human being. Sartre erroneously deduces from this idea that no objective norms of human freedom can exist, and that moral values simply amount to whatever an individual happens to choose (see Chapter Three, Section 1 and Chapter Four, Section 2). These are mistaken inferences because they rest on a distorted notion of human individuals as isolated centers of unrestricted freedom rather than as relational or communal beings, intimately tied to, constrained by, and even to a large extent defined by, their cultural settings. I have already developed this line of criticism of Sartre, and of the subjectivistic and individualistic orientation of modern thought in general. But now I want to concentrate on an element of truth in Sartre's view.

He is surely correct in saying that, in choosing for ourselves, we choose for all humankind (although it is not clear why, on the basis of his own atomistic and purely voluntaristic analysis, any individual *need* be concerned for the implications of his actions for all humankind, should he freely *choose* not to be). Sartre is also justified in holding that there is no such thing as a timeless human nature that determines, once and for all, what we are or have the capacity or responsibility to become. We can even go so far as to say that if anything is "essential" about us as human beings, it is the indeterminate character of our potentiality, as is vividly shown by our species' richly variegated lines of historical development and cultural achievement, to say nothing of the manifold forms of personal existence. Cobb speaks to the truth highlighted by Sartre when he notes that "almost any act regarded as right in one culture may be regarded as wrong in another. It is idle to appeal to human nature to settle disputes about matters of this kind" (1965:62). Cobb elsewhere observes: "There is little common human nature other than the uniquely human capacity to be shaped in history into a wide variety of structures of existence." He adds, "Here the pluralistic spirit is at work at the deepest level" (1975:136).

This pluralistic spirit is also manifested in the fact that individuals continue to shape, as well as to be shaped by, their social-historical environments. In this way they make their own distinctive contributions to an evolving process of defining humankind (or more accurately, of giving instantiations to various possible definitions of humankind), not only because they themselves are unique and genuinely free, but also because the concrete situations in which they must act always have inescapably unique traits. No two situations are ever precisely the same, even within the same cultural context, any more than any two acting individuals are the same. This does not mean that established patterns of experience or general norms for decision have no relevance to present choices; it simply means that these patterns and norms are likely to undergo constant revision as they are applied by particular persons in particular circumstances.

Thus, we learn an important lesson about ourselves from nihilism's stress on the free actions of specific persons in specific contexts and from its consequent vision of human nature as open-ended potentiality rather than as unchanging essence. This lesson remains important even though we have to balance it by continuing to acknowledge the structure and guidance given to particular decisions by the general characteristics of shared cultural environments. Because the general and the particular, the stable and the changing, work always in concert, we have no warrant for setting them in opposition to each other. This balanced picture has plenty of room for recognizing the great variety of actual and potential modes of self-formation.

We can in this way do justice to the insistence of Sartre and others that human nature is not something that can be defined in advance or in the abstract, i.e., apart from the emerging novelties of historical experience— novelties that each unique person has a hand in helping to bring into being. What the human species may at any given time appear to be, both descriptively and normatively, is subject to redefinition through what humans individually and collectively have the capacity to become. And this is not a capacity whose details admit of precise prediction; they will be made known only by the passage of time.

Once again, in yet another manner, we are reminded of a central theme of this book, a theme concisely formulated by Cobb when he writes that the "decisive characteristic of human nature is historicality, man's potentiality for being formed by history" (1965:63). I do not mean to imply with my emphasis on the historicality of human life anything like a doctrine of inevitable progress. Events of the present century show that humans have an incalculable capacity for destructiveness and evil, as well as for creativeness and good. Our potentialities do not point only in one direction but are rife with ambiguity. What I do mean to stress is the conviction that the outlooks and activities of concrete persons existing in time do not admit of reduction to some static universal or single, all-encompassing essence. This is a final, highly significant aspect of what I term the fifth lesson of nihilism: its focus on the uniqueness of the individual.

Just as there is no fixed human nature but a complex, open-ended potentiality, some of whose aspects are continually being actualized in the course of history, so there is no such thing in human experience as a static, ready-made, in-itself world. The world of our experience is not a world set against us or foreign to us. It is a world in relation to us and one always in the making. This is the sixth lesson of nihilism.

It is true that thinkers such as Sartre and Camus are deeply distressed by their conclusion that the in-itself world is not accessible to human consciousness or experience. They bemoan our inability to be at one with that world, seeing it as something ineluctably remote and strange, a standing mockery of our puny attempts to comprehend it or to enter into meaningful relationship with it. In their view, we drift beyond the world in jerry-built capsules of our own feeble invention, distanced from it by arbitrary constructs of human imagination. Our situation is thus one of unrelievable frustration and tragicomical absurdity. Their position takes for granted (despite the protestations of Sartre to the contrary) a radical separation of subject and object. The human subject is envisioned as futilely groping within its egocentric shell for an objective reality that is assumed to have nothing of the human in it and therefore to be forever beyond our grasp. Alternatively, when the objective world is thought to be within the reach at least of scientific reason, as with Russell, its true character is believed to be merely what physics describes: a system of barren facts and indifferent laws having no connection with distinctively human sensibilities, cares, or needs.

However, each of these portrayals rests on the highly dubious assumption that there is, or could be, such a thing as an in-itself, nonperspectival world, a world out of relation. There is nothing tragic or depressing about the inaccessibility of such a world, because it is inaccessible by definition. Even

Russell's world of physical science is far from being an in-itself reality. Instead, it rests heavily upon particular kinds of human questions, projects, valuations, and beliefs, as we have already seen. The researches of Kuhn (1971) and others have also shown that the world of scientific description is anything but static or ready-made. It has varied over time with changes in scientific theories, and these changes have on a few occasions been markedly discontinuous in character. Because they have been so in the past, it is likely that they will be so in the future, and probably in ways that we cannot now predict. Science, like everything else human, is characterized by an inevitable historicality. As Sartre remarks, in a pungent aphorism that aptly demonstrates this inevitability of temporal situatedness, even "the historian is himself *historical* . . . he historicizes himself by illuminating 'history' in the light of his projects and of those of his society" (1966:613).

All this being the case, it follows that there is no world radically sundered from human experience that must in consequence forever elude us; no "out there," unlived nature solely describable by steadily mounting, brick-upon-brick results of purely objective scientific research; and no such thing as a wholly independent, irrevocable past. *Everything real exists in relation.* This is a stunningly significant realization, one that the philosophy of nihilism brings home to us with compelling force.

Gregory's claim that "the most striking contribution made by existentialism is the proposition that we can and do make our own ontological world" (Brock and Harward 1984:26) applies to the nihilistic philosophy as well. In endorsing this view, I do not mean to suggest that the world is nothing but a human construct or invention. That would be to place exaggerated emphasis on one side of the relation.[15] What I mean to say is that drawing a neat line of demarcation between what we contribute to the relationship and what the world provides is impossible. Human culture and the natural order are aspects of a single fabric of experience. While it is no doubt an overstatement to speak of the ontological world as simply a human artifact, there is important truth in such an assertion that the philosophy of nihilism helps us to understand.

This realization will seem dismal as long as we cling to the notion of reality as something that must lie at one extreme of an assumed polarity of subject and object, something that must possess unalterable, entirely self-contained traits that automatically sanction certain statements or beliefs as forever true, and others as forever false. But we ought to understand instead that this rigid polarity itself is an abstract, distorted way of regarding a world that in its very nature can exist only perspectively or in relation. William James gives us an admirable rendering of the sixth lesson of nihilism (which happens also to be a statement of his own pragmatic theory of truth) when he says, "Knowledge of sensible realities . . . comes to life inside the tissue of experience. It is *made*; and made by relations that unroll themselves in time" (1967:I, 57). This theme is nihilistic only to the extent that we continue to hold to the correspondence theory of truth, to nurse the idle daydream of attaining a God's-eye view of reality, or to pine for a way of somehow extricating ourselves from the grasp of time. Otherwise, it is a valuable lesson about the conditioned character of our life in the world, and about the dependence of conceptions of that world on the subtle interweavings of experience, culture, and history.

3. THE CASE AGAINST NIHILISM

Despite these six important lessons of the nihilistic philosophy, it does not stand up as a whole under critical scrutiny and must therefore be rejected. It must be rejected for three primary reasons. I conclude this study with a review of these reasons, presenting them to the jury of my readers as a summation of the case against nihilism developed in this book.

The first reason for rejecting the nihilistic outlook is that it is grounded on certain basic assumptions that we have shown to be indefensible or at least highly questionable. When these assumptions are brought into the light of day and examined critically, the philosophy of nihilism loses most of its power to persuade. Nihilistic thinkers can therefore be faulted for not probing deeply enough and even for being guilty of a kind of intellectual laziness. Cochran's indictment of ancient skepticism holds for nihilism as well; it tends to be "an anaesthetic for those . . . wearied of thought" (1944:167).

This aspect of the nihilistic philosophy recalls an experience I had a year or so ago with one of nature's most exquisit creatures: the Western Tanager. One of these multicolored birds had flown into our garage in late evening and, unnoticed, had become trapped there when I pressed the button to bring the garage door down before retiring for the night. The next morning when I went to put our dog into his run behind the garage, I noticed the Tanager perched on my workbench, at the end of the garage opposite its main door. When I pushed the button to raise the door, the bird flew around the ceiling of the garage in panic. He then darted above the door, which was folded in against the ceiling, and not finding sufficient room to get out there, returned in a frenzy of feathers to the other end of the garage. He repeated this pattern again and again, never seeming to notice the gaping space beneath the door from which he could have escaped with ease. In similar fashion, nihilistic philosophers thrash around within the restrictive assumptions structuring their dismal view of the world, not seeming to realize that a way out might be found by questioning those assumptions or trying to conceive and assess alternatives to them.

A second reason for rejecting nihilism is that it presents a one-sided picture of human life, lavishing attention on its negative aspects but failing to take fairly into account its counterbalancing positive traits and possibilities. The nihilistic philosophy is a sustained exercise in special pleading for what turns out to be a distorted, fragmentary view of existence. Hick's rumination about "some of the existentialist writers" is especially appropriate to the nihilists:

> [T]hese writers have usually been concerned to bring out the more strained and hectic aspects of human experience, presenting it often as a vivid nightmare of metaphysical anxieties and perils. They are undoubtedly painting from real life, particularly in this anguished age, but I venture to think they are depicting it in a partial and one-sided manner (Hick, in Yandell 1973:534-535).

This attribute of nihilism helps to explain why we have so much to learn from it: a well-executed caricature often enables us to notice things that we might otherwise overlook or not sufficiently emphasize. But we should not confuse the caricature with the reality, and this is what nihilists do. There is as little faithfulness to the complexities and ambiguities of experience in their squinting cynicism, on the one side, as there is in the wide-eyed assurances of utopian dreamers, on the other.

The third reason for rejecting nihilism is stated in this chapter's epigraph, taken from Rosen's book on nihilism. This philosophy is surprisingly and ironically akin to utopianism in its anguished yearning for a perfection that, if realized, would deprive us of our humanity. To resolve all of the problems about which nihilists endlessly complain—fallible knowledge, susceptibility to pain, situatedness in time, etc.—would require the complete annulment of the conditions of our life in the world. This is not only an unreasonable demand, it also overlooks the fact that such a phantom state of "perfection" would hardly be ideal.

I have already spoken to this point in my critical discussion of the idea of heaven; I also referred to it earlier in this chapter when discussing the stable factors in the universe that make life and freedom possible, but that can also cause suffering. David Hall gets at this third criticism of nihilism when he notes the irony of wishing for a world of such complete uniformity as to be wholly intelligible. There would be an absence of significant questions in this kind of a world, just as much so as there would be in one that was wholly contingent and thus incapable of being brought under any kind of systematic interpretation. A completely uniform world would be a world without challenge or surprise. It would lack the alluring mystery that gives interest and delight to our inquiries. Physicists may sometimes complain of the complexity of the world that "greatly complicates the physicist's task" (see the quotation from D. W. Sciama, in Hall 1982:124). But Hall sees such a complaint as deliciously ironic, because did the world not possess such elusive complexity, there would be no task for physics and, hence, no such thing as physicists!

He rightly asks,

> Would the scientist truly like to rid himself and his enterprise of all significant problems? Would the astrophysicist like to solve, once and for all, the problem of the origin of the universe? Does the philosopher really desire the solution to the problem of the One and the Many? The end-state entailed by the solution of all problems is that wherein no intelligence could exist. The activity of knowing begins and ends in ignorance (1982:126).

Hall's conclusion is that "[w]e do not really want to be omniscient. Intellectual excitement results from the presumption that the answer to one question raises, in geometric progression, other equally profound questions *ad infinitum*" (1982:126).

Philosophers such as Sartre and Camus sometimes bewail our inability to attain certain and comprehensive knowledge of the world, implying an assumption of this kind of "perfection" as an ideal. But would we not be more likely to despair if we were able to attain this ideal? The flat tedium of knowing everything would make life intolerable, given life as we now experience it or are able to conceive it. There would be no intellectual adventure and little excitement of existence in the kind of simply ordered world that permitted us easily to know its every last detail—which would have to include knowing in advance all its future outcomes and thus every impending event of our own personal futures. Aristotle is right in claiming that human beings characteristically desire to know, but we should not overlook the fundamental sense in which we also take great delight in *not* knowing. As Locke shrewdly says of his own field of philosophy, "Its searches after truth are a sort of hawking and hunting, wherein the very pursuit makes a great part of the pleasure" (1959:I,7).

The price of great complexity and mystery in the experienced universe is frequent frustration and perplexity, and the impossibility of arriving at, or ever being able to know that we have arrived at, absolute solutions. But the price of living in a world that we could easily understand would be much higher. For, once that understanding was achieved, as Hall says, "no intelligence could exist." Thus, while no absolutes or final certainties are available to us, there is also no crying need that there be. While our lives are no doubt imperfect in many ways, there is no requirement that they be perfect in order to be worthwhile. In fact, a life perfect in some respects would have to be imperfect in others, so that no form of life could be perfect overall. Awareness of this necessary trade-off or tension is strikingly absent from the nihilistic philosophy. This is one of its basic flaws, a flaw that reveals a certain glaring superficiality in its outlook. It is an outlook informed by uncritical beliefs about what would constitute an ideal human situation.

These, then, are the three principal objections to nihilism with which I summarize my general case against it. I have not pretended here to be able to tell anyone precisely what the meaning of life is. Nor shall I be so presumptuous as to try to do so now, for the question admits of no single answer but of many different answers. In light of this book's analyses, we can conclude that a meaningful life is possible, even though it is not guaranteed.[16] We can assert with justification that moral obligation can be binding and real, even though its norms are not timelessly absolute. We can state with assurance that claims to knowledge can be meaningfully communicated, defended, and criticized, in spite of the lack of certain foundations and the unattainability of final consensus on all disputed questions, including some of the most basic ones. And we can confidently affirm that the world as it is, "rough edges" and all, is a suitable home for the human spirit.

Notes

Chapter 1

1. I first heard this expression from John Bash.

2. I do not share the student's conception of the nature of religious faith, but it is one that seems to be widespread. In order to make it clear when I am using the word in this particular sense, I have placed it in quotation marks. This view of the nature and role of faith is close to that of the Church Father Tertullian (c.150-c.230 A.D.), so it has a long history. Tertullian argued that the entertainment of philosophical questions leads inevitably to heresy, that only acceptance of the authority of Christian teaching can give respite from an endless round of futile searching and questioning, and that "to know nothing in opposition to the rule of faith, is to know all things" (*Prescription Against Heretics*, in Saunders 1966:343-351, pp. 347, 350). Tertullian's statement in *De Carne Christi* concerning Christ's resurrection, "it is certain because it is impossible," just makes more explicit the nihilistic tenor of this particular concept of faith (quoted Durant 1944:613).

Chapter 2

1. For more detail on the events sketched in the preceding two paragraphs see Hingley 1969, especially Chs. 4, 6, and 7.

2. The positive beliefs and hopes of the revolutionaries are discussed in Moser 1964, Ch. 2; see also Brower 1975, Ch. 5.

3. I am indebted to Dan Lyons for this example.

4. D. H. Monro notes that Russell took at least three distinct views of the nature of ethical judgments in his lifetime. See Monro 1960, in Pears 1972: 328-329.

5. Monro argues, and I think with justification, that Russell has here imported into his subjectivist theory of ethics a principle of objectivity or universality that is inconsistent with the theory itself, enabling him elsewhere to condemn moral outlooks which exhibit narrowness of sympathy as being inimical to mental growth and to claim that "democratic" ethical systems are intrinsically better than undemocratic ones for this very reason. This sounds like an argument for one kind of ethics over others, despite the fact that Russell's subjectivist theory rejects the possibility of such arguments. See Monro in Pears 1972:353-355 and Russell 1938:228-229, 260, 282.

6. London's character Wolf Larson also conceives of life in this way, as we saw. Nietzsche's influence on London is implicitly acknowledged by the mention of his name in the first paragraph of *The Sea Wolf*.

7. Some differences between Stirner's and Nietzsche's views on morality are

discussed by Patterson 1971:156-160. Perhaps the most important difference is that Nietzsche's ideal of the Superman would have been rejected by Stirner as just one more empty essence or universal external to the individual ego and thus not different in principle from Feuerbach's ideal of humanity or the traditional subservience to God. All such ideals are, for Stirner, "religious" and at complete odds with his uncompromising nominalism and egoism.

8. For a discussion of the central place accorded to the will by Schelling and Schopenhauer, and of the relations of their philosophies to that of Nietzsche, see Essay II of den Ouden 1982. In this essay, den Ouden traces the historical development from Immanuel Kant's emphasis on the moral will "as the apex of human knowing and activity" (88), through the speculations of Johann Fichte, Schelling, and Schopenhauer, to its culmination in Nietzsche's thought. I say more about this development in Chapter Ten.

9. I argue later that it is only the last of these claims that is incurably nihilistic.

10. *The Will to Power* is a posthumously published selection from Nietzsche's notebooks between 1883 and 1888. Walter Kaufmann observes that the "notes were not intended for publication in this form, and the arrangement and the numbering are not Nietzsche's" (1968:xv-xvi).

11. For my exposition of Mauthner's thought, I am indebted to Weiler 1958 and 1967, Janik and Toulmin 1973:120-133, and Kretzmann 1967:398-399.

12. Here Russell sets himself in opposition to Wolf Larson's view of human life.

13. Looking at a television commercial without sound is another example; here what is usually ludicrous in the extreme is made doubly so—something like multiplying infinity by two.

Chapter 4

1. Hazel Barnes does not quite get at Desan's point in her response to his statement and development of this problem. She notes that, contrary to what Desan terms Sartre's "repudiation of the ego," there *is* an ego in the latter's philosophy in *Being and Nothingness*, namely, one that has been created by past acts of the nihilating for-itself. She goes on to say that

Sartre never denies the existence of an active, organizing . . . individual consciousness any more than does William James, who likewise rejected consciousness as an entity. He merely insists that it is essentially a Nothingness which is individualized by its objects but never wholly determined by past objects to an extent which would prescribe what it will do with present or future ones (Introduction to Sartre 1966, p. xlv).

First, the ego of the past cannot, on Sartre's account, be active in the present; only the for-itself can. Desan's main concern in the indicated part of his book is with the absence in Sartre's philosophy of an ego capable of acting in the present. And he is right when he suggests that Sartre gives no clear or satisfying explanation of how a sheer nothingness can act or organize anything. Second, Sartre does not talk simply of the for-itself's not being "wholly determined" by past objects, but of its being totally or absolutely free, and thus of its not being determined by the past even in the slightest degree. This claim goes far beyond William James's view of the self in its relation to the past. The issue is not so much whether the self is to be viewed in substantialist terms; it is whether its freedom is to be viewed in relative or absolute terms. James believed only in a relative (though certainly significant) degree of freedom and insisted on the importance of maintaining a balanced view of the interrelation of causality and freedom, continuity and innovation. Finally, Barnes's response to Desan does not speak to the question of why the ego of the past should have the coherence and connectedness she assumes it to have, if each new stage of its emergence is one of radical freedom. Why, in other words, should there be such a thing as a connected ego at all, even in the past? The continuity of the ego through time remains, as already noted, an inexplicable mystery, one that is not resolved by Sartre's appeal to the idea of an "original project," because the power or influence of that project is something he also fails to explain in a manner consistent with his concept of absolute freedom.

2. What has been said in this section about arguments for nihilism relating to the will, where freedom is either denied altogether or becomes virtually limitless, has some affinities with Paul Tillich's association of the problem of meaninglessness with the threat of losing the unity of freedom and "destiny." See my discussion of this threat, and the accompanying references to Tillich's writings, in *Interpretive Theories of Religion*, 167-178.

Chapter 5

1. Adherents of Eastern religions would not be happy, of course, with the despiritualizing of nature that has tended to accompany the development of science and technology in the West. The point here is restricted to science's radical expansion of nature's spatial and temporal dimensions and to its implicit removal of human beings from their former place of centrality and dominance in the natural order.

2. It could be debated whether a *proper* understanding of Christianity would show it to be as relentlessly anthropomorphic as I am portraying it here. But I do not mean to enter into that debate. I am not arguing that Christianity is necessarily anthropomorphic. Like any rich tradition with a long history, it can be, and has been, interpreted in many ways. A case in point is Lynn White, Jr.'s reference to St. Francis, mentioned in the second paragraph below. Also apropos is Morris Cohen's observation that medieval thought set against "the silly and arrogant pretensions of humanity," "the great glory of God" (1964:453). This insistence on the transcendent majesty of God did go some way toward counterbalancing the anthropomorphism implicit in other aspects of medieval thought and culture. My point is simply that Christianity has tended, and on a rather wide scale, to be construed anthropomorphically, and that this strong tendency has resulted in the deep-rooted assumption now being discussed.

3. We should not push White's analogy of democracy too far. It is meant to remind us of the idea of nature as an ecosystem. It does not mean that we must assign equal moral importance to, say, a spider and a human being, or even that each species of living beings must be accorded the same moral value as the human species. Nor can the analogy in itself tell us how we ought to act in particular

circumstances of conflict between human good and the good of nonhuman individuals or species. That is another issue. What it does mean is that we should no longer assume out of hand that our good, as individuals or as a species, is all that matters, or that it matters most in all circumstances.

4. By "intrinsic" in this context I mean only values in nature which have no need of external foundation, origination, or justification to be recognized or regarded as values. I do not mean values that exist as such independently of all perspectives or apprehensions. The significance of this distinction will become apparent in Chapter Six, Section 1.

5. Alasdair MacIntyre notes the fundamental role played in Sartre's thinking by his assumption that "the lack of a sufficient reason for oneself *and* for things being as they are means an imperfection" and entails that "[w]e are in a senseless world, of which we ceaselessly and inevitably try to make sense." Sartre accepts unquestioningly, therefore, the view reflected in Thomas Aquinas's "Third Way" that the universe as a whole is radically contingent. He reasons from this view, not to the existence of God, as Aquinas does, but rather to the absurdity of all existence. The lack of a sufficient reason for things means that they "just *are* in all their nauseating fullness" (MacIntyre, in Warnock 1971:49). It is remarkable how thoroughly this second religiously based assumption, in the guise of the principle of sufficient reason, enters into Sartre's general outlook, and how crucial it is to his absurdist conclusions. This is but one more illustration of the extent to which our "secular" culture continues to be informed by ways of thinking rooted in the Christian tradition.

6. It is important to distinguish the view that things are valuable only to the extent that God confers value upon them or continues to value them, from the view that the presence of intrinsic, immanently recognizable values in the world can be best explained in terms of a Creator God. I am criticizing the first view only and do not bring the second under consideration here. The distinction between these two views was brought to my attention by Judy Schindler.

7. One indication of how deeply ingrained is our tendency in the West, even today, uncritically to identify religion with belief in God is that so astute a contemporary philosopher of religion as John Hick can insist on treating the issue of God's existence and the teachings of the great religions as though the two were the same. In his debate with Michael Gouldner, Hick leaves us with the distinct impression that lack of faith in God is lack of religious faith in general, because the religions are all "God-centered." Because for him the absence of faith in God is apparently the absence of religion altogether, atheism is said to suffer from a "basic pessimism" and to lack a "basis of hope" (see Gouldner and Hick 1983:32, 110-111). This claim is not very different from the assertions of Dostoevsky and Tolstoy that the only alternative to theism is nihilism. Hick is more judicious in his article "The New Map of the Universe of Faiths," in Cahn and Schatzi 1982:278-290, where he takes account of the obvious fact that not all religions are theistic. He still persists, however, in speaking of them all as manifesting "divine self-revelation," and as expressing various ways of experiencing "the divine" or encountering "the divine reality" (282, 284, 286).

8. The focus of this chapter has been on Christian theism, but much of what has been said could also have been said of Judaism. I have concentrated on Christianity

because it has been, and continues to be, the dominant religious tradition of the best. This does not mean that I think Judaism is unimportant or that its role in Western history is unimportant.

Chapter 6

1. Despite their assumed independence of human knowing, these meanings can continue to be anthropomorphically conceived, to the extent that they are regarded as having been created primarily for the use and apprehension of human beings. Thus, no contradiction exists between the point being made here and the assumption, discussed in the previous chapter, that nature is subservient to human beings.

2. On Newton's vacillations between a rationalistic epistemological realism, with its penchant for confident metaphysical assertion, and a restrained positivistic experimentalism, see Burtt 1954:239-240, and Ch. 7 *passim*.

3. Gottfried Leibniz assumed, I think wrongly, the intelligibility of what Philip Wiener terms "an ensemble of all points of view which only God can perceive intuitively" and which constitutes "the objective relational order of the real universe" (Leibniz 1951:x1). This assumption is the very one I now criticize, and its pervasive influence can be seen in the fact that Leibniz's concept of God's totalistic vision of the world contradicts the whole weight and tendency of the rest of his system of monads, where each monad represents a distinctive perspective on the universe. God is also portrayed as a monad by Leibniz, but because his knowledge is said to be all-comprehending and nonperspectival, he is an exception to the rest of the system.

4. These critical reflections on the notions of perspectiveless meaning and perspectiveless knowing have been stimulated by Blocker's penetrating discussions in *The Meaning of Meaninglessness*. His approach has been deeply influenced, in turn, by the writings of Martin Heidegger, especially *Being and Time*. My criticisms also owe a great deal to Ross's sustained argument, in his book *Perspective in Whitehead's Metaphysics*, for a thoroughgoing perspectival modification of the metaphysical views of Alfred North Whitehead. Both Blocker and Ross marshal much more fully than I have had space to do here the relevant arguments for a perspectivist view of meaning and reality.

5. Tillich gives a negative answer to the question too, as the following passage shows:

   Knowledge of reality has never the certitude of complete evidence. The process of knowing is infinite. It never comes to an end except in a state of knowledge of the whole. But such knowledge transcends infinitely every finite mind and can be ascribed only to God. Every knowledge of reality by the human mind has the character of higher or lower probability (1957:34).

   It is interesting to note that Tillich does attribute knowledge of the whole to God, a claim discussed and criticized in Section 1 of this chapter. The implication he draws from the claim, however, is similar to that drawn by Newton and Kant. So he does not hold up the God's-eye view of the world as an ideal of knowledge for human beings. Still—and this is perhaps the most interesting point for our purposes—he assumes that there is Someone in the universe with such an all-encompassing, inerrant view of the whole (or at least that this symbolism has great value and meaning for us). This idea leads easily into the supposition that there is such a thing as meaning-itself or meaning out of relation, i.e., the universe as seen comprehensively and nonperspectively by God. That supposition, in turn, as already seen, gives implicit but significant support to the correspondence theory of truth.

6. Tillich also gives a central role to existential doubt in his analysis of the dynamics of faith. This doubt is awareness of the risk in the act of faith, the risk that "what was considered as a matter of ultimate concern" might prove to be only "a matter of preliminary and transitory concern" and fail to make good on its promise of giving conclusive meaning and fulfilment to one's life. In that case, the hope of salvation will have been frustrated, and the meaning of one's life will have broken down. A closely related source of existential doubt is also discussed by Tillich: doubt about the adequacy of the symbolic expressions of a faith to convey the full meaning of that faith, and, in fact, awareness that they inevitably distort it or fail to do justice to it (1957:44-54, 95-98). This element of existential risk and uncertainty in the faith of finite beings like ourselves cannot be removed, says Tillich; it can only be courageously accepted. Therefore, as I have stated elsewhere, for him the certitude of faith is not absolute; it "is laced with dark strands of doubt and dread" (Tillich 1957:16-17; Crosby 1981:210). Muggeridge also comments on the element of existential doubt implicit in the act of faith when he says, "To believe greatly, it's necessary to doubt greatly." He explains his statement in this way: "The nearer you get to comprehending the true nature of our existence, the more possibility there is of being skeptical about our capacity to express that understanding" (1980:27).

7. Unlike Tillich, who locates existential certitude exclusively within the province of religion, I argue that what he calls "faith" can have secular or religious forms of expression. My way of drawing the distinction is to ask whether the faith's focus of concern is accorded the six "cosmic" functions I attribute to objects of religious interest. If not, but the six "personal" functions do apply, then I would argue that the interest has the character of a secular faith. Not only do I deny, as against Tillich, that all forms of faith are religious, but I also want to allow for the possibility of persons who lack faith, whether religious or secular. This is one way to understand what it means to be an existential nihilist. Tillich, by contrast, insists that every person has some kind of faith (see my 1981:201-202, 212-215, 233-275, 294-295).

8. High cites Wittgenstein 1969:103, 105, 205 in connection with this statement. The phrase a "comfortable certainty" is Wittgenstein's; see Wittgenstein 1969:357-358, and High 1981:259).

9. As one writer states, the authority of the scriptures of a living religion not only imposes limits but also encourages—even mandates—creative ingenuity. It not only "authorizes," in the sense of setting norms; it also "authors," in the sense of creating the climate for the emergence of innovative trends of theological thinking and new modes of self-understanding. Thus, while "theology is in part authorized by the authoritative [scriptural] given, the fact is that a number of

theologies are permissible within a particular given" (Brown 1985:26-29). Brown's article on the nature of scriptural authority is highly recommended. It and Wolterstorff's book give especially valuable background and amplification for what is said in this section about religious versions of the foundationalist assumption.

10. See my reference in the previous section to Aquinas's conviction that the blessed in the afterlife will have certain and complete comprehension of those biblical teachings that in this life are mysteries to be accepted on faith. I will have more to say later in this section about Aquinas's view of knowledge in the afterlife.

11. I should emphasize again that I am not talking here about Christianity as a system of thought. My comments are not meant to be interpretive or critical of Christianity as such but of a prominent way of thinking influenced by Christianity, a way of thinking that could well be charged with being one-sided in its failure to take into account other, counterbalancing aspects of the Christian view. Genesis teaches, for example, that the creation is good. The Psalms tell of God's riding on the wings of the wind and thundering in the heavens. Jesus observes that God's eye is on the sparrow and that he sustains the lilies of the field. The Christian doctrine of the incarnation is a model of God in the midst of earthly life, fully divine but also fully human. On the other hand, passages of the Bible such as First Corinthians 15:12-19 have been frequently interpreted to mean that without the hope of resurrection from the dead as guaranteed by the resurrection of Christ, the faith of Christians is futile and the lives of all human beings pitiable. This common interpretation implies that this life is worthless without the hope of a life to come. Romans 8:18-25, with its vision of the whole creation in "bondage to decay," groaning for its redemption even as we humans "groan inwardly" for "the redemption of our bodies," has been interpreted similarly; and so on. Is this the right interpretation? That is not the point at issue; I argue only that it has been a prevalent view in the West, and as such, an important source of nihilism in the manner I describe.

12. Smart's intent is not to criticize the traditional Christian conception of the afterlife. Rather, he wants to show that because "moral discourse is embedded in the cosmic status quo (or even more narrowly, in the planetary status quo)," and is "applied to a situation where men are beings of a certain sort," we cannot argue convincingly against the existence of God on the ground that he could have created us wholly good. He calls this line of argument the "Utopia Thesis" (Smart, in Pike 1965:112). But his analysis also has critical implications for the idea of a perfect afterlife, as I have tried to show.

13. Hick recognizes that the concept of an eternal hell with no hope of reprieve and no rehabilitory function cannot be reconciled with the goodness of God. Far from being part of a final state of perfect justice, such endless "torment could never serve any good end beyond itself, and would thus constitute precisely the kind of unredeemed evil which would make a theodicy impossible" (Hick, in Edwards 1967:III, 139). We can add that it makes no sense to think of the blessed in heaven being aware of the agonies of their fellow-creatures in everlasting hell and yet being perfectly happy.

Chapter 7

1. The concept of matter as a substantial entity in its own right was not absolutely new, of course, but only new in the context of the break with Aristotle in the sixteenth and seventeenth centuries. Leucippus and Democritus, as well as Epicurus and Lucretius, had long ago endorsed a conception of matter similar to that which became standard in the early modern era. Plato, on the other hand, held to a view of matter similar to Aristotle's. As Copleston points out in discussing Plato's theory of the forms, sense particulars, to the extent that they cannot be brought within the compass of the forms, are unintelligible and not fully real. Hence, Plato dismisses them into the sphere of the "indefinite" (*to apeiron*) or of that which is "disorderly" and "irregular," i.e., chaotic (*Philebus* 16e, *Timaeus* 30a; cited Copleston 1962:I, I, 214-215). Copleston does not note here the comparison with Aristotle, but Aristotle's concept of the material substratum as a relative factor in complete substantial reality is strikingly similar to Plato's notion of sense particulars taken apart from their participation in the forms. Both conceive matter *qua* matter as a kind of unknowable potentiality. R.G. Collingwood notes that John Dalton, in the early nineteenth century, gave an important new twist to the modern conception of matter which distinguished it from early Greek atomism. However, this twist did not alter the basic idea of matter as a substance. Democritean atomism differs from Daltonian atomism because "the Greek atoms were indivisible particles of undifferentiated matter, whereas Dalton's atoms (until Rutherford began to split them) were indivisible particles of this or that kind of matter, hydrogen or carbon or lead" (1960:18).

2. I am indebted to Blocker for this comparison of Locke and Sartre. See his 1974:89.

3. Some might contend that I have confused two separate issues: that of the nature of truth and that of criteria for assessing truth. As Rorty notes, the meaning of *true* in our language is not synonymous with the meaning of "warranted assertible" (or in our terms, satisfying the best available criteria for distinguishing truth from error). But he denies that this *linguistic* distinction has any *philosophical* importance. "Most of what passes for discussion of 'truth' in philosophy books is, in fact about justification . . . ." Attempts to make philosophical sense out of, or to demonstrate the philosophical necessity for, talk about correspondence of our statements or beliefs to external reality, as an issue over and above the procedures for their justification, have failed. These attempts have failed because they add nothing intelligible or resolvable to the discussion that the problem of warranted assertibility cannot cover (see Rorty 1980:279-295, esp. 280-282). This also seems to be precisely Bouwsma's point.

4. This view of nature ties in with the ecological perspective noted in Chapter Five, Section 2. In this perspective, human beings are seen as an integral part of the community of organisms on this planet, rather than as standing over against them in a position of ontological separateness or external dominance. The view also connects with the idea that nature, rather than God or some other nature-transcending principle, is the fundamental given in terms of which all interpretations and explanations must take place. One can hold to this view without making the assumption that natural science alone is qualified to provide reliable interpretations or explanations of natural phenomena. It can also be

endorsed without denying the importance of distinguishing between human culture and the nonhuman aspects of nature, because accounting for the emergence and distinctive role of culture can be seen as part of the task of an adequate concept of nature. At the same time, it can be recognized that concepts of nature are themselves the products of human culture and, as such, historically situated and conditioned. I discuss this last point further in Chapter Nine.

5. Leclerc assists our understanding of the seductive ambiguity of the term *nature* when he observes that the *physical*, widely regarded as the proper domain of natural science, is etymologically derived from the Greek term *phusis*, often taken by the Greeks to mean "that ultimate something in things by virtue of which they *are*, and are what they are" (1972:103; see also 48, 101-107, 315). The transition from the restricted first meaning of nature to the more inclusive second and third meanings is abetted by this sense of *phusis* in Greek thought—a sense reflected in our common use of the phrase *the nature of things*.

6. Michael Gregory makes an important point, however, when he reminds us that much of the Industrial Revolution "was the work of tinkerers, rather than scientists as such" (1984:14).

7. I am speaking here, of course, of what is often assumed to be the *ideal* of scientific explanation. To what extent practicing scientists, or existing scientific theories, approach this ideal is another issue (see my 1983:250, n. 2). The ideal is more closely approximated in physics and chemistry than anywhere else in natural science, but even in these two fields accepted explanations of natural phenomena do not always neatly instantiate it. Thus, the line between scientific approaches to nature and other kinds of approaches (such as those of philosophers) is by no means hard-and-fast. The fact that this line is often blurred gives added force to Leclerc's insistence on the need for a complementary relation between science and philosophy as far as issues in the field of the philosophy of nature are concerned.

8. These points about the background and significance of scientific reasoning must be borne in mind when considering the ideal of scientific explanation talked about earlier. They do not contradict that ideal but set it in context and clarify its character and limits.

9. The term *metaphysics*, as I use it here, does not mean *beyond physics, beyond the physical realm*, or *beyond experience*. *Metaphysics* is inquiry into generic traits of experience and the structure of their interrelations. As Whitehead puts it, the traits or categories of an adequate metaphysical scheme will be generic, not only in the sense of their extreme generality or applicability to all sorts of experiences (e.g., sensate, emotional, recollective, inquisitive, deliberative, purposive, valuative), but also in the sense of their being "indispensably relevant to the analysis of anything that happens" in experience (1926:84 note). Should we discover that we can understand some type or aspect of experience without recourse (explicitly or implicitly) to one or more of the categories of a particular metaphysical scheme, then the category or categories in question would be shown to be nongeneric, and the scheme itself would be shown to be inadequate in that respect. For a discussion of this idea as it relates to Whitehead's metaphysics, see Christian 1983:40-44.

10. Some other metaphysical approaches to nature and the place of human beings in

nature that can be mentioned as significant alternatives to the approaches of dualism or scientific reductionism are Dewey's, in *Experience and Nature*; Andrew G. Van Melsen's, in *The Philosophy of Nature*; and, of course, the pluralistic metaphysics of Aristotle. Van Melsen's philosophy of nature is based mainly on Aristotle, but he interprets the Greek philosopher's views in the context of modern science. Leclerc's prolegomena to a contemporary philosophy of nature, presented in *The Nature of Physical Existence*, are also a promising metaphysical contribution. Leclerc draws largely from Aristotle, Leibniz, and Whitehead, but he arrives at his own distinctive conclusions.

Chapter 8

1. Randall's description applies to the seventeenth century as well. This scientific ideal was inspired to no small extent, of course, by Nicholas Copernicus's *De Revolutionibus Orbium Coelestium*, which appeared in 1543. Randall notes that this work contained the "startling thought . . . that the old authorities had been found in error, and that even observation and common sense were fallible; only reason operating by mathematical calculation could be trusted" (1976:230).

2. Descartes's fascination with mathematics was matched, or nearly matched, by his fascination with machines. In his *Traité de l'Homme* (the second part of *Le Monde*, published posthumously in 1662), he draws a detailed analogy between the human body, which he regards as a machine, and the workings of elaborate, cleverly designed hydraulic mechanisms in the fountains of an aristocratic garden. He suggests that the functions of the body can also be compared with "the movements of a clock or of a mill" (see A. R. Hall 1981:193-194). In the *Discourse on Method*, he notes that every aspect of the circulation of the blood, discovered recently by William Harvey, "follows as necessarily from the very dispositions of the organs" as do the workings "of a clock from the power, the situation, and the form, of its counterpoise and of its wheels." He takes this as compelling evidence that the body is nothing but a machine (1967:I, 112). The phrase *follows . . . necessarily from* suggests the correlation with mathematical demonstrations, the importance of which is stressed by Descartes just before he goes on to make his observation about the circulation of the blood.

3. For a more detailed inspection of the role of experience in Descartes's thought, see Copleston's discussion in 1963:90-95. The heavy emphasis he placed on rational intuitions and deductive demonstrations, as against sensate experiences, got him into trouble when he developed the system of nature of his *Principles of Philosophy* (1644). A. R. Hall speaks of that work's "shadowy relevance to experience," and notes that "Cartesian physics contained a host of explanations . . . which, if they conflicted with nothing save perhaps plausibility, were confirmed by nothing." More empirically minded scientists of the next generation, such as Newton, took Descartes to task for not having (in Hall's words) "really faced the intricacies of any single phenomenon of nature," and for having "failed to tie theory . . . to the detailed facts of investigation." It was this complaint that, according to Hall, underlay Newton's famous pronouncement in the *Principia Mathematica*: "I do not feign hypotheses." See A. R. Hall 1981:115, 121-122, 106-107.

4. A version of Descartes's appeal to certainty is also contained in the empiricist

philosophies, as Dewey points out. For empiricists it is the simple data of sense which are the "objects of infallible apprehension" on whose basis the whole edifice of reliable knowledge must be constructed (Dewey 1960:65).

5. The notion of a discrete, purely present or durationless moment of awareness is, however, a patent fiction. We never experience a present not heavy with the felt influence of the past or not shot through with anticipations of the future. That great celebrant of the pervasive influence of memory, Marcel Proust, states its effects on us in this way: "An hour is not just an hour, it is a vase full of perfume, sounds, projects, and moods. What we call reality is a certain rapport between our sensations and the memories that encircle us at the moment" (1949:35). Richard Morris also reminds us

   that the subjective present is not a mathematical instant. If it were, we would not be able to hear a clock go 'tick-tock.' The fact that we hear the 'tick' and the 'tock' as a unit, not separately, seems to indicate that they are both contained within the psychological present. Similarly, if the subjective 'now' had zero duration, we would not be able to hear musical rhythms.

   Morris adds that "if the 'now' were an instant, we could not perceive motion. At best, we could only observe that a moving body occupied different positions at different instants of time" (1984:146-147). This last sentence exactly asserts Descartes's view of motion, as will be seen shortly.

6. I speak here of the *result* of Sartre's philosophical outlook in *Being and Nothingness*, not of his *intent*. It is a result which follows primarily (as seen in Chapter Four, Section 2) from his emphasis on radical freedom. Sartre is well aware that "[o]nce we have confined the Present to the Present we will never get out of it." And he explicitly criticizes Descartes (and Kant) for starting "from the presupposition of a time which would be a form of division and which itself dissolves in pure multiplicity." He states, moreover, that "finality is rightly said to be causality reversed—that is, the efficacy of the future state," implying a connectedness of the present with the future (1966:151-152; 160-162). But he tends to be so preoccupied with this "efficacy of the future state," i.e., the sheer openness of future possibility and the unrestricted role of human freedom in the face of that possibility, as to downplay in the extreme the efficacy of the past. By refusing to allow that accumulated effects of the past (including one's own past choices) can impose insurmountable constraints on present acts of freedom (including the range of meanings and possibilities we are capable at a given moment of attributing to the past), thus necessitating that these acts be in all cases ones of partial, rather than total freedom, Sartre also denies by implication any predictable outcome to our present acts, i.e., any calculable, cumulative, constraining effects of these acts on future choices. In that case, not only has connectedness of the present with the past been brought into question, but also the present's connectedness with the future, and we are brought back to yet another version of time (and self) as a mere multiplicity of detached moments.

7. The element of circularity I have discussed is that of relying on the certitude of one's substantial existence to prove the existence of God, and then relying on God

to give assurance of one's continuing existence in the face of the fallibility and uncertainty of memory and anticipation.

8. The main symbol of this precision and certainty of deductive reasoning, for which Roquentin longs, is the song *Some of These Days*. Each time the recording of this song is played, the notes follow after one another with a strong and reassuring necessity, a "metallic transparency" of clear and distinct certitude. Life, by contrast, is disjointed and radically insecure; and our claims to knowledge, shot through as they are with elements of uncertainty, convention, and contingency, are at the farthest remove from the crystalline necessity of the song. Here Roquentin shows himself to be a Platonist or Cartesian at heart, bitterly disappointed that knowledge in those two philosophies' sense of the term has proved impossible to achieve and assuming that this is the only important sense of the term (see Sartre 1964:34-35). At the end of *Nausea*, he abandons his aspiration to know, realizing its futility, and devotes himself to writing a novel, symbolizing his determination to come to terms with the idea that the best human beings can do is to invent a world for themselves by their individual acts of freedom.

9. There is a considerable difference, however, between what Descartes's method calls for and the extent to which he is able or willing to apply it to his own cultural traditions, as will be seen below. This difference is glaringly evident in his statements about the unimpeachable authority of divine revelation. In this respect, in actual practice, his stated view of the past is not different from that of Luther, despite the implications of his announced method.

10. I allude, of course, to Miguel de Cervantes Saavedra's *Don Quixote de la Mancha*, which first appeared in complete form in 1615.

11. What is said here about religion also holds for secular forms of faith. On the notion of secular forms of faith, see Chapter Six, note 7.

12. Descartes's statement that "theology points out the way to heaven" is reminiscent of Galileo. In his Letter to the Grand Duchess Christina, Galileo commends the claim of Cardinal Baronius that the Christian scriptures are to be relied upon for finding how to go to heaven, but not for understanding how heaven goes. The latter task is one to be independently undertaken through the method of physical science. See Nelson, in Gingrich 1975:364-365, 371, n. 11.

13. Descartes is equally vague and inconclusive on the whole question of values, including the specific contents of moral obligation, in his last published work, *The Passions of the Soul* (1649).

14. I owe this image to Francis Bacon. See his *Novum Organum*, Aphorism xcv; in Burtt 1939:67).

15. The sense of irony is heightened when we reflect that all the conclusions arrived at by Descartes's employment of his method must, by this reckoning, be deemed ultimately unreliable, including his conclusions about the nature of God! Our way of thinking, bound as it is to the standard of clear and distinct ideas and to the inconceivability of there being alternatives to these ideas, must be totally different from God's and, therefore, far removed from his perception of reality. This consequence knocks the correspondence conception of truth into a cocked hat,

particularly to the extent that it aspires, on the basis of indubitable propositions, toward a God's-eye view of reality.

16. I was going to add here that any such abridgment of the divine freedom would be, for Descartes, *impossible*, but the meaning of this term in this context is no longer clear. Its unclarity is one measure of the absurdist tendency implicit in the role he assigns to God's will.

17. Comte, in a manner similar to Skinner and Monod, dreamed of a society constructed on scientific principles and presided over by scientific experts. Fontenelle and Saint-Simon also had this vision. Fontenelle proclaimed that "[t]he geometric spirit is not so bound up with geometry that it cannot be disentangled and carried into other fields. A work of morals, of politics, of criticism, perhaps even of eloquence, will be the finer, other things being equal, if it is written by the hand of a geometer" (*Oeuvres Completes*, 1818, *Preface sur l'utilite des mathematiques et de la physique*, I, 34: quoted Randall 1976:254). I have not, of course, begun to list all the thinkers who have shared in Descartes's adulation and attempted universalization of scientific method. William Leiss notes, for example, that "[m]en like [Etienne Bonnot de] Condillac, [Jean le Rond d'] Alembert, and [Antoine Nicholas, Marquis de] Condorcet brought to completion the idea that a single method could be applied in all the sciences, a method that was as valid for the study of society as it was for the investigation of nature" (1974:78).

18. Carnap's "Die physikalische Sprache als Universalsprache der Wissenschaft," and Neurath's "Protokollsätze," to which Passmore refers in these pages and from which the quotations are taken, were both published in the journal *Erkenntnis* in 1932. While their universalization of natural science and its method continued to find able philosophical defenders well into the 1940s, the tenability of their position has been progressively eroded by a series of fundamental criticisms by professional philosophers and is not widely endorsed among philosophers today (for some of the details, see Passmore 1966, Ch. 16). Nevertheless, Carnap's and Neurath's general attitude toward natural science— the attitude of Descartes in modern guise—continues to inform our cultural outlook at many levels.

19. "In Descartes the anti-Existential bias is most conspicuous," says Tillich. "Man becomes pure consciousness, a naked epistemological subject; the world (including man's psychosomatic being) becomes an object of scientific inquiry and technical management. Man in his existential predicament disappears" (1953:131).

Chapter 9

1. This sentence and the preceding one also make evident an overlap of a source of nihilism discussed in Chapter Six with the third and fourth philosophical sources, namely, the search for certain foundations. This search, in turn, as I have noted, has the aim of attaining a nonperspectival, timeless, God's-eye view of truth, which extends the connection to yet another source of nihilism explicated in Chapter Six. It is ironic that the subjectivity of the isolated individual comes

widely in the modern period to be regarded as the only sure avenue to completely *objective* truth.

2. Cf. for example Hume's claim that

> all the sciences have a relation, greater or less, to human nature; and . . . however wide any of them may seem to run from it, they still return back by one passage or another. Even *Mathematics, Natural Philosophy, and Natural Religion*, are in some measure dependent on the science of Man; since they lie under the cognizance of men, and are judged of by their powers and faculties (1980:xv).

The science of man, in its turn, is erected on the foundation of contents and principles to be discovered through a sustained process of introspective analysis.

3. Locke is not as consistently nominalistic in his epistemology, however, as Hume. Locke's term *idea* sometimes refers to what Hume calls *impressions*, i.e., particular images or appearances into which any given experience is claimed to be analyzable, while, at other times, *idea* connotes a universal concept in the mind. I note this ambiguity in Locke's use of *idea* later in this chapter, when I discuss his theory of language in relation to Hume's more resolute nominalism.

4. Hume's three principles also remind us of Newton's three laws of motion. Each set of principles or laws plays an equally fundamental role in its respective field, the science of nature in the one case and the science of human nature in the other. Despite the pronounced skeptical tendencies and conclusions of his philosophy, Hume, like Kant, seems to find no difficulty in assuming that his analysis of the workings of his own mind, or of the form and content of his own experience, applies to all human beings. He thus purports to have developed a "science of Man" or an account of the universal principles of human nature, and not just to have explored the caverns of his own subjectivity (1980:xv). The gap he discovers to be so glaring and impassable in the case of the relations between his private impressions and the world is passed over easily, and without any felt need for argument, in his announced purpose in the Preface to the *Treatise* to set forth such a science—an intent also made explicit in the rest of the book's title, which, significantly enough, is "of Human Nature," not "of Hume's Nature."

5. Leo Strauss's reflections suggest a sense in which the logic of Hegel's analysis of history would force him to more than the relatively restrained view that the absolute has reached merely its *current* pinnacle of self-understanding in Hegel's philosophy. Strauss argues that Hegel must conclude from his own reasoning that the historical "process is in principle completed" in his own time, and thus in his own philosophy; "for if it were not completed, one could not know, for instance, whether the future stages would not lead to the self-destruction of reason" (1961:146). But Hegel does claim to know that this cannot occur; so, in this sense, at least, his philosophy must be seen as an all-inclusive vision of the unfoldings of history—past, present, *and* future. Copleston contends, however, that supposing that Hegel thought that philosophy had come to an end with himself is foolish, given the German idealist's insistence that philosophy can only express the contemporary world and is therefore incapable of overleaping its own time. "Obviously," says Copleston, "on Hegel's principles subsequent philosophy

would have to incorporate absolute idealism, even if his system revealed itself as a one-sided moment in a higher synthesis." But this is not the same as claiming that there would not be any subsequent philosophy, or none markedly different from Hegel's (1985:VII, 244).

6. For a concise discussion of the ambiguities, ironies, and even comic absurdities latent in Hegel's inclination to identify the present state of self-knowledge of the absolute with his own philosophy, as well as in his idealistic, markedly anthropomorphic "apotheosis of mind," see Jacob Loewenberg's Introduction to Hegel 1929:xxxii-xxxviii. On the latter point (which, given the whole thrust of Hegel's thought and especially the cumulative view it takes of the history of philosophy itself, cannot be entirely distinguished from the first one), Loewenberg has this to say:

> The folly of drawing the whole to the scale of the part is just what the dialectical method singles out as proper food for the Cosmic Spirit. Can Hegel's idealism escape the scourge of its own method? We wonder. His method, designed as it is to chastise everything particular, must impugn necessarily the idolatrous attempt to exalt the human mind by regarding its characteristic forms of experience and discourse as the measure of the Absolute (Hegel 1929:xxxvii).

What Loewenberg says about the human mind in this statement applies *a fortiori*, of course, to Hegel's particular mind and thought.

7. That is, a critical "metaphysics" that purports to exhibit the impossibility of knowing reality-itself.

8. We have given the common interpretation to Hegel's conception of the absolute spirit, namely, that it is some kind of world-soul or God. Peter Singer rightly stresses, however, the "ambiguities and uncertainties" of Hegel's views on this subject and sketches the possibility of a very different interpretation from the one we have assumed here. According to this other interpretation, what Hegel really means by a mind that comes to self-knowledge through the march of history is the progressive development of freedom and understanding in organized human community. Humans cannot come to understanding in isolation from one another, but only through processes of experience and inquiry that are essentially social. Knowledge, to be that, must be communicable; and language, as the principal medium of communication, is social and not merely individual. So what Hegel is trying to explicate is not a hypostatized cosmic mind but a collective human mind, or perhaps even the nature of rational consciousness itself, because the latter must be understood in social, cultural, and historical terms.

Despite the attractiveness of this demythologized view (its concept of rational consciousness is similar to the one I defend later in this chapter), Singer admits that we may be forced in the end by the Hegelian texts to the interpretation we have been assuming. This interpretation is that Hegel's absolute spirit is something like God, an elevation to divine or cosmic status of Kant's transcendental unity of apperception and, thus, that his thought represents after all "a retreat into the mystical unity of a cosmic consciousness." Singer explicitly endorses this more standard interpretation later in his book when he suggests that

Robert Whittmore's "panentheistic" interpretation of Hegel's absolute spirit is "plausible, not only because it is consistent with what Hegel says specifically about God, but also because it makes sense of the dominant theme of his philosophy" (Singer 1983:73-74, 82). Hegel's stress on the social character of knowledge and language, alluded to above, is an important counter to the subjective idealistic or solipsistic tendency of his philosophy we have focused on here, a tendency whose main rootage is in the philosophy of Kant and which Hegel and other absolute idealists conceal behind a smokescreen of "the mystical unity of a cosmic consciousness."

9. What I call the *subjectivist bias* is termed the *egocentric outlook* in Saunders and Henze 1967. The authors explain that this "is the outlook of one who begins at home, with the private object (with his own private experiential data), and attempts, in one way or another, to 'go abroad'." Solipsists, subjective idealists, dualists, and phenomenalists they regard as "typical exponents" of the egocentric outlook. Their characterization of the "egocentric predicament" is also pertinent to the theme of this chapter: "This is the predicament of 'how to get out,' how to move justifiably from one's own experiential data to the existence of an external world containing both animate and inanimate entities." It is "also the problem of 'how to get outside' of the experiential data of the present moment, how to warrant one's convictions regarding one's own history and propensities" (1967:17-18). One result of the continuing struggles of modern thought with this predicament, as we are seeking to show, is the philosophy of nihilism. The predicament itself is in large measure the legacy of Descartes; its tenacious hold on the modern mind shows how long a shadow the French philosopher's speculations have cast over subsequent intellectual history, down to our own time.

10. Kant clearly has principally in mind teleological or consequentialist empirical ethical theories in presenting these arguments. Not all empirical ethical theories are of this character, however. For example, Hume's ethics turns on the notion that we can directly apprehend, and with no possibility of mistake (as long as certain stated conditions are fulfilled), the inherent and objective moral quality of an act on the basis of a commonly experienced, universal moral sentiment. See David Fate Norton's extensive discussion of Hume's moral theory in 1982:94-151, and especially Norton's interpretive summary of Hume's main line of argument for his theory, 142-143. Mill's theory, which I will soon compare with Kant's, is of course a teleological theory, so all the arguments I list here are directly relevant to it.

11. It follows from Kant's analysis that we have no moral obligations toward any part of the natural order, including even the so-called higher animals. This aspect of his dualistic outlook on human beings in their relation to nature mirrors the attitude of Descartes and the Cartesian philosophers I mentioned in Chapter Eight, Section 2.

12. Kant does claim, as I will note in a moment, that pure practical reason, unlike pure theoretical reason, gives us access to the noumenal world. But this claim tends to beg the question of the egocentric predicament, as outlined in note 9 above. That predicament is itself the product of the egocentric outlook that

Kant's ethical theory, like the epistemology of his first *Critique*, presupposes and exemplifies.

13. If his character has been *wholly* shaped by his environmental conditioning in the way that his deterministic metaphysics demands, how could it be otherwise? Mill's claim to presuppositionless scientific objectivity in his ethics seems to be in conflict with his own analysis of human action. The working out of an ethical theory must surely be included among significant examples of human action.

14. It is remarkable how little effort Mill makes in this key chapter to tie the rights and duties commonly assumed in his time explicitly and rigorously to utility. He seems simply to presuppose that we will agree with him that there is such an intimate connection, i.e., that it is so obvious as not to require detailed argumentation. Thus, human happiness can be found, for him, in unswerving commitment to those values and obligations deemed central in his own culture. He nowhere questions or defends this belief in a thoroughgoing way, despite his claim to be presenting an ethical system that is resolutely scientific and empirical in character, one grounded in examination of the supposedly universal human traits and valuations implicit in subjective awareness.

15. MacIntyre gives us another telling example of this first tendency of subjectivist theories of ethics in his observations about two recent and widely discussed attempts to ground moral values in the interests or entitlements of the isolated individual: the theories of justice set forth by John Rawls and Robert Nozick (Rawls 1971; Nozick 1974). What is lacking in both of these analyses, he contends, is consideration of the factor of moral desert. This is not at all surprising to him, for he holds "that the notion of desert is at home only in the context of a community whose primary bond is a shared understanding both of the good for man and of the good of that community and where individuals identify their primary interests with reference to those goods" (1981:233; see also Ch. 17 in its entirety). To build an ethical system from a base of isolated subjectivity or pure individualism requires that we neglect the individual's connections with, and prior responsibilities to, any existing community and, thus, that we leave out of consideration such crucial moral conceptions as that of desert which can have significance only in relation to such communities.

   MacIntyre argues systematically throughout his book *After Virtue* that the Enlightenment project of deriving ethical values from free-floating subjectivity was bound to fail, precisely because of its in-principle dismissal (or attempt at dismissal) of all cultural and social influences on human thought and experience. I am also contending for this view. While I do not quite concur with his claim (1981:59) that the concept of the individual is an "invention" of modernity (versions of this concept figure in the Sophism of the Hellenic period, for example, and are especially prominent in some forms of Hellenistic philosophy), he is right in emphasizing the leading role that has been played and continues to be played by this notion in the drama of modern thought. He is also entirely correct in his contention that the idea of the isolated individual is an abstract, artificial construction with no basis in our actual human situation.

16. Paul Feyerabend writes that it "was *Wittgenstein's* great merit . . . to have emphasized that science contains not only formulae and rules for their

application but entire *traditions*." He adds that "*Kuhn* has expanded the criticism and made it more concrete. A *paradigm*, for him, is a tradition containing easily identifiable features side by side with tendencies and procedures that are not known but guide research in a subterranean way and are discovered only by contrast with other traditions" (1978:66).

17. Dewey and Whitehead, for example, have vigorously contested this belief in their writings (see especially Dewey 1958 and Whitehead 1948, 1979). For a thoughtful discussion of the topic of natural value from an ecological perspective and a defense of the thesis that there are values in nature, see Rolston 1982.

18. James Faulconer and Richard Williams point out that for Hans-Georg Gadamer (1975), "[c]ritique of the status quo is possible within the status quo because the status quo is, by definition, itself temporal. It is not necessary; it is possible, so some possibilities can be critiqued from the standpoint given by others" (1985:1186). Any given cultural setting provides innumerable possibilities, in other words, for individual criticism and redirection of what is commonly taken for granted in that setting. There is no requirement that the status quo be criticized from some absolute standpoint, because time itself contains its own principle of transcendence, either in the direction of as yet unrealized possibilities in a tradition or in the direction of possibilities once realized in it but no longer emphasized. As Faulconer and Williams express it, "[t]he moment is, thus, itself transcendental; it has at once givenness and openness" (1985:1187).

19. In *Phenomenology of Perception* and other writings, Merleau-Ponty also stresses the mutually perceptible bodies of human subjects as a basis of their intersubjective awareness or reciprocal being-in-the-world. But he has in mind the "primordial phenomenon of the body-for-us," not the objective body of physiology textbooks (or, I might add, textbooks in behavioral psychology). Thus, in contrast to Husserl, he downplays any need for analogical inferences from objective observations of bodily behavior to the subjectivity or consciousness of others, holding that the perception of others is "anterior to, and the condition of, such observations; the observations do not constitute the perception." See 1962:352, 354; cited and discussed in Dallmayr 1981:94-95.

20. The 1985 article of Faulconer and Williams, to which I refer in note 18 above, is a valuable critique of the modern quest for certainty, with its adulation of mathematical reasoning (and thus of natural science, to the extent that science is conceived as exhibiting mathematical exactitude in its method and results)—an enterprise and ideal which, by the authors' analysis, turns crucially on the assumption that truth must be something absolute and atemporal. They also exhibit an interesting connection of the atemporal notion of truth with the Enlightenment view of time as a series of disconnected instants. "Because science, by definition, cannot take refuge in epistemological skepticism, once it assumes this view of time it cannot escape explaining things in transcendent terms," i.e., in terms of "atemporal laws, the supposed laws of reason" which are necessary and therefore cannot change (1985:1183-1184). Descartes, Newton, and others attribute these atemporal laws of temporal connectedness (or causal regularity) to a more ultimate transcendent principle, namely God. Conversely, Hume's critique of necessary (i.e., absolute, unvarying) causal connections is taken by him and others of his time as opening the way to total skepticism, a fact that in itself

reveals the tenacity and pivotal role of the assumption about the nature of truth indicated above.

This article ties in nicely with my prior criticisms of the God's-eye ideal of knowledge in Chapter Six, showing especially that achievement of intelligibility in the study of human behavior requires that we abandon the search for atemporal forms of truth and explanation. Temporal situatedness is an integral aspect of the human condition, and it must be allowed a fundamental role in our interpretations of human life. Within a hermeneutic way of understanding, such as that represented by the thought of Gadamer, "truth is how things are. But it must be remembered that things are temporal. They are temporally with us in a temporal world." Truth must therefore be seen as temporality, or as contained exclusively within temporal perspectives. Faulconer and Williams point out that the view of truth as temporality means rejection of the correspondence theory of truth, conceived as the representation of timeless principles by truthful expressions, as well as of belief in the finality of method, conceived as the orderly application of general, atemporal principles. This criticism of the finality of method applies particularly in the human sciences, exploding the dichotomous assumption that explanations of human behavior "must be given either in terms of static, atemporal entities or in terms of the imaginations of the individual" (1985:1185).

Chapter 10

1. Isaiah Berlin draws this distinction in these terms in his *Two Concepts of Liberty* (1958). His book is critically discussed in Strauss 1961:135-141.

2. Descartes's nominalistic tendencies can be observed not only in his point-instant view of time and change, requiring God to sustain the illusion of inherent temporal and causal connectedness, but also in his conviction that all conceptual relations are ultimately the arbitrary creations of God. Also nominalistic is his definition of substance as a thing that "needs no other thing in order to exist" (1967:I, 239), because this definition implies that substantial individuals existing at a given moment have no inherent, but only external, forms of relatedness to the rest of the universe. Such external forms of relatedness would presumably include space and time, including the time of the substance's own endurance, which brings us back to the point-instant view of time and change. A strand of nominalism in Kant is his unquestioning acceptance of Hume's belief that the data of sense have no internal relatedness or inherent meaning and must therefore be brought into patterns of significant relation by mental processes imposed upon them from without.

3. Grotius's individualistic view of the source of political institutions, if not so clearly of their end, is evident in his insistence on the contractual basis of the legitimate state. Such a state is created by previously isolated individuals in accordance with principles that, while divinely ordained, are fully evident to each person's autonomous reason. These principles of natural law do not depend in the least for their validity, therefore, on scriptural authority or any kind of antecedent tradition but well up independently from the consciousness of the individual. Such persons willingly band together in political institutions in response to the

call of reason that resounds in their subjective awareness. This is but one illustration of the close connection between the fourth and fifth philosophical sources of nihilism.

4. Mill cites the work of Wilhelm von Humboldt in connection with this ideal of individuality, which is closely related to Mill's notion of negative freedom. See his quotes (in English) from Humboldt's 1791 essay, *Ideen zu einem Versuch die Grenzen der Wirksamkeit des Staats zu bestimmen* (Burtt 1939:993).

5. See Randall 1976:322-325. The Physiocrats of the eighteenth century sought to develop what Randall terms "a natural science of wealth"; their program was adapted to the English economic situation by Smith. One of the Physiocrats, Dupont de Nemours, states what we are calling the idea of negative freedom when he contends that "the social laws established by the Supreme Being prescribe only the preservation of the right of property, and of that liberty which is inseparable from it. The ordinances of sovereigns which we call positive laws, can be only *acts declaratory of these essential laws of the social order*" (*Origines et Progres d'une Science nouvelle*, quoted Randall 1976:324). A prominent thinker of the nineteenth century who espouses this same view that the essential duty of the state is that of protecting the autonomy of its citizens is Herbert Spencer. "Whenever the State begins to exceed its power of protector" of individual rights, and most particularly, "the law of equal freedom," he announces, "it begins to lose protective power. Not a single supplementary service can it attempt without producing dissent; and in proportion to the amount of dissent so produced by it, the State defeats the end for which it was established . . . ." The theory "that a government ought to undertake other offices besides that of protector," Spencer dismisses as "untenable" (*Social Statics*, 1850 ed., Chs. 21, 22; quoted Randall 1976:445). For a discussion of Bentham's defense of the idea of negative freedom, see Randall 1976:361-363.

6. Two recent and highly influential examples of this orientation and focus are the social theories of Nozick and Rawls, to which I referred in Chapter Nine, note 15. Also, MacIntyre calls our attention to "a certain radical individualism" implicit in the Marxist dream of a coming classless society, rid of the restraint and oppression of institutions of government. The radically "free individual" of this future society, says MacIntyre, "is described by Marx [in the first chapter of *Capital* and elsewhere] as a socialized Robinson Crusoe; but on what basis he enters into his free association with others Marx does not tell us" (1981:243; for a similar critique of Marx, see Arendt 1959:101-102, 114-116). Lacking in the Marxist vision of the future, in other words, is an explication of the valuative basis of human community. It is assumed that complete individual freedom and absence of governmental suppression and class conflict are all that will be required for harmonious social existence.

The vision is, therefore, deeply informed by the ideal of negative freedom, a striking incorporation into Marxism of a basic tenet of liberal social theory. In the *Manifesto of the Communist Party* Marx and Engels allude to this ideal when they state that "[i]n place of the old bourgeois society, with its classes and class antagonisms, we shall have an association in which the free development of each is the condition for the free development of all" (Marx and Engels 1959:29). Of course, many important differences between Marxism and classical liberalism remain. Liberalism insists, for example, that institutions of government will always be required for the protection of individual freedoms, and thus that a just society can never be achieved or maintained without political structures and the exercise of political power. Implicit in this belief is the assumption that these structures can be more than what Marx and Engels deem them necessarily to be: "merely the organized power of one class for oppressing another" (1959:29).

If anything, then, Marxism—at least as viewed from this angle—is even more profoundly individualistic than is the bourgeois liberalism it so roundly condemns. The former brand of individualism is undergirded by Marx's unwavering trust in what Löwith calls "generic man whose existence is absolutely social" (1964:321), man who enters naturally into communal relations with no need for the protections and restraints of political power. For a discussion of Marx's strictures against bourgeois individualism, which he judged to have come to consummate and revealingly decadent expression in the philosophy of Stirner, see Löwith 1964:146-147, 245-249. See also my presentation later in this chapter of Sidney Hook's exposition of Marx's critique of Stirner. Marx's is an eschatological individualism, as it were, while Stirner's is a here-and-now individualism. The latter, according to Marx, overlooks the oppressions of government and the consequences of class dominance, thus failing to perceive the distorted ideas of self and community these factors in current society sustain. In Marx's view, Stirner not only fails to recognize these distortions but also unwittingly endorses them in his own philosophy.

7. Most new commentators in the United States take for granted, for example, that politicians from the president on down espouse positions and make decisions solely in response to political pressures or with an eye to the next election. The stance of politicians is seen as purely expedient rather than principled, and their statements of principle are analyzed almost exclusively with a view to the political advantages it is assumed they "really" have in mind. In this way, a cynical kind of moral relativism, if not amoralism, is constantly communicated to the American public. Responding to political pressures and counter-pressures is appropriate in a democracy, but political representation has another dimension as well, that of moral judgment and moral leadership, This judgment and leadership can be exercised, I argue, in the spirit of pluralism. It ought not to be dogmatic or authoritarian, but it also need not be merely relativistic, tossed about by shifting currents of political influence with no moral rudder of its own. Politicians in a democracy should guide their political constituencies toward deeper levels of shared moral insight and responsible communal action by setting the tone for constructive dialogue on pressing problems of national, regional, and local concern.

8. Strauss also assumes that these are the only alternatives. He claims that the "inadequacies" of Berlin's liberalism "arise from his wish to find an impossible middle ground between relativism and absolutism . . ." (1961:140). In Chapter Nine, I tried to show that a middle ground can be found between absolutism and relativism: the generally neglected ground of pluralism.

9. I noted in Chapter Two Russell's observation that, for Bentham, one person's pleasure is equal to another person's; this reminds us of Berlin's explication of the connection between the negative concept of freedom and relativism: all human ends must be viewed as "equally ultimate, uncriticizable." To focus upon pleasure, even the greatest pleasure for the greatest number, as the positive end of

human existence can thus become a warrant for allowing others to do exactly as they please, as long as they do not interfere with any one else's freedom in doing so. For who can better judge than the individual what is likely to bring her pleasure? In other words, what starts out as a positive conception of freedom is seen at a second glance to be just the negative conception in a slightly altered guise.

10. Gar Alperowitz gives us a good statement of the nihilistic thrust of this rampant individualism, as analyzed by Bellah and his colleagues, when he writes:

Our 'habits of the heart' . . . no longer sustain a powerful impulse toward the values of an equitable community. At the core of our consciousness we do not even know how to speak about what it means to be creatures of a common culture, tradition, history. Accordingly, we do not have ways to understand the requirements of a viable politics of mutual concern (1986:61).

We should note, however, that we still have the resources in our history and culture to recapture the commonality of concern of which Alperowitz speaks (e.g., in Judaeo-Christian visions of communal justice and social compassion; and in Platonic, Aristotelian, and Stoic conceptions of the positive responsibilities of citizens in a good society), but our habits of heart, informed in large measure by the excessive individualism of liberal social theory, stand in our way.

Alperowitz argues that the analysis given by the authors of *Habits of the Heart*, while helpful in many ways, especially that of explicating the seriousness of the problem of radical individualism, is finally too mild and too "traditional." He insists on the need to "begin to forge, first, a long-term overview, and second, a set of practical institutional proposals that might avoid the pitfalls of both traditional capitalism and traditional socialism." "A revolution in perspective must ultimately occur," he declares, and not just adjustments within traditional modes of thinking. Significant reform is unlikely to take place "without a fundamental change in the core institutions—and the dynamic operating rules and motivational patterns—of the system." A central focus of needed change largely neglected by Bellah and his colleagues, according to Alperowitz, is our economic institutions and practices and the unanalyzed assumptions underlying them (1986:64 and *passim*).

The analysis I offer here, like that of *Habits of the Heart*, is only part of the story. Although the quality and estimate of our lives certainly is affected by our attitudes and beliefs, these are also powerfully affected, for good or ill, by our surrounding institutions (which are usually in place when we are born and still present when we die). Thus nihilistic despair can arise not only from a heritage of wrong-headed intellectual assumptions but from the daily toll enacted by life amid unjust or fundamentally inadequate social institutions. More than attending to the lessons of our intellectual history and recognizing the need for changes in our ways of thinking—my emphasis in this book—is needed to cast full light on the nihilistic crisis in our time and to develop effective ways of dealing with this crisis. No analysis of nihilism can be complete that deals exclusively with its intellectual sources and neglects its social-institutional sources. In the concluding section of Chapter Four, I made a similar point about the bearing of some of the formative social experiences of the twentieth century on the nihilistic mood.

11. In the first volume of his *Critique of Dialectical Reason* (first published in French in 1960), Sartre gives much more emphasis than he did in *Being and Nothingness* to the role of the individual's material and social environments in molding (and constraining) his outlook and actions. This is part of his attempt to achieve a synthesis of existentialism and Marxism. Our references here and elsewhere in this book are to Sartre in his earlier, pre-Marxist period.

12. Toward the end of the third section of Chapter Four I discussed three important respects in which the meaning of life is tied to the experience or prospect of genuine community.

13. Speaking of life in the United States, Bellah and his coauthors note that "[b]reaking with the past is part of our past. Leaving tradition behind runs all the way through our tradition" (1985:75).

14. In his brilliant study of the social and political system of the United States, *Democracy in America* (first published in French in 1835), Alexis de Tocqueville traces an important sense in which radical individualism and collectivism have a hidden affinity with one another. Because Americans believe that "all are endowed with equal means of judging" in matters of politics and social policy (as well as in other matters, such as religion), it is natural to suppose, de Tocqueville argues, "that the greater truth should go with the greatest number." That same sense of equality that renders the individual "independent of each of his fellow-citizens taken severally exposes him alone and unprotected to the influence of the greater number." Thus, the individual's "readiness to believe the multitude increases," and unexamined common opinion becomes "mistress of the world." This tendency toward conformism and collectivist ways of thinking and acting is reinforced, de Tocqueville thinks, by the fact that, in American democracy, the public has the power of enforcing its views through law, thereby infusing "them into the faculties by a sort of enormous pressure of the minds of all upon the reason of each" (1904:II, 492-493).

15. De Tocqueville expounds on this burden and the susceptibility to manipulation by external authority it creates, in this way:

> When there is no longer any principle of authority in religion any more than in politics, men are speedily frightened at the aspect of this unbounded independence. The constant agitation of all surrounding things alarms and exhausts them. As everything is at sea in the sphere of the intellect, they determine at least that the mechanism of society should be firm and fixed; and as they can not resume their ancient belief, they assume a master (II, 504).

Such a condition of complete isolation and total responsibility to determine for oneself solutions to the deepest issues of life, says de Tocqueville, "can not but enervate the soul, relax the springs of the will, and prepare a people for servitude" (II, 504).

16. Hermann Rauschning gives a detailed firsthand account of the character and ravages of Nazi nihilism in his book, *The Revolution of Nihilism: Warning to the West*, written mainly in the winter of 1937 and 1938 and published in English translation in 1939. Rauschning was a former leader of the National Socialist

Party and ex-president of the Danzig Senate. He was forced to flee Danzig in 1935, on account of his active support of constitutionalism in the election of April of that year, and he subsequently became a bitter opponent of the Nazi regime. Some well-meaning people were sucked into the Nazi program early on, he suggests, because they "only realized after a considerable time that they had been drawn into a double existence, with fictitious spiritual, national aims, and one very real one, the pursuit of power" (1939:31).

The following descriptions from Rauschning's book capture the absolutely bureaucratic and thoroughly nihilistic nature of that program, as he had come to see it in the late 1930s.

...National Socialism brought to the top a primitive, vulgar elite under the cover of national and social aims . . . . The cream of the elite use the power they have seized to feather their nexts . . . . [They carry] into practice the new doctrine of violence, the doctrine that spiritual assets are of value for the legitimation of political power and for nothing else; such things have no intrinsic authority, no value in themselves: there is nothing that counts, except force . . . . Force is applied at all times, for the one purpose of maintaining the elite in power—and applied ruthlessly, brutally, instantaneously . . . . The true elite is entirely without scruples and without humanitarian weaknesses (30-31).

In another place, Rauschning notes that everything National Socialism does "is done in the spirit of revolutionary destruction," and that it is "destroying the elements of every spiritual order, and preventing the creation of any new one" (274-275). He argues for the fatal instability of a state that deliberately repudiates any "ethical basis" and aims solely at the perpetuation of the power and position of its ruling elite. "A totalitarian dictatorship of pure violence is possible on a basis of nihilism, but it destroys its own foundation in proportion as its principles become general among the masses." "What has now to be overcome," he continues, "is the dictatorship of violence, which draws its destructive energies from the directionless revolution, a revolution merely for revolution's sake" (118, 120). This idea of "directionless revolution," bent upon senseless, unbounded destruction, recalls the concept of political nihilism explicated in Chapter Two.

17. One such factor, for example, was the idolization of the state and stress on the "infinite necessity" of the workings of the historical *Geist*—as opposed to individual freedoms—in Hegelian idealism, a strong current of thought in Germany in the nineteenth century and on into the twentieth. The authoritarian, collectivist thrust of this philosophy resulted in no small measure from revulsion against the French Revolution's reign of terror, a revolution predicated on the tenets of bourgeois liberalism. See Kuhn 1967:311-312.

18. Kant's attempted insulation of the moral will from natural motives, propensities of character, and cultural influences can also be related to the seventh philosophical source of nihilism: the primacy of will. I will examine this connection in the next section.

19. Locke sometimes seems to want to say, for example, that moral principles are

completely reducible to matters of fact, i.e., that the goodness of an act can be calculated on the basis of the amount of pleasure it produces or can be expected to produce. But he also insists that an act is *morally* good only if God intended that it be accompanied by pleasure. In this latter case, the pleasure provides incentive to do the good, but the good does not consist in the accompanying pleasure. Whether the moral goodness of an act is then grounded in the arbitrary will of God or in some principle or principles perceived by divine reason remains unclear (see Aaron 1965:257-261).

20. This latter point conflicts with Lock's claim in *An Essay Concerning Human Understanding* about the nature and derivation of moral principles. Copleston captures the gist of Hume's criticism of the view that morality is founded on the relations of ideas, or on a type of reasoning analogous to mathematical deductions, with this statement:

> [I]t is clear, if we keep an eye on concrete moral experience, that when a man makes a moral judgment there is an element of immediacy which is not accounted for on the rationalist interpretation of ethics. Morality is more akin to aesthetics than to mathematics. It is truer to say that we 'feel' values than that we deduce values or arrive at our moral judgments by a process of logical reasoning from abstract principles (1964:Vol. V, Pt. II, 143).

Hume himself observes that "[m]orality is . . . more properly felt than judg'd of; tho' this feeling or sentiment is commonly so soft and gentle, that we are apt to confound it with an idea, according to our common custom of taking all things for the same, which have any near resemblance to each other" (1980:470).

21. In those cases where a teleological view of nature continues to be upheld, as in the thought of Hutcheson, it is not an intrinsic teleology of the type endorsed by Aristotle but an extrinsic teleology, whereby God has designed the natural world and our faculties to a good end. Belief in the presence of value in nature depends crucially, therefore, upon belief in God's providential ordering and design (see Norton 1982:89-91). Although influenced by Hutcheson in many ways, Hume strongly objects to his teleological view of nature and human nature. "I cannot agree," he states in a letter to Hutcheson written on September 17, 1739, "to your Sense of *Natural*. 'Tis founded on Final Causes; which is a Consideration, that appears to me pretty uncertain & unphilosophical" (quoted Norton 1982:149). Norton comments at one place that Hume inhabited "the world left by Galileo, Descartes, and Hobbes, and that was a world in which there seemed to be nothing, or nothing extrahuman, to which moral claims could correspond" (1982:309).

Hutcheson's view recalls the second religious source of nihilism: the assumption that if there are any values in nature, they must be externally imposed. Either values are conferred on the natural order by God, or they are entirely absent there. In the second case, they can only be located in human subjectivity. This assumption and the assumption about the dichotomy of fact and value with which it is closely linked, have become deeply rooted in the modern mind, so much so as to inhibit serious consideration of the possibility that such things as intrinsic ends or values exist in nature.

22. I say in his "basic" moral theory because there is also a utilitarian strand in
Hume's ethics, one not fully integrated with the intuitive or affective aspect of it I
shall stress here. This utilitarian strand comes out strongly in his development of
the idea of justice as an "artificial" virtue (see Hume 1980:484-501). Even here,
however, Hume argues that it is because the characters of some persons have a
tendency to promote the good of humankind that they elicit in us, through the
operation of sympathy, moral pleasure. The ultimate appeal, therefore, is still to
immediate moral feeling, and only indirectly to considerations of utility (see
Norton 1982:119; Hume 1980:577, 618-620).

23. Note also in this connection the following passages from the *Treatise*: "'Tis
evident, that when we praise any actions, we regard only the motives that
produced them, and consider the actions as signs or indications of certain
principles in the mind or temper. The external performance has no merit. We
must look within to find the moral quality." Or again: "A virtuous motive is
requisite to render an action virtuous" (1980:477-478).

24. Anthony Flew interprets Hume in this way and admits to sometimes wanting "to
describe the *Treatise* as Hume's *Language, Truth and Logic* (Flew 1966:286). The
book by A.J. Ayer (first published in 1936; second edition, 1946) to which Flew
alludes defends an emotivist theory of ethics closely resembling Russell's theory
described in Chapter Two above. Flew also says of Hume,

> No doubt he ought to have said, boldly and consistently, something like: that when we
> say *This is wrong* we are not stating anything, not even that we have certain feelings,
> but rather we are giving vent to our feelings; or that when we say *He ought to resign* we
> are again not saying anything, but instead uttering some rather devious sort of
> crypto-command. But years of labor and ingenuity have been needed fully to develop
> such fashionable and sophisticated moves (1966:283).

For Flew, then, Hume is well on the way to the emotivistic subjectivism I
described earlier as a type of moral nihilism; he simply lacked the clarity of vision
to push his theory consistently through to its logical conclusion.

25. Norton seeks throughout his book *David Hume: Common-Sense Moralist,
Sceptical Metaphysician* to counter the view that Hume's ethics rests on a purely
emotive basis. He does so by arguing for several important roles played by reason
in ensuring the right background and conditions for dependable activations of the
moral sense. One of these roles is to provide "us with a full complement of the
facts relevant to the [moral] situation." Norton goes on to state that, for Hume,
"[f]eeling a particular moral sentiment is the subjective correlate which functions
as the sign of an objective correlate, some publicly available state of affairs"
(1982:130-131). But it is just the status and reliability of such publicly available
states of affairs that Hume's empiricist epistemology calls into fundamental
question. Therefore, to point out that "it is not by sentiment alone that we
recognize" moral distinctions, and that these "sentiments depend upon reason"
(Norton 1982:130), is to safeguard Hume's theory from one kind of problem (an
emotivism unchecked by rational scrutiny) only to open it to the equally

troublesome difficulty of giving a crucial role in moral judgments to a reason the philosopher has elsewhere shown to be notoriously unreliable. The two themes of Hume's having developed a case for moral realism by insulating ethical appraisals from the critical doubts about the competency of reason that pervade the first Book of the *Treatise*, and yet of his having avoided a purely emotivistic theory by allocating an important role to reason in the ethical theory of the third Book, are developed side-by-side by Norton with no apparent recognition of their mutually contradictory import.

26. Not only does Kant's opposition between theoretical and practical reason continue the alienation of human beings from nature seen earlier in the philosophy of Descartes; and not only does Mill's ethics, when combined with his metaphysics, swallow humans into the efficient causal forces of nature viewed as a deterministic system. Both Kant and Mill also suppose that if an absolute foundation for ethics cannot be discovered in the subjectivity of the isolated individual, then complete moral relativism (i.e., moral nihilism) must result. Because, as we have seen, the individual taken apart from historical and cultural surroundings is a mere figment of philosophical imagination, their supposition, if left unchallenged, has the effect of pushing us toward nihilism. Also, to assume, as they do, that there are only the two options of timeless moral absolutism or total relativism means that failure to find a basis for the first must doom us to the second.

27. When so stated, the point might seem obvious, but there are those today who continue to dispute it. For example, Fred Plum and Donald Pfaff hypothesize that "[t]he increasing explanatory powers of the neural and behavioral sciences may eventually offer for the first time the opportunity for *a closed logical system rationalizing choices of primary values*. Naturalistic ethics, an field of ethical philosophy, deals with this possibility but is poorly elaborated." Pfaff later speaks favorably of the view that "the neural and behavioral sciences may contribute fundamentally to the understanding of values." The means, he explains, that "ethical behavior is a factual matter susceptible to scientific explanation." He is confident that "neuroscience offers the opportunity to construct logically closed arguments which rationalize our choices among values." By understanding "some of the mechanisms involved in the ethical aspects of an ethical act, and based especially on the limitations of our nervous system," we may also come to understand why we are and *should be* the ethical creatures we are" (emphasis added). Pfaff apparently thinks that to comprehend, "neurophysiologically, how the ethical aspect of an ethical behavior is generated" is the same thing as to show why it is justified. Throughout his discussion, however, such putative moral goods as biological adaptation and survival, and the primacy of the group over the individual, are simply assumed, which means that implicit ethical premises, whose crucial role he seems not to notice, are operative in his reasoning. Without these premises, the scientific solutions to ethical problems he endorses would lose most, if not all, of their seeming plausibility. What he really highlights, for the most part, are means to assumed ends rather than factual derivations of the ends themselves (see Pfaff 1983:7, 141-142; Chs. 1 and 10, *passim*).

28. Kant does struggle with this problem in his *Critique of Judgment*, but his conclusion there is to locate in human subjectivity the aspects of lived nature that

408		The Specter of the Absurd

cannot fit into the Newtonian description. These aspects are the effects of nature upon us, not traits of nature as objectively conceived. Thus, the dualistic portrayal of nature and human life that emerges from the first two *Critiques* is carried into the third one.

29. Of course, many outcomes and qualities in nature may be relatively neutral with respect to value; that is, little or no value (or disvalue) may attach to them.

30. Whitehead's *Process and Reality* and W. H. Thorpe's *Purpose in a World of Chance* are other attempts to recover something like Aristotle's immanent teleology in nature. The second book, published in 1978 and authored by a Cambridge University animal ethologist, is deeply influenced by Whitehead's work and intended to be an answer to Monod's *Chance and Necessity*. Thorpe places considerable emphasis on aspects of animal behavior he interprets as consciously end-directed or purposive, and he argues that these aspects have affected the evolutionary process. "[F]or creatures having the power to choose, experiment with, and learn about different environments, necessity need no longer be spelt with a capital N" (1978:33). Mechanistic explanations, even when combined with elements of chance, as in Monod's system, cannot capture the full meaning of nature. Thorpe contends that "habits, traditions, and behavioural inventions must have played an ever increasing role in the evolutionary story as the animals mounted the ladder of complexity. Such formative forces helped them to achieve new adjustments," aided animals in their adaptations to their peculiar niches, and "enabled them increasingly to control" the environments of those niches. This course of development "has led to man's present, and in some ways disastrous, domination of the globe" (1978:75). A metaphysical approach to nature is needed, therefore, that can explain the presence and role of telic activity in nature, and explain it more convincingly than Monod's mechanistic viewpoint does. Thorpe regards Whitehead's metaphysics as an outstanding example of such an approach (1978:104-111).

31. In addition to what I have already said about Hume's failure to convince us of the universality of his moral sentiments, see MacIntyre's discussion of this same issue. MacIntyre argues that Hume's ethics turns out to be, in many respects, a defense "of the prejudices of the Hanoverian ruling elite," and thus that, far from being universal, it is an expression of "the local morality of parts of eighteenth-century northern Europe." A symptom of this provincialism in Hume's ethics is, according to MacIntyre's analysis, the heavy emphasis Hume lays on the rights of property and inheritance. MacIntyre finds it significant that Adam Smith, who also focused on supposedly universal moral sentiments in the development of his own ethical outlook, arrived at a different catalogue of the virtues than did Hume. Appealing to the passions as the basis of a universal system of ethics, therefore, begins "a movement towards and into a situation where there are no longer any clear criteria" of moral judgment (1981:215, 218-219).

32. That this criticism can be levelled against both Hume and Kant is ironic, in view of the fact that each endeavored to apply to epistemology, metaphysics, and ethics a mode of analysis based on what he understood to be the method of natural science, as described and exemplified principally by Newton. Hume, emphasizing the empirical side of that method, sought to resolve complex phenomena into their rudimentary constituents or empirical givens (e.g., sensate

impressions or distinctively moral sentiments), while Kant, stressing the method's mathematical side, sought to identify and account for "synthetic *a priori*" principles of theoretical and practical reason. Their investigations led them to question, however, not only the primacy of science but also its epistemological (Hume) or metaphysical (Kant) dependability. In their hands, the use of the scientific method had the surprising effect of undermining the authority of science itself. That undermining was not an unmitigated disaster from their standpoint, however, because it provided a way of dealing with an anxiety that can only be described as "existential": the anxiety to accord a place of central, irreducible importance to the valuative ingredients of experience. In the schizophrenic tension between their scientistic predilections and their felt need to uphold the autonomy and absoluteness of moral norms, the systems of Hume and Kant dramatically illustrate a continuing anxiety of modern times.

33. Although den Ouden takes Kant as the starting point for his sketch of the "philosophical landscape" out of which Nietzsche's central theme of the will to power grew, he is well aware "that a more complete study would push much further back into the history of ideas" (1982:66).

34. Thus, even to speak of "ends" or "goals" is misleading. No lures of the future can exist in Hobbes' system, only pushes from the past. These efficient causal pushes can, however, create dispositions to act that culminate in actions in circumstances sufficient to make them do so. Human beings are natural machines in a mechanistic universe, and all causality, including that involved in human activity, results from contiguous impacts of moving bodies, with no vacuum or action at a distance. As Burtt expresses it, for Hobbes "[e]verything that exists is a particular body; everything that happens a particular motion" (1954:133). Obviously, there is no room for teleology in such a view of nature or of human life.

35. We can perhaps go even further than this, although neither Hobbes nor Hume does so explicitly, and say that because reasoning results from our volitions (as it must, if it is to be regarded as a type of action) and these, in turn, are causally determined, then our processes of reasoning and the conclusions we draw on their basis must also be determined. This analysis would imply an even more radical priority of our volitions over our reasons, so radical in fact, as to seem to eliminate any meaningful distinction between being causally influenced to believe something and having good (or bad) *reasons* for believing it. All so-called reasons would now have to be regarded, literally, as "compelling reasons," i.e., as mere efficient causes in clever disguise. The point holds whether we are talking about an individual's attempt to defend or evaluate the rational character of his own beliefs, or some one else's critical assessment of that individual's stated beliefs. The conclusions at which both arrive are nothing more than the effects of the efficient causal factors operative in their respective environments, heredities, and characters—the third having been shaped in its entirety by the interworkings of the other two.

36. Kant argues, in *Religion Within the Limits of Reason Alone*, that our susceptibilities to evil are greatly reinforced by life in society, and that the remedy for this plight must also be societal, namely, an "ethical commonwealth" presided over by God as righteous Judge and providing a much-needed context of

encouragement and incentive for moral renovation. These claims seem inconsistent with his stress in that same work (and elsewhere) on the radical independence of the individual human will from external circumstances or internal causal motivations, and hence, on its unmitigated culpability for the evil deeds it performs and the corrupt disposition it creates, on the one hand, and its unqualified capacity for wholesale self-reform, on the other. It is noteworthy that Kant does not finally abandon humans to their raw volitions or solitary moral exertions, showing his conception of freedom to be more circumspect and realistic than that of the Sartre of *Being and Nothingness* (although at the price of evident inconsistency). See my discussion of Kant's views on the evil influences of society, the nature and role of the ethical commonwealth, and the latter's "schematization" by historical religious communities, in 1981:89-96.

37. This aspect of the will to power also implicitly (and quite legitimately) warns against too Apollonian repressions of basic human drives or instincts, such as the sexual instinct, in the name of morality or religion. Thus, Nietzsche roundly condemns the "despisers of the body" whose "other worldly" preoccupations make them yearn to "turn away from life" and die. Creativity for him, as den Ouden comments, is not only a celebration of the creative will, but of the earth and the body as well. These are the concrete settings of our life in the world, within which our creative powers must be exercised (Nietzsche 1954:146-147; quoted den Ouden 1982:117). One of the most striking manifestations of sexual repression in Nietzsche's century was the view that the sexual instinct plays, or ought to play, no important role in the consciousness or life of women. For a discussion of adamant defenses of this view, in the face of all controverting evidence, by physicians, moralists, religious leaders, and others in the nineteenth century, see Gay 1984:153-160.

38. The romantic concept of the artistic genius is presented by Kant in his third *Critique*, when he says that "genius is a *talent* for producing that for which no definite rule can be given; it is not a mere aptitude for what can be learned by a rule. Hence *originality* must be its first property." This originality cannot be taught; it can only be exemplified in great works of art. By contrast, Kant insists that we can give definite rules for scientific theorizing, arguing

> that Newton could make all his steps, from the first elements of geometry to his own great and profound discoveries, intuitively plain and definite as regards consequence, not only to himself but to everyone else . . . . In science, then, the greatest discoverer only differs in degree from his laborious imitator and pupil, but he differs specifically from him whom nature has gifted for beautiful art (1951:150-152).

For a different view that draws scientific and artistic (as well as philosophical) creativity much more closely together, stressing their elements of commonality rather than their differences, see Crosby and Williams, "Creative Problem-Solving in Physics, Philosophy, and Painting: Three Case Studies," in Amsler 1987:168-214.

39. On the explicitly egoistic and despotic implications Nietzsche sometimes draws from his theme of the overcoming of morality by the higher man—one side of his idea of the will to power—see Schutte 1984, Chs. 6 and 7.

40. A blatant recent expression of this dream, and one that, as William Leiss comments, "simply ignores all disturbing elements," is the following passage from Earl Murphy's book *Governing Nature* (1967: 11-12).

> Man's relationship with the renewing elements in his natural environment is at an important stage in history. It appears that a total control of nature is possible in a not very distant future. Many ecologists deny this, claiming that nature is too complex to be reflected in the simulation of any computer technology. Such assertions indicate that we have not yet managed to describe nature completely. Until the subject has been fully described, it is not likely that the controller can freely manipulate it with a superiority to natural processes. But the means of acquiring that complete description are already well developed, as are the economic and social conditions that make a greater control of nature necessary (Quoted Leiss 1974:18).

Not only does this statement assume a conception of knowledge or reason as instrumental to manipulation and control, it also takes for granted the right of human beings, purely for the sake of their own interests, to exert unrestricted and ever-increasing domination over the whole of nature. Some of the consequences of this reckless mentality, both actual and potential, are vividly portrayed in such books as David Ehrenfeld's *The Arrogance of Humanism* (1981; first published in 1978), Jeremy Rifkin's *Algeny: A New Word—a New World* (1984; first published in 1983), and Rifkin's *Declaration of a Heretic* (1985). Leiss's *The Domination of Nature* (1974; first published in 1972), although more measured and restrained in its tone than the other three books, contains many of the same kinds of warning they do of dire threats to nature (and human life) posed by unchecked technological willfulness.

Leiss's book takes particular pains to spell out (drawing especially on Max Horkheimer's work) connections between the theme of the domination of nature, on the one hand, and tendencies toward elitist control of human life on the other. For example, sophisticated technology and large-scale exploitation of natural resources require highly organized social systems that are apt to make increasing use of "terroristic and nonterroristic measures for manipulating consciousness and for internalizing heteronomous needs," thus extending "the sway of society over the inner life of the person" (1974:154). Leiss also analyzes the relations between mounting violence on a worldwide scale and the Enlightenment dream of bending nature to the human will. For example, extensive technological development requires coal, oil, and other energy resources that are often located in abundance only in certain parts of the world, and this creates fierce competition for control of those parts of the world by nation-states. Such competition, in turn, helps to bring about a mutually escalating arms race among powerful states that not only further exacerbates the exploitation of nature, but also favors the ascendancy of an elite of technical and political managers who justify even the most crass manipulations of citizens and the political process in the name of national defense (156-158).

The ironic outcome of all of this is well stated by Leiss:

> [I]n the process of globalized competition men become the servants of the very instruments fashioned for their own mastery over nature, for the tempo of

technological innovation can no longer be controlled even by the most advanced societies, but rather responds to the shifting interplay of worldwide forces (158).

The sense of the once confident controller having become the controlled, and of civilization now being at the mercy of forces that, with the aid of advanced technology, threaten to sweep it to destruction, has become widespread in recent times. In extreme form, this view might be termed *historical nihilism*, i.e., an attitude of complete hopelessness about the future of humankind or of despair at the ability of humans to avert coming disaster. I believe that the prevalence of this attitude goes a long way toward explaining our current susceptibility to other types of nihilism, especially existential nihilism.

    Leiss ties together the three themes of the domination of nature, of preoccupation with techniques for the control of human life, and of global conflict as follows: "Political mastery over human nature in all its diverse cultural forms is sought in response to the intensified social conflict which in turn depends in part on a growing mastery over external nature." The relationships among these three themes are, as Leiss notes, "never unidirectional; reciprocal interaction always exists" (158-159). Enlightenment thinkers envisioned the scientific control of natural processes, and the utilization of methods of social engineering based on scientific principles, as paving the way for a new era of human existence in which social conflicts would be radically reduced. Little did they imagine the opposite effect that Leiss brings so glaringly into focus.

41. It might seem that the self would have to be dualistically conceived in order for it to play such a role, but this is not necessarily the case. The concept of the self Whitehead lays out in his *Process and Reality*, for example, is consistent with the intermediate view of freedom presented in Figures 1 and 2; but Whitehead's self is not Cartesian; that is, it does not belong to an order of reality separate from the world of nature.

42. In systems of thought in which the primacy of the will is not assumed, but it has been concluded that no universal moral principles will be discovered in the subjectivity of the individual (where alone it is believed they would have to be found), it is the emotions that have generally been granted ascendancy: hence, for example, the emotivist theory of ethics. The cases of Hobbes and Hume show a close possible relationship between emotivism and volitionism. Both of these philosophers view the volitions as urges to action that either inevitably spring from, or are indistinguishable from, basic desires and emotions. Sartre, in contrast, contends that we are entirely responsible for our emotions and that they influence us only to the extent that we freely allow them to do so. His response to the extreme position of determinism is thus to develop an equally extreme stance of his own.

Chapter 11

1. In his recent book *Science and Religion,* Rolston makes the point that the possibility of suffering comes with the gift of sentience, even in animal life. He observes that

sentience, with its counterpart, suffering, is an incipient form of love and freedom. A neural animal can love something in its world and is free to seek this, a capacity greatly advanced over anything known in immobile, insentient plants . . . . The appearance of sentience is the appearance of caring, when the organism is united with or torn from its loves (1987:288).

To be torn from one's loves is to suffer, a possibility that must be accepted if love is to exist at all.

2. Other factors were also at work in Germany's case, of course, such as humiliating defeat in war and the famous "War Guilt Clause" of the Treaty of Versailles, to say nothing of heavy reparations and extensive takeovers of territory.

3.. For a balanced discussion of animal suffering that contrasts with the sweeping denunciations of Schopenhauer on this theme, see Rolston 1987:133-146, 286-293. Rolston warns us against undue anthropomorphizing in our responses to animal pain, noting that "[a]nimals and birds typically have fewer nerve endings per surface area unit of skin . . . ." This suggests that "the level of consciousness, self-awareness, or experience, or whatever is the proper name for their experiential state, is very different from, more subdued than, less intense and coherent than our own" (139). He also notes that, although the evolutionary process involves struggle and pain, especially for some individual organisms, it subserves the good of species as a whole and is basically "prolife" in its results. Thus, "for all its borrowing and spending, little is wasted in biomass and energy" overall. Although "the element of suffering and tragedy is always there" in animal life, "especially as seen from the perspective of the local self," this element is "muted and transmuted in the systematic whole." And "for all the struggle, violence, and transition, there is abiding value" (136-137).

A third basic point Rolston makes about animal suffering is that animals with sentience and mobility "can suffer, but have more control over their circumstances. Indeed, the capacity to suffer is generally accompanied by possibilities of avoiding suffering, and some freedom and self-assertion" (136). His intent is not to explain away or minimize the problem of animal suffering, but to remind us of its positive aspects. The tragedy is there and resists glib justifications, but it is not a mere surd or an unqualified evil, as Schopenhauer believed.

Rolston also asserts that when belief in God disappears, the evil of inexplicable suffering remains, "and sometimes grows the more urgent and bleak" (187). I am inclined to take issue with the second part of this claim, because I think we may be better enabled to learn to live with and respond appropriately to the fact of suffering in the world when we do not attribute its creation to an all-knowing, all-loving, all-powerful God. For then we are not constantly tormented by the question of why such a God did not create the world differently, with far less pervasive suffering. As a result, we may be better equipped to deal with the experienced world as it is, the world as the given context of our experience for which there may be no more ultimate explanation, especially one in terms of deliberate intention and design. See again in this connection my third criticism of the Christian hope of a perfect afterlife, in Chapter Six, Section 3.

4. One does not have to be a genius or famous to live a creative and productive life.

The great majority of such lives make their contributions quietly and without fanfare, and yet with powerful effect on those around them.

5. The second claim is Hocking's, as we saw in Chapter Three, Section 4.

6. Tillich links this affirmation of life, which he calls "the courage to be," to both nature and grace. By the "biological argument," he says, the courage to be originates "in the vital power which is a natural gift, a matter of biological fate." But "[r]eligiously speaking, it is a matter of grace." In any event, "courage is a possibility dependent not on will power or insight but on a gift which precedes action" (1953:84-85).

7. MacIntyre makes this point in discussing the historical roots of existentialism. See Warnock 1971:56-58.

8. The pluralistic outlook implicit in my discussion of this third lesson of nihilism and that I explicitly defended in Chapter Nine is itself one perspective among others, one with which exponents of different perspectives, i.e., the various brands of absolutism or relativism, would vigorously disagree. Thus, to take the position of pluralism does not mean having naively to believe that pluralism is not itself a perspective, or that the pluralist can somehow transcend and neutrally assess all perspectives. There is also another possible misconception of pluralism that I should warn against. To be a consistent advocate of pluralism, one's own philosophical stance does not have to be bland and noncommittal, and thus devoid of specific content. To cite my own case, many of my personal convictions stand out plainly in the approaches, assertions, and arguments that run through this book, and it should be obvious to the reader that I am deeply committed to them. These convictions are part of my general perspective on the world, and they are in no way inconsistent with my pluralistic attitude toward other perspectives.

   Perhaps "convictional openness" would be a useful complementary term to designate the position I am arguing for, because it might help to correct a tendency to interpret the term *pluralism* as connoting a kind of vague, wishy-washy, "anything goes" outlook with no positive or firmly held commitments of its own, or criticisms of the viewpoints of others. Bernard Loomer wisely remarks that "tenativity and openness are not only compatible with deep commitment, but they are essential qualities of it" (1978:529). These two traits of mind are essential because they keep deep commitment from degenerating into intellectual arrogance. The latter might be defined as the muddled notion that intensity of belief or felt obviousness of assumption are by themselves sufficient guarantees of truth, and thus that the person or group marked by strong conviction has no need for further inquiry and nothing to learn from those who adhere to other points of view. Pluralism or convictional openness has a growing edge that intellectual arrogance lacks; the latter is smugly content with what it has already attained.

9. Not all thinkers I have associated with nihilistic themes stress the importance of human freedom. Schopenhauer, for example, is a strong defender of cosmic determinism and more consistent on this subject than is Nietzsche. But we are interested at present only in one strain of nihilistic philosophy, namely, that which gives expression to what I am calling the fourth lesson of nihilism.

10. It is of crucial importance, however, that we not make Sartre's mistake of

overestimating the extent of our individual freedom. Bernard Loomer emphasizes that

> we are not only free. We are also driven by irrational impulses and destructive compulsions. We are sometimes held fast in the vise of emotional and intellectual fixations. We are subject to the inertial power of unresponsiveness. In our insecurity and anxiety we often cling to the good that we have rather than risk it all for something greater. If we are cornered in one of life's dark alleys we may see with our own horrified eyes the rise of the furies within us. In our felt entrapment we may have the depressing feeling that our civilized attitudes are a veneer that camouflage the hidden demons that mock at our pretensions (Loomer, in Sibley and Gunter 1978:533).

He also notes that the "demons who swell within each of us may not be solely of our own creation. They may also have a communal origin. There are socialized demons or communal shadows" (533; see also 534-535).

11. Such experience and counsel is often, of course, contained in texts.

12. Wolterstorff makes this point about those who share in the Christian commitment, showing that it would be a mistake to expect that all Christians should (or could) think and act always in the same ways.

> What I ought to be doing today by way of following Christ differs from what you ought to be doing, and from what I ought to have been doing when I was younger. Likewise, what I am obliged to believe as a follower of Christ differs from what someone else is obliged to believe, and differs from what I as a child was obliged to believe. So authentic Christian commitment as a whole, but also the belief-content thereof, is relative to persons and times (1984:74-75).

Another interpreter of Christianity, Søren Kierkegaard, perhaps has something similar to this in mind when he proclaims that "[i]t is subjectivity that Christianity is concerned with, and it is only in subjectivity that its truth exists, if it exists at all; objectively, Christianity has absolutely no existence." Or again, "The passion of the infinite is precisely subjectivity, and thus subjectivity becomes the truth" (*Concluding Unscientific Postscript*, in Kierkegaard 1951:208, 214). In other words, the truth of Christianity is realized, in Kierkegaard's view, only when it is appropriated into the concrete life of the individual and becomes for that individual, not abstract doctrines generally conceived, but the specific truth of that individual's personal existence, in all its stubborn particularity.

13. Because I am assuming here the concept of communal or relational individuals, and thus of uniquely personal ways of responding and contributing to a shared environment, it should be obvious that I am not commending a purely inward-directed, relativistic, narcissistic type of "values clarification" or "personal self-fulfillment." I am talking about encouraging persons to develop their unique potentialities and perspectives on the whole for the sake of contributing most effectively to the whole. In order for them to do this, they must be urged to learn as much about the different aspects of their own culture as they can and, in particular, to understand as fully as they can its valuative dimensions. Persons

with a highly informed cultural awareness are in a much better position to contribute creatively to the evolution of culture than are those relatively ignorant of their complex cultural heritage. It also helps immeasurably to this end to be schooled in the history, beliefs, norms, and practices of other cultures, because one may then become more conscious of creative possibilities in one's own culture.

Seen in this light, "value-free education" is an oxymoron. As a university professor, for example, I have the responsibility not only to teach my students about fundamental cultural values but also to embody those values. My embodiment of cultural values should not be slavish, because I also have the obligation to show in what I profess and how I behave that it is entirely proper for individuals to respond to these values, and to their cultural heritage as a whole, in ways that reflect their own firsthand processes of thought and backgrounds of experience. But it is not enough that a student's responses be developed in isolation. Students must also be encouraged to share their thoughts and conclusions with others, continually putting them to the test of public discussion and criticism. The classroom can be one arena for this kind of shared inquiry, but it also needs to be instilled as a habit of life.

14. The denial of a universal human nature is also a dominant theme of Stirner's philosophy, as we have seen. Hence, much of what I say here about Sartre applies to Stirner as well.

15. From the claim that the only world we can know is one in relation to us, it does not follow that this relational world must *center* on us. As I emphasized in Chapter Five, Section 2, the experienced world exhibits and sustains an extraordinary variety of forms of existence beyond the existence of human beings. The world as seen from the perspective of our current thought and experience is a world of which we perceive ourselves to be only a small part.

16. This is the central thesis of Britton's admirable book *Philosophy and the Meaning of Life*. Britton also develops four important criteria of a meaningful life that I have endorsed and drawn upon in earlier parts of this book. Thus, even though the forms of meaningful life are diverse, it does not follow that a life is made meaningful simply because one asserts that it is so or believes it to be so. Such an assertion or belief can be mistaken.

Bibliography

Aaron, Richard I. (1965). *John Locke*, 2nd edition. Oxford: The Clarendon Press.

Alperowitz, Gar (1986). "The Coming Break in Liberal Consciousness." *Christianity and Crisis*, XLVI/3 (March 3), 59-65.

Amsler, Mark (ed.) (1987). *Creativity and the Imagination. Studies in Science and Culture*, III. Newark, Del.: The University of Delaware Press; London and Toronto: Associated University Presses.

Appleman, Philip (ed.) (1970). *Darwin: A Norton Critical Edition*. New York: W. W. Norton and Company.

Arendt, Hannah (1959). *The Human Condition: A Study of the Central Dilemmas Facing Modern Man*. New York: Doubleday and Company, Doubleday Anchor Books.

Aristotle (1941). *The Basic Works of Aristotle*, Richard McKeon (ed.). New York: Random House.

Aswell, Edward C. "A Note on Thomas Wolfe." In Thomas Wolfe (1941). *The Hills Beyond*. New York and London: Harper and Brothers, 349-386.

Aurelius, Marcus (1965). *Meditations*, George Long (trans.). South Bend, Ind.: Regnery/Gateway.

Ayer, Alfred Jules (1946). *Language, Truth and Logic*, 2nd edition. New York: Dover Publications.

Baier, Kurt (1965). *The Moral Point of View: A Rational Basis for Ethics*, abridged edition. New York: Random House.

————"The Meaning of Life." In Steven Sanders and David R. Cheney (eds.) (1980). *The Meaning of Life: Questions, Answers and Analysis*. Englewood Cliffs, N.J.: Prentice-Hall, Inc., 47-63.

Ball, George (1984). Letter in *The New York Review of Books*, XXXI/13 (March 29), 48.

Barrett, William (1958). *Irrational Man*. Garden City, N.Y.: Doubleday and Company, Doubleday Anchor Books.

————(1979). *The Illusion of Technique*. Garden City, N.Y.: Anchor Press/Doubleday, Anchor Books.

————and Aiken, Henry D. (eds.) (1962). *Philosophy in the Twentieth Century*, 2 vols. New York: Random House.

Barth, John (1969). *The End of the Road*. New York: Bantam Books.

Bellah, Robert N.; Madsen, Richard; Sullivan, William M.; Swidler, Ann; and Tipton, Steven M. (1985). *Habits of the Heart: Individualism and Commitment in American Life*. Berkeley, Calif.: University of California Press.

Berger, Peter L.; Berger, Brigette; and Kellner, Hansfried (1973). *The Homeless Mind: Modernization and Consciousness*. New York: Random House.

Berkeley, George (1965). *Berkeley's Philosophical Writings*, David M. Armstrong (ed.). New York: Collier Books.

Berlin, Isaiah (1958). *Two Concepts of Liberty*. Oxford: The Clarendon Press.

Bernstein, Richard J. (1983). *Beyond Objectivism and Relativism: Science, Hermeneutics, and Praxis*. Philadelphia, Penn.: Pennsylvania University Press.

Berofsky, Bernard (ed.) (1966). *Free Will and Determinism*. New York: Harper and Row.

Beversluis, John (1985). *C. S. Lewis and the Search for Rational Religion*. Grand Rapids, Mich.: William B. Eerdman's Publishing Company.

Blocker, H. Gene (1974). *The Meaning of Meaninglessness*. The Hague: Martinus Nijhoff.

————(1979). *The Metaphysics of Absurdity*. Washington, D. C.: University Press of America.

Boethius, Anicius Manlius Severinus (1962). *The Consolation of Philosophy*, Richard Green (trans.). Indianapolis, Ind.: Bobbs-Merrill Company, The Library of Liberal Arts.

Bouwsma, O. K. "Descartes' Evil Genius." In Alexander Sesonske and Noel Fleming (eds.) (1966). *Meta-Meditations: Studies in Descartes*. Belmont, Calif.: Wadsworth Publishing Company, 26-36.

Bradley, F. H. (1969). *Appearance and Reality*. London, Oxford, and New York: Oxford University Press.

Brillouin, Leon (1964). *Scientific Uncertainty and Information*. New York and London: Academic Press.

Britton, Karl (1969). *Philosophy and the Meaning of Life*. London, Cambridge, and New York: Cambridge University Press.

Broad, William J. (1984). "U. S. Plans Massive Study of 'Nuclear Winter'." *The Denver Post*, XCIII/11 (August 12), 1C, 5C (first published in *The New York Times*).

Brock, D. Heyward and Harward, Ann (eds.) (1984). *The Culture of Biomedicine. Studies in Science and Culture*, I. Newark, Del.: University of Delaware Press; London and Toronto: Associated University Presses.

Brooks, Van Wyck (1932). *The Life of Emerson*. New York: E. P. Dutton and Company.

Brower, Daniel R. (1975). *Training the Nihilists: Education and Radicalism in Tsarist Russia*. Ithaca, N.Y.: Cornell University Press.

Brown, Delwin (1985). "Struggle till Daybreak: On the Nature of Authority in Theology." *The Journal of Religion*, LXV/1 (January), 15-32.

Brown, Harold I. (1979). *Perception, Theory and Commitment*. Chicago, Ill.: University of Chicago Press.

Burr, John R. and Goldinger, Milton (eds.) (1976). *Philosophy and Contemporary Issues*, 2nd edition. New York: Macmillan Publishing Company; London: Collier Macmillan publishers.

Burtt, E. A. (ed.) (1939). *The English Philosophers From Bacon to Mill*. New York: Random House, The Modern Library.

———(1954). *The Metaphysical Foundations of Modern Physical Science*, revised edition. Garden City, N.Y.: Doubleday and Company.

Cahn, Steven M. and Shatz, David (eds.) (1982). *Contemporary Philosophy of Religion*. London, Oxford, and New York: Oxford University Press.

Callicott, J. Baird (ed.) (1987). *A Companion to the Sand County Almanac*. Madison, Wisc.: University of Wisconsin Press.

Camus, Albert (1947). *Caligula and Cross Purpose*, Stuart Gilbert (trans.). London: A New Directions Book.

————(1955). *The Myth of Sisyphus and Other Essays*, Justin O'Brien (trans.). New York: Alfred A. Knopf, a Borzoi Book.

————(1975). *The Stranger,* Stuart Gilbert (trans.). New York: Alfred A. Knopf.

Cassirer, Ernst (1961). *The Philosophy of the Enlightenment,* Fritz C. A. Koelin and James P. Pettegrove (trans.). Boston, Mass.: Beacon Press.

Catalano, Joseph S. (1980). *A Commentary on Jean-Paul Sartre's "Being and Nothingness".* Chicago, Ill.: The University of Chicago Press.

Chappell, V. C. (ed.) (1966). *Hume: A Collection of Critical Essays.* Garden City, N.Y.: Doubleday and Company, Anchor Books.

Choron, Jacques (1963). *Death and Western Thought.* New York: Collier Books.

Christian, William A., Sr. "Some Aspects of Whitehead's Metaphysics." In Lewis S. Ford and George L. Kline (eds.) (1983). *Explorations in Whitehead's Philosophy.* New York: Fordham University Press, 31-44.

Cioran, E. M. (1975). *A Short History of Decay*, Richard Howard (trans.). Oxford: Basil Blackwell.

Cobb, John B., Jr. (1965). *A Christian Natural Theology, Based on the Thought of Alfred North Whitehead.* Philadelphia, Penn.: The Westminster Press.

————(1975). *Christ in a Pluralistic Age.* Philadelphia, Penn.: Westminster Press.

————(1982). *Beyond Dialogue: Toward a Mutual Transformation of Christianity and Buddhism.* Philadelphia, Penn.: Fortress Press.

Cochran, Charles Norris (1944). *Christianity and Classical Culture: A Study of Thought and Action from Augustus to Augustine.* London, Oxford, and New York: Oxford University Press.

Cohen, Morris (1964). *Reason and Nature*, 2nd edition. New York: The Free Press.

Collingwood, R. G. (1960). *The Idea of Nature.* London, Oxford, and New York: Oxford University Press, a Galaxy Book.

Copleston, Frederick (1962). *A History of Philosophy: Greece and Rome*, Vol. I, Part I. Garden City, N.Y.: Doubleday and Company, Image Books.

————(1963). *A History of Philosophy*, Vol. IV (*Modern Philosophy: Descartes to Leibniz*). Garden City, N.Y.: Doubleday and Company, Image Books.

————(1964). *A History of Philosophy,* Vol. V, Part I (*Modern Philosophers: The British Philosophers, Berkeley to Hume*). Garden City, N.Y.: Doubleday and Company, Image Books.

————(1965). *A History of Philosophy,* Vol. VII, Part II (*Modern Philosophy: Schopenhauer to Nietzsche*). Garden City, New York: Doubleday and Company, Image Books.

————(1966). *Contemporary Philosophy: Studies of Logical Positivism and Existentialism.* Westminster, Md.: The Newman Press.

————(1985). *A History of Philosophy,* Vols. VII, VIII, IX (3 volumes in 1: *Fichte to Nietzsche; Bentham to Russell; Main de Biran to Sartre*). Garden City, N.Y.: Doubleday and Company, Image Books.

————and Russell, Bertrand. "The Existence of God: A Debate." In Paul Edwards and Arthur Pap (eds.) (1965). *A Modern Introduction to Philosophy.* New York: The Free Press, 473-490.

Crosby, Donald A. (1981). *Interpretive Theories of Religion.* The Hague: Mouton Publishers.

————(1983). "Rychlak on Objectivity and Free Will." *New Ideas in Psychology*, I/3, 245-254.

————and Williams, Ron G. "Creative Problem-Solving in Physics, Philosophy, and Painting: Three Case Studies." In Mark Amsler (ed.) (1987). *Creativity and the Imagination. Studies in Science and Culture,* III. Newark, Del.: The University of Delaware Press; London and Toronto: Associated University Press, 168-214.

Dallmayr, Fred R. (1981). *Twilight of Subjectivity: Contributions to a Post-Individualist Theory of Politics.* Amherst, Mass.: University of Massachusetts Press.

Danto, Arthur (1965). *Nietzsche as Philosopher.* New York: The Macmil- Company.

Dauer, Edward A. (1986). "Market-Driven Law Ignores Social Values." *The Denver Post*, XCV/25 (August 25), 2B.

Desan, Wilfrid (1960). *The Tragic Finale: An Essay on the Philosophy of Jean-Paul Sartre.* New York: Harper and Row.

Descartes, René (1897-1910). *Oeuvres de Descartes*, published by Charles Adam and Paul Tannery, 12 vols. Paris: L. Cerf.

————(1967). *The Philosophical Works of Descartes*, Elizabeth S. Haldane and G. R. T. Ross (trans.). London, Cambridge, and New York: Cambridge University Press.

Dewey, John (1958). *Experience and Nature*. New York: Dover Publications.

————(1960). *The Quest for Certainty: A Study of the Relation of Knowledge and Action*. New York: C. P. Putnam's Sons, A Capricorn Book.

Dostoevsky, Fyodor (1931). *The Possessed,* Constance Garnett (trans.). New York: The Macmillan Company.

————(1933). *The Brothers Karamazov*, Constance Garnett (trans.), Avrahm Yarmolinsky (rev.); 3 vols. New York: The Limited Editions Club.

————"Notes from Underground," Constance Garnett (trans.). In Walter Kaufmann (ed.) (1956). *Existentialism from Dostoevsky to Sartre*. Cleveland, Oh. and New York: The World Publishing Company, Meridian Books, 52-82.

————(1967). *The Idiot*, Eva M. Martin (trans.). New York: E. P. Dutton and Company, Everyman's Library.

Durant, Will (1944). *Caesar and Christ: A History of Roman Civilization and of Christianity from Their Beginnings to A.D. 325*. Vol. III of Will and Ariel Durant, *The Story of Civilization*, 10 vols. New York: Simon and Schuster.

Edwards, Paul (ed.) (1967). *Encyclopedia of Philosophy,* 8 vols. in 4. New York: The Macmillan Company and The Free Press.

————and Pap, Arthur (eds.) (1965). *A Modern Introduction to Philosophy*. New York: The Free Press.

Ehrenfeld, David (1981). *The Arrogance of Humanism*. London, Oxford and New York: Oxford University Press.

Fandozzi, Phillip R. (1982). *Nihilism and Technology: A Heideggerian Investigation*. Washington, D. C.: University Press of America.

Faulconer, James E. and Williams, Richard N. (1985). "Temporality in Human Action: An Alternative to Positivism and Historicism." *American Psychologist*, XL/11 (September), 1179-1188.

Feyerabend, Paul (1978). *Science in a Free Society*. London: New Left Books.

Flew, Anthony. "On the Interpretation of Hume." In A. C. Chappell (ed.) (1966). *Hume: A Collection of Critical Essays*. Garden City, N.Y.: Doubleday and Company, 278-286.

Ford, Lewis S. and Kline, George L. (eds.) (1983). *Explorations in Whitehead's Philosophy*. New York: Fordham University Press.

Frankel, Charles (1965). *The Love of Anxiety and Other Essays*. New York: Harper and Row.

Gadamer, Hans-Georg (1975). *Truth and Method*. New York: Seabury Press.

Gassendi, Pierre (1658). *Opera Omnia*, 6 vols. Lugduni: Sumptibus L. Anisson et J. -B. Devenet.

Gay, Peter (1984). *Education of the Senses*. Vol. I of *The Bourgeois Experience: Victoria to Freud.* London, Oxford and New York: Oxford University Press.

Gide, André (1973). *The Counterfeiters; With Journal of "The Counterfeiters,"* Dorothy Bussy and Justin O'Brien (trans.). New York: Random House, Vintage Books.

Gingrich, Owen (ed.) (1975). *The Nature of Scientific Discovery: A Symposium Commemorating the 500th Anniversary of the Birth of Nicolaus Copernicus*. Washington, D. C.: Smithsonian Institution Press.

Godlove, Terry (1984). "In What Sense Are Religions Conceptual Frameworks?" *Journal of the American Academy of Religion*, LII/2 (June), 289-305.

Godwin, John (1978). *Murder U. S. A.: The Ways We Kill Other*. New York: Ballantine Books.

Goulder, Michael and Hick, John (1983). *Why Believe in God?* London: S.C.M. Press.

Gregory, Michael S. "Science and Humanities: Toward a New Worldview." In D. Heyward Brock and Ann Harward (eds.) (1984). *The Culture of Biomedicine. Studies in Science and Culture*, I. Newark, Del.: The University of Delaware Press; London and Toronto: Associated University Presses, 11-33.

Grene, Marjorie (1966). *The Knower and the Known*. New York: Basic Books.

Hall, A. Rupert (1981). *From Galileo to Newton*. New York: Dover Publications.

Hall, David (1982). *Eros and Irony: A Prelude to Philosophical Anarchism*. Albany, N. Y.: State University of New York Press.

Hampshire, Stuart (1983). "On The Trail of Nature." Review of Keith Thomas, *Man and the Natural World*, in *The New York Review of Books*, XXX/9 (June 2), 17-19.

Hartshorne, Charles (1937). *Beyond Humanism: Essays in the New Philosophy of Nature*. Chicago, Ill.: Willett Clark and Company.

Hauck, Richard Boyd (1971). *A Cheerful Nihilism: Confidence and "The Absurd" in American Humorous Fiction*. Bloomington, Ind.: Indiana University Press.

Hegel, Georg Wilhelm Friedrich (1929). *Hegel Selections*, Jacob Loewenberg (ed.). New York: Charles Scribner's Sons.

———(1954). *The Philosophy of Hegel,* Carl J. Friedrich (ed.). New York: Random House, The Modern Library.

Heidegger, Martin (1961). *An Introduction to Metaphysics,* Ralph Manheim (trans.). Garden City, N.Y.: Doubleday and Company, Anchor Books.

———(1962). *Being and Time*, John Macquarrie and Edward Robinson (trans.). London: S.C.M. Press.

Heller, Peter (1966). *Dialectics and Nihilism: Essays on Lessing, Nietzsche, Mann, and Kafka*. Amherst, Mass: University of Massachusetts Press.

Herbert, Lord Edward, of Cherbury (1937). *De Veritate*, Meyrick H. Carre (trans.). Bristol: Published for the University of Bristol by J. W. Arrowsmith, Ltd.

Hick, John (1963). *Philosophy of Religion*. Englewood Cliffs, N.J.: Prentice-Hall, Inc.

———"Evil, The Problem of." In Paul Edwards (ed.) (1967). *Encyclopedia of Philosophy,* III. New York: The Macmillan Company and The Free Press, 136-141.

———"Faith as Total Interpretation." In Keith Yandell (ed.) (1973). *God, Man, and Religion: Readings in the Philosophy of Religion*. New York:

McGraw-Hill Book Company, 529-541.

————"The New Map of the Universe of Faiths." In Steven M. Cahn and David Shatz (eds.) (1982). *Contemporary Philosophy of Religion.* London, Oxford, and New York: Oxford University Press, 278-290.

High, Dallas M. (1981). "Wittgenstein on Doubting and Groundless Believing." *The Journal of the American Academy of Religion,* XLIX/2 (June), 249-266.

Hingley, Ronald (1969). *Nihilists: Russian Radicals and Revolutionaries in the Reign of Alexander II, 1855-1881.* New York: Delacorte Press.

Hocking, William Ernest (1936). "Meanings of Life." *The Journal of Religion,* XVI/3 (July), 253-283.

Hofstadter, Albert. "On the Dialectical Phenomenology of Creativity," in Stanley Rosner and Lawrence Edwin Abt (eds.) (1974). *Essays in Creativity.* Croton-on-Hudson, N.Y.: North River Press, 113-149.

Holy Bible, Revised Standard Version (1952). New York: Thomas Nelson and Sons.

Hook, Sidney (1962). *From Hegel to Marx: Studies in the Intellectual Development of Karl Marx.* Ann Arbor, Mich.: University of Michigan Press.

Horkheimer, Max (1947). *Eclipse of Reason.* New York: Columbia University Press.

Hospers, John. "Free Will and Psychoanalysis." In Paul Edwards and Arthur Pap (eds.) (1965). *A Modern Introduction to Philosophy.* New York: The Free Press, 75-85.

Hospers, John. "What Means This Freedom?" In Bernard Berofsky (ed.) (1966). *Free Will and Determinism.* New York: Harper and Row, 26-45.

Hume, David (1957). *Dialogues Concerning Natural Religion,* Henry D. Aiken (ed.). New York: Hafner Publishing Company.

————(1975). *Enquiries Concerning Human Understanding and Concerning the Principles of Morals,* L.A. Selby-Bigge and P. H. Nidditch (eds.), third edition. London, Oxford, and New York: Oxford University Press.

————(1980). *A Treatise of Human Nature,* L. A. Selby-Bigge and P. H. Nidditch (eds.), second edition. London, Oxford and New York: Oxford University Press.

Husserl, Edmund (1960). *Cartesian Meditations: An Introduction to Phenomenology,* Dorion Cairns (trans.). The Hague: Martinus Nijhoff.

Huxley, Aldous (1958). *Brave New World*. New York: Bantam Books.

Hyman, Arthur and Walsh, James J. (eds.) (1980). *Philosophy in the Middle Ages: The Christian, Islamic, and Jewish Traditions.* Indianapolis, Ind.: Hackett Publishing Company.

James, Bernard (1973). *The Death of Progress*. New York: Alfred A. Knopf.

James, William (1920). *The Letters of William James*, Henry James (ed.), 2 vols. Boston, Mass.: The Atlantic Monthly Press.

————(1958). *The Varieties of Religious Experience*. New York: New American Library, A Mentor Book.

————(1967). *Essays in Radical Empiricism and A Pluralistic Universe*, 2 vols. in 1. Gloucester, Mass.: Peter Smith.

Janik, Allan and Toulmin, Stephen (1973). *Wittgenstein's Vienna*. New York: Simon and Schuster, A Touchstone Book.

Kafka, Franz (1969). *The Castle*, Willa and Edwin Muir, Eithne Wilkins, and Ernst Kaiser (trans.). New York: The Modern Library.

————(1978). *The Trial*, Willa and Edwin Muir (trans.). New York: Alfred A. Knopf.

Kant, Immanuel (1949). *Fundamental Principles of the Metaphysic of Morals*, Thomas K. Abbot, (trans.), Introduction by Marvin Fox. New York: The Liberal Arts Press.

————(1951). *Critique of Judgement*, J. H. Bernard (trans.). The Hafner Library of Classics, Number Fourteen. New York and London: Hafner Publishing Company.

————(1956). *Critique of Practical Reason*, Lewis White Beck (trans.). Indianapolis, Ind., and New York: The Bobbs-Merrill Company, A Liberal Arts Press Book.

————(1958). *Immanuel Kant's Critique of Pure Reason*, Norman Kemp Smith (trans.). London: Macmillan and Company; New York: St. Martin's Press.

————(1960). *Religion Within the Limits of Reason Alone*, Theodore M. Greene and Hoyt H. Hudson (trans.), Introductions by Greene and John R. Silber. New York: Harper and Row, Harper Torchbooks.

Kaplan, Morton A. (1971). *On Historical and Political Knowing: An Inquiry into Some Problems of Universal Law and Human Freedom.* Chicago, Ill.: The University of Chicago Press.

Kaufmann, Walter (ed.) (1956). *Existentialism from Dostoevsky to Sartre.* Cleveland, Oh. and New York: The World Publishing Company, Meridian Books.

———(1963). *The Faith of a Heretic.* Garden City, N. Y.: Doubleday and Company, Anchor Books.

———"Nietzsche, Friedrich." In Paul Edwards (ed.) (1967). *Encyclopedia of Philosophy,* V. New York: The Macmillan Company and The Free Press, 504-514.

Keen, Sam (1969). *Apology for Wonder.* New York: Harper and Row.

Kennan, George F. (1986). "In the American Mirror." Review of Arthur M. Schlesinger, Jr., *The Cycles of American History,* in *The New York Review of Books,* XXXIII/17 (Nov. 6), 3-6.

Kierkegaard, Søren (1951). *A Kierkegaard Anthology,* Robert Bretall (ed.). Princeton, N.J.: Princeton University Press.

Klocker, Harry R. (1983). "Ockham: A Note on Knowledge and Certitude." *Iliff Review,* XL/1 (Winter), 37-44.

Kohn, Alfie (1986). "How to Succeed Without Even Vying." *Psychology Today,* XX/9 (September), 22-28.

Kraus, Elizabeth M. (1979). *The Metaphysics of Experience: A Companion to Whitehead's Process and Reality.* New York: Fordham University Press.

Kretzmann, Norman. "Semantics, History of." In Paul Edwards (ed.) (1967). *Encyclopedia of Philosophy,* VII. New York: The Macmillan Company and the Free Press, 358-406.

Kuhn, Helmut. "German Philosophy and National Socialism." In Paul Edwards (ed.) (1967). *Encyclopedia of Philosophy,* III. New York: The Macmillan Company and The Free Press, 309-316.

Kuhn, Thomas (1971). *The Structure of Scientific Revolutions,* second edition. Chicago, Ill.: University of Chicago Press.

Kundera, Milan (1980). *The Book of Laughter and Forgetting,* Michael Henry Heim (trans.). New York: Alfred A. Knopf.

————(1984). "The Novel and Europe." *The New York Review of Books*, XXXI/12 (July 19), 15-19.

Küng, Hans (1980). *Does God Exist? An Answer for Today,* Edward Quinn (trans.). Garden City, N.Y.: Doubleday and Company.

Lang, Berel and Stahl, Gary (1969). "Mill's 'Howlers' and the Logic of Naturalism." *Philosophy and Phenomenological Research*, XXIX/4 (June), 562-574.

Leclerc, Ivor (1972). *The Nature of Physical Existence*, a volume in the Muirhead Library of Philosophy, H. D. Lewis (ed.). London: George Allen and Unwin, Ltd.; New York: Humanities Press, Inc.

————(1973). "The Necessity Today of the Philosophy of Nature." *Process Studies,* III/3 (Fall), 158-168.

Leff, Gordon (1975). *William of Ockham: The Metamorphosis of Scholastic Discourse*. Manchester: Manchester University Press; Totowa, N.J.: Rowman and Littlefield.

Lehrer, Keith (1971). "Why Not Skepticism?" *The Philosophical Forum*, II/3 New Series (Spring), 283-298.

Leibniz, Gottfried W. (1951). *Leibniz: Selections*, Philip P. Wiener (ed.). New York: Charles Scribner's Sons.

Leiss, William (1974). *The Domination of Nature*. Boston, Mass.: Beacon Press.

Lewis, C. S. (1955). *Surprised by Joy: The Shape of My Early Life*. New York: Harcourt Brace Jovanovich, Inc., A Harvest/HBJ Book.

Lewis, John (ed.) (1974). *Beyond Chance and Necessity*. Atlantic Highlands, N.J.: Humanities Press.

Locke, John (1959). *An Essay Concerning Human Understanding*, ed. Alexander Campbell Fraser, 2 vols. New York: Dover Publications.

London, Jack (1981). *The Sea Wolf*. New York: Bantam Books.

Loomer, Bernard M. "The Future of Process Philosophy." In Sibley, Jack R. and Gunter, Pete A. Y. (eds.) (1978). *Process Philosophy: Basic Writings*. Washington, D. C.: University Press of America, 515-539.

Löwith, Karl (1964). *From Hegel to Nietzsche: The Revolution in*

Nineteenth-Century Thought, David E. Green (trans.). New York; Chicago, Ill.; and San Francisco, Calif.: Holt, Rinehart and Winston.

Lubac, Henri de (1963). *The Drama of Atheist Humanism*, Edith M. Riley (trans.). New York: The New American Library, Meridian Books.

McCloskey, H. J. "On Being an Atheist." In John R. Burr and Martin Goldinger (eds.) (1976). *Philosophy and Contemporary Issues*, 2nd edition. New York: Macmillan Publishing Company; London: Collier Macmillan Publishers, 131-137.

MacIntyre, Alasdair. "Existentialism." In Mary Warnock (ed.) (1971). *Sartre: A Collection of Critical Essays*. Garden City, N.Y.: Doubleday and Company, Anchor Books, 1-58.

————(1981). *After Virtue: A Study in Moral Theory*. Notre Dame, Ind.: University of Notre Dame Press.

Marcel, Gabriel (1935). *Être et Avoir*. Paris: Aubier, Éditions Montaigne.

Margoshes, Adam. "Schelling, Friedrich Wilhelm Joseph von." In Paul Edwards (ed.) (1967). *The Encyclopedia of Philosophy*, VII. New York: The Macmillan Company and The Free Press, 305-309.

Márquez, Gabriel García (1971). *One Hundred Years of Solitude*. New York: Avon Books, A Bard Book.

Marx, Karl and Engels, Friedrich (1959). *Basic Writings on Politics and Philosophy*, Lewis S. Feuer (ed.). Garden City, N.Y.: Doubleday and Company, Anchor Books.

Mauthner, Fritz (1901-1902). *Beiträge zu einer Kritik der Sprache*, 3 vols. Stuttgart: J. G. Cotta.

————(1906). *Die Sprache. Die Gesellschaft: Sammlung Sozial-Psychologischer Monographien,* Martin Buber (ed.), IX. Frankfurt: Reutten and Loening.

————(1910). *Wörterbuch der Philosophie: Neue Beiträge zu einer Kritik der Sprache*. Munich: Georg Muller.

Meilaender, Gilbert (1986). Review of James M. Gustafson (1981, 1984). *Ethics From a Theocentric Perspective*, Vols. 1, 2. In *Religious Studies Review*, XII/1 (January), 11-16.

Meland, Bernard Eugene (1966). *The Secularization of Modern Cultures*.

London, Oxford, and New York: Oxford University Press.

Merleu-Ponty, Maurice (1962). *Phenomenology of Perception*, Colin Smith (trans.). London and Boston, Mass.: Routledge and Kegan Paul.

————(1968). *The Visible and the Invisible,* Claude Lefort (ed.). Alphonso Lingis (trans.). Evanston, Ill.: Northwestern University Press.

Mersenne, Marin (1955). *Correspondance du P. Marin Mersenne,* Tome IV. Published by Mme. Paul Tannery; edited and annotated by Cornelis De Waard; with the collaboration of Rene Pintard. Paris: Presses Universitaires.

Mill, John Stuart (1884). *An Examination of Sir William Hamilton's Philosophy, and of the Principal Philosophical Questions Discussed in His Writings*, 2 vols. in 1. New York: Henry Holt and Company.

————(1957). *Utilitarianism*, Oskar Priest (ed.). Indianapolis, Ind.: The Bobbs-Merrill Company, The Library of Liberal Arts.

Miller, Leonard G. "Descartes, Mathematics, and God." In Alexander Sesonske and Noel Fleming (eds.) (1966). *Meta-Meditations: Studies in Descartes*. Belmont, Calif.: Wadsworth Publishing Company, 37-49.

Monod, Jacques (1972). *Chance and Necessity*. Austryn Wainhouse (trans.). New York: Random House, Vintage Books.

Monro, D. H. "Russell's Moral Theories". In David Pears (ed.) (1972). *A Collection of Critical Essays*. Garden City, N.Y.: Doubleday and Company, Anchor Books, 325-355.

Morgan, Ted (1985). *FDR: A Biography*. New York: Simon and Schuster.

Morris, Richard (1984). *Time's Arrow: Scientific Attitudes Toward Time*. New York: Simon and Schuster.

Moser, Charles A. (1964). *Anti-Nihilism in the Russian Novel of the 1860's*. The Hague: Mouton Publishers.

Muggeridge, Malcolm (1980). *The End of Christendom*. Grand Rapids, Mich.: William B. Eerdman's Publishing Company.

Murphy, Earl (1967). *Governing Nature*. Chicago, Ill.: Quadrangle Books.

Nagel, Thomas (1972). "Reason and National Goals." *Science,* CLXXVII/ 4051 (September 1), 766-770.

Nellhaus, Arlynn (1985). "Elie Wiesel Uses His Books As Weapons of Truth." *The Denver Post*, XCIV/164 (December 22), 22D.

Nelson, Benjamin. "The Quest for Certitude and the Books of Scripture, Nature, and Conscience." In Owen Gingrich (ed.). (1975). *The Nature of Scientific Discovery*. A Symposium Commemorating the 500th Anniversary of the Birth of Nicolaus Copernicus. Washington, D.C.: Smithsonian Institution Press, 355-372.

Newton, Isaac (1721). *Optiks*, 3rd edition. London.

————(1953). *Newton's Philosophy of Nature: Selections From His Writings*, H. S. Thayer (ed.). New York: Hafner Publishing Company.

Nietzsche, Friedrich (1954). *The Portable Nietzsche,* Walter Kaufmann, (ed. and trans.), 2nd edition. New York: The Viking Press.

————(1966). *Beyond Good and Evil*, Walter Kaufmann (trans.). New York: Random House, Vintage Books.

————(1968). *The Will to Power*, Walter Kaufmann and R. J. Hollingdale (trans.). New York: Random House, Vintage Books.

————(1974). *The Gay Science*, Walter Kaufmann (trans.). New York: Random House, Vintage Books.

Nishitani, Keiji (1982). *Religion and Nothingness*, Jan van Bragt (trans.). Berkeley, Calif.: University of California Press.

Norton, David Fate (1982). *David Hume: Common-Sense Moralist, Sceptical Metaphysician*. Princeton, N. J.: Princeton University Press.

Noss, John B. (1969). *Man's Religions*, 4th edition. New York: The Macmillan Company.

Novak, Michael (1971). *The Experience of Nothingness*. New York: Harper and Row, Harper Colophon Books.

Nozick, Robert (1974). *Anarchy, State, and Utopia*. New York: Basic Books.

Oates, Joyce Carol (1984). "The English Secret Unveiled." Review of Hilary Spurling, *Ivy: The Life of I. Compton-Burnett,* in *The New York Times Book Review*, CXXXIV/46 (December 9), 7-9.

Ogden, Schubert (1966). *The Reality of God and Other Essays*. New York: Harper and Row.

Olson, Robert G. "Nihilism." In Paul Edwards (ed.) (1967). *Encyclopedia of Philosophy*, V. New York: The Macmillan Company and the Free Press, 514-517.

"On Death as a Constant Companion" (1965). *Time*. LXXXVI/20 (November 12), 52-53.

Ornstein, Robert E. (1977). *The Psychology of Consciousness*, 2nd edition. New York: Harcourt Brace Jovanovich, Inc.

Otto, Max C. (1924). *Things and Ideals*. New York: Henry Holt and Company.

Ouden den, Bernard (1982). *Essays on Reason, Will, Creativity, and Time: Studies in the Philosophy of Friedrich Neitzsche.* Washington, D. C.: University Press of America.

Passmore, John (1966). *A Hundred Years of Philosophy*. London: Gerald Duckworth and Company.

Paton, H. J. (1955). *The Modern Predicament*. New York: The Macmillan Company.

Patterson, R. W. K. (1971). *The Nihilistic Egoist, Max Stirner*. London, Oxford, and New York: Oxford University Press.

Pears, D. F. (ed.) (1972). *Bertrand Russell: A Collection of Critical Essays*. Garden City, N. Y.: Doubleday and Company, Anchor Books.

Pfaff, Donald W. (ed.) (1983). *Ethical Questions in Brain and Behavior: Problems and Opportunities.* New York, Heidelberg, Tokyo: Springer-Verlag.

Pike, Nelson (ed.) (1965). *God and Evil: Readings on the Theological Problem of Evil.* Englewood Cliffs, N. J.: Prentice-Hall, Inc.

Plato (1973). *The Collected Dialogues of Plato, Including the Letters*, Edith Hamilton and Huntington Cairns (eds.). Bollingen Series LXXI. Princeton, N. J.: Princeton University Press.

Popkin, Richard (1979). *The History of Scepticism from Erasmus to Spinoza.* Berkeley, Calif.; Los Angeles, Calif.; and London; University of California Press.

Proust, Marcel (1949). *À la Recherche du Temps Perdu, IX: Le Temps Retrouvé.* Paris: Gallimard.

Randall, John Herman, Jr. (1976). *The Making of the Modern Mind: A Survey of the Intellectual Background of the Present Age.* New York: Columbia University Press.

Rauschning, Hermann (1939). *The Revolution of Nihilism: Warning to the West*, E.W. Dickes (trans.). New York: Longmans, Green, and Company.

Rawls, John (1971). *A Theory of Justice.* Cambridge, Mass.: Harvard University Press.

Richardson, John (1984). "The Catch in the Late Picasso." *New York Review of Books*, XXXI/12 (July 19), 21-28.

Rifkin, Jeremy (in collaboration with Nicanor Perlas) (1984). *Algeny: A New Word—A New World.* New York: Penguin Books.

————(1985). *Declaration of a Heretic.* London and Boston, Mass.: Routledge and Kegan Paul.

Robinson, Marilyn and Kirksey, Jim (1987). "Denverite Waiting for Wife Finds She Was Fatally Hurt." *The Denver Post*, XCV/181 (January 28), 1b.

Rollin, Bernard E. (1981). *Animal Rights and Human Morality.* Buffalo, N. Y.: Prometheus Books.

Rollins, C. D. "Solipsism." In Paul Edwards (ed.) (1967). *The Encyclopedia of Philosophy,* VII. New York: The Macmillan Company and The Free Press, 487-491.

Rolston, Holmes, III (1982). "Are Values in Nature Subjective or Objective?" *Environmental Ethics,* IV (Summer), 125-151.

————(1985). "Duties to Endangered Species." *Bioscience*, XXXV/11 (December), 718-726.

————(1987). *Science and Religion: A Critical Survey.* New York: Random House.

————"Duties to Ecosystems." In J. Baird Callicott (ed.) (1987). *A Companion to the Sand County Almanac.* Madison, Wisc.: University of Wisconsin Press, 246-274.

Rorty, Richard (1980). *Philosophy and the Mirror of Nature.* Princeton, N.J.: Princeton University Press.

Rosen, Stanley (1969). *Nihilism: A Philosophical Essay*. New Haven, Conn., and London: Yale University Press.

Rosner, Stanley and Abt, Lawrence Edwin (eds.) (1974). *Essays In Creativity*. Croton-on-Hudson, N.Y.: North River Press.

Ross, Stephen David (1969). *Literature and Philosophy: An Analysis of the Philosophical Novel*. New York: Appleton-Century-Crofts.

———(1983). *Perspective in Whitehead's Metaphysics*. Albany, N.Y.: State University of New York Press.

Roubiczek, Paul (1964). *Existentialism For and Against*. London, Cambridge, and New York: Cambridge University Press.

Rubenstein, Richard (1966). *After Auschwitz: Radical Theology and Contemporary Judaism*. Indianapolis, Ind.: The Bobbs-Merrill Company.

Rushdie, Salman (1981). *Midnight's Children*. New York: Alfred A. Knopf.

Russell, Bertrand (1957). *A Free Man's Worship*. New York: Simon and Schuster, A Clarion Book.

———(1961). *Religion and Science*. London, Oxford and New York: Oxford University Press.

Sanders, Steven and Cheney, David R. (eds.) (1980). *The Meaning of Life: Questions, Answers and Analysis*. Englewood Cliffs, N.J.: Prentice-Hall, Inc.

Sartre, Jean-Paul (1964). *Nausea,* Lloyd Alexander (trans.). New York: New Directions Publishing Corporation.

———(1966). *Being and Nothingness: An Essay on Phenomenological Ontology*, Hazel E. Barnes (trans.). New York: Washington Square Press.

———"Existentialism Is a Humanism," Philip Mairet (trans.). In Walter Kaufmann (ed.) (1967). *Existentialism from Dostoevsky to Sartre*. Cleveland, Oh., and New York: The World Publishing Company, Meridian Books, 286-311.

Saunders, Jason L. (ed.) (1966). *Greek and Roman Philosophy After Aristotle*. New York: The Free Press.

Saunders, John Turk and Henze, Donald F. (1967). *The Private Language Problem: A Philosophical Dialogue*. New York: Random House.

Scheffler, Israel (1967). *Science and Subjectivity*. Indianapolis, Ind.: The Bobbs-Merrill Company.

Schoeck, Helmut and Wiggins, James W. (eds.) (1961). *Relativism and the Study of Man*. Princeton, N.J.: Van Nostrand Company.

Schopenhauer, Friedrich (1942). *Complete Essays of Schopenhauer*, T. Bailey Saunders (trans.), 7 Books in 1 Vol. New York: Willey Book Company.

Schopenhauer, Friedrich (1957). *The World as Will and Idea*, R. B. Haldane and J. Kemp (trans.), 2nd edition, 3 vols. London and Boston, Mass.: Routledge and Kegan Paul.

Schutte, Ofelia (1984). *Beyond Nihilism: Nietzsche Without Masks*. Chicago, Ill., and London: The University of Chicago Press.

Scott, Nathan A. (ed.) (1967). *The Modern Vision of Death*. Richmond, Va.: John Knox Press.

Sesonske, Alexander and Fleming, Noel (eds.) (1966). *Meta-Meditations: Studies in Descartes*. Belmont, Calif.: Wadsworth Publishing Company.

Short, T. L. (1983). "Teleology in Nature." *American Philosophical Quarterly*, XX/4 (October), 311-320.

Sibley, Jack R. and Gunter, Pete A. Y. (eds.) (1978). *Process Philosophy: Basic Writings*. Washington, D. C.: University Press of America.

Singer, Peter (1975). *Animal Liberation*. New York: New York Review Press.

———(1983). *Hegel*. London, Oxford, and New York: Oxford University Press.

Skinner, B.F. (1948). *Walden Two*. New York: The Macmillan Company.

———(1953). *Science and Human Behavior*. New York: The Macmillan Company.

———(1971). *Beyond Freedom and Dignity*. New York: Random House, Vintage Books.

Smart, Ninian. "Omnipotence, Evil and Supermen." In Nelson Pike (ed.) (1965). *God and Evil: Readings on the Theological Problem of Evil*. Englewood Cliffs, N.J.: Prentice-Hall, Inc., 103-112.

Solomon, Robert C. (1983). *The Passions*. Notre Dame, Ind.: University of Notre Dame Press.

Spengler, Oswald (1932). *The Decline of the West*, Charles Francis Atkinson (trans.), 3 vols in 1. New York: Alfred A. Knopf.

Stene, Eric (1984). "Parents of Slain Children Share Anger." *The Denver Post*, XCII/262 (April 19), 4A.

Stirner, Max (1971). *The Ego and His Own,* John Carroll (trans.). New York: Harper and Row.

Strauss, Leo. "Relativism," In Helmut Schoeck and James W. Wiggins (eds.) (1961). *Relativism and the Study of Man*. Princeton, N.J.: Van Nostrand Company, 135-157.

Tertullian, Quintus Septimius Florens. *Prescription Against Heretics*. In Jason L. Saunders (ed.) (1966). *Greek and Roman Philosophy After Aristotle*. New York: The Free Press, 343-351.

Thielicke, Helmut (1969). *Nihilism: Its Origin and Nature—With a Christian Answer*, John W. Doberstein (trans.). New York: Schocken Books.

Thompson, Barbara (1985). "Within the Timeless Gates." Review of Madhur Jaffrey, *Seasons of Splendour: Tales, Myths and Legends of India. The New York Times Book Review*, XC/45 (November 10), 33, 51.

Thorpe, William Homan (1978). *Purpose in a World of Chance: A Biologist's View*. London, Oxford, and New York: Oxford University Press.

Tillich, Paul (1951). *Systematic Theology*, I. Chicago, Ill.: University of Chicago Press.

———(1953). *The Courage to Be*. New Haven, Conn., and London: Yale University Press.

———(1957). *Dynamics of Faith*. New York: Harper and Row, Harper Torchbooks.

Titus, Harold H. (1964). *Living Issues in Philosophy,* 4th edition. New York: American Book Company.

Tocqueville de, Alexis (1904). *Democracy in America,* 2 vols., Henry Reeve (trans.). New York: D. Appleton and Company.

Tolstoy, Leo (1940). *A Confession and What I Believe*, Aylmer Maude (trans.). London, Oxford, and New York: Oxford University Press.

————(1960). *The Death of Ivan Ilych and Other Stories: Family Happiness, the Kreutzer Sonata, Master and Man,* Afterword by David Magarshack. New York and Toronto: The New American Library; London: The New English Library Limited. A Signet Classic.

Toulmin, Stephen (1972). *Human Understanding: The Collective Use and Evolution of Concepts.* Princeton, N.J.: Princeton University Press.

Turgenev, Ivan S. (n.d.). *Fathers and Sons,* Constance Garnett (trans.). New York: Boni and Liveright, Modern Library Edition.

Unger, Peter (1975). *Ignorance: A Case for Scepticism.* Oxford: The Clarendon Press.

Urmson, J. O. (1958). *Philosophical Analysis: Its Development Between the Two World Wars.* Oxford: The Clarendon Press.

Van Melsen, Andrew G. (1953). *The Philosophy of Nature.* Duquesne Studies, Philosophical Series 2. Pittsburgh, Penn.: Duquesne University Press.

Warnock, Mary (ed.) (1971). *Sartre: A Collection of Critical Essays.* Garden City, N. Y: Doubleday and Company, Anchor Books.

Weil, Eric (1965). "Science in Modern Culture, or The Meaning of Meaninglessness." *Daedalus* XCIV/1, 171-189.

Weiler, Gershon (1958). "On Fritz Mauthner's Critique of Language." *Mind*, LXVII/265 (January), 80-87.

————"Fritz Mauthner." In Paul Edwards (ed.) (1967). *Encyclopedia of Philosophy*, V. New York: The Macmillian Company and The Free Press, 221-225.

Wheelwright, Philip (ed.) (1960). *The Presocratics.* Indianapolis, Ind.: The Bobbs-Merrill Company.

White, Lynn, Jr. (1971). *Dynamo and Virgin Reconsidered: Machina Ex Deo.* Cambridge, Mass.: MIT Press.

Whitehead, Alfred N. (1926). *Religion in the Making.* New York: The Macmillan Company.

————(1948). *Science and the Modern World.* New York: The New American Library, A Mentor Book.

———(1979). *Process and Reality*. Corrected Edition, David Ray Griffin and Donald W. Sherburne (eds.). New York and London: The Free Press, a Division of The Macmillan Publishing Company.

Wilder, Amos N. "Mortality and Contemporary Literature." In Nathan A. Scott (ed.) (1967). *The Modern Vision of Death*. Richmond, Va.: John Knox Press, 17-44.

Wisdom, John (1970). *Paradox and Discovery*. Berkeley, Calif. and Los Angeles, Calif.: University of California Press.

Wittgenstein, Ludwig (1969). *On Certainty*, G. E. M. Anscombe and G. H. von Wright (eds.); Denis Paul and G. E. M. Anscombe (trans.). Oxford: Basil Blackwell.

Wolfe, Thomas (1941). *The Hills Beyond*. New York and London: Harper and Brothers.

Wolterstorff, Nicholas (1984). *Reason Within the Bounds of Religion*, 2nd edition. Grand Rapids, Mich.: William B. Eerdmans Publishing Company.

Yandell, Keith (ed.) (1973). *God, Man, and Religion: Readings in the Philosophy of Religion*. New York: McGraw-Hill Book Company.

Index of Names

Index of Subjects

Abandonment, 100

Absolute spirit, 249-253, 255, 395nn.6,8

Absolutism, 286-287, 297, 398-399n.20. *See* History; Nihilism; Perspectivism; Pluralism; Reality-itself; Relativism

Adventures, Roquentin's, 64-65, 68

Afterlife, 214, 413n.3; absence of certain goods in, 168-169, 387n.12; Christian belief in, 126-127, 163f-167; diminished confidence in as a source of nihilism, 164-166; belief in essential to a meaningful life, 4, 70-71, 166-169, 387n.11; nihilistic consequences of belief in, 169-172

Amoralism, 11-12, 17, 26, 107

Anguish, 89-90, 97, 99

Animals, absence of moral obligation to in Descartes, 213; absence of moral obligation to in Kant, 396n.11. *See also* Suffering, of animals

Anthropomorphism, 46-47, 128-131, 251, 383n.2

Archimedean point, 209-210, 212, 214-216

Arrest of life, 31

Arts, the, 134-135, 224-226, 237, 294; creativity in, as related to science, 410n.38. *See also* Novel, the

Asceticism, 29-30, 85

Assumptions leading to nihilism, 7, 117-119, 127

Atheism as implying nihilism, 4, 39-41, 43-46, 130, 133

Atomism, 388n.1; Newtonian, 247

Authority, at odds with reason, 222

Behavioral sciences, 86

Being, mystery of, 132

Being-for-itself, 79-80, 89-93, 144

Being-in-itself, 79-80, 92, 144, 180, 218, 375

Being-in-the-world, 398n.19

Being-for-others, 110, 300

Bergsonianism, 134

Bible, 278; authority of, 386n.9; claims to absolute authority of cannot be made theoretically certain, 160; no absolute theoretical certainty for interpretations of, 161; Descartes's appeal to, 227, 392n.9; existential certainty of its truth among Christians, 160-162; Kant's appeal to, 267-268; Luther's appeal to, 222; reliance on in Middle Ages, 201, 204, 278; one revelation among others, 160; verbal inerrancy of, 152, 162. *See also* Revelation

Boredom, 29, 55, 98, 357; as revealing the barrenness of existence, 67-68; of a static state of perfection in an afterlife, 167-168

Buddhism, 44, 61, 128, 268, 282-283

Bureaucracy, of the Castle, 111-114, 117, 300-302

Cartesianism, as secret history of modern West, 237

Cartesians, Newton as greatest of, 235; Port-Royalist, 213

Categorical Imperative, 264-265

Certainty, Descartes on, 207-240, 243, 390n.4; Husserl on, 254-258; intersubjective, 179; of knowledge in the afterlife, 164, 166, 387n.10; necessity of for existential meaning, 151; necessity of for knowledge, 80-82, 149-163, 176-177; necessity of for morality, 151; provided in the Bible,